The WPA Guide to 1930s Missouri

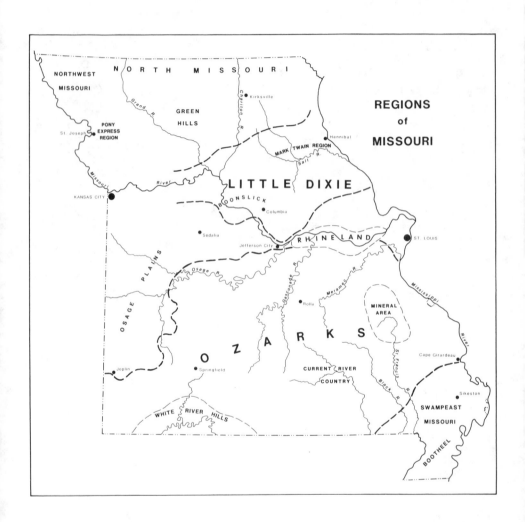

The
WPA GUIDE
to 1930s Missouri

*Compiled by Workers of the Writers' Program
of the Work Projects Administration
in the State of Missouri
With a New Foreword by Charles van Ravenswaay
and a New Introduction by
Howard Wight Marshall and Walter A. Schroeder*

UNIVERSITY PRESS OF KANSAS

Foreword © 1986 by Charles van Ravenswaay
Introduction © 1986 by the University Press of Kansas
Copyright 1941 by the Missouri State Highway Department
All rights reserved

First paperback edition, with a new foreword and introduction, published
in 1986. Originally published by Duell, Sloan and Pearce in 1941
under the title *Missouri: A Guide to the "Show Me" State*

Published by the University Press of Kansas (Lawrence,
Kansas 66045), which was organized by the Kansas Board of Regents
and is operated and funded by Emporia State University,
Fort Hays State University, Kansas State University, Pittsburg State
University, the University of Kansas, and Wichita State University

Library of Congress Catalog Card Number 86-50110
ISBN 0-7006-0292-5

Printed in the United States of America
10 9 8 7 6 5 4 3 2 1

Foreword to the Paperback Edition

On June 12, 1941, the long-awaited *Missouri: A Guide to the "Show Me" State* was published. This volume in the American Guide Series had been six years in the making. It was compact in format and convenient in size; the information it contained was encyclopedic. Its dust jacket pictured one of the last surviving Mississippi River stern wheelers, the *Ralph Hicks,* as a reminder that Missouri's location "where the rivers meet" had shaped its past and present and would continue to shape its future. The book was priced at $2.75 retail.

Now, forty-five years later, the Missouri Guide reappears to provide another generation of readers with the opportunity to learn what the State was like on the eve of World War II, when traditional ways of thinking and doing were being swept away by the onrush of change. This introduction will explain, in part at least, how the book came into being and the larger purposes it was intended to serve.

The publication of the Guide in 1941, after a long gestation period, brought pleasure to many, relief to some, and surprise to the critics, who never expected to see it, convinced as they were that the Federal Writers' Project was a foolish boondoggle of Franklin Delano Roosevelt's Works Progress Administration (WPA). Reviewers and readers gave the book a warm reception, and booksellers reported sales beyond their most optimistic predictions. Before summer's end the book had the first of at least six reprintings.

No comprehensive guide to Missouri—or to any other state—had been attempted before the Federal Writers' Project launched the American Guide Series in 1935. Earlier in the century, such books were not considered necessary or important. Nor had there been sponsors before the New Deal era to plan and supervise such an ambitious, complicated, and expensive operation. By 1935, however, conditions were right. Although the series was triggered by FDR's response to the Great Depression, other developments in American life made these guidebooks both timely and desirable.

By 1935 the automobile had replaced the plodding horse and buggy, and all-weather highways had ended the age-old hazards of travel on dirt roads. Released from those limitations, Americans were now on the move, eager not only to explore their own states but also to go far beyond to see the nation's scenic wonders and historic places, along with the natural and man-made diversions that they had read about. Travel broadened their vision and gave them a new appreciation of the size and meaning of their country, along with a deeper realization of the rapid, seemingly incomprehensible changes that were taking place. The time had come for books that reviewed, charted, and explained.

Under normal conditions, creating a State guidebook would have been difficult, but the 1930's were far from normal. Those transitional years saw profound changes in American life, brought about by the freedom of highway travel, the radio, the accelerated mechanization of farming operations, and the introduction of new industrial technologies. The Great Depression, then under way, continued with no apparent end. Added to those stresses was the drought in the Midwest, where summer brought withering heat and blasting winds, and dust storms rolled in from Kansas and Oklahoma. The news from Europe was increasingly ominous.

For millions it became a time of desperation and hopelessness: jobs were lost in the general economic collapse, and savings were swept away in bank failures. In Missouri, dispossessed black farm workers in the southeastern delta region—the "Bootheel"—and the unemployed in St. Louis and other cities created "Hoovervilles," of makeshift huts, where they were given private and public aid. Beggars wandered around the downtown city streets, something almost unknown previously, apologetically asking, "Mister, can you spare a dime?" Many of the jobless roamed the nation, pursuing rumors of possible work.

Other Americans, certainly the majority, managed to get by with varying degrees of success, although everyone was affected by the grim uncertainties of the times. Often those in real need made do with what they had and exhibited a pride that commanded respect. Self-reliance seemed to strengthen during those hard times; often I heard the comment "I don't want any charity."

On the public level there were positive developments. In Missouri the number of state parks and national forest areas steadily increased, reflecting a developing public interest in conservation, particularly of Ozark forests, streams, and the mammoth, awe-inspiring springs. The new Lake of the Ozarks, built by the St. Louis Union Electric Light and Power Company, drew many vacationers. At St. Louis, construction of the great river-front memorial to Thomas Jefferson and the nation's westward expansion got under way.

Despite the depression, traditional events continued. In Kansas City the great American Royal Horse and Livestock Show remained a major regional event. And in St. Louis, performances by the Symphony Orchestra and Municipal Opera, as well as the annual Veiled Prophets'

Ball and Parade, provided a sense of continuity. At Sedalia the State Fair remained an annual event, as did the county fairs in many communities, despite the drought and general hard times.

One remarkable development of the depression years was that in response to the increasing social and economic dislocations and to the related feeling that much of what had given life meaning and stability was being destroyed, people began searching for new ties to the past. Growing numbers visited historic buildings and traveled to see the places associated with the heroes and stirring events. The Missouri State Highway Department placed markers across the state to identify streams and towns, giving the traveler a sense of place along otherwise anonymous roads, and the State Historical Society began to erect historical markers.

The WPA guidebooks sought to stimulate the growing interest in state and national history by locating and describing historic sites and by providing capsule histories of communities along described routes, so that for residents and visitors alike, those places would have meaning beyond mere names on maps. These descriptions also noted significant historic buildings, which often were listed for the first time in the guides. In that way, many communities learned about landmarks that might otherwise never have been recognized or appreciated. In addition, the field research for the Writers' Project sometimes led to the discovery and preservation, in museums and historical societies, of significant paintings (and the identification of forgotten artists), of prints, of historical documents, and of examples of early furniture and other decorative objects made by outstanding craftsmen, items that were often little prized by their owners.

The buildings and objects that had survived from the early days helped Missourians in their search for ties with the past, in the course of which they discovered that history—great and exciting history—had taken place in Missouri as well as "back East" or "out West." Traditional music and dances, and even crafts such as weaving, quilting, and basket making, were revived. Collecting antiques, an enterprise taken up by only a few Missourians early in the century, did not become widespread until the depression years, when many people developed an interest in "old-time things" that had been scorned not long before.

From this grass-roots interest in regional history and traditional ways came the development of regional arts whose quality and creativity attracted nationwide attention. Missouri and its neighboring states were the centers of this phenomenon. While the Missouri artist Thomas Hart Benton captured the State's past and present life with his scenes of action, such writers as Josephine Johnson—many of them young and idealistic—produced works that spoke of their midwestern backgrounds and concerns. Quite different was the writing of Raymond Weeks, which was reminiscent of frontier humor; Ward Dorrance lyrically described the natural beauties of Ozark streams. In addition, scholars were making Missourians aware of their rich heritage of folklore. In 1940, songs collected by members of Missouri's Folk Lore Society were edited and published by Professor H. M. Belden; meanwhile, Vance Randolph was wandering throughout the Ozarks, recording folk songs, lore, and tales. Others collected the State's colorful place names and the remnants of the French language and French folk stories that had survived at Old Mines and Ste. Geneviève. Such efforts enriched life in Missouri during the depression years and remain as a permanent contribution.

After Roosevelt's election in 1932, federal programs were launched to give desperate people hope and work. On May 6, 1935, the President created the WPA by Executive Order, and the Federal Writers' Project was established on July 27 to provide work for jobless writers and to help them maintain their skills.

Creating an organization and establishing a program for the Writers' Project proved to be difficult, for the concept and the challenge were completely new and demanding. There was no time for reflection or experimentation. People had to be given work as quickly as possible.

In Washington, Henry C. Alsberg was appointed director of the headquarters staff. The choice was fortunate. Alsberg, then fifty-seven years of age, was an author, journalist, and editor of unusual ability. Some forty years later, a colleague, Jerre Mangione, wrote admiringly in his *The Dream and the Deal: The Federal Writers' Project, 1935-1943* of Alsberg's "inventive mind, his encyclopedic fund of information, and his literary taste." Alsberg's abiding faith in people proved to be an invaluable asset during the uncertainties and turmoil that often harassed his efforts. Although he was not a good administrator and often had difficulty reaching decisions, Alsberg's ability to inspire his subordinates contributed to the success fo the Writers' Project.

While the Washington staff was being organized, there was considerable discussion about what program the Writers' Project should undertake. No precedents existed. Mangione later recalled that ideas were presented, examined, and discarded until it was finally decided to compile a guide for each state. Alsberg and other like-minded intellectuals were enthusiastic about the plan, believing that it would create an unprecedented opportunity to "examine, for the first time in history, the country's peoples, resources, traditions, and accomplishments in great detail." These guides would do much more than help travelers get from place to place; they would also present a picture of the nation's "character," which Americans had previously ignored.

There were many problems in setting up the state offices: good writers often were poor administrators. Meanwhile, there were overwhelming political pressures to influence key appointments. In Missouri the Pendergast machine in Kansas City forced appointments that resulted in endless problems, including strikes and other tumultuous happenings that sometimes brought temporary shutdowns.

My association with the Missouri project began almost accidentally in 1938. I was then working as the business manager of my family's medical and surgical clinic in Boonville. Much of my leisure time was spent studying Missouri's history; collecting antiques, old books, and historical documents; and making a photographic survey of the state's early buildings. My collaborator in that venture was Alexander Piaget, a remarkable St. Louis photographer, whose great interest—like mine— was old buildings. Thinking that the acting director of the Missouri Writers' Project, Dr. U. R. Bell (who was then on loan from the Kentucky office), might be interested in seeing some of our photographs, I visited him. A few days later he called to ask if I could spend a few days reviewing some of the manuscript for the Missouri Guide. I agreed. Only later did I realize that he wanted to try me out: he was anxious to return to Kentucky, so he needed someone to take his place. Apparently he decided that I could do the job, for I was asked to become state supervisor of the project. My family was willing to let me divide my time between the Writers' Project and my Boonville responsibilities, so with their blessing I accepted the offer. I never regretted it.

When I took over the project in 1938, it was limping along quietly and ineffectively. It had become too small to interest either scheming politicians who were searching for jobs for friends or the disruptive hotheads who earlier had done much to give the project a bad name. In addition, when I arrived, the office staff was apprehensive because of rumors that the national organization of the Writers' Project was to be changed. In the summer of 1939, when those plans were finally announced, we learned that the Washington office was losing much of its authority and was being reduced to a technical advisory service. It did, however, retain the authority to grant or withhold the final permission to publish manuscripts prepared by the field offices. As part of the reorganization, each state project was now required to have a sponsor who would provide at least partial financial support and general supervision. In Missouri the State Highway Department took over that responsibility.

Although I was given a very small staff, limited funds, and an assignment that no sensible person would have accepted, I was also given a free hand. The overriding concern of the Washington office, and of the Democratic state officials, was to produce a Missouri guidebook that would both justify the money and time spent on it and counteract the vociferous critics of the program.

Soon after I began, I found to my dismay that much of the incomplete manuscript for the book was unusable. It was dull, full of errors, and lacking in the breadth and richness of detail that Missouri deserved. Therefore, much of the work had to be done over again—including the time-consuming job of collecting and checking information for the tours and writing or revising the essays.

My staff was small (at times I had only four people, two of whom were typists and file clerks), and in order for me to do work in the field to research the tours, I needed someone who could write, edit, and manage the office, for the flow of paperwork required by Washington was worthy of a major enterprise. Fortunately, I was able to interest Mrs. Dana O. Jensen, of St. Louis. She had been a friend for many years, and she possessed all the necessary qualifications, including high standards of literary quality and accuracy. Billie Jensen's services made an invaluable contribution to the success of this book.

Volunteer assistance came from friends who had expertise in various fields and who generously provided advice and information, particularly for some of the essays. Irving L. Dilliard, for example, an Illinoisan as well as a journalist, author, and historian, wrote with perceptive understanding about the complex character of Missourians in his essay "People and Character," something a native would have had difficulty in doing.

After the State Highway Department became our sponsor, members of that staff took over some of the routine details of the activity. They received and issued some reports, paid wages and travel expenses, and created the tour maps for the book. The department also helped to find quarters for our modest operations when we moved from Jefferson City to St. Louis for more convenient access to libraries and other research facilities. At one point in St. Louis, when our budget was fading away, we were given rent-free quarters in the Missouri Historical Society's basement storeroom, where we shared space with Admiral Peary's arctic dogsleds, a copy of Lindbergh's "Spirit of St. Louis" plane, old Indian baskets and pots, and shelves of mouldering books. We later moved to an upper floor of an abandoned factory building, where the freight elevator daily promised catastrophe and where overcoats were essential for survival in winter.

Progress on the manuscript continued, somewhat haltingly at times because of the constantly changing and uncertain funding. Our ties with the Washington office remained close, particularly during the last stages of the book. Harold Rosenberg—who soon became known as "Rosie"—came to help shape the final manuscript, to cut and tighten, and to otherwise ensure that it would conform to the format that had been established for the American Guide Series. Sometimes I complained about his long and involved sentences or that he had deleted some of my treasured passages, but such differences were minor, and we became good friends. Rosie later became a widely respected art critic.

Perhaps the most important ingredient in the making of the guidebooks was the idealism that went into them. It has been best expressed by Jerre Mangione, one of the first writers and editors on the Washington staff. He wrote about how he and his co-workers on the Federal Writers' Project had had their imaginations stirred by the opportunities. We felt, he said, that " we had never done anything of more value in our lifetime" or would never again find work that would "involve us as wholly and selflessly. . . . We had a sense of being part of a significant historical event. In a literal sense we *were* making history, for nothing like the Writers' Project or the other three federal arts projects had ever been tried by any nation anywhere."

After Billie Jensen took over operations of our Missouri office, I was free to spend much of my time checking and writing copy for the various tours. In addition to mileage and directions, the write-ups were supposed to include descriptions of the countryside and towns, of historic sites and buildings and other points of special interest, and of whatever else seemed important and would help to explain an area and its people. Before the actual drives began, much essential information was assembled through careful library research, in which I was frequently aided by staff members. The collected information, particularly references to places of historical interest, was entered on note cards, which I took along for easy reference.

Driving the routes was a fascinating experience for me: each day brought new adventures. Some were amusing, some were exasperating, and a good many considerably broadened my education. My travels were made before motels and fast-food places had begun to crowd the highways. Accommodations were sometimes hard to find, particularly away from cities and large towns. Most of my meals were taken at cafés (all small-town restaurants then seemed to be called "cafés"). Once I asked an elderly man where I might get something to eat. "Friend," he replied, "I'll tell you. There's two places here. If you eat in one, you'll wish you'd et in the other." Elsewhere I was directed to a general store, where the rotund owner, with grimy hands, obliged me by putting a slab of cheese between slices of bread and provided a bottle of orange pop to wash it down. On one hot summer day at a roadside grill I learned that iced coffee was an unknown drink in many rural communities. My order produced bewilderment and confusion from the waitress, and after several visits to the kitchen, she angrily announced, "The Boss says we won't serve it."

My travels over the state made me familiar with its different sections—its great and small rivers that had shaped history; its glaciated upland prairies in the northern portion of the state; the Ozark Mountains; and the southeast delta region, nicknamed "Swampeast Missouri," before it had been drained for farming. My assignment was to collect impressions along with facts. In doing so I learned something about the infinite variety of each region and about adaptation to those different conditions. Each region had its own pattern of trees, wild flowers, and wild creatures. Sometimes an area's unusual natural conditions produced rare features, as in Cooper County's Chouteau Springs, where tiny snails and fish have lived in the sulphur-saline water for millenniums. I puzzled as to why lizards and chipmunks were common in the Ozarks but not along the Missouri River, where I grew up.

Not surprisingly, the occupations of people living in these different regions had developed from local conditions. Ozark men found tie hacking a convenient way to earn cash, because they could get fifty cents for each tie that they delivered to a railroad collection point. I found a lone potter still working at his wheel—the last old-time potter in the state to make jugs and other crockery. Even more surprising was a rural cabinetmaker, turning out pieces like those his grandfather had made a century earlier. The descendants of Creole settlers at Old Mines were now mining tiff (barite), a mineral once considered worthless but now salable. Throughout the "lead belt," many of the mines were shut down to await better times, but the mountains of tailings alongside the mine heads testified to their former activity.

In the northern Ozarks the construction of the new Lake of the Ozarks had flooded much of the area that I had visited as a youngster. Submerged now were the Niangua River and the Hahatonka Spring, whose flow had appeared blue in its shadowy valley when seen from the Lover's Leap high above it. On a rocky crag not far from the spring was the rambling stone Hahatonka Castle, built by a romanticist long ago. In my youth it had seemed like something from a Sir Walter Scott novel, but now, near the shore of the new lake, it seemed far less grand.

At one time the inaccessibility of the Ozarks had made the region a foreign country; by the late 1930's, highways had transformed it into a vacation spot for thousands. But away from the noisy confusion of boats, cottages, and souvenir stands, something had survived of the Ozarks I remembered. On back roads, native men could still be seen squatting on their heels, as only hill people can do, silent and expressionless as they watched cars pass. Old social and economic differences also remained between those who lived on small, neatly tended valley farms and those who somehow made out on the ridges and mountainsides. I got to know some of each; they were fine people, soft-spoken and courteous, who knew wonderful old stories and songs learned from their elders. Billy Flippen—city folks might have called him a hillbilly—made a Sunday afternoon unforgettable for me by singing the plaintive "Barbara Allen" and other old ballads. His "concert hall" was a friend's barn, which a sudden shower had driven us into.

The world I found along the great rivers that flow through or alongside the State was strangely separate from the life that most Missourians knew. These restless streams have a life of their own to which the farms along their shores and the once-busy river ports are inseparably bound. In summer their roiling current flows quietly; winter may fill them with grinding masses of ice; and in some years, during the "June rise," their waters spread over their valleys from bluff to bluff. Most of the smaller river ports had become ghostly relics of the steamboat era, with empty shops and houses and elderly residents dreaming of the old days. But there was hope now that the bright new towboats, pushing monstrous barges that were beginning to dominate the rivers with such assurance, would revive river commerce. Meanwhile the unceasing battle between men and the rivers continued; during the 1930's the work boats of the Army Engineers could be seen, constantly at work repairing levees and dykes to control the shifting current.

At Cape Girardeau the cobblestone levee, with its row of handsome century-old buildings, recalled the years when "The Cape" was a major port on the upper Mississippi. Now the city had become the commercial center for southeast Missouri and for "Little Egypt," across the river in southern Illinois.

Driving south from Cape Girardeau, one leaves the upper valley of the Mississippi, which is marked by the high bluffs bordering its wide valley, and enters delta country, which physically and culturally is an extension of the Old South. Tufts of mistletoe are seen in the occasional trees, and native holly grows along Crowley's Ridge, the only elevation in that great area of flatness. When I visited there, cotton was still king, and cotton gins were evident in many places. Newer towns such as Sikeston had become the business centers, and New Madrid, founded when Missouri was part of Spain's colonial empire, had mostly memories, particularly of the most severe earthquake of record in North America, the cataclysmic earthquake of 1811–12. Signs of its devastation still remained more than a century later. Above New Madrid the Ohio River joins the Mississippi, and at New Madrid that giant stream, bordered only by lowlands, seems immense. On the morning that I saw it from the levee, the fog hung low, and the swift current moved so quietly that I could hear it lapping on the muddy shore and on the wreck of a river boat nearby, still bearing its name plate—"Sporty Days."

My travels lasted for a year or so, not continuously, for there was frequent need to return to the office, but often enough for me to follow the changing seasons in the Missouri countryside. Spring brought clouds of wild plum and dogwood blossoms and rosy-pink redbud on hillsides, while spring plowing was under way on the farms—mostly by tractor then. In late spring the first shoots of corn appeared at about the time when wild phlox, violets, and white trillium bloomed. One day in Gasconade County, I came upon a great mass of pale blue-gray camas lilies, a rare and wonderful sight. In early summer the wild roses were pink in fence rows when the wheat and oats ripened. Farmers put their grain in shocks to await threshing, as had long been the practice, and the pattern of those golden rows was a delight to see. Already, however, there was talk of huge combines that would do the cutting and threshing in a single operation. Corn harvest came in the autumn, when the red pods of sumac and the orange berries of bittersweet were among the fall colors ornamenting the roadsides. There were reports then about mechanical corn pickers that would eliminate the hand labor of cutting and piling corn stalks in orderly shocks to await the husking. The new technology—both the combines for threshing and the corn pickers—promised less work for farmers, but at the cost of things both tangible and intangible, among them the custom of having farm neighbors work together on major seasonal tasks and, along with the hard work, making them into social gatherings.

In these and other ways, traditional farming practices were being altered. The "hired man," once so necessary for farm work, was becoming as obsolete as the Missouri mule, which the farm tractor had dispossessed. That canny beast, famed as a tireless worker and for its legendary stubbornness at times, had been the friend and companion of Missouri farmers since frontier days. Change in rural life was also signaled by the radio antennas on many farmhouses and by the electric and telephone lines. Motor-driven pumps were replacing picturesque windmills.

Many old social customs persisted in the country, however, particularly those centered around neighborhood churches and schools, although it was obvious that those customs were weakening in part because of the steadily declining farm population. Few country churches still held regular services; consolidated schools were beginning to replace the one-room schoolhouses. Although many family cemeteries, dating from early times, were overgrown, church cemeteries were usually well kept and still in use. On Memorial Day, families returned to decorate graves and to read inscriptions. For the guidebook we made a special effort to locate the graves of famous people, such as Moses Austin's at Potosi and Gen. William Henry Ashley's, high above the Missouri

River near the mouth of the Lamine, a lonely site that somehow seemed appropriate for that daring explorer and fur trader.

In the 1930's, Missouri towns and cities had individual personalities that rewarded sympathetic study. Joplin, in the southwestern corner of the State had a western flavor, partly because of the large zinc and lead mines in the area, then shut down because of strikes and tragic confrontations, but more particularly because store windows displayed cowboy clothing and gear stocked for the Oklahoma ranchers. Fayette, near the center of the State, could have been a county seat in Virginia: most of its pioneer families had come from Virginia, and their cultural traditions had been continued. Hannibal, on the Mississippi, had kept the flavor of steamboating days, which its native son, Samuel L. Clemens (Mark Twain), had immortalized. At Springfield, the commercial center of the mid-Ozark region, Drury College, with its high scholastic reputation, recalled its New England Congregationalist beginnings; there, Mae Kennedy McCord delighted listeners with her weekly radio program of Ozark folk songs and stories.

Very different were Hermann, an outpost of the German-American culture, and Ste. Geneviève, where French colonial traditions were jealously guarded by its Flemish priest. At a farming village settled by German families, the priest told me that his most serious problem was his parishioners' belief in black magic. Bethel was the relic of a utopian dream. In Liberty and Independence there were reminders that the Mormons, led by Joseph Smith, had once lived in the area. Along Route 24 near Liberty and Independence (but two of the patriotic names given to Missouri towns) were Wellington, Waterloo, and Napoleon, named by forgotten pioneers with a sense of European history. The richness of Missouri's place names provides constant delight, as well as being a constant reminder of the people and cultures who had settled the state. At various places I found enclaves of descendants of Polish, Italian, Swiss-Mennonite, Germanic, French, and other immigrant groups, and of those whose ancestors had come from the Old South and the Atlantic states. Whatever their backgrounds, the Missourians whom I met were mannerly and kindly; they frequently had a rich sense of humor, which they sometimes expressed at my expense. One summer afternoon when I asked an elderly farmer in Perry County the name of an unusual tree in his yard, he looked at me—the young man from the city—shifted the straw he was chewing, and, with barely a flicker of a smile, said "I don't rightly know the common name, but the Latin name is *Pawlonia Imperialis*" (now given as *Pawlonia tomentosa*). He was right, as I found later, and I learned an important lesson.

The Guide's essays on Missouri's eleven principal cities required a great deal of looking, checking, and interviewing, but others on the staff had compiled much of the data, and I found the remaining work particularly interesting. Those cities were so different that it was a challenge to discover what made them so.

St. Louis and Kansas City, on opposite sides of the state, had few similiarities then. Kansas City was younger, smaller, somewhat brash, with a sense of purpose and direction. Its civic leaders, past and present, had given it a handsome plan of boulevards and parks. In the pleasant residential areas, many houses that dated from the early years of the century had been built in a local version of the bungalow style, their lower stories of rough-hewn limestone with frame second stories. The city had reason to be proud of its great Liberty Memorial, a monument to the dead of World War I, and its new William Rockhill Nelson Gallery of Art and Mary Atkins Museum (now the Nelson-Atkins Museum of Art). Its conservative newspapers, the *Kansas City Star* and *Times,* were widely read. Kansas City also had the beautiful new Plaza shopping center, which a local developer had designed in a Spanish-colonial style with fountains and landscaping. It was a new idea; years later, very different kinds of shopping malls would begin to appear throughout the country. The only ominous shadow over that progressive and innovative city was its ruthless political machine, which an outraged electorate would soon destroy.

St. Louis was almost a century older than Kansas City; it was also much larger and much more assured and relaxed than its hustling neighbor to the west. St. Louis's diversified economic base had brought stability and wealth. Two major universities, the Roman Catholic St. Louis University, the oldest institution of higher learning west of the Mississippi, and Washington University, founded by an idealistic New England clergyman, had long been vital forces in the city's life, as had the Missouri Botanical Garden (Shaw's Garden), the oldest botanical garden in the United States. Almost unique features of the city were the exclusive residential Places, in which through traffic is barred by handsome gates and whose affairs are regulated by an association of residents. For many years, St. Louis had suffered during the winter months from clouds of grimy coal smoke, but recently a progressive mayor had succeeded in making the city smoke free. But even so, St. Louis in the 1930's was uneasy, not only because of the depression but also from a feeling that its years of greatness were passing. It was too soon to recognize the new leadership and the new directions that were even then beginning to develop.

The Missouri guidebook was one of the last of the WPA series to be published. Shortly after it appeared, I resigned as supervisor of the project, for I had agreed to serve only until the book was produced. In 1942 I enlisted in the navy and eventually spent most of the war in the South Pacific. Mrs. Jensen succeeded me as head of the project, but plans for a Missouri picture book floundered, and she was left to close down the project. Her last responsibility was to oversee storing the office files in Jefferson City. In 1943 the Federal Writers' Project was officially terminated.

Even now, so many years after I became involved with the Missouri project, I can still feel the excitement of taking part in a great national act that rediscovered and reaffirmed faith in America during a time of fearful uncertainty.

A few months before the book was published, I wrote to Mrs. Jensen about some proofs that I had been reading and added that it left me with a strange feeling that the book was a "sort of epitaph" to a period then ending, as indeed it proved to be. I hope that the story of Missouri, which our small band created with such affection and idealism, will give today's readers not only pleasure but also an understanding of Missouri's character and traditions whose diversity and basic strengths have not been destroyed by time.

CHARLES VAN RAVENSWAAY
October, 1985

Introduction to the Paperback Edition

HOWARD WIGHT MARSHALL AND WALTER A. SCHROEDER

During the thirties, a time of severe economic conditions for the American people, much of the rural and small-town work force was out of a job; many headed up the highway to California and distant cities. As part of the New Deal, Franklin Delano Roosevelt created the so-called alphabet-soup agencies to yank us out of the Great Depression and set a new course for the nation. The Work Projects Administration (WPA) was a principal agency in this network. It represented an attempt to provide jobs and to renew goals for people dispirited by the hard times. The American Guide Series, in which this book was originally published in 1941, was but one of many WPA projects.

During the 1930's we began to look sharply at ourselves as Americans and to wonder aloud about the American ideal. Was there something essentially wrong with our still-young political system? Many people were out of work, and nearly the entire country was in a deplorable condition. There was a need to understand the dimensions of the depression and to gauge its severity.

The WPA, through its branch the Farm Security Administration (FSA), set out to interview people across the country, to photograph them, and to write about their lives and labor. The administrator of the FSA's Historical Section, Roy Stryker, recalled that the goal was to "introduce Americans to America." Thus was created the Federal Writers' Project and the concept for a series of guidebooks to each State. These guides would show us the landscape and the people around us—and perhaps bring us closer together in those difficult times.

The Missouri guide was produced under the aegis of the State's Highway Department, but the information gathering and editing was conducted by a staff led by Charles van Ravenswaay, State supervisor of the Missouri Writers' Project. Van Ravenswaay, who has written the Foreword to this reprint of the guide, is a native son, born into a family of early settlers in Boonville. He rose to become an international expert on American art and architecture, and like many Missourians now living and working elsewhere, he has remained loyal to the State.

The guide's aim was to present an unbiased view of Missouri and Missourians. As van Ravenswaay wrote in 1941: "The book is, as its title indicates, a guide, not a commentary. Every effort has been made, not to editorialize, but to present the salient facts.'' This tone, although difficult to achieve, was accomplished and assures that even today the guide is invaluable both as a guide to the State and as a mirror of the times. Because of its attention to facts, some readers will regret not finding glorification of their birthplaces, political legends, and descriptions of the majesty of the Missouri mule—the sort of braggadocio often found in today's guidebooks. Instead, readers will find honest depictions, gracefully crafted, based on field research as well as library sources.

The heart of any guidebook is the map, but today the original maps in the WPA guide are no longer adequate for locating the sites described in the text. For present-day users, then, nothing less than the official Missouri highway map is a necessary accompaniment, particularly since the network of roads has drastically changed and highways have been renumbered, relettered, and renamed.

Maps for understanding regions of the State are also important. The original guide lacked a map showing the different cultural-geographic regions of this diverse State, insiders' places and folk regions such as ''Swampeast Missouri'' and ''Little Dixie.'' The accompanying State map shows regional names currently in use. To these historic folk regions of Missouri have been added other regional designations, almost wholly invented by commercial interests or assertive governmental offices, such as the Mark Twain region, the Green Hills, and the Mineral Area. These regions, so very real in the minds of Missourians, are hard to show cartographically, because they almost always lack clear boundaries and are variously described in popular publications.

Many changes have taken place in Missouri during the forty-five years since the original publication of the WPA guide. There are new ingredients on the landscape, some chinks are now missing, and some features have been rearranged.

Gone, for example, are the historic river front in St. Louis and such obscure artifacts of local importance as the Chariton County Courthouse in Keytesville, laid waste one night by a fire. Fire also gutted R. M. Snyder's commanding bluff-top castle at Hahatonka, which figured prominently in the story of the construction of Bagnell Dam in the early 1930's. Its impressive ruins now form the centerpiece of a popular state park.

And consider the numberless log houses and brick mansions; cast-iron storefronts, diners, small-town movie houses, mills, corner grocery stores, roadside one-pump filling stations, and drugstores with soda fountains; railroad lines and depots; neighborhood saloons, shoe-factory taverns, and beer gardens; logging camps, Indian mounds, barns, covered bridges, Osage-orange hedgerows, stands of hardwood timber, root cellars, Ozark strawberry patches, rail fences, and granges; back alleys and sandlot baseball diamonds. Such words as *diner, fountain,* and *filling station* represent cultural institutions as well as slices of economic history. Just speaking those words—words that seem quaint today— reminds us of a past we have come to miss. But as we have lost these nostalgic features in the cultural landscape, we have been compensated, at least partially, by the addition of new ingredients in both city and countryside.

The give-and-take of landscape change has been visually most dramatic in the State's two largest cities. When the WPA guide was written, the real flight to the suburbs had not yet begun. Since World War II, outmigration from the centers of our cities has been greater in St. Louis than in Kansas City, so that in the mid 1980's, for the first time, the population of the City of St. Louis fell below that of Kansas City. The two-state metropolitan St. Louis area, however, retains a million-plus advantage in total population over the two-state Kansas City area.

Today we think of both of these places as sprawling multicity metropolitan areas, made up of a central city and ever-expanding suburbs. In contrast, Independence and St. Charles are treated in the WPA guide as county-seat towns in their own right, but today Missourians consider them to be integral parts of the Kansas City and St. Louis metropolitan areas, respectively. Raytown, described in the guide as a "cross-roads trading village, population 500," is, in 1985, a mature, tree-shaded middle-class suburb of 33,000 population, completely surrounded by incorporated parts of Kansas City proper.

St. Louis, which had already "turned its back on the river" during the nineteenth century, has continued its inexorable march westward. In 1940 the retail center of the city had moved westward from its nineteenth-century anchor on Fourth Street to the blocks between Sixth and Eleventh; by 1960 it had leapfrogged eight miles west to Clayton; and now, in the 1980's, the retail hub is dispersed among several immense regional shopping centers in the county. Meanwhile, the old downtown is being resuscitated with other kinds of activities. The spectacular Gateway Arch, with its fine Museum of Westward Expansion, holds tight to the spot where those old river-front buildings and empty warehouses, "the trappings of the steamboat era," once stood. A new generation of still-taller office and hotel skyscrapers is being built in the former retail district between the new Cervantes Convention Center and Busch Stadium.

Out in St. Louis County, post–World War II subdivisions for both the working class and the well-to-do have blossomed where corn and wheat once grew and cattle grazed. Yet ironically, the unrestrained spread of suburbanization into the county has preserved the survey lines of the eighteenth-century French common field of Florissant, as well as cadastral lines of Spanish land grants. The old patterns still show through, despite the encroachments of networks of new buildings, city blocks, shopping malls, and streets. A perceptive visitor to Florissant today (population 55,000) should be able to pick out from the sea of suburban tract houses the venerable white-brick church of St. Ferdinand, which served a village of fewer than five hundred when it was built in 1821.

Looking west to Kansas City, the same general picture prevails. There, the State line is almost invisible, and urban sprawl has occurred as much in Kansas as in Missouri. During the postwar years, because of lower taxes in Kansas, many upwardly mobile professionals chose to live in suburban Johnson County, Kansas, but to work in Kansas City, Missouri. Particular changes stand out in Kansas City: the rehabilitation project for the celebrated Union Station is a clear victory for the preservation of that 1914 modified Renaissance colossus; while facing it across the street stands Crown Center, a hotel and retail complex of magnificent modernist architecture, which replaced a "cluttered mass of billboards."

In Kansas City the name of President Harry S. Truman has proliferated across the landscape since the 1950's, as Mark Twain and his characters have permeated the Hannibal region. Truman's name appears and reappears on the metropolitan landscape—Truman Road, the Truman Sports Complex, the Truman Library, the Truman Medical Center, the Truman home, and the Truman family farm at Grandview—along with numerous commercial enterprises capitalizing on the fame of the favorite son.

Below the surface, Kansas City has developed its underground, mined-out limestone bedrock in several ways. In these man-made caves, humidity and temperature hardly ever change. Immense quantities of frozen foods are warehoused there in icy chambers, scientific instruments are calibrated in these naturally controlled environments, a recording studio operates underground, and organizations such as the University of Missouri store archives there.

Railroads still are important in Missouri's two biggest cities. We sometimes imagine railroads to be a thing of the past, as they may be for rural Missourians. But the presence of the railroad is still deeply felt in the cities, where, despite limited passenger service, the yards are busy with trains being hitched together to pull agricultural, commercial, and industrial goods across the country. St. Louis, which continues to be the nation's second-largest railroad center, is still considered to be a big industrial city of the East: like other distressed urban areas, St. Louis, since the 1950's, has suffered declining industrial employment. And although the major meat packers have long since dispersed to other plains cities, Missourians still regard Kansas City as a railroad-built cow town, with important rail and highway routes into the West.

One of Missouri's interesting features is that it grew up with not one but two State-dominating urban areas, peripherally located on the State's eastern and western borders. St. Louis and Kansas City continue to be competitive and divisive forces for Missourians, drawing loyalty as well as trade from the rest of the State and asking Missourians to root for the Cardinals or the Royals, but not for both. At times the geopolitical rivalry in State government between these two giants overwhelms the political process at the smallish capital city. Indeed, Jefferson City ranks a distant twelfth in population. Political power in the State has been increasingly concentrated in the two largest urban areas—while being divided between them at the same time. The reasons are, first, that their share of the State's entire population has risen to two-thirds and, second, that the political power of outstate Missouri has been eroded both by the new 1945 State constitution and by federally mandated legislative redistricting.

Beyond the two big cities, outstate Missouri is a mixture of medium-sized cities, small towns, and rural places. In the 1930's, there was a farmstead for every quarter section (160 acres) of land or less. Today it is closer to one farmstead per section (640 acres), with a proportionate loss in the farm population. Missouri's farm population of 1,125,000 in 1940 had declined to only 345,000 in 1980. Cropland acreage during that period has decreased by two million acres, most of that consisting of land that was submarginal for row crops and has wisely been reverted to pasture and woodland. Since the guide appeared, the number of farms has been cut in half, from 256,000 in 1940 to 118,000 in 1983; nevertheless, Missouri still ranks second in the nation in number of farms, being surpassed only by Texas. And along with this has come a loss of rural institutions—the schoolhouse, the general store, the church.

The arrangement of farmsteads and the rural population has likewise changed. Formerly, farmsteads characteristically were scattered rather regularly across the landscape, but farmers have relocated their new air-conditioned modern houses and mobile homes right up to the blacktop, so that the visual effect is of a spread-out string of houses. And many of the people on what seem to be farmsteads along the new blacktop are, in fact, commuters to jobs in towns or cities, part-time farmers, or exurbanites seeking a better quality of life. Today's new rural houses may be indistinguishable architecturally from houses in suburbia. They stand in great contrast to the earlier "extensive white frame farm houses and native stone barns" described in the WPA guide. These new farmsteads have access to rural water systems, mail delivery virtually to the door, and, of course, television—often conspicuous by that cultural marker of the 1980's, the satellite-dish antenna.

The services that are available in rural towns have changed in response to agricultural change. The typical small Missouri town in 1941 had a bank, an elementary school, a grocery store, a drugstore, a tavern-restaurant, a post office, a beauty parlor, a filling station or two, a movie house, a church or two, a hardware store, a lumberyard, and a machine shop. And the town was home to a few professionals—a lawyer, a doctor, a veterinarian. Today, the functions of the modern small town have diminished significantly. It is now usual to find only a combination grocery store–gas station–drugstore (we call these "convenience stores"), a hardware–auto parts store, an agricultural implement dealership, a tavern or two, and a church. Some small towns, if they are fortunate, still have a post office, but the local bank and elementary school are long gone. Many of the old buildings remain as abandoned artifacts, now the source of oral history and nostalgia, serving as an antique shop or weekend flea market, or refurbished (if only modestly) as a museum for the local historical society.

In certain strategic locations, though, small towns have grown, perhaps because they are within commuting distance of a major city, because they sit at an important highway junction, or because a significant federal project, an industry, or a recreational "theme park" has moved in.

Since the guide was first published, we have experienced an entire generation of building by the Army Corps of Engineers. The guide mentions, as being under construction, only the first Corps project built in Missouri—Lake Wappapello in Wayne County. Today the landscape has been radically altered around the nine additional Corps projects. Though these lakes were originally authorized for flood control, local citizens and politicians have recognized that these lakes are becoming increasingly important as resort and recreational areas. The lake counties in the Ozarks—such as Taney and Stone at Table Rock Lake and Miller, Camden, and Morgan at Lake of the Ozarks—have experienced a doubling or tripling of their resident population in recent years, not to mention the seasonal influx of thousands more visitors. Branson, already a tourist town in 1941 whose "business district is filled with cafés, taverns, drug stores, and novelty shops," has mushroomed and is today a congested hodgepodge of motels, restaurants, and assorted tourist attractions stretching for several miles along its radial highways.

Change in outstate Missouri would not have come so quickly if the State's road network had not been expanded and improved so impressively. In 1940, there were 7,000 miles of asphalt and concrete highways in Missouri; today that figure surpasses 32,000, and most of that increase has come on the supplementary county roads. Today, no place in Missouri is more than five miles from a paved road or blacktop.

The "unmarked, dirt road, impassable when wet," that we encounter in reading the WPA guide is no longer a hurdle to be negotiated in order to reach an out-of-the-way site.

Nevertheless, those roads of the 1930's answered a growing interest in touring by automobile. "Automobile tourist camps," as they are called in the guide, began to appear at strategic points along the major roads. These rustic accommodations of detached buildings, highly individual in design and built of local materials, have since been replaced by standardized motels, often part of a national chain.

As in the other WPA guides, the fifteen numbered "tours" of Missouri are not laid out as round trips. If a traveler were to set out from Lancaster on Tour 8, for example, he would end up at Thayer, on the opposite side of the state, some 352 miles away. Thus, the tours in this guidebook are actually organizational devices to catalog and describe the features of the State.

Today as much as ever, this guidebook lends itself to exploring the State vicariously, if not actually following one of its numbered tours from start to finish. The guidebook has a flavor of adventure, of traveling an unknown road to discover and learn about half-forgotten places with their special histories. There is today a marvelous reawakening of interest in investigating the State's wayside points of interest and its urban architectural landmarks. This trend is apparent in the popularity of journalistic accounts of back-road trips, of photographic books depicting Ozarks scenes and Missouri River towns, and of ethnic celebrations in St. Louis, Bethel, and Hermann. The guidebook addresses this interest by combining a sense of place—geography—and a sense of time—history—whether the particular topic is the experiment of founding a free society in the prairie town of Liberal or the vicissitudes of resource mismanagement in the Ozark timber industry.

Missouri is as much a middle State today as when the guide was written. It is sometimes considered the farthest west of the eastern states and at other times the farthest east of the western states. Its governor participates fully in the conferences of the midwestern and of the southern governors. The guide helps to explain this middle position by tracing the ethnic origins of its settlers and the cultural institutions that they established in Missouri.

Missouri also remains a middle State in terms of economic and social development. "All things considered," the guide concludes, "Missouri's place in the national family seems neither exceptionally high nor exceptionally low." Although in 1980 the State ranked eleventh in the value of its bank assets, it was thirty-fifth in per capita personal income. It was nineteenth in the divorce rate and thirty-sixth in the abortion rate. These rankings show Missourians to be "middle-of-the-roaders," an image suggested in Irving Dilliard's introductory essay, "People and Character," written forty-five years ago.

Missouri is a wonderfully diverse State. It merits the honest depiction of its various places that so far only this guide has provided. It is pleasant to contemplate that a new generation will have the opportunity to explore the State's many urban nooks and rural crannies, thanks to the guidebook's reappearance in paperback.

One challenge to the student of Missouri's heritage today is that swift and numerous changes have taken place all around us. The old recipe of Missouri life continues to be rewritten and given new ingredients. We encounter and hope to understand the alteration and perhaps waning of familiar legends and traditions of Missouri, such as St. Louis blues and Kansas City jazz, barbecue and country ham, the hand-pieced quilt, old-time fiddling, wooden-johnboat building, basket making, and storytelling. Many of the traditional facets of the personality of Missouri are in a state of flux, yet they remain valuable.

We also encounter exciting and demanding scenes, not yet developed, with the rising influence of new groups such as the Asians and Hispanics, each with its own important traditions. Perhaps a future guide will direct us to a Lowland Lao neighborhood in St. Louis or to a Cinco de Mayo celebration in Kansas City. For now, though, the *WPA Guide to 1930s Missouri,* like a good family album with jottings under the snapshots, helps us to understand who and what we are.

University of Missouri-Columbia
October, 1985

A Selected Bibliography

The original field research materials amassed under Charles van Ravenswaay for the WPA Missouri guide project are housed in the Western Historical Manuscripts Collection at the University of Missouri-Columbia (a joint project of the university and the State Historical Society of Missouri). These materials are available for study and use by the public at any of the university's four campuses (Columbia, Kansas City, Rolla, St. Louis).

The references listed below represent a selected updating of the guide's original bibliography (see pp. 596–611). A good deal of work and publishing, of course, has taken place since 1941. Thus, this list is only suggestive. For specific research needs and a more extensive bibliography (available without charge by enclosing a stamped self-addressed mailing packet), contact the Missouri Cultural Heritage Center, University of Missouri (Columbia, Mo., 65211).

Benton, Thomas Hart. *An Artist in America.* 4th revised edition. Columbia, University of Missouri Press, 1983.

Caldwell, Dorothy J. (ed.). *Missouri Historic Sites Catalog.* Columbia, State Historical Society of Missouri, 1963.

Callison, Charles. *Man and Wildlife in Missouri: The History of One State's Treatment of Its Natural Resources.* Jefferson City, Missouri Department of Conservation, 1981.

Chapman, Carl H., and Eleanor F. Chapman. *Indians and Archaeology of Missouri.* Columbia, University of Missouri, Missouri Handbook No. 5, 1972.

Christeson, R. P. (ed.). *The Old-Time Fiddler's Repertory.* Columbia, University of Missouri Press, 1973, 1984. 2 vols.

Conroy, Jack. *The Disinherited.* Westport, Conn., Lawrence Hill, 1982 edition of 1933 original.

——. *The Weed King and Other Stories.* Edited by Douglas C. Wixson. Westport, Conn., Lawrence Hill, 1985.

Denison, Edgar. *Wildflowers of Missouri.* 3d edition. Jefferson City, Missouri Department of Conservation, 1978.

Downey, Bill, *Tom Bass: Black Horseman.* St. Louis, Saddle and Bridle, Inc., 1975.

Erlich, George. *Kansas City, Missouri: An Architectural History, 1926-1976.* Kansas City, Historic Kansas City Foundation, 1979.

Gallaher, Arthur, Jr. *Plainville Fifteen Years Later.* New York, Columbia University Press, 1961.

Gerlach, Russel L. *Settlement Patterns in Missouri: A Study of Population Origin.* Columbia, University of Missouri Press, 1986.

Greene, Lorenzo J.; Gary Kremer; and Anthony Holland. *Missouri's Black Heritage.* St. Louis, Forum Press, 1980.

Keller, Walter D. *The Common Rocks and Minerals of Missouri.* Columbia, University of Missouri Press, Missouri Handbook No. 1, 1961.

Marshall, Howard Wight. *Folk Architecture in Little Dixie: A Regional Culture in Missouri.* Columbia, University of Missouri Press, 1980.

———, and James W. Goodrich (eds.). *The German-American Experience in Missouri.* Columbia, Missouri Cultural Heritage Center, 1985.

Meyer, Duane G. *The Heritage of Missouri.* St. Louis, River City Publishers, 1982.

Mott, Frank Luther (ed.). *Missouri Reader.* Columbia, University of Missouri Press, 1964.

Nagel, Paul C. *Missouri: A Bicentennial History.* New York, W. W. Norton, 1977.

Ohman, Marian M. *Encyclopedia of Missouri Courthouses.* Columbia, University of Missouri Extension Division, 1981.

———. *The History of Missouri Capitols.* Columbia, University of Missouri Extension Division, 1982.

Peterson, Charles E. *Colonial St. Louis: Building a Creole Capital.* St. Louis, Missouri Historical Society, 1949.

Primm, James Neal. *Lion of the Valley: St. Louis, Missouri.* Boulder, Colo., Pruett Publishing Co., 1981.

Rafferty, Milton D. *The Ozarks: Land and Life.* Norman, University of Oklahoma Press, 1980.

Ramsay, Robert L. *Our Storehouse of Missouri Place Names.* Columbia, University of Missouri Press, Missouri Handbook No. 2, 1952, 1982.

Randolph, Vance. *Ozark Folksongs.* Columbia, University of Missouri Press, 1980. 4 vols.

———. *Ozark Superstitions.* New York, Columbia University Press, 1947. Reprinted as *Ozark Magic and Folklore.*

———, and George P. Wilson. *Down in the Holler: A Gallery of Ozark Folk Speech.* Norman, University of Oklahoma Press, 1953.

Reddig, William M. *Tom's Town: Kansas City and the Pendergast Machine.* New York, Harper & Row, 1953; Columbia, University of Missouri Press, 1986.

Reid, Loren. *Hurry Home Wednesday: Growing Up in a Small Missouri Town, 1905-1921.* Columbia, University of Missouri Press, 1978.

Schroeder, Walter A. *Bibliography of Missouri Geography: A Guide to Written Material on Places and Regions of Missouri.* Columbia, University of Missouri Extension Division, 1977.

―――. *Presettlement Prairie of Missouri.* Jefferson City, Missouri Department of Conservation, Natural History Series No. 2, 1981.

Settle, William A., Jr. *Jesse James Was His Name; or Fact and Fiction Concerning the Careers of the Notorious James Brothers of Missouri.* Columbia, University of Missouri Press, 1966; Lincoln, University of Nebraska Press, 1977, paperback.

van Ravenswaay, Charles. *The Arts and Architecture of German Settlements in Missouri: A Survey of a Vanishing Culture.* Columbia, University of Missouri Press, 1977.

West, James. *Plainville, U.S.A.* New York, Columbia University Press, 1945.

FOREWORD

The Missouri Guide Book fills a long apparent
need by providing, in convenient form, a record of
communities large and small as they appear to the
native of the State. The traveler equipped with a
copy of The Guide Book will enjoy an insight into
the history, customs, and general characteristics of
our towns and cities denied the uninformed visitors.

Within this volume also is found information
presented objectively and dispassionately, through
which may be traced the rise of the arts, the sciences,
industry, agriculture, architecture, and other phases
of Missouri's cultural, social, and economic development.

As Governor of Missouri, it is fitting that I
express the appreciation of this State to the Federal
Work Projects Administration for creating The Missouri
Guide Book. As a project, it provided useful employment for many writers; as a publication, it promises
to publicize the many attractions of our State and to
stimulate a wholesome interest among Missourians in
their native State.

Lloyd C Stark

Governor

MISSOURI STATE HIGHWAY DEPARTMENT,
STATE-WIDE SPONSOR OF THE MISSOURI WRITERS' PROJECT

FEDERAL WORKS AGENCY
JOHN M. CARMODY, *Administrator*

WORK PROJECTS ADMINISTRATION
HOWARD O. HUNTER, *Acting Commissioner*
FLORENCE KERR, *Assistant Commissioner*
B. M. CASTEEL, *State Administrator*

Preface

Missourians are notoriously skeptical; they want the facts. *Missouri: A Guide to the "Show Me" State* attempts to carry on the tradition. It presents as many facts about the State as the limited wordage permitted. Because the State is unusually rich in history, because its resources, its people, and its heritage are extremely varied, it has been necessary to make a somewhat arbitrary choice from the wealth of collected material which might have been included. Minor details had to be omitted, descriptions curtailed, interesting legends discarded, for no single volume has covers wide enough apart to contain all the people, places, and things that make up the story of Missouri.

In collecting material for the book, members of the project have had an opportunity to pioneer in the study of certain phases of Missouri's development. Field research has revealed architectural, art, folklore, and music survivals, and historical details hitherto unexplored. The sifting and selection of this material has been a delicate task, more particularly because family, county, and State histories do not always agree, even on such matters as dates; in describing and interpreting events they frequently vary widely. Particularly is this true of historians of the early period of exploration and of the turbulent Civil War years in Missouri. Undoubtedly among the readers of *Missouri: A Guide to the "Show Me" State* there will be some who can shed additional light upon the material presented. Suggestions from these will be welcomed, for through them future editions of the book can be improved.

The book is, as its title indicates, a guide, not a commentary. Every effort has been made, not to editorialize, but to present the salient facts. The book represents in a very real sense a collaboration of the people of the State. Historians, teachers, librarians, and technical experts from every county have given invaluable assistance. Just as important has been the interested co-operation of farmers, business and professional men, old settlers, county officials, newspapermen, and the many individuals who have kindly lent private papers and put up with visits to their homes that this book may be as complete a guide as possible to the State of Missouri.

It would be impossible for the editors to list here all who have contributed toward the making of this book. To some few, however, particular credit is due. The staff of the Missouri Highway Department, official sponsor of the book, has made useful criticism, read endless copy, advised, encouraged, and shown unfailing interest. Maps for the volume were made by John A. Bergman, who was "borrowed" from the Highway Department. Members of the various Chambers of Commerce throughout the State have ferreted out facts, taken pictures, provided statistics, and checked copy with never-ending energy. The staffs of the St. Louis Public Library, the St. Louis Mercantile Library, the St. Louis Art Museum, the Missouri Historical Society, and the State Historical Society of Missouri have given efficiently and courteously whatever assistance was asked.

In addition, gratitude is due the following for their services as consultants and technical advisors: Irving L. Dilliard, of the St. Louis *Post-Dispatch,* who read a large part of the copy, and who wrote the essay on People and Character; Professors Courtney Werner, L. F. Thomas, Frank M. Webster, and W. G. B. Carson, and Assistant Professor John Francis McDermott, all of Washington University; Dean Frank L. Martin, and Professors H. M. Belden, Walter D. Keller, C. T. Pihlblad, Jonas Viles, Maurice G. Mehl, and Jesse E. Wrench, and Assistant Professor M. M. Brashear, all of the University of Missouri; Charles E. Peterson, and John A. Bryan of the National Park Service; Stella M. Drumm, of the Missouri Historical Society; Dr. Kate L. Gregg, of Lindenwood College; Thomas B. Sherman, of the St. Louis *Post-Dispatch;* Paul Alexander, of the Paris *Mercury;* E. A. Mayes, of the State Park Board; Jewell Mayes, Commissioner of the Department of Agriculture; William W. Anderson, of the Missouri State Planning Commission; Irwin T. Bode, of the Missouri State Conservation Commission; Earl H. Shackelford, of the Department of Labor and Industrial Inspection; W. M. Brandt, Secretary of the Central Trades and Labor Union; Martin A. Dillmon, of the St. Louis *Union Labor Advocate;* Richard Pilant, of Granby; Monsignor Charles L. van Tourenhout, and Mr. and Mrs. Jules F. Vallé, of Ste. Genevieve; Francis P. Douglas, of the **KMOX News Room,** St. Louis; Major Albert Bond Lambert, McCune Gill, and Donald D. Parker, of St. Louis; Dr. Edgar Anderson, Geneticist of the Missouri Botanical Garden; the Reverend C. J. Armstrong, of Hannibal; Will Morsey, of Warren County; Mrs. Robert S. Withers, of Liberty; Professor Carl E. Schneider, of Eden Seminary; Professor W. G. Polack, of Concordia Seminary; Harry R. Burke, of the St. Louis *Globe Democrat;* L. A. Kingsbury, of New Franklin; Hazel Price, of Glasgow; Ovid Bell, of Fulton; Mr. and Mrs. Clyde H. Porter, of Kansas City; J. L. Ferguson, of Warrensburg; Edward Sowers, of the

Excelsior Springs *Standard;* Robert McCormick Adams, of Webster Groves; Clarence E. Miller, of the St. Louis Mercantile Library; James Anderson, of the Native Sons of Kansas City Missouri; Judge North Todd Gentry, of Columbia; Paul I. Wellman, of the Kansas City *Star;* John R. Wallace, of Lexington; Robert H. Johnson, of Palmyra; S. A. Burgess, Historian of the Reorganized Church of Jesus Christ of Latter Day Saints, at Independence; and Dr. and Mrs. Herman von Schrenk, of Florissant.

Project workers in many branches of the Division of Public Activities Programs of the WPA have contributed to the interest and factual accuracy of the book. Particular gratitude is due Dr. U. R. Bell, of the Kentucky Writers' Project, and Gene Holcomb, of the Mississippi Writers' Project, who assisted in an early period. We also thank James W. Gilman, Parker T. van de Mark, and James R. Phelan of the Illinois Writers' Project, for their help in the first stages of the book, and the Missouri Historical Records Survey, which did much to make the Guide possible. The sketches which enliven the pages of the Guide were provided by the Missouri Art Project, under the direction of James D. McKenzie. The loyal interest of Eunice L. Stacer, Dorothy Faye Davis, Alma M. Gilbert, Jessie Eckles, and Werner Genot, of the Missouri Writers' Project, carried them through what must frequently have been not only exacting but exceedingly tedious work. The never failing assistance of Billie S. Jensen, project editor, who patiently served as advisor and critic, is gratefully acknowledged.

Final work on the Guide was done with the editorial co-operation of Harold Rosenberg, of the WPA Writers' Program.

CHARLES VAN RAVENSWAAY
State Supervisor
Missouri Writers' Project

Contents

Part I. The General Background

Part II. Principal Cities

Part III. Tours

Part IV. Appendices

Illustrations

"OLD MISSOURI"
(*Between pages* 32 *and* 33)

Stump Speaker
Panel from Missouri Mural, by
  Thomas Hart Benton
Pioneer Life in Missouri
Interior of Flatboat
Col. Daniel Boone
Massacre of Mormons at Haun's
  Mill

Jesse James' Reception
Portrait of Dred Scott
The Battle of Lexington
Jefferson City
St. Joseph
Louisiana Purchase Exposition
Missouri Dawn, by William E. L.
  Bunn

Mark Twain at Hannibal

THE MISSOURI AND THE MISSISSIPPI
(*Between pages* 62 *and* 63)

The Missouri River
Up Stream on the Mississippi
The Levee at St. Louis
Kansas City
St. Louis Levee
Municipal Docks, St. Louis
"Sternwheeler"
The Grand Republic

Interior of the Grand Republic
Modern Excursion Boat
Steamboat and Eads Bridge, St.
  Louis
Airview of the Mississippi
Lock and Dam across Upper Missis-
  sippi
Flood Control

Flooded Farmland

INDUSTRY
(*Between pages* 92 *and* 93)

Strip Coal Mining, Macon
Electric Shovel Loading Lead Ore
Ore Train
Chat Piles
Zinc Mine
Sheffield Steel Plant

Wine Vats, St. Louis
Champagne Cellar, St. Louis
Bottling Beer
Brew Kettles
In a St. Louis Shoe Factory
Loading a Ceramics Kiln

Maps

General Information

Railroads: Atchison, Topeka & Santa Fe Ry.; Alton R.R.; Chicago, Burlington & Quincy R.R.; Chicago Great Western R.R.; Chicago, Milwaukee, St. Paul & Pacific R.R.; Chicago, Rock Island & Pacific Ry.; Kansas City Southern Ry.; Missouri-Kansas-Texas Lines (Katy); Missouri Pacific Lines; Quincy, Omaha & Kansas City R.R.; St. Louis-San Francisco Ry. (Frisco); St. Louis Southwestern Ry. (Cotton Belt); Wabash R.R. Railroads entering the State only at terminals: At St. Louis—Baltimore & Ohio R.R.; Chicago & Eastern Illinois Ry.; New York Central System (Big Four); Illinois Central System; Illinois Terminal R.R.; Louisville & Nashville R.R.; Mobile & Ohio R.R.; New York, Chicago & St. Louis Ry. (Nickel Plate Road); Pennsylvania R.R.; Southern Railway System. At Kansas City—Union Pacific R.R.

Highways: Five major highways cross the State from N. to S., five from E. to W., two from NE. to SW., all paved. A network of roads brings every point in the State within ten miles or less, airline, of a national or State highway. Federal gasoline tax 2½¢, State, 2¢; additional tax in many incorporated towns.

Bus Lines: Affiliated Greyhound Lines; Missouri Transit Lines; M. C. Foster Bus Line; Missouri, Kansas & Oklahoma Trailways; Missouri Pacific Trailways; Missouri-Arkansas Coach Lines; Santa Fe Trailways; De Luxe Motor Stages; Tri-State Transit Co.; Crown Coach Lines; Jefferson Transportation Co.; Interstate Transit Lines; Burlington Trailways; Kansas and Oklahoma Coach Lines; All-American Bus Lines; Arkansas Motor Coaches; numerous small lines throughout the State.

Air Lines: American Airlines (New York to Los Angeles) stop at St. Louis en route SW. and W.; Mid-Continent Airlines at Kansas City and St. Joseph; Transcontinental & Western Air, Inc. (New York to Los Angeles) at St. Louis and Kansas City; Chicago and Southern

Air Lines (Chicago to New Orleans) stop at St. Louis; Marquette Air Lines (St. Louis to Detroit) headquarters at St. Louis; Braniff Airways at Kansas City. Charter service available at St. Louis, Kansas City, Columbia, Hannibal, Jefferson City, Joplin, St. Joseph, Springfield, and other points.

Waterways: Barge and towboat service is maintained on the Mississippi River from St. Louis. Barges run N. to the Illinois River, thence to Chicago. The Missouri River is navigable from West Alton, Mo., to Kansas City, Mo., with barge service maintained. The Streckfus Company and the Golden Eagle Packet Company, operating from St. Louis, maintain excursion steamboat service on the Mississippi from spring until fall.

Traffic Regulations: Motorists govern their own speed, consistent with safety, to environs of cities and towns. Highways are well marked. Each city and town makes its own traffic regulations; speed limit signs are usually posted at corporate limits. Drivers—minimum age 16—must have license from their home State. Watch for signs along highway warning of "open range" (country in which livestock is permitted to run free). Extreme caution should be used in passing school busses. Detailed information available from State Highway Department, automobile clubs, and chambers of commerce.

Accommodations: Acceptable meals and living quarters, from large hotels to small tourist and trailer camps, in all sections. Hotel or camping facilities at most State Parks, National Forests, and other recreational areas. There is one dude ranch, open all year, 4 m. west of Birch Tree on US 60, then north a short distance on supplementary route M.

General Tourist Service: Local chambers of commerce, the State Chamber of Commerce at Kansas City, automobile clubs, hotels, and service stations supply maps and information on travel, resorts, accommodations, and road conditions. The Ozark Playgrounds Association, Joplin, and the Lake of the Ozarks Association, Lake Ozark, provide information on the Ozark recreational region. Traffic regulations may be obtained from the State Highway Department; game laws from the State Conservation Commission; and State park information from the State Park Board, all at Jefferson City.

Climate and Equipment: In summer, light clothing is worn in every section, although nights in the highlands are cool and topcoats are useful. In winter heavy clothing is necessary in all parts of the State.

Equipment for hiker, hunter, swimmer, or picnicker may be obtained in all cities and near most recreational areas.

State Parks: Alley Spring (Shannon County), from State 19 on State 106; Arrow Rock (Saline County), from US 40 on State 41; Dr. Edmund A. Babler Memorial (St. Louis County), from US 50 on State 109; Bennett Spring (Laclede and Dallas Counties), from US 66 on State 64; Big Lake (Holt County), from US 59 on State 111; Big Oak Tree (Mississippi County), on County A; Big Spring (Carter County), from US 60 on State 103; Chesapeake (Lawrence County), on State 14; Crowder (Grundy County), from US 65 on State 6; Cuivre River (Lincoln County), from US 61 on State 47; Lake of the Ozarks (Miller and Camden Counties), from US 54 on County D and S; Lewis and Clark (Buchanan County), from US 59 on State 45; Mark Twain (Monroe County), from State 26 on State 107; Meramec (Franklin County), from US 66 on State 114; Montauk (Dent County), from State 32 on State 119; Montserrat (Johnson County), on US 50; Pershing (Linn County), on US 36; Roaring River (Barry County), from State 37 on State 112; Round Spring (Shannon County), on State 19; Sam A. Baker (Wayne County), from State 34 on State 101; Sequiota (Greene County), on US 60 and US 65; Van Meter (Saline County), from State 41 on State 122; Wallace (Clinton County), from US 69 on State 121; Washington (Washington County), on State 21; Fort Zumwalt (St. Charles County), on US 40.

State Wild Life Refuges: Deer Run (Reynolds County), on State 21; Indian Trail (Dent County), from State 19 on State 117.

State Reservation (not developed): Rockwoods (St. Louis County), from US 66 or US 50, on County B.

Federal Wild Life Refuges: Squaw Creek (Holt County), State 118; Swan Lake (Chariton County), county roads from US 36; Mingo Swamp (Stoddard County), State 51.

National Forests: Clark, in southeastern portion of State, consisting of the Meramec, St. Francois, Wappapello, and Fristoe divisions; Mark Twain, in the south central portion of the State, consisting of the Gasconade, Gardner, Pond Fork, and Table Rock divisions (*see State Highway Map*).

Other Recreational Sections: Arcadia Valley (Iron County), State 21, 32, and 70; Black River Region (Reynolds, Wayne, and Butler

Counties), US 60 and 67, and State 21 and 53; Eldorado Springs (Cedar County), US 54, and State 64 and 82; Excelsior Springs (Clay County), US 69 and State 10; Gasconade River Region (Pulaski, Phelps, Maries, Osage, and Gasconade Counties), US 50, 63, 66, and State 17, and 28; Lake Taneycomo (Taney County), US 65, and State 76, 80, 86, and 123; Osage River Region (St. Clair and Cedar Counties), US 54, and State 13, 64, and 82; and the Shepherd of the Hills Country (Stone and Taney Counties), State 13, 39, 44, 80, and 86.

Fire Prevention: Fire hazard is considerable in both wooded areas and prairie regions. Tourists and campers are warned against dropping lighted matches and cigarettes. State law and national forest regulations require that fires be controlled, and all campfires extinguished before leaving.

State Hunting and Fishing Laws (digest): Licenses to hunt and fish are required of all persons over 17. Combination hunting and fishing permit, $2.50; hunting permit, $2; fishing permit, $1. Additional fees for non-residents of Missouri. Licenses obtainable by residents of St. Louis at License Collector's office at City Hall, and at leading sporting goods stores; by non-residents, at City Hall only. Outside St. Louis, from county clerks and appointed agents. Information on open and closed season, bag limits, etc., supplied where license is obtained.

Liquor Regulations: State law requires closing of liquor establishments from 1:30-6 a.m. weekdays; midnight Saturday to midnight Sunday. Municipalities may shorten hours of sale. By package only in cities under 20,000. Sale to minors forbidden.

Miscellaneous: Digging in archeological sites, picking flowers, or chopping trees in State and national forests and parks is prohibited; also the destruction of trees and shrubs along highways. No formations or geological specimens may be broken from caves in State parks.

Admission to Private Houses: Only a few houses in the State are maintained as museums and open to the public during stated hours. The majority are "open upon application," that is, by invitation of the owners. These Missourians are happy to receive the courteous visitor, even though he may be a stranger, provided that he appears at a reasonable hour, preferably in the mid-afternoon, and does not stay too long. Houses described in this book as "private" are not open to the public.

What to Eat in Missouri: In Missouri, as in other States where entertaining in one's own home is a tradition, the food in private homes generally excels that in restaurants. Local cookery is a happy blend of various racial traditions. The French have contributed intricate sauces and soups, and the wide use of vegetables and native herbs. Certain families still serve *crêpes* on the proper feast days, and croquignoles. German immigrants have introduced cheese cake, potato cakes, wienerschnitzel, smoked sausage, and an endless variety of Christmas cookies. The South has added beaten biscuits, pork sausage, smoked hams, spring greens, and corn dodgers. River catfish is frequently served, as well as Ozark trout and bass. Several varieties of exceptionally fine apples, Jonathan, Grimes Golden, Red and Golden Delicious, and the piquant "Lady Apple," can be purchased from roadside stands in many portions of the State.

Calendar of Annual Events

JANUARY

No fixed date	at St. Louis	American Artists Exhibit
No fixed date	at St. Louis	Orchid Display, Missouri Botanical Garden

FEBRUARY

First	at St. Joseph	Clover and Prosperity Conference
No fixed date	at St. Louis	Golden Gloves Boxing Tournament
No fixed date	at Kansas City	Hospital Charity Ball
No fixed date	at Kansas City	Better Homes and Flower Show
No fixed date	at Springfield	Creative Arts Conference for Southwest Missouri High School Students

MARCH

Seventeenth	at Rolla	St. Patrick's Day Celebration
Last week	at Columbia	State High School Basketball Tournament
Late	at St. Louis	Mississippi Valley Kennel Club All-Breed Dog Show
No fixed date	at Kansas City	National Intercollegiate Basketball Tournament
No fixed date	at St. Louis	Ozark A.A.U. Boxing Championship
No fixed date	at Kansas City	International Food Fair
No fixed date	at St. Louis	Greater St. Louis Flower and Garden Show
No fixed date	at Kansas City	Beaux Arts Ball
No fixed date	at Springfield	All Ozark Artists Exhibit

APRIL

Third	at St. Joseph	Pony Express Commemoration
First week	at Cape Girardeau	Midwestern Folk Drama Festival
Midmonth	at Columbia	State High School Debate Tournament
Third week	at Jefferson City	Missouri Rural School Exhibit
Last week	at Joplin	Fiesta
Last week	at Columbia	Missouri Interscholastic Week
No fixed date	at Springfield	Southwest Missouri High School Students' Music Festival
No fixed date	at Columbia	Missouri State Historical Society Meeting and Banquet
No fixed date	at Kansas City	Negro Fashion Show
No fixed date	at Kansas City	Sportsmen's Horse Show and Exposition
No fixed date	at St. Louis	Fontbonne College Horse Show

MAY

First Sunday	at St. Louis	Flower Service at Christ Church
Fourth-tenth	at Warrensburg	National Music Week
First week	at Columbia	University of Missouri Journalism Week
Early	at St. Joseph	Apple Blossom Festival
Pentecost Monday	at Warrenton	Schuetzenfest
Third Sunday	at Starkenburg	Pilgrimage to Shrine of Our Lady of Sorrows
Last two weeks	at St. Louis	Iris Show at Missouri Botanical Garden
Twenty-sixth-twenty-seventh	at Poplar Bluff	Ozark Jubilee
Last week	at Joplin	Smile Girl Contest
No fixed date	at Excelsior Springs	Midwest Bridge Tournament
No fixed date	at St. Louis	Spring Horse Show
No fixed date	at Cape Girardeau	May Festival
No fixed date	at St. Louis	Hole - In - One Golf Tournament
No fixed date	at Kansas City	Heart of America Good Will Golf Tournament
No fixed date	at Springfield	Rodeo

JUNE

First Sunday	at St. Louis	Rose Garden Display at Missouri Botanical Garden
First Thursday after Trinity Sunday	at Ste. Genevieve	Feast of Corpus Christi Procession
First Sunday after Trinity Sunday	at Florissant	Feast of Corpus Christi Procession
Commencement week	at Druesdale Farms near Columbia	Christian College Horse Show
Last week	at Arcadia	Methodist Assembly (three weeks) begins
No fixed date	at St. Joseph	Municipal Opera
No fixed date	at St. Louis and Kansas City alternately	Missouri Golf Championship Tournament
No fixed date	at Grain Valley	Sni- A - Bar Farm Demonstrations

JULY

No fixed date	at Kansas City	Kansas City Golf Open Tournament

AUGUST

First week	at Vichy	Revival Meetings at Church of God Camp Grounds
Last two weeks	at Sedalia	Missouri State Fair
Third week	near Stockton	Fox Hunt
No fixed date	California	Moniteau County Fair
No fixed date	at Kahoka	Clark County Fair
No fixed date	at St. Louis	Water Lily Display at Missouri Botanical Garden
No fixed date	at Dover	"August Meeting" of the Christian Church
No fixed date	at Butler	Little Bit and Bridle Show
No fixed date	at St. Louis	Municipal Rowing Regatta
No fixed date	at Charleston	Watermelon Festival

AUGUST OR SEPTEMBER

No fixed date	at Eldon	Lake of the Ozarks Horse Show

SEPTEMBER

First week	at Fulton	Horse and Cattle Show and Street Fair
First week	at St. Joseph	Four-State Harvest Festival
Second Sunday	at Starkenburg	Pilgrimage to Shrine of Our Lady of Sorrows
Early	at Jackson	Homecoming Celebration
Twelfth-fifteenth	at Kearney	Missouri Valley Fox Hunters' Association Fox Hunt
No fixed date	at Kansas City	Guadelupe Fiesta (Mexican Colony)
No fixed date	at Kansas City	Outdoor Art Fair
No fixed date	at St. James	Grape Festival and Homecoming
No fixed date	at Concordia	Fall Festival
No fixed date	at Excelsior Springs	Mulesta

SEPTEMBER OR OCTOBER

No fixed date	at Springfield	Ozark Empire Fair (regional)

OCTOBER

First	at Mountain Grove	National Egg Laying Contest (52 weeks) begins
First week	at St. Louis	National Horse Show
First week	at St. Joseph	Baby Beef and Pig Show
First Sunday	near Salem	Convention of Christian Harmony Singing School
First Tuesday after first Monday	at St. Louis	Veiled Prophet's Parade
Night after parade	at St. Louis	Veiled Prophet's Ball
Twenty-sixth	at St. Louis	National Home Show
Last week	at Columbia	Farmers' Week, College of Agriculture, University of Missouri
No fixed date	at Cape Girardeau	Southwest Missouri Teachers' Association Convention
No fixed date	at Benton	Neighbor Day
No fixed date	at Joplin	Tri-State Kennel Club Show
No fixed date	at Lake of the Ozarks	Fishing Rodeo

No fixed date	at Kansas City	American Royal Horse Show
No fixed date	at Farm Valley	Sni - A - Bar Farm Demonstrations

NOVEMBER

First	at Taos	All Souls' Eve Graveyard Procession
First Sunday	at St. Louis	Chrysanthemum Shows, Missouri Botanical Garden and Jewel Box
Thanksgiving (odd year)	at Columbia	Homecoming Football Game
Twenty-second	at St. Joseph	Christmas Parade
Late	at St. Louis	Automobile Show
Thirtieth	at Hannibal	Mark Twain's Birthday Celebration
No fixed date	at Kansas City	Automobile Show

DECEMBER

Sixth	at Taos	Feast of St. Nicholas Celebration
Thirty-first	at Ste. Genevieve and Old Mines	La Guignolée Festival
Thirty-first	at New Hamburg	German New Year Festival
Late	at St. Louis	Silver Skates Tournament
No fixed date	at St. Louis	Poinsettia Displays, Jewel Box and Missouri Botanical Garden

PART I
The General Background

People and Character

by IRVING L. DILLIARD

THE spare Ozark hillman, with his rabbit gun and dog, is a Missourian. So is the weathered open-country farmer; the prosperous cotton planter; the subsistence sharecropper with his stairsteps family; the drawling sawmill hand; the scientific orchardist reading his bulletins from the fruit experiment stations; the lead miner; the hustling small-town merchant; the Kansas City business man; the St. Louis industrialist with one eye on Jefferson City and the other on Washington; the smiling filling station attendant who talks to everyone crossing the continent; the silent riverman who lives in a shanty boat and sees almost nobody—all are Missourians. Most of them say "neether," some say "nuther," and a few in the fashionable residential sections affect the Atlantic seaboard's "nyther."

Missourians have come from unnumbered places—from the State's unusually large group of bordering neighbors: Illinois, Iowa, Nebraska, Kansas, Oklahoma, Arkansas, Tennessee, and Kentucky; from Ohio, Pennsylvania, New York, and New England. They have come from the Carolinas and from Virginia—Howard County is a "Little Virginia"—and there are other counties which are transplantations of peoples and habits of life from the Mother South. Missouri has fifth and sixth and seventh generation stock, as permanent as the rocks everywhere in its boundaries. But it also has, if to a much lesser extent, migrants here today and gone tomorrow.

The State is an amalgam of Old World ingredients. It is German at vine-draped Bethel, immaculate Hermann, quiet Washington with its bright gardens, and Dutzow which the Berlin Emigration Society founded in 1832. German customs prevail in the white frame houses of New Hamburg, and Altenburg today is not unlike the religious colony which 600 Lutheran Saxons established more than a century ago. Westphalia keeps the name of the solid folk who settled along the Big Maries River. Waldensians developed Verona, and Bavarians built the homes on the hillside at Rich Fountain. Ste. Genevieve, St. Louis, and Old Mines are French in origin. Hawk Point is Bohemian. Taos is Belgian; Vienna, Irish. Other communities have Scotch-Irish, Welsh, Swiss, and Portuguese backgrounds. The wines of Rosati are pressed from grapes tended by Italians. St. Louis has its Dago Hill, its Kerry Patch, its Baden and German South Side; its Czechs and Bohemians,

3

its families from the changing subdivisions of the Balkan peninsula; its closely packed, happy-go-lucky Negro sections, exulting in Joe Louis, and proud of Marian Anderson and Paul Robeson and swingband leaders.

The countryside of Missouri is as varied as its people. It is the half-wild, rugged, valley-cut Ozark plateau worn down from ancient mountain heights, where darkness drops quickly on cabin dooryards. It is the rich delta of the "boot heel," where great cypress trees are still coming down to make cotton acreage on the State's last agricultural frontier. It is blue-grass pasture and rolling orchard and the checkerboard of wheat and corn prairie. It is eroded bluff country which follows the waterways and the alluvial bottom land that fringes them. It is far-spreading areas marked by towering remains of mining operations, vast mountains by day and ghostly shapes in the moonlight. It is mile on mile of municipal asphalt and two-family flats and apartment houses, of stores, and office buildings and warehouses.

Missouri is a network of great rivers and magnificent streams. The Father of Waters washes every inch of the eastern boundary from Keokuk to below Caruthersville. The milk chocolate Missouri goes ceaselessly about its age-old task of transporting the sunrise slope of the Rocky Mountains to the Gulf of Mexico. Always cold, the turbulent Current River falls seven feet to the mile. Here, too, flow the misnamed Black River, bright and clear, with its fishing pools and stave mills; the Gasconade, blue-green and bluff-walled, favorite subject of artists and photographers; the Grand River, the White, the Big Piney, the Little Piney, the St. Francis, the Meramec, the Osage, named for the Indians who lived along its banks in the 1700s.

Missouri has mighty springs that start rivers full grown, and dazzling caves which underground watercourses sculptured eons ago. Big Spring near Van Buren, rushing from its limestone cliff, is one of the great sights of outdoor America. In the first room of Meramec Cavern 300 automobiles may be parked. Through Missouri Caverns the Lost River searches its way to the light. In other caves are wonderful chambers, and stalagmites and stalactites hundreds of feet underground.

In Maytime the wild crab blooms in Missouri. June and July see the tasseled corn reaching higher at the end of each day. Its Indian Summer is the best in the world—when minted pumpkins are piled among the fodder tepees and sheep crop the late grass and the woods are scarlet and gold and purple and brown; when the valleys are filled with white mist in the mornings and steeped with blue haze as the sun sinks. Missouri has zero weather, too, and driving, swirling, drifting snow from the Northwest that covers fences and hides rural mail boxes and packs in the city streets. It has high wind blowing dust from Kansas and Oklahoma; long weeks of drouth when gardens droop and pastures turn brown and ponds recede. It has day after day of soaking rain which sends rivers on rampages and bottom dwellers to higher ground.

Doves and quail and pheasants are at home in Missouri, and ducks and geese and great flocks of strutting turkeys; flashing cardinals and screaming bluejays, larks and thrushes and scores of songsters; circling hawks and wheeling buzzards. Black bass and fighting smallmouthed bass, goggle eye, rainbow trout, perch, blue gills, crappie, and channel cat are caught in its streams, where turtles sun themselves on logs and bullfrogs croak after dark. In its woods are rabbits and squirrels, muskrats and raccoons, opossums and minks and foxes; also occasional bobcats and now and then a wolf. Deer are on the increase. Saddle and draft horses are raised on model breeding farms, and Missouri's mule, tough-skinned hybrid holding its own as a beast of heavy burden even against the coming of machinery, is world famous. The intelligent Missouri hound dog is known to sportsmen throughout the Nation.

Hickory and elm and cedar stand around Rolla; oak and pawpaw and cottonwood between Cane Creek and Cabool; cypress and maple and gum below Poplar Bluff; pine and hawthorn and redbud and dogwood along the Henry Shaw Gardenway; sassafras and sumac on countless hills. Acres of peonies spread around Sarcoxie; roses and dahlias and four o'clocks crowd the German gardens at Washington; blazing hollyhocks blow in the wind on Cardiff Hill. And the State is everywhere daubed with wake robin, skunk cabbage, bluebells, wild hyacinth, bloodroots and Jack-in-the-pulpit in spring; with larkspur, pale blue chickory, cornflowers, and black-eyed Susan; with Queen Anne's lace, dog fennel, pennyroyal, golden rod, and mallows in summer and autumn.

Missouri's eating is as good as it comes. Boone County ham steaks and red ham gravy, ham baked in milk, barbecued ribs and backbone, authentic country sausage and genuine head cheese; fried chicken and baked chicken and chicken pie and dumplings and chicken soup, eggs from the henhouse and bacon from the smokehouse; sauerkraut with squabs, and turnips with spareribs, spring greens from the yard and roadside, and green beans with fat pork—bush beans as long as they last and then long pole beans until frost. Missouri tables are loaded with dish on dish of berries—strawberries, blackberries, raspberries, floating in cream; with Jonathans, Grimes Goldens, Winesaps, Black Twigs, Delicious; apple pie, apple cobbler, apple strudel, baked apples and fried apples; homegrown tomatoes and watermelons and horseradish grown in the country's horseradish center; an endless number of pickles, always including pickled peaches and "end-of-the-garden"; vast varieties of jellies and preserves; persimmons sweetened and whitened by frost; popovers, wheatcakes and honey, piping hot biscuits and melting butter and molasses; fruit shortcake always with biscuit dough; cornbread from yellow meal without so much as one grain of sugar.

Missouri has given American politics some of its most characteristic types: "Old Bullion" Thomas Hart Benton and his *Thirty Years' View;* "Silver Dick" Bland going back to Congress election after election from the Ozarks to work for free coinage of silver; Edward Bates, Lincoln's trusted Attorney-General; and Franklin P. Blair, battling the hated "test oath." The corncob pipe and linen duster of Francis Marion Cockrell, Confederate soldier, were known to the Senate from 1875 to 1905. "Gum Shoe Bill" Stone voted against the declaration of war in 1917. Champ Clark occupied the Speaker's rostrum during the World War years, while James A. Reed laid on the lash from the Senate floor. Whisky Ring scandals, Ed Butler and the Boodle Ring, Tom Pendergast in Kansas City, are other configurations familiar in the American political scene; as well as Lloyd C. Stark and Maurice M. Milligan leading an aroused citizenry against bossism. So, too, William Henry Hatch devoting his eight terms in the House of Representatives to creating the Bureau of Animal Husbandry and government-maintained agricultural experiment stations. Behind these personages lies the frontier democracy which George Caleb Bingham painted and upon which Mark Twain meditated.

Missouri's literature has been rich and varied—*Tom Sawyer,* and *Little Boy Blue; The Crisis, The Shepherd of the Hills, The Voice of Bugle Ann,* and *West of the Water Tower. Reedy's Mirror* introduced American readers to Lord Dunsany and Conrad and Galsworthy, and presented for the first time such native writers as Zoe Atkins, Fannie Hurst, Edgar Lee Masters, John Gould Fletcher, Sara Teasdale, Julia Peterkin and Orrick Johns, many of them Missourians. William Torrey Harris' *Journal of Speculative Philosophy* printed the first English translations of works of Hegel and Fichte and Schelling, and afforded the setting for the literary debut of John Dewey, William James and Josiah Royce.

Missouri journalism has included Elijah P. Lovejoy, the abolitionist editor who became a martyr in the cause of freedom; Carl Schurz of the *Westliche Post;* Joseph B. McCullagh of the *Globe-Democrat,* who pioneered in war reporting during the Civil War; Joseph Pulitzer, who crusaded through his *Post-Dispatch,* and William Rockhill Nelson, who built up and beautified his city with the *Kansas City Star.* Henry M. Stanley, Augustus Thomas, and Theodore Dreiser worked as reporters in St. Louis where a young man named Fiorello LaGuardia obtained an assignment to tell St. Louis newspapers about the war in Cuba. Many rural newspapers have been models of their kind, and these include a fascinating group of names— The Clinton *Eye,* The Ashland *Bugle,* The Tarkio *Avalanche,* The

Eminence *Current Wave,* the Jackson *Cash-Book,* The Illmo *Jimpli-cute,* and the Linn *Unterrified Democrat.*

The people of Missouri keep their heritage in play-party games, candy pullings, pie socials and box suppers and wiener roasts. They have barn dances with fiddlers sawing away by lamplight; auctions, carnivals, medicine shows, home-comings, old settler gatherings, and family reunions with cousins and uncles and aunts from far and near. They bring the products of their skill to county fairs, specimens from field and orchard and barnlot and housewife's kitchen. They fill cathedrals and fashionable churches and village meeting houses; they go to revivals and Sunday School picnics and prayer meetings. Now neon-lighted movies are everywhere, but showboats are still playing *Over the Hill to the Poorhouse.* Fourth of July at Edgar Springs finds a speaker extolling the virtues of democracy, and the crowd participating in the hog-calling contest, the horseshoe-pitching tournament, and the races. Scott County's annual Neighbor Day has a baby show, contests, and exhibitions. At the yearly singing convention at Cedar Gap folks come down from the hills with baskets of food to chant the hymns of their fathers through the whole of a June day. Masked revelers celebrate La Guignolée at Ste. Genevieve; German families at Washington eat herring salad on Christmas Eve so they "will never be in want."

Missouri's places remember people of many kinds of importance. In Franklin a youth named Kit Carson tired of work in a saddlery shop and ran away across the Santa Fe Trail. In Columbia thirty-one-year-old Abraham Lincoln wooed Mary Todd in 1840. Arrow Rock and its old tavern come down from covered wagon and ox-team days. Ed Howe drew the portrait of Bethany in his *Story of a Country Town.* In Springfield, where the streets are aisles of gold in autumn, Wild Bill Hickok served as a Union scout, and in the Battle of Wilson Creek General Nathaniel Lyon was killed. Boonville has Thespian Hall, oldest theater building west of the Alleghenies; and Washington its zither and corncob pipe factories. Independence had hardly recovered from the Mormon warfare when it was in the midst of the guerrilla raids of the Civil War. In Lexington inscriptions on cemetery stones record migrations from the Atlantic seaboard and across the Atlantic. The grave of "Peg Leg" Shannon of the Lewis and Clark expedition is in Palmyra. St. Joseph saw William H. Russell start his colorful, if unsuccessful, Pony Express, and was the scene of Field's poem, "Lover's Lane, St. Joe." At Lebanon a preacher named Harold Bell Wright began to write his stories.

Mark Twain was born in a cabin in the hamlet of Florida; "Black Jack" Pershing on a farm near Laclede; George Washington Carver, Tuskegee's great research scientist, of slave parents near Diamond Grove; William Pope McArthur, hydrographer, first surveyor of the

Pacific coast, in Ste. Genevieve; Tex Rickard and Courtney Ryley Cooper in Kansas City. Bishop Quayle was born of Manx parents in Parkville; Thomas Hart Benton, the artist, in Neosho; the Neibuhr brothers in Wright City. The list of native sons and daughters expands and became more varied, including Victor Clarence Vaughan, distinguished medical educator, conductor of the first American bacteriological laboratory, born at Mount Airy; Ginger Rogers, and the turfman, Samuel Clay Hildreth, born in Independence; Marion Talley, born in Nevada, Rupert Hughes, born in Lancaster; Glenn Frank, born in Queen City; James Cash Penney, chain-store magnate, born near Hamilton; F. W. Taussig, who ferried the Mississippi on the way to his chair in economics at Harvard; Bernarr McFadden, born near Mill Springs; and Cole Younger and Robert Dalton and Jesse Woodson James.

Men from other soil have since the beginning joined in making Missouri what it is. Father De Smet carried his faith into the wilderness. White-haired Daniel Boone rounded out here his long life on the frontier. Dr. John Sappington dispensed his anti-fever pills to Missouri malaria victims; and Audubon tramped the forest in search of new birds. Young Robert E. Lee built jetties in the Mississippi to save St. Louis Harbor; and U. S. Grant was stationed in Missouri posts. John Wilkes Booth played stock on the stage of Ben De Bar's theater; while Washington University's Greek and Latin teacher, Sylvester Waterhouse, urged business men to develop the inland waterways. Louis D. Brandeis began practicing law a stone's throw from the old courthouse in St. Louis. Thorstein Veblen, taking refuge in the University of Missouri, wrote his mordant criticism of modern social institutions.

The history of America speaks through the things and events that have made Missouri—through the creak of high-wheeled wagon trains grinding up the Boon's Lick Trail; through Portage des Sioux still renting common fields it obtained from the King of Spain; through the black-robed missionaries and bushwhackers, jolly flatboatmen and impetuous duelists on Bloody Island; the frontier library of August Chouteau with volumes of Rousseau, Diderot, and Voltaire brought from France. Along these shores the *Natchez* raced the *Robert E. Lee;* and here Louis Sullivan built his pioneer skyscraper, the Wainwright Building. Carl Wimar's Indian paintings, Joe Jones' murals of wheat harvests, Carl Milles' green sculptures of the meeting of the Mississippi and the Missouri, call to mind at one time the State and the country as a whole. Enormous shoe factories, huge department stores, Kansas City's great Union Station and vast livestock market; co-operative creameries, closely tended kitchen gardens, basket and chair-bottom weavers, tobacco fields, patches of cane for molasses, and cross-roads country stores, join Missouri to the life of Eastern big cities, the cattle-raising West, and the rural South. George Graham Vest moved a jury with his eulogy to the hound dog "Old Drum"; and, today, in a typical metropolitan setting, 10,000 persons listen to *The Chocolate Soldier* at the moonlight-flooded stadium of the St. Louis Municipal Opera. From Maine to California, Americans have sung Missouri's "Joe Bowers," "St. Louis Blues," "Frankie and Johnny" and "Way Down in Missouri."

Missouri is the delight of those who fancy place names. Among its offerings are Pumpkin Center, Jonesburg, Grubville, and Owls Bend; Charity, Hope, Wisdom, and Worth; Fair Play, Freedom, Liberty, and Loyalty. Clever, Handy, Noble, Peculiar, and Wise; Liberal and Radical, Sleeper and Pioneer, Novelty and Competition, Joy and Romance; Advance, Half Way, Eight Mile, Ten Mile, and Seventy Six; Sinkin, Sank, Aid, Rescue, Success, and Safe; Ponder, Kidder, Braggadocio, and Huzzah; Boss, Gang, Racket, Foil, and Paydown; Solo, Cyclone and Hurricane; Protem, Veto, and Stet; Elijah, Cato, Napoleon, and Venus. Also Bearcreek, Birdsong, and Blue Eye; Deepwater, Doe Run, and Hawk Point; Musselford, Pansy, and Red Bird; Bado and Bem, Dawn and Day, Impo and Ink; Luna, Lupus, and Lutie; Neck, Nixa, and Nonsuch; Tiff, Timber, and Torch; Yancy, Yarrow, and Yount; Zalma, Zebra, and Zeta; Chloride and Cooter, Lonejack and Low Wassie, Mammoth, Minimum, Enough and Enon.

Missouri has wealth and beauty, but it is not Utopia. It has dreary slums in its large cities and tens of thousands of poverty-stricken families in its rural sections. It has underpaid workers in small industries, and it has pathetic farms on thin, eroded land which should be in pasture, timber, and fruit. It has a multitude of one- and two-room country schools which could give better service if they were consolidated. It has too many children at the low end of the living scale. It has its share of selfish partisans in politics, feathering their own nests in city halls, county courthouses, and the State capital. It could profit by many kinds of legislative reform—criminal code, electoral, structure of the State Government. It sees much of its talent siphoned away from its towns and smaller cities to the metropolitan areas, and in turn drawn from the State itself to the seemingly greener fields which lie East or West. Many of its most promising young men and women go to other States for their college training and do not come back. Its State University at Columbia often develops outstanding teachers and scholars and then loses them to other institutions which pay higher salaries.

Yet Missouri has a proud record of getting things started in education in the New World west of the Mississippi—the first State university; Jesuit St. Louis University, oldest school of college rank;

Lindenwood, the first girls' school, and Culver-Stockton, the first co-educational institution. Susan Elizabeth Blow opened America's first public kindergarten in St. Louis in 1873. In St. Louis Calvin Milton Woodward launched the world's first manual training school in 1880. John R. Kirk's Normal School at Kirksville pioneered in the idea of the consolidated school. Slave-born James Milton Turner, going away to Oberlin as a boy before the Civil War, returned to open the first Negro school in the State after emancipation. And medicine and surgery have taken long strides at Washington University's medical center.

All things considered, Missouri's place in the national family seems neither exceptionally high nor exceptionally low. Although it is third in daily newspaper circulation in proportion to population, it is twenty-ninth in book store business; if it is twelfth in encyclopaedia sales, it is thirty-second in national magazine circulation; it is eighteenth in amusement receipts and only thirty-fourth in college and university library expenditures. It is seventeenth in literate population, twenty-first in physicians, dentists, and nurses in ratio to its population, twenty-fourth in average school salaries, thirty-second in farms on hard-surfaced roads, forty-third in rural population in local library districts.

If Missouri may judge its future by its past, progress is as certain as the cream-white petals of the dogwood trees on its hillsides every April. Missouri may not lead the parade of American democracy, but neither will it bring up the rear. Many of its people are at work on accumulated social tasks and they are surveying others with equal determination to make things better. They and their fathers have done much, but a great deal remains to be done by them and their children. St. Louis' recent conquest of smoke has given fresh hope to many blighted American cities. Kansas City's political rejuvenation is proof that cities can rise up and throw off the yoke of municipal bossism. The adoption of State constitutional amendments which take wild-life conservation out of politics and lift the State judiciary from the mire of partisan nominations and elections demonstrates the responsiveness of the people at large to urgent State needs. Missouri has its head up and is looking to the front. A history such as it has is a heritage to be guarded, developed, expanded, and continuously shared with the world.

But our definition of Missouri, however detailed, cannot be complete. Missouri will not be catalogued. It cannot be written down. Missouri is many intangible things—spring in Florissant Valley, apple blossom time at Marionville, a flaming July sunrise on the deep blue of Lake Taneycomo, a leisurely float down the Current River, and black-bass suppers around open fires on willow-screened sandbars. It is tale-swapping in a woodland camp as baying foxhounds follow the scent through the brush on frosted October hills.   It is firelight and unhurried talk of friends in the room, wind calling down the chimney and wood smoke on the night air.   It is living so that life tastes good each day.   It is—Missouri.

Land of Missouri

MISSOURI, with 3,784,664 inhabitants, covering 69,420 square miles, is tenth among the States in population, and eighteenth among the States in area, being 3,000 square miles larger than the whole of New England. Bounded on the north by Iowa, on the east by the Mississippi River, and Illinois, Kentucky, and Tennessee, on the south by Arkansas, and on the west by Oklahoma, Kansas, and Nebraska, it averages about 282 miles from north to south, and about 335 miles in width. The southeast corner of the State thrusts deep into Arkansas; and on the east, the Mississippi cuts off a small piece of Kentucky.

GEOLOGY

During the Archeozoic and the Proterozoic eras, representing the earliest stages of the earth's history, Missouri's igneous rocks were formed by solidification of molten magma, or subsurface lava, which provides the base of the entire continent. These rocks lie at depths as great as 3,600 feet in the vicinity of St. Louis, and extend into the earth for distances of 20 to 40 miles. They are exposed on the surface only in southeastern Missouri, where they form the low range of the St. Francois Mountains.

When the last of the rock-forming lava had hardened, the St. Francois Mountain area was slowly thrust upward to a height of about 2,000 feet above sea level, carrying with it the region now known as the Ozark Highland. Following the Ozark uplift, a long cycle of erosions began, carving the steep canyons and narrow valleys characteristic of southern Missouri today. Near the end of the Proterozoic era, about 500,000,000 years ago, the St. Francois Mountains gradually sank to their former level and were submerged by southern seas that swept over nearly a third of the continent.

The arrival of the seas opened the long Paleozoic era, important in Missouri because most of the rock strata above the igneous rocks were deposited during this time. Beginning with the Cambrian period, the seas advanced again and again, some of them from the Gulf of Mexico, others from the Arctic regions, but each bringing great quantities of fine and coarse materials gleaned from adjacent lands. Sea-dwelling organisms added shells, and other sediment was produced by the chemical precipitation of mineral matter dissolved in the water.

Under the pressure of successive layers of deposits, these materials gradually hardened into rock strata. Most of the stratified rocks are limestones, dolomites, and cherts of organic and chemical origin, but there are also conglomerates, sandstones, and shales. The different layers, each composed of the materials characteristic of the time in which it was formed, may be seen in the sides of various railroad cuts, cliffs, and embankments.

Throughout the uniformly warm Paleozoic era the shallow seas teemed with life. In Cambrian times, the trilobites, creatures distantly related to crayfish, were common, and some marine snails and brachiopods (marine animals with bivalve shells) existed. The remains of shellfish of various kinds built considerable thicknesses of limestone. In the Ordovician period, the cephalopods, ancestors of the nautilus and the devilfish, appeared. The Devonian fishes, principally sharks and lungfish, emerged in the fourth period. Crinoids, popularly known as "stone lilies," reached maximum abundance and variety during the subsequent Mississippian period. Growing in densely populated colonies of great extent, on flexible stalks at the bottom of the clear, shallow Mississippian sea, the crinoids probably looked much like fields of waving grain. Their remains form the major ingredient of Burlington limestone, the predominant surface rock that lies in a broad belt around the Ozark region, curving westward and southward from St. Louis to the vicinity of Springfield. Large groups of crinoids are in the study collections at Washington University in St. Louis.

Near the close of the Devonian period, probably about 300,000,000 years ago, a great fracture appeared in the earth's crust from the Mississippi River near St. Mary's (see Tour 7b) westward to the vicinity of Weingarten, and thence northwestward to the St. Francois-Ste. Genevieve County boundary, near Lawrenceton. The movement of the earth's crust thrust the rock along the north side of the fracture upward to a maximum of 1,000 feet, creating what is known as a fault plane. After a long interval, probably in post-Pennsylvanian time, a vertical movement of the earth's surface produced a great fracture across the fault plane, and thrust up the rock on the south about 2,000 feet. Faults may be observed at several places in Missouri, but the fault zone crossing Ste. Genevieve County is the most extensive in the Upper Mississippi Valley.

The last Paleozoic period of which there is a record in Missouri was the Pennsylvanian, which began perhaps 250,000,000 years ago. The Pennsylvanian is considered an important period because it was during this time that most of the coal of Missouri was formed and immense quantities of lead, zinc, and barite ores were deposited. The shales, sandstones, and limestones of the period cover more than a third of the State. The land was low and poorly drained at this time, permitting vegetation to accumulate on the swamp bottoms, layer upon layer, to be gradually converted into coal strata. At the same time, the subsoils of the swampy, tropical jungles, robbed of their minerals by the roots of coal-forming forests, were gradually altered to refractory, or fire, clays. These clays underlie much of St. Louis and are found in abundant deposits in central Missouri (*see Tour 15a*). During this time, also, the first insects appeared—giant cockroaches and dragonflies, many times the size of their modern descendants. Small, bare-skinned amphibians, comparable to some present-day salamanders, crawled over the land, leaving footprints in soft shale beds. Many of these prints have been discovered during excavation for roads and buildings in the vicinity of Kansas City. The beds of fossils in Ste. Genevieve County have been termed by Dr. Stuart Weller, of the University of Chicago, "a veritable Garden of Eden for the aggressive geologist," because they offer the most varied assortment in the Mississippi Valley. Dr. Weller established a camp for students here in 1915 (*see Tour 7b*).

In other parts of the United States, large seas were characteristic features of the Permian history, the last period of the Paleozoic era, but there is no record of their having invaded Missouri. At the beginning of Permian time, Missouri was exposed to a long period of erosion. The land was low, however, so that a comparatively small amount of rock was worn away. At the end of the Permian period, the continent thrust up the Appalachian Mountains along the Atlantic Coast. Probably at this time, a great force exerted in the area from Texas to Michigan folded a portion of the Mississippi Valley into a series of parallel wrinkles or anticlines. The Illinois anticlines accumulated large quantities of petroleum, formed from the fatty tissues of marine plants and animals. Large areas covering similar formations in northwest Missouri were leased for possible oil drilling in 1938 and 1939.

The era following the last period (Permian) of the Paleozoic era is known as the Mesozoic; it probably began about 190,000,000 years ago. The mountains shut off moisture-laden winds, and the heart of the North American continent was converted into a desert. Sea creatures disappeared and new species thrived. These were the reptiles, including dinosaurs, pterodactyls, and swimming reptiles. At the close of Mesozoic time, the Ozark region was lifted slightly, forming a broad dome, again highest in the St. Francois Mountain area. This uplift initiated a cycle of erosion, which produced the present radial drainage pattern in southern Missouri.

The Cenozoic era, which followed the Mesozoic, began probably about 55,000,000 years ago and continued through the close of the Ice Age, some 50,000 years ago, to the present. For Missouri, most of the Cenozoic era was a time of uninterrupted erosion, which attacked the rocky surfaces, forming the beginning of the major stream valleys of the Mississippi Valley, including the Ozark Highland. A broad area of southwestern Missouri, extending northwest of Springfield, was leveled to the high plateau known as the Springfield Plain.

Since the first, or Tertiary, period of the Cenozoic era, most of Missouri's magnificent rock formations have been created—caverns, springs, and associated geological phenomena, as large as any in the Mississippi Valley. The limestones and dolomites cropping out in the Ozark hills are soluble in acid, and when rain and snow waters impregnated with vegetable acid percolate down they dissolve the rock, creating channels which in time become caverns and the courses of underground springs and river systems. "Undercut" cliff caves are carved by rivers in any kind of rock, but the upland caverns are restricted to limestone regions where the climate was once moist. In one stage of cave formation, the chambers are filled with water and are gradually enlarged. Sometimes when the rooms are exceptionally wide, the roofs are so thin they collapse, producing the large sinkholes so numerous in the State. In the second stage of cave formation, the caves are open and full of air. Groundwater, charged with mineral matter dissolved from the rocks above, drips from the caverns' ceilings. Through evaporation, mineral matter is precipitated, forming clusters of stalactites, stalagmites, and other formations. The majority of these deposits are dripstone or cave onyx, also called Mexican onyx, which is frequently used for wainscoting, soda fountains, and other decorative purposes.

Fish and salamanders have lived in some underground pools for so many generations that blind and colorless species have evolved. The caves have also yielded the bones of extinct human races. In a cave near Sullivan, Missouri, where the roof collapsed hundreds of millions of years ago, forming a deep sink, a swamp developed and coal accumulated to a depth of more than 100 feet. Similar sinks near Rolla contain clays that have been leached of soluble materials, leaving fine refractory diaspore clays. The pyrite in central Missouri sinks has had the sulphur removed by solutions, leaving small deposits of hematite iron ores. Typical zinc deposits of the Joplin district are cave-formed sinks filled with angular fragments of white flint cemented with zinc minerals. Before the roofs collapsed, large calcite crystals were formed, some two feet long, tinted from white to honey color, amber, pink, and amethyst.

Probably after the close of the Pliocene epoch, the earth's surface folded in the St. Francois Mountain area, thrusting the entire region up in a broad dome to a height of approximately 1,800 feet. This folding stretched the earth's crust in the adjacent Mississippi Valley region, producing fractures in the bedrock which initiated a long period of fault activity, creating the broad lowlands of southeastern Missouri.

Kentucky, Tennessee, and Arkansas (*see Tour 7c*). In the vicinity of New Madrid, the Mississippi River begins its heaviest depositing of silt, and, as this accumulates along the river bed and the flood plains south of here, its weight causes minor faulting from time to time, lowering the flood plains and maintaining the river bed nearly at sea level. The New Madrid earthquake, during the winter of 1811-12, was an aftermath of early faulting.

Following the St. Francois uplift, streams and winds attacked these rocky heights, and, after many years, all the layers of Paleozoic rock were worn away, leaving the ancient granites and porphyries exposed as the highest points in Missouri. From the St. Francois hills, rivers and streams have carved in all directions steep-walled valleys in the sedimentary rock, creating the rugged contour of the Ozark Highland, which, with its caves and rock outcrops, underground rivers and giant springs, is one of the most attractive regions in the Middle West. The soils over most of the southern half of the State are residual, formed by the slow chemical decay of the bedrocks, and are not as fertile as the transported loess and glacial soils north of the Missouri River.

Near the close of Tertiary time, in what is known as the Pliocene epoch, the climate of North America gradually became colder. Beginning with the Pleistocene or Quaternary (last of the Cenozoic era), possibly 1,000,000 years ago, great glaciers from the Arctic regions came as far south as the Missouri River, grinding and crushing the country and forming rolling prairie lands with wide, shallow stream valleys. Over the prairies, the glaciers deposited a rich drift soil composed largely of finely ground limestone, shale, and sandstone, together with boulders and fragments of granite, schist, gneiss, and quartzite. Vegetable and animal remains have given this soil a rich black color.

Four great ice sheets advanced over the northern part of the United States, but only the first two are definitely known to have reached Missouri. The first, or Nebraskan, glacier, several hundred to several thousand feet thick, advanced as far south as the Ohio and Missouri Rivers. After a warm interglacial period, the Kansan Glacier covered parts of northern United States, remaining thousands of years before beginning to retreat to the north. At its melting, the mouth of the Missouri was choked with ice, forcing the river to overflow, probably into the Meramec Valley, and to empty into the Mississippi south of St. Louis. The Missouri also carried a large amount of water from the northern Rocky Mountains, and must have been a mighty torrent several times its present size. The glaciers left a thick, heterogeneous rock waste, which roughly marks the limit of their advance. In lower Frenchman's Hollow in the northeastern part of Ste. Genevieve County, Dr. Courtney Werner discovered a four-foot boulder of granite that was probably brought in by a small iceberg from the southern lobe of the third, or Illinoian, glacier. Pieces of fossil coral from Pike County, Missouri, were carried by the ice to St. Louis County. After the melting of the glaciers, tremendous dust storms covered bluffs and uplands along the Mississippi and Missouri Rivers with a thick layer of fine yellow or buff-colored soil, known as loess. In some places, the loess reaches a depth of 70 feet.

During the Pleistocene period, mammalian fauna reached its richest variety in North America. Species of tremendous size inhabited the continent for thousands of years, retreating southward when ice covered the country, and thriving farther north during the warm interglacial epochs. Horses, elephants, musk oxen, peccaries, elk, reindeer, and many other groups that lived during the Ice Age were extinct by the time the human era opened. Skeletons of true elephants of several kinds have been unearthed, and thick beds of mastodon remains have been discovered near Kimmswick, on the Mississippi River. In 1901, Professor William Henry Holmes of the American Bureau of Ethnology wrote of them: " . . . they are the most wonderful I have ever seen— it is a page out of the history of the world that has no substitute." Horses were not known to the American Indians until brought here by the Spaniards, but the genus *Equus scotti,* which disappeared not long before the coming of man, was abundant during the Ice Age. A beaver seven feet long ranged from Missouri to the Atlantic Coast, and several species of bison much larger than those of the present day once lived in herds on the Western prairies. Most unusual were a twenty-foot ground sloth and a twelve-foot armadillo, which migrated from the Argentine pampas through Central America. There are indications that the earliest peoples were contemporaneous with some of the Pleistocene mammals, but this has not been proved.

TOPOGRAPHY AND CLIMATE

Missouri includes portions of four physiographic provinces: the Glacial, or Northern, Plains, a great expanse of generally level land, extending across the State north of the Missouri River; the Ozark Highlands, between the White River and Missouri River drainage basins, which cover most of the area south of the Missouri River; the Great Plains, a broad V-shaped wedge, penetrating the central western part; and a splinter of the rich, flat Mississippi River Plain that reaches into the southeastern corner.

The Glacial Plains are composed of the Black Prairie, Rolling Prairie, and Flat Prairie regions. The Black Prairie, in the northeastern part of the State, is Missouri's most typical example of early glacial-deposit topography. Predominantly agricultural, it forms part of the Corn Belt.

The Rolling Prairie, in north central Missouri, is drained by the Grand and Chariton Rivers, whose tributaries for long distances flow nearly parallel with the trunk streams. Erosion has created a series of almost parallel north-to-south divides and wide, shallow valleys, somewhat resembling the ridges of a washboard.

The Flat Prairie, in northeastern Missouri, has only a thin veneer of glacial deposits. The surface, smooth in the central part, is irregularly broken by ravines slanting to the bordering rivers. Here and there, a few low-rolling hills indicate the former presence of the ice sheet. The soil is heavy and sour in most areas, and the flat surfaces handicap drainage to such an extent that the agricultural system is shifting from crop farming to livestock, except where glacial soils prevail. Coal and fire-clay mining are typical of certain sections.

In the western part of the State, an extension of the Great Plains, commonly called in Missouri the Scarfed, or Osage, Plains, has the monotony of the flat prairies, but is broken by low rounded hills, with steep slopes toward the Ozark dome and very gradual ones away from it. The best use of the land agriculturally is for forage crops. The soils developed on the coal measures, sandstones, and shales are poor.

In southeastern Missouri, below Cape Girardeau, are the fertile black lowlands of the Mississippi Embayment, an extension of the Gulf Coastal Plains. These are divided into flood-plain belts, representing both the present and former courses of the Mississippi River, and are separated by the low, flat-topped ridges known as Crowley's Ridge, Sikeston, Dunklin, and Scott County hills. The flat inter-ridge belts were at one time covered with extensive swamps, some of which remain to the present day.

The St. Francois Mountains, in the eastern part of the Ozark Highlands, create a more truly mountainous landscape than any others in Missouri. The many knobs or peaks of these irregular ancient masses have been exposed by the wearing away of the younger sedimentary rocks. Pilot Knob is a striking example. The odd-shaped "potato" or "elephant" rocks at Graniteville and elsewhere were formed by a type of weathering called exfoliation, or the scaling off of sharp corners and edges of once rectangular blocks. The basins, depressions, or valleys between the knobs are commonly floored with layers of sedimentary rocks. Some of the major rivers, such as the St. Francis and the Current, rush from basin to basin through narrow but deep water gaps or bluffs of igneous rocks, locally called "shut-ins."

To the north, west, and south of the St. Francois Mountains is a broad, undulating upland, which forms the tortuous divide between the Missouri and White River drainage basins. This region has many subterranean streams, with accompanying sinkholes and springs. The eastern portion is often referred to as the Big Spring Country because of its great blue springs, such as Big, Round, Alley, and Meramec. Big Spring, with an average daily flow of 600,000,000 gallons, is the third largest in the United States (*see Tour 6a*). Along the southeastern border, the plateau terminates abruptly at a low rocky slope. The western border rises as a range of hills and forms the eastern boundary of the Springfield Plateau, a more level land devoted to the raising of wheat and cattle.

The Springfield Plateau, or Old Plains, is commonly called a structural plain, because the easy westerly slope of its surface practically coincides with the dip of the underlying Burlington limestone. Although the eastern rim of the plateau averages 1,300 feet above sea level, the surface is gently undulating, with low divides and broad valleys. The limestone rock has yielded a deep, rich, residual soil that has been increasingly utilized for grain crops, dairy stock, and poultry farms.

The White River rises in northwestern Arkansas and crosses into southern Missouri, where it flows through a series of intricately dissected rock terraces that extend northward to the Springfield Plateau. Many of its south-flowing tributaries have eroded the terraces so completely that the twisting divides are knife-edge ridges separating steep-sided coves. A typical rugged section, now famous as "The Shepherd of the Hills Country," lies north and west of Lake Taneycomo, an artificial reservoir and power site.

Near the center of the State, bordering the Ozark Dome, is a belt of rugged hills produced by the drainage lines of the Mississippi, Missouri, and Osage Rivers. Here, the usual ravine type of ruggedness is intensified by cuesta escarpments, or steep faces of rock. The sections along the Missouri and Mississippi Rivers have been rounded and smoothed by a mantle of loess. Where large tributaries from the highlands cut across the hills, flood plains divide the belt into numerous segments. The sprawling, octopus-shaped Lake of the Ozarks, with a length of 129 miles and a shoreline of 1,300 miles, was formed by the impounding of the Osage River by the Bagnell Dam, and the consequent flooding of the deeply eroded valleys.

Water covers 680 square miles of the State's area. The maximum relief from valley floor to hilltop is approximately 1,500 feet. The highest point above sea level, Taum Sauk Mountain (1,771.7 feet), and the lowest point, near Cardwell (230 feet), are both in southeastern Missouri. Including a 500-mile frontage on the Mississippi, Missouri has more than 1,000 miles of navigable waterways.

There are 133 known spring localities in Missouri, and nearly 500 springs suitable for drinking water or fish propagation. Besides these, Missouri has 27 mineral springs, the waters of which are saline, sulphuretted, or chalybeate.

Because of its size and its interior position, Missouri has a considerable range of temperature. The northwestern portion has an average annual temperature of 50 degrees; in the southeastern area it is 60 degrees. July, with an average temperature of 77 degrees, is the hottest month; January is coldest, with an average of 30 degrees. These are average temperatures, however, and mean little in a State where even the natives find the weather confusing. Ordinarily, brief periods of intense summer heat are followed by a mild Indian summer that lasts well into November, and then, after occasional periods of bitter cold, the long and lovely spring season begins. But there have been years when no rule held good; snow in May, cold in July, and summer heat in mid-January. The coldest temperature ever recorded in Missouri was 40 degrees below zero; the hottest, 117 degrees above.

The average precipitation for the State is about 40 inches, with some rain or snow falling on an average of 110 days. The southeastern area has the heaviest rainfall, with an annual average of about 48 inches; the northwestern area averages about 32 inches. The rainfall is fairly well distributed throughout the year, but is usually heaviest in the spring. In the last 65 years, 10 severe droughts have occurred, but few have been State-wide. The wettest year on record (1927) brought a precipitation of 55.06 inches; the driest year (1901) had 25.28 inches. Snowfall averages from about 21 inches in the northern section of the State to about 16 inches in the southeast, but snow rarely stays on the ground more than a few days.

Northwest winds prevail during the winter; during the remainder of the year, the air movement is largely from the south and southeast. The average wind velocities are least during the summer and early fall, varying from 7 to 9 miles per hour. In the winter and spring months higher velocities are recorded, averaging from 10 to 12 miles per hour. Missouri falls within a medium classification in respect to storminess. For each area of 10,000 square miles, the average frequency of tornadoes is about one a year. The most serious in the history of the State were the tornadoes that damaged St. Louis areas in 1896 and in 1927.

FLORA

Wide differences in Missouri's climate, soil conditions, geological history, and topography give its flora interesting variations. Out of some 2,281 different species listed by Palmer and Steyermark (*Flowering Plants of Missouri,* 1935), 10 per cent are estimated to be importations. Some of these, such as the day lily, Queen Anne's lace, horehound, catnip, motherwort, bouncing Bet, and matrimony vine, were brought in by settlers, who cultivated them for their medicinal or ornamental value, and have since escaped from the gardens to "go native." As settlement has increased, more and more plants have been introduced, many of them accidentally by the railroads and other transportation facilities; these are generally first seen along the rights of way; occasionally, however, like the white- and yellow-flowered sweet clover, they spread rapidly over vast areas.

Missouri has a generous number of plants of State-wide distribution. Black willow, sycamore, red cedar, American elm, many kinds of oak and hickory, ash, walnut, hazelnut, linden, and certain kinds of maple grow in nearly every county. Of the flowering or fruit-bearing trees, honey locust, dogwood, redbud, sumach, hackberry, persimmon, pawpaw, and the wild plum, cherry, and crab apple are the most frequent. Blackberry, raspberry, strawberry, grape, gooseberry, and elderberry grow wild throughout the State. A number of edible greens are also common: many mustards, dandelion, purslane, lamb's quarter, and cress. These, and sometimes even slick thistle and poke shoots, are boiled with the ubiquitous "side meat" of the Ozarks to make the "greens and pot likker" which is so popular with the hill folk. Mint of many kinds, bergamot, pennyroyal, jimson weed, self-heal, wild ginger, snake root, May apple, toothwort, and ginseng are among the State-wide herbs of medicinal or utilitarian value. Chicory can be used as a coffee substitute.

Besides the common wild flowers, the goldenrod, milkweed, spiderwort, sweet William, and "roses red and violets blue"—to say nothing of white and yellow—Missouri has many less familiar ones. Where picnickers and tourists have left them alone, there are lovely white bloodroot, columbine, verbena, shooting star, and Jack-in-the-pulpit. Trumpet vine and bittersweet twine up the trees, and the sunnier spots are brilliant with cone flower, orange butterfly weed, and orange puccoon. Asters in almost infinite variety, blue lobelia, mullein, Venus's-looking-glass, and Indian tobacco grow in most counties. And then, of course, there are the socially undesirables—poison ivy, purple nightshade, beggar's-lice, plantain, Spanish needle, burdock, and nettles.

Missouri's State flower is the hawthorn, a shrub with delicate flat clusters of white apple-like blossoms in the spring, followed by small edible fruit. Unfortunately, since there are nearly 200 kinds of hawthorn in Missouri, it is extremely difficult for the ordinary flower lover to recognize the official species, *Crataegus mollis*.

The flora of the southeastern lowland is probably the oldest and the most uniform in the State, some of it having apparently existed since early Tertiary times; it is characteristically of the Gulf Coastal type, and the region as a whole has Lower Austral combined with the southern phase of Carolinian plant life. In a few remaining swamps of this region grow bald cypress, pumpkin ash, corkwood, water locust, swamp cottonwood, bitter pecan, tupelo, and overcup oak. Below them are many lovely water plants: shining pondweed, American frogbit, spider lily, thalia, lady's-eardrops. Along the water edge are found red iris, pale manna grass, beak sedge, and many other aquatic varieties. On slightly higher ground, the flora is more varied. Yellow pine is the only coniferous tree in this section, but white hickory, sweet and black gum, winged elm, and white ash grow in the unflooded parts. Mistletoe and Christmas holly flourish in the southeastern area, as do giant cane, moonwort, swamp rose, wisteria, blue indigo, red-flowered buckeye, rattlesnake master, purple gerardia, green haw, and many others. Several rather rare orchis grow here: green wood, showy, yellow-fringed, and purple-fringed.

Crowley's Ridge, the only real elevation in the southeast, bears many eastern species not found elsewhere in the neighborhood. Among these are beech, Spanish oak, tulip tree, cucumber tree, and even an occasional scarlet oak and beaked hazelnut. Celandine poppies, golden seal, white baneberry, beech drops, and prickly gooseberry also grow here.

The Ozark region has the most complex and varied flora in Missouri. The valleys have mostly been cleared for cultivation, but on the slopes the original, rather stunted, oak-hickory forests, mostly of the Carolinian type, survive. The flora is between the austral and boreal phases, with the southern species predominating. Most of the herbaceous plants here are those commonly found from the Appalachian Plateau to the Central Plains, but in the more protected spots are some northern species, while on the western slopes and in rocky glades, western or southwestern varieties predominate. Elsewhere in the region, especially where some unusual ecological condition prevails, plant colonies not related to the general flora of the region are found.

Throughout most of the Ozarks, red or black oak, scrub elm, chittim wood, hawthorn (*Crataegus collina*), and witch hazel are common; also ferns and bracken in great variety, Virginia creeper, climbing milkweed, and yellow honeysuckle. Probably no section in Missouri is richer in flowers. Here grow Dutchman's pipe, hepatica, wild wood's hydrangea, goatsbeard, false blue indigo, butterfly pea, snow-on-the-mountain, passion flower, wood's angelica, and starry rosinweed. The sunny yellow coreopsis, the holly-like 'possum haw, wild heliotrope, dogbane, and false foxglove will reward the seeker, as will yellow lady's-slipper, Solomon's seal, and adder's-tongue. Here too grows grindelia, a gum plant which is used internally as a specific for bronchitis and asthma, and externally as a cure for poison ivy; and sassafras, which provides both a flavoring and a tonic.

The Iron and St. Francois Mountains and the surrounding sandstone areas have mostly an acid type of soil and furnish a favorable habitat for many oxylophytes (humus plants). Most of the forests are stunted. Pine and some red cedar grow here, together with a few of the trees more commonly found in the southeastern section, such as Spanish oak, black and sweet gum, and willow oak. The dominant flora of the area, however, is Alleghenian-Ozarkian. The rosy azalea is typical of the ericaceous plants of the region. Here are exquisite purple-fringed orchis, nodding wild onion, adder's-mouth, cancer weed (salvia), blue curls, flax, and saxifrage, which is well named "the rock breaker."

Perhaps the most interesting Ozark subdivision is the rugged area bordering the White River. The uplands have a typical Ozark flora, but along the bluffs and the steep-sided tributary valleys, and on the bald knobs, many rare plants are found. The valleys are so steep that the character of the flora depends largely on the exposure. On the north and northeast exposures the flora is mostly Appalachian; here grow butternut, yellow wood, nettle tree, sugar maple, and hydrangea. The south and west exposures, especially on the high bluffs, have, in contrast, mostly a southwestern flora. Twisted and fantastically gnarled junipers cling to precarious footholds in the rock. The smoke tree, one of the rarest of American trees, grows here, sometimes to the unusual height of 35 or 40 feet. Soapberry, Missouri currant, and the succulent vine, *Cissus incisa,* are also found.

On the bald knobs along the White River, where very few plants can adapt themselves to the peculiar conditions of the open slopes, a few species have almost a monopoly, presenting spectacular masses of color when in bloom. Almost the only tree that grows here is the juniper, but low shrubs like the pasture rose, acacia, and buckbush are fairly common, as are, too, short-lived annuals and deep-rooted perennials, such as tall larkspur, large-flowered evening primrose, purple-bracted horse mint, pink and yellow cone flower, and purple beardtongue. Most of the flora in these regions is southwestern, with some intermingling of eastern Appalachian. The small cane which grows in the southeast is found here, but under very different conditions. This is also true of the red oak, the fringe tree, and, most remarkable of all, the supplejack or rattan vine, which usually grows in swamps as a thick vine, whereas here it is more shrub-like. Other plants found on the bald knobs include adder's tongue, false aloe, flame flower, helmet flower, blazing star, and blue dogbane.

In limestone and dolomite, and occasionally in sandstone or chert areas, an exposed rock surface will sometimes prevent the encroachment of trees and shrubs. Such bare spots are known as glades, and in them also the flora is quite distinct, especially in the chert glades, which include sorrel, yellow-flowered stonecrop, St. John's-wort, prickly pear, wild petunia, portulaca, and the dainty phacelia. In the limestone and dolomite glades, umbrella wort, widow's cross, western wallflower, wild hyacinth, the sumach, which is locally called polecat bush, Indian bread root, and the edible ground plum are commonly found.

Ozark flora merges very gradually into the prairie flora. Before cultivation destroyed it, forest growth of the general Ozark character covered the prairie stream banks. The unglaciated prairie just north of the Missouri River, and near its confluence with the Mississippi, closely resembles the Ozark region in flora.

The glaciated prairie across most of northern Missouri, and in small areas of St. Louis, Saline, Cooper, Lafayette, and Jackson counties, was once covered with a never-ending succession of grasses and perennial herbs, most of which were legumes or composites. C. J. Latrobe, who traveled west from Arrow Rock in 1832, describes them: "God has here with a prodigal hand, scattered the seeds of thousands of beautiful plants. . . . When the yellow suns of autumn incline over the west, their mild rays are greeted by the appearance of millions of yellow flowers . . . which seem to clothe the undulating surface of the prairie with a cloth of gold." Characteristic prairie flowers are white anemone, meadow rose, turtle-head, white snakeroot, and river-bank grape. But in the northwestern part, along the loess-covered bluffs of the Missouri River, grow thimble-weed, locoweed, wolfberry, and wild licorice, as well as many unusual grasses. Because the loess hills erode rapidly, and are extremely dry, the forests have not encroached upon them as they have upon the flora of other sections. In the loess hills of Atchison and Holt counties are found some plants from the northwestern plains that grow nowhere else in Missouri.

There were originally very few trees in the prairie region, but here and there along stream borders were cottonwood and black willow, yellow oak, cork elm, box elder, quaking aspen, black haw, and choke cherry. Introduced timber at the present time provides many woods patches.

Along streams and in areas of low relief, particularly in the glaciated prairies, salt springs and salt licks sometimes occur. These impregnate the surrounding soil with alkaline salts, producing an unusual flora. Narrow-leaved cattail, water starwort, horned and fennel-leaved pondweed, three-square, bulrush, red spear scale, knotgrass, and barnyard grass are among the plants common to these salty areas.

In recent years, Missouri has become increasingly interested in preserving her rich heritage of flora. Educational programs attempt to make the public conscious of its floral wealth and to prevent wanton destruction. Horticulture societies, garden clubs, and flower shows maintain the public interest in beautifying the State. Shaw's Garden in St. Louis, together with its arboretum and wild-flower garden at Gray Summit, disseminates information pertaining to all forms of plant growth, care, and preservation (*see St. Louis, and Tour 5*). The

United States Government has bought 3,319,939 acres of depleted forest and submarginal lands in Missouri, out of which the Clark and Gardner national forests have been created. They operate under the United States Forest Service, in co-operation with State and local commissions, and maintain a program to improve the timber, reduce fire hazards, and beautify the State and its highways.

FAUNA

Missouri's first white settlers found an almost fabulous number of birds and animals. Some of these have now entirely vanished; the rest are becoming constantly rarer. The great herds of buffalo which once ranged as far east as the Mississippi, and even invaded the Ozark hills, are gone, the last having been seen in 1850. Holt County saw the last great concentration of elk in 1841, when at least 500 were killed by Indians. Black bear, that once prowled throughout Missouri's forests, were extremely rare by 1880. Panther are thought to be extinct, though people occasionally "think they saw" one. The antelope that once swarmed over the western prairie have been gone since 1840. The badger, fairly common as late as 1850, have likewise been driven out or trapped.

The incredible early flocks of birds have met the same fate. The passenger pigeons, whose flight literally blackened the skies, have not been seen since 1890. The little green paroquets with yellow heads, which once made the sycamores they loved "look like Christmas trees," are lost to the State. One was seen in 1904, another in 1905, and both were promptly killed. The Eskimo curlews, whistling and trumpeter swans, and whooping cranes, if they exist at all, are now extremely rare. An occasional water turkey, once plentiful, is still found in the southeastern swamp area.

So great was the early stock of wild life that the State did not become conscious until the 1870's of the depletion caused by hunters and settlers, and by lumbering and land cultivation. The first conservation law, passed in 1874, provided for a closed season on deer and the better game birds and forbade the netting of birds. The passage of the so-called Walmsley Law in 1905, however, marked the first real step toward preserving the State's animal life; it established closed seasons, a system of licenses, and a State appropriation. This law, variously altered, is still the basis of the State conservation regulations. Perhaps the biggest step was the provision in 1936 for a conservation commission. In spite of the establishment of State reservations, and of efforts to restock or introduce species, however, game is still decreasing in Missouri, with the exception of typical farm game such as quail, rabbit, and skunk.

A number of animals and birds are common to most sections of Missouri: cottontail rabbits, western fox, squirrel, opossum, common muskrat, raccoon, and a few mink and red fox. Civet and skunk are found everywhere except in the southeastern swamps, where the high water table prevents their burrowing. Of the game birds, the eastern bobwhite and the mourning dove are State-wide. Mexican quail and ring-necked pheasant have been introduced in great numbers, but, in spite of the thousands of dollars spent, neither species seems to be increasing. Among the transient or rarer game birds are the common Canada goose, mallard, blue-winged teal, wood duck, mud hen, woodcock, plover, and ruddy duck.

The State boasts an unusually large variety of songbirds, because of its generally mild climate. The bluebird, official State bird, has a cheerful whistle, and its bright back and orange breast make it attractive. Of the 400 species of non-game birds in the State, the most frequent are the bullfinch, cardinal, mockingbird, woodpecker, and the quarrelsome blue jay. Indigo bunting, whippoorwill, Baltimore oriole, and goldfinch are fairly general in the more rural sections, and occasionally loon, snipe, and killdeer are seen, and even, at rare intervals, a "Great God woodpecker."

Among predatory birds, seven or eight varieties of hawk, three or four of owl, and the common crow are general throughout the State. The northern bald eagle is frequent in the Ozarks and occasionally visits larger streams in other sections. Several kinds of buzzard are common, but these are scavengers rather than predators.

Relatively few predatory animals are now common in Missouri. Probably the most troublesome, and certainly the most numerous, are stray dogs and cats. The practice of abandoning these pets in the woods has led to their multiplying alarmingly. Wild dogs will attack cattle and deer, as well as small animals, and the cats destroy young animals and birds. It is estimated that cats kill not less than 12,000,000 birds a year in Missouri, to say nothing of the eggs they destroy. Of the native predators, the red fox, the eastern gray wolf, which is now common only in the southern parts, the coyote of the north and west, and the fast disappearing bobcat of the southeast are most frequent.

The most malicious predator, as any hiker can testify, is the minute insect known as the chigger, which looks like a tiny grain of red pepper. It burrows under the skin, causing itchy swellings of some duration. Although malaria-carrying mosquitoes still remain in the southeastern swamps, they are disappearing as drainage progresses.

Of the harmless snakes, the most frequent are water, garter, ribbon, black, and bull snakes. The venomous-looking puff adder is in reality quite harmless. Copperhead, rattlesnake, and the very rarely seen cottonmouth moccasin are the only dangerous serpents in the State.

There are no poisonous lizards, but fence lizards, swifts, and blue-tailed skink are numerous. Terrapins are common; both hard- and soft-shelled turtles are abundant. Occasionally, the curious-looking alligator turtle is seen.

Fish, like other wild life, have decreased, but buffalo, cat, and German carp are still abundant. Of the many game fish, bass, crappie, and brook trout are common. So, too, are shad, drum, jack salmon, perch, sunfish, and bullhead. Crayfish, mussels, and eels abound in most waters, and, along the less-traveled streams, giant bullfrogs also are found. Perhaps the most curious of the stream dwellers is the ferocious-looking "water dog," or aquatic salamander, which, appearances to the contrary, is entirely harmless.

Quail, raccoon, and civet, tree-denning rodents and fur bearers, and bank burrowers live in the northwestern prairie section, which has a deep, rich loess soil and is widely cultivated. This is the only section in which the Great Plains muskrat is now common. The greater prairie chicken, or grouse, are sometimes found. The region of the northern river-breaks has a more stable wild life, especially birds, because of its many streams and the fact that the poor soil affords less cultivation. The most important waterfowl flyway in the central States lies along the Chariton river-bottom lake country, though in recent years it has been somewhat reduced by dredging. The northeastern prairie is more richly wooded and has a more varied edge growth than the other prairie sections, so that the region is one of the best game habitats of the State. The New York weasel and occasional Wisconsin gray fox are found here.

The western prairie, the most typical in the State, is covered largely with brush and grasses; it therefore affords little protection to larger wild animals. The jack rabbit, the long-tailed weasel, and the northern coyote live here, as do prairie chicken.

The western prairie merges gradually into the Ozark Highland. Along this border, fur-bearing animals are more frequent than elsewhere. Where the Ozarks merge with the northern prairie, the river bottoms afford large trees, and a rich soil supports both cultivation and heavy edge cover. Gasconade County in this section is the best deer range in the State. The State's few beaver are found in Dent County. Grey fox also inhabit this area and the central Ozark Plateau to the south; in the latter, too, are Northern bald eagle, wild turkey, and the very rare eastern ruffed grouse.

Most of the southeastern region was once a swamp, but at present drainage has permitted cultivation of some 50 per cent of it. The 5 per cent of timbered area is still frequently under water, so that aquatic game is abundant. On the slight elevations, good cover and a rich supply of food supports some animals, including the only remaining otters in the State. The uncultivated portion is a tangle of cutover timber and brush, excellent for all game except burrowers and such open-field birds as quail and doves. Southern grey squirrel, swamp rabbit, eastern grey wolf, and the fast disappearing bobcat are found in this section.

Archeology and Indians

THE traces of primitive peoples found throughout Missouri have long attracted widespread interest and speculation. These remains chiefly consist of village sites, earthworks or tumuli, pottery, various types of stone implements, and decorative objects in stone, shell, pottery, or metal. Many of these were produced by the Indians of historic times; others, by earlier Indian cultures.

Indian village and camp sites are often identified by the presence of stone tools and weapons, and chips and flakes of chert or flint. In some instances, fragments of pottery and animal bones, and beds of ashes indicate the past location of wigwams and huts. In St. Louis, Franklin, Morgan, and Saline Counties are well-defined localities where the Indians quarried the materials needed for tools and weapons. Near Leslie, an ancient mine of the red and yellow oxides of iron used by the Indians for paint has been discovered; its tunnels extend to a depth of 20 feet or more and are so narrow that only small persons could have used them.

Earthworks or mounds are still numerous, although many have been obliterated. These include conical mounds, pyramidal and effigy mounds, and embankments and fortifications. Although mounds are found throughout Missouri, the greatest number, and those of the largest size, occur in the most fertile and accessible areas of the State, particularly along the Missouri and Mississippi Rivers, and in the southeast. Most of these mounds are from 4 to 5 feet in height, and from 30 to 50 feet in diameter. Many appear singly; others in various types of groupings.

The majority of the mounds are conical, built of earth, or of earth combined with stone. These were usually depositories for the dead, but burials were also made in pyramidal mounds, and, more rarely, in effigy mounds. Mounds along the Missouri River often contain rectangular or circular vaults of stone or sometimes of logs. Within these, bodies were either stretched at full length or partly doubled up. At times, apparently, the bones were deposited after the flesh had disappeared. It is known that in certain southern tribes, during historic times, a special group had the task of removing the decayed flesh from the bones in preparation for this type of burial.

The mounds in southeast Missouri are largely concentrated in an area from six to ten miles wide, extending south from Cape

Girardeau to northern Arkansas. Many of these are conical, but others are square, oblong, or of various other shapes, some of which suggest the effigy mounds, having the outline of an animal or reptile form, found elsewhere in the Mississippi Valley. Probably more than one culture flourished here before the arrival of the Europeans. The many remains indicate occupation by an agricultural people over a considerable period of time. The largest Missouri mound is in Pemiscot County, not far from Caruthersville (*see Tour 7c*). It is 400 feet long, 250 feet wide, and 35 feet high, with an approach from the south end leading up to the top. The north end is 15 feet higher than the south end. The sides seem to have been covered, originally, with burnt clay from three to four inches thick, with split cane laid between the layers. Near New Madrid is an example of the flat-topped mound, 150 by 200 feet, and 35 feet high, constructed of some sort of soft brick. Other flat-topped mounds have been found elsewhere in the State. Temples, the houses of the chiefs, or other public buildings seem to have been built on these.

Embankments or enclosures, found in various parts of Missouri, are among the most interesting of the prehistoric remains. These are often called "fortifications," but so little is known of the purpose for which they were built that the title is at best a questionable one. No two seem identical in outline; examples have been found which are circular, square, oblong, octagonal, or irregular. Near Hoberg, in Lawrence County, is a triangular enclosure 500 feet long, protected by a 2½-foot ditch on the outside. In Dade County, the so-called Indian Fort consists of 2 semicircular embankments, about 150 feet in diameter on the inside. Near by are 2 other semicircles, 600 feet long and now about 2 feet high, with a clearly noticeable ditch a foot deep on the outside. Between the ends of the inner semicircle are 2 mounds 10 feet in diameter and 2 feet high. The most interesting enclosure found in Missouri is in Van Meter State Park in Saline County. It is located on the top of what was formerly the south bank of the Missouri River, near the eighteenth century villages of the Missouri and Little Osage Indians. Similar to Fort Ancient in Ohio, it is 1,300 feet long and averages about 300 feet in width. It is well preserved and has, in places, a double ditch.

Missouri Indian pottery is classed as either "grit" or "shell," according to its temper or binding material. Many of the examples that have been found were evidently intended for domestic use. Other pieces, more decorative, were probably made for burial, religious, or purely ornamental purposes. The latter type is carefully and delicately finished and of many unusual forms, such as the slender, bottle-shaped jar, seemingly peculiar to the southeast Missouri area, and the so-called effigy pots, made in various human or animal designs. The pottery ranges in color from a rich black through all shades of brown and gray, white and terra cotta tones. The patterns are either raised or incised or painted. Excellent pottery collections are exhibited in the museum of the Southeast Missouri State Teachers College, Cape Girardeau, and the Missouri Historical Society, St. Louis.

Almost every type of arrow and spear point, from the tiny bird points to spears over a foot in length, has been discovered in Missouri. Knives, scrapers, hoes, and axes are also abundant. Discoidals, used in an Indian game, have been found. The presence of *metates* or grinding stones indicates how widely corn was grown. Flint was chiefly used in the manufacture of smaller objects: arrow and spear points, and scrapers, hoes, and similar tools. Granites and other igneous stones were used for the larger and coarser implements. Tomahawks of hematite ore are frequently seen.

Stone carvings of animals, and even of the human head, have been found in southeast Missouri mounds. Dunklin County yielded a cache of sheet-copper objects embossed with eagles, double-eagles, and what appears to be a man-eagle. These objects, as well as specimens of obsidian, copper, conch-shells, and—from a later period—iron tomahawks of European manufacture, suggest an extensive primitive commerce.

At least two main types of culture were present in the Missouri area. These are known as the Woodland and Mississippi cultures. The Woodland is distinguished by the use of pottery tempered with grit and fashioned in only one shape; burials in low mounds, generally without grave articles, and with the body flexed; coarsely chipped arrow points with stems; and grooved axes. Characteristics of the Mississippi culture are shell-tempered pottery in a variety of shapes; bodies arranged in an extended position, in low mounds built up by successive burials; articles buried with bodies; the use of very small and finely chipped arrow points. Different remains, including those of the Hopewell culture found in western Missouri, indicate, however, that a number of variations of these main cultures, or other distinct Indian cultures, have been present in Missouri. The earliest so far located is the "Bluff Dweller" culture, found in the caves and rock shelters of Taney, Stone, Barry, McDonald, and Newton Counties. These primitive cave and rock shelter dwellers had not learned the use of the bow and arrow, but they did weave baskets and mats and fine garments of feathers. A bone decorated with the picture of a mammoth (now in the Capitol Museum, Jefferson City) was found in Jacob's Cavern, three miles east of Pineville.

Prehistoric inhabitants of Missouri were long thought to have been of some ancient and distinct race, later displaced and perhaps exterminated by the Indians of historic times. Our knowledge of this early period is still fragmentary and confused, but the crafts, burial customs, and traditions of the later Indians indicate a close cultural relationship to the prehistoric group, rather than a new race. It is known that some of the tribes inhabiting the Gulf States, such as the Yuchi, Creek, Chickasaw, and Natchez, were still using and probably constructing mounds when De Soto passed through that territory in 1540-1. The Quapaw of Arkansas were also using them; and there is evidence that the Cherokee and Shawnee were mound builders. Blue Mound in Vernon County, Missouri, was for more than a century the burial place of the Osage, and as late as 1874 members of the tribe returned each year to mourn there.

Much of our confusion regarding the prehistoric period comes from the fact that the Indians found in Missouri by the first European visitors appear to have been themselves recent immigrants. Migrations among the Indians seem to have extended over a considerable period of time. They were probably induced by the increasing pressure of certain Eastern and Northeastern tribes, by the spread of French and English settlement, and by the distribution of European weapons among the Eastern tribes. Shiftings continued until near the close of the nineteenth century, when the frontier had disappeared and the remnants had been harried into reservations. Many of these migratory tribes passed through Missouri, as evidenced by a few place names, and various half-remembered tales.

The tribes occupying Missouri during the Colonial period represented two main linguistic groups. The Sauk, Fox, and Illinois tribes who dominated the northeastern portion of the State belonged to the Algonquin family, the most numerous of the North American Indian groups. The remainder was occupied by various Siouan tribes: the Oto, Iowa, Osage, Missouri, Quapaw, Kansa, and others. In general, the two groups were hereditary foes, although the various individual tribes were constantly shifting their alliances.

Of all the Indians living within Missouri during historic times, none excited the interest or admiration of the whites more than the Osage. When the first French explorers visited the region late in the seventeenth century, this tribe was living near the mouth of the Osage River. Before 1718, one group moved up the Osage to establish its villages near the headwaters of the stream. These became known as the Great or Big Osage, or, Pa-he'tsi, the "campers on the mountains." The rest of the tribe, together with their cousins, the Missouri, moved westward up the Missouri River into the present area of Saline County. Because of their village site in the Missouri River bottom, they were called the Little Osage, or, U-tsehta, the "campers in the low lands."

The Osage men were of impressive height, averaging six feet or more. Audubon considered them as "well formed, athletic and robust

"OLD MISSOURI"

STUMP SPEAKER, A Painting by Bingham

PANEL FROM MISSOURI MURAL, State Capitol,
Jefferson City, by Thomas Hart Benton

PIONEER LIFE IN MISSOURI IN 1820

INTERIOR OF FLATBOAT (1827)

COL. DANIEL BOONE

MASSACRE OF MORMONS AT HAUN'S MILL

JESSE JAMES' RECEPTION

Missouri Historical Society

PORTRAIT OF DRED SCOTT

THE BATTLE OF LEXINGTON

The State Historical Society of Missouri

JEFFERSON CITY (1855)

ST. JOSEPH

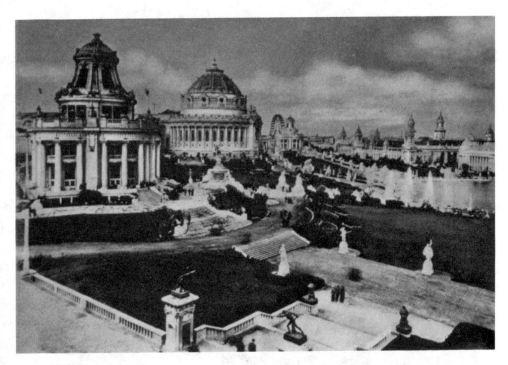

**LOUISIANA PURCHASE EXPOSITION,
ST. LOUIS** (1904)

MISSISSIPPI DAWN, by William E. L. Bunn

**MARK TWAIN AT THE TIME OF HIS LAST VISIT
TO HIS OLD HOME IN HANNIBAL**

men of noble aspect." The feats performed by their runners were remarkable, and indeed, it was not uncommon for the Osage to walk 60 miles in a day. Their war parties traveled great distances. They aided in the relief of the French at Detroit in 1712; and Che-to-ka, or Whetstone, a Little Osage, claimed that he was at Braddock's defeat with all the warriors that could be spared from the villages.

The ordinary dress of the Osage men included a breechcloth of blue or red cloth secured by a girdle, and a pair of leggings made of dressed deerskin, concealing all the leg except a small portion of the upper thigh. Unornamented moccasins made of dressed deer, elk, or bison skin, and a blanket to cover the upper portion of the body, completed the costume. The women wore moccasins, leggings of blue or red cloth, a piece of blue cloth draped around the waist, and another piece of cloth draped over one shoulder.

The villages of the Great Osage were laid out irregularly, and contained small cone-shaped huts and larger oblong structures. The latter, described by Z. M. Pike in 1806, were about 20 feet wide, and varied in length from 40 to 100 feet, in width from 15 to 20 feet. They were made of a framework of poles covered with a matting of woven rushes. Smoke from the fires made in the center of the lodge was allowed to drift through apertures left in the roof for that purpose.

The Osage subsisted chiefly through hunting, but they annually raised small crops of corn, beans, and pumpkins. The men hunted from May until August, returning in time to gather the crops left unhoed and unfenced during the summer. Late in September, the fall hunts began; these continued until about Christmas. The Indians then remained in their villages until February or March when the spring hunts commenced; first the bear, then the beaver hunt.

Those who were more fortunate in the hunt provided for the destitute, and it was customary to send provisions to the lodges of the poor, the widows, and the fatherless. This spirit of consideration was reflected in the government of the Osage. Although authority was nominally vested in a small number of chiefs, usually hereditary, no important decision was ever made without consulting the warriors in council. There was no regular code of laws, but rather a tacit understanding of the right to command.

Conspicuous among the various Indian tribes for their general sobriety, the Osage remained for more than a century but little changed by their association with white traders and visitors. "You are surrounded by slaves," old Chief Has-ha-ke-da-tungar, or Big Soldier, once remarked to a white friend. "Everything about you is in chains, and you are in chains yourselves. I fear if I should change my pursuit for yours, I too, should become a slave."

The Chouteau family of St. Louis had exclusive trading privileges with the Osage until about 1795, when they were transferred to Manuel Lisa. In 1802, through the influence of Pierre Chouteau, a group of the Great Osage moved south to the Arkansas River, where Chouteau retained their trade. In 1808, the United States government established a military and trading post, Fort Osage, near the present town of Sibley in Jackson County, to supply the Indians with goods and to protect them from the northern tribes. Some of the Indians set up their lodges near the fort, and the friendly relations thus established were preserved during the War of 1812, although the fort was abandoned for a few years. In 1821, the United Foreign Missionary Society established Harmony Mission about three miles northwest of Papinsville to educate and Christianize the Osage (*see Tour 10b*). Four years later, the Osage surrendered the remainder of their lands in Missouri and Arkansas, and by 1837, all had moved into Kansas.

The Sauk and Fox Indians, who claimed as their hunting grounds all the territory north of the Missouri River and east of the Grand River to the Mississippi, carried on a war for many years against the Missouri. Although the date of their entry into the State is not clear, the Sauk and Fox were in undisputed possession of the north Missouri area early in the eighteenth century, and often attacked their enemies south of the Missouri River. They displaced the Peoria, found by Marquette and Jolliet at and near the mouth of the Des Moines, and forced them southward. Later, the Peoria, greatly reduced in numbers, established villages near St. Louis and Ste. Genevieve, seeking the protection of the whites against their relentless enemies.

According to Black Hawk, the Sauk or Sac, and the Fox—variously known as Outagamie, Outagamiouek, and Musquakee, and nicknamed Renard (Fox) by the French—lived originally along the St. Lawrence River. Both tribes were of Algonquin stock. The pressure of the Iroquois slowly forced them westward. Emigrating independently, they eventually met at Green Bay, where they formed a lasting alliance. Intensely savage, rude in manner, and of a roving disposition, these tribes were constantly at war with their Indian neighbors and with the French, and proved a severe hindrance to French colonial trade on the upper Mississippi. Expeditions were sent against them in 1717, 1728, and 1734. The last, commanded by Nicholas Joseph De Noyalles, started for the Des Moines country from Montreal in August. After a somewhat dispirited war, an indecisive peace was arranged the following year.

The principal villages of the Sauk and the Fox in 1804 were within the present State of Missouri, south of the Des Moines; they had other villages in the present area of Iowa and Illinois. Their mode of living was somewhat similar to that of the Osage. The Sauk and Fox winter hunt began in the late fall after harvest and continued until March or

April, when the tribe returned to their villages to plant their crops.
Their agriculture was more extensive than that of the Osage. They
cultivated land near the Mississippi and raised as much as 8,000 bushels
of corn, besides beans, pumpkins, and melons. During the summer,
the younger men went on a hunt, leaving the women in the villages
to weave rush mats and bark corn-bags, and the older men to dig and
smelt lead at the mines in their territory. Lead produced during a
season reached 5,000 pounds. Their surplus products, including furs,
they sold to white traders. This commerce was long controlled by
the English, although the Spanish traders in St. Louis secured some of
it; after the acquisition of the Louisiana Territory by the United States,
it was absorbed by St. Louis merchants.

American settlement forced other tribes westward. Many of these
were encouraged to settle in Missouri by the Spanish authorities, who
hoped in this manner to form a bulwark against the unremitting raids
and thefts of the Osage, and against the possibility of American invasion.

The most important of these tribes were the Shawnee and Delaware,
who began emigrating to southeastern Missouri as early as 1784. In
1793, Baron de Carondelet authorized Don Louis Lorimier to establish these tribes in the province of Louisiana, on the Mississippi between
the Missouri and the Arkansas. Subsequently, the Spanish government
authorized Lorimier to induce them to make a settlement in the Spanish
territory. The Indians' hatred of the Americans, who had conquered
them through the victory of General Wayne and the Treaty of Greenville (1795), made Lorimier's task an easy one. In 1797, these Indians
were reported moving into Missouri in large numbers.

The settlements of the Shawnee and the Delaware were principally
made between Cinque Hommes and Flora Creeks above Cape Girardeau.
The tribes were accustomed to act together in important matters, but
they established separate villages. The largest Shawnee village contained about 400 inhabitants, and was built on the top of a hill above
Apple Creek, near the present site of Old Appleton. The Shawnee
usually called their villages Chillicothe, or Chilliticaux, the word meaning "a place of residence." Pierre Menard says they named their town
Chalacasa, after their old town on the Scioto. Their houses were of logs
constructed in the French style (see Architecture). The Shawnee were
active, industrious, and good hunters. They were also good farmers,
cultivating fields of corn, pumpkins, melons, and potatoes, and raising
cattle, hogs, and horses. When they first settled in Missouri they had
frequent wars with the Osage, but by 1802 peace was secured. They
were attentive to dress and used great quantities of vermilion and black
to paint their bodies on feast days. They were unusually careful of
their children.

Among the various Shawnee groups who settled in Missouri was one band of about 24 warriors of which Lewis Rogers, a white man taken prisoner in childhood, was chief. During the early Kentucky Indian wars, Rogers commanded a marauding party of the Ohio River, plundering boats and murdering the owners who resisted. Following General Anthony Wayne's victory, Rogers prudently decided to move into Spanish territory with his loot. Here he developed an interest in white culture and co-operated with his white neighbors, living at various places, including Bridgeton, the Fourche à Courtois in Washington County, and Franklin County south of Union, where he died. A comparatively wealthy man, Rogers offered money to any white man who would marry his daughter; after the marriage he deferred payment of the promised dowry, saying he would see if the man proved a worthy husband (*see Tour 1*).

Among the Shawnee who settled on Apple Creek was Peter Cornstalk—Nerupenesheguah—son of the celebrated Cornstalk of the Dunmore war, a war chief and a fluent and powerful speaker. At the age of 80, he was a conspicuous defender of Shawnee interests in their lands west of the Missouri State Line. A sister of Tecumseh—Teceikeapease—who married a Canadian Frenchman at New Madrid about 1808, and other members of the Tecumseh family, also lived here, as did a brother of the white renegade, Simon Girty, completely Indian in his dress, habits, and manners.

About 1808-9, these Indians became possessed with the belief that witchcraft was practiced among them and consequently burned to death some 50 women within 12 months. The charges against the women were usually based upon the report of some one who claimed he had seen the alleged witch in the form of an owl or some other bird, or in the form of a panther or beast of the forest. The frenzy was suddenly quelled by the appearance of Tecumseh, who was then busy with his plans to form a vast confederacy of all Indians, to check the advance of the white settlers.

Despite the fact that the Spanish government, and later the American government, granted the Indians title to their lands, the Shawnee and Delaware slowly moved west before the advance of the whites, establishing villages successively on White River and Castor River. They also set up a village on the present site of Bloomfield in Stoddard County, and another near the present site of Kennett. In 1806, the Delaware had villages on White River near Forsythe, on James' Fork, and on Wilson's Creek, in present Greene County. In addition, Shawnee and Delaware villages were located on the Meramec and Current Rivers, on the headwaters of the Gasconade, and at other points in the interior.

In the treaty made at St. Louis in 1815, the American government ordered all whites to move from the Shawnee and Delaware lands, but the measure was only of temporary relief, for ten years later the encroachment of white settlers compelled these tribes to sell their Spanish grant and leave the State for a home farther west.

The first groups of Cherokee to immigrate into Missouri came at an early date. According to an old tradition, after the first treaty had been made with the white people, Yunwiusga'se'ti (Dangerous Man) foresaw the end, and led a portion of the tribe westward. After the Revolutionary War, some of the Cherokee who had fought with the British requested and were granted permission to settle in Spanish territory. A settlement was made on the St. Francis River, where other Cherokee groups joined them. From time to time this tribe waged war against the Osage, and the Sauk and Fox. The latter directed their attention toward their "ancient enemy, the Cherokee," and met them in battle near the Meramec. Black Hawk records that although the Cherokee were in superior numbers they lost 28 warriors, whereas the Sauk and Fox lost only 3. In 1838, after a forced sale of their lands in Tennessee and Georgia, the Cherokee Nation was moved west into present Oklahoma. This exodus, in which they were driven with unpardonable severity by a United States Army detachment, resulted in the death of more than 4,000 of the 16,000 Indians who began the journey. Many of the Cherokee made the long journey on foot, crossing the Mississippi River at or near Cape Girardeau during the winter, and passing through southern Missouri by way of Springfield. This trail was subsequently known to the Indians by a word in their language meaning the Trail of Tears.

During the 30-year period following the Louisiana Purchase, the tribes living in Missouri relinquished their claims to Missouri lands by a series of treaties, and moved south and west into the Kansas and Oklahoma region. The first of these treaties, entered into November 3, 1804, between the United States and the Sauk and Fox at Portage des Sioux, was, according to Black Hawk, made without authority having been given the chiefs who negotiated it. Ill feeling among the Indians over this treaty, which ceded an extensive territory, caused a schism between the Sauk and Fox, and was the alleged cause for the depredations on white settlers during the War of 1812.

In the treaty made by the United States at Fort Osage in November 1808, with the Great and Little Osage, a boundary was agreed upon, extending south from Fort Osage to the Arkansas River. In this manner the Osage claim to Missouri lands was extinguished, with the exception of the area now comprising the western tier of counties south of the Missouri River.

The series of treaties with the Sauk and Fox, made at Portage des Sioux following the War of 1812, confirmed and ratified the treaty of 1804 (see History and Government). Four years later, the Kickapoo, in the treaty of Edwardsville, ceded territory in Illinois and Indiana to the United States, and in return were granted lands in southwestern Missouri. Although the title was granted the Kickapoo and their heirs forever, and was confirmed again in 1820, they were forced to move west of the Missouri State Line by the treaty made at Castor Hill, St. Louis County, in 1832. At Washington in 1823, the Sauk and Fox relinquished all remaining claims to lands in Missouri, and the Iowa gave up all claims to the same territory, part of which had been their immemorial hunting ground. The Great and Little Osage relinquished their remaining lands in Missouri in 1825, and, at the same time, a similar treaty was concluded with the Kansas Indians, whose claims had principally embraced Jackson and Cass Counties. During the same year, the Shawnee relinquished their Spanish grants in exchange for land west of the Missouri border, and four years later, the Delaware, at a council held at James' Fork of the White River, were removed to the Delaware reservation in the fork of the Missouri and Kansas Rivers. A final treaty was made in 1832 with the last remnant of the Delaware and Shawnee in southwest Missouri. This treaty, together with one four years later, known as the Platte Purchase, by which the Sauk, Fox, and other tribes ceded the area in northwest Missouri, ended all Indian titles and claims within the present area of Missouri.

History and Government

THE story of Missouri has been shaped by the location of the State at the meeting point of the Missouri, the Ohio, and the Mississippi Rivers, and by the diversity of its surface features—prairies, alluvial plains, and Ozark uplands. Its geographical position has given the region a dramatic importance in the history of national expansion, while its topography has tended to divide its people, its economy, and its political interests along sectional lines that have often resulted in confusion.

French colonial trade and exploration spread south and west along the water highway of the St. Lawrence to the Great Lakes in the opening half of the seventeenth century, and, after a pause, spilled beyond into the valley of the Mississippi. The journey in 1658-59 of Pierre d'Espirit and Medard Chouart, French-Canadian traders, confirmed vague stories of the country beyond Lake Michigan, for these men discovered the "great river that divides itself in two," one branch flowing from the west, the other southwards toward Mexico. In 1673, Louis Jolliet and Father Jacques Marquette made a voyage of exploration down the Mississippi, thinly veiling with missionary zeal the hope of their backers for the discovery of the Northwest Passage, or perhaps the gold mines of Quivira. The latter aim was not encouraged by events, but the men learned from the Indians that the Missouri came a great distance from the northwest, and Father Marquette wrote that he hoped by this river to discover the route to the Western Sea.

On his exploration of the Mississippi in 1682, Robert Cavelier de la Salle was likewise assured by Indians that the Missouri was the route to the Pacific. La Salle suggested that the Missouri was the main stream, and the Upper Mississippi only a tributary. When he reached the mouth of the Mississippi he claimed the entire valley for France, and in honor of the King it came to be known as Louisiana. Thus, without the inhabitants of the territory knowing anything about it, France gained a great empire, and European domination of the region began.

It proved to be a domination not by government officials, but by fur traders and missionary priests who, by the close of the century, had explored much of Missouri, mapped and named many of its streams, and made peace with its Indians. It was, at its best, a vague sort of rule, depending more on the good will of the natives than on any force

of arms. The trader carrying wares to his Indian customers had little
need for a permanent residence. The priests established only semi-
permanent missions on their circuits, and those not often. One such
mission, however, St. Francis Xavier (1700-03), at the mouth of the
River des Peres within present St. Louis, was Missouri's first white
settlement.

A section of Upper Louisiana, extending roughly from the Alleghenies to the Rocky Mountains, came to be called the Illinois Country
because the early French explorers found the Illinois Confederation of
Indians along the Mississippi River. During prehistoric times, Indians
had mined small quantities of lead in present Missouri and Illinois.
Specimens of ore were shown the early French explorers, and the
existence of deposits along the Meramec, the Osage, and the Lamine
in present Missouri, were well known. In 1700, LeSueur, a French
mineralogist, investigated the mines of the Illinois Country. On the
bases of his reports, Le Moyne d'Iberville petitioned the French king
for a concession of the lead mines in southeast Missouri. His petition
was not acted upon, since lead held no interest for the almost bankrupt
French Court. In 1710, however, a report that large quantities of
silver existed in that region was fostered by government officials. Two
years later, Antoine Crozat, a French banker, was granted a 15-year
trade monopoly of Louisiana. He immediately instructed his representative, De la Mothe Cadillac, to open the silver mines in the Illinois
Country. Late in 1714 Cadillac was shown samples of silver ore said
to have come from southeast Missouri, but when he visited the Illinois
Country the following spring he learned that the ore had come from
Mexico. At Mine la Motte, named in his honor, he dug for silver
but found only lead. Nevertheless, he reported that an abundant silver
mine had been discovered, and sent several kegs containing ore supposedly extracted from that mine to France. Miners and supplies were
subsequently sent to Louisiana to exploit the silver, but they never
reached the Illinois Country.

In 1717 Crozat surrendered his patent, having incurred heavy
losses. Soon afterward the Company of the West, reorganized in 1719
as the Royal Company of the Indies, was established in France. In
1719 mines were opened here at Mine la Motte and on Mineral Fork
of Big River. Governor Bienville reported that rich silver mines had
been found, and the company's stock soared. Early in 1720, Philip
Renault, agent of the Company of the Indies, arrived in the Illinois
Country with about 50 miners and some slaves. Under his vigorous
supervision prospecting and mining in southeast Missouri expanded,
but he found no precious metals. A few months after his arrival, the
"Mississippi Bubble" burst, and the bankrupt company withdrew
Renault's credit. Harassed by debts and by a desultory war between

the Fox Indians and the French, Renault continued mining lead until 1744, when he returned to France.

Although French investors lost heavily, the activities of the Company of the Indies greatly aided the Missouri region. Trade with the Indian tribes increased. Etienne de Bourgmond had traveled up the Missouri as far as the Platte River in 1714, keeping an accurate log of the journey, and becoming the idol of the Indian tribes along the way. Six years later, when a Spanish military expedition of about 60 entered French territory, they were massacred in the territory that is now Nebraska by Indians friendly to the French. As a safeguard against further Spanish trespasses, and to strengthen relations between the French and the plains Indians, De Bourgmond established Fort D'Orleans (1723-28) on the Missouri River in present Carroll County. In 1720, Charles Claude Du Tisne explored southwest Missouri, where he visited the Osage Indian villages.

About 1750, some Creole families from Kaskaskia, in present Illinois, moved to the west bank of the Mississippi, and the settlement of Ste. Genevieve developed along the bank of the river. Trade with Canada and New Orleans increased. In 1762, the New Orleans firm of Maxent, Laclede & Company received a monopoly of the fur trade on the Mississippi in the area between the Missouri and the St. Peters Rivers. In 1764, Pierre Laclede, directing the company's activities, assisted by young Auguste Chouteau, established St. Louis as his headquarters. Within a few months the village received official notice that by secret treaty on November 3, 1762, France had ceded its colony west of the Mississippi, and the city of New Orleans, to Spain. By the Treaty of Paris (1763) at the end of the French and Indian War, France lost Canada and her possessions east of the Mississippi to England. Missouri's strategic position at the crossroads of this international boundary gave the region a new prominence, which resulted in rapid development.

In 1765, St. Ange de Bellerive, the commander of Fort Chartres, the French capital of Upper Louisiana, surrendered his fort and the territory east of the Mississippi to British officers. Awaiting the formal transfer of the colony west of the river to Spain, he removed with his garrison to St. Louis, which thus became the capital of Upper Louisiana. St. Ange remained civil and military head until the arrival of Spanish officials in 1770.

The laws and customs of Paris, which had governed the colony during the French regime, remained essentially unchanged under the new government. In theory, Spanish was the official language, and Spanish officials with Spanish titles were substituted for French; but actually, many Frenchmen were appointed to offices in Upper Louisiana, and of course French was the native language of the inhabitants. During the entire Spanish period, the only new laws of consequence were those providing for the acquisition of lands and regulating dower and intestate inheritances.

The government of Upper Louisiana was not complicated. A lieutenant governor was appointed by the governor general at New Orleans to superintend the affairs of the entire territory extending from the Arkansas River to the Canadian Line. The lieutenant governor's authority was extensive, although his decisions could be appealed to the governor general. All land cessions had to be approved in New Orleans. For the more convenient direction of purely local affairs the settlements along the Mississippi were divided into districts, each with a commandant appointed by the lieutenant governor and responsible to him. Before the close of the Spanish period, five such districts were formed in the Missouri area: St. Charles, St. Louis, Ste. Genevieve, Cape Girardeau, and New Madrid. For the most part, the officials seem to have been well selected and the laws impartially enforced.

Settlement and the fur trade increased under this government. Laclede and other enterprising merchants with headquarters in St. Louis extended their operations far up the Missouri and Mississippi Rivers. Their increasing profits made St. Louis the commercial and cultural center of the upper valley. Meanwhile, resident priests were withdrawn from the British villages of the Illinois Country and sent to the growing Spanish settlements. The Creoles on the east bank, already dissatisfied with being subjects of Protestant England, were further disgruntled by this, and many of them moved into Spanish territory.

The inhabitants of Upper Louisiana were primarily fur traders, rather than colonists. They suffered from no land hunger, and their settlements were in reality widely scattered trading posts whose very existence depended upon friendly relations with the Indians. A unity with the natives was consequently one of the major policies of the government, especially since the revenue of the colony was insufficient to support a large army. From the first, the French and Spanish in this area, unlike colonists elsewhere in America, adopted the practice of recognizing the Indians' land claims and of living on the friendliest terms with them. None of their villages was fortified against the Indians, yet, so far as is known, very few Creole colonists were killed by Indians during the entire Colonial period. The Spanish neither took nor needed any military precautions until the British and Americans threatened invasion. Then St. Louis was stockaded, and forts and blockhouses were built throughout the territory.

Life in the colony was seriously disrupted by the American Revolution. The authorities at St. Louis aided George Rogers Clark in the conquest of the territory northwest of the Ohio River, and rallied to defeat a combined British and Indian attack on St. Louis in 1780. This was a significant victory of the American Revolution, for it consolidated the defense of the frontier against British expeditions and Indian raids, at the same time that it preserved the Mississippi-Ohio route for supplies to the American army. However, the enthusiasm with which the French residents of the Northwest Territory and the Spanish officials in the Missouri Territory had greeted the struggle of the colonies was soon destroyed by the harsh and disorganized government established in the territory won from the British. Even before the close of the war, great numbers of Creole families moved west across the Mississippi.

When peace came in 1783, England relinquished her possessions east of the Mississippi to the victorious Americans, yet for almost ten years she continued to occupy posts in the ceded area. Her fur traders, operating from Canada, poached on both American and Spanish territory, and gave increasingly serious competition to St. Louis merchants, who were forced to buy from them at least a portion of their goods for trading.

To Spanish officials the Americans constituted a threat at this time, for they had pushed their settlements across the Alleghenies to the very banks of the Mississippi, and there was no longer a barrier of wilderness between them and the Spanish colony. The territory was too large and too sparsely settled for defense against serious invasion; consequently the Spanish supplemented their military defenses with diplomacy. Like France and England, Spain was involved in various intrigues with American citizens to separate the western territories from the United States. As an additional measure, Spain adopted the policy of encouraging Americans to become Spanish citizens in the territory.

Circumstances aided this plan. The main revenue of the American settlements in Kentucky, Tennessee, and the Ohio River Country came from furs and agricultural products sold on the international market. The Mississippi was the highway to that market, and Spain controlled the Mississippi. This control she exercised arbitrarily, opening or closing the river to American trade without regard to official promises. The Americans were angry over their own government's failure to settle the issue, and many found it expedient to move into Spanish territory, where as citizens they could use the river without restrictions.

There were other advantages to moving across the Mississippi. Spain's land policy was far more liberal than any ever established by the English or American governments. Not only was land granted free on the basis of the settlers' individual needs, but no land taxes were assessed, and settlers without funds were given supplies and equipment. Spain even relaxed her restrictions against Protestants entering the territory. Moreover, slave-holding families were welcomed, and these came in increasing numbers after the passage of the Ordinance of 1787, by which the United States prohibited slavery in the Northwest Territory. Thus, long before Missouri became a part of the Union, slavery was an established institution there.

Spain also fostered various colonizing schemes. New Bourbon became a refuge for the French Royalists whose settlement at Gallipolis had failed, and Colonel George Morgan's grandiose plans for New Madrid were for a time encouraged by the Spanish. Nor did Spain neglect the Indians. As the various tribes were forced westward by advancing American settlement, Spain granted them land in her territory. Louis Lorimier, an Indian trader who had been in the pay of the British and who had led more than one raid on Kentucky villages, was permitted to enter Spanish territory, and lands in southeast Missouri were granted him and his Shawnee and Delaware Indian friends. Spain hoped that Lorimier's Indian colony would serve as an additional bulwark against American aggression, and at the same time would put a stop to Osage Indian raids along the Mississippi. These Osage raids were an omen of the trouble to come as American settlement pushed westward, for the Americans, who had already established villages along the Missouri, the Meramec, the Big River, and the St. Francis, settled their score with the Indians without regard to Spanish policy or Indian rights.

In 1795, by the Treaty of San Lorenzo, free navigation of the Mississippi River below the thirty-first parallel was reaffirmed, and New Orleans was opened to Americans as a port of deposit and export. Five years later, Napoleon, dreaming of reviving the French colonial empire, forced Spain to return New Orleans and the Louisiana Territory to France. No formal transfer was made for almost three years, and Spanish officials remained in charge, but the change in owners aggravated American uneasiness over foreign control of their chief highway. When the Spanish authorities in New Orleans abruptly closed the port to Americans in 1802, the frontiersmen demanded that the matter be decided once and for all, either by purchase or by force. Ministers were consequently sent to France to negotiate with Napoleon for the purchase of New Orleans. To their surprise, they were offered the entire Louisiana Territory, for Napoleon was preparing another war on England. On April 30, 1803, a treaty was signed by which the United States purchased Louisiana for $15,000,000.

The Western settlements were delighted, but the people of the East had some doubts about the purchase. Many feared that the addition of so vast a territory would destroy the original balance of the Union by giving too much power to the trans-Allegheny region. The treaty was ratified, however, and Lower Louisiana was formally transferred to the United States on December 20, 1803. On March 9, 1804,

Captain Amos Stoddard, acting as agent for both the French Republic and the United States, received Upper Louisiana from the Spanish officials in St. Louis at a formal ceremony. Stoddard thus became governor of the territory, but he retained the commandants and other Spanish officials, and the laws and customs of the province were not altered.

The boundaries of the Louisiana Territory were not clearly defined in the treaty. When Congress established Upper Louisiana as the District of Louisiana in 1804, it was described as extending from the thirty-third parallel to the Canadian line, and from the Mississippi indefinitely west. This vast area was put under the control of the Territory of Indiana, of which Benjamin Harrison was then Governor. The three judges of the Indiana Territory, who were appointed a legislative body, supplemented the old Spanish laws with new ones reflecting Anglo-American mores and procedures, but the last of the Spanish laws was not abrogated until 1825. The old Spanish districts were continued as administrative units under the new government. Each was provided with a commandant, a court of common pleas and quarter sessions, a recorder, and a sheriff, and provisions were made for appointing justices of the peace, constables, and coroners for each neighborhood.

The new government was well received at first, but dissatisfaction soon arose. The people of the territory objected to the new taxes, the swarm of officials thrust upon them, the endless delays, and, most of all, the location of the seat of government in Indiana. In the fall of 1804, the various districts sent representatives to a convention in St. Louis, where they drafted a memorial to Congress requesting specified changes.

Congress responded by passing the Act of 1805, which divorced the Louisiana District from the Indiana Territory, and set it up as a separate territory with a government of its own. Officials, appointed by the President of the United States, consisted of a governor, a secretary, and a legislature—the last composed of the governor and three judges, who were empowered to establish inferior courts and prescribe their jurisdiction, and to make all necessary laws. Provision was made for forming new districts as the need arose, and for appointing additional magistrates and civic officers. The first governor appointed was General James Wilkinson, but his administration was so bitterly opposed that on March 3, 1807, he was replaced by Meriwether Lewis, who was both well known and popular in the territory.

Three years earlier, President Jefferson had sent Lewis and William Clark on an expedition from St. Louis up the Missouri River to the headwaters of the Columbia, and from there to the Pacific, to gain first-hand information about the almost unknown western half of the Louisiana Purchase. After two years, Lewis and Clark had returned, their expedition a success. Additional information about the newly acquired land was obtained by Zebulon M. Pike, who explored the Upper Mississippi and traveled through the southwestern portion of the territory during the same period.

As governor, Lewis proved efficient and impartial. Realizing that trouble with the Indians was inevitable, he reorganized the militia and prepared for the coming crisis on the frontier. An Eastern depression had caused heavy immigration to Missouri. Settlement had consequently pushed farther and farther into the immemorial hunting grounds of the Indians, and a cycle of raids, murders, and acts of revenge had begun. As early as 1808, open war was threatened when the Osage, the most powerful tribe in Missouri, began making retaliatory raids on American settlements. General hostilities were averted by a treaty made the same year, by which the Osage gave up part of their Missouri lands on the understanding that the United States would in return help them to fight off their enemies, the Sac and Fox Indians. To cement this bargain, Fort Osage was established in present Jackson County as a United States' trading post. Other tribes proved less tractable; in 1811, fighting broke out with the tribes along the Upper Mississippi, and the territorial militia was mustered.

In terms of men killed and battles fought, the Indian War in Missouri was insignificant. It was serious mainly because it coincided with the War of 1812, in which England aided and partly directed the activities of her Indian allies. News of the declaration of war with England reached St. Louis in July of 1812. At that time only 178 soldiers of the regular army were stationed in Missouri. Requests for additional Federal aid were generally ignored, and the frontier was forced to defend itself. Forts and blockhouses were built to protect the major settlements; Fort Mason on the Mississippi and Fort Osage on the Missouri were abandoned as untenable. Captain Nathan Boone's mounted rangers patrolled the Missouri River, but the center of military activity was at Portage des Sioux in St. Charles County. Occasionally, there were skirmishes elsewhere, and isolated families were murdered. Alarms and rumors, fears and uncertainty spread throughout the territory.

The end of the war did little to relieve this condition, for the Treaty of Ghent forbade all military activity "pending treaty-making with the Indian allies of the English." Thus, while the Indians were free to move, Missouri was hamstrung by international agreement. The boldest and most disastrous Indian attacks of the entire war occurred in 1815, during the six months between the Treaty of Ghent and the signing of the first Indian treaties. Côte sans Dessein, Loutre Island, Cap au Gris, Femme Osage, and the Boon's Lick Country, among other places, were attacked. In July 1815, United States Commissioners

Auguste Chouteau, General William Clark, and Ninian Edwards began treaty conferences at Portage des Sioux with the representatives of 19 tribes. The following year, treaties were made in St. Louis with ten other tribes who had failed to appear at Portage des Sioux, and the War of 1812 was at last at an end in Missouri.

With the path of Westward migration open, and the Indian danger removed, settlers flocked to the territory. Speculation and the expansion of credit mushroomed the value of land; towns were enthusiastically platted and counties were organized. In 1818 Missouri petitioned Congress for authority to frame a constitution prior to admission as a State.

The request, ordinarily a routine matter, precipitated a national crisis. The Northern faction in Congress was particularly anxious that the existing balance between free and slave States should be maintained; consequently they fought to have Missouri created as a free State. After months of debate, the South threatened to refuse Maine's application for statehood unless Missouri was allowed to frame a constitution. Permission was thereupon granted, but with the proviso that slavery should be prohibited in the Louisiana Territory north of 36 degrees and 30 minutes north latitude. An election of delegates was promptly held in Missouri, and on June 12, 1820, the Constitutional Convention met in St. Louis. In 32 days a document was drawn up which briefly defined the respective powers of the governor, the general assembly, and the judiciary. The governor was to be elected for a single four-year term. He was authorized, with the consent of the senate, to appoint a secretary of state, an auditor, and an attorney general, each to serve for four years, and a chancellor, and judges for the supreme and circuit courts, all of whom were to hold office on good behavior. The bicameral general assembly was to have a house of representatives limited to 100 members, and a senate with a minimum of 14 and a maximum of 100 members. The representatives were to serve for terms of two years, the senators for four years. The judicial power of the State was to be vested in a supreme court having jurisdiction over the court of chancery (abolished in 1822), and the circuit courts. Every free white male citizen who was 21 years of age or over, and who had lived in the State for 1 year and in the county for 3 months, was to be allowed to vote. Federal and State officials, and priests and ministers of any religious group, could not be elected to the general assembly. Slavery was recognized, but the emancipation of slaves was permitted, and laws provided for their humane treatment, and gave them the right of counsel, trial by jury, and parity of punishment with white persons.

The constitution was immediately put into effect. On July 19, 1820, David Barton, president of the convention, issued writs for the election of State officials and of a United States representative. Alexander McNair, backed by the "honest farmers," was elected governor in a campaign which evidenced the growing resentment of the rural districts toward the St. Louis clique of lawyers who had been in control of the territorial government. The legislature elected David Barton and Thomas Hart Benton as United States senators.

To Missouri's surprise, when the constitution was returned to Congress for final approval the old debate over the admission of the State was revived. The North, still fighting to prevent the extension of slavery, seized as a basis for argument a clause in the constitution which required the legislature to pass a law prohibiting free Negroes from settling within the State. After much controversy, the Missouri compromise resolution was adopted, by the terms of which Missouri was to be admitted to the Union and the constitution accepted, on the condition that the State legislature would, "by a solemn public act," declare that the offending clause pertaining to free Negroes would never be carried out. The Missouri legislature, well aware of the absurdity of the situation, made the required declaration, and on August 10, 1821, President Monroe proclaimed Missouri's admission into the Union.

Meanwhile, in 1819, the depression which followed the Napoleonic Wars had reached Missouri. In June 1821, the legislature announced a moratorium on land debts. This gave only partial relief, however, because of the condition of the currency. The Bank of St. Louis (1816-19) and the Bank of Missouri (1817-21) had both failed, and Missourians were suspicious not only of banks, but of all currency issued by banks. In an effort to save the State from a barter system, the legislature established loan offices empowered to issue paper based on the credit of the State, but most officials and merchants refused to accept this money. Eventually, both the moratorium and the loan offices were adjudged unconstitutional.

Prosperity gradually returned. The overland trade with Mexico, begun in 1821, provided both specie and an important new source of income. The introduction of steamboat traffic on the Missouri River, at the same time, lowered freighting costs and increased the volume of shipments. The western terminus of the trade was pushed upstream from Franklin to Independence, and, eventually, to the great bend in the river. The opening of the Missouri River also expanded the St. Louis companies' fur business, the most important in the State. While the Santa Fe traders were marking the pattern of national expansion to the Southwest, the fur traders, the "most significant group of continental explorers ever brought together," were investigating routes to California and the Northwest. Thus Missouri's interests lay for some time outside the boundaries of the State. It was not until after the

Civil War, when the West was carved into States and the frontier trails were destroyed, that Missourians turned their attention primarily to their own territory.

One result of overland trade and expanded steamboat traffic was the rapid settlement of western Missouri. In 1836 the Indians relinquished their title to the Platte Country, a strip of land extending along the Missouri River north from present Platte County to the Iowa Line, and the following year it was added to Missouri. Since the Platte strip thus became slave territory, its acquisition was in violation of the Missouri Compromise of 1820. Settlers swarmed into the area, and within a decade tobacco and hemp culture, thriving on slave labor and cheap water transportation, were firmly established. In 1831, Joseph Smith, Prophet of the Mormons, revealed that Independence was to be the Mormon Zion, and thousands of his followers moved into the area. Most of the Mormons were from the North, and opposed to slavery. This, together with their clannishness, their church secrets, and their rapid increase in number, which soon gave them political supremacy, aroused the anger and fear of their neighbors. Within a few years, the Mormons were driven into Clay County, and from there, in 1836, into Daviess and Caldwell Counties. In 1838, during guerrilla fighting between the Saints and other settlers, Governor Lilburn W. Boggs ordered the militia either to exterminate the Mormons or to drive them from the State. In the spring of 1839, the last of them moved from Missouri into Illinois.

With the increase in trade and settlement, several new institutions made their appearance. The Bank of Missouri, chartered in 1837 for 20 years, provided the first sound public banking facilities in Missouri. The territorial law had encouraged education, and the enabling act of 1820 had set aside land for schools; in 1839 the State made its first important provisions for education: laws were passed creating the office of State Superintendent of Common Schools, establishing permanent school funds, and setting up the State University.

By the early 1840's, wagon trains were regularly leaving western Missouri for Oregon, and, shortly thereafter, for Utah and California. War with Mexico broke out in April of 1846, and when the Army of the West was organized, it consisted chiefly of Missourians. Colonel Stephen W. Kearny was put in command, with Colonels A. W. Doniphan and Sterling Price in charge of the First and Second Regiments of Missouri Mounted Volunteers. Under their leadership, the army marched overland to Santa Fe and occupied New Mexico, where they set up a provisional government with Charles Bent, another Missourian, as governor. Doniphan then continued southward, to complete a phenomenal drive of 3,600 miles, without quartermaster, postmaster, commissary, uniforms, tents, or formal military discipline.

The acquisition of New Mexico and California again brought the slavery question to the forefront. Under the law of Mexico, these territories had been free. The South now urged the extension westward of the Missouri Compromise line of 36 degrees and 30 minutes, so that all lands south of it should be slave territory. The Missouri legislature, however, drew up the Jackson Resolutions, in January 1849, instructing the Congressional representatives of the State to insist that Congress had no right to decide the boundaries of free or slave areas, and that new territories should have the power to settle the question for themselves; the resolutions also intimated that in the case of conflict Missouri would stand with the South. Missouri's United States Senator, Thomas Hart Benton, spokesman for the West and advocate of free land, refused to accept the resolutions, on the grounds that they were the expression of a minority group which contemplated secession. Benton's devotion to the Union was complete; he would do nothing that might endanger its solidarity. His crusade against the resolutions caused a split in the Democratic Party in Missouri, and ended his 30-year career as Senator. In 1850 a national compromise was reached on the admission of the new territories. California was to be admitted as a free State; other territories were to be organized without Congressional legislation as to the slavery issue; slavery was to be prohibited by law in the District of Columbia; and stronger fugitive slave laws were to be passed.

The Act of Congress organizing the territories of Nebraska and Kansas in 1854 included clauses repealing the Missouri Compromise of 1820 and leaving the issue of slavery to be decided by the individual States. It was obvious from the first that Nebraska would choose to be a free State; Kansas, on the other hand, was uncertain, and a struggle to influence its position began. The North, fearing that if Kansas became a slave State the balance of power would swing to the South, organized the Emigrant Aid Society and other colonizing groups to finance free settlers in Kansas. Southern sympathizers in Missouri viewed this activity with alarm. If the "Yankee slave-stealers" got a hold in Kansas, they might well advance on Missouri.

Bryant, Whittier, and other New England authors began a vigorous propaganda campaign against Missouri and the South, in which they were aided by Horace Greeley and a number of correspondents sent out by Eastern papers to report on the Kansas-Missouri situation. The pro-Southern newspapers had only one reporter covering the district along the border, where conflict was most strenuous, and he suffered from that great detriment to effective propaganda, a sense of humor. In the battle of words, Missouri and the South came out second best.

Actual strife began in Kansas with the election of March 30, 1855. Thousands of pro-slavery Missourians, principally from the western part of the State, crossed into Kansas, where they elected a territorial legislature which immediately legalized slavery in the territory. Although this Missouri vote was illegal, the government so elected was accepted as official by the Federal Government. The Northern faction retaliated by forming a rival legislature which attempted to seize power by force, and petitioned Congress to admit Kansas as a free State.

Open warfare broke out all along the Missouri-Kansas border. Pro-slavery Missourians rallied to the support of the Kansas government which they had elected. In the guise of a posse summoned by the United States Marshal, a group of them, nicknamed Border Ruffians by Horace Greeley, joined forces with the Kansas militia. In November of 1855 they entered Lawrence, the capital of the free-State group, and burned the hotel and some houses, destroyed the press, and arrested several of the free-State leaders. For this act John Brown, the fanatical abolitionist, retaliated by killing five pro-slavery settlers on Pottawatomie Creek. Assassination for the holding of opinions had begun. Before guerrilla warfare was more or less ended in 1858 by the combined effort of the Federal, and the Kansas and Missouri governments, some 200 people were killed, and $2,000,000 worth of property was destroyed.

For a few years there was comparative peace along the Missouri-Kansas border, but the issues involved had not been settled. The Dred Scott decision in 1857 had made a major conflict inevitable, since, basically, it confirmed the contention of the States Rights advocates in declaring that Congress had no right to pass laws regulating slavery, and that the States alone could legislate upon the matter. "Now freedom and slavery," as Dr. Culmer points out in his *A New History of Missouri*, "opposed each other everywhere without an arbiter in the government of the United States."

The much publicized border war had given Missouri a reputation for lawlessness, and as a staunch supporter of the South. As a matter of fact, however, the average Missourian expressed himself for a compromise of national differences, until the outbreak of war forced him reluctantly to take sides. In 1860, the various beliefs of the minority who owned the 114,930 slaves in Missouri were represented by a politically strong pro-Southern faction. Half of the slaves were in 12 counties, and two-thirds of them were in the area along the Missouri River. The pro-Union group, likewise a minority at first, consisted largely of the 160,541 foreign-born in the State, most of whom lived in the district about St. Louis. They were for the main part workmen, and their opposition to slavery was strengthened by the fact that they had had to compete with slave labor. The struggle between these radical minorities to force Missouri to take sides brought a serious schism in a State where racial, religious, and economic differences were already very acute. The split, often affecting small towns and even families, gave the Civil War in Missouri a peculiar horror.

Claiborne F. Jackson was inaugurated as Governor in January, 1861. In his inaugural address he commented on the rise of the Republican Party, which seemed to him to be attempting to end, rather than restrict, slavery. He therefore recommended that a State convention be called to sound out the will of the people on the issue. In February an election of delegates was held, with startling results. Not one pro-slavery delegate was elected; a majority of 80,000 votes went to the Northern faction. When the convention met, it recommended the compromise of the secession question, and then recessed, but did not disband. The citizens of the State were still undecided, though feeling ran high. Frank Blair, political heir of Thomas Hart Benton, co-operating with the Federal Government, organized the pro-Union forces in and around St. Louis, where the United States Arsenal was situated. On May 3, the pro-Southern State Militia established Camp Jackson on the outskirts of St. Louis, with an eye, perhaps, to the supplies in the arsenal. A week later, Federal troops under the command of Captain Nathaniel Lyon forced Camp Jackson to surrender, but the soldiers were set upon in St. Louis by Southern sympathizers, and 28 persons were killed. Despite the intense feeling which the episode aroused, another attempt at compromise was made. On June 11, Governor Jackson offered concessions, but after Captain Lyon abruptly ended the meeting by declaring war, Jackson returned to Jefferson City, and called out 50,000 State troops "to repel the invasion" of Missouri. Lyon followed in hot pursuit. Jackson moved the State government from Jefferson City, but on June 17 his troops were defeated in the Battle of Boonville. Poorly supplied with arms or ammunition, they retreated southward in disorder. Later, pro-Southern troops won victories at Carthage (July 5), at Wilson's Creek (August 10), and at Lexington (September 13).

In October, pro-Southern members of the legislature met in Neosho and passed an act of secession on the basis of which Missouri was soon after admitted into the Confederacy. Already the pro-Union State Convention had reconvened, however, and with the support of the Federal Government and troops had summarily deposed Jackson and the refugee representatives, and had set up a provisional government with Hamilton R. Gamble as governor. Thus was Missouri saved for the Union, escaping military rule and the problems of reconstruction from outside the State after the war.

General Sterling Price made an effort to organize a Confederate campaign in Missouri, but any chance for concerted pro-Southern action ended when he was defeated in March, 1862, at Pea Ridge, Arkansas.

After that the Civil War in Missouri degenerated into raids and deeds of revenge by guerrilla bands.

In the summer of 1861, the Federal Government had authorized the formation of volunteer Kansas companies. These groups were commanded by James Lane, Dr. Charles R. Jennison, and James Montgomery, all former leaders of the free-State faction in territorial Kansas. In the guise of Federal troops acting to weed out Confederate activity in southwest Missouri, these Jayhawkers, Kansas Freebooters, or Gallant Knights (depending on the prejudice of the observer) raided and burned towns, looted, and murdered with a free hand. Many Missourians had gone off to join one or the other army, but guerrilla bands, under such men as William C. Quantrill, Cole Younger, and Bill Anderson, were soon organized for defense and retaliation. Though for a time Southern sympathizers in Missouri took heart from the brilliant military maneuvers of these groups, and especially of Quantrill's, the guerrillas never had sufficient strength to strike at Federal control, and their depredations merely prolonged the miseries of the State.

In August of 1863, Quantrill captured Lawrence, Kansas, the abolitionist capital, burned 185 buildings, and killed about 150 inhabitants. In an effort to curb such bushwacker raids, General Thomas Ewing, commanding the Headquarters District of the Border, issued on August 25 his famous Order No. 11, which commanded the evacuation, with certain areas exempted, of Cass, Jackson, Bates, and part of Vernon County within 15 days. As a result, the raiders were scattered into central and southern Missouri, while the innocent inhabitants of the proscribed counties suffered.

Late in 1864, General Sterling Price made another attempt at a Confederate campaign in Missouri. He brought his troops up from Arkansas, through Pilot Knob, and toward Kansas City. He was defeated at Westport after a three-day battle, and the Civil War was practically over in Missouri.

In all, 1,162 battles or skirmishes were fought in the State, 11 per cent of those fought in the nation, and more than occurred in any other State except Virginia and Tennessee. Missouri provided a total of 40,000 troops to the Confederacy and 110,000 to the Union. The Western Sanitary Commission, organized in 1861 through the effort of Dr. William G. Eliot, St. Louis educator and minister, provided hospital and medical service for much of the Mississippi Valley. To expand its services, railroad cars and steamboats were used as traveling hospitals. Public and private groups in the Middle West donated more than $4,000,000 in money and supplies to support the Commission, which, besides giving care and equipment, kept a register of the sick, wounded, and dead, aided refugees, and established several homes for soldiers, and a home for soldiers' children in St. Louis.

The Union faction in the State had split into Moderate and Radical Republican groups, each striving for control of the new State government. On July 1, 1863, the Moderate leaders obtained the passage of an act of emancipation under which slaves would be freed July 4, 1870. The Radical faction, however, took control in the election of 1864, and at once called a constitutional convention which abolished slavery immediately and unconditionally. Missouri was thus the first of the slave States to free its slaves. The convention's next move was to draft a new constitution, put in force July 4, 1865, which provided for generous aid to public schools, regulated corporations, and prohibited further aid to railroads, since by this time Missouri was disillusioned about government subsidies to railroads. These measures were overshadowed, however, by the extremist "Test Oath," designed to keep the Radical Republican minority in power by providing that no one could vote, hold State office, preach, teach, or practice law in the State of Missouri who could not take oath that he had never in any way aided or sympathized with the Confederate cause.

To insure the approval of this constitution an ordinance was passed limiting the franchise to those who could take the Test Oath. All judges of the supreme, circuit, county, and legislative courts of record, all court clerks, circuit attorneys, sheriffs, and county recorders were to vacate their offices May 1, 1865, and their places were to be filled by appointment of the Governor for the remainder of their terms. When the supreme court judges refused to vacate on the grounds that the ordinance was unconstitutional, they were ousted by force. Ministers, priests, and nuns engaged in teaching were arrested, and in some cases fined or imprisoned. A Registry Act passed in 1865 provided that a superintendent elected in each county should be the sole judge as to who was qualified to vote; three years later, the office was made appointive.

There was, of course, opposition to these measures, but the Radical Republican government ignored it and went ahead with its reconstruction program. Some 27,000 Missouri citizens had been killed, much private property had been destroyed, and whole counties devastated. The slaves freed in 1865 represented an investment loss of about $40,000,000. Railroads, highways, bridges, and public buildings had been damaged. Taxes were the highest in Missouri's history. The Radical government set up a Bureau of Immigration which encouraged settlement, particularly of Europeans, in the State. It created the Department of Agriculture, and employed a State entomologist; it drew funds from the general revenue for the support of Missouri University and of Lincoln Institute for Negroes at Jefferson City; it established normal schools at Kirksville and Warrensburg. On the other hand, it permitted the sale of railroads foreclosed by the State at less than the interest due on the loans, so that the State treasury realized less than 20 per cent on the debts.

In 1866 the United States Supreme Court declared unconstitutional the clause of the Test Oath which disqualified professional men from practice, and four years later voters approved an amendment abrogating the entire oath.

Meanwhile, under the leadership of B. Gratz Brown and Carl Schurz, a German immigrant who had lived in Missouri only two years, a Liberal opposition to the Radical faction was taking shape in the Republican Party. In 1869 Schurz defeated the Radical Republican candidate for the United States Senate, and the following year Brown was elected governor of Missouri. The Liberal Republicans then formed a joint State ticket with the revived Democratic Party, and won a complete victory over the Radical Republicans in the election of 1872. Once the power of the Radicals had been broken, however, the Liberal Republican Party disintegrated, and the Democrats began a long period of domination in Missouri.

In 1875, 60 Democrats, 6 Republicans, and 2 Liberals met in Jefferson City and drafted a new constitution, which was adopted the same year. Under it, not less than 25 per cent of the general revenue was to be devoted to maintaining public schools. The governor's term, and that of nearly all other State officials, was lengthened to four years, with the provision that the governor and treasurer could not succeed themselves. A "home rule" charter left special legislation in cities of more than 100,000 to local vote. A State railroad commission was created to regulate rates and shipping conditions. Tax restrictions were placed on State and local governments, and towns and counties were forbidden to issue bonds for any purpose except public improvement. With some amendments, this constitution is still in use.

Conditions in Missouri had changed greatly during the war years. There was no more frontier; the old outfitting days were over, the Santa Fe trade was lost. The fur trade and steamboat traffic were dying. The new railroads were diverting business from the old river towns to wide areas far from the waterways. Tenant farmers had replaced slave labor, and the great hemp and tobacco plantations were destroyed. St. Louis, grown prosperous on war supplies and as a railroad terminus, was a sprawling city, ambitious to become the capital of the United States. Kansas City had developed as a market for the new States of Kansas, Nebraska, and Texas. The lead mines of southeast Missouri, and the lead and zinc mines of southwest Missouri were in the first flush of their rapid expansion. Industry had begun to concentrate in the cities, and there was rivalry between the rural and urban centers. With no Western empire to explore or conquer, Missourians for the first time concentrated all their vitality on their own State.

With a few exceptions, such as the town of Liberty, where the Confederate flag was flown on the court house until nearly 1870, Missourians soon forgot their war differences. Some of the former bushwhackers, however, could not settle down to normal existence. Turned outlaw, they continued to harass the countryside; between 1866 and 1882, crimes attributed to them included 14 bank robberies, the Kansas City Fairgrounds' robbery, and many stagecoach and train holdups. In 1882, Governor T. T. Crittenden began a campaign to end their depredations. Jesse James, most notorious of the bandits, was murdered by one of his lieutenants (*see St. Joseph and Tour 10A*), and his band was broken up.

As industry grew in the cities, foreign laborers were brought in, with the result that wages fell. At the same time, the cost of living increased. The resultant social unrest was reflected in Missouri in the strike of 1877, and in subsequent walkouts. These attempts to correct abuses by means of organized opposition the workers supplemented with the political support of social legislation. The Greenbacks and other social reform parties sought a remedy for the Nation's ills in inflation. Missouri's prophet of this theory was Richard P. Bland, "Silver Dick," who introduced the bill providing for free and unlimited silver coinage which Congress passed in 1877, but which was later modified, and finally repealed in 1893. In the campaign of 1896, in which the "free silver" issue was revived as the main plank in the Democratic platform, Bland was narrowly defeated for the presidential nomination by William Jennings Bryan. In the general election, the Nation repudiated both Bryan and "Silver Dick's" economic theories.

When the United States went to war with Spain, Missouri sent 1 light battery company and 6 regiments of infantry, 8,109 men in all. Only the battery company and one of the infantry regiments saw actual service, but having contributed to the success of the war, Missourians increased their demands for reforms at home. A succession of governors had warned against the menace of uncurbed big business, but nothing had been done about the matter. When the St. Louis streetcar workers staged a violent strike in 1900, William Marion Reedy summed up the situation in the statement: "The disgrace, the tragedy, the horror of the situation in St. Louis is all due to politics." Soon afterward, Joseph W. Folk, St. Louis circuit attorney, began an investigation. He discovered that, under machine leadership, "boodling" city officials had accepted bribes to grant some $50,000,000 worth of city franchises and other municipal privileges for about one-tenth of their value. According to Lincoln Steffens, in *The Shame of the Cities*, St.

Louis at this time offered an unusual variation on the familiar pattern
of municipal corruption, for leading business and professional men
joined forces with officials to loot the city's assets.   On the basis of
Folk's evidence, 39 men were indicted, but, to quote Steffens again, "the
whole machinery of justice broke down under the strain of the boodle
pull," and few of them were ever punished.   Folk, however, followed
the trail of corruption to the State government.   In 1903, the Grand
Jury of Cole County reported that legislative corruption "had been the
usual and accepted thing . . . without interference."   The lieutenant
governor resigned, and several members of the general assembly were
indicted.

In the midst of this turmoil, St. Louis prepared to celebrate the
centennial of the Louisiana Purchase.   Early in 1904, the World's Fair
opened, its elaborate French-rococo buildings spreading over the wide
area of Forest Park.   All but one of the States and Territories in the
Union had exhibits, and 62 foreign nations were represented.   The
sacred shrines of Jerusalem and the native villages of many savage
tribes were reproduced, and a fabulous art collection was displayed.
The Fair was a financial success, and served to advertise the State
widely; for Missourians it was a never-to-be-forgotten event.

In 1904, Folk was elected Governor, and his four years in office
were notable for industrial and social legislation.   The State-wide
primary law was passed.   A railroad law established a maximum freight
rate and a passenger rate of two cents per mile.   Anti-lobby, anti-trust,
child labor, public utility, and factory inspection laws were passed.
Direct legislation by initiative and referendum was adopted.   Attorney
General Herbert S. Hadley conducted a dramatic prosecution of the
Standard Oil Company and of other trusts and combinations for violat-
ing the State anti-trust laws.   As a result, Hadley became the next
governor of Missouri.   His administration fostered better roads, wider
education, and penal reforms, and encouraged new industry.

In the presidential campaign of 1912, Hadley was suggested as a
compromise candidate for the Republican Party, which had split into
two factions.   When Theodore Roosevelt became the champion of the
Progressive faction, however, Hadley threw his support to Taft, and so
destroyed his own chance for the candidacy.   At the same time, another
Missourian was figuring importantly in the Democratic convention.
Champ Clark, then serving his ninth term in Congress and his eighth
year as speaker of the House, ran for the presidential nomination, but
was defeated at the last moment by opposition from Bryan.   The candidacy went to Woodrow Wilson.

Between 1916 and 1920, when Frederick D. Gardner was Governor of Missouri, a tax board and a State prison board were created,
the contract system at the State penitentiary was abolished, and a

mothers' pension was provided. Missouri shared in the general World War prosperity, and aided in the national defense. The State over-subscribed its quotas in all five war loans, and enrolled 140,257 soldiers, one-third of them volunteers. Provost Marshal Enoch H. Crowder of Grundy County drew up and directed the activities of the Selective Service Act (the draft). General John J. Pershing of Linn County commanded the American Army in France. On April 24, 1917, the Missouri Council of Defense, for 21 months the supreme authority in the State, was organized under the direction of Dean F. B. Mumford of the University of Missouri. When the National Guard was called to service, 10,000 citizens were sworn in as a Home Guard. By June 1, 1919, Missouri's casualties totaled 11,172.

The depression which followed the war was felt heavily in Missouri, where farm values crashed and many banks, especially in rural sections, failed. In the hope of bettering conditions, Missouri shifted its politics and elected a Republican State government, with Arthur M. Hyde as Governor. In 1921, nine amendments were added to the constitution. One of these authorized road bonds of $60,000,000 to "pull Missouri out of the mud." The highway system which was subsequently developed provided the basis for the most significant economic changes in Missouri life since the Civil War (*see Transportation, and Industry, Commerce, and Labor*). Further legislative reforms were attempted by a Constitutional Convention in 1922-23, but with the exception of six amendments, the convention's suggestions were rejected by the voters.

Notable social reform measures enacted during the 1920's included pure food and drug laws, milk inspection, and further regulation of industry and corporations; also provisions for the protection of dependent children, and for more scientific treatment of the socially maladjusted. In 1928, an additional bond issue of $74,000,000 for State highways was authorized.

Since 1932, Missouri has co-operated in the social programs of the Federal Government, and has established Algoa Farms near Jefferson City as a model intermediate penal institution for older first offenders. During the administration of Governor Lloyd C. Stark (1936-40), reform was again of paramount interest. In 1938, more than 100 members of the Pendergast political machine of Kansas City were indicted for vote frauds in the city elections and for income tax evasion. Convictions followed in rapid order. Once given an opportunity, Kansas City repudiated the machine government. On June 13, 1939, the legislature approved a bill authorizing State control of the Kansas City police department.

Instances of corruption, such as the Kansas City scandal and the earlier St. Louis boodling ring, have been minor in the State. Since pioneer days, the idealism of the average Missourian has been an important political factor.   Both the city and the rural press have made every effort to fight corruption.   Modern highways, railroads, and air lines have tended to integrate the State, and to break down the racial and cultural barriers which have existed in the past.

Agriculture

PRIOR to the Louisiana Purchase, agriculture in the territory now embraced by Missouri was of the simple pattern which the French colonists had brought from Canada to Illinois and thence across the Mississippi. The Creole practice was a blend of individual and collective farming. Each group cleared a large common field and carefully fenced it against Indians and animals (*see Ste. Genevieve*). The *Grand Champ* of Ste. Genevieve in the fabulously rich Mississippi River bottom comprised several thousand acres, in which each family owned at least one long, narrow strip of land stretching westward from the river, the tenure being similar to that of French-Canadian fields along the St. Lawrence River today. To provide pasture and wood lot, a second tract of land, the "commons," was reserved near each village.

This half-collective system of farming and the productivity of the soil laid the basis for a leisurely way of life almost unique on the frontier. Once planted, the growing crop was given no further attention until harvest. "All the husbandry required," Henry Brackenridge comments in his *Recollections,* "is to stir the ground slightly before it is sown, which will alone suffice to produce an excellent crop."

The principal crops of this fertile region were corn, pumpkins, and spring wheat. Oats, barley, beans, watermelons and muskmelons, peaches, apples, tobacco, cotton, hogs, and other products were also raised for local consumption. Grist mills were established in many villages and dairy products found a wide market. Brandy and cider were commonly made from peaches and apples, and a red wine from sweet grapes.

In 1794, Ste. Genevieve and New Bourbon produced 30,980 minots (a minot was about 39 liters) of corn alone, as compared with 20,150 grown by other French settlements of Upper Louisiana; 2 years later, they produced 46,190 minots. One reason for this increase was that trading occupied less of the settler's time here than in the St. Louis and St. Charles districts.

As settlement progressed, Spain offered every inducement to immigrants. To the French-Canadians in Illinois she promised, in addition to large land grants, a barrel of corn, an axe, a hoe, a scythe, a spade, a hen, a cock, and a two-months-old pig for each family. When this policy failed to draw enough settlers, land grants and commercial privileges were granted to American settlers who would turn Catholic and swear allegiance to Spain.

Following the transfer of Louisiana in 1804, immigrants swarmed into Missouri, settling at first in the southeastern portion of the territory and, after the War of 1812, westward along the fertile Missouri River valley. To some, it seemed as though Kentucky, Tennessee, and Virginia were breaking up and moving West; other settlers came from the middle States and a sprinkling from "Yorkdom and Yankeedom." Many were attracted to the Boon's Lick Country by such legends as, "If you plant a tenpenny nail there at night, hit'll sprout crow bars by mornin'."

The Federal and State governments slowly evolved a land policy to satisfy the demands of these settlers. Wavering and uncertain, this policy was a series of concessions to the popular urge for more and cheaper land. It encouraged speculation and overexpansion, permitted soil waste by careless agricultural practices, and led inevitably to an alternation of depressions and jubilant good times. On the other hand, it made possible the settling of the entire State within a single generation, and aided the building of roads, bridges, schools, and railroads.

In 1805, the United States government established a Board of Commissioners in Missouri to pass on the Spanish land titles, which involved about 1,721,485 arpents (.85 of an acre) of land. Although the majority of the titles were clear, many had been incompletely made, or were fraudulent. Successive Congressional acts eventually recognized most of the claims, although the issue was not closed until 1870.

A series of earthquakes beginning in 1811 rendered untillable much of the land in the New Madrid area. In 1815, Congress issued loose certificates to the settlers in this region permitting them to take up an equal amount of land anywhere in the Boon's Lick Country. The result was pandemonium. Speculators bought up many of the certificates; swindlers laid false claims. Later, it was asserted that there were five times as many New Madrid claims as there had been heads of families in the earthquake area.

Meanwhile, Missouri's land boom continued, produced in part by the heavy immigration which reached its climax in 1819. At Franklin, in January, 1819, almost any good quarter brought from $4 to $12 an acre, an enormous price for that time. During the same period, improved lands around St. Louis were selling for $20 an acre. By the fall of that year, however, the Eastern depression which followed the close of the Napoleonic wars spread westward to Missouri to create a near-panic among both farmers and speculators. Congress consequently passed laws to relieve those who had purchased land on credit by extending the time of forfeiture and reducing the payments. In addition, Governor McNair granted in 1821 a moratorium for a two-

and-a-half-year period, which was known as the stay law. This, however, offered only partial relief to the debtor landowners. The Missouri legislature therefore passed an act providing for the establishment of a Loan Office for the issue of interest-bearing paper money based on the credit of the State, in an attempt to furnish a satisfactory currency and to enable landowners to borrow at a fair rate of interest. Most merchants and officials refused to accept these notes, however, and both their issue and the stay law were subsequently ruled unconstitutional.

Other efforts were made to relieve the farmers. Agricultural societies, organized during 1821 and 1822 in St. Louis, St. Charles, and Franklin, planned fairs and factories to furnish a market for home products, but their immediate effect was slight. The crisis was already passing and free land was abundant. Any man could "squat" on the public land, and by the frontier code such occupation was generally equivalent to ownership.

During the worst days of the depression, an overland trade route, opened from Franklin in the Boon's Lick Country west to Santa Fe, New Mexico, provided an outlet for Missouri foodstuffs and brought silver and gold, mules and horses into the settlements. This trade was, perhaps, the greatest single factor in the settlement of western Missouri. It established Missouri as a supply base for the flour, beef, pork, and other foodstuffs needed by the expanding empire of the Far West.

The gradual return of prosperity increased the demand for land. A bill formulated by Thomas H. Benton in 1824 was finally passed in 1842, granting 160 acres to settlers who should establish themselves under carefully guarded terms as to residence and cultivation. Much of the less desirable land in Missouri was eventually sold for 12½ cents an acre. Not until the early 1920's was all the government land in Missouri occupied.

The frontier agriculture of the American settlers was in marked contrast to that of the Creoles. Many of the first settlers were "families whose roving, inconstant mode of living [was] not suited to a permanent settlement," and who formed, as Duke Paul of Württemberg observed in 1823, "the transitional link between civilization and the unrestrained wilderness." Occasionally, they raised "a patch of corn" and some pumpkins and beans, but on the whole they were nomadic hunters rather than agriculturalists. The more permanent Missouri frontier farmers either occupied Spanish grants or New Madrid claims, or "squatted" on the public lands until the government patented their titles. At first, the danger of Indian attack and the need for mutual assistance in the clearing of land and building of homes fostered a co-operative social organization somewhat similar to the Creole type. In the Boon's Lick country during the Indian

THE MISSOURI
AND THE MISSISSIPPI

Piaget Studio

THE MISSOURI RIVER

UP STREAM ON THE MISSISSIPPI

Piaget Studio

THE LEVEE AT ST. LOUIS

KANSAS CITY

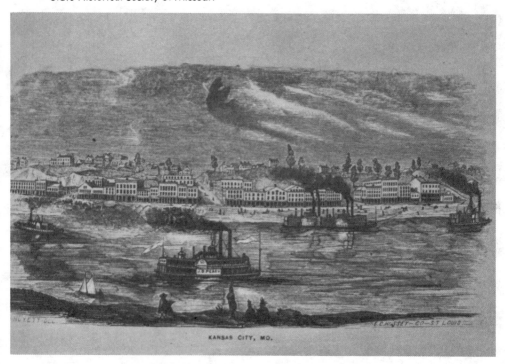

KANSAS CITY, MO.

Farm Security Administration; Vachon

ST. LOUIS LEVEE

MUNICIPAL DOCKS, ST. LOUIS

W. C. Persons

"STERNWHEELER"

Piaget Studio

THE GRAND REPUBLIC, Built in Pittsburg, 1867, and was the largest steamboat in the world.   Burned 1877

INTERIOR OF THE GRAND REPUBLIC

MODERN EXCURSION BOAT ON ST. LOUIS LEVEE

A MISSISSIPPI RIVER STEAMBOAT AND EADS BRIDGE, ST. LOUIS

U. S. Army Air Corps

AIRVIEW OF THE MISSISSIPPI AT ST. LOUIS

LOCK AND DAM ACROSS UPPER MISSISSIPPI AT ALTON, ILLINOIS

U. S. Army Engineers Corps

FLOOD CONTROL, A Lumber Mattress Is Constructed as Revetment

FLOODED FARMLAND AFTER A MISSISSIPPI RAMPAGE

troubles, great common fields were cultivated under the protection of guards sent out from the fortified cabin groups which supplanted isolated dwellings. With the coming of peace, however, the settlers took up the typically American system of individual farming.

The country was naturally suited to agriculture. "There is no part of the western country that holds out greater advantages to the new settler than the Missouri Territory," states an immigrants' guide of 1820. "Here the trees are not more abundant on the upland than would be necessary for fuel and for fences. They naturally stand at a sufficient distance from each other to admit a fine undergrowth of grass and herbage." During the first winters, many families along the Missouri River pastured their livestock on islands, or in the low bottoms whose rank growth of rushes (*Equisetum hyemale*) provided excellent forage. Wheat, corn, rye, barley, and buckwheat were planted from the first, and as the turmoil of the frontier period gave way to permanent settlement, orchards, vineyards, and vegetable gardens were developed.

Despite the general fertility of the soil, the early Missouri farmer had his troubles. Wolves prevented sheep raising in certain districts. A Mrs. Spencer of St. Charles County reported that during frontier days "wild cats and catamounts" sometimes ate holes in the shoulders of her cows. Swarms of locusts and army worms appeared to "cut down and devour every green thing." Droughts were recurrent. After 1850, the great herds of Texas cattle driven north to market through southwest Missouri spread the "Spanish, or Texas fever" to Missouri stock, and thousands died before the borders were closed to the contaminated cattle after the Civil War. In 1858, Vernon County stockmen alone estimated their loss for that year at more than $100,000.

Marketing their produce constituted another major problem. In the absence of good roads, most products were shipped by boat on the Missouri and Mississippi Rivers. In 1815, James Barnes of Boon's Lick took a flatboat of nine "different kinds of wild meat, besides honey, corn, potatoes, onions, furs, hides, deer and elk horns, etc.," to New Orleans. Such flatboating was not expensive, but it was extremely slow (*see Transportation*).

Early production was limited by poor equipment. Some farmers cultivated their land with a mattock hitched to a horse. In the absence of harrows, the ground was sometimes dragged with brush. Trace chains of cow hide and plow lines of hemp were common. Sacking pins, sacking needles, and pitchforks were of wood. Harness hames were often made from the crook of an elm tree, and wagon wheels were fashioned by sawing off sections of a log from four to six inches wide.

Along with the crudity of early agricultural methods went a wealth of superstition. A common farm saying advised, "If you would not scowl on a mug of sour or musty cider, grind and press your fruit in fair weather, when the wind blows from the N.W., and never put the juice in foul casks." One farmer testified that having washed the exposed roots of weak peach trees in warm, soapy water, "the next year they bore abundantly." Salt was considered by some to be an excellent manure. To rid barns of rats, a piece of dog's tongue plant was bruised and laid in the barn. A letter to the *Missouri Farmer,* published in St. Louis, in 1841, recommended the use of a "large warty toad" to cure a fistula on a horse: "Rub its back slightly over the effected part, and continue to rub it thus for an hour, by which time the toad will be dead and should be buried."

Nonetheless, there was some scientific farming in Missouri from the earliest settlement. Families from Kentucky, Virginia, and Tennessee brought with them slaves, adequate tools, and a wide knowledge of farming as a capital industry. Many experimented with the possibilities of Missouri soil and climate. Perhaps the earliest of these experimenting gentlemen farmers was John Hardeman, a Tennessee lawyer, who laid out a formal garden on a tract of land in the Missouri River bottom just west of Franklin. He collected trees and shrubs, flowers, vegetables, berries, and grains from various parts of the continent, and endeavored to discover those best suited to Middle Western culture (*see Tour 3*).

The common belief that "corn won't grow where trees won't," together with the danger of prairie fires and the lack of wood, had caused most of the early settlers to shun the prairie region in favor of the forested river bottoms. In 1826, General T. A. Smith, a Virginian who had come to Missouri after the War of 1812, purchased a large tract of land on the Saline County prairies near present Napton, which he named Experiment Farm. Here he succeeded in exploding the theory that prairie land was unfertile. William Muldrow performed a similar experiment in northeast Missouri, with results that, according to Wetmore, in his *Gazetteer of Missouri* (1837), "produced a new era in the State, and ever since intelligent farmers have regarded a prairie farm as the best in the world, provided they can procure at no great distance, timber enough to fence it."

The Southern type of plantation developed in Missouri mainly along the Missouri and Mississippi Rivers, where the soil was particularly suited to the cultivation of hemp and tobacco. These were the only portions of the State in which slave labor proved profitable. In the period before the Civil War, the plantations were centers of a highly cultured life. In 1849, St. Louis received from this section 49,000 bales of hemp, ranging in price from $80 to $130 a ton. Glasgow served as the port for back country Chariton and Howard County farms, shipping during that year 380 tons of hemp and 5,230 hogsheads and 4,047 boxes of tobacco. Wheat, apples, pork, lard, hides, cattle, and other farm products from these areas found an increasing American and foreign market.

In areas where the soil was not fertile, or where the distance from water transportation made shipping charges prohibitive, stockraising became an important industry. *Steele's Western Guide Book and Emigrant's Directory* (Buffalo, 1838) proclaimed Missouri:

> The country for raising cattle, horses, hogs and sheep. Vast herds of cattle are raised on the western borders of the State; and thousands are there slaughtered and the meat salted and exported by way of New Orleans to the eastern states, or to the West Indies; whilst the tallow and the hides preserved in a dry state, are sent to the tanneries in the upper part of the Valley, or to the eastern cities. The extensive prairies of this entire region, will make it always the land of great pastoral wealth. From this part of our country, the markets of Philadelphia, Baltimore, and other Atlantic cities, will derive many of their supplies, whilst our shipping will here receive its salted and jerked beef.

Thoroughbred stock was imported in the 1830's including Alderney and Jersey cattle, Shorthorn, and Aberdeen-Angus, a black beef-type cattle with short legs, and a short, wide head. By 1850, the center of the State's cattle industry shifted to the southwestern prairies. The cattle were driven to Missouri river ports, particularly Boonville, for export to market. Soon the Ozark region also began to ship salted meats, cured hides, tallow, and lard. Warsaw utilized the Osage River to export bacon, hams, shoulders, lard, pork, hides, and leather.

After the Civil War, settlers took up much of the grazing land in the Ozarks; and the construction of railroads having overcome the earlier transportation difficulty, grain cultivation more or less supplanted cattle. Gradually, the State's livestock farming region became a large "T," the vertical bar of which extended along the Missouri River from St. Louis to Kansas City, and the horizontal from Kansas City north to St. Joseph and south almost to the Arkansas Border. St. Joseph in particular during the period 1850-70 took advantage of the high beef prices in California, Colorado, and other portions of the West to purchase and drive there great herds. Introduced even earlier than the breeding of fine cattle was the breeding of fine horses. Thoroughbred stock was brought from Kentucky, Virginia, and New York, and often from England. Race tracks were laid out in many communities by Kentucky and Virginia immigrants almost before churches and schools were built. The popularity of the sport encouraged the breeding industry, which still flourishes, particularly in Callaway, Audrain, Moniteau, and Jackson Counties.

In these central Missouri counties, the raising of mules became a major industry following the introduction of jacks and jennets from

New Mexico. An expedition returning to Howard County in 1823 brought back 400 mules, jacks, and jennets; in 1832, Captain Dent & Company returned with "about 1,300 mules, 17 jack asses, 35 she asses." Mules, valued at first only as pack animals for the long overland trains, soon proved superior to either oxen or horses for heavy farm work.

The pioneer farmers saved their own seed and grew their own seedlings, but as the country was settled, stores and nurseries developed, supplying seed and plants from the East and abroad. One of the most interesting horticultural innovations was the Osage Orange, originally found on the Kansas plains and used by the Osage Indians for the making of bows; Pierre Chouteau planted a few trees in St. Louis County in 1799, according to his letter to Thomas Jefferson in 1804. In the 1850's, the tree began to be cultivated as a hedge by prairie farmers, and it now forms a characteristic feature of the Missouri landscape.

The heavy German immigration (about 1830-70) brought to Missouri many farmers trained in scientific methods, particularly in various phases of horticulture. Through their efforts, the cultivation of fruits and berries, particularly of apples and grapes, became a major industry. Grape production for wine, including the Isabella, Catawba, and Morton's Virginia grape, became the most important activity of the German communities near Hermann. The soil was warm and well drained, and the bluffs afforded protection from unseasonable frosts. In 1848, Hermann produced 10,000 gallons of good-quality wine which sold at $1.50 per gallon; by 1856, production had been increased to 100,000 gallons. Although prices soon fell, grape culture remained profitable and Missouri wines became famous. Smaller vineyards were developed in and near Boonville, St. Louis, St. Charles, and Ste. Genevieve, where "some very good grapes have long been cultivated by the old French inhabitants."

Experiments with grape culture were also made in various parts of the Ozark plateau, where Swiss, Italian, and German immigrants successfully planted vineyards. In 1867, Hermann Jaeger, a Swiss resident of Newton County, crossed Virginia grapes with the wild Ozark variety. By 1870, he had 50 acres of hardy and productive vines on his farm near Neosho. Learning a few years later that French vineyards were being destroyed by phylloxera, or grape louse, he suggested to the French government the use of cuttings and seeds from the wild grapes of the Ozarks as new roots for their vines. The offer was accepted, and within 3 years Jaeger sent more than 17 carloads of cuttings to France, and was given the cross of the French Legion of Honor. In 1868, George Hussmann began publishing in St. Louis

The American Grape Culturist, the only periodical in the United States at that time devoted solely to grape culture and wine making.

German improvements were adopted by progressive American farmers. Annual fairs, publications of various types, and the manufacture of mechanical aids increased. By 1840, most counties had agricultural societies which held spring and fall meetings and exhibitions. In 1855, the St. Louis Agricultural Society combined with the Mechanic's Fair Association, and for many years they held successful joint fairs; in 1857, they offered over $16,000 in premiums, including prizes for essays on such subjects as "On Rearing and Managing Cattle." Among the various types of farm machinery displayed were plows, cornplanters, threshing machines, corn-cutting machines, portable hay presses, corn shellers, and reapers and mowers, many made in Missouri on Missouri patents. Representing specialized agricultural and horticultural interests were such organizations as the St. Louis Horticultural Society, established in 1847, the St. Charles County Wheat Growers' Association, and the Annual Wine Fair in St. Louis. The Missouri State Horticultural Society, organized in 1859, and incorporated by an act of the legislature in 1893, is today a progressive association of fruit growers.

Newspapers and magazines early discussed problems of increasing and preserving fertility; around the 1850's, articles described methods of subsoil plowing and terracing, hybridization, manuring, and the uses of agricultural chemistry. In 1851, Joseph Ormrod, a Scotchman of Cooper County, solemnly warned against soil depletion resulting from "the miserable system of farming steadily pursued by eight-tenths of all the farmers of this country since its first settlement; a system which proceeds upon the principle of taking as many crops from the land with as little manure as possible—until the productive powers are exhausted, and then emigrating to some part of the country where they can apply the same practice to the new soil.

"And so they build canoes and railroads, and bring from the West millions of bushels of grain, and send not one fertilizing atom back to restore the lands, and in this way we shall bye and bye make the fertile prairies—barren." The most vital of the agricultural publications was *Colman's Rural World,* edited by Norman J. Colman (1827-1912), who in 1889 became the first U. S. Secretary of Agriculture.

The State urged the founding of a school of agriculture for several years before Congress granted lands in Missouri for this purpose in 1862. Eight years later, the college of agriculture was opened as a department of the University of Missouri. The State Board of Agriculture, established in 1863, was organized in 1865; serving on it were a group of German immigrants who had for more than 20 years urged scientific farming methods. The first report of the board in 1866 found agriculture in Missouri to be in a transitional state: "A system of depletion, a constant drawing of wealth from the soil with little or no effort to secure continued fertility" had forced the adoption of a program "of improved agriculture, which recognizes the great law of nature that the soil cannot continue to give without being replenished." The board advised deeper plowing, under-draining, careful selection of seed, improvement of stock, the development of dairying and cheese-making, more sheep raising, and the use of improved farming implements. Further, Missouri agriculture had been "nearly prostrated during the War . . . and . . . we have been undergoing the transition from a slave labor system to one of free labor."

Certainly, Missouri's economic pattern had been disrupted by the Civil War. Funds and resources, buildings, equipment, herds, and orchards had been destroyed. Real property values had decreased by $45,000,000 between 1860 and 1865, and taxes had multiplied; many farmers had lost their land.

Nor was it the war alone that ruined the farmers. The simultaneous growth of cities and of industry drew wealth and population from the rural areas. At the same time the construction of railroads brought a realignment of markets. Hemp culture was destroyed by the introduction of cheap substitutes, and tobacco production declined as soil depletion and the elimination of slavery made its culture less profitable.

The period of readjustment was slow and difficult, but several measures worked toward improvement. Immigration from Europe was solicited, and many farmers from the South and the North were encouraged to come West. The rapid development of the Far West gave Missouri a wider market, so that land values increased and taxes were gradually reduced. Scientific agricultural methods were encouraged by an increasing number of public and private agencies.

Farm population declined relatively, however, from 51 per cent in 1860 to 44 per cent in 1880. The Board of Labor Statistics reported a shortage of farm labor for 1884. At the same time, individual ownership of farms also showed a recession, which went farther as the supply of new agricultural lands was exhausted, and as panics followed successive periods of inflation.

The western livestock trade gradually gave way in importance to the production of grain, dairy products, poultry, and fruits. Corn has been a consistent leader since 1860; wheat reached its peak in 1880. These and oats, constituting Missouri's three major grains, attained their maximum in the Missouri and Mississippi river regions within a decade or two after the introduction of farm machinery, and there has been little variation in output since 1890.

Since the Civil War, Missouri leaders have worked for agricultural improvements. State Entomologist C. V. Riley pioneered in insect

control.   Colonel William Henry Hatch crusaded for the establishment of Federal agricultural experiment stations (approved by President Cleveland in 1887), and fought against tobacco trusts, and for
a national sanitary law with regard to infectious and contagious diseases
in domestic animals.   The annual Missouri State Fair held since 1901
at Sedalia has made important contributions.   During the 1939 fair,
prize cattle, poultry, grains, fruits, and other products of the State were
exhibited to approximately 250,000 visitors.

Some of the post-Civil War farm organizations have been active
in politics.   Most important of these was the Patrons of Husbandry, or
the Grange, which held its first national convention in St. Louis in
1873.   At one time, the Grange had nearly 3,000 local lodges.

By 1900, Missouri agriculture had taken on the general structure
it has today.   The bankrupting of many large landowners during the
Civil War resulted in the breaking up of their holdings into smaller
farms, many of which were purchased by returning soldiers or by immigrants.   In 1850, the average Missouri farm contained slightly more
than 200 acres; in 1890, 136.5.   By 1900, the average had increased
again to 146.2, and has since continued to increase.   The traditional
method of intense cultivation, largely by family labor, had begun to
give way to the cultivation of larger tracts by mechanical means.   In
1900, Missouri ranked second among the States in the number of
farms, and fourth in the total of improved acreage.   Almost one-third
of these farms were cultivated by tenants.

Despite the general diversity of Missouri's crops in 1900, livestock
was the chief product on more than half the farms in the State.   Texas
and Tennessee alone exceeded Missouri in the production of mules;
and swine, asses, and burros remained important.   With the spread of
the railroad system, butter making increased, particularly in the Ozark
areas; in 1900, Missouri produced nearly 47,000,000 pounds of butter.
Poultry, too, had increased; in 1899, Missouri ranked second in poultry and sixth in eggs.   Hay and grains provided the chief crop for
about one-fourth of the farms, Missouri ranking fifth in corn production.

The agricultural trends indicated in 1900 continued during the
period of prosperity which culminated in the inflation of farm values
during the World War.   During this period, small-grain production
was increased at the expense of corn and cattle.   Sub-marginal land was
turned to cultivation.   After 1920, the boom collapsed, and during the
early years of depression much of the land was left idle.   But by 1935,
the total acreage of Missouri farms had risen to a new high of more
than 35,000,000 acres, comprising 278,454 farms.   Between 1930 and
1935, farm incomes gradually increased, partly as a result of benefit
payments, and the number of farms mortgaged was reduced from 44.9

per cent to 36.1 per cent. The number of farm owners also grew and, at the same time, the number of tenant farmers. In 1939, despite the peak acreage, the total number of farms was almost 70,000 less than in 1900. With the passing of the drought years, production increased, and although prices were low, Missouri's crop value in 1939 rose almost 20 per cent over that of the previous year, and livestock values also showed a minor gain. Strawberries, grapes, peaches, and vegetables in the Ozark highland, and cotton in the southeastern portion of the State, have grown in importance. Cotton, the production of which is virtually limited to seven counties, is now Missouri's third largest crop. Poultry raising continues to be an important phase of farm economy, and the income from eggs remains a major item. Much of the poultry yield is from small-to-medium flocks on average-sized farms, so that the hen has been called the "mortgage lifter of the Ozarks." The Missouri State Poultry station at Mountain Grove co-operates with poultry-men by testing rations and sponsoring projects. It also distributes literature about feed, sanitation, worm and disease control, methods of culling and judging, and similar problems.

At the present time (1940), one-third of the State's population is dependent in some way on stock farms. Livestock improvement has consequently become of primary importance, and many organizations for this purpose have been developed. Among these are the Missouri Livestock Association, the Saddle Horse Breeders' Association, and the Missouri Dairy Association.

Dairying began in Missouri as a sideline, but since the development of good roads and rapid transportation, and the invention of the cream separator and the milking machine, it has become a major industry. The St. Louis region and the southwestern areas offer mild winters, abundant grass and water, and convenient markets. Organizations have been formed for the importation of registered stock, the selection of animals, and the testing of cows for butter-fat production. Typical are the activities of the Missouri Dairy Clubs, originated by the State Dairy Commission. In 1916, the first club was organized in Jasper County, which imported 105 Holstein heifers from Wisconsin. Within 7 years, it had bought 14 carloads of heifers, 8 carloads of which were purebred Jerseys.

In several parts of Missouri, interesting experiments in co-operative dairying have been made. The Missouri Farmer's Association, established in Chariton County in 1914, under the leadership of the late William Hirth, editor of the *Missouri Farmer,* has financed the building of elevators and exchanges in more than 300 towns, and has inaugurated a co-operative system for handling eggs, poultry, and cream which saves Missouri farmers hundreds of thousands of dollars annually. At Springfield, the association operates the largest co-operative creamery in the world. Locally owned co-operative creameries are at Sweet Springs, Emma, and Concordia.

Today, Missouri farmers are protected by a feed law, providing for inspection of all livestock and poultry feeds; an egg law, requiring the licensing and inspection of all traffickers in eggs; a seed law, revised in 1938, insuring the purity of seeds; a farm warehouse act, providing for the sealing and warehousing of grain on the farms where it is grown; a dairy law, providing for the licensing and inspection of milk and cream-buying stations and dairy-products manufacturing plants under the department of agriculture; and a plant and insect-pest law, insuring the inspection and certification of nurseries. In 1935, Missouri became a State-Federal Accredited Tuberculosis Free Area, all counties having had their cattle tested for tuberculosis. The office of the State Veterinarian provides for co-operation in the control and eradication of livestock and poultry diseases. In 1933, the Missouri State Department of Agriculture was created by an act of the General Assembly, to succeed the State Board of Agriculture.

Assisting Missouri farmers to utilize the most modern scientific methods is the Missouri College of Agriculture, at Columbia, which maintains county extension agents throughout the State, and home demonstration agents in two-thirds of the State, besides offering courses on all phases of scientific farming. Members of its extension staff annually give practical home instruction and counsel to 21,000 boys and girls enrolled in 4-H clubs, which are semisocial groups designed to interest youth in farming. More than 400,000 bulletins and circulars are mailed annually from the offices of the college.

A much-needed program for conservation of natural resources has also been inaugurated. Soil erosion of both sheet and gully types has seriously affected some 34,000,000 acres of what was once good farm or pasture land. In the Ozark region, water erosion is conservatively estimated to have removed 6 inches of the topsoil, in spite of the $47,-000,000 spent by land owners for flood control and drainage. Although restoration in many places is impossible, surveys have been made to determine causes and cures, and bulletins have been distributed by county farm agents, in an effort to educate the people, and to secure legislation to check further devastation.

In southeastern Missouri the largest land-development project ever undertaken without State or Federal aid has been in operation for some years. Extending along a narrow line between Cape Girardeau and the Arkansas border is a strip of land comprising some 550,000 acres, acquired under the Swamp Land Act of 1850, which was formerly considered valueless, in spite of its rich alluvial soil, because of constant floods. In 1905, however, the Little River Drainage District was organized with local capital to drain the area. Now, this rich soil is in cultivation, and the malaria-carrying mosquitoes which once caused settlers to spend more for quinine than for flour have been exterminated.

Among other causes of soil erosion are the destruction of the forests, and the common practice among farmers of burning off underbrush. Of the 15,000,000 acres of forest in Missouri, only 250,000 of virgin timber remain. This is the result of several early abuses. Toward the end of the nineteenth century, large lumber companies began operations in the Missouri forests on the "cut out and get out" policy. When the best of the timber was gone, these companies moved on. Smaller saw-mill operators contributed to the devastation by taking the best trees, and leaving only the inferior grades to reproduce. Under the common misapprehension that burning the underbrush improves pasturage, many farmers continue unwittingly to add to the destruction. Such burning destroys trees and soil humus and the protective leaf covering, so that the fertile top soil is washed away by rains. It also destroys the habitats of wild birds and animals. To conserve forest resources and prevent erosion, State laws were passed in 1931, and amended in 1934, to permit the establishment of national forests.

Since 1932, the Federal Government has been increasingly interested in farm relief. It has made provision for seed loans, payments for crop reduction, erosion control, and rehabilitation programs. In 1933, the Missouri Agricultural Advisory Council was appointed to co-operate with the Federal Farm Credit Administration to help local farmers refinance mortgages. At LaForge, near Sikeston, the Farm Security Administration has established a large resettlement project. On 6,700 acres, improved at a total cost of approximately $700,000, live more than 100 families, white and Negro. Each family has leased, for a ¼-share of the cotton produced, a tract of from 55 to 65 acres, with a 4- or 5-room house, barns, and outbuildings of prefabricated material. Each unit cost less than $2,000. Sums ranging from $230 to $1,000 have been advanced to each family for the purchase of food, livestock, and equipment. The acreage in cotton is restricted to about 50 per cent, with the remainder planted to corn, soy beans, lespedeza, and pasture crops. Large machines are owned and shared by groups of farmers; the cotton gin, blacksmith shop, and general store are managed co-operatively by the community. The financing plan for the community calls for the repayment of the original $700,000 loan within 33 years. The Osage Farms in Pettis County, established in 1938, are another government experiment to aid farmers. A 5,329-acre tract has been divided into small units, each with its own house, sold on long-term agreements.

Missouri's worst agricultural problem at present, aside from the national problem of shifting markets and economic uncertainty, is that of the tenant farmer and sharecropper. Little attention was given to the tenant problem until the census of 1880 pointed out that 25.6 per cent of the farms in the United States were operated by tenants, and that Missouri was above the national average, with 18.1 per cent of the farms operated by sharecroppers, and 9.2 by cash tenants. By 1920, there were 75,727 tenants on Missouri farms; in 1930, there were 89,076; in 1935, there were 108,023.

Tenant farming is a system whereby an owner rents his land for cultivation in return for some specified payment. Sharecropping is that form of tenancy under which an individual engages himself to provide the labor to produce and harvest a crop for a percentage of the returns from the sale of the crop. The sharecropper is the most precariously situated of the tenant class, since he is entirely dependent upon crops which may, and often do, fail.

The farm-labor problem was reflected in a sharecropper demonstration which began January 10, 1939, attracting national attention. Declaring that they had been evicted, 1,161 tenants, including many Negroes, organized by the Reverend Owen H. Whitefield, a Negro sharecropper of LaForge, Missouri, camped along the side of US 61. In March, a State organization of sharecroppers was formed. An F.B.I. investigation later intimated that the Southern Tenant Farmers Union had held out to the squatters the possibility of government grants of 40 acres of land, tools, a home, and a "dug" well. Some 500 of the "strikers" were eventually given permission by their former landlords to return to their farms; approximately 450 others were moved from the highway into swampland, which the sharecroppers named "Homeless Junction"; the remainder found homes on a 91-acre tract near Poplar Bluff, purchased with funds supplied by the Missouri Agricultural Workers Union, a C.I.O. affiliate, and other groups.

In January, 1940, a conference of representatives of landowners and tenants was called by Governor Lloyd C. Stark, and a plan was developed for the establishment of subsistence homesteads and the allotment of WPA work to supplement the earnings of day laborers in the cotton fields. The Federal Farm Security Administration has also taken steps towards rehabilitating these people, and housing, home-labor, and farm projects have been planned.

Industry, Commerce, and Labor

SOON after Father Jacques Marquette and Louis Jolliet made their voyage down the Mississippi in 1673, *voyageurs* and *coureurs des bois* (forest traders) explored the Missouri, the Osage, the St. Francis and other Missouri streams (*see History and Government*). The immediate result of these journeys was the extension of the fur trade, but with their furs these men brought back tales of vast silver deposits and hidden gold mines in the Missouri wilderness. Small quantities of copper were actually found, and fortune hunters hastened to the new El Dorado. When the illusion cleared, these turned to mining lead, the one mineral their prospecting had located. Thus were the first capital investments and the first settlers brought to the State. For over a century, the lead mines yielded no great profit, but they aided in attracting farmers, traders, and missionaries to the little villages which grew up near them.

The first permanent settlement was at Ste. Genevieve (before 1750)—a strategic location. Very shortly, the village was shipping lead, furs, salt, flour and grain, pork, lard, bacon, bear grease, feathers, and other products to distant markets.

The fur trade expanded rapidly under the domination of French trading monopolies. In February of 1764, Maxent, Laclede & Company established St. Louis as a "company town," and leading fur merchants began to operate from that center. Laclede soon controlled the Indian fur trade of the Missouri, the upper Mississippi, and the nations near La Baye, Lake Michigan, and along the Illinois River. After his death in 1779, much of Laclede's trade was carried on by the Chouteau brothers. During the British occupation of the territory east of the Mississippi (about 1765-80), however, French and Spanish traders were largely restricted to the Mississippi below the Des Moines, and to the Missouri. When St. Louis traders again attempted to expand their activities into the upper Mississippi and Great Lakes region, they met with vigorous competition from John Jacob Astor's Northwest Company, and the British Hudson's Bay Company. In 1794, Lieutenant-Governor Zenon Trudeau promoted the Spanish Commercial Exploration Company to exploit the fur trade of the upper Missouri. This company combined the capital and energies of leading St. Louis merchants, and was subsidized by the Spanish government. According to Auguste Chouteau, Sr., the average annual proceeds from the furs

74

sold by St. Louis merchants between 1789 and 1804 were $204,750, more than half being from deer and beaver.

The lead industry experienced little change until near the end of the Spanish regime. Some lead was used locally, and irregular shipments were made to New Orleans, but profits were small, and work was sporadic. The high cost of transporting the lead from the mines to Ste. Genevieve prevented any large scale mining. In general, the mines seem to have been worked only from after the August harvest to just before Christmas, and few if any of the miners lived at the "diggings."

In 1798, just before the close of the Spanish period, improved mining and smelting methods were introduced by Moses Austin, one of the insatiable, roving frontier capitalists who "knew a good thing when he saw it." Austin came from Virginia in the winter of 1796-7 and visited Mine á Breton, which had been worked for several decades. Impressed with the richness of the deposits, he obtained a Spanish grant of one square league. The following year he began operations, bringing workmen and equipment from Virginia. Austin sold much of his bar lead and shot in Ste. Genevieve and Kaskaskia, but he also sent some directly to New Orleans, Louisville, and the Ohio River markets. Permanent settlements at the mines now grew rapidly, despite the constant threat of Osage Indian raids. Outside capital was attracted, and after nearly 50 years of haphazard efforts Missouri's lead industry became profitable.

Specie was scarce on the frontier. Paper money issued by various banks, even though regarded with suspicion, enjoyed a wide circulation, and Mexican silver coins, brought to Missouri after the opening of the Santa Fe Trail, were common for many years. Most prevalent, however, was the barter system, used until long after the Louisiana Purchase. The best-selling furs, beaver and shaved deer skins, were a standard of value, a pack of the same kind of skins having a definite weight and a fairly definite price. A pound of shaved deer skins was worth about 40 cents. According to Captain Amos Stoddard, in 1804, a 100-pound bundle of beaver skins was worth $189, lynx $500, otter $450, marten $300, a buffalo robe $6, and a bear skin $3. For small transactions, Missouri Colonial merchants issued a currency redeemable in shaved deerskin and other produce called "peltry bon," or "good for furs." Among other products taken in trade were tobacco, beeswax, potash, maple syrup, salt, feathers, bear oil, venison, fish, wood, and lead. Many of these items were processed before being shipped outside the area.

In return for these country products the merchant supplied necessities, and luxuries imported from the East or South, many of which had come originally from Europe, Asia, or the West Indies. Thus, cotton material from England, sheeting and blankets from Russia, coffee from Brazil, tea from China, sugar from Cuba, steel from Germany, laces and silks, books and fine porcelain from France, and wines and liquors from many nations, found their way to Missouri. The examination of a page in any frontier merchant's day-book shatters the illusion of primitive pioneer tastes.

When the Louisiana Territory was transferred to the United States in 1804, St. Louis was the center of the government, and controlled the fur trade and investment banking; Ste. Genevieve was the lead shipping point, and an agricultural center. Settlers began to arrive in great numbers, bringing with them new needs. Villages boomed overnight; speculation piled upon speculation; unconfirmed land titles were bought and sold many times; business was chaotic and unsettled. Important landowners and early investors in the fur trade and the lead industry found the value of their holdings tripled and quadrupled.

In 1808, Moses Austin and Samuel Hammond laid out Herculaneum at the mouth of Joachim Creek, in Jefferson County, as a lead shipping point, and began to manufacture shot in towers built on the high bluffs (see Tour 7b). In 1819, Herculaneum shipped half the lead produced in the State, and Ste. Genevieve suffered accordingly. Other inland areas were developed. It was not, however, until after the Civil War that large companies were formed. The southwest Missouri mines, first opened about 1850, grew to importance during this period. The St. Joseph Lead Company, which was soon to dominate the southeast Missouri field, was incorporated in 1864.

The fur trade likewise saw changes. The single trader gave way to large companies with resources sufficient to outfit many hunters and agents, and to lobby for favorable legislation. Although the Chouteau family remained important, particularly through their control of much of the Osage trade, the industry in St. Louis seems to have been dominated by Manuel Lisa. In 1809, he aided in organizing the St. Louis Missouri Fur Company, his partners including Pierre and Auguste P. Chouteau, William Clark, Pierre Menard, Andrew Henry, and others. This combination changed in form and membership from time to time, but under Lisa's direction the St. Louis merchants retained their independence. John Jacob Astor made tentative arrangements with some of them as early as 1817, but not until 2 years after Lisa's death in 1820 did he establish in St. Louis the branch of the American Fur Company known as the Western Department. This, with his success that same year in having the United States trading factory system (Government trading posts) abolished, gave Astor a virtual monopoly of the United States fur trade.

Meanwhile, other Missouri fur traders had developed new areas. Some of these were independent, working on a shoe-string capital and enduring terrific hardships and dangers; others formed companies. William Henry Ashley formed a fur company which opened to exploration and trade the great middle area of the Far West. During the period 1822-6, Ashley's proceeds totaled $250,000. In 1826, he sold out to Smith, Jackson, and Sublette, who pushed the trade through the mountains to the Pacific Coast, from California to the Columbia River.

In 1834, when Astor withdrew from what he sensed to be a dying industry, his interests in the Western Department were purchased by his former St. Louis partners, who organized the firm of Pratte, Chouteau, and Company. Subsequently reorganized as P. Chouteau, Jr., and Company, the firm was continued until about 1866. The fur trade declined rapidly with the settlement of the West and the decimation of its wild life, but it did not die. About 1880, certain furs, such as coon and skunk, until then of little value, began to be shipped directly to St. Louis commission houses. In 1914, the Fouke Fur Company received the United States government appointment to dress and dye all the United States Alaska sealskins. These two factors have helped St. Louis to continue as the center of the raw-fur market in America, though the trade is no longer one of the major ones of the State.

During the Colonial period, leading residents in Missouri had had agents in Montreal, or more often in New Orleans, who sold their produce and sent in supplies. Later, when the Ohio River was opened to traffic and Pittsburgh developed as a forwarding point for Eastern merchants, most of the trade followed this route. Up to the Civil War, Missouri dealers went at least once a year to purchase goods in Philadelphia, New York, or Baltimore, where prices were lower, even with the additional shipping cost, than they were in St. Louis. Merchandise was shipped overland by four-horse freight wagons to Pittsburgh, where it was loaded in keelboats for transportation to St. Louis. In 1820, more than $8,000,000 worth of goods was sent from Pittsburgh to the West, much of it coming to Missouri.

As settlement progressed, a new type of merchant developed, a restless group of frontier capitalists directing their interest to anything that would yield a profit. They bought goods or bartered it for country produce of export value, started manufacturing enterprises, and speculated in land. Everywhere, they clamored for sound banks and money, good roads and public improvements, law and order. John Beauchamp Jones, himself a merchant at New Franklin and Arrow Rock during the 1830's, describes the class:

> He is the agent of everybody, and familiar with every transaction in his neighborhood. He is the counselor without license and yet invariably consulted, not only in matters of business, but in domestic affairs. . . . Every item of news, not only local, but from a distance, as he is frequently the post-master, and the only subscriber to the paper . . . has a general dis-

semination from his establishment, as from a common center, and thither all
resort, at least once a week, both for goods and intelligence.

Christian Wilt, who came to St. Louis from Philadelphia in 1810, was
typical: he established a general store in St. Louis, with branches at
Ste. Genevieve, Herculaneum, and New Hartford; opened factories in
St. Louis for the manufacture of red and white lead, selling much of
his product to the glass works of Pittsburgh and the potteries of Ohio;
operated a distillery on L'Abbé Creek in Cahokia, Illinois; made shot at
New Hartford; and manufactured soap and candles in St. Louis. The
Lamme family had stores in Liberty, Franklin, Columbia, and Independence, a tobacco factory at Franklin, and a steam flour mill and a
paper mill at Columbia. Robert and James Aull owned an interest in
three steamboats, and operated a saw and grist mill, and stores in four
towns, besides dabbling in the Santa Fe trade, and fulfilling contracts
for Fort Leavenworth, emigrating Indian tribes, and Western Army
troops.

When the merchant of the 1800's escaped the pitfalls of too easy
credit, transportation losses, and the problems of fluctuating values in
bank notes, his profits were high. In 1840, with a total investment of
more than $8,000,000 in retail business in Missouri, the average store
served more customers and employed more capital than the average
retail store in the East.

The Santa Fe trade that made possible most of this wide merchan-
dising began during the depression which followed the close of the
Napoleonic Wars. This depression reached the Missouri frontier in
1819, resulting in the decline of land values, the failure of the first
banks, and business stagnation (see Agriculture). Two years later,
when the pinch was sharpest, William Becknell and a party of Boon's
Lick Country men made the first profitable expedition to Santa Fe. The
Mexican War for Independence had opened the area to American commerce, and the success of Becknell's expedition led to the development
of an immense trade, which continued until the railroads had crossed the
plains after the Civil War. The introduction of steamboat transportation on the Missouri River made it possible to bring freight relatively
quickly and cheaply to Franklin, "the last outpost of civilization."
From here, pack and wagon trains were used to haul the goods overland. In 1823, merchandise carried to the Southwest was valued at
$12,000; in 1843 it amounted to $450,000. This trade, together with
that developed with California, Oregon, and Utah, was perhaps the
most significant factor in Missouri commerce during the middle years
of the century. Liberty, Lexington, Independence, Kansas City, and St.
Joseph soon succeeded Franklin as the "last outfitting points before
jumping off to the West." Much of this commerce, in contrast with

the monopolistic fur industry, was carried on by small traders, but large freighting companies were also organized. A single firm—Russell, Majors, and Waddell—had at one time 4,000 wagons and 40,000 oxen carrying goods from St. Louis to Sacramento and other points. St. Joseph in particular profited from the Western demand for supplies. In 1849, the total value of the stock of goods in St. Joseph stores exceeded $400,000. When the establishment of mining camps in California developed a boom market for Missouri beef cattle, St. Joseph became the center of the trade (*see Agriculture*).

Manufacturing in Missouri began with the mills, distilleries, rope-walks, and meat packing establishments developed to reduce the freight-age of raw products before exporting, and with handicraft industries which produced clothing, furniture, earthenware, and other items for a local market. Capital was supplied by merchants, and the introduction of the factory system thus accompanied the growth of Western markets. The period 1820-40 saw an abrupt shift from the primitive handicraft system to that of modern industry.

With the opening of farms along the Missouri River and in the upland prairie country, grain production, and horse, mule, and swine raising, became of primary importance. Grist mills were often built before churches or schools, and, after the introduction of the steam engine, nearly every river port became a milling center. By 1840, the 64 steam flour mills and 636 grist mills in Missouri were annually producing 49,363 barrels of flour. Ten years later, 19 St. Louis mills were producing about 500,000 barrels. Boonville, St. Charles, Hannibal, and Cape Girardeau likewise developed early as milling centers. Other grains were used in distilleries and breweries; by 1840, Missouri was turning out half a million gallons of whisky annually, and, in 1850, ranked fifth in beer, with 172,570 barrels for that year.

The tobacco industry was destined to become one of the most important in the State, with local tobacco factories, producing cigars and chewing and smoking tobacco, utilizing only a fraction of the 9,067,913 pound crop in 1840. Other Missouri industries listed by the census of that year include meat packing, woodenware and earthenware, tanneries, and carriage and wagon making. A saddle company, Moore and Porter, of Boonville, offered in 1839 "a general assortment of . . . Spanish, Quilted, Shaftered and Plain Saddles. Also a general assortment of Saddle bags, Gentlemen's Travelling Trunks covered with seal and deer skins, Bridles, Martingales, Harness, Hames, Collars etc."

The growth of publishing reflected the frontier thirst for reading matter; in 1808, Missouri had one newspaper; in 1840, there were 40. By 1860, Missouri ranked fifth in the nation, her 154 papers issuing annually 30,000,000 copies.

Lumbering camps were established in the pine area along the headwaters of the Gasconade River as early as 1818; and as late as 1852, the Gasconade Valley was still an important source of pine, although the Arkansas border was then beginning to be exploited. Much of this timber was hauled by ox-team to Springfield, or to the Osage River ports for shipping. Lumber production, valued at $70,355 in 1840, increased to $9,000,000 by 1860. Similar increases occurred in brick and lime. The manufacture of small arms, soap, candles, furniture, clothing, gunpowder, and rope grew in importance. By 1840, Missouri industry and trades employed 11,100 workers.

Iron deposits were worked in Franklin, St. Francois, Washington, Phelps, and Madison Counties, and coal deposits in St. Louis and the north-central Missouri counties. A small furnace was established on Stout's Creek near present-day Ironton about 1815, using ore from Shepherd Mountain and wood from the hills for fuel. In 1825, the State legislature granted a petition for aid in manufacturing iron, and the following year the "Springfield Iron Furnace and Forges" near Potosi began operation. In 1828, the company advertised: "Bar Iron for sale and castings of every description may be had equal to any made in the western country. Constantly on hand, Salt kettles, Mill irons, Wagon boxes, Furnace Grates, Lead moulds, and a general assortment of Hollow Ware, Pots, Kettles, Ovens, Skillets, etc."

Iron Mountain, in Madison County, long thought to be of solid ore sufficient to supply the world for a century, became the most important source of iron in Missouri. In 1836, a company was formed. Using nearby limestone for flux, and wood from the forested knobs for fuel, the ore was mined and smelted on the spot, then shipped overland to Ste. Genevieve for export. The Ste. Genevieve, Iron Mountain and Pilot Knob plank road was begun in 1851, but before it was finished the St. Louis and Iron Mountain Railroad was chartered. Completed in 1858, this railroad carried the iron to St. Louis.

The presence of coal was first noted in Missouri before 1810. It was mined before 1840, the first mines being in St. Louis County; others were opened later in Randolph, Audrain, Ray, Lafayette, and Barton Counties.

The development of railroads between 1835 and 1860 changed the pattern of Missouri commerce. Because the routes lay east and west, not north and south with the Mississippi, Missouri became allied with the industrial East and was released from her dependence upon the South. This change was emphasized by the investments of Eastern capital in Missouri industry, so that by the outbreak of the Civil War, most of Missouri's industrial trade had been diverted from New Orleans to the East.

Union forces won control of industrial St. Louis and the southeast mining area early in the struggle, but agricultural Missouri was the battlefield for opposing forces throughout the war. St. Louis profited by serving as the western supply base for a million troops. The Chief Quartermaster spent $180,000,000 in that city for supplies, transportation, and incidental expenses. St. Louis commerce and industry had an unprecedented growth. The custom's receipts for the port of St. Louis jumped from $98,609.73 in 1861 to $654,583.21 in 1865.

Missouri's difficult reconstruction period was eased by the tide of Western trade, and the continued growth of Missouri's population. Sylvester Waterhouse, in his *The Resources of Missouri* (1867), states that, in 1866, 50 St. Louis boats carried freight valued at $6,500,000 to Montana alone. In the same year, the overland freight from Fort Leavenworth totaled $50,000,000, of which approximately $35,000,000 went to New Mexico. At the close of the 1860's, Missouri industry, concentrated principally in St. Louis, totaled $206,231,499—a 500 per cent increase over that of 1840.

A diversified group of industries based upon local production of iron and coal had been well developed at the outbreak of the war. Missouri ranked sixth in the national production of pig iron, and the manufacture of agricultural implements, steam engines, machinery, and castings had become important. Architectural ironwork for many Missouri buildings of this period was cast in Missouri foundries. Iron production jumped from 100,000 tons before 1850, to 316,000 tons in the 1870's. Since the Lake Superior iron region has been developed, many of the Missouri mines have closed down, but the importance of St. Louis foundry products has not diminished.

Retailing methods underwent a change, as the railroads and the development of "traveling salesmen" made it unnecessary for small merchants to make annual purchasing trips to the East. The concentration of wealth in urban centers made possible the department store, with its wide assortment of merchandise for all tastes and pocketbooks. The department store idea is inherent in the small-town "general store," but the older department stores in Kansas City and St. Louis originated as small dry goods stores, which gradually expanded.

Chain stores, concentrating on a limited number of low- or medium-priced standardized articles, originated in the East; they spread as automobiles and highways opened ever wider markets. Among the pioneers was James Cash Penney (1875-   ), son of a Hamilton, Missouri, Baptist minister; he began his vast chain with a small store in Kemmerer, Wyoming (*see Tour 3*).

The co-operative activities of the Missouri Farmer's Association, planned and launched by William Hirth of Columbia about 1914, which began with retailing goods to members at wholesale prices, now include the processing and sale of farm produce. With an annual turnover totaling as high as $100,000,000, the M.F.A. is a vital economic force throughout Missouri and neighboring States (*see Agriculture, and Springfield*).

Since 1900, urban concentration has increased, and large corporate industries have grown up. Milling and brewing, meat packing and the leather industry, the manufacture of farm implements and machinery, and of various cast-iron and steel products, and the development of chemical and medical industries have proved of growing importance.

Of particular significance is Missouri's continued importance in Western and Southwestern markets. Within the State, the railroads have given rise to agricultural marketing and manufacturing centers like Springfield, the largest primary poultry market in the world. Dairy produce plants, creameries, cheese and butter factories, and canneries have been built in the smaller towns.

The cheapness of power and of railroad transportation and the recent introduction of trucks have made possible the development of mines, particularly of nonferrous ores, hitherto considered of little value. Mineral production increased from the depression low of $29,345,000 in 1932, to $52,446,000 in 1937. Among quarry products have been the large sandstone deposits found in the St. Peter, La Motte, and Roubidoux formations. Sand from the Ozark streams is used in sand-blasting; that from the St. Peter formation is used mainly for glass making, as it is nearly pure silica. Other Missouri sands are used in sandpaper, scouring soaps, and pottery glazing. The silica deposits at Crystal City, first successfully used in the manufacture of glass by the American Plate Glass Company in 1871, are now controlled by the Pittsburgh Plate Glass Company. Clay deposits ranging from high grade fire clay to shales and clays suitable for brick, tile, and cement have been discovered in large quantities in many parts of the State, and plants manufacturing firebrick, tile, and other products have been developed in Mexico, St. Louis, Hannibal, and Cape Girardeau. Nonplastic, flint fire clay is found in east-central Missouri; associated with this clay occurs a material which is nearly 75 per cent alumina. Mines of tripoli, asphalt, and other minerals have been opened in southwest Missouri. Tripoli is a form of porous rock used in making paint, tooth powder, and cleansing material; recently, it has also been used for insulation in building construction. The discovery of barite, or tiff, which is used in the manufacture of paints and enamels, heavy drilling sludge, linoleum, rubber goods, and as a paper filler, has opened a new industry in southeast and central Missouri. More than half of the barite produced in the United States comes from Missouri, and of this some 75 per cent comes from Washington County. Other minerals produced in lesser quantities in Missouri are copper, nickel, cobalt, antimony, tungsten, and arsenic.

Coal production has constantly increased in importance. Coal deposits underlie nearly 25,000 square miles in northwestern Missouri, several of the seams being of commercial thickness. In the central area, most of the coal mines are of the shaft type, but in Callaway, Randolph, and Barton Counties, strip or open pit mining is common.

Since the first oil wells were drilled in Jackson County in the 1860's, considerable interest has been shown in possible oil deposits in the State. Many wells have been sunk, particularly in the western and northern sections, where there is an underlying Pennsylvanian formation, but so far none has produced any appreciable quantity of oil or gas.

Early lead miners in the southwestern district found a strange dark substance adhering to the lead ore. Under the unscientific refining methods of that period, this "blackjack" was thrown into the chat heaps, which were subsequently utilized by railroads for ballast, and by counties for road building. It is estimated that $10,000 worth of the material per mile was used on the chat-graveled roads about Joplin before it was realized that the foreign substance in the lead was zinc of a high quality. Subsequently, the chat was scientifically processed in specially built mills, and it is estimated that some of the old waste heaps have produced as much as $100,000 in zinc and lead concentrates.

Since 1910, the richer deposits of zinc in Oklahoma and Kansas have made the southeastern Missouri zinc fields less important. Production dropped from 128,589 short tons in 1910 to 20,600 in 1937, but the processing of metals has continued to make Joplin an important industrial center. Until recently, processing was done by small independent companies, but during the depression years many of these firms were absorbed by larger corporations, and today the industry is largely controlled by the Eagle-Picher Corporation.

Next to lead and zinc in importance is limestone, of which several types are found in Missouri. Burlington limestone, important as a building material and for the manufacture of quick lime, is found around Carthage, Phenix, Louisiana, and Hannibal. The St. Louis limestone which overlies the Burlington in the St. Louis district is used for rubble. The limestone outcrops around Ste. Genevieve, however, are of the highest quality, and are suitable for the manufacture of lime. The limestone in Pike County is employed in rock-wool manufacture, a fast-growing modern industry.

Deposits in the vicinity of Carthage and Phenix contain marble of exceptional quality, which is widely used in the State; the Missouri State Capitol at Jefferson City is built of it. The most widely used Missouri rock, however, is the red granite found in the Graniteville area of southeast Missouri. At present, it is shipped everywhere in the United States. The Thomas Allen monument, at Pittsfield, Massachusetts, is a striking shaft sculptured from a single block weighing 42 tons.

Missouri has 21 rivers with a fall great enough to produce electricity. Of these, several have been harnessed. Forsyth Dam, in the southwestern section, impounds the White River to form Lake Taneycomo; a small hydroelectric plant here generates electricity for the Shepherd of the Hills country. More recently, a large dam has been built across the Osage River to form the Lake of the Ozarks. Here, water-run turbines generate a maximum of 210,000 horsepower. Missouri has 16,000 miles of streams, with an estimated potential of more than 600,000 horsepower; of this, only a little more than a third is at present being developed.

With the modern trend toward big cities, 70 per cent of the State's manufacturing is done in St. Louis and Kansas City. St. Louis ranks eighth among the industrial areas of the nation, is the largest manufacturing center west of the Mississippi, and has a widely diversified industry, including boots and shoes, beer, electrical machinery, medicines, and printing and publishing. Kansas City, the eighteenth industrial city in the United States, is the second largest meat-packing center, and ranks first in shipments of cattle. Important also are flour, bread, and prepared foods. St. Joseph, Missouri's third industrial city, has the largest pancake-flour factory, and the largest animal serum and vaccine plant in the world.

The remarkable growth of Missouri industry in the decade following the World War ended with two-thirds of Missouri's population resident in towns and cities, and two-thirds of Missouri's workers employed in manufacturing, mining, and the trades. Production by 1929 reached the total of $1,885,470,000 and provided work for 200,411 employees. Cities were growing rapidly, and Missouri's industrial lords were as busy as those elsewhere, weaving combinations of corporations, super-corporations, and holding companies. Manufacturers of farm machinery, however, were alarmed by the decline of farm values and products (see Agriculture). As farm values and incomes decreased, bank failures rose; in 1923, one; in 1926, seven; in 1929, thirteen; and in 1931, ninety-one. Emigration from farms and small towns to the cities grew alarmingly.

Within four years after the stock market crash of 1929, industrial production fell to less than half that of 1929, with a corresponding growth of unemployment. By 1935, however, industry showed some recovery, the total value of Missouri products reaching $1,205,877,000, with 162,144 workers employed.

LABOR

From the time of the first settlement of Missouri until the closing of the last frontier area in the middle of the nineteenth century, opportunities for individual betterment gave reality to the theory of liberty and equality for the free citizen. The persistent shortage of labor on the frontier gave craftsmen and laborers an independent power in bargaining for employment. Contracts for the building of houses and for the making of various items, as well as agreements in the fur-trade and mining industries, were carefully detailed as to the respective responsibility of employer and employee. On occasion, these matters were also the subject of legal regulation. For example, the Missouri territorial laws for 1804 protected river boatmen against cruelty or negligence on the part of the owner, and the boatmen were, in turn, responsible for the loss of boat or cargo through their negligence, and were liable for "misbehavior" or refusal to do their duty. Laws also regulated the indenture of orphans, providing minimum educational requirements, though not restricting the age or hours of work.

During the 1830's, Missouri's population increased more than 173 per cent, yet the demand for labor remained in excess of the supply. Between 1835 and 1836, the price of laying bricks advanced from $3 to $5 a thousand, and the wages of common labor advanced from 75¢ to $1.75 a day. The pay of iron workers advanced from $2 to $3 a day, that of carpenters from $1.50 to $2.25 a day, and other wages increased in like proportion. In 1836, there was a wide demand for the ten-hour day, though the master craftsmen attempted to uphold their traditional right of setting the hours of labor, frequently as high as fourteen. The shortage of workingmen and the general prosperity enabled most workers to obtain shorter hours.

The period of prosperity was abruptly ended by the panic of 1837. Salaries dropped from 50 to 75 per cent, and unemployment appeared. The change was not quietly received by workmen. The cabinet makers demanded an advance of 20 per cent in wages and a written contract with their employers. The plasterers formed themselves into a society and attempted to secure a wage increase. According to the journal of Henry B. Miller, who aided in organizing the group, notice was served to employers "that if they were not willing to give the wages . . . the group would turn out against them and not lift a trowel until they gave $2.50 per day and no less. . . . Some of the hands did not get the wages but the majority did."

These and other activities on the part of St. Louis workmen resulted in the organization of trade unions before 1840 by the journeymen laborers and mechanics. According to Russell M. Nolen in "The Labor Movement in St. Louis Prior to the Civil War" (*Missouri Historical Review,* October, 1939), these first unions were not revolutionary in their programs; they were interested in the general welfare and in the advancement of all laborers. Having the sympathy of both the press and the general public, their demands for higher wages and shorter hours were often successful. Collective bargaining and the strike proved effective weapons, and picketing and the boycott may have been known.

By 1842, the depression had spent itself and the surge of Westward migration was already creating a new Missouri prosperity which exceeded that of the 1830's. More than 11,000 of Missouri's population of 383,702 in 1840 were employed in manufacturing and the trades; by 1850, the number increased to 15,000 in industry alone, ranking Missouri eighth in production.

Missouri had now passed the frontier period, and the most productive free land had been occupied. An increasing stream of immigrants was adding to the available supply of labor. The majority of these were Germans, who found employment in the factories of St. Louis. With an ever-growing surplus of labor available, an increasing need was felt for the organization of unions, in order to maintain the earlier position of workers in relation to employers. The European worker, more experienced in labor problems than his American neighbor, gave direction to organization among Missouri workers. For the first time, a sense of the implications of the new industrial situation appears in the activities of unions, and in the writings of the period. A meeting of journeymen bricklayers, held in St. Louis in March 1840, resolved that against the encroachments of capital "we are honor bound to resist . . . as a duty to ourselves, our families and our posterity." Whereupon, the members pledged themselves to maintain "The Ten Hour System."

On July 2, 1840, the workingmen of St. Louis united in favor of the ten-hour law. A committee was appointed to interview the candidates for governor concerning their attitude towards the proposed law. At the same time the workers repudiated connections with any political party. In 1841, however, the mechanics and workingmen of St. Louis formed an organization to secure favorable legislation, and took an active part in that year's election. In this and subsequent campaigns, the journeymen, who were "political tyros," used the ballot awkwardly. They were easily scared by abuse, and saw with bitterness their efforts compromised or destroyed by professional politicians. A workingman's ticket was defeated in 1842, and after the election of 1843, when labor failed to place its own candidates in the field, and prosperity increased, labor campaigning declined.

Summing up the problems of industrial growth, Micajah Tarver, lawyer and senior editor of the *St. Louis Western Journal,* asserted in October, 1848, that "when land has been taken up, those born to no other inheritance than that of labor . . . are left to struggle unsupported against the powers of wealth and intelligence."

Prosperity was again disrupted by a panic in 1857, which, introduced in Missouri by the failure of the St. Louis banking house of James H. Lucas and Company on October 6, 1857, soon spread throughout the State. Wages were reduced 30 to 50 per cent, and prices dropped rapidly. On October 11, the *Missouri Republican* predicted that 10,000 men would be out of work and in want during the coming winter. Unemployment aids were suggested, and the statement was made that "The worker does not want alms, but . . . Labor." Some advocated moving surplus laborers to the country, particularly those who had been tempted to the city by the high wages of prosperity; others urged a plan of public works. But the only action taken was the appointment of a general association for the relief of the poor. This body was scarcely successful in obtaining funds, but industry revived sufficiently, early in 1858, to re-employ many workers. By 1860, prosperity had been revived and the unions of St. Louis became inactive.

The census of 1860 shows 114,930 slaves in the State, and 160,541 foreign born (the majority German). Most of the slaves were owned by 5,070 slaveholders resident in 15 counties. Less than 100 slaveholders were found in 53 counties, and 1 county, Douglas, had none. The slave system was not fundamental to Missouri prosperity, nor was it adapted to Missouri agriculture generally. Missouri workingmen took no united stand on the slave question despite the activity of Illinois and the Kansas abolitionists. In the election of 1860, Lincoln received a plurality of 700 votes in St. Louis. The laboring classes were divided, and the Lincoln plurality was due almost entirely to the vote of the German residents in the city, who as a group opposed slavery.

At the beginning of the Civil War, laborers were on the side of compromise, and mass meetings were called in Richmond, Louisville, Cincinnati, and St. Louis to condemn a resort to arms. Soon, however, military needs created a tremendous momentum in industrial development. The consequent rise in employment and wages was also accompanied by a rapid increase in prices. The movement to equalize wages with the increased cost of living gave trade unions a greater impetus than they had ever had before.

In 1861, some English miners in the Belleville tract in Illinois called colleagues from their own State and from Missouri to a convention in St. Louis, under the leadership of Thomas Lloyd and the "silver-tongued" Daniel Weaver. "The American Miners' Association" was formed at this meeting, with Lloyd as president and Weaver as secretary. The latter declared the object of the organization to be not merely "pecuniary but to mutually instruct and improve each other in knowledge, which is power, to study the laws of life, the relation of Labor to Capital, politics, municipal affairs, literature, science, or any other subject relating to the general welfare of our class." Other labor organizations were formed in Missouri during the war. In 1863, four were in operation; in 1864, there were nine.

To stimulate the immigration of workmen from Europe, the Missouri legislature in 1865 established a Board of Immigration, providing for publicity funds and for agents to be stationed in the Eastern States and in Europe to aid and advise immigrants. Upon the request of the board, Sylvester Waterhouse, a Washington University professor, prepared a pamphlet, *The Resources of Missouri* (St. Louis, 1867), which proclaimed that "Missouri needs able bodied men . . . the labors of myriads of workmen." As a result, many workers prepared to work for any wage came to Missouri. This cheap labor, combined with the post-war depression, weakened the unions as well as the American Miners' Association.

The St. Louis unions were dominated by German-speaking people whose leaders attempted to apply socialist theories to the organization of workingmen. The editor of the *Missouri Republican* in 1878 solemnly stated that St. Louis seemed to outsiders "the very center of communism in this country." Before long, many of the Missouri unions were nationally recognized, and the Workingmen's Party of the United States was active here.

In 1877, conditions were almost normal, and labor was quiet. Consequently, a strike during that summer came as a complete surprise. On July 22, a railroad strike began in Pittsburgh, Pennsylvania, and immediately spread throughout the Nation, to affect not only the railroads, but most other types of business. The East St. Louis railroad employees joined the strike on July 23. The conduct of the striking railway employees was exemplary throughout. A resolution cautioning all the men against the use of liquor was enforced by strikers patrolling the saloons. Other groups guarded railroad property and freight.

In St. Louis, meetings of the Workingmen's Party of the United States endorsed the "general uprising of labor in assertion of its rights," and expressed sympathy for "the railroad employees who have had their wages cut down to starvation prices." The St. Louis employees of the Missouri Pacific, and the St. Louis, Kansas City & Northern were induced to join the strike, although their previous demands for wage increases had been met. Meetings and parades were held and the fear of rioting caused Mayor Overstolz to appeal for aid to suppress possible disorder. A committee of safety was therefore appointed, composed of General A. J. Smith, General J. S. Marmaduke, and other Civil War veterans. Sheriff John Finn summoned a posse of 5,000 men. On July 27, mounted police, patrolmen, and citizen militia set out to capture the leaders of the strike, who had set up headquarters in Strube's Hall at Fifth Avenue and Biddle Street. Seventy-three men were arrested as leaders; others escaped and were picked up later. By July 30, the strike was over in St. Louis. Action was taken, also, at St. Joseph and in Kansas City, where 300 railroad strikers took possession of the

Union Station and were supported by strikers in other industries of the city.

Although in many cases better wages and a shorter working day were achieved, the principle of collective bargaining was not generally accepted by the employers. The strike, however, demonstrated the strong organization of the workingmen of the State and their knowledge of their power. Public and private property had been protected, no one had been seriously injured, and the mail trains had been permitted to operate.

Alarmed by the militia organized during the strike, and the subsequent unfavorable publicity, labor attempted to achieve its ends through negotiation and political means. In St. Louis, the Workingmen's Party, a newly formed political group unrelated to the national group of that name, disclaimed any connection with the "Internationalists," or communists. In the election of 1878, they organized their voters in an effort to elect favorable candidates. In this they were not successful, but they polled more votes than the leading parties had anticipated. In 1880 and 1884, despite the affiliation of the labor groups with the Greenback party, their efforts were again defeated.

With the strengthening of the local unions came the desire for a national labor organization. In January, 1879, a general assembly in St. Louis of the Knights of Labor—organized in Philadelphia in 1869 —adopted the motto, "All for One, One for All." The Knights exercised nominal control over organized labor in St. Louis until 1887, although many of the trade unions had by then withdrawn.

Three labor factions had meanwhile developed in St. Louis: the Central Labor Union, the St. Louis Trades Assembly, and the *Arbeiter-Verband,* which represented most of the German-speaking local unions. This division of forces was recognized as a disadvantage in collective bargaining, however, and in 1887, the three groups united to form the St. Louis Trades and Labor Assembly. A decade later, the present name—The St. Louis Central Trades and Labor Union—was adopted. The new organization applied for a charter of the American Federation of Labor, formed two years before; it was granted September 1, 1887. The third annual convention of the A. F. of L. met in St. Louis in 1888, with Samuel Gompers presiding. Three years later, at a convention held in Kansas City, the Missouri State Federation of Labor was organized.

The Missouri Bureau of Labor Statistics, organized in 1879, served both labor and industry as a clearing house for information. The new bureau investigated labor conditions and presented its findings in annual reports. The report for 1881 made searching inquiries into the method of industrial payment, health and sanitation conditions, and child and convict labor. Recommending that all wages be paid in cash, the report called attention to the payment of many workers in "script" for the purchase of goods in company stores, which charged as much as 15 per cent and more above average retail prices. The bureau reported that few health and safety measures were found in use, and that most workmen who were injured were discharged or received no disability compensation. The penitentiary had been leased to a group in 1873 for $1,000 a year, and then subleased to a manufacturing company. "The convicts were ill-treated, badly clothed, fed and bedded, often going for weeks without a change of linen. Many were so near naked they had to be kept in their cells with not even blankets to cover with." Mutiny had resulted. Conditions reported among children working in mines and factories shocked the legislature into action; laws were passed prohibiting any male under 14, and any female, from working in mines.

In 1883, the Missouri Bureau of Labor Statistics was enlarged; and in the years that followed, official recognition was given to labor problems. Although many of the first laws were loosely written or poorly enforced, successive revisions or supplementary acts gave them strength. In 1927, the bureau of 1883 was abolished and the Department of Labor and Industrial Inspection was created, one of whose duties was to enforce the laws regarding sanitation, health, and the safety of employees.

Although the eight-hour day had been provided by legislative act in 1867, it was made ineffectual by the provision that it did not "prevent parties to any contract for work . . . from agreeing upon a longer or shorter time," and other features. Most acute was the situation of the St. Louis streetcar conductors and drivers, who worked from 16 to 18 hours daily. In 1881, these workers struck for a 12-hour day, and a pay increase to $2 a day for the conductors and $1.75 for the drivers. A compromise was reached calling for 12½ cents an hour for the drivers and 15 for the conductors. Four years later, another strike was called, which lasted three weeks but was lost after police intervention. Other strikes held during this period were more successful. Significant among these was the strike of shopmen of the Missouri Pacific Railroad in 1885 against repeated wage reductions. The strike was well-organized, and indicated that labor had learned from its previous efforts. Missouri and Kansas railroad officials agreed to restore the earlier wage scale and to pay for overtime work. A 30-day notice prior to discharge or pay reduction was also provided.

Legislative action of increasing scope and effectiveness accompanied labor activity during the closing years of the century. The laws of 1891 provided better sanitation and health conditions for children in industry, and 2 years later attendance at school between the ages of 8 and 14 was made compulsory; administration of the law, however, was left largely to the discretion of each community. The law of 1881 providing that each county court appoint inspectors for the mines in its community was superseded in 1889 by the appointment of a State mining inspector by the governor. That year, too, a Board of Mediation and Arbitration was provided to handle strikes or lockouts. Additional safety and health laws were passed in 1899 and revised in 1901. Their enforcement was made the responsibility of a factory inspector.

The "script" system was eliminated by the laws of 1895, which required that wages be paid in lawful United States money. The lien laws of 1889 and 1895 secured for labor the priority of wage claims. During the 1890's, laws were passed against blacklisting, intimidation during elections, and, of particular significance, against requiring "any employee to withdraw from any trade union"—thus recognizing the right of labor to organize. Employers became responsible for negligence resulting in accidents to employees. Laborers and mechanics on public works, convicts, silica miners, and laborers in other forms of mining and smelting work, were limited to an eight-hour day. Railroad employees, foremen, and others were limited to nine hours. Regulations also attempted to prevent sweat-shops and the system of wage assignments. Laws were on the books against threats, lockouts, bringing armed forces into the State for police duty, and blacklisting of employees.

Since 1900, the growth of labor unions has been accompanied by a steadily increasing number of legislative acts. Many strikes have been held, some of historic significance. Among these was the strike of the St. Louis streetcar employees in the spring of 1900, following the consolidation of all the street railway lines. The strike, which was settled and then begun again after the discharge of strikers, involved union recognition and the closed shop. According to William Marion Reedy's description of the strike in the St. Louis *Mirror,* officials shifted responsibility, until the sheriff was ordered to form a citizens' posse. About 1600 men were drilled and armed. Strikers were shot and property was damaged. In summing up the results, Reedy says, "This strike has won though it has failed. The Company practically recognized the Union Labor principle. . . . The men were betrayed into rejecting a victory and choosing a defeat. The strikers were identified with lawlessness chiefly through the incapacity or chicanery of small politicians."

For the next 18 years the St. Louis traction system was non-union. On February 2, 1918, after a period of organizational activity, the motormen and conductors struck for recognition of the union, and five days later achieved their demands. Since that time, negotiations have won gains for the employees. At present, St. Louis is one of the few American cities in which the traction union has a closed-shop agreement with the company. With nearly 4,000 members, the St. Louis streetcar men's union is today the largest single union in Missouri.

In 1906, some workers in a St. Louis company were discharged for refusing to work more than nine hours a day. Their union called a strike when the company refused to negotiate. The strike was endorsed by the local labor council, as well as by the A. F. of L. Samuel Gompers offered to discuss a compromise, but the president of the company declined the invitation. According to Herbert Harris's *American Labor,* when Gompers' efforts failed, the company was placed on the "unfair to labor" list in the A. F. of L. official organ, the *Federationist,* in May 1907. Sales dropped from $1,000,000 a year to about $150,000. Thereupon, the company procured an injunction in the District of Columbia for the "cessation of concerted action." Gompers, asking why the Sherman Act was not enforced against the trusts whose anti-social doings had provoked its passage, was charged for contempt and sentenced to a year in prison, together with other A. F. of L. officials. The case was "kicked along in the courts for months," finally ending in a hasty peace made by the new president of the company.

As early as 1916, organized labor in Missouri had 915 unions, with 110,412 members, of which 105,181 were men and 5,231 women. All were affiliated with some national or international organization. During the World War, prosperity swept the State. The census for 1920 recorded a great urban growth and a decrease of population in rural areas. At this time 48.1 per cent of the population over 10 years of age, or 1,317,160 people, were workers. Employees of manufacturing concerns totaled 330,883 of this number, and agricultural employees represented 396,863.

Perhaps the outstanding reform measure of the post-war years was the Workmen's Compensation Law of 1925. In the ten-year period ending December 1937, a total of 806,415 accidents were reported, and sums of $26,629,850 in compensation and $12,279,760 in medical care were paid.

Following the financial panic of 1929, industrial employment dropped from 370,787 in 1930 to 141,196 in 1933. The number of strikes rose, and a new development appeared in labor organization. The American Federation of Labor had organized only the skilled crafts, yet with the improvement of machinery, the proportion of craftsmen to unskilled laborers declined steadily. To organize the latter, units of the Committee for Industrial Organization, now the Congress of Industrial Organizations, were formed. At approximately the same time, the national government came to the aid of the States by a program for absorbing unemployment in the Works Progress Administration, the Civilian Conservation Corps, the Public Works Administration, and other agencies. The American Federation of Labor finally

INDUSTRY

Missouri State Highway Department; Pohl

STRIP COAL MINING, MACON

ELECTRIC SHOVEL LOADING ORE IN A FLAT RIVER LEAD MINE

ORE TRAIN IN A FLAT RIVER LEAD MINE

Missouri State Highway Department; Pohl

ZINC MINE, SOUTHWEST MISSOURI

CHAT PILES IN THE LEAD BELT

Frank Eberle

SHEFFIELD STEEL PLANT, KANSAS CITY

CHAMPAGNE CELLAR, ST. LOUIS

American Wine Company

WINE VATS, ST. LOUIS

American Wine Company

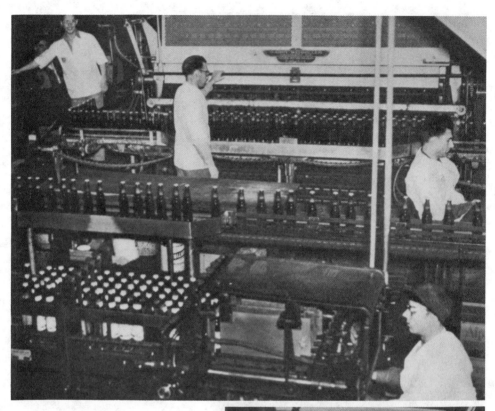

Columbia Brewing Company

**BOTTLING BEER IN A
ST. LOUIS BREWERY**

BREW KETTLES, ST. LOUIS

Anheuser-Busch Brewing Company

PAIRING AND INSPECTING UPPERS ON AN ARMY ORDER IN A ST. LOUIS SHOE FACTORY

St. Louis Post-Dispatch

LOADING THE KILN IN A CERAMICS MANUFACTORY, MEXICO

Mexico Refractories Company

expanded its activities to include the unskilled laborer, giving labor two powerful bargaining agencies.

In 1935, conditions began to improve. In that year, 162,144 workers were employed by Missouri industries, and the National Labor Relations Act became law. During the first year following its enactment, the 14th regional office, of which Missouri is a part, handled 240 cases involving 80,558 workers, belonging to both major labor groups. Of the firms concerned, 152 were located in St. Louis and 14 in eastern Missouri.

Outside of the urban centers, several groups which, through isolation and disorganization, had not had a voice in early labor development also attempted to form unions. These included the lead and zinc miners in southwest Missouri, the tiff miners of Washington County, and the sharecroppers of the cotton country of "swampeast Missouri." These people are in the main of Anglo-American stock, families which within the past half-century have come from the Tennessee, Kentucky, or Ozark hills to find employment. In southeast Missouri, the immigration of whites, together with groups of Southern Negroes, has taken place chiefly since the drainage of the swamps and the opening of the area to large-scale cotton farming. The Creole and Anglo-American population of Washington County has been augmented since 1930 by a steady immigration of families seeking occupation in the digging of tiff. A tiff miners' strike, the first Washington County had known, called in 1935, affected some 2,600 of the 3,600 workers in the area. The introduction of machinery had reduced the price of tiff to $3.50 a ton and the strikers demanded a rise to $5.50 a ton. In a few weeks a compromise was reached, increasing the price to $5 a ton.

In 1935, the International Union of Mine, Mill, and Smelter Workers, a C.I.O. affiliate representing employees of the Eagle-Picher Lead Company and its subsidiary in the Tri-State mining area, struck to obtain recognition. Prior to 1933, many unsuccessful efforts had been made to unionize the area. Employment in the mines was irregular, other types of work were not generally available, and living conditions were generally subnormal. When the strike was called, the Eagle-Picher Company immediately shut down its mines and smelters. Soon after, the company-directed Blue Card Union was organized, as a back-to-work movement. According to the National Labor Relations Board report (1939), violence began in the district almost immediately after the strike started and continued for nearly two years. The Blue Card Union, later affiliated with the A. F. of L., took over the task of local law enforcement, and an elaborate organization was formed whereby "squad cars" patrolled the highways and mines. The N.L.R.B. eventually ordered the Eagle-Picher Company to allow its workmen to join any union they pleased, and stipulated that "new employees hired after July 5, 1935, the effective date of the act, are to be dismissed to the extent necessary to make room for the employees discriminated against and ordered reinstated."

Health and living conditions are other problems of the mining area, especially "miners' con," silicosis which develops into tuberculosis. In 1937, the national death rate from pulmonary tuberculosis was 49 per 100,000; in Jasper County, Missouri, the rate was 130.5 per 100,000, the result not only of silicosis but of malnutrition.

By 1939, industrial labor in the State had reached some degree of stability, but the farm labor problem was still serious. At present the sharecroppers have a union, and various State and Federal agencies have formulated plans for their assistance (*see Agriculture*). Other groups, too, never before organized—school teachers, newspapermen, office workers, cab drivers, building service employees—have recently formed unions.

Transportation

THE story of Missouri's land and water routes includes that of the people and towns that grew along them, tuned to the echo of the flatboatmen's bugle, the whistle of the steamboat, or later, the snorting and puffing of the railroad engine. Present-day truckers, bus drivers, engineers, and airplane pilots, belong to a tradition begun by the Creole *coureurs des bois,* the gargantuan flatboatman, the steamboat pilot, the pony expressman, and the earlier railroad man; they, too, are fast becoming folk types as clearly defined as their predecessors, with a lore and jargon, "laws" and traditions of their own.

From the time of the first exploration of the Missouri region in the 1670's, the French and Spanish colonial traders, explorers, and government officials used the canoes of the Indians called *pirogues*—craft hewn from tree trunks, slender, swift, and easy to handle. Generally, they were made of cottonwood, which is comparatively easy to work; yet it took 4 men, swinging their adzes for 4 days, to make a medium-sized canoe about 20 feet long. The largest *pirogues* were about 30 feet long, with a 3½-foot beam and a mast amidship, with a square sail. These, often used for the shipping of furs and produce, were divided into compartments 4 to 6 feet long, with bulkheads cut in the solid trunk. Sometimes two *pirogues* were lashed together, with poles to hold them steady, and this craft, also outfitted with a square sail, was rowed by oarsmen at the bow and steered at the stern by a heavy oar with a wide blade.

As freighting increased, larger boats were developed. Those used for upstream traffic were long and slender like the French and Spanish colonial *bateau,* and the keelboat which succeeded it. The latter was capable of carrying from 15 to 30 tons of goods. The cargo box, where freight was stored, rose about 4 or 5 feet above the deck, and extended to within 10 or 12 feet from each end of the boat.

Progress upstream depended on muscle power. Oars were used in deep water, but in the shallow waters that made up the greater part of the journey the boat was propelled by setting poles. Fifteen-inch walks ran along the gunwales, and the boatmen, pressing the poles firmly against the river bottom, would double themselves forward and tramp from bow to stern, laboriously pushing the craft ahead. As a man reached the after end of the footway, he pulled his pole from the mud, ran forward, and again took his place at the head of the sweating crew.

95

In swift water, and when it was possible to walk along the river bank, a *cordelle* (little rope) was used. This was a line, often a thousand feet long, which was made fast to the mast. Most of the hands jumped ashore, took up the *cordelle,* and bucked the boat against the current. Sometimes the men were forced to make a path as best they could through the willows along the bank; often, they followed a well-defined towpath. So valuable were these towpaths to river traffic that all Spanish land grants specified their reservation for public use. At times, men on the gunwale would catch the limbs and brush along the shore and thus drag the boat ahead; this method was called "bush-whacking." By a combination of such devices, the keelboat was slowly worried upstream against the swift and changeable current. Ten miles was considered a good, average day's travel; 18 miles a day was deemed worthy of record. A voyage from New Orleans to St. Louis often took months.

The downstream journey was much less difficult. In 1802, the usual trip from St. Louis to New Orleans required about 25 or 30 days. Huge, square-cornered, flat-bottomed craft, variously called "flat-boats," "Kentucky flats," or "broadhorns," were built to carry the bulky downstream freight. These were simply oblong arks "very nearly resembling New England pig-sties," with roofs slightly curved from the center to shed rain. Generally they were about 15 feet wide and from 50 to 100 or more feet long, with a capacity of from 20 to 70 tons. Their freight charges were not high, and families often used them in descending the rivers. Piled with furniture and "cattle, hogs, horses, sheep, fowls and animals of all kinds," these flatboats were reminiscent of Noah's Ark. They were never brought back, but were broken up at their destination and sold for timber, the crews returning by keelboat, by land, or, later, by steamboat.

Downstream traffic greatly exceeded traffic upstream. Figuratively, all rivers led to New Orleans. The Mississippi was the connecting link; down its current swept Missouri furs, lead, salt, iron, and food-stuffs; upstream were poled and tugged necessities the frontier could not produce.

Out of this traffic emerged the professional flatboatman, whose job it was to get his cargo past shoal water, snags, Indians, and river pirates. The work and its dangers demanded a "combination rubber ball, wildcat, and shrieking maniac." These were rough and hardy men, as Mark Twain recalled, stoically suffering terrific handships, heavy drinkers, elephantinely jolly, foul-witted, and prodigal, yet, in the main, honest and faithful. It is told that, on landing, the strongest man in a crew would put a red feather in his cap to challenge anyone on shore, to the accompaniment of such verbal tauntings as that quoted in *Life on the Mississippi:* "Whoo-oop! I'm the old original iron-jawed, brass-mounted, copper bellied corpsemaker from the wilds of Arkansas! Look at me! I'm the man they call Sudden Death and general destruction. . . . I take nineteen alligators and a bar'l of whiskey for breakfast when I'm in robust health and a bushel of rattlesnakes and a dead body when I'm ailing. . . . Lay low and hold your breath, for I'm about to turn myself loose!" Only steam could defeat the flatboatman.

The first steamboat on the Mississippi, the *New Orleans,* left Pittsburgh for New Orleans in October of 1811. It made the trip despite the New Madrid earthquake, during which the current reversed and great chunks of land caved into the river. The sixth boat on the Mississippi, the *Zebulon M. Pike,* was built at Henderson, Kentucky, in 1815, and was the first to ascend the river beyond the mouth of the Ohio. Its hull was built on the model of a barge, and in rapid current the power of its one boiler had to be augmented by the use of poles. Yet, when the *Pike* arrived at St. Louis on August 9, 1817, it had made the trip from New Orleans in one-fifth the usual time. This voyage inaugurated a new era in Missouri transportation. Two years later the *Independence* proved the Missouri River to be navigable for steamboats by making the trip from St. Louis to Franklin, Chariton, and return within 21 days. During the same year the *Western Engineer,* one of the strangest of river boats, was built and equipped for Long's Expedition to the upper Missouri. The bow was shaped like the head of an immense serpent, from whose gaping mouth poured smoke and flame. The vessel moved up the river to the terror of the Indians, eventually reaching a point seven miles below Council Bluffs, the highest point reached by steamboat at that time.

The trip from St. Louis to St. Joseph, a distance of about 500 miles, sometimes took as long as that from New Orleans to St. Louis, for snags, shifting currents, and sandbanks prevented night travel. Often a boat never reached its destination. Navigation hazards, numerous on the Mississippi, were multiplied on the Missouri. With changing sandy channels, steamboats grounded as many as a dozen times a day. When the Missouri was at low-water stage, navigating it was "like putting a steamer on dry land, and sending a boy ahead with a sprinkling pot."

Half-submerged trees impaled the boats, over-strained boilers exploded, fires swept through the hulls, yet for every boat that met disaster, two others were launched. Many of the steamboats earned their cost within a year, for they were the swiftest as well as the most luxurious form of transportation. The majority were splendid structures, with double decks and interiors with gilded decorations, mahogany woodwork, and red plush upholstering. The *Natchez,* remembered for its race in 1870 against the *Robert E. Lee,* cost $200,000; the latter broke all records in making the 1,210-mile upstream run from New Orleans in 3 days, 18 hours, 14 minutes.

But for all their finery, the boats brought land-hungry settlers and traders in such numbers that their cabin floors were frequently carpeted with sleepers. Often, a missionary held a prayer meeting at one end of a boat's deck, while a gambler, with ruffled shirt, gaudy vest, Paris boots, and easy manners, plied his trade at the other. The boat would stop at a landing, a handful of people would go ashore, and soon another settlement would rise in the wilderness.

The steamboat pilot replaced the flatboatman as the outstanding figure of the rivers. Sharp-eyed, quiet, and alert, he belonged to a race apart. Often a pilot earned as much as $1,000 a month—more, Mark Twain observed, than a preacher did in a year. About the pilots, the captains, and their boats grew a lore as rich as the gargantuan stories of the flatboatmen. There was the boat "a-loaded down with ile an' bound for Noo Orleans" that caught fire and made a blaze so hot, "hit dried up the river." No less wonderful was the *Jim Johnson,* with its awesome captain who weighed 750 pounds and had but one eye; this boat was so big it took all summer to pass Boonville, and had to have rubber joints to get around the bends in the river.

Meantime, along the Mississippi River and on each bank of the Missouri, the wheels of Westward-bound traffic were cutting major land routes through the wilderness, widening the area of settlement into the back country, and carrying the commerce of the rivers on across the plains.

Missouri's land transportation developed more slowly and less spectacularly than that of its rivers. The streams were the first highways; but there existed from the earliest days of exploration a well-worn system of inland Indian trails, and natural pathways marked by the trampling of buffalo herds and other animals. Because these trails followed the easiest and most direct routes, many of them became the first roads used by European settlers, and, in turn, our modern highways.

The first road developed by white men in Missouri is thought to have been the trail between the mines in the southeast and Ste. Genevieve, over which, early in the 1700's, plodded pack trains loaded with lead. By 1772, a road of sorts cut across country between St. Louis and the site of the later village of St. Charles. Soon after 1789, military necessity prompted the Spaniards to mark *El Camino Real,* or the King's Highway, between New Madrid and St. Louis, by way of present-day Sikeston, Cape Girardeau, and Ste. Genevieve (*see Tour 7*). Despite its imposing name, the highway was often almost impassable to wagons and carriages, and a trip over it was scarcely less arduous than one upstream by flatboat.

Following the Louisiana Purchase, increased settlement brought new roads. One of the first and most important of these was the Boon's Lick Trail, which was the first east-west highway across Missouri, and which served as the trunk from which branched the great trails to the Far West. In 1819, it reached Fort Osage; in 1825, President John Quincy Adams appointed three commissioners to continue the road southwest to Santa Fe. Eventually, pack and wagon trains for the Southwest, California, and Oregon blazed other great transcontinental routes, bringing trade and settlement to Missouri.

By an act of the General Assembly in 1822, each county was made responsible for the maintenance of its roads, and all free males between the ages of 16 and 45 were required to maintain the roads within their districts. Later acts granted the right to build toll roads or bridges. Occasionally, as at New Franklin in 1839, lotteries were chartered to raise funds for road building. Yet even horseback travel remained difficult at times. One traveler commented that "if the mud does not get quite over your boot tops when you sit in the saddle, they call it a middling-good road."

What bridges there were, were heavy framed "covered bridges," of which only a few remain in the State. Ferries were established at some river crossings. At St. Louis, as early as 1797, Captain James Piggott lashed *pirogues* together, mounted a wooden platform upon them, and charged $2 to transport a horse and driver across the Mississippi. Somewhat later, Hall's Ferry, a roofless flatboat arrangement, propelled at first by a horse-driven treadmill, crossed the Missouri in St. Louis County. On smaller streams, boats were rowed or poled back and forth. Ferries were licensed by the county courts, who regulated their charges.

About 1849, enthusiasm developed for plank roads, and about 50 companies were chartered; in 1861, Congress granted all plank-road companies the right-of-way through government lands. Out of 17 such roads built in Missouri, the State's first major attempt at hard-surfaced roads, all charged tolls, except the two-mile Lafayette County Plank Road, completed south of Lexington in 1853. One of the most important, and the longest constructed in the United States, was the 42-mile thoroughfare between Ste. Genevieve and Iron Mountain, which was chartered in 1851; it was used primarily for the hauling of ore. The planks wore out rapidly, however, or warped till they resembled rockers, and the roads were abandoned within a few years in favor of macadam. Another plank road, from Cape Girardeau, was so much used by Federal cavalry and artillery during the Civil War that it became useless.

As roadways were made passable, public transport by stagecoach and wagon train supplemented that by steamboat. Taverns were built at the main stagecoach stops, rivaling each other in food and liquid refreshment. News was exchanged, messages were sent to absent ones, and the coach moved on. For travel across the plains, various schemes were tried; perhaps the most fantastic was the "wind-wagon," built in 1853. This was a vehicle with wheels 12 feet in diameter and a large sail, intended for freight transport. With this outfit, there would be no horses or oxen to feed, or to be stolen by Indians. On its trial trip, the "wind-wagon" got up a fair speed under a favorable wind, but proved unmanageable and crashed into a ditch.

By this time, railroads had caught the popular imagination. Fifty-nine delegates from 11 counties met in St. Louis, April 30, 1836, to recommend the construction of 2 Missouri lines, and to petition Congress for a grant of 800,000 acres of public lands to encourage these enterprises. Soon after, the legislature incorporated about 18 railroad companies, all of which collapsed with the panic of 1837. With returning prosperity, the boom revived and was stimulated by a national railroad convention held in St. Louis during October, 1849 (see St. Louis). Thirteen states were here represented by nearly 1,000 delegates, who proclaimed their interests to be national rather than sectional, and who advocated the construction of a transcontinental railroad. The Hannibal and St. Joseph Railroad, now a part of the Burlington system, was incorporated in 1847; the Pacific Railroad, now a part of the Frisco lines, in 1849; two years later, the North Missouri Railroad, now a part of the Wabash system, was chartered. Soon other lines were projected. Plagued by tottering credit, among other difficulties, the railroad companies received State and Federal aid in grants of funds and lands, and activity proceeded according to the rhythm of these transfusions. The first railroad construction was begun in St. Louis by the Pacific Railroad, July 4, 1851. The following year passenger service was started to Cheltenham, five miles away. Although begun later, the Hannibal and St. Joseph Railroad, completed in 1859, was the first to reach Missouri's western border. During the same year, a junction was effected between this line and the North Missouri at Macon. Meanwhile, south of the Missouri River, the Pacific had pushed construction to Jefferson City in 1855, to Syracuse about 1860, and—with work interrupted by the Civil War—to Kansas City in 1865. The St. Louis and Iron Mountain Railroad, designed to open the rich mining area of southeast Missouri, was completed to Pilot Knob before the end of 1858. By 1860, these and other lines had completed 796 miles of track within the State.

Out of the combination of these railroads with the trails that led beyond them grew the spectacular travel routes to the Far West. The fight to establish mail delivery to California threw the contract in 1857 to a company headed by John Butterfield. To pay for the semiweekly transportation of mail, Congress made a $600,000 annual appropriation. Butterfield established his line with its eastern termini at Memphis and St. Louis, and its western at San Francisco. Mail and passengers were carried from St. Louis to Tipton on the newly constructed Pacific Railroad, and there transferred to stage coaches which swung on a great arc through Springfield, to meet the Memphis stage at Little Rock, Arkansas, and from there on through Preston, Texas, to San Francisco. The distance covered was nearly 2,800 miles. The postage rate was 20¢ an ounce for letters; the passenger fare was $100 in gold. The line had more than 100 Concord coaches, 1,000 horses, and 500 mules, and employed 750 men.

Almost simultaneously with the beginning of the Butterfield line in 1858, John M. Hockaday inaugurated a stage line from St. Joseph to the army posts of Utah. A year later, the completed Hannibal and St. Joseph Railroad linked this route with the East. Then, on April 3, 1860, the brief but colorful Pony Express was launched by Russell, Majors, and Waddell. This picked up the mail from the railroad at St. Joseph and raced it westward on horseback (*see St. Joseph*).

The railroads instituted a new phase of Missouri's development. The steamboat and the early overland trails had carried settlement and commerce chiefly to sections adjoining the rivers—even today, two-thirds of the State's population live in the one-third of its area that adjoins the Mississippi and Missouri. Most of the important lanes across the State traversed the same region, and connected St. Louis on the east with Kansas City, Westport, Independence, and St. Joseph on the west. The first trans-State railroads widened this area, and by establishing western terminals in the river towns added to their importance as breaking points of transportation. For a time, the steamboat, the prairie schooner, and the railroad all poured their traffic through these booming western cities. In 1857, there were 729 steamboat arrivals at Kansas City. By the end of the Civil War, however, the Missouri River trade was dying. Mississippi River commerce declined soon after. But the war, which hastened the end of river traffic, proved the railroads' superiority in speed and service, and their ability to open new areas to settlement.

The period immediately following the Civil War was one of wild railroad promotion. Small systems were chartered, promoted, sometimes built, then sold or abandoned, almost always with a heavy loss to investors. Nevertheless, during this time some of the major rail systems of today got their start. By 1865, most of the large systems new serving the State either were in service or under construction, and some measure of order was beginning to appear. In 1878, Kansas City opened the second union station in the world.

As commerce forsook the waterways, once-important river towns, such as LaGrange, Glasgow, and Lexington, went into decline, a few passing out of existence. New towns sprouted along the railroad lines, to serve as shipping and trading points for inland agricultural districts. The railroads themselves built such towns as Moberly and Sedalia, and gave others, such as Hannibal, renewed life through the establishment of shops and other service adjuncts. The lines transported lead, zinc, and iron from the southeastern and southwestern mines, and grain and livestock from the prairies. Wheat, oil, and cattle were brought across the State as Oklahoma developed, and the railroads supplanted the old Texas cattle trails.

Still little changed in more than a century, the central Ozark upland, an area almost as large as Maine, was penetrated by comparatively few railroads, some counties being without a single line. The hills made road-building difficult, and the few inhabitants came and went over mountain trails which often were impassable to any but horseback travel.

The development of this section, as well as the growth or decline of others, has been the result of modern highway construction induced by the development of automobile travel. After the plank-road craze, the building of hard-surfaced roads languished. The main country lanes were kept in repair chiefly to provide access to the railroads. Automobiles brought a new need. The first automobiles were introduced into Missouri about 1891. Twenty years later, 16,387 were registered. Busses and trucks began to operate even before the general extension of the highways. In 1939, there were 141,609 trucks and 591 Public Service Company busses registered in Missouri.

In 1907, the State recognized the importance of highway improvement by appointing a State Highway Engineer as a member of the Board of Agriculture to advise counties in the construction of county highways which would eventually form part of the State system. Six years later, a Highway Commission was created. Under the Hawes Law of 1916, the duties and powers of the commission were increased. With the $60,000,000 bond issue voted in 1920, and the Centennial Road Law of 1921, the modern period of highway construction began: construction and maintenance passed from the control of the counties, in whose hands it had remained since the territorial period, into the control of the State. Further highway improvement was made possible by funds produced from automobile license fees and gasoline taxes. These funds were insufficient, however, to meet the rapidly expanding needs, and a second bond issue, providing $75,000,000, was voted in 1928. Today, 15,491 miles of State and national highways crisscross Missouri, 8,306 being major highways, 7,185 supplementary roads. No spot in the State is more than 10 miles from a highway. A Highway Patrol, established in 1931, enforces the law, and aids motorists in trouble.

Modern highway traffic has produced economic and social effects as far-reaching as those of the steamboat or the railroad. It has destroyed community barriers and opened isolated portions of the State for development and recreation; it has built new towns and sapped the trade and population from old centers. Out of this traffic have grown new points of view, a new jargon, and new types as distinctive and colorful as those of an earlier period. The jalopy and the hitch-hiker are universal; the gas station has added a new architectural feature; the "tourist camp" a new kind of inn.

Within recent years, there has been a revival of river traffic. Passenger service is limited to the summer excursion packets out of St. Louis; but since 1912, when Congress appropriated $20,000,000 to improve the Missouri River from Kansas City to its mouth, an intensive program for dredging and marking both the Missouri and the Mississippi channels has been carried on by United States Army engineers. Federal barge lines have pointed the way for private systems, which are experiencing a renewal of trade. Much slow freight out of Kansas City and St. Louis—grain, coal, steel, and similar products—moves by river now.

Missouri, "air-minded" almost from the first, is a center for aviation both because of its central position and because the State has no natural hazards to air traffic, such as mountains or dangerous air currents. As early as 1830, a device for propelling balloon craft by means of an endless screw was registered in St. Louis. In 1859, a year before the Pony Express, Captain John Wise, a scientist of Pike County, made a balloon flight from St. Louis to study the upper air currents, traveling the 1,150 miles to Henderson, New York, in 39 hours and 50 minutes, a record which stood for 50 years. The Louisiana Purchase Exposition, held in St. Louis in 1904, sponsored an air meet, at which $150,000 in prizes were offered—the first important prize money ever offered for an aeronautic event. Unfortunately, the only entrant was the great French pilot, Albert Santos Dumont, who brought his tiny airship across the ocean in a box, but was unable to fly because the gas bag was damaged.

By 1907, the St. Louis Aero Club had been organized, with Major Albert Bond Lambert, born in St. Louis in 1875, as secretary. An ardent aircraft enthusiast since his early youth, an expert balloon pilot, and friend of Orville Wright and of Santos Dumont, Major Lambert had, from the first, a visionary's belief in the possibilities of the new invention. Through his efforts, the newly formed Aero Club sponsored the first international balloon races in 1907, for which he served as referee. Captain H. E. Honeywell, crack designer, builder, and pilot of balloons, took many of the prizes. It was Lambert who first saw the possibility of air mail, and who first urged the military use of aircraft. In 1916 he was appointed naval observer on the battleship *Utah,* and the following year he served in the World War as Commanding Major of the Signal Corps, in the aviation section. In 1919, he became secretary of the Aero Club of America.

In 1908, the first dirigible meet was held in St. Louis. Two years later, the first international aviation meet in the United States was held at Kinloch Park, between Ferguson and Florissant. The Wright Brothers sent all six of their planes, and the famous French pilot, Le Blanc, brought his Bleriot monoplane from France. In all, nine planes entered the meet, to set several records. Le Blanc established the then remarkable record of 60 miles an hour; Hoxie (or Hoxsey), the daredevil of the air, took a balloon up one mile, and, assisted by a strong tail-wind, broke the long-distance record with a non-stop flight to Springfield, Illinois, a distance of nearly 75 miles. A world's endurance record for planes was also established at this meet—one hour and ten minutes of continuous flight. Experiments conceived by Major Lambert apparently included the "bombing" with pointed weights of dummy battleships of painted canvas set up in the park; trying out anti-aircraft guns; and the organization of the first military signal corps attached to aviation. President Theodore Roosevelt attended the meet, and made his first plane flight with Hoxie as pilot. Eighty automobiles accompanied the president to the park, bringing the comment: "This speaks well for St. Louis."

Also in 1910, the second International Balloon Race was held in St. Louis. In 1911, the Pioneer Aeroplane and Exhibition Company was licensed by the State, and another meet was arranged for Kinloch Park. During the latter year, St. Louis sent two young men to be trained as pilots by the Wright Company, which had a virtual monopoly of planes, pilots, and instruction. Flying was still, primarily, an exhibition pursuit, but in October 1911, the first air mail ever carried was flown from Kinloch Park to Fairgrounds Park in St. Louis.

When five St. Louis pilots offered themselves and some broken-down planes for military service in 1916, the Government established the first aeronautic corps of the United States Army. The following year, Honeywell designed several balloons for military use, and the Missouri Aeronautical Society began the systematic training of army pilots.

Shortly after the establishment of Lambert Field in 1920, regular mail service was established between St. Louis and Chicago. In 1923, the new field was enlarged and improved to accommodate the Pulitzer Air Races, which cost $300,000, and drew a record crowd of 140,000 spectators, 92 planes and the airship *Shenandoah* taking part.

At about this time, Charles A. Lindbergh, Jr., an unknown barnstorming pilot who had been moving about the country in his Jenny plane taking up passengers at $5 "a good ride," came to St. Louis, where an air meet was in progress. He watched the newer planes with a covetous eye. In his book, *We,* he says he would willingly have given the summer's barnstorming profits "in return for authority to fly some of the newer types . . . which would roar up into the sky when they were pointed that way, instead of having to be wished up over low trees at the end of a landing field."

At the St. Louis meet he sold his Jenny, and, after a short period of teaching and barnstorming in and out of St. Louis, enrolled as a Flying Cadet in 1924. As a second lieutenant, he returned to St. Louis and to barnstorming, occasionally doing some teaching, and even stunt flying for a circus. He was for a time instructor for the Robertson Aircraft Corporation in St. Louis, for whom he flew mail on the St. Louis to Chicago route. He was made first lieutenant at Lambert Field.

A group of St. Louis business men were persuaded to back his long-dreamed of flight across the Atlantic Ocean, and at 8 A.M., May 20, 1927, he left Roosevelt Field, New York, in the *Spirit of St. Louis.* The flight captured the imagination of the world, and gave final proof of the practicality and dependability of the airplane. In St. Louis it provided the necessary impetus for the passage of a $2,000,000 bond issue to make Lambert Field a municipal airport under the official name of Lambert-St. Louis Flying Field (*see Tour 1*).

Kansas City has become an air center of increasing importance, with a Municipal Airport in North Kansas City. Nearly every city of any size in Missouri has an airport of some kind. Six commercial air lines maintain scheduled service at St. Louis, Kansas City, and St. Joseph, and charter service is obtainable at most secondary cities.

Newspapers and Radio

D URING the early summer of 1808, a prospectus was circulated in St. Louis announcing the plan to establish Missouri's first newspaper. Its author, Joseph Charless, concluded his notice with a declaration of his faith in the freedom of the press. "It is self evident," he states, "that in every country where the rays of the Press is [sic] not clouded by despotic power, that the people have arrived at the highest grade of civilization . . . The inviolation of the press is coexistent with the liberties of the people, they live or die together." Charless spoke with earnest conviction, for he was a native of Ireland who had been forced to flee his country for his part in the Irish Rebellion of 1795.

Charless had come to St. Louis late in 1807 or early in 1808. Here he rented the north room of the old Joseph Robidoux house, ordered type from Louisville and a Ramage press from Pennsylvania, and on July 12, 1808, published the first number of the *Missouri Gazette*. The paper, issued to 174 subscribers, was printed on foolscap sheets 8 by 12 inches, with 12 columns in all. For the benefit of French residents in the community, part of the paper was printed in their native language. Subsequent editions were "regulated by the arrival of the mail." The subscription price was $3 a year in cash or $4 in country produce.

Charless' independent editorial policy brought trouble as well as rewards. The paper's circulation increased, but it aroused the opposition of many St. Louisans. Five or six of these, variously armed, attacked him in his office during February of 1814, "Mr. C. defending himself as best he could with his shillaly." When intimidation failed, a group of Charless' enemies raised funds in 1815, to establish a rival paper, the *Western Journal,* and imported Joshua Norvell from Nashville to edit it. Charless greeted the appearance of the *Journal* by reasserting: "I shall preserve the liberty of the Press as long as I am able to control one," and two years later added "Truth without Fear," to his masthead.

In spite of other attempts upon his person, and threats to burn the office, Charless continued to publish the *Gazette* until September of 1820. Two years later his son Edward took over the paper under the title, *Missouri Republican.* On September 20, 1836, it became a daily, two years after the first daily in the State, the St. Louis *Herald,* was established. Successive editors continued the policies established by its founder, and no Missouri newspaper played a more significant role in the development of the State. It was continued from 1888 as the St. Louis *Republic,* until purchased by the *Globe-Democrat* on December 4, 1919.

The first newspaper to be published west of St. Louis was the *Missouri Intelligencer and Boon's Lick Advertiser,* established at Franklin on April 23, 1819, by Benjamin Holliday. This paper, a weekly, consisted of four 8-by-18-inch pages, with five columns to a page. Its price was $3 a year if paid in advance or $4 if at the end of the year, "the former being preferable." After several changes in ownership, the paper came into the possession of Nathaniel Patten, who moved it to Fayette in 1826, and to Columbia four years later, where it was published until Patten sold it in 1835. For these peripatetic early labors, Patten is known as the pioneer of Missouri's country journalism. The outstanding quality of his papers was the then novel one of counterbalancing politics with news. Eventually, the paper became the *Missouri Statesman,* published by William F. Switzler and Y. J. Williams.

By 1820, there were five papers in Missouri, all essentially "hometown" organs, filled with extracts from foreign and domestic newspapers, quotations from well-known authors, and contributions by local poets. Editorials and letters to the editor were signed with such stentorian pseudonyms as "Veritas," "Publicus," or "Aurora Borealis." The advertisements of "Fresh goods just received by steamboat," "Stray Cow Found," or "My wife Sarah has left my bed and board . . ." were often of more interest than the general news, and compensated in part for the lack of information.

During the presidential election of 1828, national issues and leaders occupied much of Missouri's attention. The newspapers, like the people, decided either for Andrew Jackson, Democrat, or for John Quincy Adams, National Republican or Whig. Thomas H. Benton's St. Louis *Enquirer* was pro-Jackson with fervent eloquence. Patten's pro-Whig *Missouri Intelligencer* adopted as its motto: "The American system and its friends, throughout the Union." After the national election, the principal issues became those of slavery and of the Mormons. These furnished rich material for opinionated editors. Until the Civil War, almost every paper, with the possible exception of the *Independent Patriot,* devoted one-third of each issue to the virtues of the political views held by the editor, and much of the remaining two-thirds to the vices of the opposition. Little if any tolerance was in evidence.

In 1832, a year after Joseph Smith had revealed Independence as the divinely chosen site for the Mormon's temple, *The Morning and The Evening Star,* a Mormon paper edited by W. W. Phelps, began publication in that town, devoting itself exclusively to "publishing the revela-

tions of God to the Church," and denouncing the "ungodly Gentiles."
On the same press was printed the *Upper Missouri Advertiser,* a paper
used to promote this section of Missouri as the revealed place of the
future City of Zion. Resentment against the Mormons grew. In 1834,
a group of anti-Mormons seized the press and type and threw them into
the Missouri River. Some driftwood harvesters later raised the press,
and it was subsequently used by the *Upper Missouri Enquirer,* established at Liberty by Robert N. Kelly and William H. Davis, January
11, 1834. In 1845, the press was sold to William Ridenbaugh, who
established the St. Joseph *Gazette.* Afterward, a Captain Merrick is
said to have taken it to Denver, where he started the first paper published in Colorado.

About 1833, a number of St. Louis business men furnished Elijah
Parish Lovejoy with $1,200 to buy press, type, and equipment for the
publication of the St. Louis *Observer,* a weekly. As editor, Lovejoy
published strong, sincere editorials on the sins of slavery, intemperance,
and "popery." In October, 1835, while Lovejoy was absent, the publishers were told by a group of citizens that the paper must stop all
controversy upon the subject of slavery. The publishers replied that
the paper's policy would be determined by the editor upon his return.
Lovejoy immediately wrote an editorial stating that he would write
and speak what he pleased as long as he remained alive. A mob then
wrecked the establishment, driving Lovejoy to Alton, Illinois, where
he later was killed by a pro-slavery mob.

As settlers continued to pour into the State, other towns were
founded and newspapers established. At Jefferson City, Calvin Gunn
established the *Jeffersonian* in time to print the proceedings of the first
meeting of the general assembly at the new State capitol (1826). The
growth of Hannibal brought with it the establishment of the Hannibal
Commercial Advertiser in 1837, and, during the 1840's, Joseph P.
Ament moved his *Missouri Courier* from Palmyra to that thriving river
port. About 1848, Ament employed as "printer's devil" 13-year-old
Sam Clemens, the future "Mark Twain," who soon became an office
favorite and, as Miss Minnie Brashear says, "a sort of sub-editor."
When the telegraph was extended to Hannibal during the last year of
the Mexican War, Sam was put in charge of the war extras. In 1850,
he left the *Courier* to work with his brother Orion on his newly established *Western Union,* a weekly Whig paper. Two years later, when
this paper combined with another local organ to become the Hannibal
Journal, Sam became assistant editor, and set about enlivening the paper
with new features and spicy local articles. In spite of Mark Twain's
later ungenerous comments, Orion seems not only to have recognized
and encouraged his brother's talents, but to have had amazing patience
with his many newspaper indiscretions. During Orion's absence in

September of 1852, Sam climaxed a summer's jousting with the editor of a rival paper by publishing a crude woodcut he had made of that gentleman's abortive attempt to commit suicide over a love affair by wading into Bear Creek. Later, Mark Twain reported, perhaps incorrectly, the results: "Higgins dropped in with a double-barreled shotgun early in the forenoon. When he found that it was an infant (as he called me) that had done him the damage, he simply pulled my ears and went away; but he threw up his situation that night and left town for good."

While Orion was out of town during March of 1853, Sam published a poem called "Love Concealed," with the subtitle, "To Miss Katie of Hannibal." This in intent was harmless enough; but the subtitle was too long for the column, and Hannibal was reduced to "H—l," with startling results. "For once the Hannibal *Journal* was in demand," Mark Twain recalled, "and . . . actually booked the unparalleled number of thirty-three subscribers." Later 17-year-old Sam made his debut as editor of "Our Assistant's Column," writing spicy comments and puns on local happenings, notices of spiritualistic activities, bits of satire on human foibles, and ambitious "selected material." On May 26, 1853, he left Hannibal for St. Louis, where he hoped to earn money for a ticket to New York. Orion seems to have missed his assistant; late in September, he sold the *Journal* to William T. League.

The difficulties of establishing newspapers in the eastern portion of the State were multiplied in the western cities of Liberty, St. Joseph, and Kansas City, where editors' enthusiasms were all too often dampened by unexpected handicaps and an uncertain public temper. At Liberty, the *Upper Missouri Enquirer* was succeeded by several short-lived papers before the *Tribune* began its long and distinguished career in 1846. John Dougherty served as editor on the *Tribune* from 1847 to 1888. The St. Joseph *Gazette,* established in 1845, became a daily in 1857, under the direction of P. S. Pfouts and J. H. B. Cundiff.

At Kansas City, a paper begun in 1851 failed within two years. In 1854 a second weekly, the *Enterprise,* was established. The following year, this paper was purchased by Colonel Robert Thompson van Horn, under whose dynamic editorship it became the champion of Kansas City's civic growth. Van Horn changed the name to the *Western Journal of Commerce,* and in 1858 began daily publication. In 1922, the *Journal* was combined with the *Post,* which had been established in 1906, to form the *Journal-Post,* now the Kansas City *Journal.* Another vigorous editor, William Rockhill Nelson, was responsible for the establishment in 1880 of the Kansas City *Star,* which in 1901 acquired the *Times* (*see Kansas City*).

A number of foreign-language newspapers did notable work between 1835 and 1900 in helping immigrant groups to adjust themselves. The first of the German-language papers was the *Anzeiger des Westens,* first issued as a weekly on October 31, 1835, by Christian Bimpage, and changed to a daily in 1846. In 1850, the paper came into the possession of Henry Boernstein, who, in Poland, had studied medicine, served as a soldier, written editorials for newspapers, composed plays, and been a stage manager and actor. In Paris he saw the fall of Louis Philippe, but fled the country when Napoleon III came into power. In St. Louis, he undertook to rule the then rising emancipation movement, wrote a scandalous book, *The Mysteries of St. Louis,* and assumed the management of the German Theater. His influence waned, however, when he set himself up as a political boss, showing an arrogant and dictatorial spirit.

The most influential German-language newspaper was the *Westiche Post,* founded in St. Louis by Carl Daenzer in 1857. Much of its success was due to Dr. Emil Preetorious, co-editor in 1862 and editor in 1864, and to Carl Schurz, who served as editor for a short time following his arrival in St. Louis in 1867. Born in Cologne, Prussia, Schurz had been a newspaper editor at the age of 19, and later a participant in the revolution of 1848. Two years after arriving in Missouri, he was elected to the United States Senate, where he served one term. Among the journalists employed by Schurz was the young reporter, Joseph Pulitzer.

The daily *Amerika* was founded in 1862 by the German Literary Society, with Anthony Hellmich as editor. By 1880, there were 19 German papers published in Missouri. As immigration slackened, however, and the older German families became "Americanized," the papers' usefulness began to pass. The last among them was the *Westliche Post,* which suspended publication in 1938.

Other foreign language newspapers were less hardy. A number of French journals sprang up in St. Louis between 1844 and 1893, prospered briefly, and then succumbed, many of them because of popular resentment to their predominately socialist and anti-Catholic views (*see Religion.*) The most successful, *Le Revue de l'Quest* (1854-64), established by the French Literary Society of St. Louis, was conservative in tone and independent in politics (*see Literature*). The *Polish Eagle,* perhaps the first Polish newspaper in America, was established at Washington in February, 1870, moved to near-by Krakow in 1871, and discontinued about 1872.

Missouri's first advertising agent appeared in 1846, and the first newspaper directory in 1869. Today, it is estimated that over $200,-000,000 are annually expended in newspaper advertising in Missouri. The first Sunday newspaper made its appearance in St. Louis when the *Republican* was issued on September 8, 1854. Despite consternation among the religious, and denunciation from the pulpit, Sunday papers were successful from the start.

P. H. Murray, editor of the St. Louis *Advance,* was the first Negro newspaper publisher in Missouri. The *Advance,* which he established in 1880, advocated the industrial education of the Negro. There are now three weekly Negro newspapers in St. Louis; the *Argus,* the *American,* and the *Call,* the latter being printed in Kansas City and shipped to St. Louis. Negro newspapers in Missouri have brought about no outstanding innovations, but they have grown steadily in size, coverage, and circulation.

The story of Missouri's newspapers contains many names outstanding in the history of national journalism. Januarius Aloysius MacGahan was a St. Louis newspaperman who molded reportorial style and method. After 1868, he became famous as a correspondent in the Franco-Prussian War and the Paris Commune. He journeyed to the Oxus with the Russian army, and later investigated Turkish atrocities. More widely known was Henry M. Stanley, whose first work as a newspaperman was with the St. Louis *Democrat* (now the *Globe-Democrat*). His dispatches to this paper covering the Indian peace treaties of 1867 won him a commission to Europe, and the assignment to find Livingstone in Africa for James Gordon Bennett's New York *Herald.* O. O. McIntyre (1884-1938), New York columnist, was born—Gallipolis, Ohio, to the contrary—in Plattsburg, Missouri.

Eugene Field is usually remembered as a poet, but he was essentially a newspaperman. He worked on various papers throughout the Middle West: the St. Louis *Journal,* the St. Joseph *Gazette,* the Kansas City *Times,* and the Denver *Tribune.* Later, in Chicago, he published his "Sharps and Flats," in the Chicago *Morning News.* This column, if not the first, was certainly one of the earliest and best of its type. Joseph B. McCullagh, the "Little Mac" of Eugene Field's verse, was managing editor of the St. Louis *Globe-Democrat* for many years, and had a lasting influence on newspaper writing and methods. Theodore Dreiser, who worked for him during 1892-93, first as a reporter and later as drama critic, appraised him as "a real force, a great man," whose "robust personality" and "powerful, brilliant editorials" gave his journal international fame. "The whole of Europe," Dreiser recalls, "as well as America, was combed and reflected in order that his readers might be entertained and retained . . ."

During the same period, two other St. Louis editors were making journalistic history. William Marion Reedy (*see Literature*) worked on the *Missouri Republican* for a time, and then became a free-lance reporter. He found his true field, however, as editor of the St. Louis *Mirror.* He remade critical journalism in the United States by taking it from the academic groves to the market place—and even to the night clubs. Hungarian-born Joseph Pulitzer, failing to satisfy his desire for military adventure in Europe, came to the United States to serve in the Union army during the Civil War. In 1865, he arrived at St. Louis, where he worked as a reporter on the *Westliche Post.* His incisive mind and personal fearlessness soon made him a dominant figure in the State. In 1878, he merged the St. Louis *Dispatch* and the St. Louis *Post* to form the present *Post-Dispatch.* Later, he purchased the New York *World,* and in 1887 established the *Evening World.* He found ample subject matter in the lush corruption of St. Louis and New York, and did not hesitate to flay the national government on larger issues.

Similar in spirit in some respects was William Rockhill Nelson, Kansas City reformer, whom Henry Haskell describes as having "a temperament that was a combination of Lorenzo the Magnificent and Jim Hill, with a dash of St. Francis, Nietzsche and Oliver Cromwell. Wherever Fate happened to plant Nelson, he hoisted his flag and took charge." Nelson, who pioneered with a two-cent newspaper, had an instinctive appreciation for the sort of human stuff that the average individual likes to read. "The wife decides the paper the family will have," was Nelson's observation, and his paper was designed to interest her. At the same time Nelson had definite ideas about how and where Kansas City needed improvement, and these he followed up through the pages of his paper against any and all opposition.

George Hearst, a contemporary of Nelson and a native Missourian, inadvertently became the founder of a powerful chain of newspapers. In 1880, Hearst, who had made a fortune in western mining, took over the San Francisco *Daily Examiner* on a debt. Seven years later, his son, William Randolph Hearst, became manager of the newspaper and made it the first of his present chain.

From the beginning, the rural press has been a vital factor in the life of the State. Among the many vigorous editorial personalities have been Jacob Sosey, who established the *Missouri Whig* (now the Palmyra *Spectator*) in 1839, and whose family still owns and operates the paper; E. W. Stephens, editor for 35 years of the Columbia *Herald;* Robert Morgan White of the Mexico *Ledger;* H. J. Blanton, editor of the Paris *Appeal;* and William Southern, Jr., editor of the Independence *Examiner.*

On May 17, 1867, a group of editors, meeting in St. Louis, formed the Missouri Press Association. Jesse W. Barrett, who in 1862 had founded the Canton *Press,* one of the five oldest family newspapers in the State, was its first president. At first, it aimed to promote fraternity among newspaper men and to break down personal animosities. Soon, the Association saw the possibilities of creating standard conditions for the industry, and a variety of business and publication problems were taken up. Once the editors had learned to work together, the organization began a program for public improvement. In 1922, it was incorporated, and employed a full-time field manager. It is a non-profit organization, supported by assessments and dues from its members. The Missouri Women's Press Club, an affiliate of the National Federation of Press Women, was organized on May 5, 1937.

As Missouri has been a pioneer in other journalistic enterprises, so, too, it has been a pioneer in journalistic education. In 1908, one hundred years after journalism crossed the Mississippi River, the first school of journalism in the world to grant a degree was founded at the University of Missouri, with Walter Williams, former editor of the Columbia *Herald,* as dean. This new division of the university began classes on September 14, 1908, with a staff including, besides Mr. Williams as professor of history and principles of journalism, Silas Bent, assistant professor of theory and practice of journalism, E. H. Evans, student assistant in newspaper making, and Charles Griffith Ross, instructor in journalism. Ross remained on the faculty until 1918, when he became chief Washington correspondent for the St. Louis *Post-Dispatch.* He was awarded the Pulitzer prize for newspaper correspondents in 1932, and the University of Missouri presented him with a medal for work in journalism. At the end of the school's first semester, Silas Bent resigned and Frank L. Martin of the Kansas City *Star* was appointed to his position. When Williams was made Dean Emeritus shortly before his death in July, 1935, Martin became dean of the school. One of the school's achievements is the Columbia *Missourian,* which began publication as a city daily on September 14, 1908. The paper is issued under the direction of the faculty of the Missouri School of Journalism, with students as reporters, copy readers, and advertising solicitors. The University gives annual awards for distinguished service in journalism, many of which have been won by Missourians.

Recently there has been a tendency towards consolidation on the part of major city newspapers. An important example has been the St. Louis *Star-Times* combination, formed in 1932. The *Star* had its origin as the St. Louis *Sunday Sayings,* established by Charles E. Meade, Charles A. Gitchell, and James E. Munford, in 1884. The *Times* is said to trace its beginning to 1829.

Besides the award to Charles Ross, six Pulitzer prizes for distinctive journalism have been given to Missouri newspapers and newspapermen. Two have gone to members of the Kansas City *Star:* A. B. McDonald in 1931, and Henry J. Haskell in 1933. The other four have been bestowed upon the St. Louis *Post-Dispatch.* The first, in 1926, went to Daniel Fitzpatrick, political cartoonist. The following year, the award for distinguished reporting was won by the late John T. Rogers, crime reporter, whose sources of information in the underworld enabled him to furnish the *Post-Dispatch* with almost incredible "beats." In 1929, the late Paul Y. Anderson won the same award for his success in reopening the Teapot Dome oil-lease scandal. Anderson, who has been praised as a "reporters' reporter," was elevated to the Washington staff after long years of distinguished general assignments. From January, 1938, until his suicide a year later, he served as Washington correspondent for the St. Louis *Star-Times*. The *Post-Dispatch* itself, under the editorship of O. K. Bovard, received the Pulitzer prize in 1937 for its exposure of wholesale fraudulent registrations in St. Louis.

RADIO

In recent years, radio has become increasingly important as a means of purveying news, advertisements, and entertainment. Missouri has 15 commercial broadcasting stations, 6 of them in St. Louis. WEW, the St. Louis University station, formerly known as 9YK, went on the air April 26, 1921, as a more or less experimental station, confining its broadcasts to weather reports at 10 a.m. In September of that year, it added daily market reports. Among other early stations were KSD, WIL, and KMOX of St. Louis, and WDAF and WHB of Kansas City.

KFUO, the Concordia Seminary station, was dedicated December 24, 1924, and broadcasts the Gospel according to the Lutheran Church. It is not a commercial station, and carries no advertising, being maintained by contributions.

KGPC, the St. Louis Metropolitan Police station, began operation August 12, 1930. Three dispatchers are on duty at all times, receiving calls for police, ambulance service, or the Humane Society. The St. Louis *Star-Times* station, KXOK, began broadcasting in 1938.

Missouri has several "firsts" in radio broadcasting. On Christmas Eve, 1922, KSD broadcast from the Old Cathedral in St. Louis the first midnight Mass to be put on the air. This was made possible by special permission from the Vatican. On June 21, 1923, the voice of a president of the United States was heard over the air for the first time, when Warren G. Harding delivered a speech in St. Louis. The speech was one of the earliest network programs and was broadcast also by WEAF in New York and WCAP in Washington. The first broadcast of a news event was that of the Dempsey-Carpentier fight in Jersey City, July 2, 1921, which was put on the air by the St. Louis *Globe-Democrat* in co-operation with the Benwood Company. On December 6, 1923, the voice of President Coolidge addressing Congress came over the telephone wires from Washington and was broadcast from St. Louis. KSD was the first station in Missouri to provide completely air-conditioned studios; first to install high fidelity broadcasting equipment; and first to operate an experimental high frequency station. This station also participated in the first broadcast from a moving train, and in the establishment of two-way transmission between a dirigible and a radio station. These and other Missouri pioneer experiments in radio preceded the formation of the National Broadcasting Company, America's first regular radio network. KWK and KSD of St. Louis are affiliated with NBC. KMOX is the key station in the Greater Mississippi Valley for the Columbia Broadcasting System, and many network programs originate there.

Station W9XAL in Kansas City is an experimental television station operated in connection with the First National Television School, the first school of its kind in the Southwest.

The St. Louis *Post-Dispatch,* in December, 1938, announced the first regular broadcasting by short wave of specially prepared facsimile newspapers, daily and Sunday at 2:00 p.m., from station W9XYZ in the KSD studios. The paper so transcribed consists of nine pages, a little less than one-fourth the size of a regular newspaper, and is illustrated with photographs. At present this phase of radio activity is in the experimental stage. The 15 existing receiving sets have been placed in the homes of members of the radio staff, the farthest of which is 12 miles from the studio. Nonetheless, this may prove to be one of the most important "firsts" in either the radio or the newspaper world.

Religion

MISSOURI has known the swaggering boast that "God will never cross the Mississippi," the simple piety of Daniel Boone's "I always loved God ever since I could recollect," and the fine-spun controversies of theologians. It has been made Christian according to the tenets of various sects, by the sermons of learned traveling missionaries and of backwoods preachers. As a frontier, it drew "the irreligion of the times," and it has known the sweep of Protestant revivals and of fanatical "new" religions.

Before the close of the seventeenth century, French missionary priests from Canada visited the Missouri region to convert the Indians. The Jesuit mission of St. Francis Xavier was maintained near the mouth of the Des Peres River in present St. Louis from 1700 until 1703, and shared honors with the chapel built in Fort D'Orleans (1723-28) in present Carroll County, as one of the first church buildings within the State.

The first permanent church in Missouri was established at Ste. Genevieve about 1755. Before that time, the religious needs of the settlements of lead miners and salt workers in southeast Missouri were ministered to by a visiting priest from Kaskaskia or Cahokia, on the east side of the Mississippi. When the post on the Mississippi grew into a village, "the curé of Cascakies found himself obliged to go there to administer the sacraments, at least to the sick." Father Francois P. Watrin reported in 1764, "When the inhabitants saw their houses multiplying, they asked to have a church built there . . . Means were found to place at Sainte Genevieve a special curé . . . only a few years ago." The new curé was not permitted, however, to remain long in charge of his new parish. After 1763, when France formally transferred the territory west of the Mississippi to Spain, and the territory east to Protestant England, all priests were recalled from Upper Louisiana.

The following year Father Sebastian Meurin, missionary at the Kaskaskia mission from 1742 until his banishment, obtained permission from the Superior Council at New Orleans to return to Upper Louisiana as curé of Ste. Genevieve, in view of the possible migration of French families from British territory into Spanish. Because Father Meurin was sick and aged, and his limitless parish was settled by many diverse peoples, his office was a difficult one. Aided, however, by a unique papal dispensation to marry unbaptized persons, and by a generous share of French good sense, he developed for frontier life a frontier religion.

Despite the wisdom of Father Meurin and his successors, contemporary records indicate how uncertain was their influence. Father Meurin wrote to the Bishop of Quebec in 1768 that following British confiscation, the church property in Kaskaskia had been sold to Jean Baptiste Beauvais, who thereafter used the sacred vessels in his house. "My continual reproaches to him on that score," Father Meurin concludes, "have kept him away from me and the sacraments for three years." When Bishop Flaget visited Ste. Genevieve in 1814, he found families who had not come to the sacraments for twenty, forty, and even fifty years. "My God," the good Bishop exclaimed, "how much this visit was wanting here."

The religious disinterest of the cultured French families in Missouri was reflected in their enthusiasm for such liberal writers as Rousseau, Diderot, Voltaire, and even Thomas Paine and Thomas Jefferson, both of whom many considered advocates of the Anti-Christ. John Francis McDermott points out in "Voltaire and the Free Thinkers, in Early St. Louis" (*Revue de Littérature Comparée*, Paris, October, 1936), that one-fourth of the library of Auguste Chouteau, one of the founders of St. Louis, consisted of titles proscribed by the Index. Under the influence of these liberal writings many of the French residents of Missouri, though nominally Catholic, "considered all religion as priestcraft, necessary perhaps for the ignorant, superstitious and vicious, but wholly unnecessary for a gentleman—a philosopher." This point of view, recorded with shocked surprise by the Baptist missionary, John Mason Peck, seemed doubly odious to early Protestant ministers because of the subtlety and the gracious French manner with which it was expounded. The church modified its attitude to suit its parishioners. "The Priests are very indulgent," Frederick Bates wrote from St. Louis to his sister in 1806, "and when they cease, on any occasion to be so, the People withhold those contributions which are necessary for their support."

It was not until the arrival of Bishop DuBourg and the Jesuits in 1818, and of Mother Duchesne and other religious groups, that a Catholic revival was inaugurated. The new religious movement was reinforced by the coming of many pious Irish and south German families between 1830 and 1870. Freethinking, however, did not completely die away in St. Louis for many years. Most of the early French language journals published in Missouri were anti-Catholic and socialistic in policy, and after the Civil War a portion at least of the French freethinkers combined with the German students of Hegel and other philosophers to edit for more than thirty years the *Journal of Speculative Philosophy* (*see Literature*).

Catholic Spanish officials took a lesson from the liberal French policy in their treatment of American immigrants. Spain needed settlers to protect her territory against the Indians, and against any possible expansion of the United States. She preferred these settlers to be Catholic, but when French Catholics failed to come in sufficient numbers, she welcomed Protestant Americans, under the nominal provision that they embrace the Church. "The privilege of enjoying the liberty of conscience is not extended beyond the first generation," wrote Governor Don Manuel Gayoso de Lemos in an ordinance of September, 1797. "The children of those who enjoy it must positively be Catholics." But Lieutenant Governor Don Zenon Trudeau, at St. Louis, a man of "unaffected piety and wholly disinterested," promised the new settlers the private practice of any religion they pleased, and proceeded to stretch the law until it cracked.

In 1794 the Reverend Josiah Dodge from Nelson County, Kentucky, visited his brother, Dr. Israel Dodge, on Saline Creek near Ste. Genevieve. In February he preached what was probably the first Protestant (Baptist) sermon west of the Mississippi River. Two years later the Reverend John Clark, a Methodist who later became a Baptist minister, probably the first Protestant minister to enter Upper Louisiana for the express purpose of preaching to American settlers, began visiting settlements in the St. Louis area. Senor Trudeau discreetly waited until Clark had fulfilled his appointments; he then issued a commandment that the Protestant preacher must leave Spanish territory or be imprisoned. Perhaps heartened by Trudeau's liberality in this instance, the Reverend Thomas Johnson, a Baptist preacher, visited the Cape Girardeau district in 1797. Here he baptized Mrs. Agnes Ballew in the waters of Randall Creek in what is said to be the first Protestant baptism west of the Mississippi River. In the fall of 1803, when it was well known that the country had been or was about to be ceded, the Reverend Samuel Weyberg, a minister of the German Reformed Church, came from North Carolina to the District of Cape Girardeau upon the invitation of Colonel Frederick Bollinger. He established preaching places in the vicinity of Jackson, in the homes of Daniel, Philip, and John Bollinger, and Peter Ground. Although he was characterized by the Reverend Timothy Flint as "an educated man but a notorious drunkard," Weyberg seems to have done effective work. Certainly, he was the first resident Protestant minister in Missouri, although his congregation was not organized into a church unit until later.

In spite of the activities of such occasional ministers, the early American settlers, like the French, were often freethinkers or even atheists. The educated were familiar with the works of Paine, Jefferson, Rousseau, Locke, and Bacon; the uneducated were in rebellion against the class-bound formal churches of the East. Most of the great number of immigrants who flocked to Missouri after the Louisiana Purchase in 1803 were intent only upon finding economic freedom in the new territory. They had neither the subtlety of the French, nor the tolerance of the Spanish. They wanted no hindrance from man or God, and they said so.

Protestant churches were not introduced into Missouri without opposition. In 1817 the Reverend John Mason Peck stated that in St. Louis the "Anglo-American population were infidels of a low and indecent grade. . . . Their nightly orgies were scenes of drunkenness and profane revelry. Among the frantic rites observed were the mock celebration of the Lord's Supper and burning of Bibles. . . . The boast was often made that the Sabbath never had crossed, and never should cross the Mississippi." In 1834 the *Western Examiner* was established in St. Louis for "the investigation of the credibility and general tendencies of the Christian Religion." The editor, John Bobb, prophesied that "perhaps, ere another century, the now prevailing system of religion will be numbered among the exploded superstitions of past ages."

However violently expressed, these were nonetheless minority opinions. Once the turbulence of the first wave of immigration had passed, the more stable settlers, aided by the rising popularity of religious revivals, encouraged the establishment of Protestant churches. Many, however, objected to the missionaries sent by Eastern congregations who feared the rise of religious individualism on the frontier. Joseph Charless, in the *Missouri Gazette* for April 8, 1816, expressed the general resentment: "It is said that these intended *shepherds* are taught to propagate the doctrine of union of churches and state, and to discountenance republicanism." The West had not forgotten that the Eastern states had refused them aid during the War of 1812. Yet, despite the frontier's suspicious resentment, missionaries came in increasing numbers. Mostly well trained men who quickly adapted themselves and their teachings to frontier conditions, they proved a valuable stabilizing force on the frontier. They opposed the emotionalism of camp meetings, and stressed the need for an educated ministry supported by salaries.

The Protestant churches met their first success in the rural areas settled by Anglo-American families, where from the first small meetings had been conducted in private homes by lay ministers or elders. The traveling missionaries organized these groups, and attempted through church control to regulate the conduct of their members. According to the testimony of early records, they held church trials on charges of immorality, working on Sunday, selling "Bror. Beman an unsound mare," and other sins. Blue laws were thus introduced on the Missouri frontier. The Cooper and Howard County court records, like those of other counties, list many arrests for "laboring on the Sabbath," "swearing," "gambling and playing at cards or billiards," and "being idle."

Of the Protestant churches, the Baptist and the Methodist were the most successful on the frontier. Ever an exponent of religious liberty, the Baptist church readily adapted itself to the frontier dislike of salaried ministers, and formal theology, vestments, or ritual. The Methodist doctrine of "free grace, free will, and individual responsibility," naturally appealed to the democratic frontiersmen, who liked to believe that they were masters of their own destiny.

The Reverend Daniel Green, a Virginian, organized the first Baptist group in Missouri in the Tywappity Bottom in 1805, and the following year established the now discontinued Bethel Church, near present-day Jackson. Fee Fee Baptist Church, established in 1807 in St. Louis County near the present village of Pattonville, has had a continuous existence. The Mount Zion Baptist Church was established in Boon's Lick about 1812. In 1817, John Mason Peck and James E. Welch, Baptist missionaries from the East, began advocating the establishment of Protestantism in St. Louis and throughout the State. About 1818 five Baptist churches formed the Mount Pleasant Association.

When the Reverend John Travis arrived in 1806 to take up his duties as preacher for the Methodist "Missouri circuit," to which he was assigned by the Ebenezer Meeting House in Green County, Tennessee, he found the Cape Girardeau and Meramec circuits already organized. The first Methodist church west of the river had been organized about 1806 at McKendree, not many miles from Bethel Church. This site, known as the "Old Camp Grounds" because early Methodist camp meetings were held there, was the center of the Cape Girardeau circuit. The restored chapel, constructed of great hewn poplar logs, is still used occasionally by a Methodist congregation.

Although lay ministers may have organized a church before his arrival, the pioneer among Presbyterian missionaries was the Reverend Salmon Giddings, whose labors for a time were wholly itinerant. Giddings searched the settlement along the Mississippi River for former members of the Presbyterian church. A group of these he brought together August 12, 1816, to organize one of the first Presbyterian churches west of the Mississippi River, in Bellevue Valley, 10 miles south of Potosi, where four Presbyterian elders from a church in North Carolina had settled in 1807. The elders "did not, as many others have done, hide their light under a bushel, but bore it with them to their new home."

The Protestant Episcopal faith was established in Missouri with the organization of Christ Church in St. Louis, in 1819, by the Reverend John Ward. The missionary bishop, Jackson Kemper, was first rector. In 1844, the Reverend Cicero Hawks became the first bishop of Missouri.

Elders Thomas McBride and Joel H. Haden of the Christian Church (Disciples of Christ) had begun their missionary tours by 1817. In that year McBride organized the Salt Creek Church in Howard County, perhaps the first Christian Church in Missouri. During the following decade, a large number of ministers of this denomination came from Ohio and Kentucky. Among them was T. M. Allen, whose gifts were exercised principally in Boone and neighboring counties.

Many of these first ministers were educated men, but the majority were self-taught frontiersmen whose greatest assets were unlimited zeal, an ability to sustain the hardships of frontier life, and a keen understanding of the people. Not only were they "marvelously effective preachers," but they also organized the frontier churches to meet the problems created by a constantly shifting population. The Methodists platted the western country into districts and circuits. The preacher arrived at each of the specified points on the circuit at fairly regular intervals, the presiding elder appeared at longer intervals, and, once each year, the bishop came to preach, ordain, and hold sacraments. Between these visits, the laymen who did not go on circuits preached in their own localities. In Callaway County the first Methodist settlers held meetings in private houses. Services were held in the home of Samuel Miller for thirty years, and the one-room cabin was often filled with people who had come from long distances to hear the preaching. "The men," according to *Pioneer Families of Missouri* (Bryan and Rose, 1876), "would bring their guns and dogs with them. The guns were stacked in one corner of the house, while the dogs remained outside and fought. On one occasion the dogs treed a catamount during services, which were immediately closed so that all could go and witness the fight."

The Baptists formed an association of churches, each church cooperating with, but independent of, the others, and all belonging to a convention. Traveling from appointment to appointment along the country roads, the ministers were easily recognized by their manner of dress. They generally wore "straight-breasted coats, high standing collars, long waistcoats, and the plainest of neckties." Suspenders were a little known luxury. Many ministers affected the additional touch of a special hairdress: "about midway between the forehead and the crown of the head the hair was turned back and permitted to grow down to the shoulders." Joseph Brown of Callaway County—"a steam doctor and an ironside Baptist preacher—wore a long buckskin hunting shirt, reaching almost to his heels." No less singular was the Reverend Jabez Ham, who organized New Providence Church on Loutre Island, Montgomery County, in 1826. A large, stout man, he often added emphasis to his opinions by the use of his fists. However primitive his theology, his sincerity and directness made it effective. He was a famous hunter and his sermons, he often pointed out, were like an old shotgun loaded with beans which, when it went off, was almost sure to hit somebody somewhere.

Because the frontier was not accustomed to paying taxes, or to supporting any social enterprise, it was difficult to make the people provide for their ministers. The Reverend Timothy Flint made several observations on this point. "The backwoodsmen," he said, "care little about ministers and think less about *hireling* ministers, and several well-intentioned farmers preach to small assemblies in the neighborhood." The Methodist church, however, agreed to salaries for circuit riders and settled preachers. The first salaries were $64 a year. Later they were increased to $80, then to $100, with allowances made for travel and family. The ministers also were permitted to peddle approved books on biography, history, travel, and philosophy. Collecting their salaries and the money for books ordered often proved difficult. The itinerant minister preached a positive, individualistic theology. The value of his guidance was, however, reduced by the passionate excesses of the camp meeting.

At first in the urban centers, then in the small towns and rural areas, a number of ministers fought sheer emotionalism in church services, and gradually their influence was felt among the clergy and congregations. Yet even now the so-called "protracted" meeting has not passed from existence. Many are still held in the small white frame churches that dot the rural scene. Very often the annual meetings are held in "brush arbors," not because the congregation does not own a church, but because an arbor is much cooler. Virtually everyone in the vicinity, regardless of his beliefs, attends. There is usually a "preaching" in the afternoon, supper on the grounds, and another "preaching" at night. Like the old frontier meetings, each service tends more towards a dramatic display of emotion, movement, and sound than a solemn worship.

The early camp meeting left the worshippers in an argumentative and belligerent state of mind. No tolerance was shown when Joseph Smith, the prophet of the Mormons, attempted to find in Missouri the land of promise and the place for the Mormon Zion. Large numbers of Mormons followed Smith into Missouri in 1831, and settled extensive areas near Independence. Here, in the "land beautiful" described in the Book of Mormon, they organized their Missouri Zion on a collective plan, and, in contrast to the haphazard development of other frontier communities, ordered their lives upon a social rather than an individual basis. Their economic success, combined with their ability to control local elections, aroused the hostility of their neighbors. In 1833, the Mormons were forced to give up their Zion and move into Clay County. Their persecution was condemned by many Missouri newspapers, but the crusade against them increased in violence, and in 1839 the Mormons were driven into Illinois. It was not until much later, when the branch of their church now known as the Reorganized Church of Jesus Christ of Latter Day Saints was organized, that the Mormons became sufficiently strong to re-establish themselves and build their temple at Independence.

Missouri was the refuge for three kinds of Germans: liberals forced to flee reaction in Germany; conservatives who felt their beliefs were crumbling before the heresy of the liberals; and such dreamers as Dr. William Keil, whose dramatic communistic experiment at Bethel included a new religion—his religion—as well as a new economy. So it was that to Missouri were transplanted many of the elements that made for religious confusion in Germany. The Germans who came to Missouri during the early 1830's were mostly intellectual liberals who, according to Carl E. Schneider in *The German Church On the American Frontier* (St. Louis, 1939), had left the fatherland to escape the tyranny of a priest-ridden state. Obsessed by memories of German consistories and synods, these political refugees loudly objected to all forms of organized religion. Among those who rose above the petty bickerings of the day was Frederick Muench, who pointed out that it was necessary to distinguish between the essence of religion and its incidental forms. Through his publications, both in English and in German, he counselled against inherited prejudices and dogmatism.

During the same period, former members of the Reformed Evangelical Church of Germany began to form congregations in Missouri. The first two churches were organized at Friedens (*see Tour 3A*), and at Femme Osage, St. Charles County, in 1834-35, by Hermann Garlichs, a gentleman farmer, who had been invited to serve as pastor. By 1840, despite the heavy German migration, the few scattered congregations were still unorganized. In that year the *Kirchenverein des Westens* was formed at Mehlville, St. Louis County. The avowed purpose of this loose association was to control the qualifications of ministers, to develop educational institutions, and to furnish mutual aid and assistance. Its immediate use, however, was to combat the opposition of an orthodox Lutheran group which had arrived in Missouri the preceding year.

These orthodox Lutherans were about 600 Saxons who had come to America seeking religious freedom, because in Germany the rising influence of liberal Lutheran and Catholic groups had caused them to fear that they could not long "retain, confess, and transmit to their descendants" their orthodox faith. Under the leadership of "Bishop"

Martin Stephan, former pastor of St. John's Church in Dresden, they established the Missouri towns of Altenburg and Wittenburg. Appreciating the need of a college for the education of their children and their clergy, they established Concordia Seminary at Altenburg in 1839. In 1849 the school was moved to St. Louis.

Since the Catholic revival instituted by Bishop DuBourg and the various religious orders who established themselves in Missouri, the Roman Catholic church has continued its work with no lessening of vigor. A diocese to embrace the State was established in 1826, with St. Louis as its cathedral city. In 1847 Missouri became an archdiocese. As the Germans settled on the prairie along the Boon's Lick Trail and through the rocky hills of the central section, priests were sent to them. In the shadow of many Roman Catholic churches parochial schools were built. A second diocese was established in 1880, with Kansas City as the cathedral center.

The slavery issue was the last large frontier problem which concerned the Protestant churches of Missouri. Until about 1850 the slaves enjoyed, theoretically, an equal status with the white members of the congregation. They attended services with the white people, and the church attempted to regulate their lives as it did the lives of other persons. When slavery became a national issue, however, the Protestant churches were no longer able to justify the fact that some members of the congregations kept other members in bondage. In the 1840's, pro-slavery members of the Methodist, Baptist, and Prebyterian denominations split with their national organizations and formed organizations of their own. Today, the Presbyterians are divided into the Presbyterian Church in the U. S. A., the Presbyterian Church in the United States (Southern branch), the United Presbyterian Church, and the Cumberland Presbyterian Church. The Baptist denomination is divided into the Northern and Southern Conventions. In 1938, at a joint conference, the Methodist Episcopal Church, South, and the Methodist Episcopal Church, North, voted to reunite into one national organization.

After the Civil War, Missouri's religious life was affected by the organization of Negro churches, the spread of church-supported schools and colleges, and the growth of large cities. Before the war, Negroes had few churches of their own. When they obtained their freedom, one of their first acts was to form churches, organizations, and rules of procedure. Today, they have churches belonging to the Methodist, Baptist, Roman Catholic, and other denominations.

Expansion after the Civil War transferred social and economic power from farms to small towns and cities. As the cities grew, the churches there were enabled to increase their memberships substantially, to give more thought to social problems, and, by means of their new financial strength, to accomplish many social reforms. Home and foreign mission programs were extended, and local church educational institutions were broadened. Many of these institutions were of college rank; others were planned to educate younger children. With the growth of the public schools, a large number of the denominational schools disappeared.

The development of large trade centers had one other effect on religion in Missouri. During the Spanish regime, no Jews were permitted in the territory, but following the Louisiana Purchase Jewish families soon came to St. Louis. In 1836 the first Jewish services were held in St. Louis, and soon afterwards a congregation, mostly of German and Polish immigrants, was formed. The congregation of B'nai B'rith, or the Sons of the Covenant, was next formed, and members of this group later organized the congregation of B'nai El. Partly influenced by the liberal doctrines developed in certain German-Jewish centers, a group of the B'nai El congregation withdrew in 1867 and established the first reformed Jewish Church in Missouri—Shaare Emeth. Dissenting members of this group in 1886 organized the congregation of Temple Israel, which, with its parent church, has long been an important Middle Western center of liberal thought on social and political as well as religious questions. Following the Civil War, congregations of Jewish people were formed in Kansas City, St. Joseph, Sedalia, and elsewhere. The Jews brought with them an established program of social work among the needy of their own people.

According to the 1926 survey of the Bureau of Census the total number of churches in Missouri was 7,303, of which 645 were Negro. The combined church membership was 1,881,278, and of this number 82,207 were Negroes. The total value of Missouri churches was placed at $110,022,697, with the average value of an urban church estimated at a little more than ten times that of the average rural building. In the State as a whole the Southern Baptist had the most churches, 1,764. The Roman Catholic membership was the largest, with 517,466 members. The Baptist had 270,925 members, and the Methodists, 231,285.

Sports and Recreation

THOUGH Missouri offers sports of almost every modern variety, the affections of its native population are still held by fine horses, good hound dogs, and a likely fishing spot. Even in Colonial times good racing and breeding horses were imported. Horses created an immediate bond between the French settlers and the Southern families who poured into the territory after the Louisiana Purchase, bringing with them their racers and their traditions. Interest in the sport soon spread. In October of 1812, St. Charles County sportsmen (soon to be busy with Indian warfare) held two-day races on the "Mamelle Tract" near St. Charles. The rules provided that "the fastest horse (running fair) wins the money." Six years later the Jockey Club of Franklin, in the Boon's Lick County, was holding regular three-day races on the "Welches Tract," offering sizeable purses for two, three, and four-mile runs. This club, through successive reorganizations, continued for at least 20 years. Alphonso Wetmore, who attended the Franklin races in 1823, satirized the event with an "epic" poem beginning:

> Hushed be the world! with all its noisy din!
> Franklin! Thy sports I proudly usher in,
> Midst clouds of dust, and spirit stirring rhymes,
> That swell our eyes, and annals of our times.

Race tracks were laid out in nearly every city and crossroads village, to the dismay of the Protestant ministers who had been sent to Missouri from New England. "The first Sabbath that I preached in St. Charles," the Reverend Timothy Flint wrote in despair, "before morning worship, directly opposite where worship was to take place, there was a horse race." To Reverend Flint and people of like mind, these frontier sports were the Devil's snares, against which they "wrestled mightily," and, it may be added, effectively. The owners of some of the tracks, as at Franklin and Springfield, "got religious minded," and destroyed them. The Columbia course was bitterly assailed as a "center of immorality." At present, with the exception of the annual Missouri State Fair races, and those held at various county fairs, horse racing in Missouri is negligible; of more importance are the auctions and shows held wherever fine horses are raised in the State. Of particular interest are the shows at the annual American Royal in Kansas City, and the various St. Louis horse shows.

Among other frontier sports were cock fighting, goose pulling, and fist fighting. Goose pulling was vigorous. A goose with its neck greased was suspended by the feet from a bar; the contestants then took turns riding at a gallop under the bar, attempting to wring the goose's neck in passing. The one who was successful won the goose. Fist fighting was even more popular. Every neighborhood had its champion. Contests between flatboatmen and wharfmen in the river towns were so constant that arrests for "creating a public affray . . . rioting . . . endangering the lives of the residents" were frequent. Other athletics included foot racing and high jumping, often as part of public celebrations, particularly on the Fourth of July.

Rivalry in marksmanship was, naturally, keen on the frontier, and shooting matches were probably the most common sport among men. Most popular was the "beef shoot." A writer in the *Missouri Republican* for April 29, 1837, describes the contest: "A bull's eye, with a center nail, stands at a distance variously from forty to seventy yards and those five who, at the close of the contest, have most frequently *driven the nail,* are entitled to a fat ox divided into five portions." The fifth portion was the hide and the tallow, and this was the most valuable part. Most of the marksmen could "drive the nail twice out of every three trials." A modern descendant of this sport is the popular "Turkey shoot" at Thanksgiving time.

Increased settlement and changing social attitudes introduced amusements "more to be watched than participated in." Modern Missourians, however, have not lost their love for the out-of-doors. The States's generally mild climate, and the wealth of woods and rivers, provide every type of outdoor sport, except those requiring open surf, high mountains, or sustained winter. Particularly attractive is the rugged Ozark region, an area as large as the State of Maine, with its woods and streams, lakes and giant springs. Here, one may obtain a guide and a blunt-nosed, flat-bottomed boat for one of the famous "john-boat forays," or "float trips," down the Black, White, Osage, James, Big or Little Piney, Gasconade, Meramec, Current, or Niangua Rivers. One may swim or paddle, rent a motor boat, or go aquaplaning on the Lake of the Ozarks, or Lake Taneycomo, both artificially impounded lakes of exceptional beauty. Speedboat racing is common on the Missouri and Mississippi, and even on quiet sections of the Big and Meramec Rivers. A St. Louis Municipal Rowing Regatta is held each August on the Mississippi. From St. Louis, it is possible to take steamboat excursions on the major rivers throughout the summer months.

Fishing is excellent in nearly all of Missouri's rivers and lakes; this is one sport which modern civilization has not disrupted. Giant catfish are frequently taken, especially in the Mississippi and Missouri, fish weighing 50 pounds being not unusual; the largest ever recorded in Missouri weighed 150 pounds. "Noodling," or catching fish with the bare hands, is an exciting sport still carried on in the Ozarks, although it is now illegal. Catfish are frequently caught on trotlines, or by "jugging." In the latter method, large sealed jugs or cans with lines attached are set afloat; the jug bobs when a fish is hooked. In contrast with these methods is the fishing with barbless hooks favored by some master anglers.

Gigging is popular, especially on the clear Ozark streams. Gigging parties sometimes float down a clear stream at night carrying a bright light, often a gasoline lantern or a fire basket of flaming pine knots. The gigger is stationed at the bow, armed with a two- or three-pronged spear, with which he strikes fish resting on the bottom. Giant frogs may be gigged, or picked up with the aid of a bright light, along most of the less frequented Ozark stream beds.

"Jumping" and "bumping" bass is practiced at night, or in the day time when a rapid rise muddies the stream and leaves only the water among the weeds at the bank partially clear. In night "jumping," the boat, with a light in it, is allowed to drift along the edge of the weeds. The feeding bass and "skip-jacks," believing themselves trapped between boat and bank, may jump into the boat. In "bumping," a boat preferably 20 to 25 feet long is run upstream, the stern against the bank, the bow outward at an angle of about 30 degrees. The boatman slaps the half-muddied water between boat and bank sharply with the flat of his paddle. Often, bass that have taken refuge in the weeds will jump into the boat. Formerly, screens of wire or tow-sacking were raised on the outstream side of the boats, but this is now prohibited by State law.

Trout and other game fish may be taken at Bennett Spring State Park, where there is a hatchery, and on lower Roubidoux Creek near Waynesville, Crane Creek, Hahatonka, Little Piney near Yancey Mills, and at many other places throughout the Ozarks. A fishing "rodeo," in which anglers from all States compete, is held each October at the Lake of the Ozarks.

Hunting in the State is similar to that in the Middle West generally. Rabbits are numerous, and are hunted for sport or profit. Squirrels, equally common, may be taken in season. Raccoon and opossum are plentiful in some sections. A few times in recent years, a three-day license for deer has been issued, but at present (1940) there is no open season. Fox hunting is a popular sport in central and southwest Missouri. This is not, however, the English variety, with pink-coated hunters on horseback. The sport for Missourians is not a matter of social standing, nor is the object to catch the fox. The fun consists in gathering in the woods, listening to the belling of the dogs on the trail; there is not a hunter but can distinguish the voice of his dog and know when he is leading the pack. The deep-rooted love for a hound dog has not died out; field trials in trailing, pointing, flushing, and retrieving are held throughout the State for hunting dogs of various breeds. The chief quarry for bird hunters in Missouri is quail. There is no open season on the State's few pheasants, but ducks and geese pause here in their seasonal migrations, and occasional wild turkeys are found in the more remote sections.

Hiking trips are popular throughout the State, and Youth Hostels provide inexpensive stopping places. Bicycling trips and horseback riding can be arranged for in most localities, and excellent highways make picnicking or exploring by automobile a favorite pastime. Recreational areas are being developed in many parts of the State, largely by the Work Projects Administration, the Civilian Conservation Corps, and the National Park Service (*see General Information*). Some of the resorts offer a wide variety of comforts and amusements, but for the sportsman or nature lover whose tastes run to solitude and a more rugged type of vacationing, Missouri still has vast sections of almost virgin territory.

Kansas City and St. Louis offer museums, theaters, indoor and outdoor swimming pools, roller and ice skating rinks, dance floors, night clubs, and amusement parks. Skeet shooting, bowling, and table tennis have become increasingly popular in recent years. Most of the smaller cities also offer these. Well-organized systems of city parks provide golf courses, tennis, badminton, and handball courts, baseball and softball diamonds, archery ranges, and, sometimes, even special spots for model-ship racing and kite flying. The huge and excellently equipped St. Louis zoo attracts hundreds of thousands annually. City-directed playgrounds in Kansas City and St. Louis offer well-balanced programs of games, dancing, and handicrafts for children. Golf can be played practically the year round. Skiing, tobogganing, and ice skating are possible out doors for only brief periods, except in the extreme northern parts of the State.

Even the smallest town usually has a baseball team, and in the rural sections croquet and horseshoe pitching are common sports. Nearly every high school and college in the State has its basketball and football team, and sometimes a soccer and field-hockey team as well. A State high school basketball tournament, held each March in Columbia, attracts tremendous crowds. The football season is generally climaxed each Thanksgiving Day by games between traditional rivals.

Among the professional sports, baseball leads in popularity. In St. Louis the two major leagues are represented by the Cardinals and the Browns. The Cardinals won the world series in 1926, 1931, and 1934, and many of its stars have won the annual "most valuable player" award. Kansas City and many of the smaller towns have minor league ball teams. In recent years softball has become increasingly popular, perhaps because it can be played by both men and women; admission prices are low, and the games are generally held at night, when families may attend.

St. Louis supports a professional football team, and a soccer team which won the challenge cup event in 1932, 1933, and 1934. Indoor cold weather sports have been developed in recent years. Besides skating rinks, St. Louis and Kansas City have excellent ice-hockey teams, and exhibition skating draws large crowds.

Boxing was at a low ebb in Missouri for some time, as wrestling continues to be, but both sports are reviving. The Golden Gloves Tournament and the Ozark A.A.A. meets have popularized boxing in recent years. John Henry Lewis, former lightweight boxing champion, won his title in St. Louis in 1935.

Folklore and Folkways

MISSOURI'S ways are the comfortable, homely ways, and the memories of half a dozen national strains are preserved in its lore and its customs. In the open country of northern and western Missouri, the expansive days of "before the war" still color life and thought. Much more deeply rooted in the past, dialects, manners, and traditions that recall medieval England survive in the hills of southern Missouri. Midway between are the placid small towns along the Missouri and Mississippi Rivers, where still exist the languages and fashions of living brought from Germany and France a century and a half ago. Of no single region can it be said: "This is Missouri"; for the State's lore and ways were formed from all.

The majority of Missourians have a way of speaking that is probably peculiar to the State. The difference lies partly in dialect and verb forms, but more in intonation and inflection, perceptible, yet evading precise description. The State's name to outsiders may be pronounced "Mis-sour-y," but here it is "Miz-sour-a"; "fire" often become "far," and sometimes "fawr." The Missourian's inflection has neither the rapid precision of the North, the languid drawl of the West and Southwest, nor the soft fluidity of the deep South. Perhaps it partakes of characteristics of each, forming a type of its own. There are, however, noticeable variations in different sections within the State. Educated St. Louisians claim to speak English with less sectional individuality than persons of other localities. Yet outside this cultural and social circle, there is in general use the "St. Louis dialect," a compound of corruptions and inflections borrowed from the foreign born that contrasts sharply with the softer speech elsewhere. In Old Mines, Ste. Genevieve, and other French settlements of southeastern Missouri, approximately 85 per cent of the population speaks a Creole dialect, basically the French of the eighteenth century, but containing a blur of Spanish, English, and Indian words. German, often archaic in its form, is primarily the language of Hermann and of some other Missouri River towns.

Although much has been made of the survival of old English words in Missouri speech, this is exceptional rather than general. Preserved by the descendants of early immigrants from Kentucky and Tennessee, an occasional Old-World word crops up here and there in the hill country, current in one locality, unknown a hundred miles away.

Missouri speech, rather, is flavored with homely metaphors and similes that reflect rural and early-day life. Such ruralisms throw the surviving archaic expressions into high relief, intensified by a native talent for understatement. "Daunch," an English word of the fifteenth century, appears in corruption; and only an occasional person will know, when a hill woman complains, "We'unses shore air dauncey," that she means, depending on the locality, "We certainly are fastidious about our food," or, "We surely are unaware of what is happening," or, "We feel utterly listless." Few, however, will remain in doubt, when a farmer observes, "He lit a shuck out o' thar, I tell yuh, a-makin' mo' racket 'n a jack-ass in a tin barn," that someone left in a hurry and with much noise. Cool and foggy weather is referred to only in some places by the Elizabethan term, "misling"; in the hills, an illegitimate child may not be otherwise mentioned in mixed company than as a "woods colt"; and a bull is a "male brute."

Negro idiom and dialect have preserved such old English phrases as "ruinate" for "ruin" and "disremember" for "forget," and these have attained general usage over the State. The Negroes also have enriched speech with expressions peculiar to themselves, such as the phrase "in all my born days," meaning "in all my life." Negro cooks will sometimes demand the right to "tote" (carry home left-over food) as part of their wages. More recent and perhaps less valuable has been the development of the "cat language" among the Negroes of the cities, a streamlined mixture of metaphor and slang. Definitely a folk expression, it has many variations, and a Kansas City Negro may entirely fail to understand that his St. Louis friend's observation, "That sure is a fine vine you-all are under," is an admiring comment upon his apparel. In any case, Negro parlance has added much more to Missouri speech than have the French and German tongues of the socially isolated communities.

Although their tales have little currency outside their own settlements, the French and German populations have contributed much to folklore. Local raconteurs at Old Mines are especially fond of medieval French animal stories and tales of magic. In more than tales, though, Old-World culture lingers in various spots about the State. At both Florissant and Ste. Genevieve, the Host is borne through the streets in a solemn and colorful ceremony at the observance of Corpus Christi in June. Christmas is celebrated with firecrackers in the southwestern part of Missouri, and at Old Mines and Ste. Genevieve the celebration of *La Guignolée* marks New Year's Eve (*see Ste. Genevieve*), as masked revelers make the rounds of homes and business places, singing a song centuries old (*see Music*). In the foreign quarters of Kansas City and St. Louis, elaborate funeral processions wind through the streets, with lugubrious brass bands at their heads; and weddings, quite as spectacular as the funerals, are celebrated at morning Mass and followed by rounds of feasting and merrymaking. Sometimes, an Italian mother-in-law presents the bride with a handful of rice or a black hen, both symbols of fruitfulness. In a few German communities, wedding guests are charged an admission fee, and the "inviters" call at the door of each prospective guest, praising the entertainment to be offered at the wedding.

It is, however, the farmer of Anglo-Saxon stock who has most influenced the State and its life. Almost any utilitarian occasion becomes social as well, if a few persons gather. Each community has its annual fair, at which livestock is exhibited and judged, as are farm and home products. These fairs, climaxed by the annual State Fair at Sedalia, are always well attended, providing a meeting place for friends, as well as a focus for agricultural and home interests. Of scarcely less social importance are the picnics and homecomings held each summer at various small towns—usually two or three in a county; in the hill country, the Fourth of July picnic is the big event of the year. On these occasions, a small carnival comes to town, square dancing and fiddling contests are held, and hot dogs, hamburgers, and soda pop from dusty stands lend variety to the enormous lunches unpacked from cars and wagons. But the carnival attractions are of far less interest to the crowds that flock in from the country than the meeting of friends from a dozen miles or more distant who have not been seen, perhaps, for months. Auction sales, held when a farmer decides to leave the neighborhood, are also always occasions for social contact. Many who attend have no intention of buying. They come merely for the show put on by the auctioneer, and for the chance to visit.

In the late fall, the farmer looks forward eagerly to "hawg-killin' time." The neighbors gather early in the morning to help with the killing, the scalding, scraping, cutting, and salting of the meat. The livers, hearts, and kidneys are sometimes boiled together, more often cooked separately, for the feast held at noon. Ribs and sliced side meat are fried, and a truly gargantuan meal is eaten. When the men have finished their tasks, the work of the women is just starting. Meat is ground for sausage, and head cheese, scrapple, liver sausage, and other concoctions are prepared.

Box suppers and pie suppers are given at various churches or school houses. Only pies, golden brown, fruity, and appetizing, are brought to the pie suppers, but for the box suppers the girls prepare elaborate boxed lunches, each trying to outdo the others in ornate trimming and sumptuous content. At suppertime, usually at the conclusion of a program or an amateur play, the pies or boxes are auctioned off to the highest bidder, the man who buys one eating supper with the girl who prepared it. Although none is supposed to know to whom the boxes or pies belong, a girl and her beau are seldom separated, but the man may have to pay an outrageous price if rivals or practical jokers suspect the owner and bid against him. There is always pride in the price, however, since it is an index of the girl's popularity, and the money goes to some worthy fund.

Pie suppers are particularly frequent during political campaigns, when the candidates are expected to attend—and to bid. Less financially exacting, but of more importance politically and socially, are the rallies and "speakings" accompanying political campaigns in rural districts. In many counties, notably in Howard, the candidates organize a joint speaking circuit. The ladies of the local church seldom overlook the financial possibilities of an ice cream supper, and, "given fair weather and a good crowd," the evenings are often more social than political.

Funerals in the country are always well attended, as are weddings and charivaris—"shivarees," in Missouri parlance—and all primarily for the same reason: the opportunities they provide for visiting. Such activities as an occasional corn-husking, church picnics and socials, candy-pullings, all-day singings, and dances also offer social intercourse.

The country dance is most common in the Ozarks, though found in many other parts of Missouri. Although quite sharp divisions exist economically, and often educationally, between the ridge dwellers and the valley farmers, the average hillman distinguishes only between two classes of people—the natives and the "furriners." The "furriners" are all those who live outside the hills, and they are seldom welcome at a native dance. The affair is usually held at a farm home, seldom that of a better-class farmer, often one where cracks appear in the rough-sawn, native-oak floors. The dancing here, of course, is not the suave fox-trot and waltz, nor the jitter of the urban sections and the prairie farmlands, but the stamping, swinging shuffle of the square dance. A coal-oil lamp on a high shelf dimly illuminates the one room where the dancing goes on. In a corner sits the orchestra, one man with a fiddle, another with a mouth organ, and perhaps one with a mandolin. The fiddler calls the dance in a high pitched voice, his accent in cadence with the music:

> First couple balance to the couple on the right,
> Cheat or swing, do jest as you like;
> *Swing yore partners!*
> *Ladies to the right and a right hand acrost;*
> Look out girls, so you won't get lost.
>
> Hain't been drunk since away last fall,
> *Swing your partners and promenade th' hall!*
> Promenade eight till you get straight,
> *Swing that gal like you're swingin' on a gate!*

In the next room, a group of half a dozen gather around the table, playing pitch with a deck of dog-eared cards. From the kitchen doorway, half a dozen girls and young men stare at the couples who are dancing. Out in the yard still others gather about a bottle or a jug of corn whisky. The guests shift from one diversion to the other, and the merrymaking goes on until almost dawn.

But many Ozarkians have religious scruples against dancing, and believe the fiddle to be the instrument of the devil. For them, the fast-disappearing "play-party" is a substitute; often it is a dance in reality, but there is no orchestra. The players provide the music by singing, and the others clap their hands in rhythmic accompaniment. One of the favorite "plays" is "Weevily Wheat," performed to the words and tune of an old Jacobite ballad:

> Oh I don't want none o' yore weevily wheat,
> An' I don't want none o' yore barley,
> But I want some flour in half an hour
> To bake a cake for Charlie.
>
> Oh, Charlie he's a fine young man
> Oh, Charlie he's a dandy;
> Charlie likes to kiss th' gals,
> And he can do it handy!

The game is one of the old English survivals. The "Charlie" referred to is Bonnie Prince Charlie, the Stuart pretender to the throne of England in 1745, of whom the Scots sang. The players form two separate lines facing each other, the boys in one, the girls in the other. The boy and the girl at the opposite ends of each line swagger to the center and "swing," return to their places, and are followed by the next couple. The verses are timed so that the swinging occurs with the last line of each stanza.

Another game is "Four in the Middle," which, like "Weevily Wheat," may be continued indefinitely. Each boy chooses a girl, and the players form a circle around one of the couples. After singing a verse of the song, the boy and girl in the center each choose another partner, thus placing two couples within the circle. Singing to the tune of "Skip to My Lou," the players dance "right and left," and as the last stanza is sung, the first couple leaves the center of the circle. The second couple now chooses another couple and the game continues as before.

The "play-party" is but one of the picturesque customs of the hills. In the matter of courtship, a young hillman may do a little "tom-cattin' around," but when he "sets up" to a girl, he usually intends to marry her. Thereafter, for the girl to be seen talking to another man is to invite disrepute, and even bloodshed. If a boy and a girl attend church together, it is considered, in some places, tantamount to an engagement announcement. Sometimes a boy and a girl sit up together all night in the cabin of the girl's parents, but usually the mother and father are sleeping in the same room. As was customary among all pioneer American groups, the girls usually marry early, and frequently have large families. Divorce is rare, although, occasionally, a wife goes on an extended "visit" to her parents. The men and boys have much leisure time, compared with the women, who are occupied with household and agricultural duties the year around. In some families, even the splitting and carrying-in of firewood, and the milking, are considered "woman's work." For a man to participate in any form of woman's work is to invite at least the jocularity of the neighbors. The "greater family," which includes all near relatives by birth or marriage, survives among the hill people, and is dominated by the patriarch, who is imbued with an intense loyalty to his home and family. None the less, the hill dweller is an individualist. For a long time it was impossible to effect co-operative activity among the Ozark dwellers for agricultural programs or other purposes, but this age-old resistance is being gradually broken down.

The Missourian in the remoter districts attends religious services with a zealous earnestness, but even his religion has, to some extent, the function of enriching a barren social life. Yet the doctrinal side is important, too. Bitter quarrels sometimes occur over the use of musical instruments at religious services, or because some visiting minister has remarked that he "looked up at the hills and saw God." The hillman is faithful to the "old-time religion" of his forefathers, which permitted unrestrained expression for emotionally undernourished lives. Ministers frequently preach a "hell-fire-and-brimstone" gospel as sensational as that of the earliest circuit riders (see Religion).

Much less numerous than in former years, the occasional camp meetings are still important events in the lives of rural dwellers, since they provide the people with a solid week of social intercourse, a chance to "camp out," and, incidentally, their fill of sizzling admonition from the revivalist. For the women, camp meeting means more work than at home, since most of the day is filled with baking pies and cakes and cooking meals. Cooking is done in community fashion, and the meals are community affairs, served in the open on long board tables. The children run wild, and the men loaf peacefully, whittling, pitching horseshoes, or playing mumbly-peg. In the evening, everyone gathers for the revival, where the congregation is often aroused to the point of hysteria.

Religious fervor makes the devil a very real personage, and anything awe-inspiring or not easily understood is usually connected with him. Perhaps this explains why, not only in the Ozarks but all over the State, his name crops up so frequently. A bend of the Gasconade

River, overlooked by a majestic bluff, is "The Devil's Elbow"; a cavern near Columbia, whence issue cold drafts even in summer time, is "The Devil's Icebox"; a steep Ozark hillside of barren rock is "The Devil's Slide"; a formidable sharp ridge is "The Devil's Backbone."

The devil, of course, has a great deal to do with manifestations of the supernatural, but there are other, less commonly accepted influences. Most people in the Ozarks know that in some cave near Springfield 20 pony loads of silver lie buried, abandoned by the Spaniards; but, though numerous searching parties have sought it, the wealth is under a curse and has never been found. Then, there was the case of the northern Missouri farmer who, believing his dog had rabies, cut off his head. When he returned later to bury the body, it had vanished. About a year afterward, he saw the head of the dog apparently suspended above the doorway of his house; it retreated and came forward several times, as if signaling him to follow, but he refused to leave the house. Later, the body of the farmer's youngest son was found in a near-by brook, and from that time, it is said, the dog's head appeared to warn the family if any of its members was in danger. Along the Mississippi River, early morning mists are sometimes believed to be the ghosts of persons drowned in the stream. In the same section a giant headless dog appears, and ghosts of Civil War soldiers battle nightly for gold that once was hidden in an old tree. Even these, though, are less dreadful than the wraith of the desperado who, on dismal nights, formerly promenaded the road between the tree where he had been hanged and his unquiet grave.

The hanging tree has long since died, because any tree on which a man has been hanged will wither and die, just as will any tree which has been struck by a hoop snake. The hoop snake, locally held to be the most poisonous of all reptiles, will take its tail in its mouth and roll toward its victim faster than the swiftest horse can run. It can even roll uphill, and fortunate indeed is he who can escape it. But, if any snake is killed, there is always a chance for the victim to recover from its bite if part of the snake's carcass is bound over the wound. If a child steps on a rusty nail, he must grease the nail and lay it away to prevent infection. If a person afflicted with tumor will stroke a dead man's hand, the tumor will disappear. Warts can be disposed of in innumerable ways, one of which is to place a pin under a rock so that the first person who steps over the rock will acquire the warts.

The body of superstitions is encyclopedic, although many are sectional or even individual. It is an ill omen to see a cross-eyed person, especially at the intersection of two pathways. A bird flying into a house is a sure sign of death in the family, but a redbird perched near by is a good omen. To be assured that an absent lover will think of his sweetheart, she must turn his picture upside down. If two spoons are accidentally placed together on a table, there will soon be a wedding, and if a single person is seated between a married couple at dinner, he will become engaged in the near future. In some sections it is believed that the initials of one's future mate will appear on a handkerchief placed on growing wheat on the night of April 30. Many mothers conscientiously bite their babies' fingernails, believing that if they are cut with scissors the children will become thieves.

Weather is forecast by signs common to agrarian peoples of all times. Some are pure superstition; some are based on fact or shrewd observation. For many Missouri farmers, ground-hog day is February 14, not February 2. Pleasant weather is assured if clouds move rapidly or rabbits are seen in unprotected places. Pigs running about with sticks in their mouths and creating an unusual disturbance foretell a storm. In time of drouth, a snake killed and turned belly-up on the top of a fencepost will bring rain. And, of course, any vegetable whose fruit grows above the ground must be planted in the light of the moon; any whose fruit grows underground, such as potatoes, must be planted in the dark of the moon.

Witchcraft has largely passed. The most famous Missouri master, Guinea Sam, of Boonville, disappeared years ago in a puff of blue smoke, after being beaten in a "conjuratin' contest wif a St. Louis voodoo." Here and there, some person who has supposedly sold his soul to Satan retains a reputation for practicing the black art—selling charms, telling fortunes, finding lost articles, and peddling remedies compounded of mysterious herbs. In the last, the "witch" steps into the province of the numerous "herb doctors," who roam the woods seeking ginseng, bloodroot, golden seal, May apple, and other plants with which to dose the countryside.

Traces of voodooism linger among the Negroes, especially among those of the cities and of the cotton industry. It is not the voodoo worship of Haiti, however, but a curious compound of that cult with the Protestant religion, faith healing, fortune telling, and any other form of mumbo-jumbo which happens to appeal to the practitioner. The belief that an enemy can be destroyed by placing a spell upon a waxen image of him has not entirely passed. One method of invoking such vengeance is to hold the image over the fire, repeating a spell as it melts. Sometimes Negroes are troubled to find a mysterious "goofer dust" (dirt from a grave) sprinkled in their yards, as a charm to drive them from the neighborhood.

Negro lore has preserved many of the beliefs centering about the supernatural commonly held by the white settlers of the late eighteenth century. For instance, a horse can see ghosts, and so may the rider if he looks straight forward between the horse's ears. A cat should not be allowed in the room with a corpse, nor in a room where a baby is sleeping, for it will suck the baby's breath. Negro tales, including ghost stories, and legends about the Indians, are current in many localities. Bluffs known as "Lovers' Leap" are found in the proximity of almost every town in Missouri, with accompanying tragic tales of frustrated Indian lovers.

Literature

BOON'S LICK residents showed an eagerness for literary greatness when they included among their Fourth of July toasts in
1817: "The Territory of Missouri—may it become the Nursery of Literature." In his *Missourian Lays and Other Western Dit-
ties,* published at St. Louis in 1821, Angus Umphraville saluted the
great English writers and then blandly inquired:

> Why not Missouri claim
> Illustrious bards of equal fame?
> Why may she not with Albion vie
> In such a generous rivalry?

The wide variety of subjects represented in the libraries of Missouri Colonials indicates breadth of interest. Literary development,
however, was hampered by the lack of leisure and of a local press.
Henri Peyroux de la Coudrenière, Commandant of Ste. Geneviève
(1787-96) and friend of Thomas Jefferson, made plans to bring a press
to Ste. Geneviève, and the will of his brother Pierre, who died in 1795,
lists a "box with type."

Although composed without strictly literary intent, the descriptions
of the region's topography, social life, flora, fauna, mineral resources,
and Indian inhabitants recorded by Missourians in journals and
official reports are a sincere and evocative reflection of the place and
the period. The journals of Étienne de Bourgmond (1714 and 1723),
Auguste Chouteau's account of the founding of St. Louis, and Pierre-
Antoine Tebeau's narrative of Loisel's expedition to the Upper Missouri (1795) are written in an unaffected style, with consistent enthusiasm, and portray an era whose historic importance their authors
appreciated.

Journals by members of the expeditions led by Lewis and Clark
(1804-06), Zebulon Pike (1805-07), Wilson P. Hunt (1811), and
Major Stephen H. Long (1819-20) also gave the world a picture of
the Western country. There were, too, papers of scientific comment, by
John Bradbury, the English botanist, and Thomas Nuttall, the famous
naturalist, both of whom accompanied Wilson P. Hunt's expedition.
In similar vein was *A View of the Lead Mines of Missouri* (1819), by
Henry Rowe Schoolcraft, geologist and ethnologist. Henry M.
Brackenridge's "Journal of a Voyage up the Missouri River," as first
published in his *Views of Louisiana* (1814), is accurate and well writ-

ten, a classic of its kind. Washington Irving used it as a source in his *Astoria* (1836).

So much for Missouri's pre-Umphraville literature. The men who created it were primarily concerned with assembling data; none of them intended to vie with Albion. Yet from the facts themselves arose the picturesque Western types, the colorful frontier idiom (which Eastern critics found vulgar), and Western plots, either of heroic adventure, or of the kind of humorous exaggeration known as "whopper stories." Few writers could resist a language of the quality spoken by Isaac van Bibber, Jr., a relative of the Boones, in his appeal at Loutre Lick for volunteers for a Rocky Mountain expedition: "Who will join in the march to the Rocky Mountains with me, a sort of high-pressure-double-cylinder-go-it-ahead-forty-wildcats-tearin' sort of a feller? . . . Wake up ye sleepy heads . . . Git out of this brick kiln . . . these mortality turners and murder mills, where they render all the lard out of a feller until he is too lean to sweat. Git out of this warming-pan, ye hollyhocks, and go out to the West where you may be seen."

Alphonso Wetmore was the first writer to depict Missouri in terms of the Missourian. During the early 1820's, he was stationed as Army Paymaster at Franklin, where his vignettes of frontier life appeared in the *Missouri Intelligencer* under the pseudonym of "Aurora Borealis." These include his interviews with Mike Shuckwell, the mountain trapper, who appeared in Franklin with his pet bear; a satire on the Franklin races; and other local items. His *Gazetteer of the State of Missouri* (1837) consists of practical geographical data generously interlarded with sketches and anecdotes and concluding with a series of short stories. His heroes, Joe Jopling, Jonas Cutting, the comic Yankee frontiersman, Mr. Gall Buster, and other fictitious backwoodsmen, are a rough-and-ready lot with bear grease in their whiskers:

"Are you afraid of snakes, when walking barefooted near these rocky points, where they may be rattlesnake dens?"

"No stranger," was the ready reply. "I generally steps over them."

"Are they numerous in this region of country?"

"There is a right smart sprinkle of snakes in these parts. I and my brother-in-law went out snaking a few days ago, and we killed three hundred and fifty rattlesnakes, and two yearlin' copperheads, and it warn't a very good morning for snaking, neither."

"You would intimate then, that you get a better haul when the weather is favorable?"

"Yes, we cords 'em up sometimes."

Among Wetmore's contemporaries were Gottfried Duden and Nathaniel Beverley Tucker, each of whom was heard far beyond the borders of Missouri. Duden, a German scholar, lived in St. Charles County, 1824-27. His *Report* (1829) describing the beauty of Missouri and its vast resources drew thousands of German immigrants to the State between 1830 and 1870 (*see Tour 1A*). Tucker, a Virginian who came to Missouri in 1815, won acclaim with *George Balcombe* (1836), a swift-moving story of frontier life. "*George Balcombe*," wrote Edgar Allan Poe, "we are induced to regard upon the whole, as the best American novel . . . its most distinguishing features are invention, vigor, almost audacity, of thought."

Between 1818 and 1826, Tucker was judge of the northern circuit of the Missouri Circuit Court. An ardent believer in States Rights, his expressions on the political issues of the times were many and emphatic. The *Partisan Leader,* said to have been begun while he lived at Florissant, Missouri, was published in 1836 at the behest of Southerners who thought it would influence the presidential election of that year. Bearing the fictitious date of 1856, this most widely read of Tucker's works forecast events of the Civil War with uncanny accuracy.

The lack of a public press had meanwhile been rectified. In 1837, James Ruggles of St. Louis established *The Western Mirror, and Ladies Literary Gazette,* edited by Mrs. H. A. Ruggles, probably the first venture of this kind in the Middle West; it appeared for 9 months. The following year Wetmore and Charles Keemle established the *Missouri Saturday News,* which in its brief life contained various "Original Essays" and "Selected Tales" by Missourians. In the *Western Journal,* published in St. Louis (1848-56), appeared "The Life and Times of George Rogers Clark" and other articles by Mann Butler, a resident of St. Louis from about 1845 until his death 10 years later. Butler is best known as a Kentucky historian. The *Journal* also published articles on art appreciation, modern literature, and "The North American Indians"—the last by J. Loughborough, of St. Louis. A greater stimulus to Western literature, however, was Charles Keemle's *Weekly Reveille,* published in St. Louis from 1844 to 1850. Sketches, stories, and anecdotes of Western life appeared in it in rich profusion. Its columns provided an outlet for the tall tales of John S. Robb and the sketches of Joseph M. Field, whose "Death of Mike Fink" is recognized as the definitive obituary to this semi-legendary keelboatman.

In 1846, Robb published *A Sketch of Squatter Life, and Far West Stories,* which he dedicated to Charles Keemle, who had attracted him to Western subjects. In his preface, Robb states that the West "abounds in incident and humor. I have wondered why the finished and graphic writers of our country, so seldom sought material from this inviting field."

The success of these and other publications gave encouragement to an increasing number of Missouri authors during the 20 years preceding the Civil War. During the Mexican War, John T. Hughes recorded the story of his regiment in *Doniphan's Expedition* (1847), and Josiah Gregg told the tale of overland trade in his *Commerce of the Prairies* (1844). Solomon Franklin Smith, early-day actor and producer, recounted his amusing theatrical ventures in *The Theatrical Apprenticeship* (1846), *The Theatrical Journey-Work* (1854), and *Theatrical Management in the West and South for Thirty Years* (1868). As a storekeeper in New Franklin and Arrow Rock in the early 1830's, John Beauchamp Jones gathered material for his *Wild Western Scenes* (1841), which proved immensely popular. Despite its sentimentality and its florid style, the book has deservedly won a place as a minor frontier classic because of its broad humor, vigorous incident, and excellent local color. Jones' *The Western Merchant* (1849) is a record of his Missouri experiences. In the same central-Missouri region David H. Coyner, a Virginia journalist, found material for *The Lost Trappers* (1847), an account of an heroic journey through the Far West, which has long been—perhaps unjustly—discredited. Father de Smet (1801-73), of Belgium, who came to Missouri in 1823, established missions among the Pottowatomie, the Sioux, the Blackfeet, and other Indian tribes, his work taking him through the entire Northwest and Great Plains region. His writings, among the most interesting of the frontier, include *Letters and Sketches* (1843), *Residence Among the Indians of the Rocky Mountains* (1843), and *Western Missions and Missionaries* (1857).

Jesse B. Turley, a Santa Fe trader and a friend and former Missouri neighbor of Kit Carson, suggested to the famous hunter that he write his life story. Carson, who was scarcely literate, dictated his autobiography to Turley about 1856. Dr. DeWitt C. Peters edited the manuscript, which appeared in 1858 as *The Life of Kit Carson*.

Among contributions of immigrant German scholars is *A Journey to the Rocky Mountains in the Year 1839,* by F. A. Wislizenus, St. Louis physician, which contains scientifically interesting reports of flora based on the observations of Dr. George Englemann, who wrote *The Cactaceae of the Boundary* (1850) and helped found the Missouri Botanical Garden (*see St. Louis*).

Other Missouri writings of this period include the scholarly *Life of John Randolph of Roanoke* (1850) and *The Life of Thomas Jefferson* (1854), by Hugh A. Garland; the scandalous *Mysteries of St. Louis* (1851), by Henry Boernstein, German author and journalist. *Thirty Years' View* (2 vols., 1855-56), by Senator Thomas H. Benton, an account of his political career, was widely read.

Louis R. Cortambert (1808-81), who lived in St. Louis from the 1830's until the Civil War, is estimated by some critics to have been the most talented French writer in the country. He was an advanced political thinker, and an ardent disciple of Thoreau. From 1854 until about 1860, he edited the *Revue de l'Ouest,* founded by the French Literary Society of St. Louis, of which he was president. His books include *Voyage au Pays des Osages* (Paris, 1837), *L'Histoire de la Guerre Civile Américaine* (Paris, 1867), and *Réligion du Progrés* (New York, 1884).

The Civil War reduced the literary output of Missourians to such partisan items as *My Cave Life in Vicksburg, with Letters of Trial and Travel* (1864), whose author, "A Lady of Quality," was Mrs. James M. Loughborough, a native St. Louisan and the wife of a Confederate officer; and *A Brief Narrative of Incidents in the War in Missouri* (1863), by the Reverend Henry M. Painter, a vitriolic attack on the Union by a Presbyterian minister who had been "banished" to Boston for his supposed pro-Southern activities in Boonville.

In the year the conflict ended, Mark Twain (Samuel Langhorne Clemens, 1835-1910), whose career as journeyman printer, steamboat pilot, reporter, and assistant editor (*see Newspapers, and Hannibal*) had taken him from Hannibal, Missouri, to St. Louis, New York, Philadelphia, Keokuk, Cincinnati, and eventually Sacramento, published a humorous tale, *Jim Smiley and the Jumping Frog,* in the *New York Saturday Press.* The war-worn public responded instantly to the Westerner's wit: the story was reprinted throughout the country. Twain's first book, *The Celebrated Jumping Frog of Calaveras County and Other Sketches,* appeared in 1867. Among his works dealing with the West are *Roughing It* (1872), which describes his wanderings in this region; *Life on the Mississippi* (1883), which harks back to his steamboatin' days; and the classics, *Tom Sawyer* (1876) and *Huckleberry Finn* (1884), which have a Missouri and Mississippi Valley background.

Mark Twain's robust language came from the vitals of Western life. American writers have found it easier to write of America since his day. Passages like the following from *Huckleberry Finn* cleared the way for the development of a fluid prose related to common speech and plain people:

> Once or twice of a night we could see a steamboat slipping along in the dark, and now and then she would belch a whole world of sparks up out of her chimbleys, and they would rain down in the river and look awful pretty; then she would turn a corner and her lights would wink out and her powwow shut off and leave the river still again; and by and by her waves would get to us, a long time after she was gone, and joggle the raft a bit, and after that you couldn't hear nothing for you couldn't tell how long, except maybe frogs or something.

The world of childhood is the especial sphere of Eugene Field, poet and columnist, whose "Little Boy Blue" and "Wynken, Blynken and Nod" have endeared him wherever English is spoken. Born at St. Louis in 1850, son of one of the lawyers who pleaded the case of Dred

Scott, Field was an eccentric fellow, fond of practical jokes and given to whimsies of many kinds. He began his career on the St. Joseph *Gazette;* later he worked in Missouri for the St. Louis *Journal* and the Kansas City *Times.* From 1883 until his death in 1895, he wrote "Sharps and Flats" for the Chicago *Morning News,* a column that set the capstone on this branch of journalism.

Most of Field's verse was gauged to popular consumption, and was, consequently, as ephemeral as last week's newspaper. Sentiment was his main stock in trade, particularly the sentiment aroused by little "tykes." To escape monotony, he resorted to Dutch, Old English, and other dialects, a device that brought more penalties than rewards. His books included *A Little Book of Western Verse* (1889), *With Trumpet and Drum* (1892), and *A Second Book of Verse* (1892).

American thought was appreciably influenced in the post-Civil War period by the "St. Louis movement," an upsurge of philosophical activity created largely by Henry C. Brokmeyer (1828-1906) and William Torrey Harris (1835-1909). Brokmeyer, a Prussian versed in Hegelianism, came to Warren County, Missouri, in 1854, where, sickly and impoverished, he lived until 1858. In that year, William T. Harris, of Connecticut, who had begun teaching school at St. Louis in 1857, brought the distressed philosopher to St. Louis. Here, his health improved, Brokmeyer translated Hegel's *Larger Logic* and tutored Harris in the German master's system.

In 1866, Harris and Brokmeyer organized the St. Louis Philosophical Society, with Brokmeyer as president. In the following year, Harris established the *Journal of Speculative Philosophy* (1867-93), which had as its motto: "Philosophy can bake no bread but it can give God, Freedom, and Immortality." This publication was the first to introduce American intellectuals to the important works of Hegel, Fichte, Schelling, and other European thinkers. In turn, it was the outlet for the first philosophical papers of William James, John Dewey, and Josiah Royce.

Harris, although the author of 479 books, won his chief fame with his annual reports as Superintendent of the St. Louis Public Schools (1868-80). In 1880, he moved to Concord, Massachusetts, to join the group of Concord philosophers. He hoped to succeed Emerson as the leader of the great idealistic movement, but in this he failed completely.

Chief among those identified with Harris and Brokmeyer in the St. Louis movement were Adolph E. Kroeger, Denton J. Snider, Dr. Alexander De Menil, George H. Howison, and J. Gabriel Woerner. Kroeger (1837-82), German-born newspaperman who had come to St. Louis in 1858 as corerspondent for the New York *Times,* wrote prolifically for the *Journal of Speculative Philosophy* and translated many works of the German philosophers. Snider (1841-1925), author, linguist, and lecturer, is perhaps best known for his ambitious "psychologic" system, reared on a creaking Hegelian framework. A prodigious worker, he also published commentaries on Dante, Homer, Goethe, and Shakespeare. Dr. De Menil's important contributions include *The Literature of the Louisiana Purchase Territory* (1904).

Among the many books by Missourians in the nineties were *Bayou Folk* (1894), *A Night in Acadie* (1897), and *The Awakening* (1899), 3 novels of Creole life by Kate O'Flaherty Chopin (1851-1904); *The Columbian Historical Novels* (12 vols., 1897), by John R. Musick (1849-1901), a Kirksville lawyer who wrote 26 novels; and *How Thankful Was Bewitched* (1894), a novel by Professor James K. Hosmer (1834-1927) of Washington University, whose earlier works included several historical studies and 3 biographies. Although commonly identified with Atchison, Kansas, E. W. Howe (1853-1937) spent his boyhood in Gallatin; near-by Bethany was the prototype of the Twin Mounds described in his *Story of a County Town* (1883).

In 1899, Winston Churchill, born at St. Louis in 1871, published the extremely popular *Richard Carvel,* a story of the Revolutionary War period. This novel, together with *The Crisis* (1901), and *The Crossing* (1904), in which Churchill drew heavily on his Missouri background, quickly made him the "foremost novelist of his day." *The Crisis* sold 320,000 and *Richard Carvel* 420,000 copies within a few months of publication.

William Marion Reedy (1862-1920), son of a St. Louis police captain, did much to stimulate Midwestern literature in the opening years of the twentieth century. He first worked as a reporter on the *Missouri Republican,* but finding the newspaper world too narrow, he became a free-lance writer, contributing frequently to the *Sunday Mirror* of St. Louis, then chiefly a society newspaper. The owner, James Campbell, became interested in Reedy, and in 1896 made him a present of the paper, which, as *Reedy's Mirror,* became an intellectual weekly of Nation-wide fame. Reedy was an excellent critic, with a genius for finding and encouraging talented young authors. Indeed, his present importance rests largely upon the tremendous influence he exerted over the writers and thinkers of his time, although his own literary ability may also prove lasting. His books include *The Imitator* (1901), a novel, a group of essays, *The Law of Love* (1905), originally appearing in the *Mirror,* and *A Golden Book and the Literature of Childhood* (1910). Buried in the 30 volumes of *Reedy's Mirror* are his articles, essays, and editorials, dealing with matters political, religious, social, ethical, artistic, and cultural. These range from quieter critical comments to his "The Story of a Strike" (1901), in which he indicted the incompetence and dishonesty of St. Louis politics with a furious, terrible scorn.

It was Reedy who advised Edgar Lee Masters to write his *Spoon River Anthology,* which first appeared in the *Mirror.* It was he who, through the *Mirror,* first popularized Galsworthy, Conrad, Cunninghame Graham, and the Sitwells in America. Among the young American hopefuls whom he encouraged were Zoë Akins, Orrick Johns, Homer Croy, Sara Teasdale, John Gould Fletcher, John Hall Wheelock, and Fannie Hurst. The latter, born at St. Louis in 1889, is well known for her short stories and novels, particularly *Humoresque* (1918), *Lummox* (1923), and *Back Street* (1931). Johns, also of St. Louis, wrote *Asphalt and Other Poems* (1917), and *Black Branches* (1920); his prose includes *Blindfold* (1923) and *Time of Our Lives* (1937). Croy, born on a farm near Maryville, Missouri, in 1883, is a skilled interpreter of the Missouri rural scene. His earlier stories of adolescent boys, *Boone Stop* (1918) and *Turkey Bowman* (1920), give no hint of the realism employed in his widely read *West of the Water Tower* (1923) and *R.F.D. No. 3* (1924).

Sara Teasdale's (1884-1933) rise to prominence as a poet dated from the publication in *Reedy's Mirror* of her blank verse monologue, "Gunevere," in 1907. Among her subsequent works are *Helen of Troy and Other Poems* (1911), *Rivers to the Sea* (1915), *Love Songs* (1917), and *Flame and Shadow* (1920). Zoë Akins, born at Humansville in 1886, also published her early poetry in *Reedy's Mirror.* *Interpretations* (London, 1911), her first volume of poems, included "I Am the Wind," which has been set to music. Miss Akins later moved to New York, where she became one of the country's foremost dramatists. Among her successful plays are *Déclassée, The Varying Shore, The Greeks Had a Word for It,* and *The Old Maid,* Pulitzer prize winner in 1935.

This impressive list of contributors to *Reedy's Mirror* does not by any means, however, include all of Missouri's early twentieth century writers. The State had grown up; the frontier was no more, and city life had taken on a conventional pattern. The result was a literary searching for new material and backgrounds. This freshness was found in the Ozark region, where a rich vein of customs, dialects, and folklore lay ready. John Monteith pioneered in the movement with his novel, *Parson Brooks* (1884), which portrayed the Missouri hillman with honesty and restraint. It remained, however, for Harold Bell Wright to make the region the subject of best sellers. The heartthrobs of *Shepherd of the Hills* (1907) and *The Calling of Dan Matthews* (1909) were shared by millions. Wright's depiction of the hill people has been criticized as superficial, but the dialect is more accurate than is generally supposed.

Notable among contemporary writers associated with the Ozarks is Vance Randolph, who lived at Pineville for ten years studying the hill people, their speech, manners, and work. To date, he has written *The Ozarks* (1931), *Ozark Mountain Folk* (1932), *From an Ozark Holler* (1933), and *Camp on Wildcat Creek* (1934). Randolph also aided Thames R. Williamson in gathering material for *The Wood's Colt* (1933), a swift-paced tragedy which is authentic in spirit and idiom. Among others who have employed an Ozark milieu are Ralph McCanse of Springfield, whose long narrative poem, *The Road to Hollister* (1927), protests against the ludicrous way the hillbilly is sometimes treated; Dennis Murphy, who won the poetry award of *Kaleidescope* in 1928 with *The Boy With the Silver Plow;* and Mac-Kinlay Kantor, whose novel, *The Voice of Bugle Ann* (1935), gives an accurate picture of Missouri fox hunting. Rose Wilder Lane, the novelist, has lived in Mansfield since 1920. Her contributions to Ozarkana include short stories, and the novels, *Hill Billy* (1926), *Cindy* (1928), and *He Was A Man* (1925).

Rupert Hughes, the popular novelist, short story writer, and music critic, was born at Lancaster in 1872. Among his stories with a Missouri setting are *The Whirlwind* (1902) and *You Hadn't Ought to Go* (1920). John G. Neihardt, a Missourian by adoption, and now a resident of Branson, holds a secure place in American poetry with *The Song of Hugh Glass* (1915), *The Song of Three Friends* (1919), an epic of Mike Fink the keelboatman, and *The Song of the Indian Wars* (1925). Casper S. Yost, editorial writer for the St. Louis *Globe-Democrat,* is the author of *A Successful Husband* (1907), *Patience Worth* (1916), and other books. Raymond Weeks (1868-), also a Missourian by adoption, draws upon the background of the Missouri River "Dixie belt" for his short stories. In his *The Boys' Own Arithmetic* (1924) the problems are stated in the form of entertaining sketches. Despite his comment that few would read his *The Hound-Tuner of Callaway* (1926), because it contains no duels, broncos, wildcats, or typhoons, the book has attracted considerable attention. In spirit, Weeks belongs to the frontier, with his quiet, incisive humor, his tall stories, and his never-ending delight in the world and the people about him.

Several modern writers are identified with Missouri by birth rather than by product. Of these the most famous perhaps, though in widely separated fields, are T. S. Eliot, Dale Carnegie, and Courtney Riley Cooper. T. S. Eliot, born at St. Louis in 1888, the grandson of the founder of Washington University, has lived in England for many years. His long poem, *The Waste Land,* won the *Dial* prize in 1922 and excited international comment. His critical essays and his editorship of *The Criterion,* London, have had a profound effect upon contemporary literary values. He has also written several verse plays. Dale Carnegie, more properly a lecturer than a writer, was born in Nodaway County and attended school at Warrensburg. His *How to Win Friends and Influence People* is the *Gone With the Wind* of self-improvement literature. Courtney Riley Cooper, a Kansas Citian, wrote many popular novels and short stories.

Most of Missouri's younger writers are earnest craftsmen whose narratives tend toward the social document, a trend almost world-wide at the present time. Representative of this group are Jack Conroy, Martha E. Gellhorn, Josephine Johnson, and Elizabeth Seifert. Conroy makes a profoundly stirring case for the underdog in *The Disinherited* (1933) and *A World to Win* (1935). The life of the professional man, rather than that of the laborer, is the preferred domain of Mrs. John Gasparotti (Elizabeth Seifert), who, like Conroy, is a native of Moberly. *Young Doctor Galahad* (1938), her first novel, won a $10,000 prize offered by Dodd, Mead & Company; she is also the author of *A Great Day* (1939) and *Thus—Doctor Mallory* (1940). Martha E. Gellhorn evidences her social-mindedness in *What Mad Pursuit* (1934), *The Trouble I've Seen* (1936), and *A Stricken Field* (1940), a novel of horror laid in Czechoslovakia. Josephine Johnson's *Now in November,* a story of farm folk stretched on the economic rack, won the Pulitzer prize in 1935. She later published *Winter Orchard* (1935), a book of sketches and short stories, *Jordanstown* (1937), a disturbing picture of social conflict, and *Year's End* (1937), a collection of poems.

Among other Missouri writers of the present day are Kansas Citians Louise Abney, Paul I. Wellman, and Henry Haskell. The works of veterans Carl Crow, George Creel, Glenn Frank, Temple Bailey, Mary Margaret McBride, and Rose O'Neill have enjoyed a wide circulation. Most promising of the younger writers as a portrayer of the Missouri scene is Ward Allison Dorrance of Columbia, whose fine prose style and sympathetic understanding of the Missouri background have attracted attention in *Three Ozark Streams* (1937), *We're From Missouri* (1938), and *Where the Rivers Meet* (1939).

The Theater

MISSOURI'S theater had its beginning in efforts to relieve the tedium of frontier life. In 1814, the entertainment-starved settlers of St. Louis flocked to watch the self-styled magician, Eugene Leitensdorfer, erstwhile soldier of fortune, spy, bird-catcher, Capuchin monk, Jewish rabbi, and Mohammedan dervish, who was at that time making a tour of the West. After him came Brown's Mammoth Circus for a week's stay, with its weary, bedraggled performers and moth-eaten animals. These were a far cry from the drama, but they were enough to whet the appetite, and to encourage the organization of an amateur dramatic club.

On the night of January 6, 1815, a heterogeneous group, such as could scarcely have been gathered outside the frontier, sat on the hard benches of the first St. Louis theater, an old building which had served as blacksmith shop, a church, and a courthouse. In the candlelight flickering upon the improvised stage, they watched Missouri's first theatrical productions: *The School for Authors* and *The Budget of Blunders,* played by a "group of St. Louis young gentlemen," the Roscians. Within the year, a rival society, the Thespians, was flourishing. Both groups used the old building, christened "The Theatre" by the Thespians. The Roscians were not long important, but for almost 20 years the Thespians functioned, sporadically it is true, but none the less effectually. They staged plays, and fostered appearances by traveling companies, combining, with true frontier versatility, the functions of drama league, little theater, booking agent, and impresario. In their theater was played what was probably the first professional engagement in Missouri: the performance of William Turner and his wife, Sophia, February 17, 1818, in *Isabella, or The Fatal Marriage.*

In 1819, the drama in St. Louis was emancipated from the old blacksmith shop with the opening of the New Theater, a frame building seating 600, designed by Isaac H. Griffith. At this time, three persons prominent in the history of the Midwestern theater became identified with the Missouri stage—Noah M. Ludlow, Samuel Drake, and John H. Vos. These men carried on the struggle begun by the Thespians. Vos was a house painter "of good education" who came with his wife from Kentucky to St. Louis in 1818. He shortly became interested in the theatrical life of the city, and joined forces with the Turners. It was under his management that the New Theater was opened. All was not smooth sailing, however. In January, 1820, Vos was in such reduced circumstances that the Thespians sponsored a benefit performance for him, which included "the much-admired petit comedy called *The Jew and the Doctor"* and the "laughable farce of *The Toothache."* Ludlow was a native New Yorker who, in the course of a varied career, had joined in the East the theatrical company of "Old Sam" Drake, with whom he toured Tennessee and Kentucky. After leaving Drake's company, he entered into correspondence with Vos, and organized a company of his own, which he brought from Tennessee to St. Louis by packet in 1820. Within a few days, he and Vos struck up a partnership, and took over the New Theater, where they began with Mrs. Centlivre's *The Busy Body,* and O'Keefe's musical farce, *The Poor Soldier,* followed by *The Castle Spectre,* and *The Rival Soldiers.*

At the same time, Drake, possibly unaware of Ludlow's activities, brought his three sons, two daughters, and five assistants, all of whom were experienced actors, to St. Louis by steamboat from Louisville. Ignoring Ludlow and Vos, he presented his own bill in the ballroom of Bennett's City Hotel, there being no second theater. The "Kentucky Company," as Drake's troupe was called, offered a variety of plays: *The Jealous Wife, The Adopted Child, The Secrets of Milford Castle.* Thus St. Louis, long starved for entertainment, found itself suddenly with a superfluity. The little town being unable to support two theaters, the rivals were forced to combine, under Drake's management. The joint company did not prosper, however, despite favorable press notices. Since Drake, Ludlow, Vos, and most of their families were actors, quarrels arose over casting; in addition, the weather was unseasonable, and times were hard. At the end of the season the company gave up. Ludlow subsequently attempted to play the near-by towns, but this venture also failed. At St. Charles, where the house grossed $7.50, the audience complained of his charging a price as high as that of a recent vaudeville act, which included both a monkey and a tightrope walker! Ludlow returned to Nashville, and St. Louis returned to amateur entertainment.

The Thespians carried on in the New Theater until 1825, after the demise of the professional companies. In that year they equipped an old salt warehouse, and christened it the *Old Salt House Theater.* Two years later, James H. Caldwell of New Orleans leased this theater, and advertised performances daily except Sunday, a program much too ambitious for the times. The theater closed after a few weeks; but brief as it was, Caldwell's venture is important in Missouri's stage history, for he inaugurated the practice of featuring individual actors.

It might be interesting to examine for a moment the frontier taste in theatrical entertainment. Farce seems to have been most popular,

with melodrama a close second; in 1828, a critic complained in the press
that melodrama was driving comedy from the stage. Shakespeare seems
to have been a perennial favorite. Tableaux of all kinds met with
enthusiastic acclaim. Visiting celebrities received due welcome. Indeed, when the famous Viennese dancer, Fanny Elssler, came to St.
Louis on her grand tour of the United States in 1841, one writer
sneered that "nothing but Fanny Elssler's legs" would draw a house.
The scenery for those early productions was extremely crude; most
often it was made by some actor in the company. Lighting was even
cruder, oil lamps or candles being the only means of illumination. The
theaters were unheated, small, and poorly ventilated, and the benches
were hard.

Inevitably, an interest in the theater developed an interest in play-
writing. Would-be authors became so numerous that managers took
refuge behind committees appointed to pass on manuscripts. Most of
the contemporary plays produced were "literary," and heavy with moral
sentiment. The infrequent plays based on frontier life generally failed.

Among the earliest of successful plays by Missouri authors was *The
Pedlar,* a farce of doubtful literary merit but rich in local color, by
Alphonso Wetmore, an Army paymaster (*see Literature*). The story
centered about a Yankee peddler, Nutmeg, whose pack would have
shamed a modern five-and-ten-cent store, and his successful wooing of
Old Prairie's "nut brown" niece, Pecanne. The following is from
Act I, Scene I:

> NUTMEG: My sweet little mermaid, what have you there?
> PECANNE: Stockings; do you wish to buy them?
> NUTMEG: Yes, my dear little wood-nymph, if you will take merchandise.
> PECANNE: What have you? O! (a lantern) by the powers of love, the
> very thing my Uncle is in want of. I'll give you this whole
> bundle for it.
> NUTMEG: Here, take it; and this cup, and a kiss to boot. (Kisses her.)
> PECANNE: What a sweet breath! He don't chew tobacco, I'm sure.
> (aside)

Religious opposition to the theater began early and continued
vigorously in Missouri. In a letter written in 1816, Bishop Flaget
opposed St. Louis as the seat of the new diocese because the city had a
theater. In 1851, the Reverend William Greenleaf Eliot, the liberal
Unitarian who founded Washington University, condemned attendance
at the theater as unduly exciting and therefore bad for youth.

The theater, however, became increasingly popular. Gradually, the
early amateur groups were replaced by professional organizations.
Ludlow returned to St. Louis for several engagements, and eventually
raised by subscription $30,000 for a theater building in the city. Soon
after, he formed a partnership with Sol Smith, an experienced comedian
and manager of itinerant troupes, who had come to St. Louis from the

East. This partnership dominated the Missouri theater for the next 16 years, and also operated theaters in Mobile and New Orleans.

They took over the Old Salt House Theater, although Ludlow pronounced it "a miserable apology for a theater," and a "wretched affair, dirty, illy contrived, and poorly provided with scenery." Construction had begun on the new building, when the Old Salt House burned down, leaving the partners without a theater. The new structure was consequently rushed to completion, and the New St. Louis Theater, on the southeast corner of Third and Olive Streets, was dedicated with appropriate ceremonies on July 3, 1837, Ludlow presenting his stand-by, *The Honeymoon.* Said by some authorities to have been the first theater in the country with individual seats in place of benches, the New St. Louis was hailed as the outstanding playhouse of the West.

Eastern road companies had begun to tour a Western circuit bringing world-renowned stars of the day. Because St. Louis was known as "a good show town," the leading artists came here: Ellen Tree from England, in 1838-39; Jenny Lind, under the management of P. T. Barnum; Mlle. Celeste, so popular that seats were sold by lottery.

The theater of Ludlow and Smith exemplified the strange mixture of the elegant and primitive prevailing in mid-nineteenth-century Missouri. When Ellen Tree came for a second engagement, with her husband, Charles John Kean, a performance of *Romeo and Juliet* had to be stopped while the hero and heroine solemnly swabbed the oil lamps. Lesser players had to be extremely versatile. An applicant for a $30-a-week job as a scene painter remarked that he had heard the firm spoken well of, "a rare thing with managers, nowadays," and presented as an extra inducement to being hired the fact that he played character parts—harlequin, monkey, wild man, old man, and Indian. Yet, despite its crudities, the theater prospered. When Junius Brutus Booth played an engagement in 1846, he preferred a one-third share of the receipts to a guarantee of $100 a night and a third of the receipts on the customary last night benefit. Incidentally, he drew a sharp public reproof for appearing on the stage intoxicated on his opening night.

In 1851, John Bates opened a theater in St. Louis, ending the Ludlow-Smith monopoly. The next year, the St. Louis Varieties Theater opened. Both shortly passed into the hands of Ben DeBar, a protégé and successor of Ludlow and Smith.

Meanwhile in the smaller communities throughout the State, such as Jefferson City, where the only professional drama was an occasional visit by a traveling company, amateur theatrical groups were being developed. Palmyra organized a Thespian Society in 1836; it flourished until 1842 or 1843, when the theater was converted into a packing house. In Boonville a Thespian Society, organized about 1838, brought the versatile Mrs. Riley to its log theater. Nineteen years later, it erected the large, white-columned Greek-Revival Thespian Hall, now said to be the oldest surviving theater building west of the Alleghenies. Liberty, Columbia, Lexington, and Hermann had early theaters. The Thespian Society at St. Joseph performed the comedy, *The Prisoner at Large,* in 1845, the year of the town's incorporation. In 1854, two German residents of Hermann lugged scenery and costumes from their own theater across the hills to near-by Washington, where they organized the *Theaterverein.*

One of the most colorful developments in the history of the Western theater was the showboat. At first, these boats offered only vaudeville or circus entertainment, but their repertoire soon included popular melodramas. When the steam calliope which signaled the approach of a showboat was heard, all the town gathered on the water front. The showboat would tie up at the wharf with banners flying; then, members of the cast, a band, and often the crew would parade to advertise the play. The popularity of the showboat continued until well after the Civil War. When the *Floating Palace* came to St. Louis in 1852, 2,500 crowded aboard, and many paid a dollar to watch the performance through the windows. Even the decline of water traffic did not spoil the showboat business. Fourteen showboats were in operation as late as 1925, and at least one appeared at St. Louis in 1937. The *Goldenrod,* no longer plying the rivers, remains at St. Louis the year around, offering the melodramas popular since Victorian days.

In Kansas City, the only early showhouse was Frank's Hall, still standing at the northwest corner of Fifth and Main Streets. In 1871, Colonel Kersey Coates opened the $105,000 Coates Opera House. This was the finest theater west of the Mississippi River, until the Tootle Grand Theater was built a few years later at St. Joseph. Road shows extended their itinerary to include Kansas City and St. Joseph, bringing such players as Edwin Booth, Lawrence Barrett, Emma Abbott, and Mary Anderson. Amateur and professional dramatics flourished simultaneously in Kansas City. The Kemble Club, an amateur group, staged several plays, and the more ambitious Lawrence Barrett Dramatic Club produced *Richard III, Romeo and Juliet, Twelfth Night,* and *Julius Caesar.* In 1883, the Gillis Theater and the Music Hall opened, and in the next two decades ten more professional theaters appeared. Joseph Jefferson, Sarah Bernhardt, Mrs. John Drew, and Fay Templeton appeared at the Gillis, but as the center of Kansas City shifted, the theater descended to a second-class musical tab-show house. It was rebuilt after a fire and explosion in 1923, and now is given over, between vice crusades, to burlesque.

In Joplin, at the one-story frame theater that preceded the Blackwell Opera House, a miner without the cash price of admission could exchange a wheelbarrow load of lead ore at the box office for tickets for himself and family. Springfield and other secondary cities built theaters that were almost luxurious; smaller towns had "opera houses" which, despite the splendor of their names, were often simply second-floor rooms equipped with a stage.

The post-Civil War period was the golden age of the professional stage, which saw the erection of half a dozen theaters at St. Louis and the transformation of Uhrig's Cave, on the site of the present Coliseum, from a beer storage house to the city's first summer concert garden. Theater attendance became almost as customary as attendance at to-day's motion pictures. In the cities, stock companies stayed for a season, charging 10, 20, and 30 cents for admission; lesser companies toured the small-town opera houses, and—after the turn of the century—the summer "airdome" theaters.

This period of great theatrical interest produced Missouri's out-standing early playwright, Augustus Thomas. Born in St. Louis in 1857, Thomas first earned his living as a newspaper reporter, and then became identified with the McCullough Club, an amateur dramatic group in St. Louis. In 1888 he went to New York to become press agent for Julia Marlowe. His first play, *The Burglar,* was completed the following year. *In Mizzoura,* which appeared in 1893, was his most successful work. His plays were well constructed, and were important in their day because they helped to free the American stage from European domination.

Now that showboats seldom visit the river ports, tent shows provide entertainment for the small towns. Representative is the Princess Stock Company, which has made a regular Missouri circuit for more than 35 years, presenting old and new plays with equal sincerity, principally to "family" audiences. The traditional music and entertainment between acts, the candy with prizes, the "diamond ring given away free on Saturday nights," and the friendly banter of "Toby," a favorite in the towns he has visited for more than a generation, all add flavor to these performances.

With the development of motion pictures, legitimate theaters in Missouri grew dark, as elsewhere; at present, St. Louis and Kansas City have but one each. Most of the old theater buildings have become motion picture houses. A few, like the Gillis at Kansas City, and the Garrick, which was built at St. Louis for the World's Fair crowds of 1904, have switched to burlesque. Since 1919, St. Louis has had a successful annual summer season of light opera in the outdoor Munici-pal Theater in Forest Park (*see St. Louis*); and in very recent years, the Playgoers has built up a subscription list large enough to make St. Louis a profitable show town for the big New York and Chicago companies. Aside from these, Missouri's drama has returned largely into the hands of amateurs.

In the summer of 1912, members of the St. Louis Artists' Guild founded The Players, a writing and acting group. Its best-known member has been Zoë Akins, who wrote several of its first plays. In Kansas City, 2 years later, 50 persons prominent in the social life of the city organized the Comedy Club, chiefly for their own amusement. These groups have stimulated or sponsored numerous amateur organizations, which today present plays of professional caliber in both cities, as well as "little" theaters in a number of Missouri's secondary cities. At Kansas City following the World War, two amateur theatrical groups, the Harlequin Players and the Little Theater, were formed, the latter eventually merging with the Comedy Club. Later came the Blackfriars and the Provincials, chiefly interested in presenting plays by Missouri or Middle Western writers. The Provincials are still active. The vigorous Civic Theater and the Children's Civic Theater were followed by the Resident Theater, which produces Broadway successes with professional guest stars.

At St. Louis, the success of The Players prompted the growth of an organization separate from the Artists' Guild. The result was The Little Theater, established in 1926, which strives to develop new talent and to bring a wide range of plays to its stage. It offers an annual prize of $250 for the best original play submitted. Another amateur group, the Mummers, organized in 1927, has established a reputation with a variety of plays from Greek tragedy to Sinclair Lewis. Thyrsus, a Washington University organization, forgetful of Founder Eliot's anti-theater pronouncements of 1851, gives both student and professional plays. Another Washington group, the Quadrangle Club, sponsors an annual musical comedy in which the book, the music, and the production are by students. Such people as Fannie Hurst, Gus Haenchen, Morris Carnovsky, and Melville Burke have been active in these clubs. A dozen other "little theater" enterprises have come into being in recent years. In the St. Louis Outdoor Civic Theater, organized in 1938, St. Louis actors perform on a profit-sharing basis.

Drama has become part of college curriculums. A new Washington University course, co-operating with the St. Louis School of the Theater, leads to a Bachelor of Science degree in education, with a major in dramatics. The Missouri Workshop, of the University of Missouri, presents plays in which much of the casting, staging, and directing is done by the students. Stephens College, also at Columbia, in 1937 engaged Miss Maude Adams as professor of the drama. Several teachers' colleges, besides maintaining student theatrical organizations, have carried their work nearer to the people through folk festivals. Actors from this and other States gather at Cape Girardeau each spring, to present plays written by high school and college students in an annual contest conducted by the Southeastern Missouri State Teachers College. In 1934, the first National Folk Festival was held in St. Louis, directed by Sarah Gertrude Knott. An annual Ozark Folk Festival brings together many Missouri groups.

In the same category are the pageants staged for various town anniversaries and similar occasions. Probably the best known of these is the Veiled Prophet celebration in St. Louis, which has been held early each October since 1878. The celebration begins with a parade of elaborate floats expressing some chosen theme, and this is followed by dancing and street revels. The culmination of the celebration is a formal ball at which His Mysterious Majesty, the Veiled Prophet, picks with pomp and ceremony a Queen of Love and Beauty to reign over St. Louis social life for the coming season. One of the most pretentious pageants ever given in Missouri was the Pageant and Masque of St. Louis, presented in 1914, for which Thomas Wood Stevens wrote the pageant, and Percy Mackaye the masque. In 1921, the centenary of statehood afforded an opportunity for a spectacular celebration at Sedalia, produced on a 600-foot stage at the State Fair. In 1935, Ste. Genevieve held a bicentennial pageant lasting 4 nights and attracting an estimated 35,000 out-of-town visitors.

Numerous Missouri players have established national reputations on stage and screen. These include Sol Smith Russel, born in Brunswick; Mrs. Louis James and Mary Hall, who played Shakespeare; and Robert T. Haines, once Mrs. Fiske's leading man. Nettie Gallagher became leading lady for David Warfield and later for Otis Skinner. Among other stage and screen celebrities whom Missouri claims by either birth or residence are Wallace and Noah Beery, William Powell, Walt Disney, Buddy Rogers, Ellen Drew, Jean Harlow, Jeanne Eagels, Ginger Rogers, Grace Hopkins, who for several seasons was leading woman for Thomas W. Keene, and Stanislaus Stange, a dramatist and librettist as well as an actor.

Music

THE songs of the French voyageurs were the first civilized music heard in Missouri. As these adventurers pushed their canoes up uncharted Western streams in the eighteenth century, they timed their paddle strokes to the ringing "Chanson du Nord," or to ballads such as the one recorded later by John Bradbury, English botanist, which began:

> Beyond our house there is a pond,
> Fal lal de la,
> There came three ducks to swim thereon;
> All along the river clear,
> Lightly my shepherdess dear,
> Lightly, fal de la.

By 1780, a local event, the repelling by the French of a combined British and Indian attack on St. Louis, had been commemorated in the song "Chanson de L'Année du coup," said to have been written by Jean Baptiste Trudeau, a St. Louis schoolmaster. Celebrating the traditional courage of all defenders,

> When the enemy first appeared,
> To arms we ran, no one afeared;
> Townsmen, traders, grave and gay,
> Bravely to battle and win the day,

the song unjustly accuses of cowardice Fernando de Leyba, Spanish acting lieutenant-governor of Upper Louisiana, and ends on a jubilant note of French victory.

Thomas Ashe, visiting the Creole settlement at Ste. Genevieve on a summer's evening in 1806, found the inhabitants gathered about their dooryards, "the women at work, the children at play, and the men performing music, singing songs, or telling stories . . ." Between numerous special occasions for group festivities, such as balls and holy or feast days, the music-loving Creoles gathered night after night for the pure joy of singing together. They sang of the tragedy of a mother who unknowingly murdered her son in "Le Retour Funeste"; of the trials of love in "L'Amant Malheureux" and "Belle Rose"; and of a more reflective theme in "Le Juif Errant." Of all these old French songs, perhaps the most familiar today is the ancient "La Guignolée," still sung by masked revelers on New Year's Eve at Ste. Genevieve and Old Mines. The Creoles contributed little to the development of modern music, but they had a great influence on the cultural history of the State.

When the Anglo-Americans surged across the Mississippi River after the Louisiana Purchase in 1803, French melodies were engulfed in the musical literature of the American frontiersman, which, though essentially naive, encompassed the range of human emotions. Typical early songs are "Lord Thomas and Fair Annet," a variation of an English seventeenth-century ballad, the tragedy of hard-hearted "Barbara Allen," and "The Three Butchers," a story of female treachery concluding:

> She wrung her hands and tore her hair
> And hung her head and cried,
> "If I'd a-knowed it was Johnson,
> Before I'd a-did it I'd a died."

The folk mind of the pioneer bred new songs on new subjects, preserving in the old ballad form the memories of Fourth of July celebrations, of political campaigns, and of other significant events. The trials of "Joe Bowers from Pike" (*see Tour 7a*) caught the tempo of the California gold rush decade, and introduced a new type of American literature. An unknown Howard County Negro summed up the conflicts of the Civil War in these lines:

> God Bless the whole kepoodle
> Hail Columbia Yankee Doodle
> We're fightin' for the happy land of Canaan.

The ballad, "Jesse James," with its famous ending,

> O Jesse had a wife, a mourner all her life
> And the children they were brave,
> But the dirty little coward that shot Mr. Howard
> He laid Jesse James in his grave,

was a folk tribute to a character whose career expressed the trying post-Civil War era. Similarly, the famous "Frankie and Johnny," with its endless accretions and variations, reflects with genuine pathos some of the qualities of urban living. More recently (1912), "Houn' Dog" swept the country during Champ Clark's campaign.

These songs of earlier times, and of men who have become folk-lore characters, are still sung in Missouri. One hears them frequently in the fastness of the Ozarks and in quiet towns along the Missouri River. "Fiddling" is no longer as common as it was, and the influence of the radio and the talking movie is increasingly apparent, but young people at parties, on hay rides, and about the fire at the end of a 'possum hunt, will drift from modern tunes into such old songs as "The Oxford Girl," "Maxwell's Doom," and "The Three Rogues." How long the old music will survive in memory it is impossible to estimate; some observers feel that another generation will see its end. Many of the old folk songs have been collected by the Missouri Folk-Lore Society and appear in *Ballads and Songs* (1940), edited by H. M. Belden.

The group singing of hymns, many from the *Sacred Heart,* a popular early hymnal, is still common in Missouri. The custom is most extensively preserved in the Ozark Highlands, where "singings" are held in the small white churches on the hillsides. Often the groups are organized into "schools," which meet regularly for all-day singings under the direction of a leader who, like the old circuit rider, travels from community to community, instructing the younger generation in the basic fundamentals of tone length, pitch, and tone shape. The Christian Harmony Singing School is an example of this type of musical expression. It was organized in 1858, and each October holds an all-day singing at the Mount Hermon Church in Dent County. As popular as the singings are the "sociables," at which fiddlers' contests are often held and singing games played (*see Folklore and Folkways*).

Very early in Missouri's history as a State, in trade centers such as St. Louis and St. Charles, and, later, Fayette, Lexington, and Liberty, there were families who had brought to their new homes the traditions of cultivated music. In 1818, A. C. van Hirtum "late from Amsterdam, Organ Factor and Professor of Music on the piano-forte," advertised classes at St. Louis, where a short time later Mme. Marie Victoire Adelaide Le Masurier de Perdreauville, formerly lady-in-waiting to Marie Antoinette, opened an academy for young ladies, offering lessons in both vocal and instrumental music. Early newspapers carried occasional notices of concerts; music became a standard subject in female schools; two individuals in the St. Louis Directory of 1821 were listed as musicians. Not until the 1830's, however, when German immigration into Missouri increased, did an interest in formal music become general. Among the German farmers, tradesmen, and artisans who settled in the State was a gifted group of German intellectuals. Notable among these were Johann Weber, former Court Councilor of Coblenz, William Robyn, and Charles Balmer, each of whom made a distinctive contribution to the development of music in Missouri.

Johann Weber arrived in St. Louis in 1834, bringing with him a rich library of the compositions, many with full orchestral scores, of Bach, Beethoven, Gluck, Handel, Haydn, Mozart, Palestrina, Pergolesi, and others. Through his enthusiasm and that of other members of his talented family, the St. Louis Sacred Music Society was organized. Meanwhile William Robyn, through his friendship with Wilson Primm, conservator of French traditions in St. Louis and an amateur musician, had become teacher of music at St. Louis University. Robyn organized and trained the St. Louis Brass Band, and later served as conductor of the St. Louis Musical Society Polyhymnia. Charles Balmer came to

St. Louis as accompanist to Madame Caradori-Allan, the celebrated singer. A more prolific composer than either Weber or Robyn, Balmer, in partnership with C. Henry Weber, opened a music store and music publishing house (1848), which became one of the largest in the West. Through this firm new compositions, many of them by Missourians, were made available to the public.

The organizations formed by these and other men between 1830 and 1840 may be properly regarded as the ancestors of the St. Louis Symphony Orchestra, though the line of succession is devious. By 1839, as a result of the awakened interest in music, the J. C. Dinnies Company of St. Louis was able to advertise for sale Italian, German, and French violins, clarinets, trombones, bassoons, guitars, triangles, bass viols, trumpets, various types of flutes, flageolets, fifes, bass and snare drums, and "pianofortes from the most celebrated manufacturers." Gradually, under the patronage of the church, the theater, and the schools, various choral societies and instrumental music groups sprang up. By 1880, however, St. Louis' musical population had centered its diffused interest in the St. Louis Choral Society, parent organization of the St. Louis Symphony Society. Second oldest in the United States, the St. Louis Symphony Orchestra has in recent years ranked among the best in the country. Its directors have included among others Alfred Ernst, Max Zach, Rudolph Ganz, and, since 1931, Vladimir Golschmann.

The history of the Kansas City Philharmonic Orchestra follows a similar pattern. Around the time of the Civil War, musical interest in Kansas City was stimulated by the work of Frederick Schattner and Philip Johns, musicians from the group of German intellectuals who played so vital a role in all Missouri's cultural history. The work of these men, however, resulted in no lasting organization. Attempts in the early 1890's to establish a symphony orchestra and a string quartet also were unsuccessful. Not until 1932, when the Co-operative Orchestra was organized, did the efforts of Kansas City music lovers achieve any lasting results. The following year the Co-operative Orchestra became the Kansas City Philharmonic, with Karl Kreuger as director.

Many other towns and cities in Missouri, such as Jefferson City and Fulton, have little symphonies—organizations whose members receive no pay. Of these the Sedalia Little Symphony, organized in 1935 and directed by Abe Rosenthal, is outstanding.

Opera and musical comedy have always been warmly received in Missouri. The appearance of Mrs. Rowe's "Grand Melodramatic Opera of *Guy Mannering*" in 1828, and the occasional presentation of such works as Auber's *Masaniello* and Weber's *Der Freischütz* created an early enthusiasm for this musical form. During the 1850's, the old Varieties Theater in St. Louis held several amazingly successful opera seasons. Arditi, whose "Kiss Waltz" was composed in St. Louis, Brignoli, the Italian tenor, and numerous other stars and companies kept alive this early enthusiasm until 1919, when the St. Louis Municipal Opera was established. Since its opening, this famous institution has had audiences aggregating more than 10,000,000 persons (*see St. Louis*). A Grand Opera Association, organized in St. Louis in April, 1939, is underwritten to present opera on a non-profit basis. The Civic Music League each year brings to St. Louis a series of well-known concert artists, dancers, and musicians.

The works of Missouri composers appeal to a wide range of musical tastes. Compositions and compilations of songs appeared as early as 1821, when Allen D. Carden's *Missouri Harmony or a Choice Collection of Psalm Tunes, Hymns and Anthems* was published in Cincinnati. A number of schottisches, marches, polkas, waltzes and galops, often with local dedications, appeared all through the 1850's. Representative of these are "The St. Louis Gray's Quickstep," the "Missouri Grand March," the "Missouri Belle Polka, inscribed to the Young Ladies of Christian College," and an ambitious suite, the "Belles of Missouri Quadrilles."

Among the first Missouri composers to win general recognition was Carl Valentine Lachmund, born in Boonville in 1857, who studied under Moszkowski and Liszt, and was the only American pupil for whom Liszt wrote a recommendation. In New York, Lachmund became a concert pianist, conductor, teacher, and composer, being best remembered perhaps for his "Japanese Overture." Other Missouri composers include Robert Goldbeck, protégé of Alexander von Humboldt; Jessie Love Smith Gaynor, known for her compositions for children; Dorothy Gaynor Blake, her daughter; and Constance Owen Faunt Le Roy Runcie, granddaughter of Robert Owen and versatile composer of songs, chamber music, and symphonic compositions.

Another group has written music inspired by literary masterpieces. Samuel Bollinger based his dramatic overture, "Pompilia and Caponsacchi," on Browning's *Ring and the Book;* Richard S. Poppen received favorable notice for his opera, *Robin Hood;* Ernest Richard Kroeger has written overtures based on "Sardanapalus," "Endymion," "Thanatopsis," "Atala," and Thomas Moore's "Lalla Rookh," and has also composed "Ten American Sketches," in which he portrays the character of the American Negro and Indian, and gives impressions of mountain and prairie life. Carl Busch, long associated with the development of music in Kansas City, is also known as a composer. John J. Kessler, born in St. Louis in 1904, probably Missouri's most distinguished living composer, has produced a symphony, three symphonic poems, chamber music, a concerto for piano and orchestra, and a quintet for piano and strings.

Many popular song writers from Missouri, among them Theron

Bennett, Ted Browne, Gus Haenchen, and Earl Haubrich, have produced national hits. Some of the early songs by these men were published in St. Louis by the Victor Kremer Music Company, the Buck and Lowney Music Company, and the John Stark Music Company.

Missouri has had few musical publications. The short-lived *Polyhymnia; A Musical Anthology for the Piano,* edited by William and Henry Robyn in 1851, was followed by the popular *Kunkel's Musical Review* (1879-1902). The only musical journal to attain genuine distinction was *The Clef,* published in Kansas City from 1913 to 1915, and edited by Laura Valworth Lull. Rupert Hughes, a native of Lancaster, Missouri, won early recognition by his essays in the *Criterion,* and his books *Musical Guide,* and *Contemporary American Composers'* (1900). An unusual but nonetheless effective contribution to the history of music was Henry Robyn's invention of a press and five-type system which made it possible for the blind to set type and print text and music in Braille.

Musical education throughout Missouri has been furthered by the Federation of Music Clubs, organized in 1918, and by the Missouri State Teachers Association. Excellent music courses are offered in the various schools and universities, with the Swinney Conservatory of Music at Central College, Fayette, and the Kansas City Conservatory of Music outstanding in the field. Religious groups at liturgical centers such as Conception Abbey, near Conception Junction, and at the Convent of O'Fallon, have won recognition for their studies of Gregorian chants.

Since 1936, the WPA Missouri Music Project, under the direction of Elmer Schwartzbeck, has further stimulated an interest in and a knowledge of music by the organization of teaching projects, bands, and orchestras in Kansas City, St. Louis, Jefferson City, and Sedalia. Project units conduct classes in schools, give demonstration programs in both rural and urban communities, and assist in organizing orchestras, bands, and choral clubs. The work of the St. Louis project is typical: during 1939 and 1940, the three St. Louis units—the Little Symphony, the Brass Sextet, and the Colored Dance Orchestra—played more than 1,500 engagements to a combined audience of approximately 1,500,000 persons.

Within the development of American music, but independent and sometimes quite oblivious of it, the American Negro has slowly evolved a mode of musical expression known as jazz, which some critics—chiefly European—have come to accept as the only distinctly American contribution to music. The origins of jazz lie deep in the experience of the Negro people, extending back into their slavery days, or possibly, as many scholars believe, to their life in Africa. Certainly the subtle and intricate rhythms suggest a racial memory, a long sustained overtone of African drums.

Early in their American experience, Negroes began to produce a folk music about their labor in the fields and on the river fronts, weaving elements of white ballads into their own unconstrained harmonies. These songs, and their religious music, the vast literature of Negro spirituals, are choral in nature, achieving their effects through a simplicity of melody and the subtle repetition of melodic phrases.

In Missouri, as elsewhere, religious groups of Negroes have sung from the earliest times such familiar spirituals as the beautiful "Were you there when they crucified my Lord?" and the plaintive "Every time I feel the spirit moving in my heart, I will pray. . . ." To express his more personal melancholy and dejection, the Negro sings "the blues." The blues are, originally, casual and spontaneous inventions. The singer merely sings a phrase stating the theme, and then repeats it while he thinks of another line. Hundreds of blues songs have been created, and as soon forgotten, throughout the South, particularly along the Mississippi. Occasionally, however, some musical listener will repeat and embellish a phrase that pleases him. Later, others will take it up. Thus the sorrow of some lone cotton picker or wharfhand becomes, eventually, part of the living body of Negro music. When W. C. Handy, composer of the famous "St. Louis Blues," published his collections of blues songs, he acknowledged that they were little more than notations of themes picked up in his wanderings along the river.

When instruments became more easily available to Negro musicians, this folk music entered a new stage, that of jazz and—recently—swing, which has been described most succinctly as "collective improvisation." Although these styles may have originated in New Orleans, and have reached their most perfected form to date in Chicago, their gradual evolution was brought about by countless anonymous musicians on their journey north along the river.

From 1895 until 1905, St. Louis was the home of a group of gifted Negro musicians, some of whose work has become part of the repertory of jazz bands everywhere. Among these were Scott Joplin, who came to St. Louis from Sedalia, wrote the "Maple Leaf Rag" and other brilliant and difficult compositions, and died in wretchedness and insanity; W. C. Handy, dean of American jazz composers, who wrote the "St. Louis Blues," "Beale Street Blues," "Aunt Hagar's Blues," and others; and Tom Turpin, who, according to E. Sims Campbell, was "swinging and playing the blues years before white America recognized them." Turpin was a pianist and a prolific composer. Incessantly engaged in the production of new works, he received constant rebuffs from publishers, who declared the bass runs, quixotic chords, and grace notes of his compositions too difficult for the average player

—finding them perhaps, as Campbell did, "as intricate as Bach." In 1896, Turpin succeeded in finding a publisher and the "Harlem Rag" was followed by the "St. Louis Rag," "The Buffalo," and others. Meanwhile, in excursion boats cruising up and down the river, in river-front saloons, in honky-tonks and bawdy-houses, unknown Negro musicians, most of them natural players with no knowledge of written music, began experiments with free orchestration, leaped from conventional arrangements to an individualized expression, and reached the extreme of decorative elaboration known as "sewing an overcoat on the button."

How many of the names prominent in swing music are associated with Missouri is difficult to say. The life stories of many of these musicians have not been told in written form, but are passed by word of mouth from player to player, from city to city; for musicians are, by virtue of their trade, nomadic.

Coleman Hawkins, tenor saxophonist from St. Joseph, Missouri, has been judged by some critics to be without a superior in instrumental technique. M. Hughes Panassie, connoisseur of swing music, finds "no more intelligent playing than Hawkins'," adding that he "would really have to be a virtuoso because the melodic line of his solos is sometimes so complicated that without an impeccable performance they would be very sorry affairs. The variations he plays are among the most complicated in the whole field of hot interpretation." The same critic has observed in the recording of Ben Moten's orchestra, late of Kansas City, "the atmosphere of an actual performance by a great swing band." "Count" Basie, born in New Jersey, received his first important notices in Kansas City, where the ingenious showman, Cab Calloway, took out his union card. Basie, a brilliant pianist, invents his propulsive solos against the beautifully integrated music of an orchestra that consistently produces distinguished improvisation. "Red" McKenzie of St. Louis, white jazz singer, has been called by some critics one of the two best white singers in the field of swing. Possessed of an unusual voice, of "beautiful somber cast," McKenzie uses it to create instrumental effects. Still playing the excursion boats in and out of St. Louis, as he has for more than 20 years, or beating fantastic rhythms out of pianos in black-and-tan cafés, is Fate Marable, who brought Louis Armstrong up the river, and was the leader of one of the first swing bands.

Jazz music, in spite of the virtuosi who employ it as their medium, still is, as Wilder Hobson has remarked, an essentially folk expression, an untutored music, spontaneous, and free of the constraints of convention. To many, especially to those whose tastes have been conditioned by the musical standards of the white man's music halls, the intricate structure of swing music, the constant invention and variation, and the new prominence in solo work of instruments that have heretofore been used only to supply contrasts, constitute sheer chaos. Others, especially the Europeans, find in swing music the vitality of new forms and fresh combinations, the challenge of a new idiom.

Art and the Crafts

ISSOURI'S first artists were the housewives, blacksmiths, potters, carpenters, and itinerant portrait and sign painters who, without formal training, succeeded in combining the "useful with the agreeable." Only recently has a maturing public judgment come to appreciate the best of this handwork as a folk expression constituting a genuine indigenous art. Since 1937, the Missouri WPA Art Project, under the direction of James MacKenzie, has employed artists to record examples of these pioneer creations.

Of all the early Missouri folk arts, perhaps none was as generally practiced nor as highly developed as the making of coverlets ("coverlids") and quilts. The coverlets were hand woven of wool, or of wool, linen, and cotton, colored blue, red, green, yellow, brown, or black with dyes made from roots and berries. Variations of a square geometrical motif were most popular, but flowers, turkeys, eagles, and peacocks were also common. The early quilts, frequently of exquisite needlework, often reveal a striking originality of color and design. Stylized appliqué patterns based upon natural forms—the tulip, ivy, grape, oak, and maple leaf, and others—vied in favor with the earlier all-white quilts embroidered in almost microscopic stitches. Other "female arts" included cross-stitch and needle-point embroideries, samplers and pictures, arrangements of wax flowers and fruits, decorations and jewelry woven of human hair, fruit and flower groups painted on velvet, and various types of ornamental beadwork.

The village blacksmith, who was often gunsmith, locksmith, and implement maker as well, made ironwork of traditional design. Hinges and locks unmistakably French remain on the older houses in Ste. Genevieve. German artisans produced many strap and pad hinges, locks and wrought-iron latches, and elaborate wrought-iron crosses and grave fences.

A pottery was established in Ste. Genevieve before 1777, and as settlement spread nearly every community boasted at least one pottery manufacturing jars, jugs, pitchers, milk pans, flower pots, urns, and even lard lamps and pig banks. Tile stoves were made at the New Florence pottery in the late 1880's.

Examples of early stone carving consist mainly of gravestones, including several at Hermann with Classic detail of cameo-like delicacy, and some at Zell of Gothic and of eighteenth-century German-baroque design.

During the Colonial period, cultured settlers brought into Missouri portraits, paintings, miniatures, and portfolios of engravings and sketches of European origin. Paintings and religious objects, salvaged from the French Revolution, or presented by benefactors such as Louis XVIII of France and the Baroness de Condite de Ghysinghem of Flanders, found their way to the Roman Catholic churches in Missouri. German Lutheran groups also brought their treasures. These importations encouraged an early appreciation of the fine arts.

Paxton's *St. Louis Directory for 1821* indicates that frontier leaders understood the importance of these collections. "It is a truly delightful sight to an American of taste," says Paxton, "to find in one of the remotest towns of the Union a church decorated with the original paintings of Rubens, Raphael, Guido, Paul Veronese, and a number of others by the first modern masters of the Italian, French, and Flemish schools. The ancient and precious gold embroideries which the St. Louis Cathedral possesses would certainly decorate any museum in the world."

In the same period, an increasing number of artists, both European and American, came west to sketch and paint the Indians and "the inconceivable grandeur" of the country. Titian Ramsay Peale (1800-85), and Samuel Seymour, an English-born Philadelphia engraver and landscape artist, were members of Long's expedition up the Missouri in 1819-20. Seymour was to "furnish sketches of landscapes . . . distinguished for their beauty and grandeur . . . miniature likenesses, or portraits of distinguished Indians and . . . groups of savages engaged in celebrating their festivals, or sitting in council." Charles Alexandre Lesueur (1778-1846), a talented French artist, visited Missouri in 1826, and sketched many villages and frontier scenes. The Swiss artist, Charles Bodmer (b. 1805), accompanied Maximilian Prince of Wied, on his tour of the West (1832-34). Rudolph Friedrich Kurz (1818-71), of Bern, Switzerland, sketched old buildings in St. Louis and Indian groups near St. Joseph in the late 1840's; and Frank Blackwell Mayer paused to sketch in St. Louis and Clark County, Missouri, in 1851.

Peter Rindisbacher, the meticulous recorder of Wisconsin Indian types, settled on a farm near the present village of Mehlville. Also a resident was Paulus Roetter (1806-94), who sketched Missouri scenes, and nautical and botanical specimens for Louis Agassiz and Dr. George Engelmann. Charles Deas (1818-67) of Philadelphia wandered to St. Louis in the early 1840's, after having sketched Indian types in the upper Mississippi and Missouri River regions, and according to his own testimony found in that city all that "a painter can desire in the patronage of friends and general sympathy and appreciation." He remained in St. Louis until his death in 1867, painting, among other subjects, *Long Jake,* the mountain hunter, *The Indian Guide, The Voyageur, The Trapper,* and an epic canvas of Clark's meeting with the Shawnees at the Council of North Bend during the Revolutionary War. In his latter years, according to Henry T. Tuckerman's *Book of the Artists,* Deas was confined to an asylum, yet "his talent even when manifest in the vagaries of a diseased mind, was often effective; one of his wild pictures, representing a black sea, over which a figure hung, suspended by a ring, while from the waves a monster was springing, was so horrible, that a sensitive artist fainted at the sight." Surrealism, it would seem, also existed on the frontier.

The interest in the frontier exhibited by both Easterners and Europeans was exploited in panoramic views of the Mississippi River. These forerunners of the motion picture, painted on long strips of canvas, were exhibited by unrolling them before the audience, usually to the accompaniment of running comment. Six panoramic views of the Mississippi are known to have been painted, five by St. Louis artists. One of the first was exhibited in Boston in 1839 by John Rowson Smith (1810-64), who had been a scene painter in a St. Louis theater as early as 1832. This panorama was destroyed by fire, but by 1844 Smith completed a new picture "four miles in length," which he successfully exhibited in America and abroad.

Most widely known of the Mississippi panoramists was John Banvard, who displayed his work in Eastern cities and in Europe in 1847 and thereafter. Probably the most talented was Henry Lewis (1819-1904), who came to St. Louis from England in 1836; he began work on a panorama of the upper Mississippi in 1848, and completed it the following spring with the aid of four assistants. "We went to see it in the same spirit that we are wont to ramble through the living forests," comments the editor of a St. Louis periodical in October, 1849. The panorama, *A Tour of the Eastern and Western Hemispheres,* painted in St. Louis about 1858 by Eduard Robyn, brother of Henry and William Robyn (*see Music*), reflects the artist's training as a lithographer. The canvas was discovered by the Missouri Writers' Project and is now in the Missouri Historical Society in St. Louis.

The earliest portrait painters to visit St. Louis were itinerant French artists who came up from New Orleans during the summer months. The first professional portraitist known to have resided in Missouri was Francois M. Guyol, who advertised in the *Missouri Gazette,* March 5, 1812, that he "executes *Portraits* in oil colours, also in *Miniature* and assures an exact resemblance. He paints *Profiles* (à la quarrelle) [sic] for five dollars, including the frame." Evidently, the artist did not depend entirely upon his art, for the advertisement concludes: "Lessons given in Architecture, Planimetry, plane and spheric Trigonometry, Algebra, with Drawing, and Fortification so as to prepare them for an entrance into the engineer corp of the United States Army."

In 1819, an artist who exhibited in St. Louis a traveling "Museum of Wax Figures and large Paintings" with patriotic subjects advertised "Profiles correctly taken and framed." The following year, the St. Louis *Missouri Gazette* proudly announced the completion of M. Basterot's painting of "the vow of Ste. Genevieve consecrated by St. Germain, bishop of Auxerre and St. Loup, bishop of Tours," for the church of Ste. Genevieve. "It is," the editor notes, "the first original historical picture the Missouri region can boast of. . . ."

Chester Harding came to Missouri in 1819 to paint a portrait of the aged Daniel Boone. An engraving was made of this portrait by James Otto Lewis, and about two hundred copies were sold locally. The portrait itself was later cut down, only the head being preserved; so that this engraving, of which a copy, perhaps unique, is in the Missouri Historical Society collection, is now the sole key to the original painting. Lewis was commissioned by the Indian Department from 1823 to 1834 to make portraits of Western Indians, an early instance of Federal patronage of the arts.

Although the work of these early artists possessed a sort of sporadic relation to Western life, George Caleb Bingham (1811-79) was the first to attempt a serious interpretation of the region. Brought to Missouri at the age of eight, Bingham was self-taught during the first period of his career. In 1834, he met Major James S. Rollins, Columbia attorney, who became his life-long patron and sympathetic friend. The following year he opened a studio in St. Louis. Bingham's genre paintings have been compared with the work of European painters of the seventeenth century, and it is possible that the artist saw and studied the work of foreign masters in St. Louis collections. St. Louis University owned at that time various Spanish paintings of the seventeenth century, as well as *The Cobbler* and *The Knife-Grinder*, attributed to Teniers.

From 1837 to 1856, Bingham divided his time between Missouri and the East, where he studied at the Pennsylvania Academy of Fine Arts in Philadelphia, and painted portraits in Washington. His most significant work of this period is a series of genre paintings of Missouri subjects which began to appear about 1845. In the early 1850's, he painted a group depicting typical phases of a Missouri political campaign. Keenly observant, his social appraisals were always mellowed by a rich sense of humor.

Missouri was not slow to recognize Bingham's talents. Nearly every Missouri family of consequence "sat to Mr. Bingham." The Mercantile Library of St. Louis commissioned important works. In

1851, the editor of the *Western Journal* (St. Louis) commented enthusiastically: "BINGHAM—well known in the East as the Missouri Artist and being 'par excellence' the American Artist, has come to spend the winter in St. Louis. BINGHAM'S style is one which is now rapidly forming a School of pure American Art. He has no occasion to copy the old masters. He himself is a master—one of the new masters." The *Journal* also published woodcuts of Bingham's paintings by the St. Louis engraver, G. A. Bauer.

Other artists shared with Bingham the growing appreciation for the arts. Among these were Manuel Joachim De Franca (d. 1865), of Portugal, a fashionable artist in St. Louis; Miss Sara M. Peale (1800-85), daughter of the artist, James Peale, who painted, among others, Thomas H. Benton and Lewis F. Linn; and William Coggswell, who came to St. Louis about 1858, and Matthew Hastings (1834-1919), primarily portrait artists, although Hastings is chiefly remembered for his caricatures and his pictures of frontier scenes. George Fall painted portraits in Fayette for a short time during 1846, and in 1869, Charles P. Stewart made a prosperous visit to Columbia.

The general interest in Western subjects was reflected in the demand for inexpensive lithographed town views and Missouri scenes, and in various types of commercial art used by book and music publishing firms. In 1840, the St. Louis *Republican* published a series of colored views of St. Louis, "painted from nature and drawn on stone by J. C. Wild." Work by other artists, nearly all of them German, followed. Perhaps the most talented Missouri lithographer of this period was Eduard Robyn. His work, published by various St. Louis firms, includes colored views of Washington and Hermann.

Harriet Hosmer (1830-1908), Massachusetts sculptress, came to St. Louis in the fall of 1850 to study anatomy at Dr. McDowell's Medical School. Later, she executed a commission for the Mercantile Library Association, her *Beatrice Cenci*. Her statue of Thomas Hart Benton was unveiled in Lafayette Park, St. Louis, in 1868. During this period, James Wilson MacDonald (1824-1908) was studying in St. Louis under Alfred Waugh, completing in 1854 his first work in marble, a bust of Thomas Hart Benton.

Other artists who worked in Missouri at this time are Alban Jasper Conant (1821-1915), whose work has a severe, almost photographic quality; Joseph R. Meeker (1827-69), one of the first to paint the southeastern Missouri bluffs along the Osage and Gasconade Rivers, and the lead mining region of southwestern Missouri; and Thomas Satterwhite Noble (d. 1907), who specialized in character studies, particularly of Negroes. Noble's *The Last Sale of Slaves—St. Louis Courthouse,* a favorite exhibition piece for many years, is now owned by the Missouri Historical Society.

In 1841—two years after its invention was announced in Paris—the daguerreotype was in use in Missouri. That year Messrs. Moore & Ward advertised in St. Louis that they were "prepared to take daguerreotype likenesses in a superior style, which, being the reflected forms of the subjects themselves, far surpass in fidelity of the resemblance, anything which can be accomplished by the eye and the hand of the artist." John H. Fitzgibbon, who opened his St. Louis studio in 1841, made regular trips West to photograph Indians and frontier scenes. In 1877, he established the *St. Louis Photographer and Illustrated Monthly Journal,* which became "the exponent of photographic art for the great valley." In time, the effects of photography were felt, and the lucrative field of portrait painting was virtually destroyed.

Next to Bingham, the most important Missouri artist in the middle years of the nineteenth century was Carl Ferdinand Wimar (1828-62). Wimar came to Missouri in 1843, and studied under Leon Pomarede, a panoramist for whom he worked. An unexpected legacy enabled him to study in Düsseldorf from 1852 to 1856 under Emanuel Leutze, after which he returned to Missouri. Wimar was one of the first artists in America to recognize the value of photography as an aid to painting. In 1858, he went on the first of a series of trips to the Far West, to make photographs and sketches of Indians. His last work was the murals in the dome of the old St. Louis Courthouse, in which he combined classical allegories with historical events.

Missouri was now no longer an isolated region. The growth of the railroads and the great prosperity of the 1850's made extensive contact with the East and with Europe possible. Missouri artists went abroad to study, and brought back copies of the old masters and original canvases. Painters of the Western scene were influenced by the schools of Düsseldorf, Weimar, Munich, and Paris. The closer contact with foreign cultures encouraged a wide interest in the arts. In 1846, the St. Louis Mercantile Library Association began assembling a permanent art exhibit. Commissions were given to well-known Missouri artists and a representative collection was gradually acquired.

Beginning in 1857, loan exhibitions of art were an annual attraction of the St. Louis Agricultural and Mechanical Association Fair. In the same year, Boonville dedicated Thespian Hall, with one room as an art gallery. In 1859, a committee headed by Manuel J. De Franca assembled a notable collection for the St. Louis Fair.

A museum of art was first advocated in St. Louis in 1851. In 1860, largely through the efforts of A. J. Conant, the Western Academy of Art was established, with Henry T. Blow as president, and Ferdinand T. L. Boyle, a New York artist, as director. The Civil War disrupted this society, however, and scattered its collection.

Following the Civil War, the taste of the art world seems to have undergone a change; the catalogue for the art exhibit at the St. Louis Agricultural and Mechanical Association Fair for 1879 apologizes for the fact that "most of the contributions are the products of native art," but assures the public that this art "has been highly spoken of by English and French critics"—the collection included such eminent American painters as W. M. Chase, P. P. Ryder, George Inness, and the best Missouri artists. The exhibit of 1894 was devoted largely to French impressionists. By 1899, however, public interest had swung back to native art. According to the catalogue for that year, the exhibit consisted "principally of the work of American artists. It is a gratifying fact that, as the years go by, it is less and less necessary to go abroad for art works worthy of satisfying the demands of critical and discriminating amateurs." Five years later, the handbook of the Artists' Guild exhibit at the World's Fair, St. Louis, declared: "There is no doubt American art . . . is gradually evolving in different localities distinct characteristics." Regional art was on its way.

The prophet of the new order was Halsey Cooley Ives (1847-1911), a designer and decorator who came to St. Louis as an instructor in the Polytechnic School in 1874, and almost immediately became the leader of local art activities. In 1875, he instituted a free evening drawing class at Washington University. This expanded rapidly, and paintings and art objects were collected. In 1879, the university incorporated the St. Louis School and Museum of Fine Arts as a separate department, with Ives as director. One of the first such schools in the Middle West, it immediately became a focal point for the art enthusiasts of the region. As teacher there, Ives moulded the development of many Missouri artists. Shortly, it was obvious that the enlarged school must have more adequate quarters. Wayman Crow, long a patron of the arts and a friend of Ives, consequently erected a building on the corner of Nineteenth and Locust Streets in 1881 which he deeded to the University as a memorial to his son, Wayman Crow, Jr., who had died in 1878.

In the meantime, Ives and his friends were instrumental in establishing a number of art groups, associations, and exhibits. The Art Society, founded in 1872, was followed in five years by the St. Louis Sketch Club, organized by the artist J. R. Meeker. In 1886, a group of Sketch Club members organized the St. Louis Artists' Guild. Professional as well as social in purpose, the guild has proved a meeting ground for artist and layman, and a vital force in St. Louis.

In 1877, Hercules L. Dousman of St. Louis built a wing onto his residence to house his art collection. This gallery was open to the public on certain days, but did not fill the need for a city museum. A building was erected, however, for the St. Louis World's Fair of 1904, which assembled an excellent exhibit of paintings from 26 nations, one of the most notable collections shown in the Midwest up to that time.

In 1907, St. Louis voted to support by public tax a permanent museum in this building "to aid in developing a national artistic conscience—the consciousness of national motive or inspiration in art . . ." (*see St. Louis*).

The integration of art interests in Kansas City followed much the same pattern as that in St. Louis. With the close of the Civil War, and the development of Kansas City as a major shipping center, came a desire for the amenities as well as the necessities of life. In 1870, George Bingham moved to Kansas City. He had studied at Düsseldorf between 1856 and 1859, and after his return had become involved in Civil War questions. In the years that followed, he held various political jobs until 1877, when he was appointed professor of art at the University of Missouri. During this time, Bingham painted numerous portraits, but many of these lack the vigor of his earlier period. Occasionally, he painted landscapes; *Order No. 11,* a melodramatic portrayal of General Thomas Ewing's Civil War order to evacuate the Missouri counties along the Kansas border, also belongs to this period. The popularity of an engraving of this painting did much to preserve his memory. In Kansas City, Bingham divided his time between art and politics, until his death in 1879. He is buried in old Union Cemetery.

Other artists made Kansas City their home for varying periods—Frederic Remington, John Mulvaney, George Colby, and others. A sketch club of artists and laymen was organized about 1885. This group organized the Kansas City Art Association and School of Design, opened in January, 1888, with Lawrence S. Brumidi of the National Academy of Rome as director. Drawing was taught in Kansas City public schools before 1870, and a number of early clubs and groups brought training in arts and crafts to children and amateurs. In 1906, the Fine Arts Institute was organized, and has since increased its attendance and its activities.

William Rockhill Nelson, owner and editor of the Kansas City *Star,* became champion of the movement to secure a museum for the city. With a collection of copies of old masters purchased in Europe, he opened The Western Gallery of Art on West Ninth Street in 1897. The collection was later transferred to the Board of Education and increased from time to time by further donations from Nelson. Other groups brought contemporary paintings to Kansas City. Efforts to vote a bond issue for a museum were, however, defeated. Upon his death Nelson provided for the construction and endowment of the present William Rockhill Nelson Gallery of Art. Additional funds from the estate of Mrs. Mary McAfee Atkins were utilized for the Atkins Museum of Fine Arts wing (*see Kansas City*).

Recently, smaller communities have also developed art centers. St. Joseph organized an Art League in 1914, and Joplin in 1921, to sponsor lectures and exhibitions; Sedalia has an art gallery.in the public library. The State Fair at Sedalia, like many county fairs, has offered annual awards for the best portraits, oil paintings, and woodcarvings presented.

No artist has been able to support himself in Missouri through painting alone, and many have inevitably been drawn to larger cities. Among these was Paul Cornoyer (1864-1923), who studied in Paris and gained recognition in the East, but who returned to St. Louis to teach, and painted many of his best pictures there. James Carroll Beckwith (1852-1917), born in Hannibal, and Leopold Seyffert (b. 1887), of California, Missouri, became prominent New York portrait painters. Oscar E. Berninghaus, born in St. Louis in 1874, drifted to New Mexico about 1900, to become one of the founders of the Taos art colony. He has maintained contact with St. Louis through his annual designs for the Veiled Prophet's parade, and various commissions. Richard E. Miller (b. 1877), chiefly known for his portraits, studied in the St. Louis School of Fine Arts and worked for a St. Louis newspaper before going to Paris.

Several well-known cartoonists and illustrators have done their work in Missouri. The caricatures which Joseph Keppler (1838-94) drew for *Puck* revealed a sense of satire unrepressed by the primness of nineteenth-century America, and introduced a new type of humor. Two years after his arrival in 1867, Keppler, a Viennese, established the first of his humorous publications, the St. Louis *Die Vehme,* which failed after a year and was succeeded by *Puck.* When this also failed in 1872, Keppler moved to New York, where he re-established *Puck* in 1879. The magazine had an exuberance and a flavor that made it an immediate success. Its jibes were chiefly directed against Tammany and the Republicans, but at no time was it purely partisan. All forms of graft, extravagance, and injustice were ridiculed in its pages. Keppler's spiritual successor, Daniel Robert Fitzpatrick (b. 1891), a native of Wisconsin, has contributed biting cartoons to the St. Louis *Post-Dispatch* since 1913. George McManus, born in St. Louis in 1894, drew his first comics for the St. Louis *Republic,* then went to New York, where he originated the bellicose "Maggie" and her long-suffering husband, "Jiggs."

Missouri has produced several well-known illustrators. Charles M. Russell (1864-1926), who as a youth left St. Louis to become a Montana cowhand, achieved fame in the 1880's as a portrayer of life in the Old West. McClelland Barclay (b. 1891) and Hugh Ferriss (b. 1889) began as illustrators in St. Louis, but moved to New York early in their careers.

Missouri sculptors who have attained prominence are Howard Kretschmar, Robert Bringhurst, Victor Berlendis, and George J. Zölnay. John Rogers (1829-1904) first began modeling his familiar, homely groups while working as a mechanic in Hannibal. Frederick Cleveland Hibbard, born in Canton in 1881, studied at the Chicago Art Institute and later moved to New York. His group at Hannibal, *Tom Sawyer and Huck Finn,* and his *Madonna of the Trail* are widely known. Walker Hancock, born in St. Louis in 1901, studied in St. Louis and later in Rome, and is now instructor in sculpture at the Pennsylvania Academy of Fine Arts; he is represented in St. Louis by his *Zuni Bird Fountain* in Forest Park, and other works.

In the twentieth century the rapid growth of cities, agricultural unrest, and finally the World War and its febrile aftermath laid new problems before the world. American artists have grappled with all the "isms" of European art, but have tended to return to the native scene for subject matter. The deepening depression of the 1930's intensified interest in the local life; Missouri wheat fields and Missouri people appeared in the many new murals decorating public buildings. Recognizing themselves and their neighbors in these canvases, Missourians have felt closer to their artists than ever before. Although many artists have contributed to this movement, it has been dominated in Missouri by Thomas Hart Benton, grandnephew of Senator Thomas Hart Benton and son of a member of Congress, who was born at Neosho, a hill town on the fringe of the Ozarks, in 1889. After a period at military school, Benton worked on a Joplin paper as cartoonist, then studied at the Chicago Art Institute. He joined the general migration to Paris, but after four years returned to New York, exhausted and disillusioned. He served as a draughtsman in the army, but, still seeking his proper style, continued to examine his own background, and the qualities of the old order. In 1931, he was selected to interpret "contemporary America" on the walls of the New School for Social Research in New York, a commission that made him famous. Two years later, he painted the Indiana mural at the Chicago World's Fair. Then, commissioned to execute murals for the Missouri State Capitol, Benton dipped boldly into the historic stuff of Missouri, and crowded his design with Frankie and Johnny, Huck Finn and Nigger Jim, the James Boys, a political rally, a country kitchen—with ugliness and simplicity, dignity and corruption. When the mural was completed, Benton was charged with "deliberate insult and painting a lie." The controversy that followed provoked much discussion and absurdity, and proved highly stimulating to Missouri's art.

Equally vigorous in his depiction of the Midwest is Joe Jones, who once summarized his autobiography as "Born St. Louis 1909. Self-taught." Son of a house painter, he finished Benton Grade School in St. Louis at 14, ran off to California, and returned to paint houses with his father until the depression put the family on relief. Jones then began painting pictures. Soon he interested members of the St. Louis

Artists' Guild in his work, and opened an art class for the unemployed. In 1935, his first one-man show was held in New York, where he has since achieved a growing reputation.

Other artists living in Missouri at the present time have achieved fame in varying degree. The number is, in fact, so great that no proper evaluation of their work is possible here. *Who's Who in American Art* has 148 listings for Missouri. A summer art colony has sprung up in Ste. Genevieve, attracting several noteworthy artists. Clubs, schools, and museums, and the Missouri WPA Art Project have been working incessantly to bring art closer to the daily life of Missourians.

Architecture

IN THE medley of Missouri's architectural heritage may be seen a visible expression of the national groups which have formed her history. It is the sum of these styles rather than a single "Missourian" type that is the chief architectural interest of the region. Here is the "palisadoed" house of the early French, the half-timbered German house, the American log cabin in all its variety, and the formal Classic-Revival house.

THE CREOLE BUILDER

The first French buildings in Missouri of definite record were those constructed (1723-28) at Fort D'Orleans on the Missouri River in present Carroll County. The fort group contained officers' quarters, a chapel, a store, a powder magazine, a forge, an icehouse, and the houses of the chaplain, the tool maker, and the commandant—the last of upright logs set in the ground, the roof thatched with prairie grass. In the years before the chimney was added, De Bourgmond, the Commandant, was forced to build his fires "in the center of the house as the Indians do," the smoke finding its way through a hole in the roof. Hungry dogs made necessary a fenced chicken yard, and the kitchen garden as well as a "big" and a "little" garden of formal French plan were similarly protected.

Ste. Genevieve, which has preserved more examples of French Creole architecture than any other city in the Mississippi Valley with the exception of New Orleans, was described as follows in Henry M. Brackenridge's *Views of Louisiana* (1814): "Although there is something like regularity of streets, and the houses are built in front of them, they do not adjoin, while the gardens, orchards, and stables, occupy a considerable extent of ground. Each house with its appurtenances, has the appearance of one of our farmyards . . . These tenements are generally enclosed with cedar pickets, placed in the manner of stockades, and sometimes with stone walls."

The French house as built in the eighteenth century villages along the Mississippi and Missouri presents an interesting combination of Canadian and West Indian French architectural styles. In form, the Missouri Creole house is Canadian, and, more remotely, Norman in outline. The distinctive wide porch or gallery (*galerie,* or "garli" as one hears today) is West Indian in origin, and was undoubtedly added as a compromise with the Missouri summer. The proportions vary from the simple house of 12 by 13 feet to the St. Louis Laclede-Chouteau mansion, 95 by 55 feet. All had the grace and the air of plausibility which distinguished an architectural type evolved spontaneously in response to actual needs.

According to Charles E. Peterson in *A Guide to Ste. Genevieve* (1940), at least three types of construction were used by French builders in Missouri:

(1) The *maison de poteaux en terre* (house of posts in the ground) was built of timbers set upright and fastened together only at the top. Above ground, the posts were squared, and when built of rot-resisting cedar made a sound structure. This style may have derived from early Spanish settlements on the Gulf Coast; it is also similar to certain Indian constructions. It is, apparently, unknown in France and Canada. Examples of this type, once the most common of all, can be seen in Ste. Genevieve, and perhaps elsewhere in Missouri. A related form was the *maison de pieux* (stakes) *en terre,* a cruder type in which the posts were left round. In Ste. Genevieve it was chiefly used for outbuildings.

(2) In the *maison de poteaux sur solle* (house of posts on a sill), the massive squared posts are set on a sill supported by a stone foundation, or occasionally, as farther south, on wood blocks, to remove the frame from the dampness of the ground. This type required more skill to build, but was generally more durable.

Spaces between the posts were filled with clay and grass (*bouzillées*), as in Louisiana, or with stone and mortar (*pierrottées*), as in Normandy. Almost always, the walls have a marked inward slope. Exterior walls were sometimes plastered, sometimes left bare, sometimes *encanellé* (covered with split saplings set obliquely), as on houses at Old Mines, and then whitewashed. The *galerie,* on one or on all four sides of the building, varied in width from four to eight feet.

(3) The *maison de pierre* (stone house), introduced from Canada and France at an early date, was not popular in Ste. Genevieve, but was often used in St. Louis. Laclede's stone warehouse, the first building in the village of St. Louis, was begun in 1764. The cellar was dug with corn hoes by Indian squaws, who used the wooden trenchers in which they prepared their food for carrying away the earth.

Thatching was the first roof covering, and to support the steep hip roofs, heavy hewn timbers forming Norman trusses were used. Thatching proving impractical, however, in the hot, dry summers, the North American shingle (*bardeau*) was introduced, permitting wider, less sharply pitched roofs. Wooden crosses were often added to ridges and gates.

Floor plans were of at least two general types—the very old arrangement of a row of rooms end on end, and the more compact scheme two rooms deep. In the larger houses, the central hall or living room was the "family room" from which the other rooms opened. The appearance of such a *salle* in one of the larger St. Louis houses is described by Theophile Papin in the *Annals of St. Louis:* "There were no carpets on the deal floor, but instead there was a polish of wax so hard wrought and lustrous that . . . the flames of the yawning chimney piece at the farther end, and the dotting lights of the bracketed wall sconces, shone fitfully on the vast platform as if from a monster mirror. Nor were the walls papered, but their embellishments were even more effective . . . with . . . robes of young buffaloes, singularly enormous mooseheads, bear, otter, and beaver skins, and here and there in contrast with several valuable groups of Indian war implements, a bird's nest hung cunningly, with its perching bird, in the wall space."

The kitchen, although often in the basement of the larger houses, was not always part of the main building. Often, it occupied an *appentis,* or lean-to, built as an addition to the rear or to one side of the house. Occasionally a section of the *galerie* was enclosed, making a room which is called today a *bas-cote.* The interesting stone kitchen of the Bolduc house in Ste. Genevieve is of this kind. Sometimes the kitchen was a separate building—the "summer kitchen" of the Americans—service to the dining room being maintained by the younger Negro servants.

With the exception of a few doors, the woodwork found in the Creole houses is similar to that of contemporaneous American houses, being fashioned probably by the same craftsmen. Glass was used early; the Guibourd house in Ste. Genevieve still has two pairs of casement windows similar to those found in Canada and Louisiana. Hardware and nails for Creole houses were imported at an early date, and three wrought-iron door latches found in Ste. Genevieve show a close affinity to those of Quebec. The interior walls were often plastered and whitewashed, and in more luxurious homes were sometimes frescoed or painted in panels, as in the Laclede-Chouteau house; but the ceilings were left open to show the carefully shaped beams (*soliveaux*), with their beaded moulding, and the attic flooring. Shrines and tall wooden crosses on inscribed stone pedestals added to the European appearance of the early settlements.

The immigration which began about the time of the American Revolution, and reached its full tide after the War of 1812, destroyed most of the Creole architectural traditions. Charles Dickens, visiting St. Louis in 1842, found that "In the old French portions of the town the thoroughfares are narrow and crooked, and some of the houses are quaint and picturesque, being built of wood, with tumble-down galleries . . . and an abundance of crazy old tenements with blinking casements, such as may be seen in Flanders. Some of these ancient habitations, with high garret gable windows perking into the roofs, have a kind of French shrug about them; and being lopsided with age, appear to hold their heads askew, as if they were grimacing in astonishment at the American improvements . . ." But seven years after Dickens' visit, much of the French section was destroyed by fire, and two generations ago, the last house of the French type in St. Louis was pulled down.

THE LOG CABIN

Like many of the Creoles, the first American settlers in Missouri used logs or hewn timbers, but they laid their logs horizontally to form the walls. This form of construction, common for centuries in North European countries, was introduced into North America by the Swedes and Finns who settled on Delaware Bay in 1638 and by the Germans who first came to Pennsylvania about 1683. Two major types were widespread in eighteenth century Missouri: the log cabin, of unhewn logs with V-shaped corner notchings and the ends of the logs projecting, said to be the Swedish type; and the hewn-log house, with squared timbers and neatly mortised, smooth-cut corners credited to the Germans. With Missouri's tide of German immigration, the hewn-log house had a fresh introduction into the State.

The log cabin, since it could be built with less labor, was commonly found on the first line of frontier settlements. Few boasted windows, and many were left with unchinked walls, whose generous cracks admitted both light and air, and, where no chimney was built, provided an outlet for smoke. The flexibility of the log cabin is suggested in the story of William Brown of Montgomery County: he built his cabin under the high bluffs along the Missouri, so that he could cut his firewood on the bluff and roll it down to his front door; when the wood gave out, rather than haul some, he moved his house to the foot of the next wooded bluff. Near Boonville, in 1819, John Mason Peck, Baptist missionary, ". . . found a cabin, about twelve feet square, made of rough black jack poles, as any stout man could lift, with a sort of wooden and dirt chimney. Very little 'chinking and daubing' interfered with the passage of the wintry winds between the logs . . . the floor was the earth, and filthy in the extreme; and the lodging-place of the inmates were a species of scaffolds around the walls, and elevated on forks."

In contrast were the hewn-log houses erected by many frontier settlers as soon as circumstances permitted. Often, the ingenious builder had no other tools than a broadaxe, a frow, and, sometimes, an auger, drawing-knife, and cross-cut saw. The permanence of these "roomy, tight and comfortable" structures is indicated by the large number that have survived throughout Missouri. In some portions of the State, log houses and cabins are still being built.

The most distinctive feature of the hewn-log house is the carefully fitted corners. Although individual builders developed many variations, "saddle," "dovetailed," and "square" cornerings are the most frequently seen in Missouri houses. Of the three, the dovetailed joint was the most difficult to produce, but, like the saddle joint, it was permanent, being "self-locking." The square corner, or "flat end," as it was sometimes called, and its variant, the "halved" cornering, were popular, but required the use of spikes to hold the timbers in place.

"Raising" a hewn-log house was a neighborhood event. Often, the owner himself felled the trees and squared the timbers, but at times the house was entirely the product of neighborhood co-operation. If the dwelling was small, it was "run up" in a day, thus permitting a dance to "warm the house" the same evening. Occasionally, there was trouble: at one house-raising in St. Charles County the size of the crowd caused the floor to break, and the dancers fell into the cellar.

Larger houses required two or three days' labor. The work was carefully divided, so that the various materials were ready as needed. One group, the choppers, felled the trees and cut them to proper lengths. A man with a team hauled the logs to the site of the house, where they were squared. Four duly elected "corner-men" notched and fitted them. When the timbers were completed, the walls were raised. The average single-room house required from 30 to 40 logs for the walls.

Carefully selected, straight-grained trees (usually walnut or oak) were felled and split for clapboards. These clapboards were about four feet long and from five to eight or more inches wide, with one side generally thicker than the other. About 400 were needed to cover the roof of a house 16 by 18 feet. Puncheons for the floor were split from trees about 18 inches in diameter, in lengths about half that of the surface they were intended to cover. The flat, exposed surfaces were smoothed with a broadaxe, and well pinned down with wooden pins on wooden poles or "sleepers," so that they would not "rock, nor shake, nor rattle." Often, however, they were omitted, at least temporarily, well-packed earth serving as a floor.

A doorway about three feet wide and sometimes no more than five feet high was cut in one side and framed with three-inch timber. The door itself was of puncheon or, preferably, of walnut or oak planks. A similar, but wider, opening was made for the chimney. The earliest chimneys were of "wattle and daub," interwoven sticks and withes covered with clay. The face and back of the fireplace were covered with flat rocks, well plastered with mud, and the interior of the chimney carefully "muddied" to the top "to secure the house against the fier." However well "secured," this type of chimney was a fire-trap, and was replaced as soon as possible by one of stone or brick. Openings for windows were covered with glass or, if none was obtainable, with greased cloth or paper. Shutters made either of puncheon, sawn plank, or clapboards were common.

When the walls were the height of a man, the builders "drew them in" with smaller logs to make the "pitch of the roof." Clapboards, each row slightly overlapping the one below, were laid over these logs, and held in place by spiked-down weight poles. A variant of this rather clumsy form of roofing was a frame or ribbing of poles, called "rafts" if unsplit, rafters if hewn.

The finished house was made weather tight by stuffing the spaces between the logs or timbers with "chinking" (or "chunking") of stones, or of oblong pieces of split heart-wood set in slanting rows and "muddied," or daubed both inside and out with loam or clay mixed with straw, grass, and lime, to form an insulation. Ornamental features sometimes included small panes of glass set in the door to give additional light, and wooden locks, latches for the doors and shutters, and capacious mantel shelves.

Essentially, the log cabins and hewn-log houses were single room dwellings. Additional rooms were added, however, forming either a two-story structure or a row of rooms. In Missouri, the Southern double log house of two rooms, separated by an open passageway and covered by a common roof, was popular. The open passage, or "dogtrot," usually without a floor, served as a sitting and dining room in warm weather, and as a dancing place. It contained the ladder or steep box stairway leading to the loft, which was often the sleeping room of the children in summer, as well as the general storeroom. In the double house, one of the enclosed rooms commonly referred to as "the house" or "the big house," was the center of family life; the other was usually reserved for guests. Porches or galleries, front and back on the better houses, formed as distinctive a feature as those on the houses of the Creoles.

Various outbuildings supplemented the frontier house. Among these were the log barn, the corn crib for grain storage, and the spring house, used for refrigeration. Many Southern settlers in Missouri had a summer-kitchen, a capacious smokehouse, and slave cabins. These out-buildings were of horizontal log construction, and, with the exception of the corncrib and sometimes the barn, were generally of hewn logs, chinked and daubed like the main house. Surrounding the house, the barn lot, and the cleared "patches," was a "stake-and-rider" or "worm fence" of split railings.

GERMAN ARCHITECTURE

Although German families from North Carolina and Pennsylvania settled in Missouri during the eighteenth century, the majority came when the State was no longer a frontier but a region of settled communities. They brought with them a medieval architectural tradition, which they modified to suit the conditions of their new country. Thus in every German settlement of Missouri are found half-timbered houses, whose walls contain a skeleton of carefully squared and fitted timbers which served as a decorative contrast to the whitewashed plaster filling. Various types of wall filling were used. In the Muench house (about 1835), in Warren County, the spaces were covered with a woven basketwork of split hickory strips between horizonal staves, filled in with a mixture of clay and grass which became as hard as mortar. Where lime was available, the spaces were filled with a mixture of lime, gravel, and sand, and surfaced with a coating of fine plaster. The weather-boarding which now makes many of these houses hard to recognize was added to provide additional insulation.

Often the front doors are "Dutch," built in upper and lower sections in true Palatinate style. Sometimes, the interior doors have the American six-panel design, but more generally they have the German diamond paneling, or some of its variants. Though German settlers may have used a thatching of straw for their first roof coverings, shingles soon became popular. At Altenburg, and perhaps at Loose Creek and elsewhere, the local brickmakers made roofing tiles of the German type in soft shades of red. Some of the roofs show a decided overhang.

Related to the half-timbered house, and closely resembling certain types of American frame house, are the buildings of combined brick and half-timber construction, or of a framing with weatherboarded brick nogging. In the old tannery at Bethel (about 1850), the timbers are carefully hewn, and the principal upright supports are set into the walls of the lower floor, although they do not extend to the foundation. The brickwork of the second floor was originally plastered and may have been weatherboarded.

Early German settlers along the Missouri and Mississippi Rivers frequently built their homes of the excellent limestone abundant there, usually of a soft buff color. Architecturally, these houses show either a medieval or a Renaissance influence. The medieval tradition is evidenced in steeply pitched roofs, ponderous walls, and the use of single heavy lintel stones above doors and windows. The Renaissance influence appears in houses with slightly rounded archways, less steeply pitched roofs, and round-topped dormer windows. The windows in both types are characteristically small and low set, leaving a wide band of wall surface between their tops and the cornice line. Usually, these houses are one-and-a-half or two stories high, and have central halls.

In the Ruskaup house, near Drake, a large "family room" occupies the left half of the house. The right half is divided into sleeping rooms, with ceilings of rough-hewn, exposed beams, and with built-in cupboards and shelves. Other houses exhibit beamed ceilings carefully dressed with beaded mouldings, similar to those used in Creole and American houses in an earlier period. In some, the ceiling is boarded, and decorated with an elaborately painted "hex" mark—sometimes ornamented with flowers and German words—which was supposed to ward off witchcraft and evil spirits. It was probably once common throughout the State, but few examples have survived. Low, heavily paneled doors are set deeply in the thick stone partition walls, some of which are of whitewashed, uneven clay plaster. In Perry and St. Charles Counties, the stone houses are seldom of more than a story-and-a-half, and generally have a series of rooms rather than a central hall arrangement. To many of these, galleries have been added in the Creole manner. Sometimes, the basement is a full story high, so that the front door is at the top of a long flight of wooden steps.

Around Hermann, where brewing and wine making were important industries, many of the houses are built over vaulted cellars, whose thick walls and heavy, simple arches have a medieval character. Similar to these cellars are the ruins of the old breweries sometimes found in the hillsides, with their great arched wall openings.

Stone sheds, smoke-houses, barns, and similar outbuildings, and sometimes stone fences surrounded the early stone dwellings. Frequently, stone was used also for the huge, barn-like mills of that time.

Most impressive of the stone buildings are the many churches, among the earliest of which is the charming St. Joseph's Catholic Church at Zell, Ste. Genevieve County, which was begun in 1848 by Father Angelo Hypolite Gandolfo. The original barrel vaulting has been covered by a flat ceiling and a square stone tower has been added to the front, but the rest is unchanged in its gaunt bulk. Father F. X. Weiss, a native of Alsace, added the stone parish house and perhaps the convent school and stone wall surrounding the church yard in the early 1850's. The near-by stone churches of Baden and of Bloomsdale date from a slightly later period. At Altenburg are the original stone church dating from 1845, and the more interesting Trinity Lutheran Church, with its prim side galleries and simple pulpit and altar, built in 1867. The traditional German designs have also been preserved in the later stone churches of Ozora, Taos, and Starkenburg. In contrast with the medieval-style stone churches are the red-brick, Gothic-Revival structures built mostly between 1860 and 1900, and often locally designed.

German brick houses in Missouri follow contemporary German designs rather than the Renaissance form of the earlier stone and half-timber houses, with their pilasters, ornate windows and doors, balanced façades, quoins, and elaborate cornices. From Germany came the modified mansard roof and the gambrel with the lower slope often bell-shaped, which characterized some of the frame and brick houses of the later German settlers in Hermann, Washington, parts of St. Louis and St. Charles. Particularly in Hermann and Washington, the houses are built directly on the street, affording additional garden space in the rear. Occasionally, the gable end of the house fronts the street, with the entrance deeply set in a thick brick wall. Double, heavily paneled doors with wrought-iron latches, occasional ornamental lintels of classic design in stone, brick, or wood, and fan-shaped lights in the gable end are identifying ornamental features. The simple early cornices were soon superseded by elaborate brickwork, evidently individually designed by the builders.

Between 1855 and 1880, Germans of St. Charles County constructed and perhaps originated, a distinctive type of one-and-a-half story brick house with a long, sweeping roof which ended abruptly over a generous front gallery, somewhat in the style of the early Creole houses. Found in no other portion of the State, this type of house is a practical and attractive adaptation to the Missouri climate, and represents one of Missouri's few claims to architectural originality. Although sometimes painted gray, the walls are more often left the natural, soft red of the brick, thus forming a pleasing contrast for the universal white trim, green shutters, and weathered shingle roofs.

Some mention must be made, too, of the generous barns, whose vigorous, clean-cut designs often afford more interest than the houses to which they belong. Like those in Pennsylvania, these barns show an architectural descent from the barns of Upper Bavaria, the Black Forest, and Switzerland, except that they are seldom attached to the house.

Perhaps the most interesting of Missouri barns are those on the prairie of north Morgan County, where a group of Swiss Mennonites settled shortly after the Civil War. These often measure 100 by 40 feet, and sometimes rise 40 or 45 feet to the roof ridge. The basement walls are stone, and those of the superstructure are of vertical boarding, in keeping with Swiss and German precedent. The framing throughout is of heavy, hewn timbers carefully pinned together. The lower or basement floor is divided into stalls, sometimes with outside doors. These entrances are protected by the distinctive forebay, or overhang, which extends some five or ten feet beyond the wall of the lower story. Entrance for a team and wagon is gained over a causeway through tall, double doors.

In Gasconade and Franklin Counties, the barns, although smaller, are of impressive stone construction. Generally, these are so built into the hillsides that the slope acts as the necessary embankment. Win-

HISTORIC BUILDINGS

Piaget Studio

THE OLD CATHEDRAL OF ST. LOUIS, ST. LOUIS
(1831-34)

**BIRTHPLACE OF JESSE JAMES, NEAR EXCELSIOR
SPRINGS** (log ell c. 1822)

**SPRING HOUSE (c. 1810), DANIEL BOONE HOME-
STEAD, ST. CHARLES COUNTY**

Piaget Studio

Piaget Studio

OLD COLONY TANNERY, BETHEL (c. 1850)

**INTERIOR, FIRST HOME OF CONCORDIA SEMINARY,
ALTENBURG (1839)**

**HOLMAN HOUSE, CALEDONIA
(c. 1818)**

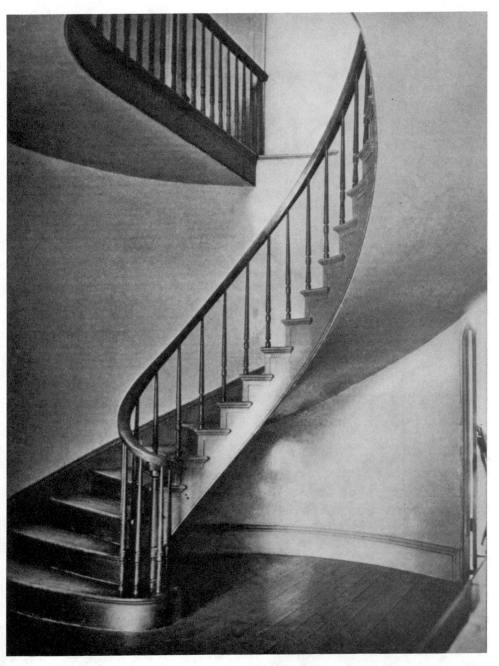

**STAIRWAY, LOCKE HARDEMAN HOUSE
NEAR ARROW ROCK (c. 1840)**

CARL STREHLY HOUSE, HERMANN (c. 1860-65)

WATHEN-RANNEY HOUSE, CAPE GIRARDEAU (1839)

Piaget Studio

RALLS COUNTY COURTHOUSE, NEW LONDON
(1857-58)

DRAWING ROOM, SELMA HALL, near Crystal City
(1854, reconstructed 1939)

dows illuminate the interiors, and often the gables are decorated with ventilation slits and stones bearing the name of the builder and the date of construction.

INFLUENCES FROM THE EASTERN STATES

The American settlers in Missouri brought with them the traditions of the East and, more remotely, of England. Their first homes were, necessarily, adaptations of the log house, but as their resources, families, and pretensions grew, these were replaced by buildings of frame, brick, or stone, usually designed by the owner with the aid of the local carpenter, or "undertaker," as the term was in those days.

From the beginning, frame houses with skeletons of heavy hewn timber, like those of New England and Virginia, were popular. Occasionally, an enterprising mill owner offered to prefabricate frame houses for the settlers. David Delauney advertised in September of 1819 that whoever desired to "secure houses framed and put together at the mill, will have them done to order with the best materials and delivered at his landing . . . together with shingles &c., at very reduced prices . . ." Nogging of brick and mortar often filled the spaces between the framing of the walls, creating an effect strikingly similar to the medieval English half-timbered house.

Durham Hall, an impressive frame mansion built by Moses Austin at Potosi about 1798, was the most important American house erected in Missouri during the Colonial period. A photograph made shortly before it burned in 1871 shows a front two-story portion with a four-columned portico, and a one-and-a-half story rear wing with low eaves, dormer windows, great brick chimneys, and 30-pane windows. Also traditional in form is the Holman house near Caledonia, built by William Woods, with the assistance of a "Yankee carpenter," before 1818; it is a one-and-a-half story "salt-box" frame house, with several features unusual in Missouri, including interior walls sheathed with wide boards. In many of the early houses, the stairway is built into a wall or added to the exterior under the shelter of the gallery. Above the large fireplace openings are, generally, narrow mantel shelves, and the space on either side of the wide chimney is filled by cupboards. The ceiling beams, often carefully dressed, are frequently left exposed.

Similar in design and arrangement are the stone buildings dating from the same period. Many of the two-and-a-half story stone houses of Cape Girardeau and St. Charles Counties, with their generous windows, heavy end chimneys, and center doorways, suggest a Pennsylvania ancestry. Earliest among these in point of design, if not date, is the Matson house at Defiance, St. Charles County, a two-room structure on a high basement, with an attic story. Its walnut woodwork and wainscoting, mantel shelves, and paneled cupboards suggest Kentucky or Virginia antecedents. In the near-by Nathan Boone house (before 1820), the walnut woodwork exhibits carved sunbursts and other classic details.

Brick construction was introduced into Missouri soon after the Louisiana Purchase, although bricks were used in chimneys before that time. The earliest surviving example is the Price building in Ste. Genevieve (about 1804), a two-and-a-half story building. Brick buildings were erected in St. Louis in 1812, a year after brick had been advertised at "$3 per thousand as they come and $6 if picked." Clay suitable for brick was found in nearly every part of Missouri, and many brick makers and masons were itinerants who burned the bricks needed on the site of the building. In 1830, a Mr. Middleton of Saline County had his "commodious residence" built by two of his slaves, one a mason, the other a carpenter. Most of the brickwork of Howard County houses dating from the period 1830-60 was done by two slaves, whose master hired them out to builders.

The dwellings built by immigrant Virginians and Kentuckians in the Missouri River Valley consist chiefly of one-and-a-half story brick houses of two to four rooms, with a generous frame or log wing. Their interior fittings were similar to those of the American frame houses, with hidden stairways and chimney cupboards, much decoration being lavished on cupboard doors and mantels.

Woodwork details, such as delicately fluted columns, carved swags, and sunburst motifs, were often copied by Missouri builders from books by the Eastern architects Asher Benjamin, Benjamin Shaw, Minard Lafever, and others. Many of the entrances are relatively simple in design, with wide six- or nine-paneled doors and a rectangular transom. A few examples, however, have either a simple semi-circular fanlight, or an elliptical one with elaborately leaded design, as originally in the John Jackson house (1828) near Glasgow.

Greek-Revival designs were being introduced into Missouri, and other fashionable trends followed in swift succession. Missouri's first important architect, Joseph C. Laveille (d. 1842), of Harrisburg, Pennsylvania, advertised himself in St. Louis in 1820 as an architect and practical builder of "long experience in the principal cities and towns in the United States." In partnership with George Morton (1790-1865), he built the first St. Louis Courthouse and did much work for the city preparing "skids for steam boats" and "making sundry coffins for paupers." In 1830, the firm designed the Cathedral of St. Louis, the first important Greek-Revival building in Missouri, completed four years later. It is of tawny limestone with a four-columned Tuscan portico and a square stone steeple.

The Italian Renaissance style introduced by Italian priests influenced building in portions of Missouri, suggesting itself in the Church of St. Joachim at Old Mines (1828), and more clearly exhibited in the stone facade of the third church of Ste. Genevieve (1831-37). Its most literal expression, however, is found in the Vincentian Church of the Assumption at St. Mary's-of-the-Barrens, near Perryville, begun in 1827, as a reproduction on a reduced scale of the Vincentian mother church of Monte Citorio in Rome. Renaissance designs were also followed in Jesuit buildings, such as the original St. Louis University group, and the stone seminary of St. Stanislaus at Florissant, completed in 1849.

For some time, Classic-Revival remained the accepted type for public buildings. Following the burning in 1837 of the first State capitol at Jefferson City, the design for a new two-story edifice by A. Stephen Hills, an English architect, was approved. This latter building also burned in 1911, and was replaced by the present capitol (*see Jefferson City*). Even more impressive was the St. Louis Courthouse, designed by Henry Singleton and begun in 1839; the completed building is largely the work of Robert S. Mitchell, appointed architect and superintendent in 1851. In 1859, the original low dome was replaced by one of Renaissance design supported by a wrought-iron framework, developed from Mitchell's design by William Rumbold. This use of structural iron was then novel in the United States; the dome of the national capitol at Washington was not completed until two years later. The Courthouse, completed in 1862 at a total cost of $1,199,871, was at that time the finest building in the trans-Mississippi River region.

County courthouses also favored Greek temple designs; nearly all had porticos of Doric or Ionic columns. Of similar derivation were many Protestant churches of the period. The Second Presbyterian Church in St. Louis, designed by Lucas Bradley, St. Louis architect, and built in 1841 at a cost of $42,000, was the most expensive church in the State. Of those which survive in the small towns, the Presbyterian Church at LaGrange (1848), the church at Newport, Franklin County, and the Christian Church at Troy (1859) are notable. Their red-brick walls and white trim, double entrance doors, long three-section windows, and occasional brick pilasters on the façades, give the style a charm which later country church architecture has not equalled.

To a greater extent than in parts of the East and the South, Missouri country builders preserved certain eighteenth century traditions until past the middle of the century—long after the Gothic-Revival and Italianate designs sponsored by a brilliant group of St. Louis architects were introduced into the State. As a result, local Classic-Revival architecture divided the field with other styles. The signature of the type— the temple portico with its familiar row of white columns—could be seen here and there, but the style never became popular for dwellings.

More characteristic of Missouri homes was the one- or two-story portico the width of the entranceway, with Tuscan, Doric, or Ionic columns supporting either a pedimented gable or a flat roof. On many smaller houses, particularly on the long, narrow St. Louis houses of that period, the portico was eliminated in favor of a recessed entranceway with a trim of Tuscan or Corinthian pilasters. Generally, the doorway in these was embellished by a rectangular transom with side lights, glazed with frosted or blue or red overlay glass cut in floral designs.

The interiors of these houses indicate the changed social life of the time. Even in unpretentious homes, the rooms are larger, the hallways more spacious. The stairways, delicately spiral, U-shaped, or, more rarely, double, are lighted by a "belvedere," or "prospect room," a raised skylight on the roof top, a feature that became increasingly popular in the succeeding period. The mantels and woodwork exhibit broad, plain surfaces with simple moulded trim, to make an effective background for the crowded, ornate furnishings of the period. Many rooms have elaborate plaster cornices and ceiling medallions, from which hung prismed chandeliers fitted for candles, oil, or, later, gas.

In contrast to the Classic-Revival architecture is the romantic Gothic-Revival style, first developed in England and consistently used in Episcopalian churches in Missouri. The original Christ Church Cathedral in St. Louis, probably the first of this type in the State, was completed about 1838. It was poorly constructed, however, and in 1859 the present Cathedral, designed by Leopold Eidlitz, New York architect, was begun. It was completed in 1867, and the tower added in 1910. Brick churches, such as Christ Church at Boonville (1846), and the church at Lexington built several years later, like English seventeenth century country churches, have square or octagonal towers, long, narrow windows, and steeply pitched roofs. Construction was occasionally of frame, as in the church at Ironton, whose walls are sheathed in vertical boards to create the illusion of added height, and whose pointed gables and tiny casement sashes represent the ultimate development of Gothic architecture in Missouri.

Commercial and public buildings, like some surviving in the older section of St. Louis, also followed Gothic designs. Particularly interesting was the St. Louis Central High School, designed by William Rumbold, which was built in 1856 and abandoned in 1893. With its Tudor lintels, corner towers with bulbous tops, and long windows of Gothic tracery on the stairways, it was an excellent illustration of Gothic-Revival design in Missouri.

During the second half of the nineteenth century, architecture, like every other phase of Missouri life, experienced great confusion as a result of the rapid growth of population and wealth and particularly of industry. The population of cities doubled and quadrupled in a decade;

property values mushroomed; the gardens and lawns of an earlier period were covered with sunless rows of buildings. A bewildering series of architectural revivals brought in the designs of the French and Italian Renaissance, and of the Gothic, the Queen Anne, the Romanesque, and the Colonial periods. At the same time, industry and science were inexorably forming an architecture of their own through the use of new and often better materials, particularly metal and glass. The gradual introduction of furnaces, plumbing, gas, and electricity made architectural change a necessity.

George Ingham Barnett, St. Louis architect, was born in England in 1815, studied under Sir Thomas Hines in London, and in 1839 came to the United States, where he remained in New York for several months before coming west. His first buildings in St. Louis include a row of three-story brick and stone apartments of English Regency design. He applied Italian Renaissance to Dr. Charles A. Pope's Medical College (1848) and to Henry Shaw's country home (1849); his break with Classic tradition is more clearly shown in Shaw's town house (1850) which is square, with a flat roof and heavy ornamental cornices. It is of brick, with stone quoins and window trim, and single-paned, rather large windows. The slightly recessed entranceway has tall, heavily decorated double doors. Sometimes houses of this type were further embellished with wrought-iron or open-work stone balconies.

During the 1850's, many of these sprawling Italian Renaissance country houses, with flat roofs and square corner towers, were built about St. Louis. Barnett again used this style in the design for a great house built for Ferdinand Kennett on the Mississippi River bluffs at Selma, which was completed in 1854 at a cost of $125,000. Gutted by fire in 1939, the house has been restored.

The great fire of 1849 destroyed most of St. Louis' downtown section, and the buildings were largely replaced by structures of Renaissance design. Perhaps the most interesting was the Allen-Collier building, a five-story brick structure which, when completed in 1850, was perhaps the tallest in the city. The elongated Renaissance arch in the decoration on the façade anticipates similar treatment on later skyscrapers. The following year, work was begun on the monumental stone Custom House, completed in 1859.

These St. Louis buildings had an immediate influence throughout the State. Brick courthouses with rounded windows, flat roofs, bracketed cornices, and cast-iron balconies are found at Troy, Kahoka, and Buffalo. In Howard County, Brannock Hall at Central College (1856), designed by Solomon Jenkins, is of the same type. Ten years later, John Aldridge designed Lewis Library at Glasgow, with its interesting recessed entranceway and cast-iron double stairway.

Introduced slightly later were the French Renaissance designs resembling the Italian, revived and made fashionable during the Third Empire. On these, the flat Italian roof is replaced by the French mansard, in reality an additional story disguised as a roof with dormer windows. Iron balconies were common.

These architectural trends were interrupted but not diverted by the Civil War. Peace stimulated the growth of St. Louis, Kansas City, and other urban centers, but the interest in Classic-Revival was as dead as the hopes of the Confederacy, and French and Italian Renaissance styles became increasingly popular. The rows of prim houses built in St. Louis at that time, no matter how plain or ornamented their façades, nearly all wear mansard roofs as a patent of architectural respectability. The wealthier residential areas show a sharp struggle between license and restraint, as witnessed by such extremes as the garish "Cracker Castle," designed in 1869 by C. B. Clarke, for J. O. Pierce, who made a fortune selling hardtack to the Union Army, and the elegantly formal early houses in Vandeventer Place. On buildings in smaller towns sprawling porches with fussy jig-saw trim were tucked on the front, or wrapped around three sides like a ruffled apron. Another style popular for country houses was the Swiss chalet type introduced into Missouri before 1861. These, usually of brick or stone, have long, low eaves, and tiny balconies.

Commercial architecture, in the meantime, was beginning to experiment with structural iron. The ore deposits of Iron Mountain, and of Franklin and Phelps Counties were feeding a growing number of foundries which years before had commenced casting balconies, handrails, lintels, gratings, and other items, mostly in Classic-Revival design. An expansion of these iron manufactures now took place. Iron instead of wooden joists were used in the Courthouse in St. Louis, and in Thespian Hall at Boonville slender, cast-iron columns support the theater ceiling. Soon, entire fronts were made of cast iron. As real estate prices rose, buildings grew steadily taller, and more and more iron was used structurally to strengthen the masonry walls. The three-story Booth-Papin Building in St. Louis (1872) had a front of thin cast-iron columns between large windows. Five years later, the Thomas Gantt Building was remodeled with a new front which combined cast-iron supports and large windows. The effort was no longer to reproduce Renaissance designs; architects strove only for a light, strong framework which would permit generous-sized windows. These buildings, separated by a generation from the modern skyscraper, were pioneers in functional design.

Of equal significance as an architectural achievement and as an engineering feat was the construction (1867-1874) of the graceful Eads Bridge across the Mississippi River at St. Louis. This was one of the first uses of cast and wrought iron to solve an engineering problem of this kind. Four years later, General William Sooy Smith's Missouri River bridge at Glasgow, the first all-steel railroad bridge in the world, proved the structural value of this material.

Asa Beebe Cross, who established his office in Kansas City in 1857, was, as John A. Bryan points out in his *Missouri's Contribution to American Architecture* (1928), an architectural pioneer in the western part of the State. The following year he designed the Classic-Revival Wornall house, but his later designs turned toward current Renaissance and Romanesque trends. The Keith and Perry Building (1887), the old Courthouse (1892), and the first Union Station, which he designed with his partner, William E. Taylor, are examples of his later work in Kansas City. At St. Joseph, a group of architects established offices before 1870, and one of these, P. F. Meagher, designed the beautiful stone Gothic-Revival Corby Memorial Chapel near St. Joseph (1871-72). In 1869, Edmond Jacques Eckel, a young graduate of the Ecole des Beaux Arts of Paris, visited St. Joseph and decided to establish his office there; he contributed many buildings of French Renaissance design to St. Joseph, as well as to other cities in the Middle West.

Henry van Brunt, one of the original members and a president of the American Institute of Architects, opened an office in Kansas City in 1887, with Frank M. Howe as his partner. His talent found expression in such buildings as the Electricity Building at the Chicago World's Fair, the old Bryant Building, and the Emery, Bird, Thayer Dry Goods Company Building in Kansas City; the last bore the architectural innovation of bands of ornament instead of the usual heavy overhanging cornice. This same treatment also appeared in the Kansas City Club (1888), a modern adaptation of Romanesque design, with a rounded corner.

The trend championed by Van Brunt both in his designs and his writings was carried on in St. Louis buildings, where H. H. Richardson of Boston and Louis Sullivan of Chicago developed the new manner. In 1886, Richardson designed the massive stone John R. Lionberger house in Vandeventer Place, and the rambling, shingled, Henry S. Potter house, with its air of comfortable informality. Richardson's influence upon St. Louis architecture was mainly felt, however, through George F. Shepley, who, born in St. Louis in 1860, had, after completing his studies, entered Richardson's office.

In his *Autobiography*, Sullivan describes his reactions to the new steel-frame construction. He says he recognized immediately that "the new form of engineering was revolutionary, demanding an equally revolutionary architectural mode. That masonry construction, insofar as tall buildings were concerned, was a thing of the past to be forgotten, that the mind might be free to face and solve new problems in new functional forms." In 1890, Sullivan and Adler, Chicago architects, were commissioned to design the ten-story St. Louis Wainwright Building. Sullivan produced a structure with a sheer vertical sweep from the string-course above the second floor to the spandrels and cornice above. Simplicity in the major lines is combined with rich detail. The influence of the Wainwright Building was immediate and lasting. His designs for the Union Trust Building and the St. Nicholas Hotel, both built in 1893, show an equally fresh interpretation. Less well known, but perhaps from the standpoint of sheer design Sullivan's finest work in Missouri, is the Wainwright Tomb in Bellefontaine Cemetery (*see St. Louis*), completed in 1892.

Despite the implications of Sullivan's Missouri buildings and of the work of Van Brunt, Missouri architects continued to find irresistible the popular interest in revived designs. The Gothic, the French Renaissance, the Queen Anne, and the Colonial were adapted in new homes, business buildings, garages, factories, and churches. Anachronisms like the St. Louis Union Station (1893-94), inspired by the Romanesque gates of Carcassone, France, and the French Classic designs which dominated the St. Louis World's Fair of 1904, sprang up in prominent places. Yet out of the confusion came some notable adaptations of traditional designs to modern needs. For instance, William B. Ittner's St. Louis English-Tudor school buildings reveal a careful study of educational needs and problems.

The increasing demand for taller business buildings, however, worked in favor of the line of development suggested by Sullivan's Wainwright Building. In 1908, the firm of Howe, Hoit & Cutler (formed shortly after Van Brunt retired) planned a 14-story building with a skeleton steel frame, the first of its type in Kansas City, for R. A. Long, Kansas City "lumber king."

During the 1920's, the skylines of both Kansas City and St. Louis were slowly altered by the erection of groups of skyscrapers. Straight vertical shafts were varied by "stepback" designs, and the lingering nostalgia of Gothic, Romanesque, or Classic "icing" disappeared before the gradual realization of the beauty of sheer weight, mass, and line. On small business structures, however, and in domestic and religious architecture, the variety of "isms" grew more bewildering.

After 1929, the pinch of the depression halted construction and sobered Missouri architectural desires. The effect of this interlude was first noticed in the growing demand for "planned cities" to provide for changing needs. Both in St. Louis and Kansas City, slum areas have been cleared away to provide sites for an impressive group of public buildings. In the designs of these structures, the break with the eclecticism of the previous decade is clearly seen, and where Classic columns and ornaments are used, they are given contemporary application.

Today, the emphasis is more and more upon the functional; modern design looks toward the ultimate purpose of the building, with an eye to the best use of the newer materials, structural glass, metal, concrete. This trend is notable in the Kansas City Municipal Auditorium, designed by Hoit, Price & Barnes, Alonzo Gentry, and Voskamp & Neville. St. Mark's Episcopal Church in St. Louis, designed by the firm of Nagel & Dunn, and completed in 1938, employs modern materials and construction methods to an even greater extent. The restrained color, the dull blue windows with their themes from present day life, and the heroic figure of St. Mark on the facade are fresh and interesting in their application. Smaller public buildings and private homes have also recognized the desirability of the new style. Harris Armstrong, Kirkwood architect, has introduced several such buildings, among them the Cori residence in St. Louis County, and the Shanley Office Building. Very significant, too, are the post offices, courthouses, and school buildings being erected in many smaller towns throughout the State. An original American architecture is slowly evolving, aware of the past, but alive to the needs and spirit of the present.

PART II
Principal Cities

Cape Girardeau

Railroad Stations: E. side Main St., between Independence and Merriwether Sts., for St. Louis & San Francisco R.R. (Frisco Lines).
Bus Stations: 129 N. Fountain St., for Dixie Greyhound Lines, Inc., Schofield Bus Line, Arkansas Motor Coaches; 220 N. Fountain St., for Arkansas Motor Coaches; Metropolitan Cafe, 417 Broadway, for Prost Bus Company, Tri-States Bus Company.
Municipal Dock: Foot of Themis St., for Eagle Packet Co.; summer excursion service only.
Taxis: 15¢ one passenger, 5¢ each additional, any place in city.
Traffic Regulations: Speed limit 20 m.p.h.; one-way traffic on Fountain St., between Bellevue and Themis Sts.

Accommodations: Three hotels; lodging houses and tourist camps.

Information Service: Chamber of Commerce, 225 Broadway; Auto Club of Missouri (AAA), 328 Broadway (members only).

Radio Station: KFVS (1400 kc.)
Motion Picture Houses: Three.
Swimming: Fairgrounds Park, N. side of Broadway, West End Blvd., to Perry Ave., adults 25¢, children 15¢.
Golf: Hillcrest Golf Club, 3 m. W. of city limits on US 61, 9 holes, 25¢.
Tennis: Fairgrounds Park, N. side Broadway, West End Blvd., to Perry Ave.
Football: Houck Stadium, Bellevue St. at Broadway.

Annual Events: May Festival, Southeast Missouri State Teachers College; Convention, Southeast Missouri Teachers Association, Southeast Missouri State Teachers College, Oct.

CAPE GIRARDEAU (347 alt., 19,426 pop.) overlooks the Mississippi River from a rock ledge 150 miles downstream from St. Louis. Site of two colleges, the town has been for more than a century the educational and commercial center of southeastern Missouri. In a region where change is slow and tradition solid, the city has managed a gradual transition from river trade to industry. At present it has shoe and cement plants, sawmills, and miscellaneous small factories.

The city begins at the granite-paved municipal wharf. West of the levee, across the railroad tracks, is Water Street, once the business center of the town, but now merely three blocks of weathered brick structures facing the river. Where Water Street ends, Murtaugh Park, a slender ribbon of landscaped greenery, stretches southward for two blocks along the river. St. Vincent's Church, overlooking park and stream, is a white landmark visible for miles. The business district, dominated by the solemn Court of Common Pleas Building, is concentrated on Main Street and Broadway, along the bluff slopes and flat upland paralleling the river. Wedged between newer structures on the business streets are the mellowed houses of earlier days. About this heart of the old city has grown a modern community of broad streets, suburban business areas, and the frame and brick cottages of industrial workers. To the northwest, on the heights near the Southeast Missouri State Teachers College, is the more pretentious residential area.

Cape Girardeau was first settled by American families from North Carolina, Tennessee, and Kentucky; later the community attracted many German settlers. Both the Southern and German traditions are still in evidence. A few Classic-Revival residences, erected by pioneers who grew rich on frontier trade, remain in the older parts of the town. Elsewhere, houses suggestive of the German influence stand flush with the sidewalks; these are usually of one-and-a-half stories, but some are two-story structures with cast-iron balconies that break the primness of the unornamented façades.

Tradition says that missionary priests erected a rude cross on the *Cape de la Croix* (now Gray's Point) south of the city in 1699. About 1720, a French ensign named Girardot (or Girardo), stationed at Kaskaskia as early as 1704, is thought to have settled on "the Cape," a rocky promontory north of the present city on the Cape Drive Parkway. Maps as early as 1765 designate this point on the river as "Cape Girardot" or "Girardeau." Verified history of the area begins about 1786, when Louis Lorimier and a band of Shawnee and Delaware Indians moved across the Mississippi into Upper Louisiana, then Spanish territory. After several years spent at the Big Shawnee Spring near the present town of St. Mary's, Lorimier moved to the present site of Cape Girardeau about 1792, where, as Spain's trusted agent in Indian affairs, he was granted large tracts of land, and exclusive Indian trading privileges. Instead of platting a town, Lorimier founded an independent trading post with his wife, Charlotte Pemanpieh Bougainville, a half-blooded Shawnee. Later, the District of Cape Girardeau was organized, with Lorimier as commandant; in this capacity he aided the Spanish colonial policy of encouraging Anglo-American immigration by offering virtually free, tax-exempted land.

Andrew Ramsay and his family settled in the district, and were soon followed by others from Kentucky, Virginia, Tennessee, and the Carolinas. These brought with them their slaves, their long rifles, and their traditions of frontier communal life. The German families from North Carolina introduced Protestantism into the territory. Lorimier's Red House occupied the present site of St. Vincent's Catholic Church. Near by was a spring, about which Lorimier's Indian relatives and friends often camped. Along the *Rue de la Charette,* which followed the river bank, were the shops of Steinbeck & Reineck, Michael Quinn and other merchants; of Solomon Thorn, gunsmith; of John Risher, John Patterson and Charles Seavers, blacksmiths; and of David Wade, a carpenter who also sold hand-sawn lumber. Regular shipments of furs, salt pork, lard, beef, cotton, and bacon were sent on flatboats down the river.

When Lieutenant-Governor De Lassus arrived at Cape Girardeau in November, 1804, en route to New Orleans, after having formally surrendered Upper Louisiana to the United States, Lorimier saluted his old friend with ten shots which he fired, in lieu of a cannon, from a hole bored in a tree. Lorimier accepted the change in government with good grace, and even donated 4 acres of land, timber, $200 and 30 days' labor, toward the construction of public buildings. His post was designated as the seat of government for the district, and about 1806 a town was platted. Among the public buildings was a small log jail with a dungeon and a somewhat more comfortable "debtors' room." Later, a Grand Jury reported that prisoners "have so frequently . . . escaped punishment by passing through the jail, that the idea of imprisonment is publicly hooted at." However, there was no "hooting" at the local courts. Horse stealing was punished by 30 lashes on the bare back, and expulsion from the district. There were those who felt, however, that life in the town was not strict enough. One woman wrote early in 1807: "Cape Girardeau is a very beautiful place but it is very wicked. There is no chance to hear the Gospel preached without going 10 miles over a wretched road to a small Chapel. The main way the men spend their Sundays is in drinking and gambling, horse racing and chicken fighting."

The growth of the town was halted abruptly when the United States Land Commission rejected Lorimier's Spanish land title, thus invalidating all titles to lots in the city. In 1815, the county seat was moved to Jackson, and Cape Girardeau declined. In 1836, however, some 25 years after Lorimier's death, the United States recognized his title, and the town experienced a rebirth.

Cape Girardeau's location on the first high point above the confluence of the Ohio and the Mississippi gave it strategic importance in the river trade, which, between 1815 and the Civil War, partially compensated for the loss of political prestige. Logs were floated down to the sawmills, and flour mills sprang up beside the abundant sources of water power. Pork-packing houses were established along the levee. In 1843, Vincentian priests opened St. Vincent's College for young men. In 1849, the Presbyterians organized Washington Female Seminary in the old log building of the Ellis Hotel, and advertised classes in "all polite branches of learning, including playing the guitar." The first newspaper, the Cape Girardeau *Patriot,* began struggling through seven years of publication in 1836.

During the Civil War, Cape Girardeau was more important as a post to guard communications than as a military objective. Union soldiers occupied the town in July of 1861, erected fortifications at the four approaches to the town by river and road, and repulsed a Confederate attack on April 17, 1863. The war affected Cape Girardeau mainly through the cessation of river traffic, and the spoliation of the back country by raiding troops and guerrillas.

Flour milling promised to bring new life, once the war ended. But in 1873, when Cape Girardeau's flour was taking first prize at the Vienna World's Fair, the St. Louis and Iron Mountain Railroad, completing its line southwest, passed the city by, and tapped the district that had been carrying on its trade by way of the river. Even the establishment of the Southeast Missouri State Teachers College in Cape Girardeau that year could not offset this blow.

In 1880, Louis Houck (*see below*) organized the Cape Girardeau Railway Company. On the condition of completing the road from Delta to Cape Girardeau, a distance of 15 miles, by January 1, 1881, he was offered the property of an earlier railroad which had failed. When it became apparent that the rails could not be laid in time, an ingenious device was worked out. At the end of the completed track, workmen laid a temporary one by taking up the rails which the engine had passed over, and laying them again in front. Houck brought the train into town ten minutes before the deadline, expecting a great demonstration. But Cape Girardeau was quiet; the inhabitants had gone to bed.

The new railroad stimulated growth, and soon other lines were extended. In 1902, Houck organized the Gulf System, now absorbed by the Frisco lines, thus placing Cape Girardeau on the main line between St. Louis and Memphis.

Within recent years, flour milling has passed from Cape Girardeau, but modern industry, attracted by a dependable labor supply, has come in with the railroads and the revival of river traffic. Today, the city has a large shoe factory, a cement mill, sawmills, an electrical appliance factory, and a miscellany of other plants. The Federal river improvement program has its work headquarters for the district in Cape Girardeau. The $11,000,000 Little River Drainage Project, which redeemed 540,000 acres of tributary agricultural country to the south, added to Cape Girardeau's importance. In 1928, a $1,600,000 bridge was completed across the Mississippi, opening new trade territory and bringing an increase in population.

POINTS OF INTEREST

The COURT OF COMMON PLEAS BUILDING (*open 8-5 weekdays*), Spanish St. at Themis St., is a two-story gray brick building of modified Classic-Revival architecture, in a park which crowns the high ground west of the waterfront and is reached by a flight of 59 steps from Spanish Street. A tower surmounts the structure, and a portico the full height of the façade relieves its severity on the east. Erected to replace the log building dating from 1805, the central portion of the present courthouse was built in 1854 on land originally donated by Louis Lorimier. The north and south wings were added in 1889. Cells in the basement held Civil War prisoners, some of whose names are legible on the walls. In addition to the court of common pleas, the building houses city offices.

Northwest of the building is the CONFEDERATE MEMORIAL FOUNTAIN, erected by the Women's Relief Corps in 1911, a round, cast-iron fountain surmounted by the statue of a Confederate soldier.

During the summer months, the shallow basin of the fountain is used as a wading pool.

ST. VINCENT'S CHURCH (*open 5:50 a.m. to 6 p.m. daily*), NW. corner Main and Williams Sts., facing Murtaugh Park and the Mississippi River, is a stuccoed brick and stone structure of Gothic-Revival design, built in 1851 to replace a stone chapel destroyed by a tornado. Many details from the earlier church are said to have been incorporated in the present structure. The church houses relics of SS. Paul, Peter, Andrew, and Vincent.

SITE OF LOUIS LORIMIER'S RED HOUSE, NE. corner William and Spanish Sts., is marked by a massive red-granite boulder. Bronze plates inset on the east and west sides commemorate, respectively, Louis Lorimier's residence in Cape Girardeau, and *El Camino Real,* the Spanish military road opened in 1789, which followed Spanish Street after entering Cape Girardeau on Sprigg Street.

ST. VINCENT'S COLLEGE (*private*), 201 Morgan Oak St., is housed in a rambling three-and-a-half-story stuccoed brick building. The central portion of the building was erected in 1843, the southern wing was added in 1863, and the chapel and auditorium in 1871. The school, now a junior seminary which trains boys for the priesthood, was founded as St. Vincent's Academy in 1838 by Father J. Brands. Five years later, when the college buildings were completed, the professors and students of St. Mary's College at Perryville were transferred there, and the Preparatory Seminary and Novitiate were moved to St. Mary's. On the night of January 4, 1848, the steamer *Seabird,* tied up to the river bank near the college with a cargo of powder, caught fire and exploded, greatly damaging the college buildings. They were again injured by the tornado of 1850. In 1857, the college was converted into a seminary for candidates for the priesthood.

The SHERWOOD-MINTON HOUSE (*private*), 444 Washington Ave., a two-story, stuccoed brick house of modified Greek-Revival design, is now used as an apartment house. It was built as a 12 room home by the Reverend Adriel Sherwood, pastor of the Baptist Church, in 1846. During the Civil War, the house was occupied by Mathew W. Moore, lawyer and publisher of the *Cape Girardeau Eagle.* Later, the house was used as a military hospital. During 1870-71, it was occupied by a Presbyterian girls' school.

FORT D, NE. corner Locust and Fort Sts., constructed by Union troops in 1861, consists of earthworks and a moat surrounding a small parade ground. The fort has been preserved as a public park.

During March of 1861, Union forces occupied Cape Girardeau, and Forts A, B, C, and D were built at strategic points commanding the approaches to the city. Fort A was built at the east end of Bellevue Street, Fort B on the grounds of the present Southeast Missouri State Teachers College, and Fort C at the end of Sprigg Street. Fort D was one of the major defenses of the town at the time of General John S. Marmaduke's attack on April 17, 1863, which ended in Marmaduke's retreat to Jackson.

Between periods of duty, the soldiers at Fort D bowled with 32-pound cannon balls on an alley arranged in the center of the parade ground. During the winter, many of the men dug rooms in the bluff overlooking the river, finding these quarters more comfortable than tents.

SOUTHEAST MISSOURI STATE TEACHERS COLLEGE (*open 8-6 weekdays*), Normal Ave. between Pacific St. and Henderson Ave., a four-year, state-owned, coeducational institution, is housed in a group of two- and three-story buildings, constructed of white limestone in varied but harmonious architectural styles. Dominating the group is a three-story, domed administration building of modified Greek design. Here is housed the HOUCK COLLECTION of statuary, reproductions of masterpieces from an exhibition at the Louisiana Purchase Exposition at St. Louis in 1904. The Library Building, a structure of modern functional design dedicated in 1939, contains a museum in which are displayed the notable THOMAS BECKWITH COLLECTION of Indian artifacts and pottery, a record of prehistoric Indian culture in southeastern Missouri; the DUCKWORTH COLLECTION of fossils, micro-fossils, and shells; and the DR. A. T. CHATHAM COLLECTION of firearms.

The LORIMIER CEMETERY, Fountain St. at Washington Ave., on the crest of a hill overlooking the Mississippi River, contains the graves of many early Cape Girardeau residents. The unusual "triple" Scripps monument (about 1825), commemorates William and Ann Scripps and their daughter Grace. Near by is the grave of Alexander Buckner (1765-1833), a member of the State Constitutional Convention (1820), and a United States senator (1830-33).

The gravestone of Louis Lorimier records that "Major Louis Lorimier, a native of Canada and first settler and commandant of the post of Cape Girardeau under the Government of Spain . . . departed this life the 26th of June, 1812. Aged 64 years and 3 months. . . ." Charlotte, his "consort," the daughter of a Shawnee chief, "departed this life on the 23rd day of March, 1808, aged 50 years and 2 months, leaving 4 sons and 2 daughters"; her stone also bears a Latin verse, probably composed by Bartholomew Cousin, Lorimier's secretary, which reads in translation:

> She lived the noblest matron of the Shawnese race,
> And native dignity covered her as doth this slab.
> She chose nature as her guide to virtue,
> And with nature as her leader spontaneously followed good,
> As the olive, the pride of the grove, without the planter's care,
> Yearly brings its fruit to perfection.

Lorimier played an interesting and at times vital part in the history of the Upper Louisiana country. Born on the Island of Montreal in 1748, he and his father were engaged in Indian trade in Ohio as early as 1769. During the American Revolution he was a violent Tory; in 1778, he led a band of 40 Shawnee and Miami Indians in a raid on Boonesborough, Kentucky, and captured Daniel Boone. After the

Revolution, his anti-American activities helped to produce discontent among local Indians and British loyalists, resulting in a British-supported Indian War. Following the overwhelming defeat of the Indians and the capture of his trading post, he moved into Upper Louisiana, where he and his Indian allies were welcomed by Spanish authorities, who wished to use the Shawnee and Delaware Indians to protect Spanish settlements against raids by the Osage.

Northeast of the Lorimier memorial is the GRAVE OF LOUIS HOUCK, historian and railroad builder. Born in St. Clair County, Illinois, April 1, 1841, Houck spent his youth in Belleville, Illinois, receiving his early education in his father's printing office. From 1858 to 1859, he attended the University of Wisconsin; in 1860, he began the publication of a German paper in Belleville. He was admitted to the bar in 1862, and soon after dropped newspaper work. In 1869, he moved to Cape Girardeau. Here he practiced law until 1881, when he entered upon his career as a railroad builder. Houck was instrumental in securing the Southeast Missouri State Teachers College for Cape Girardeau. He wrote many books, the most notable being *The History of Missouri,* published in 1908. He died February 17, 1925.

The WATHEN-RANNEY HOUSE (*opened by arrangement*), 501 N. Main St., set back from the street on a sloping lawn, is a two-and-one-half story, ten-room Classic-Revival structure of buff colored "cotton rock." At the back is a two-story brick ell. The front portico has slender Ionic columns of wood. The wide double entrance doorway, said to have been made in Louisville, Kentucky, is flanked by small columns and surmounted by a fanlight transom. On the rear ell, galleries extend across both floors. Although the house has fallen into disrepair, and interior changes have been made, much of its early beauty is preserved in the thick walls and deep windows, the hall running the length of the house, and the staircase with its Georgian decoration and walnut handrail. Alfred P. Ellis, owner of the first hotel in Cape Girardeau, built the house in 1839 for his only daughter, Maria, who married Ignatius Wathen. The stone was quarried by slaves. Designed by Edward Branch Deane, the house was for years considered the most beautiful between St. Louis and Memphis. It is now used as a rooming house.

CAPE ROCK PARK, entrance on Cape Rock Road, is a landscaped parkway containing a circle drive approximately 6 miles in length. Tables and ovens are provided for picnickers, and the drive affords many excellent views of the Mississippi River. On the "Cape," a rocky promontory overlooking the river, is a stone marker commemorating the trading post traditionally established in the vicinity about 1733 by Ensign Girardot.

The MARQUETTE CEMENT MANUFACTURING COMPANY PLANT AND QUARRY, (*conducted group tours by written application only*), south on Sprigg Street (Alt. US 61), employs an average of 300 workers in a modern plant having a capacity production of about 4,000 barrels a day.

The dark gray and bluish gray Plattin limestone from the 150-foot deep quarry (R) is transported by an overhead conveyor to the stone plant and mill (L). Here the stone is combined by a complicated process with clay from the river flood plain, iron ore, and diaspore clay to insure uniform quality. The raw materials are then converted into cement clinker in rotary kilns at a high temperature.

The plant was established as the Eagle Portland Cement Company in 1909, and was purchased by the present company in 1923. Three company-owned boats and barges transport their product.

POINTS OF INTEREST IN ENVIRONS

McKENDREE CHAPEL, 12 *m.;* The COVERED BRIDGE and MILL, Bufordville, 18 *m.* (*see Tour 7*).

Columbia

Railroad Stations: 121 Christian College Ave. for Wabash Railroad; SE. corner Broadway and Water St. for Missouri-Kansas-Texas Lines.
Bus Stations: NW. corner 10th and Locust Sts. for Southwestern Greyhound Lines, Inc., and for Missouri Transit Co.
Airport: Municipal Airport, 3 m., NW. of post office on US 40; no scheduled service; taxi fare, 25¢, driving time, 10 min.
Taxis: 20¢ within city limits; 5¢ each additional passenger.
Local Busses: Fare, 5¢.
Traffic Regulations: Speed limit 15 m.p.h. downtown, 25 m.p.h. in residential areas.

Information Service: Chamber of Commerce, Municipal Bldg., SW. corner Sixth St. and Broadway; Automobile Club of Missouri (AAA) 605 E. Broadway (members only).

Accommodations: Four hotels, tourist camps, and lodging houses.

Motion Picture Houses: Five.
Auditoriums: Brewer Field House, University of Missouri, S. side Rollins St. W. of Hillcrest Ave.; Jesse Auditorium, Jesse Hall, Francis Quadrangle; Stephens College Auditorium, S. side of E. Broadway, between Waugh St. and College Ave.; Christian College Auditorium, Christian College; University Library Auditorium; Waters Hall Auditorium, White Campus.
Radio Station: KFRU (1400 kc.).
Swimming: Municipal Pool, US 40, between Ashley and Bowling Sts., free; Commercial Pool on Ashland Road one-half mile SE., 25¢.
Golf: University of Missouri Golf Course, S. side Stadium Road at Maryland Ave., 9 holes; greens fee 50¢.
Athletics: Memorial Stadium, S. side Stadium Road between Maryland Ave. and Providence Road, for football; Rothwell Gymnasium, Rollins Ave. at Hitt St., for basketball; Rollins Field, S. side Rollins St., between Hillcrest Ave. and Maryland Ave., for baseball.

Annual Events: State High School Basketball Tournament, Rothwell Gymnasium, last of March; Annual Meeting and Banquet, State Historical Society, in April; State High School Debate Tournament, University of Missouri, Main Campus, mid-April; Missouri Interscholastic Week, high school competitions in music, athletics, literature, drama, and stenography, University of Missouri, end of April; Journalism Week, School of Journalism, University of Missouri, first week in May; Farmer's Week, College of Agriculture, last of October.

COLUMBIA (748 alt., 18,399 pop.) is primarily a college town. Clustered about campuses, dormitories, and administration buildings, and all but surrounded by college-owned recreational facilities, Columbia centers its social and economic life upon its institutions of learning. From September until June, students give it youth, vigor, and sophistication. In summer, when they have departed, Columbia reveals a sedate old age. For Columbia is old; its roots sink deeply into the traditions of a pro-slavery border State, and beneath its air of alert progressiveness, its manners are conservative.

The business area, lying within the original townsite in the approximate center of the city, extends east and west along Broadway. The red- and buff-brick buildings have had their faces lifted, and the modernized first floors contrast sharply with the wide cornices and deep-set windows above them. With thousands of students to serve, the department stores and other shops carry goods and styles unusual in a town of Columbia's size, and the city has become the shopping center for a wide area.

The University of Missouri extends across the south side of the town; Christian College is in the north-central portion; and Stephens College in the east-central section. Interspersed between the colleges are the principal residential sections, where the houses, separated by landscaped lawns and flower gardens, create an atmosphere of comfort and leisure. The majority of the dwellings are of contemporary design. Only here and there one finds a touch of the ornate trim of the architecture of the nineties, and even more rarely a house that suggests pre-Civil War days. Centered about the University on the south and west are the student fraternity and sorority houses, and a few faculty dwellings. A new residential section, Sunset Hill, lies beyond the southwestern city limits.

North of Broadway the city changes character. Here the streets are lined with small frame houses occupied by industrial and low-salaried white-collar workers. A shoe factory and the model municipal water and light plant are located in this neighborhood. Along US 40, which forms the northern limits of Columbia, is a suburban district composed of small business houses catering to the tourist trade. Also in this area are the new senior High School, the Ellis Fischel State Cancer Hospital, and the Columbia Municipal Airport.

Along Flat Branch, in the west-central part of Columbia, is the Negro community. Of Columbia's resident population, 15 per cent are Negroes, most of whom work as domestics at the colleges or in private homes. The Negroes have their own schools, churches, professional men and women, and social life, but the downtown shopping area claims most of their business patronage.

Columbia originated in the town of Smithton, which, in 1819, was established one mile west of Columbia's present courthouse by the Smithton Land Company, and named for General Thomas A. Smith, receiver of the Franklin land office. The town's financial backers chose the site hurriedly in the hope that it would be made the county seat when Boone County was organized on November 16, 1820. The new village lasted just long enough for Circuit Judge David Todd to hold the April term of court under a sugar maple tree, and then was forced by the lack of an adequate water supply to move across Flat Branch, in May, 1821, to where Thomas Duley already had a log cabin. About Duley's cabin a new town was platted, and named, for some unknown reason, Columbia. The new community then bid for the county seat and obtained it, in spite of bids from other towns, in consideration of 50 acres of land, 2 public squares, $2,000 in cash, and 2 wells. Columbia was subsequently incorporated in 1826.

Colonel Richard Gentry, in whose tavern the post office was located, was the first mayor and the second postmaster. Distinguished as a soldier and a regional politician, Colonel Gentry was also a fancier of fine horses. He had an ordinance passed prohibiting horse racing on the principal thoroughfare except on Saturday, but warning "women and children to stay off Broadway between 8th Street and Flat Branch" on that day because Columbia's horsemen had certain affairs to settle, and they needed the best street in town on which to do it. In 1837, Gentry set off with 600 militiamen to fight the Seminole Indians in Florida. In this campaign, Gentry lost his life. Senator Thomas Hart Benton used his influence to secure the position of postmistress for Mrs. Gentry, who subsequently kept the post office for 30 years. This was one of the first instances of a woman receiving such an appointment in the United States.

In 1822, the Boon's Lick Trail, originally six miles to the north, was re-routed through Columbia, affording the new town not only the profitable business of supplying the Western immigrants with necessities, but also an opportunity to display its advantages for settlement. In 1830, the town's population was 600; in 1837, it was 1,000. Recognizing the great possibilities of the town, the peripatetic Nathaniel Patten, distinguished country journalist, had moved his *Missouri Intelligencer* here from Fayette in 1830. The paper continued under various names until 1938.

A majority of Columbia's early inhabitants came from Virginia and the bluegrass region of Kentucky. True to their cultural traditions, these people put their faith in two things: democratic government and education. So vital a part has education played in Columbia that it is impossible to separate the history of the town from that of its various schools; while its schools, in turn, have been closely related to its churches. In 1823, Dr. William Jewell, for whom William Jewell College at Liberty was named, helped to establish the Baptist Church which, in 1829, fostered the Bonne Femme Academy. In 1833, the citizens of the town founded Columbia Female Academy, better known as the Lucy Wales Academy.

In the meantime, Missouri as a whole had become interested in securing a State university. Congress had made a 46,030-acre land grant, the proceeds from which, amounting to $78,000, were to be used to establish such a school. An act of the general assembly subsequently provided that the site was to be chosen in the community offering the highest material inducements, and the fight was on. Columbia chartered Columbia College in 1835, in the hope that it might serve as a nucleus for a State university; and Boone County, under the leadership of Major James S. Rollins, now known as the "father of the University of Missouri," bid for the choice of Columbia as a site. In 1837, Howard County petitioned the general assembly to make Howard College the State institution. Others entered the contest, but by 1839 the struggle had narrowed to Boone, Callaway, Cooper, Cole, and Howard Counties. The solicitation of subscriptions was conducted with the fervor of a political campaign. House to house canvassing supplemented torchlight parades and mass meetings. Although the financial panic of 1837 had made money scarce in the Midwest, it is recorded that men subscribed more than they possessed in cash, and sold their homes and their farms to meet their pledges. Edward Camplin, who could neither read nor write, gave $3,000, one of the 3 largest subscriptions. The especially appointed commission that met in Jefferson City to decide the winner on June 4, 1839, found that Boone County had won with a subscription amounting to $117,900. The contract for the first building was let for $74,494, and the cornerstone of the university was laid July 4, 1840. Thus Missouri set up the first State university west of the Mississippi River. John H. Lathrop, of Hamilton College, New York City, was appointed president, and courses began April 14, 1841, in the building used by Columbia College, which closed within a few years. The first class, consisting of two members, was graduated in 1843. Until the first State appropriation in 1867, tuition fees and local contributions supported the university— today, with a faculty of 391 and an enrollment of 7,882, the school has a biennial appropriation of approximately $4,150,000. Women were not admitted until 1869. Columbia had two girls' schools prior to this, however: Christian College, incorporated and chartered in 1851, and Stephens College, chartered in 1856.

As the Civil War drew closer, bitter controversy flared within the town, and the university was drawn into partisan agitation. President James Shannon, its second president, and an "anti-Benton" Democrat, became so politically involved in the slavery question that he resigned. By 1862, the war had all but absorbed the school. The institution was in debt, its students had joined the armies, and its building was occupied by Federal militia, although no battles were fought in Columbia.

The political proscriptions that became part of the State's organic law after the war kept Columbia in turmoil; for the State constitution of 1865 required each voter to swear that he had not aided the Confederate cause. This oath was an immediate cause of bitterness, since in 1866 all but 400 were excluded from the ballot. In 1870, Columbia, with a population of 2,236, had but 238 qualified voters. All university officials were at this time required to take the State convention's oath of loyalty.

With the return of political normalcy, Columbia resumed old activities and began new ones. A railroad was planned from the city to "some point on the North Missouri Railroad." The branch reached the main line at Centralia in 1867. The Boone County Court ordered $200,000 in bonds issued for the building of this branch line, and an additional $150,000 for the construction of 3 turnpikes, one between Columbia and Rocheport, another east to the county line, and the third connecting Columbia and Claysville by way of Ashland.

Shortly after 1900, shoe and garment factories were established. The development of the State highway system and the introduction of trucks made possible the establishment of wholesale houses. But education remains Columbia's principal business. State organizations, connected in one way or another with the university's work, have established headquarters here. These include the State Historical Society of Missouri, founded in 1898, the Missouri Press Association, the Missouri Farmers' Association, and the Missouri State Teachers Association. The university and the colleges have grown; in 1940, their enrollment exceeded 10,000, providing the city with an $8,000,000 income.

POINTS OF INTEREST

UNIVERSITY OF MISSOURI (*open 8-5 weekdays*), main entrance Elm St. at Eighth St. (catalog containing campus map obtainable at Registrar's office), includes 10 schools and colleges, housed in 40 major and approximately as many smaller buildings on campuses and experimental areas covering 800 acres. The university began with one building, which was destroyed by fire in 1892. The College of Agriculture, and the School of Mines, at Rolla, were added in 1870. The Schools of Law and Medicine followed in 1872. One of the latest of the group is the School of Journalism, established by Dr. Walter Williams, later president of the University, in 1908. This was the first school in the world to grant a degree in journalism (*see Newspapers and Radio*).

The university is divided generally into Main, or Red, Campus, and East, or White, Campus, the color designations arising from the building materials employed. The Red Campus includes the College of Arts and Science and the professional schools. The Main, or North, entrance leads through the MEMORIAL GATEWAY, distinguished by two square limestone pillars that bear the sculptured seal of the university and bronze bas-relief portraits of James S. Rollins (1812-88), "Father of the University of Missouri," and John H. Lathrop (1799-1866), first president. The cornerstone of the original University Building, salvaged after the fire of 1892, is in the west (R) pillar, where it was placed in 1915. The buildings cluster about FRANCIS QUADRANGLE, named for David R. Francis, former governor, and president of the Board of Curators (1911-21). All are of red brick trimmed with white limestone, and most are in the eclectic style popular during the seventies and eighties.

Right from the entrance is the MEDICAL BUILDING, and south from this, on an oblique line, the hospital group of three-story, intercommunicating buildings. Left from the entrance are JAY H. NEFF and WALTER WILLIAMS HALLS, twin, two-story structures in modified English Renaissance. These house the School of Journalism. In Neff Hall, students write copy and help edit the Columbia *Missourian,* one of the city's two afternoon newspapers. In Room 211 is a celebrated collection of trophies and curios, including a seventeenth century printing press and a scroll copy of the *Book of Ruth,* dating from the fifteenth century. A pair of Chinese stone lions of the Ming period, presented by the Chinese government, guard the western entrance to Neff Hall.

At the west entrance to Walter Williams Hall, a mounted stone from St. Paul's Cathedral, given by the British Press Union, bears a bronze meridian plate. A carved stone from the British House of Parliament, presented by Reuters News Agency in 1937, is at the southwest corner. An ancient Japanese granite lantern, the gift of the American-Japan Society in 1926, adorns the north entrance. South from the journalism buildings is the SCHOOL OF BUSINESS AND PUBLIC ADMINISTRATION, with the old twin-towered CHEMISTRY BUILDING to the south.

Six ivy-clad IONIC COLUMNS are in the center of the quadrangle. These, once part of the portico of the original University Building, remained standing after the fire of 1892, and have become a traditional relic of the university. Right from the columns is the ENGINEERING SCHOOL. In the tower of SWITZLER HALL, the first building added to the university, is the old University Bell, no longer in service. LATHROP HALL, the music and fine arts building, is at the rear of this group. Left from the quadrangle are the president's home, a two-story, English Renaissance structure, and three-story SWALLOW HALL, also known as the Geology Building.

JESSE HALL, the administration building, forms the southern portion of the quadrangle. This four-story structure is semiclassic, with Corinthian columns and a great dome; it houses administrative offices on the ground floor, and art exhibits, including plaster models of much of the State Capitol sculpture, on the third and fourth floors. Left from the main entrance are the original tombstones from the graves of Thomas Jefferson and of David Barton, Missouri's first United States Senator. The former monument, carved from Jefferson's own design, and first erected at his grave in Monticello, Virginia, was presented to the university by Jefferson's heirs in 1883, and commemorates his interest in Missouri, the first State made from the Louisiana Territory. The marble tablet bearing the original inscription was damaged in the 1892 fire, and is now kept in a vault. Southwest from Jesse Hall is the EDUCATION BUILDING; southeast is TATE HALL, which houses the School of Law.

Here the campus swings eastward across Ninth Street. LOWRY HALL, northeast corner Ninth and Lowry Streets, is a three-story limestone structure housing the BIBLE COLLEGE OF MISSOURI, founded in 1895. Although its credits are accepted by the university, this school is not a part of the State unit.

The GENERAL UNIVERSITY LIBRARY BUILDING, on the block bounded by Ninth and Hitt Sts. and Lowry and Conley Aves., an English Renaissance edifice in white limestone, links the nineteenth century architecture of Francis Quadrangle with the Oxford designs of the new East (White) Campus. Erected in 1915, and enlarged in 1936, the building contains, in addition to the university library, the

STATE HISTORICAL SOCIETY OF MISSOURI, which has more than 220,-000 volumes and pamphlets relating to the State's history, and boasts a larger membership than any other State historical society. The society is the repository for an extensive collection of Missouri newspapers, including files of the Hannibal *Journal*, edited by Orion Clemens and his brother Sam (Mark Twain). The collection of original Bingham paintings in the reading room on the first floor includes *Order No. 11, Watching the Cargo, Vinnie Ream,* and others. Floyd Calvin Shoemaker has been secretary and librarian of the society since 1915.

Northeast from the library, at the east end of Lowry Street, ME-MORIAL TOWER, a Gothic-type native white-limestone structure rising 140 feet, forms an entrance arch to White Campus. The Tower, dedicated as a World War memorial in 1926, contains tablets inscribed with the names of 118 students who lost their lives in the war. The illuminated clock over the archway, and the chimes were added in 1936.

East from the Tower, a quadrangle of nine native white-limestone structures in modified English Renaissance style house the COLLEGE OF AGRICULTURE, where associated sciences and home economics are also taught. MUMFORD HALL, a three-story building at the northwest corner, contains the dean's office. In CONSERVATION HALL, extreme northeast corner, is one of the few schools of wild-life conservation in the country. South from here are the greenhouses, where plant experimentation work is conducted.

SANBORN FIELD, NE. corner Rollins and College Aves., established by the Federal Government in 1888, is the oldest agricultural experimental farm in the nation. West from the field are the principal athletic facilities, including BREWER FIELD HOUSE and ME-MORIAL STADIUM, with a seating capacity of 26,000.

STEPHENS COLLEGE (*open 8:30-5*), Broadway Ave., between Waugh St. and College Ave., a junior college for girls, is housed in about 30 buildings, which, except for minor outlying structures, are divided between 4 campuses, totaling 220 acres. The principal buildings, from two to six stories in height, are of modified English Renaissance design. Stephens' country club, riding stables, and golf course are at the eastern end of Walnut Street. The school is said to have originated in the Columbia Female, or Lucy Wales Academy, which was founded in 1833 and closed in 1853. In 1856, a Baptist Female College was chartered, which in 1870 was designated as one of the State female colleges of this denomination. James L. Stephens of Columbia endowed this institution with $20,000, and its name was consequently changed to Stephens College. The school's greatest growth has been since 1912. In 1937, considerable national interest attended the appointment of Maude Adams, celebrated actress, as professor of drama. In 1939-40, the college had an enrollment of 1,646 students, and a faculty of 320.

CHRISTIAN COLLEGE (*open 9-12 and 2-4:30*), Christian College and Rogers Aves., on a 20-acre campus, is a junior college for young women, housed in 11 buildings, 7 of which are intercommunicating. The campus structures are all of brick, in a combination of Romanesque and English Renaissance styles. The central structure, St. Clair Hall, houses the administrative offices. The college was the first chartered women's college in Missouri. It was founded in 1851 by James Shannon, second president of the university, largely because his daughters were at that time barred from the university by the rule against admitting women. Today, enrollment at Christian is limited to 250; students are admitted by a selective system.

The site of BOON'S LICK TRAIL, NE. corner West Broadway and McBaine Ave., the pioneer trail that extended between St. Louis and Franklin, passing through Columbia, is marked by a red-granite shaft erected by the D.A.R. in 1913.

The J. L. STEPHENS HOME (*private*), 1403 East Broadway, is a two story brick dwelling, erected in 1843 by James L. Stephens, for whom Stephens College is named. The 12 rooms are divided by central hallways. In 1849, Stephens attended the inauguration of President Zachary Taylor, and was so impressed by the beauty of one of the White House rooms that he had the "east" room of his home redecorated in a similar fashion. The French crystal chandeliers installed then are still in use. The house later became the property of Stephens' daughter, Annie, who married Sidney K. Smith, a St. Louis attorney. After her death it was remodeled into apartments.

GORDON MANOR (*private*), 2001 East Broadway, a large, square, two-story brick house containing 14 rooms, was erected in 1823 by Captain David Gordon, who had come to the Missouri Territory in 1820 and entered a claim to several hundred acres of land on each side of Hinkson Creek, east of Columbia. After erecting a log cabin, he left his son, James M., in charge and returned to Kentucky to await the decision on whether Missouri would enter the Union as a "slave" or "free" State. When the State was declared pro-slavery, Gordon packed his family into wagons and returned to Columbia with many of his 26 slaves. Slave labor burned the brick, felled the trees, and sawed the lumber necessary to build Gordon's mansion. Here the annual State militia "musters," which often lasted 3 days, were held. Captain Gordon died in the house in 1849. Passing from one member to another, the house remained in the family for 103 years, then was sold to Stephens College.

The PRESBYTERIAN STUDENT CENTER (*open 9-5*), 100 Hitt St., is housed in a two-story, T-shaped brick structure. The house was erected by James Hickman in 1828. After his death, it was occupied first by David S. Lamme, who married Hickman's widow, then by Robert S. Barr, a Columbia merchant, and lastly by William Y. Hitt, for whom Hitt Street is named. The building is now the property of the Presbyterian Church.

The ELLIS FISCHEL STATE CANCER HOSPITAL, U.S. 40, is a nine-story structure of modern set-back design, with alternating bands of cream- and brown-colored brick. The building was begun in

1938 and completed in 1940, following a legislative enactment providing for a State Cancer Commission for the care of indigent sufferers from cancer and allied diseases. Admission is gained upon the recommendation of the court of the county in which the patient lives.

POINTS OF INTEREST IN ENVIRONS

Rocheport, 15 *m.*, Boonville, 25 *m.*, Fayette 27 *m.* (*see Tour 1*).

Hannibal

Railroad Stations: Union Station, E. side of Main St., Lyon to Collier Sts., for Chicago, Burlington & Quincy R.R., and Wabash R.R.; 501 S. Main St., for St. Louis & Hannibal R.R.
Bus Stations: Central Bus Depot, 201 S. Main St. for M. C. Foster Stages, Jacksonville Trailways, Southwestern Greyhound Lines, Inc., and Santa Fe Trailways of Illinois.
Airport: Long's Airport, 7 m. NW., junction US 36 and US 61 at W. city limits on US 61; no scheduled service.
Taxis: 10¢ to 25¢ within city limits. To Mark Twain cave 35¢.
Local Busses: 10¢ fare, 2 tokens for 15¢.
Traffic Regulation: Speed limit 20 m.p.h. throughout city.

Accommodations: Three hotels; tourist camps and lodging houses.

Information Service: Chamber of Commerce, City Hall Bldg., NE. corner Broadway and 4th St.; Automobile Club of Missouri (AAA), 119 S. 4th St. (members only).

Motion Picture Houses: Three.
Golf: Mark Twain Golf Course, 3 m. W. of junction with US 36 on US 61, 9 holes, 25¢ weekdays, 40¢ Sun.; Hillcrest Golf Course, 1 m. W. of junction with US 61 on US 36, 9 holes, 25¢ weekdays, 40¢ Sun.; Hannibal Country Club, Country Club Drive, 9 holes, $1.00 for non-residents.
Swimming: YMCA, 418 Center St., 25¢; Indian Mound Park, W. side Mc-Masters Ave., N. of Pleasant St., adults 25¢, children 15¢.
Boating: Mississippi River, foot of Bird St., rowboats $1 per day; motorboat rides 25¢.

Annual Events: Mark Twain's Birthday Anniversary, Nov. 30.

HANNIBAL (488 alt., 20,865 pop.), is best known as the home town of Mark Twain, yet it is Missouri's fourth industrial city. Along the banks of the river, with its wooded islands and background of lovely green hills, several landmarks are preserved. Occasionally, the talk of the older inhabitants recalls the days of Huckleberry Finn, Tom Sawyer, and Becky Thatcher; and the illusion of Mark Twain's "little white town drowsing in the sunlight of a summer morning" returns. Yet, it is the clatter of railroad shops and the hum of machinery that dominate the town. The rare arrival of a towboat or barge at the Municipal Wharf, or the passing of a river steamer in the mile-wide current, arouses as much excitement among the citizens on modern Main Street as among visitors who have never known a life dependent on river traffic.

Hemmed between the twin bluffs of Mark Twain's "Cardiff Hill" and Lovers' Leap, the city now extends from the original townsite, a narrow flood plain near the water's edge, westward along three valleys. The business district lies close to the water front, with Main Street, which parallels the river, and Broadway, which extends westward, the principal thoroughfares. Here—particularly along north Main Street —are several brick and frame business structures dating from the Mark Twain period. Yet even these, grimy and bedraggled from age and smoke, cannot recall to Hannibal "that look of soft and shambling picturesqueness suitable to an old river town, and essential to the 'St. Petersburg' of Tom Sawyer and Huckleberry Finn," which Julian Street describes in *Abroad At Home*.

South of the business district, along Bear Creek, are the railroad tracks and massive brick buildings of the industrial section, which has developed since the decline of the earlier river traffic. Here are the principal props of modern Hannibal: the Burlington Railroad shops, a shoe factory, a stove foundry, a railroad car-wheel plant, and lesser establishments.

Quiet, tree-bordered streets traverse the lower or eastern residential section; on the tangled dividing ridges between the valleys the houses perch at the top of long flights of steps. Westward, within what must once have been an easy buggy ride, are the homes of Hannibal's original "well-to-do" families. Set back on expansive lawns, and half-hidden by maple and sycamore trees, these houses are of the rambling types popular in the Midwest between 1850 and 1890. Near by, a less well-kept residential area mingles an impression of quiet age with the contemporary note of modern homes.

In the 1860's, when the lumber industry demanded strong, unskilled labor, approximately 40 per cent of Hannibal's population was Negro. When the lumber era passed, most of these Negroes were set adrift economically. A few remained as domestic servants, or to work in the heavy industries. Today, their descendants make up 8.8 per cent of Hannibal's population.

In past years, Hannibal was a typical Mississippi River town, and until recently it was also a typical "home town"—it took the pressure of outside curiosity to make its people conscious of the lofty stature of the Mark Twain memory. Now the town has erected a museum and scattered markers to remind the visitor that it was to Hannibal that the Clemens family moved from Florida, Missouri, in 1839, when Samuel was still a child. Here he experienced many of the incidents of Tom Sawyer's career—the river life, the cave and cemetery escapades, and the youthful romance. Here, too, he served his printer's apprenticeship as a short cut to an education.

Hannibal has also been the home of other noted Americans. Admiral Robert E. Coontz (1864-1935) was born and reared here, and is buried in Mount Olivet Cemetery. John Rogers, famed as a sculptor, modeled his first work from the clay of Lovers' Leap when he was still a mechanic in the railroad shops. Carroll Beckwith, noted portrait painter, was a native of Hannibal. Cliff Edwards, better known as "Ukelele Ike," and Egbert Van Alstyne, composer of "Memories" and

"In the Shade of the Old Apple Tree," spent their early years in this town.

Like other towns on the Mississippi, Hannibal owes its early growth to river trade. In 1818, the site of Hannibal was granted to Abraham Bird of New Madrid, in exchange for property destroyed by the New Madrid earthquake of 1811. The following year, a group of land speculators platted a town at the mouth of Bear Creek which they named Hannibal, in the classic fashion of the period. They then held a sale of lots in St. Louis. The establishment of a post road and mail service from Louisiana to Palmyra brought a gradual increase of cabins in the settlement. By 1827 Hannibal had five families; in 1830 it consisted of "thirty souls." For a time the overwhelming magnificence (on paper) of Marion City threatened to snuff out the flickering light of the village; but Marion City did not materialize, and the growth of Hannibal was put on a sound basis by the formation of the Hannibal Company, and the incorporation of the town in 1838 under trustees who sold property "at low prices, chiefly to actual settlers."

Before long, flatboats laden with Iowa grain and hemp tied up at the waterfront; hogs fattened in the back country were driven in for market; logs were floated down from Wisconsin and Minnesota and converted into boards. A pork-packing plant was established; tobacco factories, flour mills, and sawmills flourished. A schoolhouse was erected in 1830; Samuel Stone started a ferry in 1832; a library was organized; and the *Commercial Advertiser* was established in 1837. The town's growth was marked by such milestones. In 1847 the local newspaper boasted that during the past season steamboats had carried downstream from Hannibal's port freight valued at more than $1,200,000.

Fully established as a place of importance, Hannibal eased into the complacent life of a river town. Once a day, a packet arrived upstream from St. Louis and another downstream from Keokuk. Years later, Mark Twain would picture the town. ". . . the streets empty, or pretty nearly so; one or two clerks sitting in front of the Water Street stores, with their splint-bottomed chairs tilted back against the wall, chins on breasts, hats slouched over their faces, asleep . . . ; a sow and a litter of pigs loafing along the sidewalk, doing a good business in watermelon rinds and seeds; two or three lonely little freight piles scattered about the 'levee'; a pile of 'skids' on the slope of the stone-paved wharf, and the fragrant town drunkard asleep in the shadow of them. . . ." Presently, dark smoke would appear above one of the remote river points, and "instantly a Negro drayman, famous for his quick eye and prodigious voice, lifts up the cry, 'S-t-e-a-m-b-o-a-t a-comin!' and the scene changes! The town drunkard stirs, the clerks wake up, a furious clatter of drays follows, every house and store pours out a human contribution, and all in a twinkling the dead town is alive and moving. Drays, carts, men, boys, all go hurrying . . . to a common center, the wharf. Assembled there, the people fasten their eyes upon the coming boat as upon a wonder they are seeing for the first time. And the boat *is* rather a handsome sight, too. She is long and sharp and trim and pretty . . ." Ten minutes later the steamer would be under way, and "after ten more minutes, the town is dead again, and the town drunkard asleep by the skids once more."

The town began to assume its contemporary character shortly before the Civil War, when railroads from the East stopped short at the Mississippi River. Hannibal's position on the western shore suggested it as a logical terminus for a railroad to the West. In 1856, the first train of the Hannibal and St. Joseph Railroad was run westward as far as Palmyra, the county seat. Three years later, the road was completed across the State to St. Joseph. Shops for the road were established in Hannibal, and in them, in 1862, was built the world's first railroad mail car. Here, too, was constructed the *General Grant,* the first locomotive built west of the Mississippi, which made its initial run in March 1865.

During the Civil War, commerce almost passed from the river, but the new railroads already had assumed a large place in Hannibal's economic pattern. In 1871, the Hannibal (now Wabash) Bridge was completed. Of draw-span design, it was the second bridge across the Mississippi to touch Missouri shores. In 1886, the town built the State's first city-owned light and power plant, and in 1889 it established the first tax-supported library in Missouri.

When the lumber boom collapsed, and the flour mills moved away, new and heavier railroading industries moved in, and the shoe factory was established. Three miles south of town, the shale and limestone bluffs attracted one of the largest cement-manufacturing plants in the Nation. Hannibal-La Grange College, a Baptist co-educational institution, moved to Hannibal from La Grange, Missouri, in 1929. In 1935, the $1,000,000 Mark Twain Bridge across the Mississippi River was completed.

POINTS OF INTEREST

The MARK TWAIN MUSEUM AND HOME (*open 8-6 daily*), 206-208 Hill Street, adjoining buildings, contain Mark Twain memorabilia, and antiques of the Hannibal vicinity. The museum, dedicated in 1935, is a two-story stone structure designed in the manner of the old building which formerly stood on the site. The collection housed here contains an impressive number of objects associated with Mark Twain. Of outstanding interest is the group of photographs made of the author near the close of his life.

Entrance to the home is made from the museum through a covered passageway. The two-story, white frame house, built flush with the sidewalk, is representative of unpretentious Missouri houses of the pre-Civil War period. The rooms are small, the ceilings low, the box stairway ladderlike; ornament of any sort is lacking. It was a house built with slender means to fill a family's need.

The house, and the lot on which it stands, are intimately associated with the Clemens family. Shorty after moving to Hannibal in 1839, Mark Twain's father, John Marshall Clemens, bought for $7,000 the entire quarter block extending east from the alley to Main Street. Like most of his other financial ventures, this speculation proved disastrous, for he was unable to meet the payments, and creditors took over the property in 1843. It appears that one small lot in the section was saved by a St. Louis cousin, James Clemens, Jr., and on this John Clemens built the three lower rooms of the present house in 1844. In these the family lived until 1846, when John was forced to pay a note which he had unwisely endorsed for a friend—to do this, he had to sell most of the family furniture. The cousin offered to let him remain on the property for a rental of $25 a year, but with little left save a piano, this was impractical. A Dr. and Mrs. Grant, who at that time lived across the street, on the second floor of the Pilaster House, took the family in, under an arrangement whereby the Clemenses cared for the house and prepared meals. The Clemenses lived with the Grants until 1847, when they returned to their own house. In 1850, Orion, the eldest son, began an ill-starred venture as an editor. When a fire destroyed much of his equipment, he moved his plant to the parlor of the house, and there he published the Hannibal *Journal* from about 1851 until he was forced to sell it two years later. It was in this diminutive parlor, therefore, that Sam, as his brother's assistant editor, began his career as an author (*see Newspapers and Radio*). Orion added the second floor rooms to the house to give additional space.

It was about the time that the Clemenses first moved into their own house (1844) that the *Tom Sawyer* days—that is to say, the boyhood of Samuel Clemens—may be said to have begun. Most of the home incidents of the book actually happened. Sam Clemens did throw clods at his brother Henry (the prototype of Sid) for getting him into trouble about the colored thread with which he sewed his shirt when he came home from swimming; he did give pain-killer to Peter the cat. At the parlor door he saw his mother stand up to the town bully who was pursuing his daughter with a rope, with the intention of "wearing it out on her." Jane Clemens admitted the fleeing daughter, and then barred the door with her arms until the enraged father stopped swearing and threatening, and slunk off.

The house was purchased and presented to the city by Mr. and Mrs. George A. Mahan in 1912. In 1937-38, it was carefully restored and furnished with such objects and furniture as a Midwestern home in the days of Mark Twain's boyhood might have contained. Some of the furnishings were taken from the home of "Becky Thatcher," and other early Hannibal families. "Aunt Polly's" room (the front upstairs bedroom) reflects the prim tastes of its "might-have-been" occupant. Her dresses are hanging in the closet; her night gown, long and full, lies across the foot of the bed. "Tom's" room has sturdy, durable furniture, and on the bedside table is his loot from the whitewashing episode: the brass door knob, the marble, and the other trophies.

The "BECKY THATCHER" HOUSE (*open daily*), 211 Hill Street, is a two-and-a-half-story gray frame structure in which the Hawkins family lived during a portion of Sam Clemens' childhood. Sam first knew Laura Hawkins (Becky Thatcher) when her family lived in the "Pilaster House." The two children vowed never to love any one else and always to walk to and from school together. When Sam once accidentally dropped a brick on Laura's finger, it was he who cried loudest and longest.

The "PILASTER HOUSE" (*private*), SW. corner of Hill and Main Streets, named for the Greek-Revival pilasters which ornament its exterior, is a two-and-a-half-story yellow frame house of considerable architectural interest. Tradition has it that the house was ordered for erection in Marion City, but that because of a flood, it was delivered at Hannibal, and so was set up there. The building is closely associated with the Clemens family. On the first floor was McDaniel's store, where Mark Twain later said he "bought candy for more than sixty year." Rooms on the second floor were occupied by the Hawkins family during the early 1840's, and after that by Dr. and Mrs. Grant. The Clemens family lived with the Grants in this house from about 1846 to 1847. It was here that John Clemens held the meeting which brought about the building of the Hannibal and St. Joseph Railroad, and here he died March 24, 1847.

The SITE OF HUCK FINN'S HOME, 213 North Street, marked by an iron tablet, is occupied by a modern two-story frame dwelling (*private*). Here in a disreputable old house lived Tom Blankenship, Huck Finn's prototype, a scant block down the alley, but socially in the wrong direction, from the Clemens' home. Sam adopted the Blankenships outright, and he was likely to be there at any hour of the day. At night, summoned by a system of cat-call signals, Sam would slide down the roof at the back of the Clemens' house, and by means of a convenient arbor and flight of steps, join Tom and the gang.

The shed at the rear of the present house is said to date from the period of the Blankenship residence.

The JOSEPH P. AMENT PRINTING OFFICE (*private*), 315 N. Main Street, is a three-story brick building in the style of the commercial architecture of the 1840's. Its wooden cornice has recently been removed. A room on the second floor, over the "Brittingham Drug Store," once housed the *Missouri Courier,* edited by Joseph P. Ament (*see Newspapers and Radio*). In the fall of 1848—a little over a year after his father's death—thirteen-year-old Sam Clemens began a two-year apprenticeship here. The Clemens' family fortunes were at low ebb, and Sam helped out as best he could, wearing Ament's much-too-large castoff clothing, and sleeping, with the other apprentice and the journeyman printer, on a pallet on the office floor. It was on his way home from this office one afternoon that Sam saw flying along the pavement a square of paper, a leaf from a history of Joan of Arc, which changed his outlook on life and gave him the urge to write.

The JUDGE JOHN MARSHALL CLEMENS' LAW OFFICE (*private*), 112 Bird Street, is in a two-story gray frame building now in bad repair, set flush with the sidewalk. Extensive alterations during the past 50 years have left few of the original exterior features. The first floor is said to have been used for a time as a law office by Mark Twain's father, John M. Clemens. It was perhaps here that Sam Clemens, unwilling to go home one night because of some prank, came to spend the night. He describes in *Innocents Abroad* how, as he lay on the lounge, a square of moonlight from the window slowly approached a shape on the floor to reveal the dead face of a man named McFarlane, who had been stabbed in the Hudson-McFarlane feud and carried 'to the office pending the inquest. Sam suddenly decided to leave, taking the window sash with him, because, as he explained, it seemed more convenient at the time to do so.

Near by is "Wildcat Corner," the corner of Main and Bird Streets, where Sam and Tom Blankenship (the original Huck Finn) conducted a piece of high finance with a coonskin. Huck sold the skin in Selm's store for ten cents. When the clerk threw it on a pile of furs in the back part of the store, Sam climbed through an open window and retrieved it for Huck to resell. This continued until the scheme was discovered.

The CARROLL BECKWITH HOUSE (*private, except tea room*) NW. corner 4th and Bird Streets, a two-story yellow-brick house, with a comparatively recent frame addition at the rear, has been modernized until only a few traces of its age remain. Here was born Carroll Beckwith (1852-1917), portrait painter, member of the National Academy of Art, and life-long friend of Mark Twain. One of Beckwith's paintings hangs in the Garth Memorial Library, SE. corner Fifth and Church Streets.

The house was also one of the many Hannibal homes of the Hawkins family, whose daughter, Laura, was the prototype of Becky Thatcher.

CENTRAL PARK, bounded by Fourth, Fifth, Broadway, and Center Streets, is the "square" of Mark Twain's childhood. On or near the square was the school of Mr. Sam Cross which Sam attended, and in which he purposely misspelled February in a spelling bee, so that Becky might win. The square at that time was a hill covered by a jungle of plum and hazelnut trees and wild grapevines. At recess and noon hours, the children gathered flowers, climbed the trees, and swung in the grapevine swings.

At the NE. corner of the park is Frederick Hibbard's WILLIAM H. HATCH STATUE, commemorating the Hannibal attorney and congressman who fathered the Federal law establishing agricultural experiment stations (*see Agriculture*). His home, near Hannibal, was given to the State by his daughter, Sallie Hatch, and is the site of the Hatch Dairy Experiment Station, operated by the University of Missouri. Hatch (1833-96) was a native of Kentucky who came to Hannibal in the 1850's. He represented the First Missouri District in Congress from 1878 to 1895.

The ROBERT E. COONTZ BIRTHPLACE (*private*), NW. corner Sixth and Bird Streets, is a two-story yellow-brick house surrounded by an ornamental iron fence. Admiral Robert E. Coontz (1864-1935) was Chief of Naval Operations from 1919 to 1923, Commander-in-Chief of the United States Fleet, 1923 to 1925, and Commandant of the 5th Naval District, 1925 to 1928. He is buried in Mount Olivet Cemetery.

The TOM SAWYER AND HUCK FINN STATUE, Main and North Streets, is a bronze group by Frederick C. Hibbard—born at Canton, Missouri—that catches the careless dress and adventurous spirit of Mark Twain's two most famous characters. The statue was donated by Mr. and Mrs. George A. Mahan and their son. It is on a base of red granite at the south foot of "Cardiff Hill," the playground of Tom, Huck, and their cronies. Erected in 1926, the group is regarded as the first statue in America to commemorate literary characters.

The MARK TWAIN MEMORIAL LIGHTHOUSE, N. end of N. Main Street, atop "Cardiff Hill," rises 54 feet above its base and nearly 200 feet above the Mississippi River. It is of metal framework covered with sheet iron and plywood, and is surmounted by a fixed beacon. The lighthouse was dedicated from Washington, D.C., by President Franklin D. Roosevelt, when he opened the Mark Twain Centennial Celebration in January, 1935. The hilltop, easily accessible, affords an excellent view of the river and surrounding lands. The "Cardiff Hill" of the stories is in reality Holliday's Hill, named for a Mrs. Holliday who once lived at the top, and burned a lamp in her window every night as a guide for the river pilots. It was down this hill that the boys rolled the stones which startled churchgoers, and that final enormous rock which, by freak of fortune, hurdled a Negro and his wagon instead of crushing them.

LOVERS' LEAP, S. Bluff Street, rises 230 feet above the south end of Main Street. The usual legend of the Indian lovers who flung themselves from its limestone heights is told of this bluff. More authentic, however, is the story of its use by a religious group as a gathering place in anticipation of ascending to Heaven. In the early 1840's, William Miller, a New York City deist, decided that the world was coming to an end in 1843. Protestant churches throughout the country were thrown open to his preaching, and he gained a great following among a group of Hannibal and Marion County citizens. Disappointed in their expectation in 1843, the "Millerites," as the sect was called, again looked for Christ on October 22, 1844. Crops and jobs were left unattended, stores were closed, and positions were resigned, as the people prepared, as though on their deathbeds, to meet their God. Dressed in long white robes, the group ascended to the crest of Lovers' Leap, where they waited to be snatched to Heaven when the world was destroyed.

POINTS OF INTEREST IN ENVIRONS

Scenic Mississippi River Drive. Riverview Park, 1.4 *m.;* Mount Olivet Cemetery, 1.7 *m.;* Hannibal-La Grange College, 2.5 *m.;* Mark Twain Cave, 2.6 *m.* (*see Tour 3*). Site of Bates Trading Post, 2 *m.;* Hatch Dairy Experiment Station, 2.2 *m.* (*see Tour 7a*).

Jefferson City

Railroad Stations: State St. at Monroe St. for Missouri Pacific R.R.; Monroe Building, 212 Monroe St., for ticket office; North Jefferson City for station of Missouri, Kansas & Texas R.R.

Bus Stations: Union Bus Terminal, 111 W. High St., for Southwestern Greyhound Lines, Inc., Missouri-Arkansas Coach Line, Missouri Transit Co.; Missouri Pacific Bus Station, 101 W. McCarty St., for Missouri Pacific Trailways, Missouri-Arkansas Coach Lines, Missouri Transit Co.

Airport: Robertson Aircraft Corporation Field, 3 m. NW. of post office, driving time 10 min.; no scheduled service.

Taxis: 20¢ first 12 blocks; beyond by zones up to 35¢ within city limits.

Local Busses: Fare 5¢.

Traffic Regulations: 15 m.p.h. in school zones; 15 m.p.h. downtown; 30 m.p.h. in residential sections.

Information Service: Chamber of Commerce, 211 Madison St.

Accommodations: Two hotels; tourist cottages, and lodging houses; rooms scarce during biennial legislative sessions beginning Jan. 1 of odd-numbered years.

Motion Picture Houses: Two.

Radio Station: KWOS (1340 kc.).

Swimming: Chamber of Commerce Pool, McClung Park, 1200 block Chestnut St., adults 25¢, children 10¢.

Tennis: Two courts, McClung Park, 10¢; also courts at City Park.

Public Library: 210 Adams St.; open weekdays 9-9, Sun. 2-5.

Annual Events: Missouri Rural Schools Exhibit, Capitol Building, third week in Apr.

JEFFERSON CITY (557 alt., 24,268 pop.), State capital and seat of Cole County, straddles the steep southern bluff of the Missouri River. Known locally as "Jeff" or "Jeff City," the capital is named for Thomas Jefferson. The river and the direct railroad route to Kansas City and St. Louis have attracted to it a number of industries. It is, however, primarily a political city, with State government, for which it was created, its major business. Yet, at first, only the great gray dome of the capitol suggests the city's political character, for the atmosphere of its business and residential sections is that of any prosperous Midwestern trade center.

The city spreads inland across finger-like ridges and valleys that parallel the river. High Street, following the first of the ridges east and west, is the axis of the community. Compact blocks of brick and stone structures, whose low roofline is broken by the seven-story Central Missouri Trust Company Building, extend between the capitol and government buildings on the west, and the Cole County Courthouse on the east.

A block north of High Street, atop a bluff overlooking the river, the governor's mansion faces the capitol across an undeveloped (1940) park which parallels Capitol Avenue. Four blocks east of the mansion on Capitol Avenue is the State penitentiary. Below the bluffs, near the railroad tracks and along the winding river, are garment and shoe factories and the shops of the Missouri Pacific Railroad.

The residential sections lie east, west, and south of the business district. Negroes, comprising 10 per cent of the population, live in the southeastern portion of the city, in the vicinity of Lincoln University, a State-supported Negro college.

As center of Missouri's vast web of commissions, boards, and departments, Jefferson City always has had a large percentage of clerks, accountants, bookkeepers, and other white-collar workers. These groups are an important part of the city's economy, but the life of the community is mainly determined by the businessmen, professional people, and railroad and factory employees who, with their families, compose the permanent population. Many of these are of German descent, and their cultural background has blended into the character of the city.

When Missouri's first general assembly convened in St. Louis in September 1820, a five-man commission was appointed to select a site for the State capital on the Missouri River "within forty miles of the mouth of the Osage." The committee was to meet at Côte Sans Dessein on the first Monday in May 1821, and proceed with their work. Since Côte Sans Dessein, on the north bank of the Missouri River at the confluence of the Osage, was the only place remotely resembling a village within the limits prescribed by the legislature, the commission recommended it as the capital site. But speculators, swarming into the village to capitalize on an anticipated land boom, made things difficult, and the assembly instructed the commission to look further. On December 31, 1821, the self-styled City of Jefferson, a rudimentary settlement several miles upstream from Côte Sans Dessein, was selected as Missouri's capital. Until a statehouse and adequate quarters for the assembly could be erected, St. Charles served as the seat of government.

For months the city of Jefferson consisted merely of a dramshop, a foundry, and a mission in the general neighborhood of Lohman's Landing—now the foot of Jefferson Street. Major Elias Bancroft platted the site in 1822. In May of the following year, Daniel Colgan was awarded a contract to build "a good brick building, 60 feet long, 40 feet wide, two stories high, with fireplaces well finished," which was to serve as the capitol and the governor's mansion. Erected on the site of the present executive mansion, it cost $18,573 of the $25,000 appropriated.

In 1823 only two families resided at the capital. The town was incorporated two years later, yet in 1826, when the general assembly moved there from St. Charles, the community had but 31 families, a general store, a gristmill, a distillery, some tanneries, and the Rising Sun Hotel. In 1825 Calvin Gunn founded the *Jeffersonian;* in the same year he was appointed State printer, a position he held until 1843.

The capital's wavering growth during early years prompted boosters of several other towns to clamor for the selection of a new seat of government. The future status of Jefferson City consequently became doubtful and settlers hesitated to establish themselves in the town. Lots sold slowly, and the general assembly was reluctant to provide necessary improvements. Governor John Miller finally declared in his 1832 message: "If this town is not to be the seat of government, the fact cannot be too soon made known . . . if it is to remain such, it is advisable to appropriate money for grading streets and other improvements."

Governor Miller suggested that the construction of a State penitentiary at Jefferson City would aid in strengthening the town's position as capital. The legislature appropriated $25,000 for this purpose in 1833, and the prison was completed in 1836. In a letter dated June 20, 1837, Ethelbert W. Lewis, a Virginian who stopped at Jefferson City en route to Howard County, gives a vivid glimpse of the frontier legislature:

> To acquire a just idea of the drama that is acting, you must picture to yourself a room crowded with men seated in rows, with tablets placed before every man, some writing, some talking, and some appearing indifferent to everything around them. . . . You must picture every kind of mortal from the serene old statesman to the most rough-hewn backwoodsman; with now and then a pert little dandy. . . . A Mr. Wilson of Van Buren County, a member of the lower house, came to Jefferson to take his seat in the legislature. He went into the senate chamber and offered his credentials. They informed him there of his mistake and told him he belonged to the other house. He replied: D——, I came through there but thought it was a grog shop.

The capitol burned in 1837. The original State seal and virtually all of the State records were lost in the blaze. The new statehouse, a $175,000 structure on the site of the present capitol, was completed five years later. Jefferson City, meanwhile, acquired permanent aspects. Pigs still wandered at will through its hilly streets, but stage service was available and steamboats docked regularly at Lohman's Landing. These facilities enabled local industries to expand. Flour and gristmills were built and the tanneries and distilleries throve. The development of the town was further accelerated by an influx of German immigrants.

Jefferson City was incorporated as a city in 1839. The census of the following year enumerated 1,174 inhabitants, including 262 slaves. For almost a decade thereafter, progress was steady. A frightful interruption came in 1849, however, when the Mormon vessel *Monroe* stopped at the city and discharged cholera-stricken passengers. Sixty-three of them died. Throughout the next two years the plague stalked the countryside, striking down settlers and paralyzing commerce.

The trans-State line of the Pacific Railroad was completed between St. Louis and Jefferson City in 1855. The first train, carrying the president of the railroad, the chief engineer, and an excursion party from St. Louis, was due to reach Jefferson City in the afternoon of November 1, 1855. A huge celebration was prepared. When the train reached Hermann, a coachload of soldiers was attached to lend pomp to the arrival at the capital. Traveling at 25 miles an hour, the train chugged onto a temporary trestle across the Gasconade River. The first pier collapsed and 8 coaches plunged through, dragging the engine back on them. Twenty-eight persons were killed and 30 were injured. Because of this disaster, train service between the capital and St. Louis was not begun until 1856.

The commercial promise of the railroad was soon obscured by the clouds of the approaching Civil War. Following Lincoln's election to the presidency, Jefferson City became the arena in which the question of adherence to or secession from the Union was debated. Governor Claiborne F. Jackson, however, openly sympathized with the South and favored secession.

After heated discussions, the assembly decided to refer the matter to a convention. The convention voted to remain in the Union. Governor Jackson nevertheless refused to recognize Federal authority and rejected President Lincoln's call for troops. Instead, he asked for 50,000 volunteers for the State militia—commanded by former Governor Sterling Price—and marched from the capital at the head of the Home Guard to join the Confederate forces at Boonville. Two days after his departure, Federal troops led by Colonel Frank P. Blair took possession of the city, pitching camp on Capitol Hill. The nearest approach to a battle occurred in 1864, when General Price came within 4 miles of the town and announced his intention of sacking it. Artillery fire was exchanged and Confederate cannon balls fell within the present city limits. When the Union troops received reinforcements, Price withdrew, continuing westward toward Kansas City.

Jefferson City was slow in recovering from the war until the constitution of 1875 (see History and Government) restored general peace of mind. An era of expansion, beginning in the 1880's, brought substantial benefits. Printing had already become an important industry, and, in 1881, a shoe manufactory was established. A second shoe plant began production in 1884, and a third factory, now closed, was opened shortly thereafter. A drawbridge was built across the Missouri River in 1895. In the same year Sedalia made a determined effort to wrest the capital from Jefferson City. An amendment for removal submitted to popular vote in November, 1896, was, however, defeated.

Since 1900, Jefferson City has developed from a comparatively small town into the State's eighth largest city. The completion of the present capitol in 1917, following the destruction of the old statehouse by fire in 1911, ended all doubts about the city's future status as Missouri's seat of government. Industrial changes have exerted little influence on the community, for it was born of politics, and government is still its principal business.

POINTS OF INTEREST

The NEW STATE OFFICE BUILDING (*open 9-5*), SE. corner High St. and Broadway, an eight-story, limestone structure of modern set-back design, is the newest of the government buildings. Completed in 1938, it houses the more important boards and commissions, and appointive offices.

The SUPREME COURT BUILDING (*open 9-5 weekdays*), SW. corner High and Washington Sts., is a three-story brick structure of modified French Renaissance design. Built in 1907, it contains the suites of the 8 supreme court justices, the courtrooms, the offices of the State's attorney-general, and a law library, said to be one of the best in the United States, of approximately 65,000 volumes.

The STATE CAPITOL (*open at all times; guides 8-5*), N. High St. between Broadway and Washington St., towers above a landscaped park which overlooks the Missouri River bluffs. The building was designed by Tracy and Swartout, and completed in 1917 at a cost of $4,125,000, including furnishings. Built of Carthage marble, it is an adaptation of Italian Renaissance styles. Four stories rise to the lanterned dome, where a recessed fifth story extends east and west. The bronze statue of Ceres, topping the lantern, is 262 feet above the ground and 400 feet above the river. The mass of the structure is relieved by a series of engaged columns on the north and east façades, and by porticoes of free Corinthian columns at each of the elevations.

Midway of the approach to the main or south entrance, facing High Street, are Robert I. Aitken's *Fountain of the Arts* (L) and *Fountain of the Sciences* (R). The frieze over this entrance, by Alexander S. Calder, represents Missouri History; the sculptured pediment, by A. A. Weinman, allegorically depicts Missouri surrounded by other figures. The grand entrance stairway, 120 feet wide at the base, ascends to the portico, opening onto the second floor and continuing upward to the third. On either side of the stairway, at the foot, are representations of the Missouri River (L) and the Mississippi (R), by Robert Aitken. A heroic bronze statue of Thomas Jefferson, by James E. Fraser, stands on a granite rostrum in the center of the flight. The bronze doors at the main entrance are said to be the largest cast in bronze since the Renaissance.

The terrace overlooking the river on the north side of the building bears a bas relief of the Signing of the Louisiana Purchase Treaty, by Karl Bitter. Below this is Weinman's bronze *Fountain of the Centaurs*. The frieze extending under the portico on this side of the building is an allegorical presentation of the changing civilizations, by Herman A. McNiel.

Entrances to the main floor, which contains museums and administrative offices, open left and right of the main portico and from the arched passage beneath it. The interior is finished chiefly in marble. The rotunda extends upward 68 feet into the eye of the dome. The interior of the dome and the successive floor levels of the rotunda are decorated by murals depicting human progress, designed by Frank Brangwyn of London and painted by A. W. Rinechede of New York. At the east end of the main rotunda is the Soldiers and Sailors Museum, which contains, among other historic relics, the battle flags of Missouri regiments and the portraits of all Missouri governors. The Missouri Resources Museum, at the west end, has mineral, agricultural, and commercial exhibits, and one of the State's most comprehensive Indian collections.

From the rotunda, curved marble stairways lead to the inaugural balcony where Missouri governors take the oath of office, and to the governor's office. The walk of open galleries in the central section of this floor, which contains the offices of elected executives, is decorated with 22 lunettes depicting Missouri in war and Missouri in peace. Smaller lunettes above doorways along the corridors portray episodes in the State's history.

The third, fourth, and fifth floors contain legislative chambers. Fraser's bronze statues of Meriwether Lewis (L) and William Clark (R) occupy two of the niches in the corridors of the third floor. Murals by Allen True, depicting Missouri types, fill the groins of the smaller domes at the four corners of the rotunda. The senate chamber is right, the house of representatives left. Both chambers are richly decorated and lighted by superb stained glass windows designed by H. T. Schladermundt of New York. The senate lounge is in the extreme east wing. In the extreme west wing is the house lounge, the walls of which bear the controversial Thomas Hart Benton murals (*see Art*).

The fifth floor gives access to a railed ledge in the dome. The acoustics are so excellent that a whisper is easily audible across the 60-foot span. The 12 stained-glass windows of the dome above the gallery are by Thomas Calvert. A flight of 214 steps leads to the highest accessible point in the building, an outdoor observation balcony at the base of the lantern atop the dome.

The EXECUTIVE MANSION (*private*), NW. corner Madison and Capitol Sts., on a bluff overlooking the Missouri River and enclosed with an ornamental iron fence, is a three-story mansard-roofed structure of French-Italian style. It was designed by George I. Barnett and built in 1871. The massive granite columns of the portico were donated by Governor B. Gratz Brown, who quarried them from his mines in Iron County. The porte-cochère and entrance on the south were added during the administration of Governor Alexander M. Dockery. On the first floor are the entrance hall, reception parlors, library, and dining room. The second floor contains 7 bedrooms; the third floor has 6 bedrooms and a billiard room. The winding stairway is one of the finest in Missouri. With the exception of the front hall, each room has a marble fireplace. The furnishings have been brought up-to-date at various times, but many old pieces have been retained.

MISSOURI STATE PENITENTIARY (*open 9-3 Mon.-Fri., except when closed by special conditions*), main entrance State and Lafayette Sts., on a 34½-acre rocky promontory above the Missouri River, consists of a group of red- and buff-brick buildings enclosed by turreted limestone walls. The prison consists of 6 modern cell blocks and 2 dormitories, the additional buildings containing 9 factories. It houses an average of 4,200 criminals, approximately one-half of whom are employed at a wage of from $1.00 to $5.00 a month. The women's prison, known as Prison Farm No. 1, is on the east, outside the prison wall. Its original building was once the mansion of James L. Minor, Secretary of State in 1839. Purchased by the State in 1926 and re-modeled, it has been supplemented by a new cell block.

The NATIONAL CEMETERY (*open 8-5*), 1042 E. McCarty Street, is the burial place of 78 Union soldiers slain in a battle near Centralia in September, 1864. The plot was purchased by the government in 1867. Soldiers killed in the World War are also interred here. WOODLAND CEMETERY, adjoining National Cemetery on the west, includes a plot allotted to the State in which are buried two Missouri governors: Thomas McReynolds and John S. Marmaduke.

LINCOLN UNIVERSITY (*open 8:30-4:30 weekdays*), between Lafayette, Chestnut, Dunklin, and Franklin Sts., is a State-supported university for Negroes. The enrollment is about 800. On the campus overlooking the city are two administration buildings, College Hall and Memorial Hall; the home economics building, Schweich Hall; the Mechanic arts building, Damel Hall; two women's and two men's dormitories; and the president's home. Here are also the power plant, farm cottage, and other farm buildings. Missouri law requires the institution to provide Negro residents of the State with educational opportunities comparable to those offered by the State University at Columbia. Lincoln University has an extension service designed to serve teachers in rural, town, and city schools who are interested either in self-improvement or in the completion of a college course. With a 60-acre farm near the campus and a 55-acre farm near Dalton, considerable attention is given to instruction in agriculture. In connection with the farm at Dalton, the university conducts the Dalton Vocational School.

Lincoln University grew out of an idea conceived during the Civil War around the campfires of the 62nd U.S. Colored Infantry while it was stationed at Fort McIntosh, near Galveston, Texas. The 65th U.S. Colored Infantry, under Major General Clinton B. Fisk (for whom Fisk University, Nashville, Tennessee, was named) endorsed the movement. Funds were solicited, and a committee on organization was appointed on June 8, 1866. The school, called Lincoln Institute, was opened at Jefferson City on September 17, 1866, with former Lieutenant Foster as president, succeeding a school taught by a group of white women for the freed Negroes of the community. The present site was acquired in 1866. In 1879 the institute was formally transferred to the State, and has since been maintained by legislative appropriations.

POINTS OF INTEREST IN ENVIRONS

Taos, 9 *m.;* Algoa Farms, 10.9 *m.* (*see Tour 4*). Westphalia, 15 *m.* (*see Tour 8*).

Joplin

Railroad Stations: Union Depot, NE. corner Main St. and Broadway, for Kansas City Southern, Atchison, Topeka & Santa Fe, and Missouri-Kansas-Texas Railroads; SE. corner Sixth and Main Sts., for St. Louis-San Francisco Railroad (Frisco Lines); S. side Tenth St., Main St. to Virginia Ave., for Missouri Pacific Railroad.

Bus Stations: Union Bus Terminal, NE. corner Third and Joplin Sts., for Southwestern Greyhound Lines, Crown Coach Co., and Vicory Transit Lines; Joplin Bus Depot, 317 S. Joplin St., for Missouri, Kansas & Oklahoma Trailways and Santa Fe Trailways; All-American Bus Station, 315 Main Sts., for All-American Bus Lines, Inc.

Airports: Municipal Airport, 4.7 m. NE. of post office on N. Main St. Rd. (Optional US 66); no scheduled service; taxi fare 50¢.

Interurban Stations: Joplin Public Service Co., 201 E. Fourth, for half-hourly bus service to Webb City, Carterville, and Carthage, Mo.

Taxis: 10¢ per passenger.

Local Busses: Fare 5¢.

Traffic Regulations: Speed limit 20 m.p.h.; free parking downtown.

Accommodations: Hotels, lodging houses, tourist camps.

Motion Picture Houses: Six.

Radio Station: WMBH (1450 kc.).

Concert Halls: Memorial Hall, SW. corner Eighth and Joplin Sts.

Athletics: Miners' Park, NE. corner Eighth and Joplin Sts., for Western Association baseball; Junge Field Stadium, Jackson to Murphy Ave., Thirteenth and Fifteenth Sts., for football.

Golf: Schifferdecker Park, NW. corner Seventh St. and Schifferdecker Ave., 18 holes; greens fee 35¢.

Tennis: Public courts in all city parks.

Swimming: Reding's Mill Park, Murphy Blvd., at Shoal Creek, 25¢ adults, 15¢ children; Sagmount, 3 miles south on Highway 71, 25¢ adults, 10¢ children; Cunningham Park, SE. corner Twenty-sixth St. and Maiden Lane, 10¢; Landreth Park, Murphy Blvd., at Finn St., 10¢; Leonard Park, NE. corner Seventh St. and Turk Ave., 10¢; Ewert's Park (for Negroes), NE. corner Seventh St. and Murphy Blvd.; YMCA (men and boys), SW. corner Fifth St. and Wall Ave., 10¢.

Riding: Schifferdecker Park, NW. corner Seventh St. and Schifferdecker Ave.

Annual Events: Fiesta, last week in April; Annual Smile Girl Contest, last week in May; Tri-State Kennel Club Show, last of Sept. or first of Oct.

JOPLIN (1,009 alt., 37,144 pop.), built literally upon the mines that have nurtured it, is near the center of a lead and zinc belt that swings in a 30-mile crescent across the corners of three States—the greatest zinc producing area in the world. Although Joplin's business and social life is keyed to the price of these metals, the increasing importance of local agricultural products and industries has eased the pinch of the lean mining years, and given Joplin a remarkable economic stability.

Straddling the boundary of Jasper and Newton Counties, the city is spread across a high, rolling prairie that covers many ore deposits. Since their discovery nearly a century ago, the richest horizons have been "worked out," leaving a labyrinth of abandoned passages which have been filled with water to provide a firm foundation for the city. South of Joplin, the prairie ends abruptly at Shoal Creek, whose winding valley and sharp, wooded bluffs—where an extensive city parkway has been developed—introduce the Ozark Highlands.

Joplin Creek, three blocks east of Main Street, divides the city into East Town and West Town, once rival mining camps and now distinguished from each other socially and financially. In West Town, the business section extends for 33 blocks along Main Street. Commercial structures, varying in height from two to five and more stories, dominate by sheer size and numbers the rather uniform residential area surrounding it. In this "downtown" section, between Third and Eighth Streets, are the principal hotels, theaters, banks, retail stores, and office buildings. At the Tenth Street intersection, a narrow wholesale and industrial district extends along the Missouri Pacific and the St. Louis and San Francisco railroads tracks. At Twelfth Street are the municipal market buildings, the crossroads for the wholesale fruit and produce trucks of neighboring States.

Once gaudy with saloons, dance halls, and gambling rooms, Main Street is now keyed to the conventional pitch of a prosperous American business street. With the exception of a flamboyantly ornamented three-story white building, once known as "The House of Lords" and famous for its saloon and gambling tables, and a scattering of other buildings dating from the boom days of the 1870's, most of the structures have been built since 1900. It is in the incidental aspects of Main Street life that Joplin's alliance with its past and with the Southwest becomes apparent. Among the well-dressed Middle Westerners who typify the region, one sees the tall, angular Ozark type, and an occasional cowboy from the Southwest. Sidewalk conversations mix the Ozark dialect with the Texas drawl. "Marriage parlors—one flight up," are open day and night, and second-hand stores near the edge of the business districts display, among a jumble of other items, cowboy boots and pistols.

The most prosperous homes and the city's few apartment houses are here in West Town. Along tree-shaded streets are well-kept brick and frame houses much alike in size and design. Close to the business section, among the older houses, are a few of the handsome homes erected by persons who "struck it rich" during early mining days. In the far northwest, between Byers and Jackson Avenues, and Glenview and Jaccard Avenues, the Roanoke district of modern houses crowns an elevation which looks out upon old Smelter Hill, now occupied by the Eagle-Picher Lead Company's plant and the dwellings of its employees.

Except for a small area of substantial homes in the Eastmoreland district centering about Fifteenth Street, East Town is a section of smaller residences. Broadway, the original business thoroughfare, still contains a few of the narrow brick and frame buildings and residences of days long past. Close to the business district live the majority of the Negroes who compose 2.2 per cent of Joplin's population, a considerable number of foreign-born, and the Indian groups who make up 1.9 per cent of the inhabitants. In the area where early "close-in" mining was conducted, the houses are small and shabby. Beyond this district, they appear increasingly prosperous.

Outside the fringe of Joplin's residential areas are the mines, the ore mills with their immense chat piles, and the mineral processing plants. Piles of weathered rock and shallow, weed-grown depressions mark the shafts of abandoned "gopher hole" mines. Mounds of new, raw earth show where occasional small operators are taking out the less profitable ore left by larger mining companies. Once the chat piles overshadowed everything, but today many of them have been used up in highway construction.

Joplin's story revolves around the mining first of lead, then of zinc. Yet it was not lead but land that attracted the first settlers to the area. In 1838, John C. Cox, a Tennesseean, settled on Turkey Creek, near the end of what is now Mineral Avenue. A year or two later, the Reverend Harris G. Joplin, a young Methodist minister from Greene County, Missouri, staked out an 80-acre tract, on which, near a spring which still flows, he built a cabin just east of the creek that now bears his name. By 1841, a settlement had grown up around the two cabins and Cox had opened a store. Commissioned postmaster, he set up in his store the community's first post office, called the Blytheville Postoffice in honor of Billy Blythe, a wealthy and popular Cherokee who lived on Shoal Creek. Church services were held in Reverend Joplin's cabin until he returned in 1844 to Greene County, where he died three years later.

The discovery of lead in the immediate vicinity of Joplin was accidental, despite the fact that the almost pure deposits were so close to the surface that they were sometimes exposed by flooding creeks or hard rains. About 1849, David Campbell, a miner from Neosho, visited his friend, William Tingle, on Turkey Creek at the mouth of Leadville Hollow. Noticing what he thought to be an abandoned Indian or Spanish excavation, Campbell investigated. When the first digging produced more than a hundred pounds of galena, Campbell and Tingle developed the mine. Pig lead from it was hauled overland to Boonville and sold by Tingle's slave, Pete. From there it was taken by steamboat to St. Louis. In 1850, the firm known as Tingle & McKee advertised that they had a good mine and were in the process of building a log furnace.

During the year of the Tingle-Campbell strike, a Negro boy belonging to Judge Cox turned up several large pieces of ore on Joplin Creek, near the Campbell mine, while digging for fishing worms.

"Cox's Mines or Nigger Diggings" developed, and soon other strikes were made in the Joplin Creek area. Further hope of immediate development, however, was shattered by the Civil War. No major engagements occurred in the vicinity, but Jasper and near-by counties became a marching and recruiting ground for the contending armies. Foraging parties discouraged mining enterprise by taking whatever they found, including smelted lead to use for bullets.

When the war ended, the richness of deposits in the vicinity attracted national attention. Old and new mining companies began operations, and miners and prospectors poured into the region. Land was offered for lease on a royalty basis of 10 per cent of the ore recovered. Necessary equipment consisted of a pick and shovel, a windlass and ore bucket, a hand drill, and some blasting powder. Here was the poor man's chance for fortune, and a fever of small mining operations broke out.

For the most part those who migrated to the Joplin and other Tri-State mining camps had little in common with the Bret Harte characters who crowded the West in the gold rush days. Although the mining camps drew their share of adventurers, most of the settlers were of English and Scotch-Irish descent—"hill folks" from the near-by Ozarks—who came with their wives and children. Even in the "wide open" early days, family life was the dominant factor in Joplin and the other mining camps of the area. Newly arrived European immigrants have played no rôle in the Tri-State mining fields. Until recently, the development of the area has been characterized by successful individual enterprise and a lack of labor disputes.

In 1870, the Granby Company, then the largest in the area, offered a prize of $500 to the miner or company of miners who produced the largest amount of ore within a given period. E. R. Moffet and John B. Sergeant, employees of the company, won the prize. Quitting their jobs, they leased a piece of land from Judge Cox along Joplin Creek and spent most of the prize money for powder and tools. They then sank the first shaft in the valley, and having struck a rich pocket of lead ore, built smelting furnaces on the present site of the Union Depot. A few years later, when Captain E. O. Bartlett invented a process for making sublimed white lead, Moffet and Sergeant purchased the patent. With this monopoly, and the expanding prosperity of the mining field, they developed their Lone Elm Mining and Smelting Company into one of the largest in the district.

Within a year after Moffet's and Sergeant's strike, 500 men were mining lead in the Joplin Creek valley, and intense rivalry sprang up among the various companies. On July 12, 1871, Patrick Murphy of Carthage organized the Murphysburg Town Company, which purchased a tract of 40 acres west of Joplin Creek and platted the town of Murphysburg. A few weeks later, Judge Cox retaliated by platting a townsite east of Joplin Creek, between Galena and Cox Avenues and Central and Valley Streets, which he named Joplin City in honor of his old friend, the Methodist minister. Rivalry between the two new towns was immediate, and bitter. Saturday night fights became the

accepted means of establishing superiority. Between major brawls—
lead by such characters as "Reckless Bill," "Three Fingered Pete,"
"Rocky Mountain Bob," and "Dutch Pete, the bad man from Bitter
Creek"—the children fought back and forth with stones. The winter
of 1871-2 was known as "the reign of terror," and "Dutch Pete" was
its monarch. But in the early spring, J. W. Lupton, a miner, licked
the armed bully, and other law-abiding citizens were stirred to action.
Lupton was made constable. On March 19, 1872, the county court
was petitioned to incorporate the two towns under one charter and
name it Union City. This charter had hardly been granted before its
legality was questioned, but on March 23, 1873, when the combined
population was approximately 4,000, the State general assembly passed
an act re-incorporating the two towns as the City of Joplin.

Because it was generally regarded as a boom town that would soon
exploit its wealth and die, the city at first held small attraction for
the railroads. In 1875, however, Moffet and Sergeant organized the
Joplin Railroad Company, which, in 1877, completed a 39-mile branch
line connecting with the Gulf Railroad at Girard, Kansas. Two years
later, this road was purchased by the St. Louis and San Francisco Railroad. In 1882, the Missouri Pacific Railroad extended its tracks to
Joplin; four other railroads followed during the next two decades.

The railroads not only provided a cheaper method of freighting lead,
but made possible the development of the zinc industry. Joplin's growth
was immediately stimulated. The potential value of zinc had been
pointed out before the Civil War, but its extraction was difficult, the
market price was low in comparison with lead, and freighting charges
were high. Miners consequently discarded "black jack" as worthless.
Eventually, however, a satisfactory means of processing the ore was discovered, and by 1872 Joplin began to ship out zinc. The price rose
rapidly from $3 to $15 per ton. In 1880, Jasper County zinc production was double that of lead.

By 1888, the city, with an approximate population of 8,000, was
a nationally recognized lead and zinc center. But the town was young,
and sudden wealth is a heady wine. Great fortunes were made and lost
in "handkerchief-size" plots. Men plunged, either in cards or with
mining leases. Miners were paid off in the saloons (the town had 40)
on Saturday nights, and spent Sundays nursing heads cracked during
drunken brawls. The price of metal fluctuated, and it was sometimes
possible for a miner to make more by digging ore himself and selling
it to a buyer than by working for the companies. Lead and zinc were
widely accepted as money. Small boys gleaned the waste discarded by
careless and inefficient mining methods, and turned in the metal for
candy. A miner who lacked cash for tickets at the Blackwell Opera
House could exchange a wheelbarrow load of ore for family admission.
Even groceries could be purchased with lead or zinc.

Eventually, of course, the town sobered up. The business men who
had control of the city government further developed the reform measures instituted by Lupton in the seventies, and changes began to take

place in the town's commercial life. Wholesale concerns were established. The smelters moved from the more or less exhausted local mines to the rich deposits which had been discovered south and west of the city, and Joplin settled down to the buying and selling of ore, the processing of metals, and other regional industries. By 1900, Joplin had become the largest town and railroad center of the district, and diversified activities had been introduced.

During the past 40 years, Joplin has come to realize the trade possibilities of her location between the Ozark Highland and the western plains. Within a 20 mile radius are commercial quantities of milk, eggs, wheat, and strawberries. Also available, though not quite as important, are chickens, wool, mohair, corn, hay, soybeans, cowpeas, grapes, apples, and other fruit. In 1930, the total value of agricultural products in the Joplin area was $7,064,413. Five railroads, 19 motor freight lines, and 7 motor bus companies make these raw products, and the markets of the Southwest, accessible to Joplin.

Mining and its allied industries, however, are still Joplin's major interest. From 1899 to 1938 inclusive, ore shipments from the area had an aggregate value of $826,550,365. Within the past few years, the structure of the industry has changed, for the independent operators have largely been absorbed by large, corporate enterprises, of which the Eagle-Picher Company is the most important. The period of consolidation has been accompanied by the development of central mills to replace small milling units. These changes, fundamental in the mining history of the region, have accented the unrest produced by the recent depression. A strike, called in 1935 by the International Union of Mine, Mill, and Smelter Workers for recognition of the union as an agency of collective bargaining, continued in varying forms until a decision handed down by the National Labor Relations Board on October 28, 1939, brought the strikers a measure of victory.

Various factors besides location, natural resources, and good transportation facilities have combined to make Joplin increasingly important as an industrial and wholesale center. Comparatively low wages, and a stable population of which 95.5 per cent are native-born whites, have been an inducement to capital investment. In 1937, 57 Joplin industries employing 1,349 people produced goods valued at $6,719,389. Chief among these products were crushed stone, animal fats and proteins, flour, limestone, marble, creosoted and wolmanized lumber, and various lead smelter products. Three explosives plants in the vicinity provide a large item in the city's freight with a combined annual capacity of 63,000,000 pounds of powder and dynamite. Considerable ore of good quality remains underground near Joplin, and, because many citizens hope operations may someday be renewed, water has been pumped from a number of the once-abandoned mines. Large amounts of tripoli, used in the manufacture of scouring powder and in ceramics, and of dolomite, used for glass manufacture, also are produced in the area. Yet zinc is still the dominant mineral, nearly seven tons of it being mined for each ton of lead, its nearest rival in production.

POINTS OF INTEREST

SCHIFFERDECKER PARK, NW. corner Seventh St. and Schifferdecker Ave., consists of 160 acres of rolling prairie and woodland. In it are a zoo, an 18-hole golf course, and a clubhouse. The MINERAL MUSEUM (*open 9-5, free*), within the park, contains several thousand specimens of Missouri minerals: lead, zinc, iron, calcium, and silicon in various forms. A few of the specimens weigh as much as 3,000 pounds. Included also are models illustrating the history of lead and zinc mining methods, and commercial exhibits of lead and zinc products. The museum was established by Tri-State mine owners and engineers in 1930.

SHOAL CREEK PARKWAY, south of Joplin, is accessible by S. Schifferdecker, S. Main, and S. Sergeant Avenues. Covering an area of 220 acres and consisting of McClelland Park, Witmer Park, McIndoe Park, and Barr and Bartlett Park, the parkway is a landscaped area following the winding valley of Shoal Creek. Picnic tables and ovens are located at scenic spots along the blacktop-paved drives, and swimming beaches along Shoal Creek have been developed.

The J. C. COX HOME (*open by arrangement 9-4*), north end of Mineral Ave., is a one-and-one-half-story red-brick house with stepped gable ends, built in 1867. Near this house John C. Cox settled in 1838 and built his first log-cabin home. A bronze tablet on the front of the building gives the date of erection and the builder's name. North of the house is the private cemetery of the Cox family, where the pioneer and several of his children are buried.

The MUNICIPAL MARKET (*open 7 a.m. to 7 p.m.*), Main and Virginia, and Twelfth and Thirteenth Sts., is housed in two buildings separated by a narrow driveway. The older structure, with a marquee overhanging the sidewalk on Main Street, is a two-story building of modified Romanesque design built in 1912. The other, erected in 1935, is one story in height and of modern warehouse design. The market serves as a wholesale clearing house for local fruit and vegetable farmers and for truckers from the Southwest. Approximately 30,000 trucks belonging to "gypsy" truckers and retail merchants use the market's facilities in handling an annual business of almost $1,250,000. Apples, tomatoes, grapes, and strawberries are the principal produce. All business is wholesale.

The JUNGE BAKING COMPANY (*open 9-4*), 1805 Main St., occupies a group of three- and four-story brick buildings. Started as a bread bakery by August and Albert Junge in 1900, the firm began making crackers and cookies in 1904. It now employs more than 300 persons during the busy season, and distributes its products in 20 States.

EAGLE-PICHER LEAD COMPANY PLANT (*private*), Perkins St. at Maiden Lane, crowning "Smelter Hill," is a group of corrugated iron and brick structures, where much of the Tri-State ore is converted into commercial products. Utilizing lead from the company's smelters at Galena, Kansas, the plant produces pigments and alloys, including babbitt, solder, and printer's metal. In 1927, the manufacture of rock wool from smelter slag was developed, and the rock wool plant was subsequently erected. Many of the manufacturing processes are secret. The present plant, with other units of the Eagle-Picher system, is the outgrowth of the lead furnaces established by O. H. and W. H. Picher in the Joplin district in 1874. The company pioneered in the development of the Picher (Oklahoma) lead and zinc field in 1912. A merger combining the Picher Lead Company with the Eagle White Lead Company of Cincinnati was made in 1916. Other companies were absorbed, starting in 1920, to form the present extensive Eagle-Picher organization. The Joplin plant of this company produces more than 22,000 tons of lead oxide, 13,000 tons of rock wool, and 3,500 tons of metal goods and alloys annually.

JOPLIN STOCK YARDS, INC. (*open weekdays*), Range Line Rd. to Florida Ave., and south of Turkey Creek along Newman Ave., are said to be the largest truck-in yards in the world. Established in 1931 by local capital to develop an additional farm market in Joplin, they now are a center from which truckers from Oklahoma, Arkansas, Missouri, and Kansas handle approximately $400,000 in live stock monthly. Auction sales are held every Friday and regular commission sales are held daily.

Kansas City

Railroad Stations: Union Station, 2400 Main St., for Atchison, Topeka & Santa Fe; Alton; Chicago, Burlington & Quincy; Chicago Great Western; Chicago, Milwaukee, St. Paul & Pacific; Chicago, Rock Island & Pacific; Kansas City Southern; Missouri, Kansas & Texas; Missouri Pacific; St. Louis & San Francisco (Frisco Lines); Union Pacific; Wabash.

Interurban: Missouri & Kansas R.R., hourly from 9th and Main Sts., to Olathe, Kans.

Bus Stations: Union Bus Terminal, 917 McGee St., for Crown Coach Lines, Finley-Shotwell Bus Line, Interstate Transit Lines, Jefferson Transportation Co., Kansas City & Independence State Lines, Kansas City & Leavenworth Transportation Co., Odessa-Kansas City Bus Lines, Southwestern Greyhound Lines, Inc., Southern Kansas Greyhound Lines, Union Pacific Stages. Union Bus Depot, NE. corner 11th and McGee Sts., for Burlington Trailways, Crown Coach Lines, Jefferson Transportation Co., Kaw Valley Stages, Missouri-Arkansas Coach Lines, Missouri Pacific Trailways, Santa Fe Trailways, Southern Kansas Greyhound Line. Ninth St. and Baltimore Ave., for Coltharp Bus Lines. Southside Bus Station, 3200 Troost Ave., for Crown Coach Lines, Southwestern Greyhound Lines, Finley-Shotwell Bus Lines.

Airport: Kansas City Municipal Airport, Clay County, 1.6 m. via Hannibal Bridge (*free*), for Transcontinental & Western Air, Inc., Braniff Airways, Mid-Continent Airlines. Bus fare 10¢, taxi 35¢ from downtown district.

Taxis: First mile 25¢, each additional mile, 10¢.

Streetcars and Busses: Fare 10¢; 4 tokens for 35¢.

Traffic Regulations: Parking meters downtown, 5¢ for ¼-1 hr., depending upon area. Night parking ½ hr. 3-6 a.m., except in stockyards district and other posted areas. No double parking, no parking adjacent to safety zones. No L. turn, no turn at posted intersections, no U-turn at light-controlled intersections. Speed limit, 25 m.p.h. in general; 20 m.p.h. at intersections not controlled by signal lights; 35 m.p.h. on through streets. Speed limit at night, 25 m.p.h.

Accommodations: 105 hotels; apartment hotels and lodging houses with wide range of rates; tourist camps on major highways.

Information Service: Chamber of Commerce of Kansas City, Hotel Continental, NW. corner 11th St. and Baltimore Ave.; Automobile Club of Missouri (AAA) 3239 Broadway (members only); Western States Automobile Club (NAA), 3937 Main St. (members only); Travelers' Aid Society, Union Station Lobby.

Theaters and Motion Picture Houses: Music Hall in Municipal Auditorium, Little Theater in Municipal Auditorium, 13th and Wyandotte Sts.; Kansas City Resident Theater at 1600 Linwood Blvd.; Gillis Theater, burlesque, 506 Walnut St.; over 50 motion picture theaters (5 first run).

Athletics: Ruppert Stadium (American Association Baseball), 2128 Brooklyn Ave.; Bourke Field, Rockhurst College (football), 53rd St. and Troost Ave.; Pla-Mor Park (softball), 26 W. 31st St. Ter.; Pla-Mor Ice Palace (hockey), 3127 Wyandotte St.; Arena, Municipal Auditorium (wrestling, boxing, basketball), 13th and Wyandotte Sts.

Swimming: Pla-Mor Pool, 3127 Wyandotte St.; Boulevard Manor, 1115 E. Armour Blvd.; Fairyland Park, 7501 Prospect Ave.; Municipal Pools (*free*). The Lagoon, Swope Park, Meyer Blvd. and Swope Parkway; Penn Valley, 26th and Jefferson Sts.; The Grove, 15th St. and Benton Blvd.; Garrison Square, 5th St. and Troost Ave.; West Terrace, 17th and Jarboe Sts.; The Parade (Negro), 15th St. and the Paseo.

Golf: Fee Courses: Armour Fields, 67th St. Ter. at Ward Parkway; St. Andrews, 89th and Summit Sts.; South Ridge, Grandview and Red Bridge Rds.; Stayton Meadows, Sterling Ave. and US 40. Municipal Courses: Swope Park No. 1 (18 holes 50¢, except Sunday 75¢) and Swope Park No. 2 (18 holes 25¢) Swope Park. Five membership clubs.

Tennis: Over 130 public courts (*free*), supervision of Park Board, Swope Park, smaller parks, parkways, and neighborhood sites.

Riding: Clark Johnson's Tapawingo Stables, US 40 at Lake Tapawingo; Sunnyside Stables, 82nd and Summit Sts.; Blake Swope Park Stables, 7900 Oldham Rd.

Amusement Parks: Fairyland Park, 75th and Prospect Sts., usual park equipment.

Radio Stations: WDAF (610 kc.); KMBC (980 kc.); WHB (880 kc.); KCMO (1480 kc.); KITE (1590 kc.); and W9CAL (*experimental television*).

Annual Events: Better Homes and Building Exposition, Feb.; Kansas City International Food Fair, National Intercollegiate Basket Ball Tournament, March; Sportsman's Horse Show and Exposition, April; Heart of America Good Will Golf Tournament, May; Kansas City Golf Open Tournament, Country Club Fiesta, July; Guadalupe Fiesta (Mexican Colony), Outdoor Art Fair, Sept.; American Royal Livestock and Horse Show, Oct.; Kansas City Automobile Show, Nov.

KANSAS CITY (723 alt., 399,178 pop.), Missouri's second largest city, is the crossroads and market place for almost the entire western half of the United States. Two things are chiefly responsible for its stature, according to Henry J. Haskell: "The great bend of the Missouri, and Nelson of *The Star*." The former provided the reason for building the city; the latter shaped its modern development. Where the Missouri River turns north, early Western immigrants disembarked, to take up their journey on the overland trails. This gave Kansas City an initial trade advantage, which the modern town has amplified with 12 trunk-line railways, a network of modern highways, river barge lines, and air routes. To this vigorous industrial scene, the late William Rockhill Nelson, through his agitation in the *Star* and with the aid of a group of influential citizens, added a landscaped boulevard system, parks, improved residential areas, a museum, and other civic improvements.

Downtown Kansas City, extending east from the bluffs above the Kaw and south over the hills from the Missouri to Thirty-first Street, is marked by contrasts and evidences of uneven development. The intersection of Twelfth and Main Streets is the nerve center of the area. Around it are concentrated the major stores and theaters, and most of the large hotels. The new civic center, its plaza dominated by the City Hall and the Courthouse, is located a few blocks east of the intersection; southwest of it are the Kansas City Power and Light Building, tallest structure in the State (1940), and the imposing new Municipal

Auditorium. But within a few blocks of the auditorium is a row of frowsy tenements which were once the dignified houses of "Quality Hill," and within sight of a modern skyscraper, a clay bank looms raw and yellow. Between the beautifully landscaped grounds of Liberty Memorial and dignified Hospital Hill, with its impressive red-brick buildings, is a cluttered mass of billboards. As plans for civic improvement mature, however, many of these anomalies will disappear. The efforts of private builders and public officials to create a homogeneous city have already accomplished notable results, particularly in unifying the city's architecture.

In a rough circle about the downtown district are the homes of the Negroes who make up 9.6 per cent of the city's population. Most of them are employed in industrial plants, or as domestic help. They have their own business and theater district on Eighteenth Street, between Troost Avenue and Vine Street.

The railroad-threaded industrial district, the city's second major division, begins on the west within a few blocks of the downtown center, in the Kaw bottom just under the bluffs, and swings in a wide crescent two-thirds of the way around the city. From Twenty-third Street north to Twelfth Street, the Stockyards and Livestock Exchange straddle the State Line in a neighborhood of cattlemen's cafés and harness shops. In these two districts live most of Kansas City's second largest foreign group, some 3,000 Mexicans employed by the railroads and packing houses. Northward, on the flat lands toward the Kaw's mouth, the Central and Woodswether industrial districts reach to the municipal docks. Swerving northeast, back from the river front, the industrial area thins down toward the huge grain elevators in the north and east bottoms, then sheers far back from the low flood plains to pursue the bluffs into the Blue River Valley at Kansas City's northeastern tip. Thence it follows the Blue River, whose color at this point is at odds with its name, past the Ford Motor Company plant and the widely flung mills of the Sheffield Steel Corporation, to the Chevrolet and Fisher Body plants in the Leeds district beyond Thirty-first Street. South of Fortieth Street are limestone quarries.

Between this line of industries and the downtown section, the residential district extends southward. The unpretentious middle-class section, an area about nine miles north and south by four miles east and west, lies east of a line drawn roughly along Troost Avenue and Rockhill Road. Among the older houses at the northern tip, once the exclusive "Northeast" residential section, is the 72-room mansion of the late R. A. Long, lumber king; the building is now the Kansas City Museum. Between Garfield and Prospect Avenues, from Independence Avenue north to Cliff Drive, imitation Tudor castles of stone, and imposing brick houses with towers and oak floors of elaborate parquetry, have been converted into apartment and rooming houses. Here, too, is an extension of the Italian colony, separated from the larger group around Holy Rosary Church at Independence Avenue and Campbell Street by the Tracy Avenue Negro section. Kansas City's 12,500

Italians compose the larger part of its foreign born. They were first attracted here by the fevered railroad construction in the latter half of the past century, but at present they operate small businesses, work in industry, or hold minor political posts.

The internationally known Country Club district, south of Forty-seventh Street and west of Rockhill Road, which contains the city's finest homes, was Kansas City's first planned residential section. In 1908, when J. C. Nichols began its development with the encourage-ment of the tireless Nelson, this neighborhood was a confused debris of Negro shanties, trash dumps, and abandoned rock quarries. Now it is a carefully landscaped stretch of broad, winding streets which follow the natural contours of the land. The park intersections contain statuary and other art objects brought from Europe. Country Club Plaza, at Forty-seventh Street and Mill Creek Parkway, the business section of the district, has Spanish-type buildings of cream-colored brick and stucco, grouped about open park lots.

Lacing together the various sections of Kansas City is a $40,000,000 boulevard system developed from the plans of the late George E. Kess-ler. The first unit around West Terrace Park was completed in 1910, largely through the activity of Nelson and his Kansas City *Star*. To-day, it is possible to start at Sixth Street Trafficway in West Terrace Park, travel almost entirely around the city, double back through its center to the southern limits, then return to the business district, without leaving the boulevards. The Paseo, planned originally as the most elaborate boulevard, still has pergolas and sunken gardens at its northern extremity, where it traverses a once-luxurious apartment house district now occupied by Negroes, but it is of less importance today than some of the newer south-side thoroughfares.

Kansas City had its beginning in two roaring frontier settlements: the Missouri River town of Kansas, and the bullwhacking, feverish town of Westport, four miles to the south on the Santa Fe Trail. The town of Kansas originated in the post which François Chouteau, an employee of the American Fur Company, established in the Kaw River bottom, in the spring of 1821. Chouteau's post served as a depot from which the other posts of the company could be supplied and their furs collected. With Chouteau came traders, trappers, laborers, and voy-ageurs, with their wives and children—15 or 20 families in all. When a flood destroyed Chouteau's warehouse about 1830, he moved his post a few miles east to the foot of the present Grand Avenue, where Peter Roy had established a ferry in 1828.

After the *Independence* had proved the Missouri River to be navigable by steamboats in 1819, and the Indians had been removed in 1825, western Missouri began filling with settlers. Jackson County was organized in 1826, with the county seat some ten miles east of Chouteau's settlement, at Independence; this rapidly 'became the prin-cipal outfitting point for wagon freighting to Santa Fe and northern Mexico, and for emigrants to Oregon in the early 1840's. The trail to Santa Fe lay west from Independence, crossing the Big Blue River some four or five miles south of the Missouri River.

West of this ford and the long hill beyond it, John Calvin McCoy built a store in 1832, to cater to the needs of those returning from the Southwest, and to catch some of the overflow business from Independence. The following year he platted the town of Westport, offering lots to newcomers on condition that they build and conduct some kind of business. Westport merchants received their goods by steamboat at the ferry landing four miles to the north, where Chouteau had established his new post. The town soon vied with Independence as the eastern terminus of the Santa Fe Trail. Guests at the historic Harris House, which stood at the present corner of Fortieth and Main Streets, included General John C. Frémont and Francis Parkman, the author. The latter wrote in 1846: "Westport is full of Indians, whose little shaggy ponies were tied by dozens along the houses and fences. Sacs and Foxes, with shaved heads and painted faces; Shawnee and Delawares fluttering in calico frocks and turbans; Wyandottes dressed like white men, and a few wretched Kansas wrapped in old blankets, were strolling about the streets. Whiskey circulates more freely in Westport than is altogether safe in a place where every man carries a loaded pistol in his pocket."

The discovery of California gold did not provide the same impetus to Westport that it gave to other Western towns, for in 1849 Asiatic cholera, brought by the gold-seekers, broke out. When the gold rush subsided, and the railroads were extended to Fort Leavenworth, Westport had little further reason for existence.

Meanwhile, the settlement at Chouteau's Post, called "Westport Landing" by both Westport and Independence, had grown into a prosperous community. The opening of the Platte Purchase in northwest Missouri for settlement in 1836 had brought both immigrants and trade. When Ceran St. Vrain and William Bent, famous fur traders on the upper Arkansas River, began hauling their freight direct to the landing in 1845, they established a precedent which was followed by others. Soon "Westport Landing" was an active community with a thriving trade of its own. When Gabriel Prudhomme, who owned the land, died in 1838, the "Kansas Town Company" purchased his farm of 271 acres for $4,220, platted it into lots, and named it Kansas. The original town site was the land now bounded by the Missouri River, Broadway, Forest Avenue, and the section line that crosses Main Street at Missouri Avenue. A disagreement among the investors restricted development until 1846, when the company was reorganized, and another sale of lots was held. The population was then 700.

The Santa Fe trade brought new business to the village. Five or six steamboats were sometimes unloading their freight at the levee at the same time. The streets were filled with spenders, gamblers, and the roistering brotherhood of the trail. Oxen bellowed and mules brayed while lusty drivers, cursing in a dozen languages and dialects, cracked their long whips. The outbound Mexican trains were laden heavily with whisky, for which there was an insatiable demand. What loading space was left was packed with groceries, cotton goods, notions, and Indian trade goods. Returning caravans were freighted with furs, buffalo robes, dried buffalo meat, Mexican dollars, and, eventually, with rawhide sacks of gold dust. Within a period of 5 months during 1848-9, some 900 wagons started on their journey from the village. About 2,000 travelers were outfitted here in a trade estimated at $5,000,000.

When the cholera epidemic broke out, the boom collapsed, and for the next six years most of the trade went elsewhere. The population was more than halved. None the less, a charter was obtained incorporating the village as "the City of Kansas," February 22, 1853. By 1855 much of the overland trade had returned. Grand Avenue was graded and widened that year, and soon four other streets were cut through the bluffs and cross streets were opened. Gullies were gradually filled, and the sharp hills leveled. In this same year, R. T. van Horn, for more than 30 years the champion of Kansas City's development, became editor of the Kansas City *Enterprise* (est. 1854). A board of trade became the Chamber of Commerce in 1857, when the city "was in a neck-and-neck race with Leavenworth and St. Joseph for the rich prize of the great commercial metropolis of the far West." Albert D. Richardson, a New York *Tribune* reporter, found the levee "a confused picture of immense piles of freight, horse, ox, and mule teams receiving merchandise from the steamers, scores of immigrant wagons, and a busy crowd of whites, Indians, half-breeds, Negroes and Mexicans." Everything wore the accidental, transitory look of a new settlement, and there was "much stir and vitality and the population, numbering two thousand, had unbounded, unquestioning faith that there was *the* City of the Future."

Despite the seeming good times, Kansas City by 1856 had already known two years of incipient civil war. The citizens, mainly Southern sympathizers, were involved in the organization of the Kansas and Nebraska territories. Their resistance to the growth of anti-slavery interests in these areas was fanned by pro-Southern groups elsewhere who sent armed bands into Jackson County. In the spring of 1856, recruits arrived from Alabama, Georgia, and South Carolina, commanded by a Major Buford; soon others came under "Titus of Virginia, Whitfield, Jenizen, Coleman, Bell and others." Fiercely excited public meetings were held. Armed Southerners rode about town shouting "Death to all the damned Yankees." Patrons of the Gillis House on the levee, nicknamed "the Free State Hotel," because it was owned by the New England Emigrant Aid Society of Boston, slept uneasily with "revolvers under our pillows and a Sharp's rifle close at hand." The society hastily leased the building to a strong pro-slavery man.

Bands of marauders were organized to raid eastern Kansas; the Kansas "Red-Legs" pillaged and murdered in western Missouri. "Both groups acted in the name of patriotism." The outbreak of the Civil War caused the local conflict to enter a new and more desperate phase.

Agriculture and trade were disrupted; commerce was driven from the river. The town grew more and more shabby; the streets went unrepaired, the taxes unpaid. The daily news was a repetition of such items as: "Major —— yesterday killed six bushwhackers and burned three houses." "Captain —— captured three Union soldiers, cut off their ears and hung them to a tree between here and Independence." Following Quantrill's raid on Lawrence in 1863, during which 150 men were killed, the Union General, Thomas Ewing, Jr., stationed in Kansas City, issued his Order No. 11, by which the major part of the counties of Jackson, Cass, Bates, and part of Vernon, in Missouri, were depopulated. Rebel sympathizers were forbidden to follow any business within the area. A year later, Union and Confederate armies clashed on the outskirts of the city in the Battle of Westport, the "Gettysburg of the West." Again the population dropped.

Peace brought a new and strangely altered West, and for Kansas City the beginning of a period of uninterrupted growth. As C. L. Edson's ballad puts it:

> The herders and the traders and the sod corn crew
> They planted 'em a city when the world was new;
> They planted Kansas City, and the darn thing grew.

New markets opened as the frontier was pushed into the Far West. Corn and wheat and cattle from the plains supplanted the gradually dying overland commerce. In 1865 the end of the pack train and steamboat era was marked by the coming of the first railroad into the city—the Missouri Pacific—and a new geographic trump was discovered.

The natural water-level grades which the railroads followed converge at the mouth of the Kaw. As Henry Haskell points out: "take a freight car two hundred miles to the northwest, west, or southwest of that strategic point, give it a shove, and it will coast down to Kansas City. That fact determined the location of the future distributing center." Soon a network of lines developed, and along their routes farms and towns grew up. Wheat and cattle became the staple crops of the prairies. When the Missouri cattle trails were closed (*see Agriculture*) to Texas cattle, annual drives were made to the Kansas towns along the new railroad lines. In 1870 the first stockyards were built in Kansas City. Within a few years the town became the center of the trade, and packing houses were opened. At first most of the cattle handled in Kansas City were from Texas, but by 1890 Kansas and Missouri furnished the majority. Kansas City, however, never became a typical cow town. A few herdsmen brought something of the cow country atmosphere to the stockyards district, but "the boys in the high heel boots, chaps and spurs" were swallowed up in the larger life of a community busy killing hogs, handling wheat, grinding flour, and supplying agricultural implements to the grain farmers.

Kansas City developed as a grain center after the grasshopper plagues of 1874, which made necessary the shipment of corn to Kansas.

New capital was attracted. By the next year, when the westward movement of corn ceased, the eastward movement of wheat began. The trade was anchored by the erection of an exchange building in 1877, and a steady growth of elevator and milling activity followed.

The city had found its stride. A Union Depot (the second in the world) was erected in 1878, and enlarged two years later. It continued to serve until the present Union Station was opened in 1914. The Kaw was bridged in 1866, and the Hannibal Bridge—the first across the Missouri River—was completed in 1869, to be supplemented by the Armour-Swift-Burlington Bridge in 1909. The city annexed nearby Westport in 1897. Horse car lines appeared, succeeded by cable cars, and finally by the overhead trolley cars which had been invented by John C. Henry of Kansas City in 1884. A convention hall built in 1899 was destroyed by a fire a year later. Its successor was rushed to completion in 90 days, to be ready for the Democratic National Convention of 1900, which nominated William Jennings Bryan for the presidency. An era of park building and public improvements began. Kersey Coates Drive grew out of an almost impenetrable jungle. Vinegar Hill was transformed into the beginning of Penn Valley Park.

Kansas City had prospered. The fortuitous bend in the river had given it a head start; the slope of the land had provided a long lead in the race for supremacy. The herders and the traders and the sod corn crew had done their part. The city was not pretty, but it was lively in the lusty Western fashion. Even a Kansas City writer (1879) admitted the city was not "tame," but the determined spirit to make it "*the* City of the Future," which Richardson had noted a decade before, remained. Then came William Rockhill Nelson, to demonstrate what one man with a fixed idea, a stubborn spirit, and a newspaper all his own, could do.

Born in Indiana, March 7, 1841, Nelson had studied law and had been admitted to the bar, had raised cotton, done contracting for roads and buildings, and had been part owner of a Fort Wayne newspaper. In his thirty-ninth year he decided to start his own newspaper, and chose Kansas City as the most advantageous site. Thus, in 1880, he became owner and Editor-in-Chief of the Kansas City *Star*. Immediately, he began a relentless agitation for civic improvement: better streets, better homes, better buildings; parks, statuary, museums. The Star prospered. It absorbed the Kansas City *Mail* in 1882, founded the *Weekly Star* in 1890, added a Sunday edition in 1894, bought the Kansas City *Times* in 1901, and began making white paper for its own use in 1903 (*see Newspapers and Radio*). Through the daily repetition of its message, a group of influential Kansas Citians were encouraged to realize William Rockhill Nelson's ideal of a city as beautiful as it was prosperous.

The two decades that followed 1900 brought auto assembly plants and a gradually increasing variety of industries to Kansas City. Stimulated by the World War, business in horses, mules, and cattle reached new heights. Viaducts were completed connecting Kansas City, Mis-

ST. LOUIS : KANSAS CITY

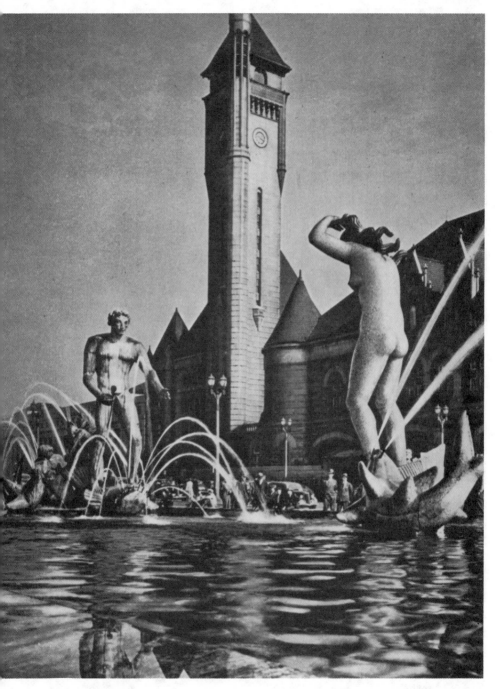

St. Louis Post-Dispatch

THE MEETING OF THE WATERS, Group by Carl Milles,
Aloe Plaza, St. Louis

CITY ART MUSEUM IN FOREST PARK, ST. LOUIS

LUCAS SUNKEN GARDEN, ST. LOUIS

Nagel & Dunn, Architects

ST. MARK'S EPISCOPAL CHURCH, ST. LOUIS

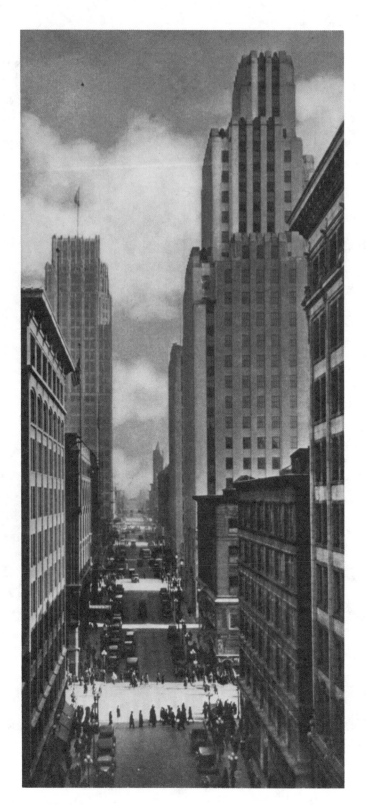

ELEVENTH STREET, KANSAS CITY

Earl Hense

**CIVIL COURTS BUILDING,
ST. LOUIS**

Charles Trefts

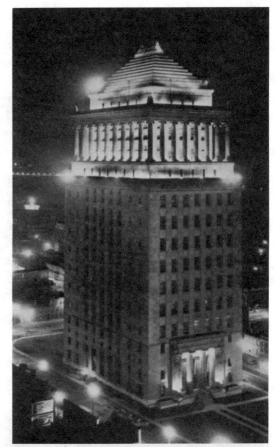

**MUNICIPAL AUDITORIUM,
KANSAS CITY**

Harkins Commercial Photo Company; Kansas City Star

**UNION STATION WITH DOWNTOWN KANSAS CITY
SKYLINE IN BACKGROUND**

HOMES IN COUNTRY CLUB DISTRICT, KANSAS CITY

Missouri Writers' Project

**WILLIAM ROCKHILL NELSON GALLERY OF ART
AND MARY ATKINS MUSEUM, KANSAS CITY**

SWOPE PARK, KANSAS CITY

Jackson Company

Municipal Theatre Association

"MUNY" OPERA—ST. LOUIS
Crowds gather nightly in Forest Park during the Summer
to enjoy performances of the Municipal Opera Company

souri, with Kansas City, Kansas. The population increased from 163,752 to 324,410.

Today (1940) Kansas City is the leading hay market and seed distribution center of the world, the second general livestock market, the first in stocker and feeder cattle, the first in horses and mules. In addition to the traffic of its railroads, more than 100,000 tons of freight are shipped annually over the Missouri River.

Kansas City can also pride itself upon many cultural achievements. It established the University of Kansas City in 1935. It is the home of many denominational and specialized schools, among them the Unity School of Christianity, a religio-ethical organization with a large following, which originated and maintains its headquarters here. The concerts of its philharmonic orchestra attract audiences from a wide region. Its William Rockhill Nelson Gallery of Art and Mary Atkins Museum of Fine Arts ranks among the foremost in the country.

Since 1931, Kansas City and Jackson County have been undergoing extensive changes under a ten-year plan, a city and county project which entails an expenditure of approximately $60,000,000 in city and Federal money. The program includes the construction of numerous public buildings, improvement of the Municipal Airport, beautification of the Liberty Memorial, and a general opening up of congested districts by broad highways and spacious parks.

POINTS OF INTEREST

1. MUNICIPAL AUDITORIUM (*open for group tours 9-4 weekdays, 1-3 p.m. Sun.*), Thirteenth to Fourteenth, Wyandotte to Central Sts., completed in 1936 as a PWA project, is an Indiana limestone structure of modern design, equal in height to a ten-story building. The simplicity of its almost windowless walls is relieved by A. T. Stewart's medallions and friezes depicting the industrial and agricultural activities of the Middle West. The $6,500,000 structure contains the Arena, with no posts to obstruct vision, seating 12,000; the Music Hall, home of the Kansas City Philharmonic Orchestra, seating 2,572; the Little Theater, seating 600; 28 committee rooms; and an exhibition hall with 3½ acres of floor space. Murals by Ross Braught decorate the stairway and the Music Hall. The building has the third largest air-conditioning plant in the United States. It is approached from the north over a wide mall and trafficway, vacated by the demolition of the Convention Hall which was erected in 1900 (*see Architecture*).

2. The KANSAS CITY POWER AND LIGHT BUILDING (*observation tower open 9-11:15 a.m., 12:30-4 p.m., Mon. through Fri., except holidays*), northwest corner Fourteenth St. and Baltimore Avenue, with 34 stories comprising 481 feet, is Missouri's tallest building. Designed by Hoit, Price & Barnes, it is constructed of steel and Indiana limestone. The structure is square at the base and tapered through setbacks, to form a tower near the top. At the thirty-second floor, small observation balconies on the four sides of the lantern-type tower afford

an extensive view of the city and its environs. In the great cage of glass crowning the tower, lights are automatically turned on by a photo-electric cell when daylight has diminished below a certain intensity. This flame-like beacon can be seen by plane at a distance of 75 miles. The LIGHTING INSTITUTE (*open 9-12, 1-5, Mon. through Fri.*), a free industrial exhibit which includes one of Edison's early dynamos, is maintained on the eighth floor.

3. The KANSAS CITY DIVISION JACKSON COUNTY COURTHOUSE (*open 9-5 Mon.-Fri., 9-12 Sat.*), Twelfth to Thirteenth, Oak to Locust Sts., a $4,000,000 structure of Indiana limestone in modern setback design, forms a unit of the new Civic Center. On the facades are carvings by Charles L. Keck, who also created the bronze statue of General Andrew Jackson—for whom the county was named—that stands before the north approach. The county jail, with a capacity of 450, occupies 3 of the upper floors. This structure, one of two Jackson county courthouses, serves the western part of the county, which was organized as a unit in 1892.

4. CITY HALL (*open 8-5 weekdays: observation gallery open 9-4:30 Mon. through Fri., 9-12 Sat.*), Eleventh to Twelfth, Oak to Locust Sts., with a height of 425 feet, dominates the Civic Center. Constructed of steel and Indiana limestone, in modern setback design harmonizing with other new structures, it was completed in 1937 as a PWA project at a cost of $5,000,000. Major episodes in the city's history are depicted in a frieze of 16 panels directly above the sixth story; those on the east and west were designed by Ulrich Husen, that on the south by Paul Jennewin, and that on the north by Walker Hancock. All the carvings were done by Ugo La Vaggi. The Council Chamber, called one of the most beautiful legislative halls in America,

---

KANSAS CITY. Points of Interest

1. Municipal Auditorium
2. Kansas City Power and Light Building
3. Kansas City Division Jackson County Courthouse
4. City Hall
5. Meyer Memorial
6. New York Life Building
7. Lookout Point
8. Kansas City Livestock Exchange and Stockyards
9. Kansas City Museum
10. Cliff Drive
11. Concourse
12. Indian Mound
13. Mercy Hospital
14. Union Station
15. Liberty Memorial
16. Penn Valley Park
17. Washington Square
18. Hospital Hill
19. Union Cemetery
20. Harris Home
21. Kansas City Art Institute
22. William Rockhill Nelson Gallery of Art and the Atkins Museum of Fine Arts
23. Swope Park
24. University of Kansas City
25. Site of the Battle of Westport
26. Alexander Majors House

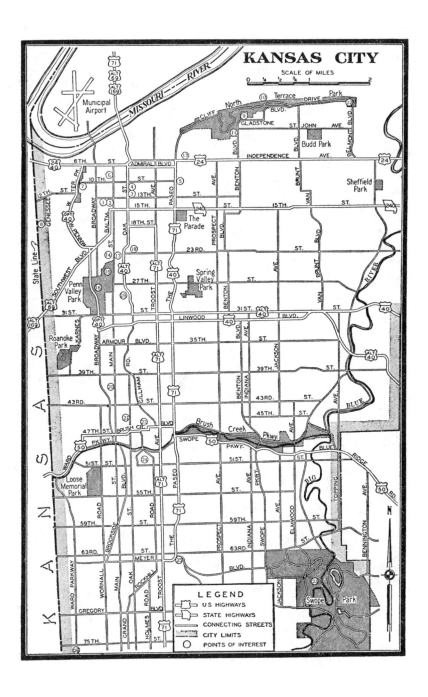

is paneled in rift-sawed oak, decorated with arabesques of bronze. At the thirtieth floor is an observation balcony with a telescope. City Hall Plaza, facing Twelfth Street and the courthouse beyond, rises in walled terraces and a series of fountain pools which cover the building's underground garage.

5. MEYER MEMORIAL, Tenth St. and the Paseo, was provided for by public subscription and dedicated June 2, 1909, in recognition of August R. Meyer's leadership in the development of Kansas City's park and boulevard system. Mr. Meyer was the first president of the park board and, with William Rockhill Nelson and George E. Kessler, provided the mainspring for the development of the system. Born in St. Louis in 1851 of German parents, Meyer's childhood was spent in Germany. Later he returned to the United States, where he worked as United States Government assayer at Leadville, prospered as a mining engineer, and came to Kansas City in 1881. A life-size bas-relief figure of Mr. Meyer, the work of Daniel Chester French, appears on a bronze panel inset on the south side of a 15-foot shaft of Tennessee marble.

6. The NEW YORK LIFE BUILDING, NE. corner Ninth St. and Baltimore Ave., Kansas City's first skyscraper, was designed by McKim, Mead & White, and built in 1890. Structural steel was not used in it, and its ten story height approaches the maximum for masonry walls.

The building is faced with granite, brownstone, brick, and terra cotta. The corners are accented by quoins. Above the third floor, the building takes the shape of the letter H. Across the south elevation are 5 arches each 33 feet high, of which the center arch, with its wrought-iron grille, forms the main entrance. Above this is a two-ton bronze of an eagle with outstretched wings poised above a nest containing two eaglets. The eagle's wings measure 12 feet from tip to tip. The group was designed by Louis Saint-Gaudens, cast in one piece, and placed in its present position in February 1891.

7. LOOKOUT POINT, West Tenth and Summit Sts., is at the crest of the palisades that tower above the west bottoms and Kersey Coates Drive. Wide stone stairs wind down the cliff from a terrace set off by balustrades and two ornamental towers. This point commands a view of the Central and Woodswether industrial districts, the stockyards, the packing plants in Kansas City, Kansas, the confluence of the Kaw and Missouri Rivers, the Municipal Wharf, and the Municipal Airport. West Terrace Park, which includes the palisades, extends south along the bluffs from Clark's Point at Sixth Street Trafficway and Pennsylvania Avenue to Seventeenth and Holly Streets.

8. KANSAS CITY LIVESTOCK EXCHANGE AND STOCK-YARDS (*open*), 1600 Genessee St., serve the packing plants of Kansas City, Kansas, and the Nation's largest horse and mule market. The EXCHANGE BUILDING, where buyers and commission firms have their offices, is in Missouri, but 64 per cent of the yards are in Kansas City, Kansas. The building, of concrete and brick, is nine stories tall and contains five acres of floor space. In the yards, which extend from

Twenty-third Street on the south to Twelfth Street on the north, and from Genessee Street to the Kaw River, are 238 acres of pens connected with the large packing house by chutes and runways and a special double-decked bridge. Of the yardage, 87 acres are under cover. Daily capacity is 70,000 cattle, 50,000 hogs, 50,000 sheep, 5,000 horses and mules. Horse and mule auctions are held each Monday in a barn at the southeast corner of Nineteenth and Wyoming Streets. At Twenty-third Street is the AMERICAN ROYAL PAVILION, erected to house the American Royal Horse and Livestock Show that began in 1878. The present building dates from 1925, when its predecessor was partly destroyed by fire.

9. The KANSAS CITY MUSEUM, 3218 Gladstone Blvd., housed in the former R. A. Long home, built in 1908 in modified French Renaissance design, crowns a promontory overlooking the Missouri River valley. The Kansas City Museum is a nonprofit, private organization, developed in 1939 for the purpose of creating a museum of science and history stressing the background of the Middle West. Through the co-operation of the R. A. Long heirs and Kansas City, the house became the property of the organization. The museum contains the Daniel B. Dyer Collection of North and South American Indian objects; the Missouri Valley Historical Society Collection of frontier source material; the Board of Education Collection covering the fields of industrial and natural science; and the William Volker Chinese and Japanese Collection.

10. CLIFF DRIVE, traversing North Terrace Park for 3.2 miles between Woodland and Belmont Aves., affords an excellent view of the Missouri River water front and the industrial district of North Kansas City across the river. This winding, scenic drive is known throughout the country for its rugged beauty. Cliff Drive Spring, in a roadside grotto 0.2 miles west from the east entrance, provides drinking water of good quality. An emergency reservoir, part of the city water system, and adjacent picnic grounds, occupy the hilltop near the western terminus.

11. The CONCOURSE, a small common bounded by Benton Blvd., Bellefontaine, St. John, and Anderson Aves., overlooks a portion of Cliff Drive and the Missouri River from its Colonnades, a semicircular portico with Doric columns. In the western part of the Concourse are tennis courts. At the intersection of Benton Boulevard and St. John Avenue stands the THOMAS HART BENTON MEMORIAL, a granite boulder dedicated in 1915 by the local chapter of the D. A. R. to one of Missouri's first United States Senators.

12. INDIAN MOUND, NE. corner Gladstone and North Belmont Blvds., in North Terrace Park, has yielded relics of archeological interest. It is believed to have been a lookout post for prehistoric inhabitants. The mound, worn by erosion, has been built up and landscaped with walks and driveways.

13. MERCY HOSPITAL (*visiting hours 2-4 p.m., Sun. only*), 1710 Independence Blvd., was founded in 1897 by Drs. Alice Perry Graham

and Katherine B. Richardson for the treatment and cure of children under 16 whose parents cannot afford regular medical fees. The best doctors of the city contribute their services; 145 beds are provided. Clinical service was rendered 14,604 children in the fiscal year 1937-38. The three red-brick buildings, trimmed with stone and terra cotta, are Georgian in style.

14. The UNION STATION, 2400 Main St., of modified Renaissance design, was designed by Jarvis Hunt of Chicago, and dedicated in 1914. The lobby, parallel to the tracks, is an imposing room 230 feet long, and 100 feet wide, with a 94-foot ceiling. The richly patterned floor is composed of Kasota, Black Belgium, and Tennessee marbles. The balconies below the great windows are traditionally used by Christmas carolers.

At right angles to the lobby is the long waiting room which extends over more than a dozen tracks below. Parking space for cars is provided in the plaza facing the Liberty Memorial.

15. LIBERTY MEMORIAL (*open 9-6 weekdays, 9-9 Sun. and holidays; elevator to observation balcony at top of shaft, 25¢; war veterans, free*), Main St. to Kessler Road, Twenty-eighth St. to Pershing Rd., of modified Greek design faced with Indiana limestone, was built to honor those who served in the World War. Provided for by a subscription totaling more than $2,000,000 contributed by 83,000 citizens, and designed by Harold Van Buren Magonigle of New York, the memorial is approached from the south along a landscaped mall with twin drives and walks extending along the broad hilltop. Veiled sphinxes guard the entrance to the paved and walled court, from the center of which rises a massive 217-foot shaft. Crowning the shaft is a bowl-like censer in which burns the "Flame of Inspiration," an ingenious effect produced by steam and colored lights, visible for many miles after dark. On either side of the shaft stand separate buildings, with huge bronze urns at the portals. Memory Hall, on the east, contains four bronze tablets honoring the Kansas City soldiers who died in the World War. On the east wall is a mural by Jules Guerin, a native of Missouri, representing the stars and stripes supported by the figure of Victory. At her right, an American soldier remembers a fallen comrade. At her left, an American sailor consoles an aged woman. In the background may be envisioned a host of marching men, and in the distance are the ruins of the cathedral of Audenarde. The 24 mural maps on the other walls were painted by D. Putnam Brinley, and depict the line of operations in France. The room also contains reproductions of the table and chairs used at the Versailles Peace Conference. The museum on the west side of the court contains war relics, trophies, and a flag shrine. Embellishing the great wall of the north approach is a symbolic frieze, 18 by 148 feet, designed by Edmund Ameteis. Below is a terraced court with stairs descending to twin pools containing illuminated fountains. At the north edge of the lawn, facing Pershing Road, is the Dedication Wall in which are set five bronze plaques, bas-relief portraits of Marshal Foch of France, Admiral

Beatty of Great Britain, General Pershing, General Jacques of Belgium, and General Dias of Italy, all of whom participated in the dedication of the 60-acre site in 1921. Construction began in 1923, and on Armistice Day, 1926, the completed memorial was dedicated by President Coolidge.

16. PENN VALLEY PARK, Twenty-sixth to Thirty-first and Wyandotte to Summit Sts., is a 131-acre tract of hills and valleys containing a lake, bathhouse, swimming pool, tennis courts, and scenic drives. The park was begun in 1897. In the northeast section, directly west of the Liberty Memorial Hall entrance and on the site of the former home of Frank Lee Wilkinson, early Kansas City lawyer, is the PIONEER MOTHER MONUMENT, sculptured by Alexander Phimister Proctor, Canadian-born sculptor who worked for many years as Augustus Saint-Gaudens' assistant. The bronze group, unveiled November 11, 1927, represents a pioneer woman holding a baby in her arms and riding one of two plodding horses, while the husband and a guide walk on either side. The late Howard Vanderslice, Kansas City grain broker and public benefactor, provided funds for the group as a memorial to his mother and his wife's mother.

On a promontory near the western edge of the park, overlooking the lake, stands THE SCOUT, a bronze Indian astride his pony, one hand shading his eyes as he gazes out across the business districts. Placed here in 1917, the figure was modeled after that of Phillip, son of Kicking Bear, an Oglalla Sioux, by Cyrus Edwin Dallin, Utah sculptor.

17. WASHINGTON SQUARE, Pershing Rd., Main St. to Grand Ave., a small landscaped park, is the setting for VALLEY FORGE, an equestrian statue of George Washington, replica of a statue in New York City by Henry Merwin Shrady. The statue was dedicated Armistice Day 1925, under the auspices of the Patriots and Pioneers Memorial Foundation who provided the purchase fund of $17,500. It was rededicated Armistice Day 1932.

18. HOSPITAL HILL, Twenty-first to Twenty-fourth Sts., and Holmes St. to Gillham Road, a landmark overlooking the business section of the city, is the location of a large medical unit. GENERAL HOSPITAL (*visiting hours 2-3 and 7-8 p.m., Mon., Wed., Fri., Sun.*), Twenty-third to Twenty-fourth and McCoy to Locust Sts., crowns the hill. Built in 1908, the red-brick buildings of the group are Georgian in style, with towers and other Gothic features. RESEARCH HOSPITAL (*visiting hours 10:30-11:30 a.m., 2-4 and 7-8 p.m.*), southwest corner Twenty-third and Holmes Sts., was the original hospital on the hill, established in 1886 as the German Hospital. It is now housed in seven buildings which blend into the general architectural scheme. GENERAL HOSPITAL NO. 2 (Negro) (*visiting hours 2-3, 7-8 p.m., Tues., Thur., Sat., Sun.*), northwest corner Twenty-second and McCoy Sts., is a seven-story structure of modern design opened in 1930, the first municipal hospital for Negroes west of the Mississippi River.

19. UNION CEMETERY, Warwick to McGee Trafficway, Twenty-seventh St. Terrace to Thirtieth St., was established about

1858 on the turnpike connecting Kansas City and Westport, and served both towns. Among the estimated 50,000 graves are those of the artist, George C. Bingham (*see Art*), and Alexander Majors (1814-1900), best known as the organizer and superintendent of the Pony Express. Here is also the grave of Elizabeth Porter (1750-1845), a native of Ireland who emigrated with her husband to Virginia before the Revolution, was captured by Indians during the war, and forced to walk to their village near Niagara Falls, where she remained until the end of the war. Mrs. Porter was the mother of Reverend James Porter, the first minister in Kansas City. Near the grave of Colonel John Calvin McCoy, founder of Westport, and surveyor of Kansas City, are the graves of his first wife, Virginia Chick McCoy, who died of cholera "after seven hours illness" in 1849, and their son Spencer, who, as a Confederate soldier, was killed at 18 in the battle of Springfield in 1863. A 10-foot granite shaft erected by the Federal Government marks the graves of 15 Confederate soldiers who died in Kansas City while prisoners of war. Also buried in this 30-acre hillside tract are about 1,200 other soldiers, many in unmarked graves.

20. HARRIS HOME (*not open*), 4000 Baltimore Ave., a two-story brick mansion, was built in 1854 by Colonel John Harris, owner of Westport's pioneer hotel, the Harris House. Originally, the Harris home stood on a terrace at the southwest corner of Westport Road and Main Street, but it was moved to its present site in 1933. Among the guests in this pioneer mansion were Horace Greeley, General Sterling Price, and General George A. Custer.

21. KANSAS CITY ART INSTITUTE (*open 9-5 weekdays, 2-5 p.m. Sun.*), 4415 Warwick Blvd., an endowed school of fine and industrial arts, is housed in a group of buildings, the first a remodeled 55-room brick residence of Flemish design. Epperson Memorial Hall, of modified late Gothic architecture, adjoins the main building in a setting of landscaped grounds. Two former greenhouses near by offer classes in painting and sculpture, ceramics, advertising and industrial design, fashion design and illustration, the graphic arts, and interior decoration. Among the school's students was Walt Disney, creator of Mickey Mouse (*see Tour 3*). Thomas Hart Benton (*see Art*) is a member of the faculty.

22. WILLIAM ROCKHILL NELSON GALLERY OF ART AND THE ATKINS MUSEUM OF FINE ARTS (*open Tues. through Sat. 10-5, Wed. 7-10 p.m., Sun. and holidays 2-6 p.m. Oct. through May; closed New Year's Day, July 4, Thanksgiving, and Christmas; admission free Sat., Sun., Wed. evening, and public holidays; all other days, adults 25¢, children 10¢*), Rockhill Road, at Forty-fifth St., occupies a landscaped 20-acre tract, the former homesite of William Rockhill Nelson, the chief donor. Completed in 1933, it is built of concrete and Indiana limestone in modified Classic design. The four facades have a series of bas-relief carvings by Charles Keck, depicting the conquest of the American West. The great central Kirkwood Hall is distinguished by 12 huge columns of black marble. The build-

ing is artificially lighted and ventilated. Titian, Goya, Reynolds, Copley, El Greco, Rembrandt, Gainsborough, Velasquez and Van Gogh are among the painters represented, and extensive collections of sculpture, pottery, and bronze from ancient Egypt, Greece, and Rome are on display. There are unusually fine departments of Oriental art, and a series of period rooms, of which the American wing is the most notable. A bequest by William Rockhill Nelson, editor and publisher of the Kansas City *Star*, has been swelled by $2,450,000 bequeathed by members of his family and his attorney, Frank F. Rozzelle, and by $700,000 bequeathed earlier by Mrs. Mary Atkins.

23. SWOPE PARK, SE. from Sixty-third St. and Swope Parkway, containing 1,346 acres, is the third largest city recreational center in the United States (1939). The natural beauty of the rocky, wooded hills and deep ravines has been enhanced by landscaping and winding drives. Near the main entrance is Shelter House No. 1, built of local limestone, with twin observation towers and rustic pergolas at either end. Six other picnic shelters are located throughout the park. East of the main shelter house is a flower garden, from which rises a 165-foot flagstaff, just south of the American Legion memorial drinking fountain. To the northeast are picnic grounds and a colonnaded music pavilion. East from the sloping mall that extends from the formal gardens are the Zoological Gardens, bear pits, and a lake for aquatic birds. Beyond the zoo lies a lagoon for boating and bathing, and the Lake of the Woods, a city fishing resort. Two 18-hole golf courses, numerous tennis courts, and children's playgrounds are among the park's recreational facilities. SWOPE MEMORIAL, near the brow of a wooded ridge overlooking the lagoon on the east, is the mausoleum of Thomas Hunt Swope (1827-1909). Designed by Wight & Wight, it is constructed of white Vermont granite, and has 12 Doric columns grouped about a bronze bas-relief plaque of the philanthropist, by Charles Keck. Swope was born in Kentucky, and came to Kansas City 30 years later, devoting himself to the real estate business and kindred enterprises. His investments met with success, and, in addition to other benefactions, he donated this tract to the city in 1896.

24. The UNIVERSITY OF KANSAS CITY, 5100 Rockhill Rd., is a nonsectarian, privately endowed coeducational institution with an enrollment of more than a thousand. The original college, which offered two years of work, was formally opened October 2, 1933. In September, 1934, a third year was added, and by September, 1935, the four-year Liberal Arts course was instituted. The 70-acre campus, the gift of William Volker, is attractively landscaped. Most of the buildings, arranged about a quadrangle, are constructed of local stone in the French Renaissance tradition. Nationally famous is the library's Robert M. Snyder collection of nearly 15,000 early American books, dealing principally with the West, which is available to the public by arrangement.

25. The SITE OF THE BATTLE OF WESTPORT, Meyer Blvd., at Sixty-third St. and the Paseo, is marked by a granite monu-

ment, placed by the Grand Army of the Republic and its auxiliaries to commemorate the struggle on that ground on October 23, 1864. This engagement, called the "Gettysburg of the West," was the largest battle fought west of the Mississippi River, and the defeat of the Confederate forces here ended the war in the trans-Mississippi region.

General Sterling Price, commanding the District of Arkansas, swept north into Missouri in September 1864, in an attempt to sever Federal lines and force the withdrawal of Union troops. Fighting began along the Big Blue River on the morning of October 22, and by evening, although numerically inferior, Confederate cavalry had succeeded in occupying Federal entrenchments. The major battle began the following morning. It involved approximately 20,000 Federal troops commanded by General Alfred S. Pleasanton, and Price's army of about 9,000 recruits from Missouri, Kansas, Arkansas, Iowa, Wisconsin, Colorado, Texas, and Illinois. General Joseph Shelby, commanding a division of the Confederate troops, occupied a strong position on a hilltop in front of Westport, and succeeded in repulsing successive attacks until an old man showed the Federal leaders a gap in the rocky ledge through which they could ascend. The fighting soon became desperate. Captain Curtis Johnson of the Kansas volunteer cavalry, and Confederate Colonel James H. McGhee met in a duel in the middle of the battle. Johnson, severely wounded, killed McGhee, and with the loss of their leader, McGhee's men broke and fled. At the same time, Confederate General John S. Marmaduke was making his last stand along the Big Blue in an endeavor to hold back Pleasanton's men. Hopelessly outnumbered, Marmaduke retreated.

The Confederates made a second desperate stand on an east and west line from the present Forest Hill Cemetery to the Wornall Road. Unable to check the attack of the combined Federal army, the retreat to Arkansas was continued. Losses during the battle totaled approximately 1,000 dead and severely wounded.

26. The ALEXANDER MAJORS HOUSE (*open by permission*), 8145 State Line, a two-story, white frame house with double recessed entrance portico, was built in 1855 by Alexander Majors, member of the overland freighting firm of Russell, Majors & Waddell (*see Tours 2 and 7a*).

The house, originally containing nine rooms, was built on land purchased by Majors' firm as a "home corral" for the oxen used in the freighting business. Below the old home was the caravan camp where the great wagon trains were made up. Lighter horse-and-mule-drawn wagons conveyed the goods from Westport Landing, and the great canvas-covered schooners were loaded here for the long trek to the West.

Alexander Majors (1814-1900) was born in Kentucky and came with his parents to Lafayette County, Missouri, about 1819. The family later moved to Jackson County. In 1848, with an outfit of wagons and teams, young Majors began carrying freight from Independence to Santa Fe. About 1855, he formed a partnership with William H. Russell, and William B. Waddell. Majors managed the road business;

the others directed purchasing and finances. During the heyday of the firm, they employed more than 4,000 men, 40,000 wagon oxen, and 1,000 mules. Shipments were made in trains of about 25 wagons each. Each wagon had 12 oxen and a teamster, and each train had additional oxen, mules, and men in reserve. Profits of the firm in 1855-56 amounted to about $300,000, but the business was hazardous, and the gains of several years would sometimes be lost in a single season.

In 1859 the firm took over the operation of a daily stagecoach from Fort Leavenworth to Denver, and the following year it inaugurated the pony express. This last venture, combined with other factors, bankrupted the company in 1861.

In 1858, when the firm obtained the government contract to freight supplies to General A. S. Johnston's army in the Mormon War, Majors moved to Nebraska City, and his home came into the possession of his eldest daughter, Mrs. Samuel Poteet, whose descendants owned it until 1910. The house is now the property of Majors' great-granddaughter, Miss Louise J. Johnston, who is restoring the building to its original appearance.

St. Charles

Railroad Stations: Foot of Tompkins St., for Missouri-Kansas-Texas R.R.; N. of St. Charles on State 94, near city limits (L), for Wabash Railroad.
Bus Stations: St. Charles Hotel, 205 N. Second St., for Southwestern Greyhound Lines, Inc., the M. C. Foster Bus Lines, Missouri Transit Co., and River View Bus Lines; 401 N. Second St., for Ferguson-Wellston Bus Company.
Taxis: 25¢ within city limits, 5¢ second passenger, 10¢ each additional.
Traffic Regulations: Speed limit 20 m.p.h. on Main St., 25 m.p.h. elsewhere. No U-turn on Main St.

Accommodations: Three hotels; tourist camps and lodging houses.

Motion Picture Houses: Three.
Swimming: Blanchette Park, entrance Randolph and Chestnut Sts., adults 25¢, children 10¢.
Athletics: Blanchette Park, entrance Randolph and Chestnut Sts., six clay tennis courts, four horseshoe courts, two baseball diamonds, free.

ST. CHARLES (614 alt., 10,803 pop.), spread upon the bluffs that overlook the Missouri River approximately 20 miles northwest of St. Louis, is a city of precipitous streets, attractive terraces, and shaded lawns. First permanent white settlement on the Missouri, and first State capital, it has a leisurely charm, rich in historic associations and natural beauty. Each of the peoples who have lived here has imprinted something of its culture on this farming and educational center. During early days, St. Charles was the funnel-mouth through which French trappers, Spanish explorers, American pioneers, and German immigrants flowed towards the western fur trade, the rich soil of the plains, and California gold. The old ferryboat landing at the mouth of Blanchette Creek in the southern portion of the town is overgrown with weeds and trees, and its existence almost forgotten; but the Boon's Lick Trail, which led west from here, following for a time the vagaries of the little stream, is still used. Progress has scarcely touched the tiny valley, so that the starting point of America's greatest highway has changed little from the time when high-wheeled covered wagons, strings of pack mules and horses, and trudging, impoverished settlers turned hopefully Westward along its route.

The business district, dominated by the copper dome of the gray stone courthouse, climbs abruptly from the river front. Higher up the bluffs, between the business section and Lindenwood College, stretch the residential streets. Here level space is prized, and the houses crowd close together. A few are modern dwellings, but many are old, with second-story balconies and green shutters. Along Second, Third, and Fourth Streets are the neat, square, jig-saw-trimmed houses of the descendants of German settlers, and several large Gothic-Revival churches. At the extreme western edge of town is the campus of Lindenwood College for women.

Although a portion of St. Charles' population finds work in the American Car and Foundry Company plant, in the brewery, shoe factory, and lumber yards, the city's economy is based chiefly upon the rich farms that surround it. The people have become almost completely Americanized, but here and there some folktale or legend, some piece of furniture or bric-a-brac, reveals a French or German heritage.

Legend and tradition confuse the story of St. Charles' beginnings. It is thought that the first settler, Louis Blanchette *dit le Chasseur* (nicknamed the hunter), a French-Canadian, came here with his Pawnee Indian wife, Angelique, in 1769, and built a cabin near the mouth of the creek now named for him. The low bluffs which form the background of the town were the first high ground west of Missouri's junction with the Mississippi. Safe above flood waters, yet accessible to the near-by fertile bottomlands, the site also afforded conspicuous trade advantages. Other French-Canadians arrived, and gradually the scattered cabins grew into a village, which took its name from the bluffs the Creoles had called *Les Petites Côtes* (the little hills). In 1781, there were but half a dozen houses, and this number was no more than doubled during the succeeding ten years The first inhabitants preferred a mode of life only slightly less roving than that of the Indians. A few engaged in farming, but the majority seem to have supported themselves by hunting, fishing, and trapping. Between 1780 and 1786, the Spanish government tried to discourage settlement west of the St. Louis district by refusing to issue or approve land grants, but the pressure of settlement westward was irresistible.

In 1787, August Chouteau surveyed the settlement, and St. Charles as a town may be said to date from that year. Soon afterward, the District of St. Charles was formed, comprising an area extending west from the Missouri River boundary of the St. Louis District, theoretically to the Pacific Ocean. Blanchette was made commandant, and his cabin on block No. 20, bounded by McDonald, Main, Missouri, and Water Streets, became the seat of this empire.

Slowly, life in the village began to change. On November 7, 1791, the church erected by the Roman Catholics of the community was blessed under the Invocation of San Carlos Borromeo, sixteenth century Archbishop of Milan. Subsequently, the settlement was known by the Spanish name, *San Carlos del Misuri,* Anglicized after 1803 to St. Charles.

In 1793, Blanchette and Angelique died, and Charles Tayon was appointed civil commandant (1793-1801). Immediately, Tayon announced that Blanchette and the original settlers held no legal title to the land, since their claims had not been approved by the governor general at New Orleans. He then granted to himself the property on which the government buildings were located, and divided Blanchette's other real estate and possessions among his own followers. The block on which the first church stood was granted to Joseph Piche and Louis Chancellier; even the old stone fort that stood on the hill 250 feet above the river was abandoned to private interests and converted into a mill. On January 11, 1797, the people petitioned for, and 12 days later received, a grant of land to be used as a common field—a large tract divided proportionally among the inhabitants (*see Ste. Genevieve*). The lots in the commons were similar in extent to lots in St. Louis; 1 arpent in front and 40 in depth.

Under Spanish encouragement, many American settlers came to the territory. Among them were the Boones—Daniel and his wife, Rebecca, their sons, Nathan and Daniel Morgan, and various relatives (*see Tour 1A*)—who arrived in St. Charles during the late 1790's. The Indian trade by which Blanchette and his fellow French-Canadians had prospered gave way to a more highly organized commerce. In May 1802, Perrin du Lac visited the settlement and noted:

> After St. Louis and Ste. Genevieve, St. Charles is the most important place . . . the results of the emigration of some families from St. Louis, who being hunters by profession came to reside there, in order to be near a country the most abundant in game. But notwithstanding the beauty of its situation, the salubrity of its air, and the richness of its soil, they have not been permitted to enjoy these advantages long. The Americans came in crowds into the surrounding country, which already contains about four hundred families . . .

In 1803, the vast unexplored West, roughly designed as Louisiana, became American territory. The following year, the Lewis and Clark Expedition, commissioned by President Jefferson to chart the course of the Missouri River and the Columbia River westward to the Pacific, stopped at St. Charles, where in spite of the daily arrival of Anglo-Americans French culture still predominated.

Two years later the expedition returned with charts and fabulous tales, and the race for empire started. St. Charles, "the last out-post of civilization," began to boom. The lone, independent trapper retreated before large, organized groups, traveling by barge. Money had come to the frontier. A hundred houses, numerous supply shops, two brick kilns, a tan yard, and several stores were erected. On October 13, 1809, St. Charles was formally organized as a village, with Alexander McNair, later first Governor of Missouri, as one of the trustees. Three years later, under the provisions of the new territorial government, the old District of St. Charles was reorganized as one of Missouri's five original counties. St. Charles remained the seat of government.

A colorful group of frontiersmen made the village their home or occasional rendezvous. Jean Baptist Point du Sable, reputed founder of Chicago, died and is buried in St. Charles. James Mackay, fur trader and explorer, apparently succeeded Tayon as Commandant of the post of St. Charles. Lewis Jones, famed for his Indian exploits, and a relative by marriage of Daniel Boone, lived here until after the War of 1812. His brother, Ben, accompanied the Astor expedition in 1811, and is credited with having saved it on several occasions. Even

Aaron Burr, planning secretly to form an independent Western Empire, came here in 1805, to confer with Timothy Kibbe, Revolutionary soldier and colonel of the local militia.

During the War of 1812 the Indians were aroused against the French and American settlers. Commercial activity was stalemated, and St. Charles and the surrounding territory required the protection of a series of forts: Daniel M. Boone's fort in Darst's Bottom; Howell's fort, Pond's fort, White's fort, and others. Though several of the outposts were attacked, St. Charles was not molested.

After the war, restless eastern farmers began to pour into the Missouri River Valley. The *Missouri Gazette* of June 9, 1819, states that 107,000 acres of public lands were disposed of in March of that year at $2.91 an acre. In the same issue a report from St. Charles observed that "never has . . . an influx of people . . . been so considerable . . . flowing through our town with their maid servants and men servants . . . the throng of hogs and cattle, the white-headed children, and curly-headed Africans." The dust of the town's streets never settled. Many of the milling throng were to become famous: General John Augustus Sutter, in whose California millrace was later discovered the nugget that precipitated the great California gold rush; Mother Rose Philippine Duchesne, who was to receive religious honors. Already known were John Mason Peck, historian and pioneer Baptist missionary preacher, who lived in St. Charles in 1816, and the Reverend Timothy Flint, Presbyterian minister and inimitable frontier chronicler, who resided here from 1816 until about 1822. Living first in a two-room log hut, for which he paid Madame Francois Duquette $12.00 a month, Flint found the old French and Roman Catholic town somewhat wanting in hospitality to his Presbyterian doctrines.

In 1820 Robert McCloud began issuing the *Missourian* on his handpress. The following year Missouri was admitted into the Union, and St. Charles, already the territorial capital, was designated as the temporary State Capital by the first legislature, which met in St. Louis. The general assembly convened on the second floor of three joined brick buildings furnished rent free by the town. The tavern-keepers maintained their reputation for fair dealing by furnishing board to the legislators at $2.50 a week, but most of them were men of small financial means and not prompt to pay. Even with pork at 1½¢ a pound, venison hams at 25¢ each, eggs at 5¢ a dozen, and honey at 5¢ a gallon, the innkeepers lost money, and had no regrets when the capital was moved to Jefferson City in 1826.

The great wave of German immigration that left so deep an impress on St. Charles was precipitated in 1829 by the publication of the enthusiastic letters of Gottfried Duden, a German scholar, who had lived in Warren County, west of St. Charles, from 1824 to 1827. Aided by the Giessen, the Berlin, and other societies, the first of the immigrants began to arrive in 1832, some having even abandoned their feather beds and heavy clothing in anticipation of an almost subtropical climate. The stream continued until 1870, when the population of St. Charles

County was approximately two-thirds German, and a local observer wrote that "the ideals of the founders of the Giessen Emigration Society, to establish a new German environment in this western part of the Union has been fulfilled, though in a manner such as we had not anticipated or dreamed."

The Germans expanded St. Charles economically as well as physically, transforming it into a freighting and shipping center for a rich farming area. Maximilian, prince of Wied, wrote in 1832: "Next morning we reached St. Charles . . . consisting of about 300 houses, where the massive church, with its low tower, had a very good appearance. The environs of this scattered village are bare, but there are many European fruit trees in blossom. Most of the houses are built of wood, but a modern part of the place is of brick." Two years later, Edmund Flagg rhapsodized in the Louisville *Journal:* "The view of St. Charles from the opposite bank of the Missouri is a fine one. The turbid stream rolls along the village nearly parallel with the interval upon which it is situated. A long line of neat edifices chiefly brick with a few ruinous old structures of logs and plastering, relics of French or Spanish taste and domination, extend along the shore; beyond these, a range of bluffs rear themselves proudly above the village crowned with their academic hall and a neat stone church, its spire surmounted by a cross."

On March 10, 1849, St. Charles was incorporated as a city. In this same year, the dust of its streets was once more stirred by a wave of restless, Westward-moving people. The California gold rush was on. But the frontier, too, had moved beyond the town; Independence, St. Joseph, Liberty, and Westport had become outposts of civilization, and St. Charles had reached its greatest period of expansion. The Civil War made near-by St. Louis the great commercial and industrial center of the State, and the railroads usurped the river's importance. In 1871, after a series of disasters that took 19 lives, the second railway bridge across the Missouri River was completed at St. Charles. At that time it was one of the longest cast-iron and steel bridges in the United States. In 1879, and again in 1881, heavily laden freight trains crashed through its spans into the river, but each time the bridge was rebuilt. Later, it was replaced by the present structure. Difficulties, almost equally great, attended the building of a highway bridge. The present structure, completed in 1904, was made toll free in 1931.

Agriculture and education have remained the chief interests of St. Charles, though a brewery and a foundry, and later a shoe factory, have been established. In 1923, with the construction of Highway 40, a portion of the trans-continental Old Trails route, modern vehicles opened the old pioneer trail to present-day commerce. Although the sale of gasoline and lunches is a poor substitute for the business St. Charles once enjoyed, new methods of transportation have created opportunities for the development of small industries and an increasing tourist trade.

POINTS OF INTEREST

OLD STATE CAPITOL (*private*), 206-212-214 S. Main Street, in the center of the business district, consists of three brick buildings joined together. When erected in 1814, the three units had identical facades, but at present only the central structure retains the original simple wooden cornice and small windows. In the second-floor rooms of these buildings was held the session of the assembly which met June 4, 1821, to pass the act required by Congress for the State's admission to the Union. The lower floors of Nos. 212 and 214 were at that time occupied by Charles and Ruluff Peck, who had a general merchandise store. Chauncey Shepard and his family lived on the first floor of No. 206.

The territorial legislature had met at St. Louis, but out-State groups preferred a more centrally located permanent seat of government, as less likely to be influenced by the powerful St. Louis clique of lawyers and business men. The offer by St. Charles of rooms rent free was therefore accepted until a permanent capital site could be chosen, and the assembly met here from 1821 to 1826. Among the legislators who used these rooms was the Honorable Jacob Groom of Montgomery County, who introduced himself on one memorable occasion as "a tearin' critter of the catamount school," and wound up his speech in support of Jackson with the declaration: "I am no book larnt man, but there is few who can beat me swapping horses or guessing at the weight of a bar. I have come here because my people voted for me, knowing I was a honest man and could make as good whiskey and apple brandy at my still as any man." Yet it might not have been of Jacob Groom that the St. Charles boys were thinking when they wrote above the speaker's chair, "Missouri, forgive them. They know not what they do."

Since 1826, business concerns have occupied the lower floors, and the upper floors have been used for residential purposes. A bronze tablet marks the north building of the group.

ST. CHARLES COUNTY COURTHOUSE (*open*), Second, Third, Jefferson and Washington Sts., built in 1903, is of native limestone with massive pillared entrances and a surmounting dome. In the corner of the courthouse yard, at Second and Jefferson Sts., a large red-granite boulder and bronze tablet marks the alleged starting point of the Boon's Lick Trail (*see Tour I*).

The LUDWELL POWELL HOME (*open on written application to the owner, Mrs. George W. McElhinney*), corner Sixth and Jefferson Sts., a three-story, red-brick house with late Greek-Revival trim, was built about 1840 by Colonel Ludwell Powell, first mayor of St. Charles. The double-deck porch along the rear ell, and the Adam-type front portico, are recent additions. The interior of the house has been changed very little and contains an interesting collection of early furnishings. The original brick slave quarters at the rear are in excellent condition.

ST. CHARLES COLLEGE BUILDING (*private*), 117 N. Third St., is a four-story, brick structure now divided into apartments. The roof has been raised a full story above the original height, and the original fanlight doorway has been altered. St. Charles College was established by Mrs. Catherine Collier and her son, George, in 1835. Mrs. Collier donated $5,000 to be used as an endowment fund, and her son purchased land and erected buildings at a cost of $10,000. Opened under the presidency of the Reverend John H. Fielding, the institution was placed under the control of the Methodist Episcopal Church in 1838. During the Civil War, the property passed into the control of other parties.

SACRED HEART CONVENT (*open 9-5*), Decatur, Franklin, Second, and Third Sts., with its entrance on Second St., is a group of red-brick structures consisting of the original building, erected in 1838, and extensive wings subsequently added. The original unit is used for administrative purposes and contains the room in which Mother Duchesne, the founder, lived. Here are preserved the relics which she brought with her from abroad, her watch, table silver, a small crucifix, and other personal objects, as well as two carved eighteenth century figures of wood, one of the Blessed Virgin and one of St. John. The room also contains furniture which she used and two paintings, *St. Francis Regis* and, on wood, the *Adoration of the Magi,* both brought from France by Bishop DuBourg more than a century ago and presented to Mother Duchesne. The large and very old carved wooden crucifix, still retaining traces of its original polychrome decoration, is said to have been stolen from Mother Duchesne's home in France during the French Revolution. Years later, a St. Louisan saw the cross in a French antique shop, and purchased it for his family chapel near Florissant. Identified later by the sawblades which reinforce it, the relic was piously carried to St. Charles. On the grounds at the left of the entrance to the building is a shrine erected by Madame Aloysia Jacquet in honor of "Our Lady of the Pillar." The first stone was blessed by the Reverend Father De Smet, and the shrine was completed about 1853. At the base of the altar is the inscription, "Pray for the Conversion of the Indians." The remains of Mother Duchesne, who was beatified May 12, 1940, and is expected to be canonized, are preserved in the vault.

Rose Philippine Duchesne (1769-1855) was born in Grenoble, France, of a family of wealthy manufacturers and eminent statesmen. She entered the religious life as a novice in the Visitation Order at the convent of Ste. Marie-d'en Haut (1797). Her father forbade her to be professed because of the political situation at the time, but consented to her remaining at the convent as a novice for two years. When the religious orders were proscribed as a result of the French Revolution, Rose Philippine returned to her home, where she worked among the poor. In 1805 she took vows in the newly founded order of the Sacred Heart, and on March 20, 1818, in charge of four other nuns of the Order, she sailed for America to perform missionary work among the

Indians. At St. Charles, the five nuns opened the first Convent of the Sacred Heart in the new world (*see Tour I—Florissant*).

LINDENWOOD COLLEGE (*open 8-5*), entrance Kingshighway at Madison St., occupies a wooded 149-acre campus encircled by a drive known as Butler Way. Sibley Hall, erected in 1856 and named in honor of the founder, has a recently added Colonial-type porch with 8 columns 26 feet tall. Ayres Hall, Butler Hall, Irwin Hall, and the administration building, Roemer Hall, are all three-story brick buildings which show Tudor-Gothic influence. The Margaret Leggat Butler Library is also of Tudor-Gothic design. Niccolls Hall, the largest dormitory, is an imposing three-story brick building with a large four-pillared portico. The Lillie P. Roemer Arts Memorial Building, the gift of the late Dr. John L. Roemer, houses the School of Music and Fine Arts.

Lindenwood, one of the oldest schools for women in the Mississippi Valley, was established by George Champlin Sibley and his wife, Mary Eastern Sibley, in a log cabin on the present grounds. In 1853 it was chartered as Lindenwood College by a special act of the legislature, which was amended in 1870, vesting the appointment of directors in the Presbyterian Synod of Missouri. Its property valued at more than $2,000,000, the college is free of indebtedness and has an endowment fund of more than $2,000,000. It is an accredited four-year college, with an enrollment of approximately 500 and a faculty of 50.

BLANCHETTE PARK, Randolph and Chestnut Sts., consists of 42 acres formerly known as the Fairgrounds. Purchased by the city in 1910, the land has been equipped with soft-ball diamonds and tennis courts lighted for night play, an auditorium for dancing, and a sunken rose garden illuminated at night when the roses are in bloom. Free band concerts are given each Thursday evening during the summer months.

ST. CHARLES BORROMEO CEMETERY, west of Blanchette Park, contains the graves of many early pioneers, among them, Jean Baptiste Point du Sable, Francois Duquette (1774-1816), Major James Morrison (1767-1848), trader, salt manufacturer at Boon's Lick, and merchant, and Rebecca Younger (1826-50), wife of Coleman Younger of Liberty, famed outlaw of the Civil War decade. A monument has recently been erected to the memory of Louis Blanchette, founder of St. Charles, the site of whose grave in the cemetery is unknown. The tablet records that Blanchette was the "builder about 1776 of the first St. Charles Borromeo (log) Church . . . In its shadows both he and his Pawnee Indian wife were buried after their deaths late in 1793. According to tradition they were removed in 1831 to the present Borromeo churchyard and in 1854 translated to this . . . cemetery."

Items for Americana are the gravestones of Sir Walter Rice and William Dugan. Rice (1799-1858) was not a nobleman, but an American whose parents, naming him for Sir Walter Scott, believed that "Sir" was a Christian name. Dugan (1803-74) was fond of drink, heedless of his wife's warnings that he would come to an unhappy end. One day his mule kicked him to death, and his wife, to point the moral of the tragedy for future generations, had the scene of the mule kicking Dugan carved on his gravestone, as well as an account of the event. His children objected to this memorial and attempted to have it removed. Failing in this, they erected a more conventional monument beside the first.

Ste. Genevieve

Railroad Stations: Front St. between Merchant and Jefferson Sts. for St. Louis-San Francisco R.R. (Frisco Lines) and Missouri-Illinois R.R.
Bus Station: 261 Merchant St. for Prost Bus Co.
Ferry: 1.6 m. N. of city limits on Main St.; passenger cars 75¢, trucks $1.
Traffic Regulations: Speed limit 20 m.p.h.

Information Service: Public Library and Historical Museum, NE. corner of Du Bourg Place.

Accommodations: Three hotels.

Motion Picture Houses: One.

Annual Events: Procession and ceremony of the Feast of Corpus Christi, first Thursday after Trinity Sunday; La Guignolée, New Year's Eve.

STE. GENEVIEVE (401 alt., 2,787 pop.) with its very old homes and business houses, its massive red-brick church and walled convent, gives reality to the French tradition that forms so much of Missouri's background. Its heart is Du Bourg Place, the public square, shady and informal, and dominated by a church and small courthouse rather than by commercial structures. Emerging from the square, with no line of demarcation, are the residential sections, whose quiet streets, with their flower gardens and boxwood framed houses, are lined with elm and maple trees. Some of the residences are the Creole upright log houses, now weatherboarded, which were erected during the Spanish regime (*see Architecture*). These have wide porches, or galéries, and occasionally their gardens are enclosed by rose-colored brick walls. In general, the meanderings of the North and South Gabouri Creeks mark the north and south, and the Old Cemetery between Fifth and Sixth Streets the west boundary of the old town. A new city of crisp modern houses and wide streets encircles the original village.

Trading center for a fertile farming district, Ste. Genevieve is also the shipping point for an excellent grade of marble and is one of the largest lime-producing towns in the State. But perhaps the best index of its life and manners is its festivals. On New Year's Eve, masked revelers dressed as Indians or blacked as Negroes shuffle from house to house, accompanied by a fiddler and singing "La Guignolée," an ancient French song with unwritten music and traditional words. At one time it was sung to solicit food and drink for the King's Ball, held on Twelfth Night; today, however, the masked singers demand only wine.

At the *Gloria* of the Mass of Holy Thursday, before Easter, when the bells are silenced, the altar boys call the congregation to service by marching around the church square three times, rattling their rick-racks (wooden rattles) and calling out, *premier coup* (first bell), *deuxième coup* (second bell), and *dernier coup* (last bell). Later, in May or June, depending on the date of Easter, the Feast of Corpus Christi is celebrated. On this day, small shrines are erected in front of the houses, and the town is decorated with flowers. At midmorning, accompanied by his assistants, the priest, bearing the Eucharist, and dressed in the most resplendent robes of his office, leads a procession through the streets. Singing children precede the parade, scattering flowers. The procession ends with a special Mass and blessing in front of the church on the public square.

As its history is recounted in Ste. Genevieve, no one knows where legends end and facts begin. Records trail off into old wives' tales, making charming, though sometimes improbable, stories of days before the 1785 flood. Some early dates, however, and several events that shaped the destiny of the town are definitely known. By 1715 Frenchmen had discovered lead at Mine La Motte, 30 miles to the southwest, and were mining it by crude means; in 1723 Philippe François Renault brought men and machinery from France, and slaves from San Domingo to work the mines. Renault abandoned his mining venture in 1744 and returned to France, but the industry which he had promoted was sporadically continued. Early maps and records suggest that families from Kaskaskia moved west across the Mississippi during the late 1740's and established farms in the fabulously rich bottom. The earliest known grants of land here were made in 1752 by Macarty, the Commandant at Kaskaskia, when 27 inhabitants owned 93 arpents (nearly 3 miles) of river frontage. Seven years later, a parish was organized at the settlement then called the "Poste de Saint Joachim." Agriculture was the primary interest of the community (*see Agriculture*), together with salt making on near-by Saline Creek, fur trading with the Indians, and lead mining. "From the earliest time," Brackenridge later recalled, "the French inhabitants of Ste. Genevieve had all been more or less engaged in the storage, purchase, and traffic of lead."

When the territory west of the Mississippi River was secretly transferred to Spain in 1762, and that east of the Mississippi to England in 1763, Ste. Genevieve became an outpost of the Spanish Empire, and its affairs were shaped by the devious colonial ambitions and fears of Spain. The discontent of the Creoles on the east bank under Protestant British rule was aggravated by the withdrawal of all priests from the colony. Spain quickly took advantage of this dissatisfaction. In Ste. Genevieve, the Creole way of living was not disturbed. For the first time, a resident priest, Father Louis Meurin, was sent to the village, armed with a unique Papal dispensation to marry unbaptized Roman Catholics. Local men were appointed to administrative posts and large grants of land were offered to settlers. Soon a steady stream of immigrants began to cross the Mississippi. Nor were they all Creoles from the east bank; many came from Canada and Lower Louisiana, to be joined later by French Royalist refugees, Americans, and Germans.

Despite its growth, Ste. Genevieve (it is unknown when this name was first given to the settlement) was not a village in the American sense. Captain Philip Pittman of the English army, who visited there in 1766, found 70 families in a settlement "about one mile in length." Even in 1782 the place was considered too scattered for defense. The unusual length of the settlement, as Charles E. Peterson points out in his *A Guide to Ste. Genevieve* (1940), suggests that it was strung out along a main road like many of the old villages in French Canada.

In spite of the lack of civic consciousness, the richness of its soil and its commercially advantageous position brought Ste. Genevieve a measured prosperity during the following 50 years. The salt workers began supplying Indians, hunters, and the settlements of the Illinois country. A profitable fur trade sprang up. Lead production was steady. Grains, meats, honey, and lard were shipped to St. Louis and New Orleans by boat. In 1772, the settlement had a free population of 264 males, and 140 females, and 287 slaves. Ste. Genevieve was larger than St. Louis.

The chief problem of the village was the annual rising of the waters of the Mississippi. In 1785, the floods reached a climax; the village was inundated with approximately 15 feet of water. Thereafter the villagers moved—over a period of years—to the high valley of the Gabouri Creek four miles to the northwest. A few houses were probably transported from the old village, and, in 1794, the old church was moved. When Duke Paul of Württemberg visited there in 1822, only "a few scattered houses" remained along the banks of the Mississippi.

Just south of the settlement was the three or four thousand-acre *Le Grand Champs,* or Big Field, in which each villager had one or more long, narrow strips of land on which he sowed his own crop (*see Agriculture*).

A garrison was established, but it was only at intervals that regular troops were stationed there. In 1778 the commandant directed that soldiers might be hired out to the inhabitants, though they were not to be given credit. There was also a jail, but a prisoner could obtain leave under escort of a soldier to attend to his business outside, and the commandant usually sent him what the Reverend Timothy Flint described as "a suitable provision of whisky to blunt the acuteness of his feelings."

In 1791, after an exciting flatboat trip from Pittsburgh, five-year-old Henry Marie Brackenridge (*see Literature*) arrived in Ste. Genevieve to learn French. He remained in the village three years, and made frequent visits later in his life. His accounts of the social life of the inhabitants, in his *Recollections of Persons and Places in the West,* are the most charming—and perhaps the most accurate—of early records. Each Sunday afternoon after Mass, the children attended the "ball," a school of manners at which the "strictest decorum and propriety" were preserved. The minuet was the principal dance. In this manner, observed Brackenridge, the people acquired grace and self-denial, that "basis of true politeness." Thomas Ashe (1806) tells of summer evenings when the people gathered in groups outside their houses, each group with its guitar player, fiddler, story-teller, or singer. As the evening advanced and the heat diminished, strolling began. Near midnight, the musicians of the village united, and the villagers "danced with infinite gaiety and mirth till past one in the morning."

Under French and Spanish government, Ste. Genevieve's "simple, gay, generous, and good-humored folk" were left to their own ways. But with the beginning of American rule, they were suddenly brought into a world filled with surveyors, clerks, recorders, lawyers, and judges, who possessed a complicated set of codes. Captain Amos Stoddard, temporarily in charge of this region, observed that the people "have yet to learn . . . the procrastinations, tricks, and impositions so successfully practiced in other territories." In 1812, when the district was organized under the territorial laws of Missouri, Ste. Genevieve continued as the seat of government. Interesting visitors came to the village, among them the Duke of Württemberg (1822), King Otto of Greece, whom General John Bossier entertained for three months in 1830, and the Prince of Wied (1832). In 1810 John James Audubon stopped briefly in the town with his business partner, Ferdinand Rozier, who became in 1827 the town's first mayor.

River trade for a time made Ste. Genevieve St. Louis' greatest rival. The village declined, however, as St. Louis grew. The fur trade moved westward, and new methods of refining salt put an end to that industry. Many of the lead miners left for other fields. By 1836 the population had dwindled to approximately 800. Then, for a brief period the development of trade and the discovery of iron in the back country brought new wealth and a larger population. A $200,000 plank road was constructed to facilitate lead transportation between Iron Mountain and Ste. Genevieve in 1851-3, but the planks wore out, and the Iron Mountain Railroad diverted the ore to St. Louis. Thus Ste. Genevieve had to fall back upon agriculture, and this was altered by the end of slave economy, and the large German immigration near the middle of the century.

The construction of the Frisco and Missouri-Illinois railroads and, recently, of a modern highway, together with the development of lime and marble industries, have given the community a measure of economic stability. The town's importance, however, is chiefly historical, although each year a few more of the old houses disappear, and the Creole language is fast dying out. Fortunately, the love of gardens and the custom of retaining ancestral homes has allowed the Germans to fit neatly into the older Creole pattern. The *Grand Champs,* privately owned, is still measured in arpents, the French equivalent of .845 acres, and is still farmed in elongated strips. Houses still have the dormer windows that suggested to Charles Dickens "a kind of French shrug," and the Roman Catholic Church remains the center of community social activity. As Ward Allison Dorrance observed in his *The Survival of*

French in the Old District of Sainte Genevieve, to see Monsignor Van Tourenhout, who insists upon wearing about town his clerical dress— *soutane, birettum,* and all—conversing with a nun under the stone arch of the old convent gate is a sight not often granted in modern Missouri.

POINTS OF INTEREST

1. The STE. GENEVIEVE CHURCH (Catholic), Du Bourg Place, casting its shadow across the square whose history is so much its own, is a massive red-brick edifice of Gothic-Revival design. Completed in 1880, it is the third building to occupy the site since the first church was moved from "Old Village" following the flood of 1785. As the first permanent church in Missouri, it played a vital part in the community. With the good sense of the early French, the priest, as Dorrance points out, "kept his blind eye to the telescope . . . and was content to have for frontier life a frontier church," doing what good he could and realizing that unbending commands in many matters would have passed unheeded. As early as 1792, midnight Mass was said with the elaborate altar and gilt cross "splendidly decorated and lighted with the largest wax candles the village could afford." Once, when a flood threatened the village, a procession was organized to drive back the waters. At the ringing of the bells, the population gathered and, "with the Holy Host, the cross, and two or three bells tinkling," solemnly marched to the river, chanting *Pater Nosters* and *Ave Marias;* thus "the waters were rebuked." When someone fell ill, the Host, preceded by the priest in his pontifical robes, was carried to the sick person's house, with all the ceremony circumstances would permit. On hearing the ringing of the bells, the villagers would hasten to join the procession. Bishop Benedict Flaget, who came from Bardstown, Kentucky, in 1814, remarked that he had been "received with the same pomp as if I had been in Paris." The Bishop lost some of his enthusiasm for this reception when he discovered that "some of the oldest and richest inhabitants have not been to the sacraments for twenty, forty and even fifty years." Before he left, however, more than 600 persons had received confirmation.

Changing social conditions brought changes within the church. At the close of the nineteenth century, "Papa" Girard, the last French *bedeau* (beadle) of the church, was one of the few remaining ties with the early French period. He awakened persons who fell asleep by a vigorous nudge of the collection box; those who made a liberal contribution were rewarded with a bow and an offer of snuff.

The most remarkable feature of the history of the parish has been its line of priests. Father Sebastian Louis Meurin came to Ste. Genevieve from France by way of Canada and several missions. Father de Saint Pierre, German by birth, came to America during the Revolution as chaplain to General Rochambeau's French army. After work among the Peoria Indians, he was appointed Pastor at Ste. Genevieve in 1789. His successor, Father James Maxwell, who was concerned with civil as well as religious matters, was the dynamic chairman of the first council of the territorial legislature, the originator of a scheme for Irish immigration to southeastern Missouri, the directing force of the Louisiana Academy, and an active influence in many other affairs. In 1804, Maxwell buried the district's commandant, François Vallé, Jr., beneath his pew, where is also the grave of Madame Vallé; he himself was buried beneath the sanctuary of the church ten years later. Father Henry Pratte, born in Ste. Genevieve in 1788 and educated in Montreal, Canada, was the first Missouri-born priest. The present pastor, Monsignor Charles van Tourenhout, has administered the affairs of the parish for 50 years. To him, more than to any other, can be credited the preservation of much of the history and many of the legends, traditions, and customs in Missouri's oldest town.

2. The HISTORICAL MUSEUM (*open 1-5 weekdays, 11-5 Sundays; 10¢*), in the center of Du Bourg Place, is housed in a one-story limestone building of modified Norman design. Dedicated in 1935 to commemorate the town's bicentennial, the museum exhibits historical and archeological relics, chiefly from Ste. Genevieve County. The collection includes Audubon and Rozier's termination of partnership agreement, dated April 6, 1811; the iron safe from the old Ste. Genevieve Savings Association Bank which Jesse James robbed May 26, 1873; and a crayon portrait of Madame Cecile Chouquette Moreau of Ste. Genevieve, said to have been made by Audubon in 1810. In one end of the building's single room is the public library.

3. EL CAMINO REAL MARKER, NE. corner Du Bourg Place, approximately 75 feet south of Merchant St., is a red-granite shaft on the route of the King's Highway of the Spanish era. The road, laid out in 1789, extended from New Madrid, through Ste. Genevieve, to St. Louis. It followed an ancient Indian path, and was probably but little better than a trail (*see Transportation*).

4. The JOHN PRICE HOUSE (*opened by permission*), rising flush with a walk at Third and Market Sts., at the SE. corner of Du Bourg Place, is a two-and-a-half-story brick structure now (1941) housing a beer parlor. The structure is of large hand-made brick laid up in

---

STE. GENEVIEVE. Points of Interest

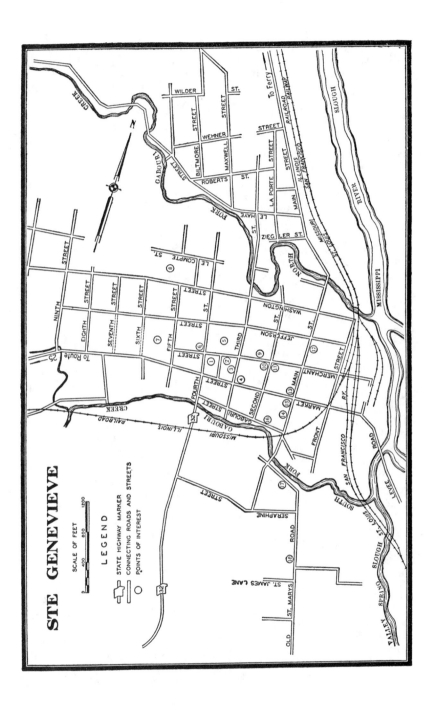

Flemish bond, with a dentil cornice similar to that on the Philipson-Vallé house. The presence of small brick in common bond at the gable ends suggests that the structure once had a hip roof.

The house was built between 1800 and 1804 by John Price, a Kentuckian. In 1798, Price and his brother Andrew were engaged in trade with Louisville and Frankfort, and during the same year Price was granted a license to operate a ferry from Ste. Genevieve to Kaskaskia for a period of six years. In 1806 Price's house was sold by Sheriff Henry ("Honest Harry") Dodge to Joseph Pratte, to settle a debt of $1,200. Dodge (1782-1867) was then beginning the career that brought him fame on the frontier: he became brigadier general of Missouri militia during the War of 1812, and was delegate to the Constitutional Convention in 1820. Indicted for treason, he thrashed nine of the jurymen; the remainder fled. Dodge served in the Winnebago and Black Hawk Wars, led an expedition to the Rocky Mountains in 1835, and was Territorial Governor of Wisconsin, and United States Senator (1848-57).

5. The SISTERS OF ST. JOSEPH CONVENT (*open 9-5 daily*), N. side of Du Bourg Place, is housed in a four-story brick building, west of which is a long, low stone building whose west side forms part of the stone and brick wall encircling the convent yard and gardens. The property was purchased in 1848 from Joseph Pratte, who used the several smaller stone buildings as warehouses for furs and merchandise. The Sisters of St. Joseph opened the Academy of St. Francis de Sales and enjoyed sufficient patronage to erect the four-story brick building in 1867. The academy was closed after the public school system was established.

6. The JACQUES DUBREUIL GUIBOURD HOUSE (*private*), NW. corner Fourth and Merchant Sts., is a story-and-a-half Creole dwelling, with walls of upright, squared logs and plaster-filled interstices, covered with white weatherboard. The long sloping roof, framed with hand-hewn timbers, covers the front and back *galéries*. Guibourd, a native of Angiers, France, went to San Domingo as secretary to a wealthy planter. During the slave insurrection there, he was saved from death by his faithful Negro valet, Moros, who accompanied his master to Ste. Genevieve. The lot on which the house stands was granted to Guibourd on June 15, 1799, and the house may have been built soon afterwards. The garden, protected by a high brick wall, is planted in flowers which were Creole favorites: lilies, lilacs, the "Crown Imperial," honeysuckle, and roses. Jules F. Vallé, a descendant of the first commandant, occupies the house, which he has restored and furnished with early furniture.

7. In the OLD CEMETERY, Fifth and Sixth Sts., and Market and Jefferson Sts., on a tree-shaded hillside, weathered gravestones record, often in French, the memory of many early residents of Ste. Genevieve. Among these are the Commandant Jean Baptiste Vallé, Felix and Odile Pratte Vallé, Jacques Guibourd, Ferdinand Rozier, Henry Janis, Vital Beauvais, J. B. S. Pratte, and Walter Fenwick. Near the Fifth Street

entrance is the monument erected by the Missouri assembly to the memory of Dr. Lewis Fields Linn (1795-1843), half-brother of General Henry Dodge, who was known as "the model senator of Missouri." Linn, a Kentucky physician, came to Ste. Genevieve in 1816, was elected to the State senate in 1830, and appointed to succeed Alexander Buckner in 1833 in the national Senate, an office he held until his death. Linn was the author of the Platte Purchase bill, and an advocate of the Oregon Territory bill. He also aided in the development of Iowa.

8. The LOUISIANA ACADEMY BUILDING (*open by permission of superintendent, Ste. Genevieve High School*), NW. corner Fifth and Washington Sts., overlooking the town from a hilltop, is an impressive two-and-a-half-story stone structure completed about 1810. The academy, organized in December of 1806 and chartered the following June, was planned as a free school for the children of poor white families and Indians. Mann Butler, pioneer Kentucky historian, was in charge of the school between 1812 and 1814. In 1818, three Christian Brothers were sent here to teach, the first Christian Brothers in the United States. The school was closed during the Civil War. The board of education now owns the grounds, on the northern portion of which the new high school, a two-story brick structure of modified Georgian design, has been erected.

9. The SENATOR LEWIS F. LINN HOUSE (*private*), Merchant St., west of Second St., is a two-story white frame house set on the edge of the sidewalk. The house is said to have been built by Dr. Linn in 1827, three years before he became Senator. With its small, many-paned windows and roof line suggesting the New England salt-box type of house, the structure is representative of those built by many of the first American settlers in Ste. Genevieve. The side entrance opens upon a garden containing many fine examples of boxwood.

10. The DR. BENJAMIN SHAW HOUSE (*open by arrangement*), SW. corner Merchant and Seconds Sts., is a one-and-a-half-story white frame house of uncertain origin. Local tradition dates it before 1820 as the home of an early physician. The woodwork appears to be American. The large double interior doors are said to have come from a steamboat wrecked near by in the Mississippi River.

Directly behind the Shaw house on Second Street is a curious one-and-a-half-story stone structure with a recessed porch, locally known as the INDIAN TRADING POST. The structure may have been the warehouse of the merchant Jean Baptiste Bossieur, and is thought to date from before 1820.

West of the Shaw house on Merchant Street is the one-and-a-half-story PARFAIT DUFOUR HOUSE (*private*), a Creole structure of upright-log construction, now weatherboarded. Dufour, a native of Detroit, and an early resident of Ste. Genevieve, seems to have lived for a time near Mine à Breton, and later at Fourche à Duclos, being interested in lead mining operations. Dufour was granted this lot by the Spanish government, and in 1789 owned a house here.

11. The PHILIPSON-VALLÉ HOUSE (*private*), SE. corner Second and Merchant Sts., is a stone structure with sharply pitched roof, dormer windows, a dentil cornice similar to that on the Price House, and many-paned windows. The stoop which once gave access to the front doorway has been replaced by the present recessed entranceway.

The house is thought to have been built by Jacob Philipson, a merchant, during his residence in Ste. Genevieve, 1811-14. Highly educated, and accomplished musicians, the Philipson brothers—Jacob, Joseph, and Simon—were perhaps the first Jewish residents of Missouri, having come there from Philadelphia in 1807 and 1808. The brothers were principally identified with St. Louis, where they became prominent merchants.

The house was purchased in 1824 by J. B. Vallé and later became the property of his nephew, Felix Vallé, who, in 1849, with John Harrison as a partner, organized the American Iron Mountain Company to work the iron deposits in St. Francois County. In 1851, Felix became a partner in a rolling mill which was for many years one of the principal industries of St. Louis. His wife, Odile, is affectionately remembered as "Mama" Vallé because of her many charities.

Diagonally across Merchant Street is the two-and-a-half-story stone ROZIER BANK BUILDING (*open*), said to have been built during the 1850's as an office for the American Iron Mountain Company.

12. The VITAL DE ST. GEMME DE BEAUVAIS HOUSE (*open by permission*), 20 South Main St., is a good example of the Creole-type house erected during the Spanish regime, although the exterior has been altered. Built by Vital de St. Gemme de Beauvais prior to 1791, the house is a long, low building with "a ponderous wooden frame," now weatherboarded, of squared logs placed upright in the ground (*see Architecture*). The sweep of the roof covers front and rear *galéries*. A massive chimney originally divided the interior into two equal parts. In one division was the dining room, parlor, and principal bedchamber; in the other was the kitchen. Each had a small private chamber at the end, and walnut floors.

The grounds originally were enclosed with sharpened cedar pickets, eight or ten inches in diameter and seven feet high. This was for protection against the pigs and cows wandering the streets and, presumably, the Osage Indians, who "on one occasion . . . left the village without so much as one horse to turn a mill." The front yard was narrow, but the back area contained a barn, stables, Negro quarters, and offices, as well as an enclosed vegetable and flower garden and a small orchard.

When Henry Brackenridge came to live in this house his French was limited to the word *oui*, but when he returned to Pittsburgh three years later, his education exceeded even his father's expectations: he remembered only "yes" and "no" in English.

13. The JEAN BAPTISTE VALLÉ HOUSE (*private*), NE. corner Main and Market Sts., is a one-and-a-half-story Creole-type dwelling said to date from about 1785. Its side walls of upright logs are set on a thick, high foundation of stone. Alterations made in the 1860's

included a change of the roof and the addition of dormer windows and numerous interior arrangements. The house was originally the home of Jean Baptiste Vallé (1760-1840), son of François Vallé, Sr., who brought his family to Ste. Genevieve from Kaskaskia before 1758 and became the richest man of the Illinois country, and the first commandant under Spanish authority.

The Spanish census for 1787 states that the establishment of "Don Juan Baptista Vallé" included his wife, 2 children, and 37 slaves. Appointed in 1804, he was the last commandant of Ste. Genevieve, succeeding his elder brother François, Jr., in this office.

14. The BOLDUC HOUSE (*opened by permission*), 123 S. Main St., a ten-room, one-and-a-half-story structure with a sweeping roof, massive chimney, and galleries on three sides, is one of the least changed of the old French houses of Ste. Genevieve. The date of erection is uncertain, and additions to the house have been made at various periods. Tradition asserts that the frame of the house was moved up from the old town, and if so, it may be one of the oldest houses in the Mississippi Valley.

Louis Bolduc, Sr., (1734-1815), a prominent merchant and slave owner, was the first owner of the house. According to an old story, he used his cellars as a storeroom for large sums of money. Once an American merchant wagered that he was wealthier than Bolduc. When he was asked to bring a half-bushel basket to measure Bolduc's silver, however, the merchant paid the bet without protest. Also associated with the old house is the story of Michael de l'Amoureux and his son Jean, as recorded by Harry Petrequin in his *Stories of Old Ste. Genevieve*. M. de l'Amoureux, a merchant of L'Orient in France, came to America in 1793, and to Ste. Genevieve some years later. One of his sons, Jean fell in love with Désirée La Chance, whose father had won the soubriquet "Lafatigue," for his indolence. When his father refused to permit the match, Jean married a Negro slave girl.

15. The MEILLEUR HOUSE (*private*), Main St. immediately north of Bolduc house, also known as the Old Convent, a two-story frame structure, was built about 1815 by René Meilleur, son-in-law of Louis Bolduc, as a private dwelling.

On June 25, 1837, five Sisters of Loretto opened in this building a school which they conducted here until 1848, when they purchased the property now owned by the Sisters of St. Joseph. The two-story brick corner building immediately to the north, now a blacksmith shop, is said to have been Meilleur's store.

16. The FRANÇOIS VALLÉ HOUSE (*private*), 167 S. Gabouri St., is a fragment, greatly altered, of the home of François Vallé, Jr. (1758-1804), who in 1783 succeeded his father, François, Sr. (1716-83) as Civil and Military Commandant of Ste. Genevieve, a position which he held until the time of his death. In 1787, he had 3 houses on this lot for his household consisting of his wife, 2 children, and 39 slaves. His son François III (b. 1779), was educated under the supervision of Gouverneur Morris of New York, at a school in New Jersey,

where he remained until 1796. In 1802 he brought a millwright from Kentucky, erected a sawmill on the River Aux Vasse, and began to supply the community with lumber.

After the transfer of the Territory, William Henry Harrison, then Territorial Governor, visited the Vallé's, and, thinking to compliment the family, appointed the son sheriff of the District. Madame Vallé was pleased, until she learned that the sheriff was also the official hangman. She at once ordered Governor Harrison from her house, and he was obliged to revoke the appointment.

17. The GREEN TREE TAVERN (*private*), 244 Old St. Mary's Road, another *maison de poteaux sur sole* (*see Architecture*), with the proportions of the interior woodwork and the reeded panels suggesting American influence, was built as a residence by François Janis in 1791. It became a tavern when the number of travelers pouring into the new territory made the entertainment of all strangers in private homes no longer possible. The sign bearing the words "Green Tree Tavern," preserved in the local museum, may have been the same that attracted the English writer, Thomas Ashe, in 1806. He found his host to be a "lively Frenchman," whose wife made coffee that equaled any that Ashe had tasted in Paris. Four years later, Brackenridge reports that the innkeeper, mistaking him and his companion for footmen in their travel-worn clothes, quartered them in an outhouse. During the night, the friend's trousers were eaten by rats.

18. The MISPLAIT HOUSE (*open by permission*), Old St. Mary's Road, a small, one-and-a-half-story Creole house, its front *galérie* almost hidden by a great box bush, seems to have come to Basil Misplait from his parents, in 1804. Originally, perhaps, the house had not more than a single room, and the roof was once hipped. For some reason the outer walls were constructed to lean slightly inward. In the rear is a stone well with a tent-shaped top over the windlass, a form which seems to be peculiarly French. South of the house, and placed at right angles to the road, is the larger, one-and-a-half-story St. Gemme-Amoureux House (*open by arrangement*). When it was built, the house had a steep, thatched, French-Canadian hip roof. When the *galéries* were added later, the roof line was altered to its present form. The original stone chimney top has been changed to brick within recent years. The construction is similar to that of the Bequet-Ribault House (*private*) near it to the south, which has walls of cedar posts planted vertically in the ground (*poteaux en terre*), and originally had *galéries* on all four sides, with whitewashed, plastered walls. Despite changes, many interesting details have been preserved, such as the *en queue d'aronde* shutters pegged with wooden pins.

Across the road from these houses is the *Grand Champ*, which extends east to the Mississippi River. The field was cultivated in the old manner as late as 1907.

POINTS OF INTEREST IN ENVIRONS

Lime Quarries and Lime Processing Plants, 1 *m.;* Site of Nouvelle Bourbon, 5 *m.;* Zell, 6 *m.;* La Saline, 7 *m.;* Ozora Marble Quarries and Camp Wrather, 14 *m.* (*see Tour 11*). Fort Chartres, 8.5 *m.;* Kaskaskia, 13 *m.* (*see Illinois Guide*).

St. Joseph

Railroad Station: Union Depot, 1200 S. Sixth St., for Chicago, Burlington and Quincy R.R., Atchison, Topeka and Santa Fe R.R., Chicago Great Western R.R., Union Pacific R.R., Missouri Pacific R.R., Chicago, Rock Island and Pacific R.R.

Bus Stations: Union Bus Depot, Ninth & Frederick, for Jefferson Transportation Co., Burlington Trailways, Santa Fe Trailways, Missouri Pacific Trailways, Rock Island Bus Lines; Union Bus Terminal, Eighth & Edmond Sts., for Union Pacific Stages; Jefferson Transportation Co., Felix St., between Fifth and Sixth Sts., for Wathena-Troy Line.

Airports: Municipal Airport, 6 m. NW. of post office on Water Works Road, left on Airport Road, for Mid-Continent Airlines; taxi fare 50¢, driving time 30 min.

Local Busses: Fare 10¢; 3 tokens for 20¢.

Taxis: 25¢ first 2 miles, 15¢ each additional mile.

Traffic Regulations: Speed limits, 20 m.p.h. downtown, 30 m.p.h. in residence section. One-way streets in congested area.

Accommodations: 28 hotels; tourist camps and rooming houses.

Information Service: Information Office, City Hall, Eleventh and Jules Sts.; Automobile Club of Missouri (AAA), SW. corner Fifth and Jules Sts. (members only); Chamber of Commerce, 209 N. Fifth St.

Radio Station: KFEQ (680 kc.)

Motion Picture Houses: Nine.

Swimming: Municipal pool, Twenty-second and Messanie Sts., adults 25¢, children 15¢; Hyde Park pool, Hyde Park Ave., at Fourth St., adults 25¢, children 15¢.

Golf: Fairview Municipal Club, Mitchell Ave., S. of Bartlett Park, 18 holes; greens fee 50¢.

Tennis: Municipal courts, between Twenty-eight and Thirtieth Sts., S. of Messanie St., free.

Annual Events: Pony Express Commemoration, Patee Park, 914 Penn St., April 3; Apple Blossom Festival, early in May; Baby Beef and Pig Show, St. Joseph Stockyards, first week in Oct., Christmas Parade, day after Thanksgiving.

ST. JOSEPH (814 alt., 75,711 pop.), which covers the bluffs that overlook the Missouri River and the grain and grazing lands of the western prairie, once bestrode the roaring trade lanes to California and Mexico. Today, it is Missouri's third largest city, and an important grain, livestock, manufacturing, and wholesale center. Here is the center of the fifth largest meat-packing industry in the world, out of which has risen a modern city of skyscrapers and chromium-plated façades. But even in the maturity of its development, St. Joseph keeps its sidewalk lounging chairs, and clings to the river and to memories of the wagon trails and the Pony Express of its early days.

The narrow streets of the retail district—suggesting the frugal French manner of city planning—follow the bottomland close to the river. This is the original townsite, with the east and west thoroughfares named for members of the family of Robidoux (locally pronounced "Roobidoo"), founder of the city: Faraon, Jules, Francis, Felix, Edmond, Charles, Sylvanie, Angelique, and Messanie. Toward the eastern end of the district, Frederick Avenue, a transformed stagecoach road, twists diagonally northeastward, past the Civic Center and City Hall, at Tenth and Eleventh Streets. Tall modern buildings dominate the section, yet here and there are quaint old structures with stone-trimmed turrets, dormer windows, and second floors that bulge over the streets.

Also along the river front, but west and south of the retail section, the wholesale and manufacturing district slopes from the bottomland down to the narrow flood plain that skirts the foot of the lower bluffs. Here are the larger wholesale houses, hulking red-brick buildings of St. Joseph's heyday, heavy with brownstone trim and arched windows, with red-granite columns fronting the entrances and spiral fire escapes overhanging the walks. Small establishments occupy former retail buildings and hotels, many with buttressed iron fronts, balconies, and porticoes. The Patee House, corner of Twelfth and Penn Streets, once considered the finest hotel west of St. Louis, now houses a shirt factory; the Edgar House, 101 Francis Street, where Abraham Lincoln visited in 1859, is now occupied by a paper box company. In South St. Joseph, near the city's limit, are the heavy industries: stockyards, packing houses, flour mills, and grain elevators.

The residential sections crown the hills and bluffs of the retail and industrial districts. The handsomest houses lie northeast of Frederick Avenue along Lovers' Lane and in the vicinity of Twenty-eighth Street, where 20 miles of tree-shaded drives swing southward from Krug Park on the north, through Corby Grove and Bartlett Park, past the Municipal Golf Course, to Hyde Park and King Hill.

East of the retail section, the brick and stone mansions of St. Joseph's opulent eighties crowd the sharp hillsides. Perched high on narrow terraced lawns, their gingerbread-trimmed turrets and dormer windows often rise above the trees that line the streets. Near the city's southern limits are the frame cottages of the industrial workers.

St. Joseph's population (1930 census) is 89.6 per cent native white. Negroes—largely descendants of early Buchanan County's 2,000 Negro slaves—comprise 5 per cent. They live in several scattered sections, with the larger number clustering about the Negro high school on Eighteenth Street, between Angelique and Sylvanie Streets. Approximately 4.8 per cent of the inhabitants are foreign-born, many of them Poles and Russians. The majority of this group are employed in the packing plants and stockyards.

Joseph Robidoux first visited the site of St. Joseph while on a trading expedition up the Missouri River in 1799. In 1826, as an employee of the American Fur Company, he was sent to establish a new post at the mouth of Roy's branch in the Blacksnake Hills. The following year

Robidoux moved his post to the south bank of this stream, now enclosed by the St. Joseph Sewer System.

Robidoux's Post, as it came to be called, was in the heart of the Indian country. The Blacksnake Hills, which extend along the Missouri almost to the mouth of the Tarkio River, were named for the Indians who once lived there. An Iowa village was east of Robidoux's Post, and six miles down the Missouri was a Fox village. Robidoux, living at peace with the Indians, shortly became a sort of wilderness king, employing some 20 Creoles who made regular trips into the Grand River country and present-day Kansas and Nebraska to trade for furs. In 1834, Robidoux bought the post from the American Fur Company for $500. Maximilian, Prince of Wied, who visited there that year, found the post to consist of two white-painted houses, and "extensive fields of maize protected by fences, and very fine cattle grazing the plain."

In the fall of 1836, the Federal Government, seeking to end the constant clashes between pioneers and Indians, made the Platte Purchase, which added to Missouri approximately 2,000,000 acres—the present counties of Buchanan, Platte, Atchison, Andrew, Holt, and Nodaway. Settlers, many of them slave holders, poured into the area from Virginia, Tennessee, Indiana, and Ohio. They found the country good for raising hogs, cattle and necessary food crops; it also proved to be excellent for hemp, which was introduced in 1840 and remained an important crop until the abolition of slavery and the introduction of cheaper fibers made its cultivation unprofitable.

Buchanan County was organized in December of 1838, and two years later Sparta was made the seat of government. The majority of the settlers, however, felt that Robidoux's Post, the principal settlement in the county, should be the county seat. After the hemp harvest in the early summer of 1843, Robidoux therefore had a town platted on the site of his settlement which he named St. Joseph, after his patron saint. Following much agitation, petitioning, and voting, St. Joseph was declared the county seat early in 1846. When Father De Smet visited the town in the fall of that year he found it in a "most prosperous condition." The "American, French, Creole, Irish, and German" settlers had already built "350 houses, two churches, a city hall, and a jail." William Ridenbaugh had established (1845) the St. Joseph *Gazette;* the Thespians were presenting plays; the Hawes & Mabie Circus had performed before the delighted inhabitants. The settlement of the Oregon Territory had swelled the immigrant tide, and St. Joseph, the last town in northwestern Missouri having direct river communication with the East, was prospering.

Staple commodities were brought upstream from St. Louis, and exchanged at St. Joseph for furs and buffalo hides. Grizzled mountain trappers from the Far West, dressed in embroidered and fringed deerskin, wandered about the streets. During the summer of 1848, Rudolph Kurz, the Swiss artist, recorded in his journal: "The bourgeois or the heads of firms, clerks and other engagees or employees of the different fur companies, crowded the streets and public houses of the town. St. Joseph is for them now what St. Louis was earlier—their rendezvous." In 1849, a daily average of 20 steamers paid St. Joseph owners the $5 wharfage fee. A plow factory, sawmills, flour mills, a pork-packing plant, foundries, and other industries catering to frontier life followed the settlers and the river trade.

In 1844, a wagon train of some 800 persons, led by General Cornelius Gilliam, had crossed the river just north of the new village of St. Joseph. Among the immigrants was James W. Marshall, itinerant wheelwright. In 1848 Marshall discovered gold at Sutter's mill, California, and the steady but moderate stream of migration became a torrent. By the middle of February 1849, several thousand adventurers had streamed into St. Joseph, bound for California. Many were from the northern States, some had even come from Europe. Because cholera had broken out in Independence and Westport, the rival points of departure for the Santa Fe Trail, a majority of the immigrants were diverted from the southern to the northern route, so that St. Joseph early took the lead as the major wagon train and supply depot. Between April and June 1849, approximately 1,500 prairie schooners crossed the river at St. Joseph. Thousands more crossed on the ferries above and below the city. Kurz records: "The city was packed so full of people that tents were pitched about the city and along the opposite bank of the river in such numbers that we seemed besieged by an army." At night gold-thirsty optimists sat about their fires, singing their song:

> Oh, the Good Time has come at last,
> We need no more complain, sir,
> The rich can live in luxury,
> And we can do the same, sir;
> For the Good Time has come at last,
> And as we are all told, sir,
> We shall be rich at once, now,
> With California gold, sir.

The "good time" had indeed come for St. Joseph. Merchandise stocks were valued at $400,000. Between March and October 1849, 123 buildings were erected, 64 of them of brick. It was fevered and ephemeral, this outfitting of wagon trains—but it left behind it the foundation of one of St. Joseph's major modern industries. The earlier immigrants (the future wheat farmers of the prairies) had needed meat. To satisfy the demand, large numbers of hogs were fattened on the corn and acorns of northwestern Missouri. In 1846, John Corby had established a slaughtering house. At the time of the California gold rush, half a dozen other houses had been established. People grew tired of eating cured pork and demanded fresh beef; this made profitable the driving of cattle to California in herds. Cows bought in Missouri for $10 a head were sold in California for $150, and St. Joseph stockmen roamed Missouri, Arkansas, and Iowa in search of cattle. In May 1853, approximately 10,000 head crossed the Missouri River here, beginning the long drive to the California valleys.

As the rush to California slackened, the discovery of gold in Colorado in 1858 precipitated a new mass migration. Charles A. Krone, the St. Louis actor, reported that St. Joseph in 1859 had the bustling appearance of a great fair, with excited travelers preparing to make the plains journey in prairie schooners, "rickety old farm wagons," and even small two-wheeled push carts. Many bore such mottoes as— "Faint Heart Never Won Fair Lady," "I Dare," "For Pike's Peak Ho." Before long many were to return, disappointed in their search for gold, hungry, ragged, and dispirited, their brave wagon boasts changed to "Prodigal Son," "Pike's Hell," "A Fool is Born."

The development of the Far West necessitated better transportation facilities than river boats and freight wagons. In 1847, the State assembly incorporated the Hannibal and St. Joseph Railroad Company (*see Transportation*). Despite the enthusiasm of a few citizens, the average St. Joseph merchant was indifferent to the proposed railway, and, it is said, contributed only enough to buy the two surveyors new suits of clothes. Federal and State grants of land and funds made construction possible. The last spike on the road—a gold one in the fashion of the period—was driven by Joseph Robidoux, February 13, 1859. The following day, the first passenger train to cross the State arrived, giving St. Joseph the tremendous advantage of being the last Western railroad terminal.

The railroad made an important connection at St. Joseph with two famous transports to the West. Nearly a year previously, John M. Hockaday had inaugurated, under government contract, a stage line to Salt Lake City, 1,000 miles away. Since the chief purpose of the line was to make a closer connection between troops in Utah and the War Department, it aimed at dependable, rather than rapid, service. On the other hand, speed was needed if California was to be saved for the Union. Out of this demand emerged the Pony Express, whose story constitutes one of the most colorful chapters of St. Joseph's history. Service was begun April 3, 1860, with St. Joseph the eastern terminus, and Sacramento, California, the western. Riders left both places on the same day. On April 14, the California rider reached St. Joseph with the western mail (*see Transportation*).

The contemporary railway mail car was a direct outgrowth of the need for a means of sorting mail quickly for the waiting Pony Express rider at St. Joseph. Incoming mail was sorted in the St. Joseph post office, placed in a pouch, and given to the rider, until William Davis, postmaster, conceived the idea of sorting the mail on the train en route. His suggestions for a railroad car were approved by Postmaster General Blair, and the first mail car was constructed at Hannibal for service on the Hannibal and St. Joseph Railroad.

For St. Joseph, as for much of western Missouri, the Civil War was merely the climax of a slowly gathering conflict. Buchanan County was predominately Southern in its sympathies; more than 2,000 slaves were owned by its citizens. When some of the slaves were aided and encouraged to escape into "Free Kansas" by crusading abolitionists, ill-feeling was intensified. In 1859, a Dr. John Doy was intercepted in his attempt to get a group of slaves out of Missouri, and the case was brought to St. Joseph. Shortly before the trial, however, a party of Kansans entered the jail, "secured" the jailer, and escaped with Doy into Kansas. During the tense spring of 1861, a pro-slavery mob headed by M. Jeff Thompson tore down the United States flag at the post office, an incident which cost St. Joseph its chance to become the eastern terminus of the Union Pacific Railroad in 1862. Thompson, then in the real estate business, later joined the Confederate army and became known as the "Swamp Fox of the Confederacy," because of his elusive military maneuvers.

Guerrilla bands, using the town for a base, spread terror over the countryside. Nearly 2,000 men went south from Buchanan County to join Confederate forces. Schools were closed and business practically disappeared until soldiers were quartered in the town. Near the end of the war, however, the general business boom which had begun in the North reached St. Joseph, and continued into the era of railroad building. Even the periodic descent of clouds of grasshoppers—stripping the countryside of everything green and chewing at the lace curtains of St. Joseph homes—could not check the resurgent prosperity. Freighting companies were organized, and the livestock industry took a new lease on life. When the war ended, Texas cattlemen began moving great herds eastward to market. Prevented from driving their cattle to the railroad at Sedalia by the hostility shown in the Ozark region to the tick-infested stock, the cattlemen came on to St. Joseph, bringing not only meat animals, but new breeding stock. A St. Joseph company built a toll and railroad bridge across the river. Completed in 1873, this served until it was superseded by the present free bridge in 1929. In the quarter-century following the Civil War, five more railroads entered the city.

By 1880, St. Joseph was at the peak of postwar prosperity. Seven years later, the livestock business demanded new and larger facilities. The St. Joseph Stock Yards Company was organized, and the yards were removed to their present location; in 1897 Swift & Company purchased the controlling interest in the reorganized company. Three other major packing houses were subsequently established here. By 1890 St. Joseph's flour mills, packing houses, and horse and mule markets were of interstate importance. With a population of more than 52,000, St. Joseph was said to be the wealthiest city per capita in the Nation. Gingerbread mansions were built, and civic improvements were instigated. By 1910 the population had increased to about 77,000.

Today (1941) St. Joseph is the world's fifth largest livestock market and its tenth largest producer of flour. Its stockyards have a capacity of 18,000 hogs, 10,000 cattle, 14,000 sheep, and 2,000 horses and mules. Its packing houses, in 1937, consumed 246,801 cattle, 78,010 calves, 518,841 hogs, and 793,887 sheep. The development of apple orchards on the loess hills of Buchanan County has made St. Joseph an important fruit-growing center. In addition to flour mills, there are a brewery, with an annual capacity of 150,000 barrels, candy factories, producing 20,000,000 pounds per year; and a school tablet and stationery supply company, a hog-cholera serum plant, and a floor maintenance plant which are the largest of their kind in the nation. More than 400 companies continue the trade that originated with a frontier fur trading post and a wagon train depot.

POINTS OF INTEREST

1. The SYLVANIE ROBIDOUX HOUSE (*open 9-5 daily: 10¢*), NW. corner Second and Michel Sts., a two-story, gray-brick building, was the third house built by Joseph Robidoux. It has 15 rooms and 8 fireplaces; its stairways are of walnut. Robidoux built the house in the 1840's as a present for his daughter, Sylvanie. George Moran, Negro impersonator, of the team of Moran and Mack ("Two Black Crows"), once lived here.

2. The JOSEPH ROBIDOUX HOUSE (*open by permission*), 219-225 Poulin St., is an unusually long one-and-a-half-story brick structure, now tenanted by Negroes. Set almost flush with the sidewalk, it has a raised stone basement and a low attic. Once a part of the extensive "Robidoux Row," the house was built in the early 1840's, and is said to be the oldest house in St. Joseph. Here the founder of St. Joseph died in 1868.

Joseph Robidoux was not only the founder of St. Joseph but one of its most colorful citizens. Careless in dress, an inveterate gambler, shrewd in bargaining and Indian diplomacy, he became the patriarch of a large, far-flung, and tumultuous clan. He was born in St. Louis, August 10, 1783, of French-Canadian parentage. His father, also named Joseph, was a prominent fur trader. Joseph, Jr., became an important trader on the upper Missouri. About 1809 he established a post at Council Bluffs, where Manuel Lisa of St. Louis, and the American Fur Company of which John Jacob Astor was the founder, were his chief competitors. Robidoux and Lisa pledged that neither would take advantage of the other in trading with the Indians. Once when a band of Pawnee Indians was expected, Lisa secretly prepared to break the pact. To appear innocent of duplicity and to prevent Robidoux from trading with the Pawnee, he went over to call on his neigh-

ST. JOSEPH. Points of Interest

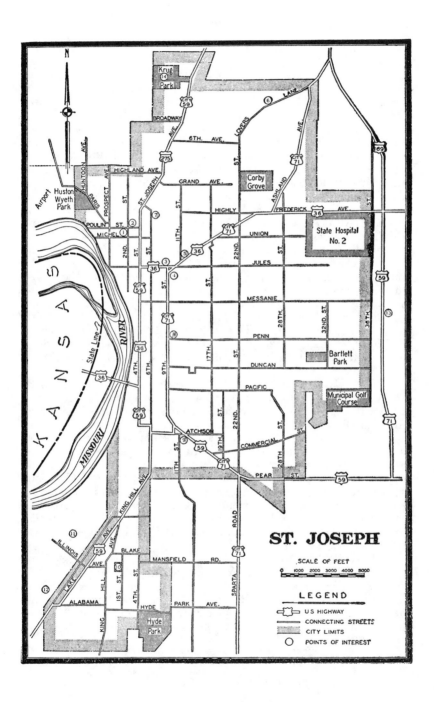

bor. Robidoux welcomed him, and proposed a toast to their friendship in champagne; then, complaining of illness, he asked Lisa to go to the cellar for the wine. When Lisa entered the cellar, Robidoux "let fall the trapdoor, rolled a cask upon it and with mocking words left his opponent imprisoned in order that he might trade alone with the Pawnees."

In 1822, the American Fur Company purchased Robidoux's interests with the understanding that he would not return to Council Bluffs within a three-year period. At the end of this period, Robidoux, who had attempted to settle down in St. Louis as a baker, announced his plan to return to "the Bluffs." Compromise seemed wiser than competition, and Robidoux was offered an annual salary of $1,800 by the American Fur Company to establish a post at the Blacksnake Hills.

3. The MARY ALICIA OWEN HOME (*open by permission*), 306 N. Ninth St., was the birthplace and life-long home of Missouri's best-known authority on Indian folklore. An old-fashioned, two-story frame structure, the house was built by Miss Owen's father shortly after he came to St. Joseph in 1844. It still houses members of the Owen family. Mary Alicia Owen (1850-1935) was interested in Indian customs from childhood. The Sac and Fox adopted her into their tribes, enabling her to learn at first hand, and later to record, their tribal dances, songs, and legends. Her largest collection of Indian relics is at Oxford, England, although some articles were given to the State Museum at Jefferson City, and the Missouri Historical Society in St. Louis.

4. The PUBLIC LIBRARY (*open weekdays*), NW. corner Tenth and Felix Sts., houses the PUBLIC MUSEUM, which contains a collection of more than 225 pistols, many of them rare, a small group of Indian relics and cliff-dweller mummies, and a number of curios.

5. The EUGENE FIELD HOME (*open by permission*), 425 N. Eleventh St., a rambling two-story brick house painted white, is on a narrow, terraced lawn enclosed by a decorative iron fence. The interior of the house has been remodeled into apartments. Eugene Field (1850-95) married Julia Sutherland Comstock of St. Joseph in 1873. In 1876, he returned to the city from St. Louis, where he had worked as a journalist, to serve as city editor of the *Gazette* for 18 months. Although known for his verse while here, Field did his best work later, in Kansas City, Denver, and Chicago.

6. LOVERS' LANE, a tree-shaded residential street winding from N. Eighteenth St., to Ashland Ave., won early fame through Eugene Field's nostalgic poem, *Lover's Lane, Saint Jo*. The poem was written while Field was in London, prevented by his youth from marrying Julia Comstock. After expressing a desire to be driving in "Lover's Lane" with a "brown eyed maiden," he continued:

> I purposely say, 'as we *snailed* along,'
> For a proper horse goes slow
> In those leafy aisles, where Cupid smiles,
> In Lover's Lane, Saint Jo.

7. The M. K. GOETZ BREWERY (*guides at office*), SE. corner Sixth and Albemarle Sts., is housed in a group of large, red-brick buildings occupying a 14-acre tract. The brewery, which has an annual capacity of 150,000 barrels, is on the site of the original plant erected in 1859 as the City Brewery by Max & Goetz. M. K. Goetz, who was responsible for the subsequent growth of the industry, was an Alsatian who came to the United States in 1854. Four years later, while enroute to California, he visited St. Joseph and decided to make it his home.

8. The PONY EXPRESS STABLES (*open by arrangement*), 912 Penn St., is a one-and-a-half story brick structure with wide entrance doors. The date of construction and the extent of subsequent alterations is not known, but tradition associates the building with the Pony Express. Service was inaugurated at five o'clock on the afternoon of April 3, 1860. "Little Johnnie" Frey mounted his pony in the old Pike's Peak stable and rode to the express company office on North Second Street, where he was given a buckskin pouch containing 85 pieces of mail. He fastened this to his saddle, and while hundreds cheered, dashed off on the first lap of the 1,975-mile trip to California. The express maintained a schedule of approximately ten days for each trip, unless news of vital importance was being carried. President Buchanan's farewell message was carried in 7 days, 19 hours; the news of Lincoln's election crossed the plains and mountains in 8 days, Lincoln's inaugural address established the record time of 7 days, 17 hours. The express demanded riders who were hardy, courageous, and schooled in the life of the plains. Among those who served were William F. ("Buffalo Bill") Cody, "Pony" Bob Haslem, Jack Keeley, and Jack Slade—the last won his greatest notice as an outlaw, but he served the Pony Express well. After 16 months of operation, the express gave way to the telegraph.

9. The QUAKER OATS COMPANY PLANT (*open 9-5 Mon.-Fri., guides*), 2811 S. Eleventh St., is a modern group of brick buildings covering four blocks. The plant, which manufactures pancake flour and breakfast cereals, is the largest of its kind in the country.

10. KING HILL, South St. Joseph, between Cherokee, First, and Lookout Sts., and Indiana Ave., rising approximately 300 feet above the river, is the highest point in the city, and one of the highest in the range of the Blacksnake Hills. In 1846, Father De Smet wrote that King Hill was the scene of the last battle of the Blacksnake Indians. "It is covered with human bones, and a line of mounds may be perceived in form of ramparts and fortifications. On that occasion the whole tribe of the Blacksnakes was destroyed." On the first summit is an observation point which affords an extensive view of the city and of the stockyards and packing plants.

11. The SWIFT AND ARMOUR PACKING PLANTS (*open 8-4 workdays; guides*), Packers Ave., W. end of Illinois Ave., consist of a great group of brick and concrete buildings strung between a network of railroad tracks and the Missouri River. Near the plants on

three sides are extensive livestock pens. Here more than 2,000 persons are employed in the slaughtering, curing, and packing of hogs, sheep, and cattle, and in the manufacture of by-products. Both companies maintain laboratories in which scientists are constantly searching for new uses of animal substances. Originally, the only items of value derived from the slaughter of livestock were meats, hides, lard, and tallow. Today, nothing is discarded as valueless; one-time waste is converted into an astounding miscellany that includes umbrella handles, dice, chessmen, tennis strings, varnish, and felt.

13. The ANCHOR SERUM COMPANY (*open 8-4 workdays; guides*), Lake Contrary Rd., at SW. edge of town, housed in a sprawling maze of brick and concrete buildings adjoining acres of hog pens, is said to be the world's largest hog cholera serum manufacturing plant. It has branches on three continents. In the immaculate buildings, serums for the prevention of diseases of hogs, horses, cattle, sheep, and poultry are produced.

13. The JESSE JAMES HOUSE (*open daily: admission free with purchase of gasoline, 15¢ otherwise*), US 71 between Messanie St., and Mitchell Ave., is a small, one-story frame cottage, recently moved to its present location from 1318 Lafayette Street and operated as a tourist attraction in conjunction with a filling station and cafe. Here the outlaw (*see Tour 10a*) lived quietly with his family as a respected, mild-mannered citizen known as "Mr. Howard." And here, on April 5, 1882, he was killed by a former lieutenant, Bob Ford, assisted by his brother Charles, who wanted the $10,000 reward. Mrs. James swore out a warrant charging them with the murder of her husband. The men were sentenced to be hanged but were pardoned by Governor T. T. Crittenden. They were subsequently released from another charge of murder in Ray County. According to early accounts, after receiving the reward, they lived in debauchery until Charles committed suicide and Robert was shot in a Colorado dance hall.

14. KRUG PARK, Savannah Road (US 275) at the northwestern city limits, is a landscaped area of 168 acres containing graveled scenic drives, picnic grounds with tables and ovens, a children's circus, and the KRUG PARK BOWL, which has a seating capacity of approximately 20,000 persons. Many public functions, including annual musical or dramatic productions which have ranged from *Everyman* to *The Mikado,* are held in the bowl. The original 61 acres of the park were donated to St. Joseph by Henry Krug; in 1936, his son, Henry Krug, Jr., donated the additional 107 acres.

POINTS OF INTEREST IN ENVIRONS

Bridlewreath Farms, 4.7 *m.;* Corby Mill Ruins, 6.3 *m.* (*See Tour 3*). Sparta Church, 3.5 *m.* (*see Tour 10*).

St. Louis

Railroad Stations: Union Station, S. side Market St., 18th to 20th Sts., for Atchison, Topeka & Santa Fe; Alton; Baltimore & Ohio; Chicago, Burlington & Quincy; Chicago & Eastern Illinois; Chicago Great Western; Chicago, Milwaukee, St. Paul & Pacific; Chicago, Rock Island & Pacific; Kansas City Southern; Missouri-Kansas-Texas (Katy); Missouri Pacific; New York Central; Illinois Central; Louisville & Nashville; Mobile & Ohio; New York, Chicago & St. Louis (Nickel Plate); Pennsylvania; Quincy, Omaha & Kansas City; Southern Railway; St. Louis-San Francisco; St. Louis Southwestern (Cotton Belt); Wabash Railways. 710 N. 12th Blvd. for Illinois Terminal Railroad Co.; Delmar Station, 6100 Delmar Blvd., for Wabash Railway Co.; Tower Grove Station, 1485 S. Vandeventer Ave. for Frisco Lines and Missouri Pacific.

Bus Stations: Greyhound Terminal, 701 N. Broadway (in Union Market Bldg.), for affiliated Greyhound Lines; Missouri Transit Lines; M. C. Foster Bus Line; St. Louis, Red Bud & Chester Bus Lines; Washington-Union Bus Lines; Belleville-St. Louis Coach Company; River View Bus Line. Trailways Bus Depot, 700 N. Broadway, for Missouri, Kansas & Oklahoma Trailways; Missouri Pacific Trailways; Missouri-Arkansas Lines; Santa Fe Trailways; Jacksonville Bus Lines; St. Louis County Bus Company; Vandalia Bus Line; M. C. Foster Bus Line; St. Clair Bus Line. All-American Bus Lines, 800 N. Broadway, for DeLuxe Motor Stages; Missouri Transit Lines; M. C. Foster Bus Line; Tri-State Transit Company. Union Bus Terminal, 600 Walnut St., for Fennessey Bus Lines; M. C. Foster Bus Line; Missouri Transit Lines; River View Bus Line; Prost Bus Line; St. Clair Bus Line; Wallen Bus Line; Washington-Union Bus Lines; St. Louis, Red Bud & Chester Bus Lines. East St. Louis City Lines Station, 3rd & Washington Ave., for East St. Louis, Ill., lines.

Airports: Lambert-St. Louis Municipal Airport at Robertson, 16 m. NW. of downtown section on Alt. US 66 for American Airlines; Chicago and Southern Air Lines; Transcontinental and Western Air, Inc., and Marquette Air Lines, Inc. Taxi from 12th St. Blvd. and Locust St., or major hotels, $1; driving time 30 min.

Taxis: 35¢ first 1¾ miles; 10¢ each additional mile; 5 passengers one fare.

Busses and Street Cars (including suburban lines): 10¢ fare; 4 tokens 35¢, good except on Page, Lindell, and Delmar busses; universal transfer except Page, Lindell, and Delmar busses. (10 a.m. to 4 p.m. special shoppers' ticket, 10¢ plus 5¢ for a round trip; weekly pass, unlimited, $1.25).

Service Cars: Individually owned and operated over scheduled routes, 15¢; 10 a.m. to 4 p.m. 10¢ except on Lindell-Waterman line; no transfer.

Sightseeing Tours: All American Bus Lines Terminal, 800 N. Broadway, for De Luxe Sightseeing Tours; scheduled tours daily.

Steamboat Landings: Streckfus Docks, foot of Washington Ave. Trips daily during summer on streamlined SS *Admiral*, 10 a.m. to 5 p.m., except Saturday "Sunset Trip," 2:30 to 7:30 p.m. Trips nightly 9 to 12 m. Eagle Packet Company Docks, 805 N. Wharf (foot of Vine St.) for 2, 3, 4, 7, and 10 day trips. Two-day trip to Hannibal, Mo., Beardstown, Ill., LaGrange Locks, Ill., Cape Girardeau, Mo.; three-day trip to Cairo and Chillicothe, Ill.; four-day trip to Ottawa, Ill.; seven-day trip to Sheffield, Ala.; 10-day trip made once each spring and during July to Chattanooga, Tenn., and once in August to St. Paul, Minnesota.

Ferry Lines: Carondelet Ferry, foot of Davis St., cars 35¢, trucks 50¢; 15 min. service.

Bridges: Municipal Bridge, 7th & Papin Sts., cars 10¢, trucks 15¢; Eads Bridge, 3rd St. and Washington Ave., cars 20¢ to 50¢, trucks 35¢ to 85¢, trailers up to $1; McKinley Bridge, 3729 N. Broadway, cars 20¢, each additional passenger 5¢; Chain of Rocks Bridge, US 66, 11,000 Riverview Drive, N. St. Louis, cars 25¢, trucks 40¢.

Traffic Regulations: Speed limit, 15 m.p.h. downtown except where marked otherwise, 20 m.p.h. in parks, 30 m.p.h. elsewhere. Left turn at light-controlled intersections on white light (replacing amber) only; R. and L. turns at all other intersections except where indicated by signs or traffic officers. One-way streets, N. and S., 6th to 9th Sts., and E. and W., portions of St. Charles St. in downtown districts. Limited parking in congested area, indicated by signs.

Accommodations: 65 hotels.

Information Service: Chamber of Commerce, 511 Locust St. (inquire here for free booklet of historic sites in St. Louis area marked by the Young Men's Division of the Chamber of Commerce); Automobile Club of Missouri (AAA), 3917 Lindell Blvd. (members only); St. Louis Convention Publicity and Tourist Bureau, 911 Locust St.

Radio Stations: KMOX (1120 kc.); KSD (550 kc.); KFUO (850 kc.); KWK (1380 kc.); KXOK (630 kc.); WEW (770 kc.); WIL (1230 kc.).

Theaters and Motion Picture Houses: 1 legitimate, 2 burlesque, 3 outdoor theaters, 1 Little Theater; more than 90 motion picture houses; 1 show boat (foot of Locust St.).

Auditoriums: Municipal Auditorium, Market St., Fourteenth to Fifteenth Sts., containing a convention hall, opera house, and four smaller halls; the Coliseum, 2608 Washington Ave.; the Arena, 5700 Oakland Ave.

Swimming: Municipal pools (suit, towel, and soap 5¢ at most pools); Mullanphy, 11th St. between Cass Ave. and Mullanphy St., open July and August only; Marquette (suit 10¢) SW. corner Osage St. and Minnesota Ave.; Fairgrounds Park, between Grand Blvd., Natural Bridge, Vandeventer, and Kossuth Aves.; Buder, SW. corner Ewing Ave. and Hickory St., open July and August only; Sherman, NW. corner Kingshighway Blvd. and Easton Ave.; Soulard, E. side 7th St. at Soulard St.; Cherokee Community Center (Negroes), 3225 S. 13th St.; Tandy Park Community Center (Negroes), SW. corner Goode and Kennerly Aves.; Adonic Center Bath House No. 5 (Negroes), NW. corner Jefferson Ave. and Adams St.; Vashon Center (Negroes), Market St. and Compton Ave.; Gamble Center (Negroes), Harrison and Gamble Sts.; numerous privately operated pools.

Boating: Forest Park Lagoon, row boats and canoes, 50¢ an hour; motor boat rides, 50¢ a half hour for one or two persons, 60¢ for three, 75¢ for four.

Golf: Forest Park (municipal), 9 holes 25¢, 18 holes 50¢; annual permit covering both courses, $10 (not good Sat., Sun., or holidays). Numerous parks and country clubs in the immediate vicinity of St. Louis offer every golf facility at nominal charges.

Tennis: 116 municipal courts, all major city parks; resident and non-resident adults or children $1 for season. Children not permitted to use courts on Saturday afternoon or Sunday. 10 courts of 116 are all-weather courts.

Riding: Free bridle paths in Forest, Tower Grove, and Chain of Rocks Parks; horses rented at near-by stables. Numerous privately operated riding academies and stables; varying rates.

Ice-Skating: The Arena, 5700 Oakland Ave. (open Nov. to March); the Winter Garden, 520 De Baliviere Ave. (open Sept. to March); 12 outdoor skating areas in parks.

Athletics: Sportsman's Park, Grand Ave. and Dodier St., for major league baseball (Browns and Cardinals); Washington University Stadium (Francis Field), N.E. corner Forsythe and Big Bend Blvds., and Walsh Stadium (St. Louis University), 5200 Oakland Ave., for football; Walsh Stadium for midget auto racing; the Arena, 5700 Oakland Ave. for ice hockey; Municipal Auditorium, Market St., 14th to 15th Sts., and the Coliseum, 2608 Washington Ave., for boxing and wrestling; Forest Park for soft ball, handball, amateur baseball, cricket, archery range, ski jump, toboggan slide, 22 picnic grounds.
Amusement Parks: Forest Park Highlands, 5600 Oakland Ave., and Chain of Rocks Park, 11,000 Riverview Drive.

Annual Events: Orchid Display, Missouri Botanical Garden, 2315 Tower Grove Ave., Jan.; American Artists Exhibit, City Art Museum, Jan. and first half of Feb.; Golden Gloves Boxing Tournament, Municipal Auditorium, Feb.; All-Breed Dog Show, Mississippi Valley Kennel Club, no fixed location, late in March; Flower Show, Greater St. Louis Flower and Garden Association, the Arena, March 18-28; Flower Sermon, Christ Church Cathedral, Thirteenth and Locust Sts., first Sun. in May; St. Louis Spring Horse Show, Missouri Riding Stables, 5200 Berthold Ave., May; Iris Display, Missouri Botanical Garden, last two weeks in May; Municipal Opera (light opera in open-air theater), 12 weeks, June to August; National Horse Show, the Arena, first week in October; Veiled Prophet Parade, first Tuesday after first Monday in Oct.; Veiled Prophet Ball (invitation only), Municipal Auditorium, night after the parade. The annual St. Louis National Home Show is held late in Oct., as is the St. Louis Auto Show; Chrysanthemum shows, Missouri Botanical Garden, and the Jewel Box, Forest Park, open first Sun. in Nov.; St. Louis Symphony Orchestra Season, Municipal Auditorium, Fri. afternoons and Sat. nights from end of Oct. to end of March; National Auto Show, the Arena, or Municipal Auditorium, usually late November; Poinsettia Displays, Missouri Botanical Garden, and the Jewel Box, Forest Park, Dec.; Silver Skates Tournament, the Arena, Dec.

ST. LOUIS (657 alt., 816,048 pop.), largest city in Missouri and eighth largest in the country, lies along a crescent-shaped bend of the Mississippi River about ten miles downstream from the convergence of the Mississippi and the Missouri. Five bridges span the augmented Mississippi, connecting St. Louis with the industrial suburbs that face it across the river.

St. Louis is a city that outgrew its past, and added half a million to its population after its early reason for existence had almost vanished. Transportation, first by river and then by rail, built up St. Louis; railroads are still a sustaining factor. But it is the city's industrial underpinning, diversified and complex, that has enabled it to survive the decline of the flatboat and the steamboat. Less than 8 per per cent of the city's labor is employed in any one industry, and two-thirds of the 312 industrial classifications of the bureau of Census are represented in this metropolitan area. Fur trade, which brought the city into being, is still carried on; St. Louis remains the world's largest raw fur market. It is one of the principal grain markets in the country, and the world's foremost producer of stoves and ranges, sugar-mill machinery, harvest hats, woodenware, brick, and terra cotta. It has several huge breweries, and until the recent trend toward decentralization it had many large shoe factories. Flippant wits used to term the town "first in booze, first in shoes, and last in the American League."

Other products of importance are drugs and chemicals, textiles, and iron and steel articles.

The plan of the city has undergone important modifications in the past 15 years, and even greater changes are contemplated. For a mile and a half along the wide brown body of the Mississippi stretches a granite paved, almost deserted wharf. Bordering this was, until very recently, a close-packed belt of empty warehouses, commercial buildings, and factories dating from the period following the great fire of 1849. Once the commercial core of the city, this section was virtually abandoned when St. Louis turned its back on the river. The heart of the present city lies several blocks to the west, and for many years the dead belt along the old levee was a problem. A solution has been found, however, in plans for a river-front plaza, commemorating Thomas Jefferson and national expansion. It is planned to preserve only those buildings of special historic significance, and work has already begun on razing the useless structures. On either side of this cleared area, however, one can still observe the stratification of a century, from the trappings of the steamboat era to the jagged towers of modern skyscrapers.

Within the memory of people still living, Fourth Street was the center of downtown St. Louis. The principle older streets run north and south, paralleling the river. As the city has grown, additions have been made at haphazard angles, so that many of the streets running away from the river spread fanwise, some following old trails that formerly converged on the levee, others originating in the demands of modern traffic.

The divorce of the city from the river was emphasized when the east-west stretch between Twelfth Street Boulevard and Fifteenth Street was chosen for Memorial Plaza, where all the new civic buildings are located. West from the end of Market Street, the main axis of the plaza, a specially lighted super-highway, with no grade crossings to complicate traffic, facilitates transportation to the suburbs at the western edge of town.

The chief business district of St. Louis extends roughly from Fourth Street almost to Grand Boulevard, and from Chouteau to Franklin Avenues. The leading retail houses are in the downtown shopping district between Sixth and Eleventh, and Olive and Washington. From the central shopping section to Grand Boulevard are wholesale dealers, printing houses, and offices of various kinds, interspersed with Negro tenements. Grand Boulevard has been called the "pain and pleasure or medico-movie" district, for between several major picture houses are office building entirely given over to doctors and dentists, a group of small taverns and night clubs, and the inevitable dime store, novelty shops, and small clothing and shoe stores. In the heart of this section is the typical St. Louis anomaly of Vanderventer Place, two blocks of brick and stone mansions, built between 1870 and 1890, ponderously facing each other across a lanscaped parkway, and shut off from the encroaching slums by carefully maintained restrictions and a firm stone gate.

Westward from Grand Boulevard in the center of the city are rows of rather heavy and over-ornamented houses, many of them given over now to boarding houses, small display rooms, funeral parlors, or antique shops. Close to Kingshighway these give way to large and fashionable apartment houses and hotels. Centering about Euclid and Maryland Avenues in this section is an exclusive shopping district where one may buy imported delicacies, rare silver or china, unusual toys, or clothes guaranteed not to be duplicated in the city. A little to the south is an impressive group of hospitals, clinics, and nurses' homes.

West of Kingshighway is the broad expanse of Forest Park, bordered by fine residential areas, especially on the north, where there are many private "places," like those in London and Paris, in which the well-to-do are guarded against the hurly-burly traffic by ornamental gates, and insured against neighborhood changes by rigid building restrictions.

Along DeBaliviere and westward on Delmar, small shops, enormous super-markets, and innumerable restaurants and eating places cater to the apartment house dwellers of the neighborhood. Directly to the north of this section is the colorful Wellston shopping center, stretched along Easton Avenue. Along the ever crowded street are open stalls for vegetables and flowers, crates of chickens and geese, and the tantalizing odors of herring and dill. Here are cut-rate stores, variety shops, credit clothing houses, furniture and second-hand dealers, shooting galleries, and delicatessens; and everywhere up and down the street, the signs of fortune tellers, faith healers, and astrologers.

Enclosing this central swath of the city are the North and South sides, which have much in common. Each is joined to the city along the business district by a slum area and Negro district; and each is settled in the main by lower middle-class and working families, predominately of German extraction. Particularly is the German element strong on the South side. Here are rows and rows of identical two-story residences and modern spruce cottages, where housewifely duties commonly include scrubbing the stone stoops and sidewalks to a dazzling whiteness. Each side has its own shopping center; the North, at Grand and West Florissant, running north to the Water Tower; the South, on Grand from Cherokee to Gravois. The German groups have athletic and singing societies, and keep many of the Old-Country customs; the older people habitually speak German at home, and many of the churches offer services in that language. Almost half of St. Louis's foreign-born are Germans.

Adjoining the South-side German community are Czech and Bohemian groups, and a fairly large Italian settlement. The Italians are settled mainly between Kingshighway and Sulphur Avenue, and Manchester Road and Arsenal Street; most of them work in the near-by clay-products plants. Here on Corpus Christi and various other religious feast days, fire crackers are set off and processions are held; on

All Souls' night, candles are lighted in the cemeteries. On Saturday night, the quick spatter of Italian may be heard in the corner taverns, where ravioli and spaghetti, garlic steaks, and sour red wine are sold.

St. Louis became a haven for Negroes during the Civil War, and today they constitute 11.4 per cent of the population. They reside for the main part in a far flung belt bounded by Chouteau, Cass, and Seventh Avenues, and Marcus Street, with the major Negro shopping districts along Franklin, Vanderventer, and Chouteau Avenues. On warm evenings they pour out of the tenements to congregate on the front stoops, or sit in rocking chairs along the streets. Sidewalk vendors sell spicy chunks of barbecued meat, hot fish, or great slices of iced watermelon, and the air is rich with laughter and the soft drawl of conversation.

The first attempt at settlement made on the site of St. Louis and —as far as is known—in the State, was the Jesuit Mission of St. Francis Xavier, established in 1700 at the mouth of the Rivière des Pères (Fr., River of the Fathers) within the present city limits. The Kaskaskia Indians from the Illinois River, and the Tamaroa Indians from their village of Cahokia on the opposite side of the Mississippi, settled here with the Fathers. Within three years, though, the Indians moved, and the mission was abandoned. More than a half-century passed before a permanent settlement was established at St. Louis.

On July 6, 1763, Maxent, Laclede, and Company of New Orleans were granted exclusive rights to the Indian trade in the Missouri River Valley and all the country west of the Mississippi as far north as the St. Peters River. On August 3, Pierre Laclede Liguest, junior partner of the firm, with some 30 other persons, left New Orleans for Fort Chartres, on the east bank of the Mississippi below St. Louis, where he stored his supplies for the winter. In December, he selected the present site of St. Louis as the most suitable location for a new post, announcing that he "intended to establish a settlement which might hereafter become one of the finest cities in America."

Actual settlement was delayed until the following spring. On February 14, Laclede sent over from Fort Chartres a party of workmen under command of 13-year-old Auguste Chouteau, to lay the foundation of the post. The village, named for Louis IX, Crusader King of France and patron saint of Louis XV, originally consisted of but five streets. Rue Royale, now First Street, faced the river, and behind it were Rue de l'Église (Church Street) and Rue des Granges (Street of the Barns), modern Second and Third Streets. Intersecting were Rue Bonhomme (Farmer Street) and Rue de la Tour (Tower Street), now Market and Walnut Streets. The village plan included La Place d'Armes, a public square for civic gatherings, between present Market and Walnut Streets, and Main and the river. Laclede built his house immediately west, across present First Street, and set aside the block where the old Cathedral is now, between Second and Third and Market and Walnut Streets, as a church site. Most of the early houses were of upright log construction (see Architecture) in the French manner. A few, more substantial, were of stone with wide verandas, and with foundations, like that of Laclede's, dug by Indians who had settled near by to live on the Frenchmen's bounty.

Just above the town and slightly to the north on the second river bank level were a group of Indian mounds, so situated as to form a rough parallelogram. The largest, at the northeast corner of present Mound and Broadway, was known as La Grange de Terre (the Earth Barn), or simply as the Big Mound, and was for many years a landmark. Excavation proved it to contain bodies and artifacts of considerable antiquity. One of Lewis Rogers' band of Shawnee (*see Archeology and Indians*) was buried in it in 1819, and until 1826 the Indians returned regularly to mourn at his grave. It was from the top of this mound that the Rector family watched for Thomas Rector's signal that he was all right after the duel in which he shot and killed Joshua Barton in 1823. All of the large group of mounds which once stood just without the wall of the original city were leveled as St. Louis grew, in spite of abortive attempts to have them preserved in a city park. Of the other mounds once scattered along the near-by bank of the Mississippi, only a piece of one at the foot of present Wyandotte Street still remains.

The village of St. Louis was nicknamed *Pain Court* (Short of Bread), but the name seems to have been a Gallic jibe at the lack of agriculture in this commercial town rather than an indication of poverty. Laclede's fur business grew within 5 years to more than $80,000 annually, and St. Louis became and remained the center of the Western fur trade. In 1765, the exclusive fur-trading privileges granted Maxent, Laclede, and Company were withdrawn by the Spanish government, and with the region open to competition new settlers, merchants, and outfitters flocked in. Expeditions were made to the many streams west and north.

Meanwhile French colonials across the Mississippi, rather than become British subjects, moved to the west side of the river, many of them settling in or near St. Louis. Among these were Captain St. Ange de Bellerive, former Commandant of Fort Chartres, and his garrison of 20 soldiers. St. Ange was the first commandant of St. Louis.

When France and Spain became the allies of the Colonists in the American Revolution, St. Louis assumed strategic military importance to the British. In June of 1779, the British General Haldimand was ordered to reduce the Spanish and American posts on the upper Mississippi. Haldimand consequently organized a group of Indians, together with some Canadian traders and their servants. Sent by various routes, these combined into a body of about 1,200 for an attack on St. Louis in May of 1780. The village was warned of the approaching enemy, however, and partially fortified itself. The attack was repulsed by some 50 soldiers and 280 townsmen, aided by a small reinforcement from Ste. Genevieve, in a battle commemorated in the popular song "Chanson de L'Année du Coup" (*see Music*). This was the second victory of the Colonists and their allies in the West. It preserved the important Mississippi-Ohio River route for the entry of American supplies, and relieved in part the danger of British attack from the West.

For a time pirates made commerce on the Mississippi dangerous, plundering and murdering wherever the opportunity offered. In 1788, however, *L'Année des Dix Bateaux* (the Year of the Ten Boats), the pirates were driven from the river by the concerted efforts of the crews of ten boats which traveled upstream together from New Orleans. After this purge, St. Louis grew rapidly. The average annual value of furs received there between 1788 and 1804 was $203,750. This increased trade made St. Louis the center of wealth and culture in the upper valley, in spite of its isolation. The well-to-do built spacious mansions and equipped them with furniture, glass, and china brought from France. They built up fine private libraries and art collections, and either employed tutors or sent their children to Europe to school.

This pleasant existence was disrupted after the Louisiana Purchase in 1803, when St. Louis became the crossroad of Westward expansion, and French and Spanish culture was deluged by a flood of American immigration. The town was overrun with adventurers, gamblers, and freethinkers who boasted that "God would never cross the Mississippi." The levee along the length of the river was notorious; street brawls were almost nightly occurrences. Such Americans of wealth and culture as came to St. Louis during this period, like the upper level of the French and Spanish residents, either withdrew into isolation, or soon found themselves participating in the more fashionable aspects of the city's hectic life. Many a gentleman lost a fortune on the turn of a card, or won one by the correct appraisal of a fighting cock. A long series of duels made Bloody Island infamous the country over. Dr. Bernard G. Farrar fatally wounded James A. Graham there in 1810; seven years later, the prominent and highly respected Thomas Hart Benton shot and killed Charles Lucas on the same "field of honor."

Men were now beginning to explore the fabulous empire of the West. James Pursley and a group from St. Louis had made a journey to Santa Fe in 1802; Lewis and Clark made their historic voyage between 1804 and 1806. St. Louis fur traders and trappers were breaking trails over a far-flung territory. In 1809 the Missouri Fur Company was organized, with a capital of $40,000, by William Clark, Manuel Lisa, Pierre and Auguste P. Chouteau, Sylvestre Labadie, and others. Competition was attempted by John Jacob Astor and his American Fur Company, through a branch established in St. Louis in 1822, but although Astor succeeded in the North and Northwest, the St. Louis group continued to control the Missouri Valley. For 40 years after the purchase of the territory this trade amounted to $300,000 annually.

Riotous independence gradually gave way to sober community life. In 1808, Joseph Charless founded the *Missouri Gazette,* the first newspaper west of the Mississippi River, and George Tompkins, later Missouri supreme court judge, established one of the first English schools. The same year, with its boundaries pushed west to Seventh Street, St.

Louis was incorporated as a village with 1,400 inhabitants. Fourteen years later it received its city charter. Between 1799 and 1840, the population increased from 925 to 16,394. Caravans of settlers, sometimes 30 to 50 wagons a day, crossed the Mississippi at St. Louis on their way to the West. The flatboats of Missouri farmers, loaded with locally grown pork, hemp, grain, apples, and flour, turned toward New Orleans in increasing numbers.

St. Louis assumed the political leadership of the State from the very beginning; the territorial legislature met in the city, as did the constitutional convention of June, 1820. As the rural sections were settled, however, friction developed between them and St. Louis. The farmers had been hurt in the depression of 1819, and they mistrusted the St. Louis clique of business and professional men who were in power. In the first election, Alexander McNair was elected governor largely by the rural vote, and shortly the seat of government was moved temporarily to St. Charles, and six years later to Jefferson City. Even at the present time, St. Louis remains curiously independent of the rest of the State; nor has the friction between it and the rural sections completely died out.

On August 2, 1817, a crude steamboat, the *Zebulon M. Pike,* pushed its way up the tawny Mississippi to dock at St. Louis after a six weeks' trip from Louisville. This was the first steamboat to reach St. Louis, the advance guard of the giant flotilla which was to transform the town into one of the Nation's leading cities. As the dockage lengthened along the bank and the boats gathered thick as flies, St. Louis spread back from the river, its population skyrocketing from 20,-000 in 1837 to 75,000 in 1850, 160,000 in 1860, 350,000 in 1880.

The first manufacturing in St. Louis was done in small shops operated by craftsmen, assisted by journeymen and apprentices, who made copperware and tinware, shoes, furniture, pottery, bricks, and other necessities. Tobacco factories began operating in 1817, and manufacturies of red and white lead pigments, tanneries, and other small plants followed. By 1850, St. Louis was well established as an industrial center. Nineteen flour mills were exporting half a million barrels of flour annually. Twelve or more foundries, using more than 7,000 tons of ore, had been developed to utilize the iron ore or southeast Missouri and the cheap Missouri and Illinois coal. Foundry products included plows designed to turn the heavy prairie sod, and other agricultural machinery, ornamental ironwork for buildings (this later included entire store fronts), and steamboat engines. Other important industries produced sheet lead and lead pipe, white lead, shot, cotton and woolen goods, and distilled products. St. Louis exported foodstuffs and manufactured goods to a tremendous market: bacon, beef, corn, flour, oats, apples, hemp, lead, and iron. The assessed valuation of St. Louis property jumped from $1,218,390 in 1818 to $16,665,145 in 1847. Optimistic St. Louisans, measuring the growth of the city, estimated it would contain a population of millions within another half century. Meanwhile, political events in Germany, combined with the stimulus of a new social restlessness, induced a heavy German migration to Missouri, starting about 1832. Before 1850, thirty thousand Germans had settled in St. Louis—professional men and scholars, skilled tradesmen, and cheap labor for the growing industries.

With industrial growth came an interest in civic and cultural activities. A Roman Catholic diocese had been organized under Bishop Rosati, an Episcopalian under Bishop Jackson Kemper, both men of exceptional intelligence; other denominations built up strong congregations. Fort Bellefontaine (1806-27) on the Missouri was replaced by Jefferson Barracks on the Mississippi as the base of all military activity in the West. A public library, an annual agricultural fair, and other civic enterprises were introduced. Social life took on a new brilliance. General Lafayette, French patriot and Revolutionary War hero, was entertained at a grand ball and banquet in Bennett's Mansion Hall in 1825. The Planter's Hotel, begun in 1837, was described by Charles Dickens in 1842 as "an excellent house, and the proprietors have most bountiful notions of providing the creature comforts." Ingenious bartenders invented the highball, Southern Comfort, and Planter's Punch. Sol Smith, Sam Drake, and Noah M. Ludlow came to make St. Louis a theatrical center. The Polyhymnia, an orchestral group, was established; Parodi and Patti sustained "their distinguished reputation in song, commanding . . . full houses and enthusiastic applause." St. Louis University was organized in 1832 from a college dating back to 1818; Washington University began 21 years later. Dr. Joseph N. McDowell established as a branch of the University of Missouri a medical school which was to become the basis of the present Washington University Medical School, and the nucleus for St. Louis's present importance as a medical center. In the 1850's, the city instituted a public school system.

This development did not escape the pains of growth. Depressions came in 1819, 1837, 1857, 1873. The course of the Mississippi changed, threatening to leave the port of St. Louis behind a sandbar; this was halted by work directed by Robert L. Lee, then a lieutenant in the United States Army, who planned and supervised the construction of jetties and revetments at the upper end of Bloody Island (1837-39). The enthusiasm of the St. Louis railroad convention of 1836, resulting in the chartering of 18 railroad companies by the legislature, was deadened by the sudden panic of 1837, which delayed construction for almost 20 years. Most serious of all were the events of 1849. On May 19, the steamboat *White Cloud* caught fire at the wharf. The flames spread rapidly to adjacent boats, which were cut adrift, thus extending the conflagration. Wharf buildings caught fire and, aided by wind, the flames destroyed 15 business blocks with a property loss variously estimated at from $3,000,000 to $6,000,000. Reconstruction was delayed by an outbreak of cholera, a plague which had visited the city once before, in 1832. Within a short period, 4,060 out of a population of 64,000 had died. Many families fled the city. Trade was at a standstill. The streets were deserted save for doctors hurrying to their patients, and the regular circuit of hearses collecting the dead.

The tragedies resulted in a renovation of the city. The area destroyed by fire contained the oldest buildings, many of them of frame or log construction, and these were replaced by more substantial buildings of brick. Streets were widened. Public health problems ignored by the growing city had been brought to general attention by the plague. The problems of sewage disposal, of contaminated water in both public and private wells, and of inadequate hospital and institutional facilities, were met by a new civic consciousness.

The 1850's brought national prosperity. The Mexican War (1846-47) had added new territory to the United States; gold had been discovered in California in 1848, and in Colorado in 1858; railroads had proved practical. St. Louis was in a position, both geographically and commercially, to benefit by the great Westward movement precipitated by these factors. The fur trade was declining, but St. Louis traders and trappers were familiar with the great Western trails, and St. Louis merchants rapidly prepared to outfit the tide of migrants with clothes, shoes, stoves, machinery, foodstuffs, tools, and medicines. The levee still hummed with the river traffic of the Missouri and Mississippi, in spite of the newly introduced railroads. The Pacific, the first railroad in Missouri, was begun in 1851; other lines followed in rapid succession, and all, with the exception of the Hannibal to St. Joseph line, had their eastern terminus in St. Louis.

At the outbreak of the Civil War, St. Louis, like many other Missouri towns, was divided in its sympathies. The old French families, and the Kentucky and Virginia families with whom they had intermarried, were nominally pro-slavery. Slavery was not profitable in an urban economy, however, and many of these families had commercial ties with the East. It was to their interest that St. Louis remain neutral, but when a choice was forced upon them, they somewhat reluctantly supported the South. These, however, were a minority group. Two-thirds of St. Louis's population of 190,500 were either foreign born or had come from anti-slavery States. The Irish and German residents, charged with the new social ideals of Europe, and at times forced to compete with cheap slave labor, were strong Union crusaders. The crisis came soon after the fall of Fort Sumter. Since the St. Louis Arsenal held the largest supply of munitions in the Middle West, each side maneuvered for its possession. Both Confederate-sympathizing State troops and Union troops drilled in the city until May 10, 1861, when General Nathaniel Lyon and Francis P. Blair, with about 10,000 German and American soldiers, surrounded the 800 State troopers at Camp Jackson in Lindell's Grove, near present Grand Boulevard and Lawton Avenue, and forced their surrender. Thereafter, St. Louis served as a base of Federal operations, and martial law and special levies of money and property made life difficult for Confederate sympathizers. Early in 1865, a constitutional convention dominated by radical Republicans met in St. Louis and drew up the Drake Constitution. Its wise provisions were overshadowed by the infamous "iron clad oath," which made it impossible for former Confederate sympathizers to vote or hold public office. This provision was declared unconstitutional four years later by the United States Supreme Court.

St. Louis not only escaped damage, but actually profited by the war. The Chief Quartermaster spent $180,000,000 in the city during the course of the conflict, and the pressure of war orders for clothing and supplies helped to bring the town's industries to maturity. In the decade 1860-70, the value of St. Louis manufacturing increased 296 per cent, with flour, paint, sugar, steam machinery, and the products of foundries, planing mills, breweries, tobacco, and meat packing establishments predominating.

The post-war years saw the decline of the steamboat beset by the railroads and the tow-barge. The blockading of the South during the war had hastened the end. The railroads opened a new route to the East, and doomed the old New Orleans-St. Louis axis which had been the Mississippi steamboat's reason for being.

Paradoxically, the period of decadence produced the largest and most luxurious craft. Two of these were the *Natchez* and the *Robert E. Lee,* which commanded national attention by their race from New Orleans to St. Louis in 1870. The greatest of all, the *J. M. White III,* with 75-foot stacks and side-wheels four-stories high, was built in 1878.

St. Louis turned to the new means of transportation without a falter in her stride, and soon railroad lines converged on the city as thickly as the boats had gathered at the wharf. Eads Bridge and the first Union Station were both completed in 1874. The bridge made Illinois coal and cheap building sites accessible to St. Louis industries. Many moved across the river to develop important chemical and metal-casting plants.

The new growth stimulated civic improvements. Henry Shaw developed, endowed, and presented to the city the Missouri Botanical Gardens and Tower Grove Park. Forest Park, purchased in 1875, is the largest of the present 68 parks, which total more than 3,000 acres. Symphonic groups had existed, at intervals, since the 1830's; the St. Louis Symphony Orchestra (second oldest in the country) was founded in 1880. The interest which St. Louis had shown in art since Colonial times found increasing expression after the 1840's in private collections and in the encouragement given local artists. The Mercantile Library Association, established in 1846, not only founded a remarkable library, but also assembled the first public collection of art objects in the city, and commissioned such artists as George C. Bingham, Harriet Hosmer, and Carl Wimar for original works. Following the Civil War, annual art exhibitions introduced "modern" artists to St. Louis. The pressing interest in political and social problems was voiced by a vigorous public press: the *Westliche Post,* the mouthpiece of Carl Schurz and other German-American intellectuals, the *Post-Dispatch,* directed by Joseph Pulitzer, the *Globe-Democrat, Reedy's Mirror,* and others (*see Literature, and Newspapers and Radio*). Various magazines were launched. Most significant was the *Journal of Speculative*

Philosophy, published from 1868 to 1893 by a group of St. Louis philosophers. Its founder, William Torrey Harris (1835-1909), was an important figure in American education..

In 1876, the Democratic party held in St. Louis the first national political convention west of the Mississippi River, nominating Samuel J. Tilden for the presidency. The following year a new charter for local government, providing for the separation of the city from the county, was adopted. Considered a model for other cities, this charter emancipated St. Louis from the control of the State legislature except by general laws.

The city experienced a financial panic in 1873, and a serious railroad strike in 1877. In the tranquil period that followed these disturbances, St. Louis merchants organized the Veiled Prophet's festival, which has been held early each October since 1878 (*see Drama*), and which yearly draws tremendous crowds of street revelers.

In 1900, the world was at peace, and prosperity had not yet moved around the corner. St. Louis, with a population of 575,238, began preparation for the Louisiana Purchase Exposition of 1904, commemorating the growth of St. Louis and the Middle West. Most of the European nations were represented, and all America moved to the tune of "Meet me in St. Louie, Louie, meet me at the Fair." The exposition, financed by the city and a group of directors under David R. Francis, a former governor of Missouri, was a tremendous success. The backers made money, the city acquired an improved water system and an art museum, and the general public became acquainted with foreign cultures and social trends—and, if legend is correct, with ice cream cones; it is said that an ingenious waffle vender at the fair first conceived the idea of packing ice cream in a waffle, and so began an American institution.

The industrial activity of the First World War period brought a new wave of prosperity, resulting in widened streets and boulevards, and new public buildings, financed in part by an $87,000,000 bond issue voted in 1926. A second bond issue of $16,000,000 was voted in 1934 for public buildings, park and playground improvements, hospitals, street widenings, grade eliminations, and sewer construction. The city suffered with the rest of the world from the recent depression period, but in the past five years the number of industries has steadily increased. The present (1941) defense program has accelerated airplane production, and given an impetus to other St. Louis industries.

POINTS OF INTEREST

1. EADS BRIDGE, Washington Ave. at the Mississippi River, the world's first steel-truss bridge, was designed by and built under the supervision of Captain James B. Eads (1820-87). Begun in 1867 and dedicated July 4, 1874, it cost nearly $10,000,000. The entire length of the graceful, three-span structure is 6,220 feet; it is 54 feet wide, and stands 55 feet above high water. The 530-foot center span and

the two 502-foot side spans, built with ribs of chrome-steel tubing were at the time of construction the longest fixed-end metal arches ever built. Both sides rest on solid rock, the west pier 91 feet and the east pier 127 feet below the high water mark. The piers are constructed of limestone below the average high water level, and of granite above. The bridge consists of two decks, the upper for highway traffic, the lower for trains, the latter connecting with the Union Station yards by a tunnel. The view of the bridge from the levee at night is particularly fine, with the lights above and the dim, arched shadows below.

The bridge was a revolutionary undertaking. At the time of its construction, engineers questioned the possibility of erecting such long spans, and the use of steel was protested. Difficulties were encountered equal to those experienced on the Brooklyn Bridge, where pneumatic caissons were used for the first time in pier construction. Since little was known about combating the effects of working under compressed air, 119 men developed "caisson disease" and 14 died of it before Eads Bridge was completed.

2. The OLD ROCK HOUSE (*not open*), SW. corner the Wharf and Chestnut St., facing the river, is a two-story limestone building with a mansard third story added in the past half century. According to *The Old St. Louis Riverfront* (1938) published by the Jefferson National Expansion Memorial staff, it was built in 1818 by Manuel Lisa, the great fur trader, for the operations of the Missouri Fur Company.

ST. LOUIS. Points of Interest

1. Eads Bridge
2. Old Rock House
3. Site of the Old Customhouse
4. Merchants Exchange
5. Old Courthouse
6. Old National Hotel
7. Old Cathedral of St. Louis of France
8. Eugene Field House
9. John Woodward Johnson House
10. Wainwright Building
11. Mercantile Library
12. Dent-Grant House
13. Civil Courts Building
14. United States Customs and Courthouse
15. City Hall
16. Municipal Courts Building
17. Municipal Auditorium
18. Soldiers Memorial Building
19. St. Louis Public Library
20. Christ Church Cathedral
21. Robert Campbell House
22. Union Station
23. Aloe Plaza
24. Lafayette Park
25. Anheuser-Busch Brewery
26. Old Arsenal
27. Maryville College of the Sacred Heart
28. Tower Grove Park
29. Missouri Botanical (Shaw's) Garden
30. St. Louis University
31. St. Francis Xavier's Church
32. Cathedral of St. Louis
41. American Wine Company Plant
42. Fairgrounds Park
43. North St. Louis Water Tower

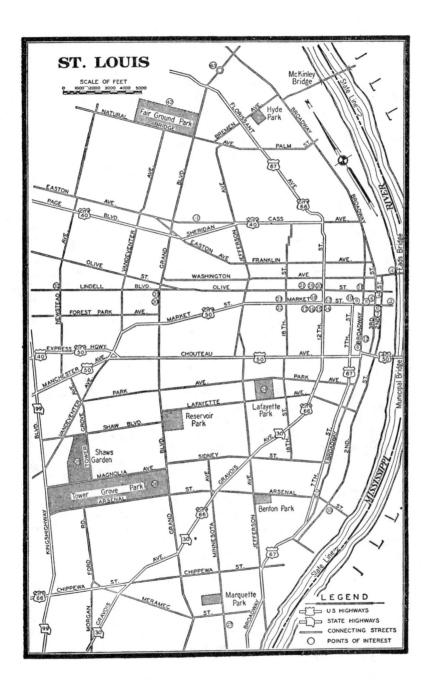

ST. LOUIS

The first steamboat reached St. Louis in 1817, and the Old Rock House was, with Brady and McKnight's warehouse, the first structure built directly on the river's edge to facilitate the new trade. Following Lisa's death, the building was used for many purposes. John Clemens had a sail rigging and tarpaulin loft on the second floor in 1851, and advertised to California emigrants that he could "offer greater inducements . . . in his line to those going that way than any other establishment in the City." Recently, it housed for a time a tavern and night club, where the philosophical could speculate on the possibilities of Manuel Lisa's ghost listening to black Anne's specialty numbers.

3. On the SITE OF THE OLD CUSTOM HOUSE, SE. corner of Third and Olive Sts., stood until 1941 what was probably the first Federal office building west of the Mississippi River. After more than 40 years in rented quarters, the Government decided in 1851 to erect its own edifice in St. Louis. The space selected was that occupied by the old Smith and Ludlow Theater, where since 1837 such famous actors as Junius Brutus Booth had appeared. The theater was torn down in 1852, and the customhouse, designed by the supervising architect in Washington, was begun. Constructed of Missouri "Barrett stone," it was of Italianate design. As completed in 1859, the building contained a post office on the main floor—with special accommodations for German patrons—the Federal courts, and the offices of the district attorney, the sub-treasury, and the customs. In 1888, the customs offices were moved to a newly constructed building between Eighth and Ninth, and Olive and Locust Sts. After the completion of the new customhouse on Market Street in 1935, the old building was largely vacant, until its demolition was begun in January, 1941, to make way for the Jefferson National Expansion Memorial.

4. The MERCHANTS EXCHANGE (*open 9-4 weekdays*), Third St., from Chestnut to Pine Sts., is a three-and-a-basement story structure of Warrensburg, Missouri, limestone in Italianate style. It was designed by Lee and Annan, and completed in 1875 at a cost of $2,000,000. When built, it was the largest trade hall with an unsupported ceiling in the United States, and it is still the largest grain exchange trading floor in the United States. It is 221 feet 10 inches long, 92 feet 6 inches wide, and 60 feet high. The central figure of the ceiling murals, which were painted by August Becker and Vincent Sciepoevich, is emblematic of St. Louis; it is surrounded by groups depicting agricultural, mineral, and industrial products of the Mississippi Valley. Until 1911, the Veiled Prophet's ball was presented in this building, and it was here that the Democratic convention which nominated James Tilden for president in 1876 was held.

5. The OLD COURTHOUSE (*open 8-5 weekdays*), Fourth St. to Broadway and Market to Chestnut Sts., is a two-story, cruciform structure of Greek-Revival design. It is surmounted by a 128-ton cast-iron dome, 198 feet high, whose design was an architectural and engineering novelty at the time of its construction. Its designer, William Rumbold, one of the courthouse architects, patented the idea in

1862. Except for the west wing, which is partly of brick, the building is constructed of hewn limestone blocks. Six Doric columns support the main porticoes at the east and west entrances. The wings center on a 60-foot rotunda which rises in four circular galleries to the dome. On the interior of the dome are four frescoes painted by Carl Wimar (*see Art*), early St. Louis artist, in 1862: on the north is *Indians Attacking the Village of St. Louis, 1780;* on the east, *The Landing of Laclede;* on the south, *De Soto Discovering the Mississippi River;* and on the west, *Westward the Star of Empire Takes Its Way.* On the fourth gallery, Wimar also painted four figures representing Law, Commerce, Justice, and Liberty. The inner dome is decorated with Wimar's portraits of George Washington, Martha Washington, Edward Bates, and Thomas H. Benton. The first mural decorations west of the Mississippi, these paintings have been restored several times, but are now in bad condition.

Designed by Henry Singleton, Robert S. Mitchell, and William Rumbold, the courthouse was begun in 1839, but many changes were made in the plans and the building was not completed until 1862. By 1845, however, the main portions of the structure had been finished, and the courthouse developed as the center of civic and legal activities during a period of important national expansion. Sergeant S. Prentiss, United States Senator from Mississippi, spoke at the Fourth Street entrance in 1840; Henry Clay attended court in the building and sold real estate from the east entrance in 1847; in 1859, U. S. Grant freed here his only slave, and made application—later refused—for the position of St. Louis County engineer. A series of meetings was held in the rotunda during 1846 to raise troops for the Mexican War, to collect funds to maintain them, and to care for the wives and children of the men during their absence. Troops were temporarily quartered here. In 1847, the returning soldiers were welcomed in the rotunda, and an impressive public funeral was held there for two officers of the Illinois volunteers who were killed in the battle of Buena Vista.

The rotunda is also associated with trans-Mississippi railroad development, for in October, 1849, the first national railroad convention met in this room. Almost a thousand delegates, representing 14 States, elected Stephen A. Douglas chairman and listened to Thomas H. Benton's impassioned speech advocating a trans-continental railroad, which ended, "There is the East. There is India."

The building is historically identified with the Dred Scott case, which did much to precipitate the Civil War. Dred Scott was born a slave in Virginia. His master, Peter Blow, brought him to Missouri in 1827, and subsequently willed him to an unmarried daughter, whom he was to help support by doing odd jobs. This arrangement proved unsatisfactory, and Dred was sold to Dr. John Emerson of Jefferson Barracks. When the doctor was transferred to Rock Island, Illinois, and from there to Fort Snelling, then in Wisconsin Territory, he took Dred with him. Both posts were in free territory and thus arose the later contention. In 1837, Dr. Emerson returned to Jefferson Barracks;

he died six years later, leaving Dred and his family as part of his trust estate, of which his widow and her brother, John F. A. Sanford of New York, were executors.

Mrs. Emerson at length moved East, leaving the slaves to shift largely for themselves. Scott, with his family, became a charge on the bounty of Taylor Blow, the son of his old master. It is probable that the Blow's instigated the first of the long series of trials which made Dred a national symbol, in an effort to have him set legally free so that they might be relieved of their sense of responsibility.

In June of 1847, the first suit against Mrs. Emerson was tried in the old courthouse. It was technically an action for assault and battery, and false imprisonment, with Dred basing his plea for freedom on the fact that Dr. Emerson had taken him into free territory. The verdict was against Dred, but in the trial of 1850, also held in this building, Dred won. On appeal to the Missouri Supreme Court, this judgment was set aside in March, 1852, in a session likewise held in the old courthouse.

Meanwhile the status of the case had been changed by the marriage of Mrs. Emerson to Dr. Calvin C. Chaffee, a physician of Springfield, Massachusetts, who was a member of Congress and an abolitionist. Not only was Mrs. Emerson's interest in owning slaves reduced, but by Missouri law her marriage disqualified her from serving as an executor of her husband's will. This left Sanford as sole executor and nominal titleholder of Dred. As the subsequent trials were between residents of different States, they came under the jurisdiction of the United States Courts. The case was so charged with national implications that from an insignificant local trial it became a test of principles in which many of the country's most prominent lawyers and abolitionists were involved. In May of 1854, the United States Court in St. Louis declared Dred and his family the property of the Emerson estate. The case was appealed to the United States Supreme Court, and on March 6, 1857, Chief Justice Roger B. Taney rendered the famous decision. Dred Scott, having been born a slave, might like any chattel be taken anywhere his master chose to go. Accordingly, he was still a slave, and had no right to sue in the Federal courts. The court declared further that no Negro could ever be a United States citizen, that the Missouri Compromise was in violation of the Constitution, and that slavery could not be prohibited in the territories of the United States. During the same year, Dred was emancipated by the voluntary act of his master and died in St. Louis, September 17, 1858.

In this building, in 1866, General Francis P. Blair contested the legality of the "Test Oath" (*see History*), and Louise Minor, a pioneer suffragist, sued in 1872 for the right to vote. Numerous distinguished attorneys practiced here: Edward Bates, attorney general in Lincoln's Cabinet; Montgomery Blair, postmaster general in Lincoln's Cabinet; General A. W. Doniphan of Mexican War fame; and many others.

Between 1930 and 1940, the building was not used as a general courthouse, but Justice of the Peace courts retained quarters there in

IN THE CITIES AND TOWNS

Missouri State Highway Dept.; Pohl

STATE CAPITOL, JEFFERSON CITY

BOLDUC HOUSE, STE. GENEVIEVE (built probably before 1785)

HERMANN HOUSE, KIMMSWICK (begun 1859)

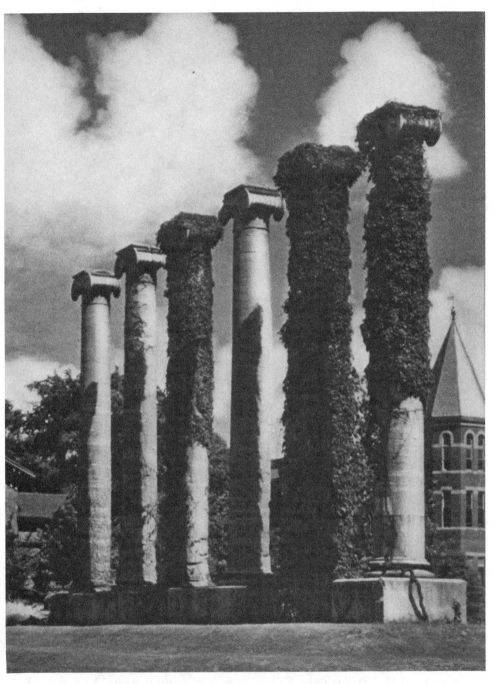

CAMPUS SCENE, UNIVERSITY OF MISSOURI, COLUMBIA
These columns are all that remain of the first building of
the oldest State university west of the Mississippi

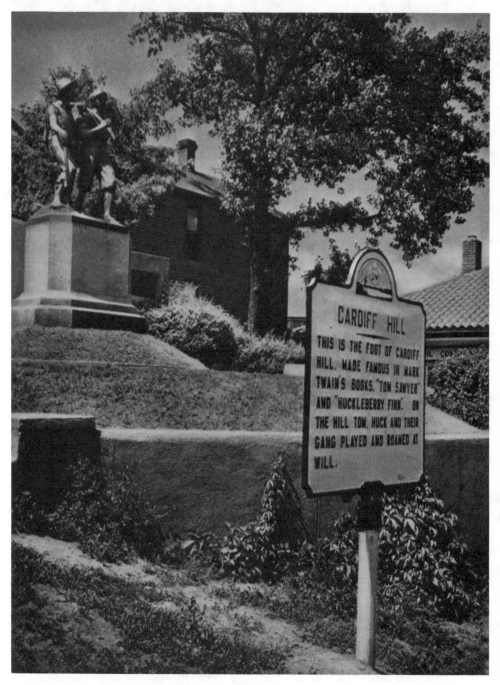

CARDIFF HILL

THIS IS THE FOOT OF CARDIFF
HILL, MADE FAMOUS IN MARK
TWAIN'S BOOKS, "TOM SAWYER"
AND "HUCKLEBERRY FINN". ON
THE HILL TOM, HUCK AND THEIR
GANG PLAYED AND ROAMED AT
WILL.

Piaget Studio

TOM SAWYER AND HUCK FINN, HANNIBAL

Kansas City Star

"OLD SETTLERS" PARADE, INDEPENDENCE

STORES ON THE SQUARE, BUFFALO

Piaget Studio

THESPIAN HALL, BOONVILLE (1857)

Piaget Studio

SCHOOL OF JOURNALISM, UNIVERSITY
OF MISSOURI, COLUMBIA

HALL OF WATERS, EXCELSIOR SPRINGS

Excelsior Springs Chamber of Commerce

Work Projects Administration in Missouri

THE COUNTY TRAVELING LIBRARY IN CONCORDIA

CIVICS CLASS IN A SPRINGFIELD PUBLIC SCHOOL

"Life" Magazine; Meith

order to hold title, as stipulated in 1823 when the site was donated for an earlier courthouse by John B. C. Lucas and Auguste Chouteau and his wife. The building is being restored as part of the Jefferson National Expansion Memorial plan. On the south façade, a bronze plate commemorates the near-by site of Fort San Carlos, important in the defense of St. Louis during the British and Indian attack, May 26, 1780. On the southeast corner of the plaza, at Fourth and Market Sts., a granite boulder commemorates the first trail west from St. Louis, the Boon's Lick Road via. the St. Charles Rock Road.

6. The OLD NATIONAL HOTEL, SE. corner Third and Market Sts., a four-story, red-brick structure, occupies an historic site. In 1818, the first Protestant Church (Baptist) in St. Louis, long the scene of Masonic celebrations and public meetings, was built on this spot. In 1831, the church and lot were sold to Thornton Grimsley, who immediately built the first National Hotel. From the Market Street entrance of that building Daniel Webster delivered an address in 1837. Sergeant S. Prentiss of Mississippi, General Robert E. Iee, General Zachary Taylor, and other famous men are said to have been guests there. This hotel was replaced in 1847 by the present structure. On October 28, 1847, "A. Lincoln and family, Illinois" stayed here while en route to Washington, where Lincoln took his seat in Congress.

7. The OLD CATHEDRAL OF ST. LOUIS OF FRANCE (*open 8-6 weekdays; 6-6 Sun.*), N. side of Walnut St. between Second and Third Sts., is a yellowed limestone Greek-Revival structure, with a four-columned Doric portico relieving the severity of the south façade. In raised gold letters on the cornice is the Latin inscription: *In Honorem S. Ludovici Deo Uni Et Trino—Dictatum A.D. MDCCCXXXIV.* Plaques on either side of the center portico bear the legend, in French and English, "My House Shall Be Called The House Of Prayer." Three plaques behind the portico repeat in English, Latin, and French: "Behold The Tabernacle Of God With Men And He Will Dwell With Them. Apoc. 24." The land has been church property since St. Louis was established. On this site, the first Mass was celebrated in 1764, and the first church, a log one, was built six years later. The present church, built in 1831-34 under the direction of Joseph Rosati, first Bishop of St. Louis, is the fourth to occupy the site. The building is of peculiar religious significance. Pope Gregory XVI, a classmate of Bishop Rosati, granted this church an indulgence usually obtained only by pilgrims visiting the seven Roman Basilicas; by special indult it may be gained by visiting the three altars here. No other church or cathedral in America is so privileged. Three very old paintings said to have been given the church by Louis XVIII are in the church: *The Madonna, Saint Bartholomew,* and *St. Louis of France.* In the sanctuary is a bell cast in 1772, the gift of Benito Vasquez, a Spanish soldier and landholder. Two hundred Spanish silver dollars were melted and cast with the other metal to sweeten the tone. The bell was formally baptized in 1774, and given the name Pierre Joseph

Félicité, for its godparents Pierre Joseph (the Spanish Lieutenant Governor) and Félicité de Piernas. The edifice is now known as The Church of St. Louis of France, the title of "Cathedral" having passed from it October 18, 1914, when the new St. Louis Cathedral was consecrated.

8. The EUGENE FIELD HOUSE (*open 8-5; ring and enter*), 634 S. Broadway, is a three-story, red-brick house, with a recessed entranceway flanked by Doric pilasters. A walled formal garden surrounds the house on the north, east, and south sides. This house, together with eleven others which formed a solid block known as Walsh's Row, was built about 1845. Threatened with destruction in 1934, it was saved through the efforts of a citizen's group and dedicated as the Eugene Field Museum in December, 1936. It is maintained by the Board of Education.

Within a year or two after their marriage in 1848, Eugene Field's parents, Roswell M., and Frances (Reed) Field, moved to this Broadway address, and here Eugene was born September 3, 1850. In 1856, his mother died and Eugene was sent to live with a cousin in Amherst, Massachusetts, remaining there until about 1869, when he returned to attend the University of Missouri. When he was 21 he received a legacy and went to Europe. He returned here to begin his journalistic career on the old St. Louis *Evening Journal* (*see Newspapers and Radio, and Literature*).

The two rooms on the first floor of the house contain important Field manuscripts, including "Flyaway Horse," "Lit-tle Mack," "Krinken," and "Lover's Lane," as well as many small items intimately associated with the author. On the second floor are articles of furniture and clothing used by Field and his wife, Julia Sutherland Comstock Field. *A Catalogue Of The Collection With Annotations,* by Jesse P. Henry (1936), may be obtained here (*10¢*).

9. The JOHN WOODWARD JOHNSON HOUSE (*open upon application*), 613 Market Street, is a two-and-a-half-story, gray painted-brick house, probably dating from the early 1830's. Built directly upon the street, it is now a rooming house with shops on the first floor. The gardens which were once beside it have long since been swallowed by the growth of the city, and the original entranceway, with its handsome elliptical fanlight, has been removed.

John W. Johnson came west from Maryland in 1808 to serve as government trader to the Sauk and Fox Indians living near the junction of the Des Moines and Mississippi Rivers. He was factor at Fort Madison, Iowa, from its beginning until its evacuation and destruction in September, 1813. In that year he became trader and agent to the Sauk and Fox tribes who had settled on the Little Moniteau River in Missouri. In 1815, he officiated in the purchase and distribution of $30,000 worth of presents to the 19 Indian tribes who made peace at Portage des Sioux (*see Tour 1, Portage des Sioux*). The following year, he became agent and factor at Prairie du Chien, where, as chief justice of the Crawford County Court, he played an important part in the early history of Wisconsin.

When the government trade was abolished in 1822, Johnson moved to St. Louis. In 1831, following the death of his first wife, a daughter of Keokuk, he married Mrs. Lucy Honeywell Gooding, a native of Maine, and soon settled in this house. Family history records that the new Mrs. Johnson opened the door one day to find Johnson's three half-breed daughters calmly awaiting admittance. "Mama say we go live with Papa," they announced. Mrs. Johnson apparently had not known of their existence, but she accepted them into the family circle. Under her care the girls became belles of St. Louis, and all married well. In 1834, Johnson became the third mayor of St. Louis. He died June 1, 1854, in his eightieth year, and is buried in Calvary Cemetery near the monument to General Sherman.

10. The WAINWRIGHT BUILDING, 105 N. Seventh St., one of the first important skyscrapers, was completed in 1891. Designed by Louis Sullivan, Chicago architect, it is an expression of Sullivan's belief that steel-frame construction demanded a new type of design to replace the classic styles then popular. The ten-story structure, faced with stone, brick, and terra cotta in rich shades of reds, has an unbroken sweep of vertical line from its base to its top story. Decoration is restricted to the narrow carved bands framing the main doors of the entrance, and to the richly designed cornice. The influence of this building on contemporary architecture was immediate. For 25 years architects used Sullivan's formula: accent by vertical lines, volume through undifferentiated façades, line by leaving the shaft of the building sheer and uninterrupted.

11. The MERCANTILE LIBRARY (*open 9-6 weekdays*), sixth floor, Mercantile Library Building, 510 Locust St., grew out of an association established in December, 1845, by eight St. Louis business and professional men. In 1851, the association erected a library building on this site. It was replaced in 1885 by the present six-story red-granite and brick Romanesque-Revival structure, which was designed by Henry S. Isaac. The library has at present (1941) a total of 170,-000 volumes, including many rare Western items, books, pamphlets, newspapers, and manuscripts. In the reading rooms are displayed the sculptured figures, *Beatrice Cenci* and *Oenone* by Harriet Hosmer, Verhaegen's *Daniel Webster,* Chester Harding's *Portrait of William Clark,* the portraits of a group of Indian chiefs by George Catlin, and other works by Missouri artists.

12. The DENT-GRANT HOUSE, SW. corner Fourth and Cerre Sts., a two-and-a-half-story red-brick house built in 1845, is now closed and in bad repair. Here, in 1848, Ulysses S. Grant, then a lieutenant stationed at Jefferson Barracks, married Julia Dent, daughter of Colonel Frederick Dent. He resided here with Colonel Dent until he completed a log cabin on his St. Louis County farm, "Hardscrabble," in the winter of 1854.

The CIVIC CENTER, surrounding Memorial Plaza, Twelfth St. Blvd. to Fifteenth St. between Market and Pine Sts., and Thirteenth to Fourteenth Sts., between Pine and Olive Sts., comprises a group of major public buildings.

13. The CIVIL COURTS BUILDING (*open 8-5 weekdays, except Sat. 8-12*), Eleventh St. to Twelfth St. Blvd., and Market to Chestnut Sts., faces the plaza's eastern extension. A 14-story, 385-foot structure of Indiana limestone, it is the city's most controversial architectural medley. The building rises in modern office-building style to a setback at the 245-foot (twelfth floor) level. There it is augmented by an Ionic Greek temple, surmounted, in turn, by an Egyptian pyramid roof with two aluminum griffins at its crest. The architectural peculiarities are partly the result of an effort by city officials to afford a higher accessible point than that reached by the near-by Southwestern Bell Telephone Company Building. Completed in June, 1930, at a cost of $4,520,000, the building houses the Civil, Circuit, Probate, and Appeal Courts, and other public offices. An observation promenade (*open 9-4 weekdays except Sat., 9-12*) surrounds the twelfth floor. At Chestnut Street, on the Twelfth St. Boulevard side, a memorial flagpole with a sculptured stone base, the work of Victor S. Holm, commemorates veterans of the Spanish-American War, Philippine Insurrection, and China Relief Expedition.

14. The UNITED STATES CUSTOMS AND COURT-HOUSE (*open 8-7 weekdays*), Market to Walnut Sts., and Eleventh St. to Twelfth St. Blvd., is a ten-story Bedford stone structure of modern setback style. Designed by Mauran, Russell, and Crowell, it was completed in 1935 at a cost of $4,500,000. The first floor walls are finished in golden-veined Ste. Genevieve marble with trim of Virginia royal black marble; the decoration of the upper floors combines Ste. Genevieve, St. Albans red, and verd antique marbles. The courtroom of the United States Circuit Court of Appeals, on the fifth floor, entirely paneled with walnut, is considered one of the most beautiful in the State.

15. The CITY HALL (*open 8-5:30 weekdays except Sat., 8-12*), Twelfth St. Blvd. to Thirteenth St. and Market St. to Clark Ave., is four stories high, replete with gables, dormers, and elaborate towerlets.

16. The MUNICIPAL COURTS BUILDING (*open 8-5:30 weekdays except Sat., 8-12*), Thirteenth and Fourteenth Sts., on Market St., is a three-story Bedford-stone structure in modified classic design. Completed in 1911, it houses the municipal courts and some of the city offices. At the rear are the CITY JAIL and JUVENILE COURT BUILDINGS.

17. The MUNICIPAL AUDITORIUM (*open 9-4 weekdays*), Fourteenth to Fifteenth Sts., and Market St. to Clark Ave., is a $7,-000,000 structure of Bedford stone in modified classic design, with eight massive columns dominating the front. It was dedicated in 1934. An exposition hall occupies almost the entire street floor; on the main floor are the convention hall, built without columns and seating 11,500;

and the opera house, seating 3,500. A stage 145 feet by 48 feet separates the hall and the opera house and can be used by either. Four assembly rooms, each seating 700, adjoin the larger halls. Gray and gold predominate in the decoration.

18. The SOLDIERS MEMORIAL BUILDING (*open 9-7:30*), Thirteenth to Fourteenth, and Chestnut to Pine Sts., a $1,000,000, 2-story structure of Bedford stone and granite in modern classic design, fills the central block of Memorial Plaza. Opened in 1938, it consists of a loggia and two museum structures, surrounded by a portico with squared columns. In the center of the loggia, beneath a mosaic ceiling, is a cenotaph of blue-black Belgian marble, bearing the names of 1,249 St. Louisans who died in the World War. The museum rooms, finished in Ste. Genevieve marbles, contain a collection of war relics and trophies. The second floors consist of assembly rooms for service organizations.

19. The ST. LOUIS PUBLIC LIBRARY (*open 9 a. m.-10 p. m. weekdays; 2-9 Sun.*), Olive to Locust and Thirteenth to Fourteenth Sts., a three-story granite structure of Italian Renaissance style, was designed by Cass Gilbert. The façades are embellished with sculptured medallions, and on the stone screens occupying the lower part of the arched main-floor windows are 30 shields bearing devices that represent famous printers. The main floor, opening off an inner lobby finished in Tennessee marble, includes the chief public rooms. Erected in 1912, the building cost $1,800,000. It now contains more than 870,000 volumes.

20. CHRIST CHURCH CATHEDRAL (*open 8-6*), SE. corner Thirteenth and Locust Sts., a limestone structure in early English-Gothic style, is the mother church of the Episcopal Diocese of Missouri. Designed by Leopold Eidlitz, New York architect, it was begun in 1859; the first service was held in the completed structure on Christmas day, 1867. The original stained-glass windows, a few of which remain, were made by Owen Doremus in Montclair, New Jersey. The Mary E. Bofinger Memorial Chapel, the gift of Captain John N. Bofinger, was designed by J. B. Legg and consecrated May 17, 1894. The tower, narthex, and doorway, designed by Kivas Tully, were added in 1911.

The simplicity of the interior focuses attention upon the imposing reredos of Caen stone, donated by Mrs. Christine Blair Graham and dedicated December 25, 1911. Designed and executed by the firm of Harry Henes & Sons of Exeter, England, in co-operation with Kivas Tully, it is 35 feet high and 30 wide, covering the entire back of the chancel. Intricate carvings tell the history of the church. Beneath the main altar are carved groups representing the Annunciation, the Presentation in the Temple, and the Resurrection. Immediately over the altar, beneath the large crucifix, is a carving of the Nativity. A descriptive booklet with a key to the figures (*50¢*) is obtainable at the Bishop Tuttle Memorial Building which adjoins the Cathedral.

Each year, on the first Sunday in May, a sermon is preached here "On the wisdom and goodness of God as shown in the growth of flowers, fruits, and other products of the vegetable kingdom." Funds for this "flower sermon" were provided by the will of Henry Shaw, founder of the Missouri Botanical Garden.

21. The ROBERT CAMPBELL HOUSE (*private*), 1508 Locust St., an ante bellum, three-story, gray painted-brick structure with stable, outbuildings, and summer house in the side lawn, primly views the modern world about it through a cast-iron fence. The long, narrow residence is the last house to remain of the many which made Lucas Place a fashionable residential area during the 1850's.

Robert Campbell, the builder, was born in North Ireland in 1804, and came to St. Louis in 1824. The following year he went to the Rocky Mountains, where he remained as an associate of General William Henry Ashley in the fur trade. When Ashley retired about 1830, Campbell and a partner, William Sublette, remained in business as the Rocky Mountain Fur Company. In 1835, Campbell returned to St. Louis, where besides continuing to direct the affairs of his fur and Indian trade, he served as president of the Bank of Missouri and later of the Merchant's Bank. In 1846, he aided in the preparation of Kearny's expedition to the Mexican War, and, in 1851, served with Father de Smet, famed Indian missionary, as representative of the United States government in the great Indian Council at Horse Creek.

Following his death in 1879, his two sons, Hugh and Hazlett K., continued to live in the home, and maintained it as it had appeared during their childhood. Both died recently, leaving an estate totaling more than $3,000,000, for a share in which several hundred people are suing.

22. UNION STATION, S. side of Market St., Eighteenth to Twentieth Sts., is a four-story Bedford-stone building of modified Romanesque design, rising at the front in a slender, 230-foot clock tower. The waiting room on the main floor, below street level, is connected with the Grand Hall above by a staircase which passes under an arch—across the 50-foot span of which a whisper is easily audible. Lighted by stained-glass windows on the south, the Grand Hall rises to a vaulted ceiling the height of the building's peaked roof. At successive floor levels the Hall is surrounded by corridors containing offices. The station and its train sheds and power house, covering more than 20 acres, were opened in 1896. They were designed by Theodore C. Link.

23. ALOE PLAZA, bounded by Market, Pine, Eighteenth, and Twentieth Sts., is dominated by Carl Milles' fountain, *The Meeting of the Waters*. Unveiled early in 1940, the 14 bronze figures of the fountain group symbolize the meeting of the Missouri and the Mississippi Rivers. The Missouri River is represented as a young woman, coyly touching up her hair. Approaching her is the eager figure of a young man, personifying the Mississippi River, with a flower in one outstretched hand. Around the two central figures are three tritons, a waterman with two great sharks, a waterwoman hauling two urchins along by the scruffs of their necks, figures of leaping fish, and small boys bearing large fish. From the mouths of the various sea creatures

water spouts high into the air, forming fascinating patterns, and, incidentally, drenching the onlookers whenever the wind blows.

Erected as a memorial to the late Louis P. Aloe, for whom the plaza was named, the fountain was financed by $60,000 contributed by Mrs. Aloe and the city of St. Louis. Carl Milles, one of America's leading sculptors, was born in Sweden in 1875. Since 1926, he has been resident sculptor at the Cranbrook Academy of Art, Michigan.

24. LAFAYETTE PARK, bounded by Mississippi, Missouri, Park, and Lafayette Aves., a landscaped area of 30 acres, is the oldest park in St. Louis and, possibly, west of the Mississippi. Then part of the St. Louis commons, it was designated as a park by the city council in 1836. For many years the St. Louis Greys, a local militia unit, drilled here. On April 25, 1870, twenty European tree sparrows (*Passer montanus montanus*) and other imported birds, were liberated in the park by Carl Daenzer and a Mr. Kleinschmidt. Less aggressive than the English sparrow, the tree sparrow has not naturalized itself rapidly and is reported (1940) found in America only in the St. Louis region, where it is abundant in restricted areas. Near the Lafayette Avenue entrance to the park is a bronze copy of Jean Antoine Houdon's STATUE OF GEORGE WASHINGTON, placed there in 1869.

Near the center of the park stands Harriet Hosmer's heroic STATUE of THOMAS HART BENTON, which was cast in bronze at the Royal Foundry at Munich and erected in 1868. The statue was unveiled by Benton's daughter, Mrs. Jessie Benton Fremont.

25. The ANHEUSER-BUSCH BREWERY (*conducted tours, 9:30-10:45 and 1:30-3:45 weekdays except Saturdays; illustrated booklet obtainable in reception rooms*), SW. corner Broadway and Pestalozzi St., occupies a group of 137 red-brick structures covering 142 acres. Most of the buildings date before 1900 and are of vigorous Romanesque design with square crenelated towers and elaborate details. Perhaps outstanding among these early buildings is the six-story, stone and red-brick BREW HOUSE, built in 1892 and designed by Widmann, Walsh, and Boisselier, St. Louis architects. Trumpeting elephants of metal top the square stone posts at the northwest gate to the Brew House yard.

The present firm had its origin in 1857, when Eberhard Anheuser purchased a small, bankrupt brewery on this site. In 1865 his son-in-law, Adolphus Busch, purchased a junior partnership, and in 1875 the Anheuser-Busch Brewing Association was formed. The chief growth of the company followed the development of a lager beer that could be pasteurized without changing its flavor, and thus could be kept for long periods of time. With this product Anheuser-Busch pioneered in bottling beer, and by 1900 had the greatest brewery in the United States. It is now (1941) the largest brewery in the world. It has a capacity of more than 1,000,000 bottles of beer every 8 hours, and a total annual capacity of 2,500,000 barrels (79,500,000 gallons).

Beermaking is a highly technical process. Basically, however, it consists of mashing barley malt in water, and draining off the liquid, or wort, which is then boiled with hops and cooled; yeast is added next, and the mixture is allowed to ferment. After several months of aging, during which a slow secondary fermentation takes place, the beer is filtered, and then bottled, canned, or put in kegs for the market.

26. The OLD ARSENAL (*not open*), entrance SE. corner Second and Arsenal Sts., consists of a group of red-brick and gray-limestone buildings enclosed by a limestone wall on the north and south sides, and by an ornamental fence made of musket barrels on the west side. The arsenal was established in 1827 on a 44-acre tract. Small arms and ammunition were manufactured here, and military supplies dispensed to the United States troops in the West. Eight of the original stone buildings erected in 1830 remain. The three red-brick buildings used as barracks were built about 1856. At the outbreak of the Civil War, Missouri secessionists planned to capture the arsenal, but they were kept from doing so by the surrender of Camp Jackson (*see History and Government*)—a victory for Union forces which proved a decisive factor in preserving Missouri for the Union. Following the Civil War, the importance of the arsenal diminished; since 1922 it has served as the St. Louis Medical Depot.

West of and adjacent to the Arsenal grounds is LYON PARK, a landscaped area approximately a block square and containing a red-granite obelisk which commemorates General Nathaniel Lyon. The area, formerly in the arsenal preserve, was set aside as a park before 1876.

27. MARYVILLE COLLEGE OF THE SACRED HEART, Meramec St. and Nebraska Ave., is a four-year corporate college of St. Louis University. In 1827 members of the Sacred Heart Order under the direction of Mother Philippine Duchesne (*see St. Charles and Tour 1, Florissant*) opened an academy for young girls in St. Louis. On December 7, 1846, this school was incorporated by the State legislature as a seminary. In 1864 the growth of St. Louis forced the group to move, and the present tract of land, then south of the city proper, was purchased. The construction of the five-story ADMINISTRATION BUILDING was delayed until the close of the Civil War. With a mansard roof and other details of the type made fashionable by the architects of the Third French Empire, the structure is notable for the original carved walnut woodwork in the public rooms and in the library, whose long, shuttered windows, walnut bookcases, and antique tables and chairs are reminiscent of French convents.

28. TOWER GROVE PARK, Kingshighway to Grand Blvd., and Arsenal St. to Magnolia Ave., is noted for the variety of its trees and the beauty and diversity of its water lilies. At various points along the central drive are the bronze statues of Shakespeare, Alexander von Humboldt, and Columbus, all executed by Baron Ferdinand von Mueller of Munich, Germany, and given to the city by Henry Shaw. Around the bandstand are marble busts of Mozart, Rossini, Wagner, Beethoven, Gounod, and Verdi, also the gift of Henry Shaw. Northeast of the Shakespeare statue are the lily ponds.

The park was originally part of the country estate of Henry Shaw

(1800-89), an Englishman who came to St. Louis in 1819. In 1840, he retired, having amassed a comfortable fortune from his cutlery business and real estate operations. After a period of travel and study, Shaw developed a plan for a botanical garden, which he carried out with the assistance of Dr. George Engelmann, distinguished St. Louis physician and botanist, and of interested friends in England and Germany. About 1866 Shaw decided to create a great park. He subsequently offered the city a gift of 190 acres and a 99-year lease on an additional 200 feet around this tract, on the condition that the city would devote $360,000 to improving the area as a public park. The proceeds of the lease were to be used for the maintenance of Shaw's Garden. His offer was accepted by the city and the park was named for Shaw's country home, called Tower Grove by Shaw because, it is said, a grove of sassafras trees stood near by. More than 20,000 trees, many of them rare species, and all of them grown in the garden's arboretum, have been planted in the park.

29. The MISSOURI BOTANICAL (SHAW'S) GARDEN (*open, except Christmas and New Year's, 8 a.m. to sunset, weekdays; 10 a.m. to sunset Sun.; guidebooks at main entrance, 25¢*), has its main entrance at Tower Grove Ave. and Flora Place. Seventy-five acres of gardens and buildings are enclosed by a white limestone wall. Modeled after Kew Gardens, London, "Shaw's" Garden contains more than 12,000 species of trees and plants, and its floral shows are nationally known. Tropical LILY PONDS, in which, besides the natural pink and blue, 17 varieties of hybrids developed by the garden are grown, lead west from the main entrance to the conservatories, display houses, and formal gardens. Here are grown great masses of rare and unusual iris, and chrysanthemums. In specially constructed houses are some of the world's rarest orchids, as well as orange and banana trees, magnolias, palms, and hundreds of plant curiosities, among them the Artillery plant which shoots seeds from its pod, the Dumb Crane, a bite of which would swell the tongue hideously, and the Crown of Thorns. Camellias, genistas, and other winter-flowering shrubs are displayed in the LINNEAN HOUSE, northwest of the main entrance, the only greenhouse remaining of those erected during Mr. Shaw's lifetime, and one of the few mid-nineteenth-century greenhouses left in the country. It is constructed of brick walls with intricate fanlights over the doorways, and has less glass than is now customary. Over the entrance are the portrait busts of three great naturalists: Thomas Nuttal, Linnaeus, and Asa Gray. The north wing of the three-story, red-brick ADMINISTRATION BUILDING was Shaw's town house. Designed by George I. Barnett in Italian-Renaissance design and begun in 1851, it was dismantled at its former site and re-erected here. The Italian marble mantels, carved in elaborate baroque designs, the wrought-iron, open-grille doors, and the main stairway, are distinctive. The BOTANICAL LIBRARY (*open 8:30-5 to research students, by application only*) is housed in the central and south wing. It contains a general collection of botanical publications, with more than 52,000 books, 82,000 pamphlets, and many manuscripts.

Included is an important group of Herbals printed between 1474 and 1670, in which descriptions are given of the character and uses of plants.

South of the Administration Building group is TOWER GROVE, Shaw's country home, a two-story brick structure above a high basement, and with a square center tower. The house, built in 1849, was designed by Barnett and Peck in the Italianate manner. To the north, near the wrought-iron entrance gates to the home, is SHAW'S MAUSOLEUM, a small octagonal structure resembling a summer-house. It contains Shaw's tomb, which is topped by Ferdinand von Mueller's carved marble figure of Mr. Shaw sleeping. To the east is a one-story, red-brick, stone-trimmed MUSEUM AND LIBRARY BUILDING (*not open*), built 1858-59, and also of Italianate design. Restored in 1930, it is now used as a lecture hall.

The garden was established in 1858 and opened to the public about two years later. Following Mr. Shaw's death in 1889, it passed into the hands of a self-perpetuating Board of Trustees, and is maintained by a bequeathed fund. The growth of the city has necessitated the purchase of a 1,600-acre tract near Gray Summit (*see Tour 5*), for use as a propagation unit, arboretum, and wild flower reservation.

In addition to the permanent displays and many seasonal flower exhibits, the Garden holds four major flower shows annually: orchids in January and February, iris in late May, chrysanthemums in November, and poinsettias in December.

30. ST. LOUIS UNIVERSITY (*open 9-5 weekdays*), administration building, 221 N. Grand Blvd., comprises a group of six red-brick and stone buildings, three to five stories high, in modified Gothic style, including the gymnasium and Sodality Hall, south across W. Pine Blvd., and the medical and dental school buildings on the 1300 block of S. Grand Blvd. The ADMINISTRATION BUILDING contains a room memorializing Father Pierre Jean De Smet, famous early missionary to the Indians. In the parlors and corridors of the building are approximately 40 old paintings, attributed to Teniers, Pieto Meacello, the School of the Master of St. Severin, de Breen, Rubens, and others. The collection was begun by Bishop Du Bourg soon after St. Louis Academy was established, and many of the paintings are said to have been taken from convents and churches deserted during the French Revolution.

Founded in 1818 as St. Louis Academy by the Right Reverend Louis William DuBourg, Bishop of Louisiana, the school was renamed St. Louis College in 1820. It was conducted for the first nine years by members of the diocesan clergy attached to St. Louis Cathedral. In 1823, Jesuit priests from Maryland organized an Indian school at Florissant, now St. Stanislaus Seminary (*see Tour 1*), and in 1827 they took over the directorship of St. Louis College. On December 28, 1832, St. Louis College received its charter as St. Louis University— the first university west of the Mississippi River. It was moved from its old site on Washington Avenue and Ninth Street in 1888. Until recently, only men were admitted, and the university granted degrees to women through a group of corporate colleges, a system that was probably unique. The university, combined with the corporate colleges, has an enrollment of 4,830 students, and a faculty of 656.

31. ST. FRANCIS XAVIER'S CHURCH, the church of St. Louis University, SW. corner Grand and Lindell Blvds., is of English Gothic design executed in St. Louis limestone trimmed with Bedford stone. It was planned by Henry Switzer, and dedicated in 1898. The stained-glass windows, by Emil Frei of St. Louis, are consonant with the design of the church. In the south vestibule is a figure in Italian marble of the Blessed Virgin, carved by Charles Gerts in 1853. Beneath it, a marble tablet records the deliverance of the students and faculty of the university from the cholera plague of 1849. According to tradition, the students promised the Virgin a silver crown for her statue if she would protect them from the plague. Although over 4,000 residents of St. Louis died from the disease, the students were unharmed, and true to their word, they purchased the crown, which is now preserved in the library of the university.

In the lower chapel of the church is the altar of the former church at old Kaskaskia, Illinois; it contains a consecrated stone said to have been used by Father Marquette for saying mass. The bells in the tower were cast at Seville, Spain, in 1789. They were brought to New Orleans by a Lutheran group and from there, about 80 years ago, were removed to St. Louis by the Jesuits. They were placed in the tower in 1914.

32. The CATHEDRAL OF ST. LOUIS (*handbook obtainable in the vestibule, 25¢*), 4400 Lindell Blvd., is a $3,000,000 gray-granite structure of developed Byzantine style, measuring 204 by 305 feet. It was begun May 1, 1907, and dedicated October 18, 1914. Work on the structure has continued steadily since that time. Barnett, Haynes & Barnett were the architects.

Three domes rise behind the two 157-foot towers facing Lindell Boulevard; only one, however, the 227-foot central dome covered with green tile and topped by a gold cross, is visible from the street. The floor plan of the cathedral is that of the Greek cross. The narthex or vestibule, measuring 21 by 90 feet, and 26 feet high, has 10 mosaic ceiling panels depicting the life of St. Louis. The nave is covered by a great dome resting upon pendentives and flanked by two semidomes. Mosaics, planned to cover the surface of the domes, are only partially completed (1940). With the exception of those in the chapels and on the sanctuary wall, which were done by Tiffany & Company, the mosaics in the cathedral were designed by Albert Oerken of Germany, and executed by the Ravenna Mosaic, Inc., and Emil Frei, Inc., of St. Louis. The entire wall space is done in banded courses of yellow Verona and Champville marbles. Two great rose windows are set in the north and south walls. The south window is predominantly blue; the north window is predominantly red, with a cross as the center motif. An interior gallery entirely surrounds the building. Detached from the nave by ambulatories are four chapels: The Blessed Sacrament Chapel, the Virgin Mother, or Lady Chapel, All Souls' Chapel, and All Saints' Chapel.   The main altar dominating the sanctuary is covered by a baldacchino 57 feet high, the dome of which is supported by 10 monolithic columns 2 feet in diameter and 20 feet in height of red Verona, yellow Sienna, Fiori de Pesco, and verd antique marbles.   The bases of the columns are of golden-black Oporto marble, and the capitals are of Trani marble.   The altar itself is of yellow Sienna marble.

FOREST PARK, Lindell Blvd. to Oakland Ave., and Kingshighway to Skinker Blvds., 1,380 acres, is the second largest natural park in any United States city.   Purchased in 1875 for $799,995, the tract was the site for most of the Louisiana Purchase Exposition (1904).   At the northeast entrance, Kingshighway and Lindell Blvds., a bronze statue of Francis Preston Blair, by W. W. Gardner, flanks Lindell Drive (R), which leads SW. past the FISH HATCHERY (R), a series of propagating pools operated by the United States Bureau of Fisheries.

33.   The ST. LOUIS MUNICIPAL OPERA THEATER (*1,700 free seats; others 25ç-$2*), an open-air theater seating 10,000 occupies a five-acre natural bowl facing Theater Drive at Government Drive. Light opera is presented here each summer during June, July, and August.   At both sides of the auditorium are roofed pergolas capable of sheltering 15,000 persons in case of summer showers.   The stage is the largest outdoor stage in the world, and is designed to facilitate the moving of massive settings.   The revolving stage in its center, also the largest of its kind, is capable of making an entire revolution in nine seconds.

The outdoor theater idea in St. Louis developed from the success of the great Pageant and Masque of St. Louis (1914) and the Pageant of Independence (1918).   The Municipal Opera was launched in 1919, opening with *Robin Hood*.   Since that time, more than 10,708,000 people have attended 1,459 performances.

Four pieces of statuary surround the theater's entrance.   A short distance west of it, is the BERTHA GUGGENHEIM MEMORIAL FOUNTAIN, a limestone *Pan* by J. A. Horchart, pipes above a lily pool; and farther west, at Lagoon Drive, stands the FOUNTAIN-ANGEL by Romanelli.   A bronze equestrian STATUE OF GENERAL FRANZ SIGEL, by Robert Cauer, at McKinley and Government Drives, was unveiled in

---

ST. LOUIS AND VICINITY.   Points of Interest

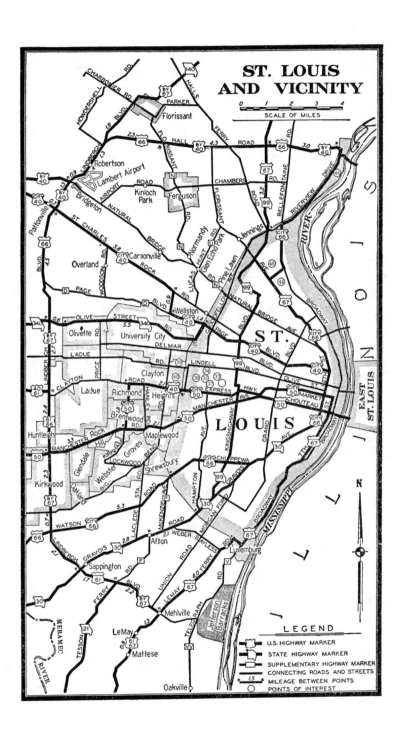

ST. LOUIS
AND VICINITY

SCALE OF MILES

LEGEND
U.S. HIGHWAY MARKER
STATE HIGHWAY MARKER
SUPPLEMENTARY HIGHWAY MARKER
CONNECTING ROADS AND STREETS
MILEAGE BETWEEN POINTS
POINTS OF INTEREST

1906 to commemorate the services of German-American Union troops in the Civil War. Near by, the CONFEDERATE MEMORIAL, a bronze group by George Zolnay, represents a Southern family sending its only adult son to battle.

34. The JEFFERSON MEMORIAL (*open 10-5, except Thanksgiving, Jefferson's Birthday, Christmas, New Year's, and the Fourth of July*), facing DeBaliviere Ave. on Lindell Blvd., is a two-story white limestone structure, consisting of two wings connected by a loggia in modified classic design. Built on the site of the main entrance to the Louisiana Purchase Exposition, the building was a gift to the city from the exposition directors. It was opened to the public April 30, 1913. In the center of the loggia is an immense marble statue of Thomas Jefferson by Karl Bitter. A bronze group, also by Bitter, on the wall of the east wing, portrays the signing of the Louisiana Purchase Treaty, April 30, 1803. The building is occupied by the Missouri Historical Society. The east wing contains the society's offices, a museum of Indian objects and Missouriana, and the library, which has a collection of rare books and important manuscripts. The west wing contains trophies and gifts received by Colonel Charles A. Lindbergh in recognition of his 1927 trans-Atlantic flight, which was financed by St. Louis interests. East of the building, a bronze group by Nancy Coonsman Hahn memorializes the women of Upper Louisiana Territory.

35. At Post-Dispatch Lake on Government Drive is the POLY-CHROME ELECTRIC FOUNTAIN, a terraced limestone formation. The water, illuminated by colored lights at night, drops from the gardens surrounding the shelter house atop Government Hill. On the flanking hillsides, 2,000 Japanese cherry trees bloom in late April or early May.

36. East of the Fountain, at Wells and McKinley Drives, is the JEWEL BOX (*open 9-9*), a steel and glass conservatory of modern setback design, facing a series of reflecting lily pools. Here the Park Department displays selections from the almost 500,000 plants and flowers grown in the surrounding 80 acres of gardens and greenhouses.

37. The ST. LOUIS ZOOLOGICAL GARDEN (*open 8-6*), between Wells, Concourse, Washington, and Government Drives, occupies a 77-acre preserve west of the Jewel Box. The ANIMAL PITS at the east and west extremities have been constructed to simulate the actual habitat of the exhibits. Between the pits are the lakes and six main buildings, predominantly of Spanish design: the LION, ELEPHANT, PRIMATE, REPTILE, ANTHROPOID, and BIRD HOUSES. North of the bird house is the largest OUTDOOR BIRDCAGE in the world, erected for the Louisiana Purchase Exposition. At its east end is a bronze memorial drinking fountain, HOPI INDIAN BIRD CHARMER, by Walker Hancock. The St. Louis Zoological Garden was established in 1913 and has been supported by taxes since 1916.

The zoo's collection is not only unusually large, but contains some exceedingly rare specimens. Every year, millions watch the absurd antics of Happy and Pao Pei (Chinese, precious jewel), the zoo's two pandas, admire the skill of the seals and sea lions at catching fish, and shudder in fascinated horror over the force-feeding of the giant boa constrictor which stubbornly refuses to feed itself. Twice daily and three times on Sundays throughout the summer months the chimpanzees and the cats give circus performances; lately, two trained ponies and a dog have been added to the troupes. Jimmy, one of the star performers in the chimpanzee show, can turn backward somersaults; another smokes cigarettes with engaging nonchalance; some ride bicycles. Major circuses have tried to hire the acts, but so far permission has never been granted.

38. The CITY ART MUSEUM (*free; open 10-5 daily except Christmas and New Year's Day. Mondays 2-9 p.m., May-Oct. A "Handbook of the Collections," 75¢, at the entrance*), a $1,000,000 building of Bedford stone in classic Roman design crowns Art Hill in the central west section of Forest Park. In front of the museum stands an heroic bronze equestrian STATUE OF ST. LOUIS THE CRUSADER, by Charles H. Niehaus, given to the city by the Louisiana Purchase Exposition Commission. Two marble figures, *Painting* (L), by Louis St. Gaudens, and *Sculpture* (R), by Daniel Chester French, adorn the buttresses of the main entrance steps. Above the portico with its Corinthian columns are statues representing six great periods of art: *Classic Art*, by F. E. Elwell, *Oriental Art*, by Harry Linder, *Egyptian Art*, by Albert Jaegers, *Renaissance Art*, by Carl Tefit, *Gothic Act*, by John Gelert, *Modern Art*, by C. T. Hannan. Two bronze griffins by A. Phimister Proctor are at either end of the base of the main pediment. Designed by Cass Gilbert and erected as the central art building of the Louisiana Purchase Exposition, the building consists of a large vaulted center hall, branching into galleries on the main floor, with a ground floor for galleries and work rooms, and a second floor for graphic arts. About a central fountain in the main hall are major pieces of statuary. Right of the main hall are a series of period rooms, and left, exhibits of the decorative arts, both notable in their fields.

Outstanding items in the museum's collection are the Medieval Rooms, a chapel and gallery of Romanesque architectural details, and a Gothic Court containing an oak stairway and galleries from Morlaix, France, of about 1500; the Hispano-Moorish Court, and the five European and five American period rooms; the James F. Ballard Collection of Oriental Rugs; and the Samuel C. Davis Collection of Chinese ceramics. The Missouri artist, George C. Bingham, is represented by a group of portraits and genre paintings. The educational department of the museum conducts a series of gallery talks for adults (*October-May, Tuesdays 11 a.m., Fridays 10 a.m.*), and "Story Hours for Children" (*October-May, Saturdays 2:30 p.m.*). A summer lecture series is announced annually. The department also makes appointments for conducted tours and special features for groups.

The museum originated in free evening drawing classes, sponsored in 1874 by Washington University (*see Art and the Crafts*). Today, tax-supported, it ranks among the best in the United States. Northwest of the museum is the heroic bronze STATUE OF EDWARD BATES (1793-1869), by J. Wilson McDonald. On the four sides of the granite pedestal are medallion portraits of Captain James B. Eads, Governor Hamilton R. Gamble, Charles Gibson, and Henry S. Geyer, Bates, a member of Missouri's Constitutional Convention of 1820, was later recipient of many State and national honors, including appointment as Attorney General to Lincoln's Cabinet in 1860. The statue was unveiled on the formal opening of the park, June 25, 1876.

39. WASHINGTON UNIVERSITY (*open 8:30-5 weekdays*), main entrance, Lindell Blvd. and Skinker Rd., comprises a group of 35 buildings occupying a 155-acre campus between Skinker Rd. and Big Bend Blvd. north of Forsythe Blvd. A Bronze STATUE OF ROBERT BURNS, by Robert Aitken, faces Skinker Road south of the entrance. Except for two white-limestone structures facing Forsythe Blvd. (L) at the foot of "the hill," as students call the main campus, the buildings are of pink Missouri granite with Bedford stone trim in Tudor-Gothic style. BROOKINGS HALL, the administration building, dominates the campus at the end of Lindell Boulevard. At night, the central towers are flood-lighted, creating a particularly effective approach. The university, now endowed with about $20,000,000, developed from Eliot Seminary, which was chartered in 1853. The present campus was occupied in 1905. The university's medical buildings, including the School of Dentistry, the St. Louis Children's Hospital, the Edward Mallinckrodt Institute of Radiology, St. Louis Maternity, Oscar Johnson Institute, and Barnes Hospital, occupy a separate campus surrounding the intersection of Kingshighway Blvd. and Euclid Ave. The university, with all branches, has an enrollment of 8,549, and a faculty of 818.

40. CONCORDIA THEOLOGICAL SEMINARY, 801 DeMun Ave., was established by Lutheran Saxon immigrants in a one-room log cabin at Altenburg, Perry County, Missouri, in 1839 (*see Tour 11*). The Evangelical Lutheran Synod of Missouri, Ohio, and other States, was organized in 1847, and in 1849 took over the seminary and moved it to St. Louis. Today (1941) the Synod owns and operates 18 colleges and seminaries in the United States, Canada, China, India, and South America. Concordia Seminary offers a 4-year theological course and has an annual enrollment of approximately 325 students.

The campus occupies a 71-acre, landscaped tract. The present group of 18 stone buildings, designed by Charles Z. Klauder in a modern interpretation of Gothic, were dedicated in 1926. Unusual color effects are achieved through the combination of red, yellow, gray, and putty-colored stone from Boulder, Colorado, and from Altenburg, Zell, and St. Louis County. Near the center of the campus is a REPLICA OF THE ORIGINAL LOG CONCORDIA SEMINARY BUILDING at Altenburg. A collection of historical documents, books, and craft objects relating to the early Lutheran immigrants has been assembled by the Concordia Historical Institute, and is housed in the ADMINIS-

TRATION BUILDING (*open upon application to the curator, Professor W. G. Polack*).

41. The AMERICAN WINE COMPANY PLANT, 3015 Cass Avenue (*open 10-12, 1-3 daily except Saturday, Sunday, and holidays; guides*), manufactures champagne and various still wines. The plant, a low, gray-stone building of modified Gothic design, was built in 1859. In that year the American Wine Company was organized, largely through the efforts of Isaac Cook (1810-86), an early Chicago merchant and office holder. The newly formed company purchased the deep stone cellars of the Missouri Wine Company, which had been established in 1832. These century-old cellars—stone-arched, cool, damp, and glistening with white mould—extend over an area almost a block square in a maze of passageways and levels 60 feet underground.

To make champagne, catawba wine from the islands of Lake Erie is blended with other three- or four-year-old wines, bottled, and placed in a room with a temperature of 80 degrees. Here fermentation is rapid and a pressure of from 100 to 125 pounds per bottle is developed. To reduce breakage, each bottle is made with an inverted base. Fermentation is followed by aging from 6 months to 12 years. Preparation for market includes the careful removal of the sediment by a riddling and degorging process, and the insertion of permanent corks. An average of more than 300,000 bottles of champagne is kept in the plant. Three varieties are made, varying from medium dry to very dry, and recently eight standard varieties of still wines have also been introduced.

42. FAIRGROUNDS PARK, between Grand and Fair, and Natural Bridge and Kossuth Aves., became a public park in 1909, having served since 1856 as the grounds for St. Louis fairs. The Agricultural and Mechanical Association which sponsored these events was chartered in December 1855, and the first fair opened October 13, 1856, with a premium list of $10,000. So great was its success that it was repeated annually, except during the Civil War. The most important event of its kind in the Mississippi Valley, the St. Louis Fair served as a clearing house for industrial and agricultural development, and its emphasis on art, music, and education had significant cultural effects. A zoological garden opened on the fairgrounds in October 1876, was the forerunner of the present zoo in Forest Park. At one time the grounds contained a race track; also an early aviation field. In October 1911, the first air mail in the world was flown from Kinloch Park to this field. The present park is a landscaped tract containing ball fields, tennis courts, and one of the largest outdoor swimming pools in the world (*suit, soap, and towel, 5¢*). The pool, circular in shape and 420 feet in diameter, is lighted at night.

43. NORTH ST. LOUIS WATER TOWER (*not open*), North Grand Blvd. at 20th Street, often called "the Old Water Tower," is a white, 154-foot Corinthian column of brick with an octagonal base of Chicago stone 41 feet in diameter. The column, erected about 1871, was used until 1912 to create pressure to move water pumped from the

Mississippi at Bissell's point, one mile to the north, to the Compton Hill Reservoir, about four miles to the south. The five-foot water pipe in the center of the column is surrounded by a spiral staircase leading to a platform at the top of the structure. In 1929 the column was equipped as an air beacon.

44. BELLEFONTAINE CEMETERY (*open 8-5*), entrance, 4947 W. Florissant Ave., covers 333.5 acres between Broadway and West Florissant Ave., and Morin and Calvary Aves. At the north corner is the grave of General William Clark of the Lewis and Clark Expedition. The WAINWRIGHT TOMB, memorializing Charlotte Dickson Wainwright (d. 1891) and her husband Ellis Wainwright (d. 1924), is considered one of the masterpieces of Louis Sullivan, Chicago architect. Completed in 1892, the grey limestone structure is surmounted by a low dome. Bands of rich and delicate carving contrasting with plain surfaces, rather than any specific decorative motif, give the tomb an unmistakable Oriental quality.

Others buried in Bellefontaine are Francis P. Blair, Senator Thomas H. Benton, Manuel Lisa, General Sterling Price, and James B. Eads. The cemetery was opened in 1850. Maps showing the location of celebrities' graves are obtainable (*free*) in the office (R), at the main entrance.

45. CALVARY CEMETERY (*open 7:30-5*), 5239 W. Florissant Ave., containing 476 acres, is the largest in St. Louis. A Catholic cemetery, it was founded in 1864. North of the entrance is the grave of General William Tecumseh Sherman, and in the east section is that of Alexander McNair, Missouri's first Governor. The cemetery also contains the grave of Auguste Chouteau, one of the founders of St. Louis, and the beautiful tomb of Thomas Biddle, Philadelphia army officer who was killed in a duel with Congressman Spencer Pettis of St. Louis in 1831. OLD ORCHARD, a two-story brick house erected by Henry Clay in 1845 and now an outing farm for orphan boys, stands in the cemetery near W. Florissant Ave.

46. CHAIN OF ROCKS PARK, 11000 N. Riverview Drive, a stretch of wooded bluffs above the Mississippi River, overlooks one of the city's waterworks plants. From points along Lookaway Drive, the park affords a wide view of the river and the Illinois environs of St. Louis.

Springfield

Railroad Stations: SW. corner Main Ave. and Mill St. for St. Louis-San Francisco R.R. (Frisco Lines); 305 N. Main Ave. for Missouri Pacific R.R.
Bus Stations: Union Bus Depot, 303 W. Olive St. for Missouri, Kansas and Oklahoma Coach Lines, McAlister Bus Lines, Fred Harvey Bus Lines, Missouri-Arkansas Coach Lines, All-American Bus Lines, A. W. Shepherd Bus Lines; Greyhound Union Bus Terminal; 460 St. Louis St. for Southwestern Greyhound Lines, McAlister Bus Lines, Crown Coach Co., Fred Harvey Bus Lines, Lea Bus Lines.
Airport: Municipal Airport, 3 *m.* E. of Post Office on Division St.; no scheduled service; taxi fare 25¢.
Taxis: 10¢ in midtown zone, 15¢ elsewhere in city limits, 25¢ in immediate suburbs.
Local Busses: Fare 5¢.
Traffic Regulations: Speed limit, 20 m.p.h. in downtown area and school zones; 30 m.p.h. elsewhere, except 40 m.p.h. on Glenstone and Sunshine Roads; traffic entering the Public Square moves to right only.

Accommodations: Thirty hotels; numerous lodging houses and tourist camps.

Information Service: Chamber of Commerce, SW. corner Walnut St. and Jefferson Ave.; Automobile Club of Missouri (AAA), 535 St. Louis St. (members only).

Radio Stations: KWTO (560 kc.); KGBX (1,260 kc.).
Motion Picture Houses: Six.
Swimming: Municipal Pools: Grant Beach, 742 W. Lynn St., Fassnight Park, 1217 S. Campbell Ave., Silver Springs Park (Negroes), NE corner Florence Ave. and Scott St., Doling Lake, NE. corner Talmadge St. and Boonville Ave. Free hours at all municipal pools daily until 4 p.m. Other hours, adults 20¢, children 10¢. YMCA, 417 S. Jefferson Ave.; YWCA, 426 South Jefferson Ave., one day membership 35¢.
Baseball: White City Park, SW. corner Boonville Ave. and Division St., Western Association and St. Louis Cardinal affiliate.
Football: Southwest Missouri State Teachers College Stadium, NW. corner Grand St. and National Ave.
Golf: Glenstone Golf Course, N. Glenstone Road between Division and Pythian Sts., 18 holes; greens fee 50¢.
Tennis: Grant Beach, 742 W. Lynn St.; Fassnight Park, 1217 S. Campbell Ave.; Washington Park, 701 E. Locust St.; Phelps Grove, Beach St. at Dollison Ave., Sanford Park, 800 N. Nichols St.; Busiek Courts, 1100 Cairo St., membership fee $10 a year, guests free.

Annual Events: Creative Arts Conference for high school students of southwestern Missouri, Drury College, Feb.; Music Festival, contests for high school students of southwestern Missouri, Southwest Missouri State Teachers College, Apr.; spring baseball training camp, White City Park, Apr.; May Day, Southwest Missouri State Teachers College, May 1; Annual Rodeo, May; Junior Chamber of Commerce Swim Meet, June; Ozark Empire Fair (regional), Sept.; "Joyland," Shrine Mosque, Dec.

SPRINGFIELD (1,345 alt., 61,238 pop.), Missouri's fourth largest city, is in the southwestern part of the State at the northern edge of the Ozark Highlands. The business district is concentrated around the Public Square, which lies near the center of the city. Within the square is the "pie," a slightly raised concrete safety zone approximately 75 feet in diameter, around which traffic moves to the right. Just north of the square is the new Civic Center, bounded by Pine Street, Boonville Avenue, Scott Street, and Jefferson Avenue, which includes a new Post Office and Federal Building, a Court House, the Social Security Building, and a modern jail. Around Commercial Street, the principal industrial and commercial district extends along a tier of railroad tracks. Here are creameries, furniture and garment factories, cooperages, chicken and egg establishments, and the railroad shops.

In 1930, Springfield's population consisted of 95.5 per cent native born whites (of which 73 per cent are native Missourians), 3 per cent Negroes, and 1.5 per cent foreign-born. The majority of the laboring class live in one-story frame cottages in the vicinity of the shops and factories. Many businessmen and professional men reside on the eastern side of the city, an area characterized by one- and two-story white frame houses fronting on landscaped lawns and shaded by huge oak, elm, and maple trees. On the southeast, expensive houses of modern design predominate.

The Negroes live north of the midtown railroad tracks, and east of Jefferson Avenue. Their homes for the most part are either the large dilapidated frame houses of an earlier day or modern cottages. Most of the men work for the railroad.

The first attempt to establish a permanent settlement in the Springfield area was made by Thomas Patterson, who brought his family up the James River in 1821 and purchased the claim of the John P. Pettijohn family. When 500 Delaware Indians arrived the next year, asserting that the government had given them southwestern Missouri for a reservation, one of the white settlers was sent to St. Louis to ascertain which claim was correct. The Indians were upheld, and a Delaware and a Kickapoo village are said to have been built on or near the present site of Springfield. Subsequently, all the white settlers abandoned the area except James Wilson, who moved in with the Indians, marrying first one then another of the Indian women. When the Delaware left the locality, he sent his third Indian wife with them, and returned to St. Louis, where he married a white woman, and purchased farm implements. He then returned to develop a farm on the creek which now bears his name.

In 1830 the Government began moving all Indian tribes westward, and a rather slow migration of white families into the region began. Meanwhile, John Polk Campbell and his brother, Madison, had left Tennessee to search for a neighbor's runaway son and to verify reports of the Ozark country. Finding the boy near Fayetteville, Arkansas, they came northward to the site of Springfield, then known as Kickapoo Prairie, and staked claims by cutting a blaze and their names on a tree near a spring approximately 400 yards northeast of the present Public Square. When Campbell and his brother-in-law, Joseph Miller, returned with their families in February 1830, they found the William Fulbright family and A. J. Burnett on the land. Burnett's cabin was near the spring on Campbell's claim, but he yielded possession when the Campbells showed their names and marks on the tree. The site was well chosen, since the spring was excellent, and important early trails were near by. Within a few months a settlement grew up.

In 1833, Greene County was organized, Campbell was made county clerk, and the county seat established in his 12-by-14-foot log cabin. Two years later, Campbell and his wife deeded 50 acres between what are now Jefferson and Campbell Avenues and Pershing and Mill Streets to the county for a townsite. The sale of lots provided funds to erect a courthouse on the Square, which Campbell had platted with the streets converging in the center, in conformity with one he had seen in Tennessee. This unorthodox plan aroused comment, which Campbell dismissed by asserting: "Well, that's the way they made 'em where I cam from."

Traditions vary as to the origin of the town's name. One account relates that Springfield was named for the former home of one of the early settlers. Another states that Campbell chose this name because there was a field on the hill, and a spring under it. The town was incorporated in 1838, and reincorporated in 1846, a year prior to receiving its charter.

Since southwestern Missouri was too much isolated by surrounding hills to develop along with the rest of the State, Springfield grew slowly. It was, however, strategically located at the intersection of the region's two most important roads, so that when heavy migration did begin, expansion was rapid. The majority of the settlers who began coming in 1850 were stockbreeders looking for good grazing and grain producing lands. By 1859, Springfield, with a population of 2,500, controlled the trade of the area. The Government land office for that quarter of the State had been established there in 1835, and the town was a depot for the Butterfield Stage Line.

When the Civil War began, Springfield's population was predominantly in favor of the South. The town's key location and commercial prosperity made it a military objective for both the Union and Confederate armies throughout the war. In the Battle of Wilson's Creek, which was fought 11 miles south of town on August 10, 1861, General Nathaniel Lyon was killed, and the Southern army won a costly victory of doubtful military value. The Confederates subsequently held Springfield until they were driven out in February 1862 by the Union forces, which retained possession, despite numerous counterattacks, until the end of the war.

Charles Butler Hickok, better known as Wild Bill, served at the Union headquarters in Springfield as scout and spy. After the war he remained here. He struck up a friendship with Dave Tutt, a former Confederate soldier and a professional gambler, but after a time the

two quarrelled. On July 21, 1865, they met on the Square, and Wild
Bill shot Tutt through the heart at a distance of 75 yards. He was
tried, defended by John S. Phelps, later governor of Missouri (1876-
80), and acquitted. The following year he was appointed deputy
United States Marshal at Fort Riley, Kansas. In 1876 he was shot
and killed by Jack McCall at Deadwood, South Dakota.

In 1870, when Springfield had grown to a town of 5,555 people, a
bitter fight developed over the extension of the Atlantic and Pacific
Railroad (now a part of the Frisco system) to within a short distance
of the city. Springfield wanted the railroad to pass through the town,
but when the line was laid out it followed the high divide between the
Missouri and White River basins, and consequently missed the Square
by one-and-a-half miles. A group of land speculators, United States
Congressman Sempronius H. Boyd, Charles E. Harwood, and John W.
Lisenby, were quick to seize the possibility for new profit. They persuaded Dr. Edwin T. Robberson, who owned the land north of town
through which the railroad would pass, to sell them a controlling interest, so that they might plat a new town. Springfield citizens immediately retaliated by organizing a company to compel the railroad to
come through the town. Delegations were sent to St. Louis and to the
Boston offices of the railroad. The speculators promised the railroad a
40-acre tract for shops, a 200-foot strip for yards, and 200 acres for a
townsite, a half interest in which would go to the railroad company, if
the line followed the original survey. Several railroad officials, including Andrew Pierce, later president of the company, came to
Springfield, and a general meeting was held. Pierce offered to bring
the railroad through the town in exchange for a $25,000 bonus and a
depot on Central Street. The majority of the citizens objected. General C. B. Holland informed Pierce that since the charter called for
a railroad to Springfield, "not to a patch of black jack brush more than
a mile away," the town would not pay the railroad a cent. Pierce then
jumped up, pounded on the table, and shouted, "I'll very soon show
you where I'll build! . . ." Immediately afterward the Ozark Land
Company was organized, with Pierce as president, and the new town
was deeded to this company. Springfield had lost the fight.

For a time, the swift rise of North Springfield alarmed the residents
of the older town, but the benefits of the railroad soon overflowed to
the original city, increasing both its population and its commerce. Drury
College was founded "between the towns" in 1873, and shortly thereafter, a post office was established in the same neighborhood. In 1881,
when the Kansas City, Fort Scott, and Memphis Railroad (later also a
part of the Frisco system) was completed, additional shops were established in North Springfield, but trackage was laid through the older
town. Gradually, the two expanding communities met; in 1887 they
were consolidated.

Aided by the railroads, Springfield's industries flourished and the
population quadrupled. The development of fruit and vegetable production on the fertile limestone soils of the surrounding plateau, and the

establishment of the Southwest Missouri State Teachers College in 1905, gave Springfield a second impetus for growth. Between 1900 and 1910 the population increased more than 50 per cent.

One-fifth of Springfield's present (1941) working population is employed by railroads. Dairying and poultry raising have been added to the agricultural pursuits of the region, and the Missouri Farmer's Association has established three of the largest co-operative plants in the United States: the Producer's Produce Company, which processes poultry products, the Producer's Creamery Company, and the M.F.A. Milling Company. Two large institutions, the United States Hospital for the Criminal Insane and the Missouri Pythian Home, have been established. The city is the national headquarters of the Assemblies of God, a strong denomination throughout the area. Within the past decade, the Ozark Highlands have been developed as a recreational area. These interests have accentuated Springfield's importance as the center of Ozark business and social life.

Of the $26,000,000 worth of manufactured and processed goods produced by Springfield's industries annually, 77 per cent comes from the farms that lie within a 150-mile radius. Ozark dairy and poultry farms furnish raw materials for Springfield's output of butter, cheese, dressed poultry, and dried eggs. The near-by grain fields and those of contiguous regions south and west supply the city's flour and feed mills, bakeries, and allied industries. Oak, hickory, maple, elm, walnut, and a small amount of pine cut on Ozark farms supply the raw materials used by Springfield furniture factories, cooperages, planing mills, and wagon factory. The stockyards of the city receive the "truck-in" shipments of the hill farmers and pass them on to larger markets; the small packing plants just east of the city redistribute some of the cattle as meat and meat products. The southwestern Ozark farmer habitually eats biscuits and white bread made of Springfield flour, and fattens his stock on Springfield feed. He usually wears Springfield overalls, uses Springfield-made harness, and hauls his produce in Springfield wagons and trailers.

POINTS OF INTEREST

The JOHN POLK CAMPBELL HOME (*open by arrangement*), 975 Mary Ave., a two-story white frame structure built in 1851, is the oldest building in Springfield. Last of the many houses built by the "founder of Springfield," it was intended by Campbell to be similar to his earlier home in Columbia, Tennessee; but he went to Oklahoma (then the Cherokee Nation) before the structure was finished, leaving the plans with a builder who had never seen the original. The contractor succeeded in reproducing the interior, but could not achieve an accurate copy of the outside. In 1861 Union troops used the house as headquarters. Later, it served as a Confederate hospital, and as a home for Union soldiers. It has been extensively altered, and moved from its original location, about 300 feet to the northwest, on

Jefferson Avenue. At present (1941) it is occupied by a descendant of Campbell.

Many stories of Campbell's vigorous personality have survived. In 1833, the year the first church was built, Campbell laid out a one-mile race track in the southeast part of the present city, then a prairie. Two years later he was "strongly drawn to religious matters," but refused to join his wife's church because, owing to some personal grudge, he did not wish to "go to heaven with Parson Joel Haden." He found a more congenial companion in another church, and soon after destroyed his race track.

The SITE OF GENERAL NICHOLAS SMITH'S TAVERN is marked by a granite table on the south wall of a two-story, gray-brick building at 222½ Boonville Avenue. The tavern, whose dates of erection and demolition are uncertain, faced the Warsaw Road, Springfield's earliest outlet, and was used as a station on the Butterfield Stage Line, which carried the first overland mail from Missouri to San Francisco in 1858 (see Transportation). The arrival of the first stage was celebrated at the tavern with a banquet, speeches, and fireworks.

DRURY COLLEGE, East Benton Ave. between Central and Calhoun Sts., and extending to Summit Ave., a four-year, coeducational institution, occupies a group of 13 buildings. Cannon used in Civil War operations flank the front approaches to BURNHAM HALL, the administration building, and at the rear a low mound outlines the now effaced rifle pits of the Union Army. The college was organized on March 26, 1873, as Springfield College. A few months later, a gift by Samuel Fletcher Drury of Olivet, Michigan, resulted in its reorganization under its present name, which memorializes Albert Fletcher Drury, son of the school's benefactor, who died in 1863. The college was founded and has been largely maintained by Congregationalists, but is non-denominational in character. It has an enrollment of approximately 400 students. The EDWARD M. SHEPARD MUSEUM (open by arrangement), on the second floor of Pearson Hall, houses a collection of fossils, insects, mineral specimens, and Indian arrowheads. Near the northern end of the campus are two small INDIAN MOUNDS.

In DOLING PARK, NE. corner Talmadge St. and Boonville Ave., is DOLING CAVE (adults 10¢, children 5¢), an improved passage winding 1,000 feet into a limestone bluff. A spring flowing from the cave feeds a lake used for boating and bathing. Within the park are playground facilities.

The MISSOURI PYTHIAN HOME (open 2-5 daily), NE. corner Pythian St. and Fremont Ave., is a three-story, limestone building of a variant Norman-English style. The grounds consist of five acres. Maintained by the Knights of Pythias, the institution houses about 100 orphans and aged widows of deceased members of the order. Motion pictures and other entertainment are presented in the auditorium.

The SPRINGFIELD WAGON AND TRAILER COMPANY PLANT (open 9-12 and 1-4 weekdays), SW. corner Chestnut St. and

Sherman Ave., largest wagon manufactory west of the Mississippi River, consists of a group of one- and two-story brick buildings with a ground area of 12 acres. The plant employs about 100 workers. The average annual production is 1,000 wagons, or about one-third of the yearly total of the horse-and-buggy days. When crops command good prices, production sometimes approaches its former peak. At other times the diminishing demand is offset by sales of auto, truck, and circus trailers. The present type of wagon is still deep-bodied, with a high spring seat, but within recent years the plant has added a new item—a wagon with high running gear, steel wheels, and pneumatic tires. This vehicle is especially adapted to the cane fields of the South, and can be used as a wagon or trailer.

The ART MUSEUM (*open 2-5 daily*), in the City Hall, 870 Boonville Ave., has a collection of paintings, etchings, and historical material.

SOUTHWEST MISSOURI STATE TEACHERS COLLEGE (*open 8-5 weekdays*), west side of National Ave., between Madison and Grand Sts., its campus extending to King's Ave., on the west, is a four-year, State-supported, coeducational institution. The buildings are chiefly three-story limestone structures of English Renaissance design. The older ones form three sides of a quadrangle, with Academic Hall, the administration building, in the center. ACADEMIC HALL was erected in 1905 and a year later the college was opened as a State normal school. The present name was adopted in 1919. The school offers a Bachelor of Arts degree and courses in business training. The enrollment is approximately 1,000 during the regular term and 2,000 during the summer term.

NATIONAL HEADQUARTERS, ASSEMBLIES OF GOD (*open 8-5 weekdays*), 336 W. Pacific St., a two-story, buff-brick building trimmed with limestone, is occupied by offices for church administration, and the denomination's publishing house. The publishing department prints 15 periodicals, including Sunday School papers and quarterlies, in addition to religious tracts and books which have an international distribution. It employs approximately 125 persons.

The church also operates the CENTRAL BIBLE INSTITUTE (*open daily*), North Grant St. at Norton Rd., a training school of the Assemblies of God. Two spacious red-brick buildings house classrooms and dormitories, with an adjoining frame assembly hall and recreation building. The annual enrollment is about 400 students.

POINTS OF INTEREST IN ENVIRONS

U.S. Hospital for Criminal Insane, 2 *m.;* National Cemetery, 4 *m.;* Crystal Cave, 5*m.;* Sequiota State Park, 5 *m.* (*see Tour 9b*). Wilson Creek Battlefield, 11 *m.* (*see Tour 6b*).

PART III

Tours

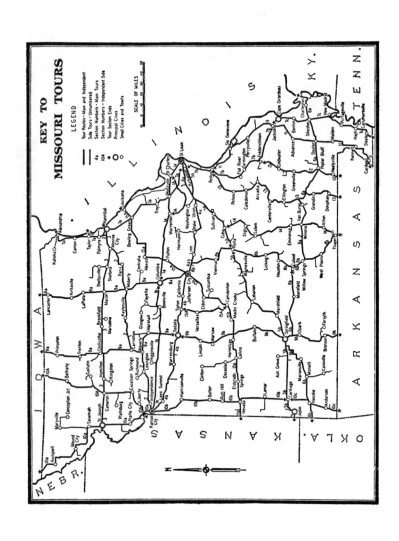

Tour 1

(East St. Louis, Ill.)—St. Louis—St. Charles—Columbia—Boonville
—Concordia—Kansas City—(Kansas City, Kans.); By-Pass US 40
and US 40.
Illinois Line to Kansas Line, 259.3 *m.*

Concrete paved throughout; two, three, and four lanes.
Route paralleled roughly by Wabash R.R. between St. Charles and New Florence junction; by Missouri-Kansas-Texas R.R. between Rocheport and Boonville; by the Missouri Pacific R.R. between Sweet Springs and Concordia; and by the Chicago & Alton R.R. between Odessa and Blue Springs.
Hotels in large cities; tourist and trailer camps throughout.

US 40, the most direct route across the State, follows in general
the historic course of western migration through the Missouri River
Valley. West of St. Louis the highway crosses the Missouri River at
St. Charles and follows the high prairie ridges to Boonville, where it
recrosses the river and continues westward through Kansas City to the
Kansas Line.

Section a. ILLINOIS LINE *to* COLUMBIA; *125.5 m.* US 40

US 40, in union with US 50 (*see Tour 4*) and US 66 (*see Tour
5*), crosses the MISSISSIPPI RIVER, 0 *m.*, from East St. Louis, Illinois, on the St. Louis Municipal Bridge (*toll, used for relief, 10¢ passenger cars, 15¢ commercial vehicles, passengers and pedestrians free*). In
ST. LOUIS, Missouri (413 alt., 816,048 pop.) (*see St. Louis*), Optional US 40 follows Chouteau Ave. to Manchester Ave., which is used
by trucks; passenger cars turn north and west around Forest Park, and
west of the city, at 16.8 *m.*, Optional US 40 meets US 66 and By Pass
US 40-67.
Right on this road, called Lindbergh Boulevard, to the Natural
Bridge Road, 1.1 *m.*

R. here 1.3 *m.* to BRIDGETON, first known as Village à Robert, or Marais
des Liards (Fr., cottonwood swamp), and later as Owens Station. Present-
day highways from St. Louis to Bridgeton and Florissant follow the general
route of the French and Spanish trails of the eighteenth century.
Bridgeton is a village of old red-brick houses shaded by giant elm and
maple trees. At the western end of the town is the one-and-a-half-story JUDGE
W. W. HENDERSON HOUSE (*private*), an imposing pre-Civil War brick dwelling with a Classic-Revival portico and a gambrel roof. Adjoining the village
on the west and northwest is the site of the former BRIDGETON COMMONS, a

1,000-acre tract granted the community by the Spanish government and confirmed by an act of Congress in 1812. In 1852 the land was leased to individuals for a term of 999 years at annual rentals varying from 10¢ to 75¢ an acre.

Among Bridgeton's early settlers was Lewis Rogers, a white man who had been captured by Indians as a child and raised as a member of the tribe. He married the daughter of a Shawnee chief and eventually became chief of the tribe himself. Following General Anthony Wayne's defeat of the Shawnee and their allies in 1794, and the treaty of Greenville, Rogers brought his tribe west across the Mississippi and settled at Bridgeton (*see Archeology and Indians*).

At 2 *m.* on Lindbergh Boulevard is the LAMBERT-ST. LOUIS MUNICIPAL AIRPORT (R), a $2,000,000 landing field of 693 acres. The field has modern hangars, flood lights, radio compass, traffic-control towers, and 4,200 feet of hard-surfaced runways which permit landing or taking-off regardless of wind direction. Besides an administration building, a meteorological station, machine shops, and every modern service, several extensive plants for the manufacture of standard planes and motors are in operation at the field. All types of passenger, express, and mail service are available.

At 3.5 *m.* is a junction with By-Pass US 67, a concrete road, which the route follows (L) to the Charbonier Road, 5 *m.*

1. Right here 0.4 *m.* to FLORISSANT (575 alt., 1,369 pop.), a loosely knit village of small gray and white frame, and red-brick houses surrounded by gardens, orchards, and barns. Named Florissant (flowering) by its first French settlers, and called St. Ferdinand by Spanish authorities, the village was known as St. Ferdinand de Florissant until 1939, when it officially became Florissant. Most of the streets were named for either French or Spanish saints. The large German immigration during the nineteenth century is represented by the slim spire of the Sacred Heart Church at the crest of the slope. In the valley, prefaced by an avenue of giant elms, is the venerable, white-painted brick Church of St. Ferdinand, or, as it is more familiarly known, "the French Church." Many of the inhabitants speak either French or German fluently.

Nicolas Hebert *dit* Le Compte is said to have "frequently been" on or near the site of Florissant as early as 1763; but a village did not develop there until about 1785. From about 1786 until the territory was purchased by the United States in 1803, François Dunegant *dit* Beaurosier was civil and military commandant of the village. The settlement of 60 houses was occasionally menaced by Indians, and in 1793 the wife and sons of Antoine Rivière, Jr., were killed near the village. Twenty years later Father Dunand records that five of his parishioners were slain. Among the Creole residents of the village were Pierre Vial, who made an overland trek to Santa Fe in 1792, Joseph Robidoux, the founder of St. Joseph, Antoine Deshetres, who as "Tonish" of Washington Irving's "Tour of the Prairies" won a sort of comic immortality, and Auguste Archambault, Howard Stansbury's guide during his trip West in 1849-50, and guide and butcher to General John C. Frémont.

The CHURCH OF ST. FERDINAND, west end of St. Francis St., is the oldest church dedicated to the Sacred Heart in the United States. The white brick building forms the center of a T-shaped group whose wings consist of the rectory and the Convent of the Sisters of Loretto. The cornerstone, which was presented to Father de la Croix by Mother Rose Philippine Duchesne (*see St. Charles*), was laid by him February 19, 1821; on November 21 of the same year the church was blessed and opened for services. It was consecrated by Bishop Joseph Rosati, September 2, 1832. The present structure replaces an old log church erected on the site about 1788. The RECTORY, a two-and-a-half-story brick building with dormer windows, was built in 1819.

In 1870, an extension of some 20 feet and a new façade of late Gothic design were added to the church. The interior of the building contains the original galleries on the right and left of the altar. The one on the left was used by Negro slaves, and that on the right by Mother Duchesne and the Sisters of the Sacred Heart, and later by the Sisters of Loretto. A white and gilt wooden tabernacle preserved in the church was made in 1789 by a local cabinetmakers for the first log building; the tabernacle in use at present, likewise white and gilt, dates from 1821. It is carried in the annual Corpus Christi procession. In the church are the paintings, *The Crucifixion, with the Virgin and St. John* (School of Rubens, C. 1604), and *St. Ferdinand* (artist unknown, thought to have been painted about 1786), which Bishop Louis William Valentine Du Bourg brought from Europe. Preserved in the altar is a life-size wax figure of St. Valentine wearing his priestly vestments and holding a chalice, also brought from France by Bishop Du Bourg. The figure contains relics of the Saint.

The CONVENT OF THE SISTERS OF LORETTO (*open*) is a two-and-a-half-story brick building with dormer windows; a simple one-story portico shelters the main entrance. The convent had its inception in 1818, when, at the request of Bishop Du Bourg, Mother Duchesne and four Sisters of the newly founded Society of the Sacred Heart arrived in St. Louis from France. Because preparations had not been completed for them in Florissant, the Sisters started a school in St. Charles; but poverty, the hardships of a rough frontier town, and the indifference of the population to their efforts, caused them to abandon it after a year. Bishop Du Bourg then arranged for the removal of the Sisters to Florissant, and the nuns set out upon another lap of their journey, which had been one of trial and discouragement from the beginning. At one time Mother Duchesne wrote: "There was a moment this month when I had in my pocket only six sous and a half, and debts besides." Of their march to Florissant with their cows, chickens, and other possessions, Mother Duchesne was able to write with some humor. The cows were "indignant at being tied, and the Sisters were forced to coax them the entire distance with cabbages." "I divided my attention," she said dryly, "between the reliquaries and the hens." The Sisters opened a school in a cabin on Father de la Croix's farm, and in May 1820, had 21 pupils. In the fall of that year, the nuns moved into the completed convent, and the first branch of the Sacred Heart Order in the United States was established. The Sisters were obliged to do all the house and farm work, in addition to teaching.

In 1828 Mother Duchesne re-established the Convent and school in St. Charles (*see St. Charles*), but she maintained a school in Florissant until 1846. In 1847, at the request of Father van Assche, six Sisters of Loretto, or Friends of Mary at the Foot of the Cross, arrived in Florissant. During the first year the hardships they endured rivaled those of the Sacred Heart Sisters, and there were days when they did not have sufficient to eat. However, through perseverance and some unexpected outside help, they eventually bcame firmly established. In 1880 they erected the academy building which they occupied for 39 years. When it was destroyed by fire in 1919, the Sisters transferred their work to Webster Groves, but they still conduct the parish school of St. Ferdinand, which was founded as a separate institution in 1887.

CASA ALVAREZ (*private*), on St. Louis St. at the north end of St. Pierre St., of horizontal log construction in the American manner, now weatherboarded, is said to have been the home of Augustine Alvarez, adjutant to the commandant of the post of St. Ferdinand de Florissant during the 1790's. The long sweep of roof ending abruptly in a front gallery is of the Missouri French design characteristic of the village. The house is now the property of Dr. and Mrs. Hermann von Schrenk, and the side garden, famed for its lilies and delphinium, is one of the stations in the annual Corpus Christi procession.

This procession begins at sundown, and is heralded by the tones of silver trumpets, as, from the Sacred Heart Church, priests, nuns, altar boys with bells, and laity with banners and lighted candles begin the march through the flower-decked streets. In the midst of the procession, vested priests carry the Blessed Sacrament in a monstrance under a silken canopy. The last stop, before the return to the church, is before an altar in the Von Schrenk garden, where a priest raises his arms in the benediction of the Blessed Sacrament, and fireworks and rockets shower the night with cascading fire. Except for a few years after the World War, the inhabitants of Florissant have decorated the town and marched with the Sacrament on every Corpus Christi since 1814.

2. Left on Charbonier Road 1.4 *m.* to Howdershell Road; L. here 0.7 *m.* to ST. STANISLAUS SEMINARY (*open Thurs. and Sun. 2-5, other days by permission*), said to be the oldest existing Jesuit novitiate in the world. The reception rooms and offices are in a four-story gray-limestone building with white Classic-Revival trim and green shutters, built 1840-49. Closely grouped about the central building and forming a rough quadrangle are the dormitories, chapel, and classrooms of the seminary. Near by are the old cemetery, and the low buildings of the winery with its deep, century-old cellars. The landscaped lawn, laid out in a simple formal plan many years ago, contains an unusual variety of trees and shrubs.

Early in 1823, two priests, seven novices, and the other members of the Jesuit novitiate at White Marsh, Maryland, established themselves in three small log cabins on Bishop Du Bourg's farm near Florissant, to complete their studies in preparation for missionary work among the Western Indian tribes. A school for Indian boys, the first of its kind in the United States, was planned by Bishop Du Bourg, to familiarize the young missionaries with Indian manners and languages "and in turn to prepare the children to become guides, interpreters and helpers to the missionaries." The enterprise was granted an annual government subsidy of $800. St. Regis Seminary began actual operations May 11, 1824, with the admission of two Sauk boys, one six and the other eight years of age. Soon other Indian boys were admitted, and the troubles of the Fathers began. The boys, accustomed to freedom, resented what was virtual imprisonment for them, and promptly ran away; but the faculty tracked them through the wilderness at one o'clock in the morning and caught them after a five-mile chase.

"The greatest difficulty the instructors had with the Indian boys," Father van Quickenborne wrote worriedly, "was in teaching them the necessity and nobility of manual labor." Working in the fields, "squaw work," outraged their pride, and was an upheaval of their entire system of social values. It was only by working in the fields with the boys that the missionaries were able to induce them to perform manual labor. Not more than 30 boys were enrolled in the school in the 7 years of its existence, and because of lack of funds and discouraging results it was closed in 1831.

During February of 1831, Father Theodore Mary De Theux became Superior of the Missouri mission and in. August of that year he established the Jesuit novitiate of St. Stanislaus. The institution was incorporated in 1870.

The SEMINARY LIBRARY (*open only to men by arrangement*) contains many books brought more than a century ago from Europe, as well as rare American imprints. Hanging in the corridors and the public rooms are paintings brought to the United States by priests of the order. Many are said to have been taken from French churches and monasteries during the French Revolution. A small CHAPEL contains the original altar, brought from France during the 1820's, on which is preserved a small, carved wooden figure of the Virgin and Child, said to be of Flemish origin and dating from the sixteenth century.

The CEMETERY south of the quadrangle, with its rows of modest white headstones, contains the graves of many early priests and missionaries. Among those buried here is Father Louis Sebastian Meurin, who said the first Mass in St. Louis, and died at Prairie du Rocher in 1777—his remains were transferred here: Father Charles Felix van Quickenborne, born in Belgium in 1788, who was buried here in 1837; Father Judocus van Assche (1800-77), who brought the Sisters of Loretto to Florissant and served St. Ferdinand's Church as pastor for more than forty years—his parishioners called him *le bon père;* and the most famous of all the Florissant priests, Father Peter John de Smet, Indian missionary and author (*see Literature*), who was born in Belgium in 1801 and ordained priest at Florissant in 1827. Father de Smet's travels totaled more than a quarter of a million miles. He made seven journeys into the Indian country, one to the west coast, nine voyages to Europe, and tours all over the

United States. He was often instrumental in making peace between the Indians and the government. He died at St. Louis University in 1873.

Westward to Wentzville the route follows By-Pass US 40.

PATTONVILLE, 17.1 m. (500 alt., 83 pop.), grew up around a blacksmith shop established here by T. T. Lucas in 1860. The FEE-FEE BAPTIST CHURCH (L) was named for Fee-Fee Creek, upon which the church was first established in 1807 by Thomas R. Musick, the first Baptist minister permanently established in Missouri. The name of the stream had, in turn, come from the nickname of Nicolas Beaugenou, who had settled upon it at an early date. The Church was moved to Pattonville in 1869 when the present red-brick structure was erected.

At 22 m., the route crosses the MISSOURI RIVER, a broad, dun-colored stream, swift and treacherous, with poplar- and willow-shrouded banks, dangerous snags of flood-washed trees, and shifting sand bars. Drifting down the Mississippi in 1673, Marquette and Jolliet heard a great roaring which they thought was produced by a rapid. They discovered instead the mouth of the Missouri. "I have seen nothing more dreadful," Marquette writes. "An accumulation of large, entire trees, branches and floating islands was issuing from the mouth of the River Pekistanoui with such impetuosity that we could not without great danger, risk passing through it." Although these explorers called the stream by the Illini Indian name, meaning "muddy water," later travelers and cartographers called it *Rivière des Missouris,* among other names, for the Missouri Indians who lived near the mouth of the stream at the end of the seventeenth century. The meaning of the word, long the subject of controversy, is probably either "the people of the big canoes," or an Illini Indian corruption of the Sioux name, *Nishudge,* meaning "smoky water."

In early days, a ferry at St. Charles served the needs of travelers. On the St. Louis County shore, on a site near the approach to the modern steel bridge which has replaced the ferry, stood a little French inn, of which Washington Irving, who visited it in 1832, wrote: "With its odd diminutive bowling green, skittle-ground, garden-plots, and arbours to booze in, it reminded us more of the Old World than anything we had seen for many weeks."

ST. CHARLES, 22.5 m. (456 alt., 10,803 pop.) (*see St. Charles*) is at the eastern junction with State 94, a black-topped road.

Right on State 94, crossing a wide tract of alluvial bottom land in the shape of a "V," at the apex of which is the junction of the Missouri and the Mississippi Rivers. The long, shallow, timber-choked lakes and swamps (R), named by the French *Marais du Croche* (crooked swamp) and *Marais Temps Clair* (clear weather swamp), are remnants of the former course of the Missouri. Large numbers of migratory birds find food and shelter here. At 14.3 m. is County H, a graveled road; left here to PORTAGE DES SIOUX, 15.4 m. (437 alt., 254 pop.), overshadowed by the massive Illinois bluffs across the Mississippi. The scattered little houses are grouped around the plaza of St. Francis Church, a Gothic-Revival structure (built 1879). Inland from the village are the COMMON FIELD granted Portage des Sioux by the king of Spain.

Many other Missouri villages had such grants during the French and Spanish regimes, but Portage des Sioux is the only one that has neither sold her land nor leased it for long terms. The rent derived from it provides a substitute for local taxes.

The origin of the name Portage des Sioux is suggested by an Indian legend recorded in Alphonso Wetmore's *Gazetteer of the State of Missouri* (1837): "The Sioux and a tribe of the Missouris being at war, a party of the former descended the Mississippi on a pillaging expedition. The Missouris . . . ambushed themselves at the mouth of the Missouri in considerable numbers, intending to take their enemies by surprise. The Sioux, being more cunning, instead of descending to the mouth of the Missouri, landed at the portage, took their canoes on their backs, and crossed over to the Missouri several miles above."

As the two-mile portage saved a river journey of some twenty-five miles, it acquired military and commercial importance. In 1799 the Spaniards erected a fort there against possible American expansion, and asked François Saucier, then living in St. Charles, to form a settlement. The War of 1812 brought prosperity to the village as the center of military operations against the Indians of Upper Louisiana. The treaty of peace with England, which required individual treaties with Britain's former Indian allies, increased Indian warfare on the Missouri frontier. During the summer of 1815, however, representatives of 19 Indian tribes came to the village to make treaties with the United States commissioners: Governor William Clark of Missouri Territory, Governor Ninian Edwards of Illinois, and Auguste Chouteau of St. Louis. These and similar treaties made at St. Louis the following year ended Indian depredations on the Missouri frontier.

West of St. Charles, By-Pass US 40 and State 94 are united for two miles (*see Tour 1A*).

Between St. Charles and Boonville, the highway follows in general the old route of the Boon's Lick Trail which led westward from St. Louis to Franklin in the Boon's Lick Country. In a larger sense, the Trail was a section of the great transcontinental highway which began at the Atlantic Ocean, and during two centuries of settlement was extended to the Pacific. Originally, the trail to Boon's Lick was probably a poorly defined animal and Indian path which the first immigrants naturally followed because it was the easiest and most direct route across country. In 1816 and 1817, the courts of St. Charles and Howard Counties had the road surveyed, but immigrants still complained that it was difficult to follow, and settlers were asked to mark the forked roads. Weekly stage service between St. Charles and Franklin was established in 1820; before long, as many as four or five coaches left St. Charles daily for the West. In 1821 the line was extended to Fort Osage in Jackson County. Hampton Ball of Jonesburg, Missouri, who drove a Boon's Lick stage in the 1840's, said, "We did not always stick to the road. There were no fences. When one track became too muddy or rough with ruts, we drove out on the prairie or made a new road through the woods."

The procession along the pioneer trail was colorful. Sturdy high-wheeled covered wagons, often brightly painted, bore the loads of furniture, china, and glassware for the new homes. On the wagon sides hung the axe, skillets, and kettles. On the seat at the front, or perhaps in the rear, rode the women and children. The men usually led the oxen or mules. The more affluent had light carriages as well as wagons. Sometimes a group of slaves formed part of the caravan from a Southern plantation, whose owner had been lured West by the promise of cheap land good for tobacco cultivation. Not all rode; many thousands patiently trudged Westward with their worldly goods in a pack. Food and shelter was obtained at the inns and taverns along the route, or from hospitable settlers, many of whom had come from Kentucky and Tennessee.

ST. PETERS, 29.5 m. (445 alt., 305 pop.), which as a parish dates from 1820, was platted as a village in 1868. The Gothic-Revival ALL SAINTS' CHURCH was built in 1874.

At 30.5 m. is a junction with State 79, which leads R. 52 miles to Louisiana (see Tour 15). The highway is a newly completed scenic drive winding among the Mississippi River bluffs.

O'FALLON, 33.5 m. (535 alt., 618 pop.), was founded in 1857 and named for Major John O'Fallon, St. Louis capitalist and director of the old North Missouri Railway. The group of Flemish-type buildings near the center of the village comprises THE CONVENT OF THE CONGREGATION OF THE SISTERS OF THE ADORATION OF THE MOST PRECIOUS BLOOD (open), mother house of an educational order noted for its embroideries.

A red-granite marker (L), 33.9 m., designates the SITE OF FORT ZUMWALT, approximately 300 yards (L) inside FORT ZUMWALT STATE PARK, an undeveloped (1940) 48-acre area. The stone chimney and ruined log room on the site are said to be the remains of a cabin built by Jacob Zumwalt in 1798 and incorporated in Zumwalt's Fort when it was built during the War of 1812.

In 1817, according to local tradition, the cabin became the property of Major and Mrs. Nathan Heald. At the outbreak of the War of 1812, Heald had been in command of Fort Dearborn, on the site of what is now Chicago. Ordered to evacuate, the white residents were scarcely out of sight of the fort when the Indians attacked them and killed practically all. Major and Mrs. Heald were captured, each by a separate band of warriors. The Major escaped, and a friendly Indian chieftain offered to deliver Mrs. Heald to him in exchange for a mule and a bottle of whisky. The trade was agreed upon, and the reunited couple came to St. Charles County, where, in 1831, they were visited by their Indian benefactor.

West of O'Fallon, the highway crosses an agricultural country rich with orchards, fields of wheat, and tree-fringed acres of corn, timothy, alfalfa, and oats. French and—after the Louisiana Purchase in 1803—American settlement began in the river bottoms and spread to the uplands. Between 1830 and 1860, large numbers of German families were induced to settle in St. Charles County by the writings of Gottfried Duden (see Tour 1A).

At 41.5 m., where By Pass US 40 becomes US 40 westwards, is a junction with US 61 (see Tour 7) on the outskirts of WENTZVILLE (675 alt., 752 pop.), which was founded in 1855 and named for the chief engineer of the St. Louis, Kansas City & Northern Railway. During the 1870's, Wentzville was a tobacco manufacturing center. Here George W. Myers, of the firm of Liggett and Myers, R. B. and C. C. Dula, J. T. and John H. Drummond, Paul Brown, and many others later identified with the country's leading tobacco companies started in the business.

WARRENTON, 57.5 m. (943 alt., 1,254 pop.), seat of Warren County since 1835, was named for General Joseph Warren, Revolutionary patriot killed in the Battle of Bunker Hill. CENTRAL WESLEYAN COLLEGE (open), east end of Main Street, has an average enrollment of 140. It was established by a group of German Methodist ministers at Quincy, Illinois, in 1852, and reorganized at Warrenton as the Western Orphan Asylum and Educational Institute in 1864. In 1884 the orphanage was made a separate institution and named Central Wesleyan Orphans Home. Central Wesleyan College offered both a high school and a liberal arts college course until 1939, when it became a two-year junior college. Its seven red-brick buildings are shaded by magnificent trees.

In the Square near the center of Warrenton are the red-brick one-story CIRCUIT CLERK AND RECORDER'S OFFICE, built 1868-9, and the WARREN COUNTY COURTHOUSE, built 1871. The latter, a two-story red-brick structure of Italianate design, has a one-story portico with cast-iron Corinthian columns. A two-story SHERIFF'S OFFICE AND JAIL, built 1908, completes the group.

At Warrenton is a junction with State 47 (see Tour 1A).

The farming village of JONESBURG, 68 m. (900 alt., 422 pop.), was named for James Jones, a North Carolinian, who built a log house here in 1828. Six years later he established the Cross Keys Tavern, a familiar stopping place on the Boon's Lick Trail. A red-granite MARKER (L) commemorates the building. Two granddaughters of Innkeeper Jones live almost directly across the street from the site and have on display many relics of the tavern, including the walnut post-office box. The town was not platted until 1858, when the building of the railroad gave it importance as a shipping point for the adjacent farm community.

A red-granite marker (L), 76.7 m., designates the SITE OF PETER DAVAULT'S TAVERN, built on the Boon's Lick Trail in 1828. The back wing of the present two-story frame building belonged to the original tavern.

The two-story red-brick SYLVESTER MARION BAKER HOUSE (open by permission), 80.4 m. (L), built 1853-55, has a wide central hallway and rooms 18 feet square. During Bill Anderson's pillage of Danville (see below), a group of his men visited the house, searching for Mr. Baker, a United States Marshal and a Union sympathizer. He was not at home. "When Mother told them she had no money in the house," relates Miss Anna Baker, who with her brother, Sam Baker, still lives in the dwelling, "they pulled a feather bed into the middle of the first floor bedroom and set it on fire. One of the raiders, however, returned for a pistol he had left in the house and put out the fire in order to save his weapon. By this accident the house was saved."

DANVILLE, 80.5 m. (800 alt., 63 pop.), is the ghost town of the Boon's Lick Trail. The site was selected in 1834 as the seat of Montgomery County, and soon became a thriving community with a brick courthouse and several taverns. The Civil War, however, brought calamity. On the evening of October 14, 1864, while a group of men stood in the square discussing the posting of pickets, Bill Anderson with about 80 of his guerrillas galloped into the village. The leader swung to one side and shouted, "Fire on them!" Two men were killed; the others scattered. "Some of the citizens, armed, rallied to the block house for defense," but the bushwhackers soon fired the structure, and continued shooting residents thought to be Federal sympathizers. Homes and stores were looted. Eighteen buildings were burned in the village, including the County Clerk's office containing the county records. Danville never recovered. The commercial importance of the Boon's Lick Trail passed when the North Missouri Railroad was built, and Montgomery City, on the railroad to the north, gained Danville's advantages. The county seat was moved there in 1924.

The CHAPEL OF THE DANVILLE FEMALE ACADEMY (L), a weathered Classic-Revival church built in 1859, is all that remains of a school established by Professor James H. Robinson in 1856. At the time of Anderson's raid nearly a hundred girls were attending the school. A group of the bushwhackers ordered them out in their night clothes, but refrained from firing the buildings when several girls called out, "We're rebels!" Soon after the raid, the school was closed. The long redbrick FULKERSON TAVERN (R) was built about 1840. The L-shaped, two-story, gray frame SEE-NUNNELLY TAVERN (R), with its wide paneled door and multi-paned windows, is the only old building on the village square. Built shortly after 1837 by Jacob See, a Virginian, it was a well-known stop on the Boon's Lick Trail. In 1852, See gave the tavern to his son-in-law, Daniel Nunnelly. Between Danville and Mineola, the highway curves sharply to the south, and the prairie gives way to a procession of wooded hills. Below, hidden by the long, curving hillside, is Loutre River.

The village of MINEOLA (Ind., healing waters), 83.5 m. (965 alt., 86 pop.), is a straggling group of frame stores, a stone blacksmith's shop, and a gasoline station or two. The town was not platted until 1879, but the mineral waters of LOUTRE LICK (L), together with the Indian trails along the route of the Loutre River, gave the location an early importance. A grant of land which included the Lick was made to Colonel Nathan Boone by the Spanish government before 1800. In 1812 the Thomas Massey family leased a portion of Boone's grant and built a cabin in the valley. During the spring of the following year, Fox or Pottawatomie Indians attacked the family, and young Harris Massey was shot at his plow in the "little cleared patch." In 1815 the Boone grant was purchased by Major Isaac van Bibber, adopted son of Daniel Boone. With the development of the Boon's Lick Trail,

Van Bibber built a two-and-a-half-story, rambling frame tavern (1821). No early Missouri stopping-place was more renowned. A man of "garrulous and speculative philosophies," the Major once explained to his guests his theory of the recurrence of all events every 6,000 years. The following day, his guests said they would pay their bill when they came around again 6,000 years later. "No," he firmly replied, "You are the same damned rascals who were here 6,000 years ago and went away without paying your bills, and now you have got to pay before you leave."

LOUTRE (Fr., otter) RIVER, 83.7 *m.*, winds between high banks to its union with the Missouri River at Loutre Island. About 1807, some Kentucky families settled on Loutre Island. In February 1812, Fort Clemson was built there for protection against the Indians.

In the vicinity of WILLIAMSBURG, 91.5 *m.* (840 alt., 83 pop.), platted in 1837, the comparatively thin limestone soil is more adapted to grazing than to cultivation. Stock raising and horse breeding are the principal occupations of the Kentucky and Tennessee farmers who have made the region their home.

The name of KINGDOM CITY, 104.4 *m.* (800 alt., 12 pop.), a group of roadside cafés and overnight cabins, perpetuates a famous Callaway County incident. In October 1861, the Pike County militia, under the command of General John B. Henderson, prepared to invade Callaway County, a Confederate stronghold. Callaway's Colonel Jefferson F. Jones assembled three or four hundred old men and boys, and armed them with squirrel rifles, muzzle-loading shotguns, and at least one "cannon" made of a painted log. This show of resistance induced the Union commander to agree to refrain from invading Callaway County, if Jones would promise to disband his force. Both kept the agreement, and this independent action caused Callaway County to be known as "The Kingdom."

Because Callaway County residents were strongly Southern in their sentiments, they were disfranchised. Nonetheless, they elected, and sent across the Missouri to the capital, representative after representative, each of whom was rejected as promptly as he presented his credentials. The procession of would-be assemblymen continued until the franchise was restored.

At Kingdom City is a junction with US 54 (*see Tour 15*). At 124.5 *m.*, US 40 joins US 63 (*see Tour 8*), with which it is united to COLUMBIA, 125.5 *m.* (713 alt., 18,399 pop.) (*see Columbia*).

Section b.   COLUMBIA to KANSAS LINE; 133.8 m.   US 40

West of COLUMBIA, 0 *m.*, US 40 traverses the low hills of historic Howard County to cross the Missouri River at Boonville, where it leaves the valley of the Missouri and crosses the prairie upland to Kansas City.

A red-granite marker (R), 5 *m.*, indicates the SITE OF THE VAN HORN TAVERN, built about 1820 by Ishmael van Horn. Originally an open dog-trot separated the two lower rooms, but when trade increased a long wing was added and the dog-trot was made into a hall. In 1914 the tavern was moved to its present location (300 feet north of the farmhouse), and converted into a barn:

A pile of pressed cane and a low brick "boiling down" vat with a sturdy shelter mark W. W. SWANSTONE'S SORGHUM MILL (*open*), 11.3 *m*. (R), one of many in central Missouri. Nearly every farm has its patch of cane. From late summer through early fall, the slim naked stalks, carefully stripped of leaves, are cut and hauled to the mills to be pressed of their thin, green juice. Originally kettles were used for boiling down the juice, but now a long, shallow metal pan built over a low brick stove makes the work easier. The technique is simple, but variations in boiling time, stirring, and skimming result in distinctively flavored products. "Vintages" and makers have distinct reputations with local epicures, for whom the hot-biscuit-with-plenty-of-butter test is final.

At 14 *m*. is a junction with a graveled road.

Left here to ROCHEPORT, 1 *m*. (596 alt., 396 pop.), a senescent river town. A ferry was established near here by John Gray in 1819, and by 1820 Arnold's Warehouse was in operation. The town was platted in 1825. During the exciting presidential campaign of 1840, the Whigs held a State convention here. Rocheport later suffered from recurrent cholera epidemics, and, during the Civil War, from constant plundering. Bill Anderson and his bushwhackers called it "our capital." The inscription, "H. W. 1844," carved in the cobblestone gutter on the west side of Main Street, near the railroad tracks, marks the high water level of a flood of 1844.

The red-brick ROCHEPORT COMMUNITY HALL, in the northeastern portion of the town, built as the Rocheport Baptist Church in 1860, was recently restored and presented to the community by C. Q. Chandler of Wichita, Kansas, a former Rocheport resident. The ROCHEPORT MILL (R), at the north edge of town, in 1872 replaced an earlier mill destroyed by fire.

At 15.2 *m*. is a junction with a faintly marked dirt road.

Left here a few hundred feet to the old Fayette and Rocheport road, where Federal troops were ambushed by guerrillas. Throughout the Civil War, Federal troops held the strategic central Missouri area, but their authority was often disturbed by Confederate or bushwhacker raids. The dramatic forays, and, at times, barbarous cruelties of Bill Anderson and his men became legendary. Born in Randolph County, Missouri, Anderson moved with his parents and two sisters to Johnson County, Kansas, where it is said he lived quietly as a farmer in 1862. According to Hampton B. Watts, a member of his band, the tragic deaths of Anderson's sisters in Kansas City, after their arrest and imprisonment as Confederate sympathizers, and the murder of his father, caused him to "take up arms against his government." During September 1864, Howard County was his headquarters. Learning that Captain Parks, stationed at Boonville, had crossed the river with 100 men "to capture or to kill Bill Anderson," he deployed his men behind the brow of the hill on the old Rocheport Road. Parks and his men entered the narrow, tree-shadowed lane. When they had passed, the guerrillas, "yelling like Comanches," attacked the rear of the marching column. The rout was complete.

Entering the valley of the Missouri River, the highway curves past a graveled turnout and a red-granite MARKER (L), 22 *m.,* commemorating five of the seven or more forts built by the settlers of the Boon's Lick Country during the War of 1812.

At 24 *m.* is a junction with State 5, a concrete road.

Right on State 5, the route approximates that of a plank road built from New Franklin to the Missouri River about 1856. In 1833 the legislature granted a charter for a lottery to raise funds for a railroad on this mile-long route; successive acts provided that the lottery funds be used for a macadamized or plank road. The road was never kept in repair, but the lottery was a great success. In spite of later anti-lottery laws, the charter was sold to a St. Louis speculator in 1842, and until 1877 the Missouri State Lottery was flamboyantly profitable.

NEW FRANKLIN, 1.3 *m.* (597 alt., 1,144 pop.), lies entirely along the crest of the Missouri River bluffs. Laid out by James Alcorn, a Revolutionary War soldier, in 1828, the town has had its principal growth since the building of the Missouri-Kansas-Texas (Katy) Railroad shops at Franklin Junction, one mile southwest.

North of New Franklin, State 5 winds leisurely through a fertile, rolling upland of apple orchards, corn and wheat fields, rolling green pasturelands, and patches of tobacco. Here a softer inflection, a gently broadened "a," the use of "cousin" more often than "mister," and a generous courtesy, introduce the "little Virginia" that is Howard County, the heart of the Boon's Lick Country.

The white-brick SCOTT-KINGSBURY HOUSE (*open by written application*), 2.9 *m.* (L), was built about 1835 by William Scott. The Kingsbury Orchards (R), producing Jonathan, Grimes Golden, Ben Davis, and Delicious apples, were established in 1871 by the late R. T. Kingsbury. Texas, Oklahoma, and Kansas were early markets. The success of this orchard led to the planting of others along the Missouri River bluffs.

MOUNT PLEASANT CEMETERY (R) is on the site of Mount Pleasant Baptist Church, said to have been organized in 1812.

Almost hidden by giant lilac bushes and maple and honey locust trees at the crest of a high, rolling hill is LILAC HILL (*private*), 11.4 *m.* (L), perhaps the most distinguished house of Federal design in Missouri. Built of red brick, it has tall chimneys at the end of each wing and a gracious fanlight doorway. Kentucky-bred Judge Alfred W. Morrison, who built the house about 1832, held many public offices, among them that of State treasurer (1851-61): he resigned from the latter rather than take the test oath of allegiance to the Union.

FAYETTE, 12.5 *m.* (661 alt., 2,608 pop.), seat of Howard County, is centered by a red-brick courthouse. Organized January 13, 1816, Howard County is known as the "Mother of Counties." From it were formed all or part of 36 Missouri and 10 Iowa counties. Fayette, designated the county seat in 1823, became its political and social, but not its commercial, center. A group of brilliant politicians made it their meeting place—Governors Reynolds, Miller, and Jackson, Judge Abiel Leonard, and General John B. Clark. The county was further strengthened politically by early wealth and a relatively large population. The St. Louis *Evening News* of June 3, 1832, called it a "Delphic region in the matter of politics, especially with the Democratic party of Missouri. . . ." Of Missouri's first 15 governors, 8 lived at one time or another in Howard County.

Fayette became a business center following the decline of Glasgow as a river port and the development of good roads. The character of its stores, as well as its jigsaw trimmed houses, show that the community's principal growth dates from the 1880's.

CENTRAL COLLEGE, north end of Main St., is a co-educational, four-year school. Fifteen brick and stone buildings of modified Classic and Gothic design are at the center of a landscaped 42-acre campus. Successor to a series of Howard County schools which began with Franklin Academy in 1820, Central College was established in 1844 as Howard High School by Reverend William T. Lucky. Within a year it was made co-educational, and came under the control of the Missouri Annual Conference of the Methodist Episcopal Church, South. Enrollment jumped from 80 in 1844 to 312 in 1853, more than 3 times the State university enrollment of that time. Four years later, the high school was reorganized as a college and opened with two separate branches: Central College for men, and Howard Female College, later called Howard-Payne College. In 1922, these were re-united as the present Central College. BRANNOCK HALL, a three-story brick structure, was occupied during the Civil War by Federal troops, who kept their horses on the first floor and used the second and third floors as barracks. The STEPHENS MUSEUM OF NATURAL HISTORY and the HISTORICAL AND ARCHEOLOGICAL MUSEUM (*open by permission; see curator*) are housed on the third floor of Science Hall. The varied collections include a notable group of bird skins and mountings, and the tombstones of Daniel and Rebecca Boone, and of Captain Sarshall Cooper (1763-Apr. 16, 1815), leader of the Boon's Lick settlers during the War of 1812.

MORRISON OBSERVATORY (*open by permission*), west of the campus in Fayette City Park, was established in near-by Glasgow in 1874 with funds given Pritchett School Institute by Mrs. Berenice Morrison-Fuller, now of St. Louis. At that time it was the largest observatory west of the Mississippi River. Pritchett College was closed in 1922, and in 1935 the observatory was moved to Fayette. The JUDGE ABIEL LEONARD HOUSE (*private*), a two-story, red-brick structure with one-story portico and fanlight entranceway, was built about 1835 by Judge Abiel Leonard (1797-1863), lawyer, political leader, and Missouri supreme court judge. Behind the house are the original brick slave cabins.

North of Fayette, at 13.8 *m.* (L), on a wide, shaded lawn, is the two-story white frame CLAIBORNE FOX JACKSON HOUSE (*open by permission*), said to have been built about 1847. Jackson (1806-62), whose three wives were daughters of Dr. John Sappington, served as governor of Missouri (1860-62), and as a leader of Missouri Confederate groups. SYLVAN VILLA (*open by permission*), 23.1 *m.* (R), built by Captain William D. Swinney in 1832, was once the center of a large plantation. Life in the old red-brick house during the period immediately after the Civil War is described in *Plantation Life in Missouri* (Glasgow, Mo., 1939), by Mrs. Berenice Morrison-Fuller, who spent her childhood here.

GLASGOW, 25.4 *m.* (622 alt., 1,490 pop.), sprawls along the ridge and down the sharp slopes of the Missouri River bluffs. Paralleling the river is the main business street, where an occasional building with elaborate brick cornice, iron balcony, and small-paned windows suggests the pre-Civil War days when bales of hemp and barrels of tobacco and apples crowded the wharf. The residential streets are cut deep in the loess bluff slope, and rock and brick retaining walls box the grades.

Named for James Glasgow, a St. Louis merchant, the town was laid out in 1836 after three earlier attempts to establish a river port in the vicinity had failed. Since it was on the border, and its citizens were divided in their sympathies, Glasgow suffered during the Civil War. Federal troops occupying the town surrendered to Generals John B. Clark and Joseph Shelby, October 15, 1864, after a severe bombardment. Two nights later, Bill Anderson rode in, in search of Colonel Benjamin Lewis, a Union sympathizer. "I'll hound him," he had said, "and make an example of him." Colonel Lewis was seized and subjected to a long series of tortures and indignities before he was finally ransomed by a relative. The injuries he received are said to have caused his death.

The decline of river traffic brought an end to Glasgow's early prosperity, although the town has continued to serve the needs of the surrounding community. The change from the old order was marked by the construction of the Chicago & Alton Railroad Bridge, 1878-79. This five-span structure across the Missouri River, built under the supervision of General William Sooy Smith, was the first all-steel railway bridge in the world. Engineers predicted that steel would be too rigid to withstand vibration or would become brittle in cold weather and break. The span held firmly, however, until a new bridge was built in 1922.

The LEWIS LIBRARY BUILDING (*open Tuesday 3-5, Tuesday evening 7-9, Saturday 3-5*) is the oldest building used continuously as a library in Missouri. Built in 1866 and endowed by Colonel Benjamin W. Lewis, Sr., it is a two-story brick structure enclosed by a cast-iron fence with double gates. Curved cast-iron stairways lead to the two reading rooms and library on the second floor. In the library room, furnished with the original shelves, desks, and chairs, is a portrait of Colonel Lewis by A. J. Conant, St. Louis artist.

LEWIS COLLEGE (*open*), SE. corner of Market and Third Sts., a two-story red-brick structure built 1848-49, has a Classic-Revival façade of brick-work pilasters. The first floor was designed for an Odd Fellows hall, and the second floor for the class rooms of the Glasgow Female Seminary. The dormitory adjoining the college was built in 1852. Following the decline of the seminary, the buildings were used for several years by Pritchett School Institute. In 1869 they were sold to Lewis College, which used them until about 1882, when the college was moved to the Colonel Benjamin Lewis mansion, which formerly stood north of the town.

At 25 *m.* on US 40 is a junction with State 87, a graveled road (R), and with an unmarked dirt road (L).

1. Right on State 87 to the SITE OF OLD FRANKLIN (L), 0.5 *m.*, platted on the Missouri River bank in 1816. Five years later the town occupied a unique position as head of the Santa Fe Trail. Within a few years it had a population of several thousand, a town patrol for the regulation of slaves, a library, a race track, an agricultural organization, and a "cultivated society," which included Meredith M. Marmaduke, General Duff Green, General Thomas A. Smith, Claiborne F. Jackson, Nathaniel Beverly Tucker, Dr. John Sappington, and others. George Caleb Bingham (*see Art*) and Kit Carson, hunter, trader, and trapper, knew Franklin as the home of their childhood. Carson, the son of a Revolutionary War soldier, was born in Kentucky. In 1811, at the age of two, he was brought to the Boon's Lick Country. Seven years later his mother apprenticed him to David Workman, a Franklin saddler. It was from Workman's shop that he ran away in 1826 to join a group starting for Santa Fe.

In 1821, a small party of traders, headed by William Becknell, left Franklin for New Mexico. The success of this commercial venture opened the Santa Fe Trail, which was for 50 years the line of American expansion in the West and Southwest. Cheap steamboat transportation at length caused the establishment of outfitting points farther up the Missouri River, and with the rise of Lexington, Independence, and Westport, Franklin's glory began to fade. In 1823 the county seat was moved to Fayette, and 20 years later Franklin had almost entirely disappeared. Alfalfa, wheat, and watermelons now flourish on the approximate location of the "metropolis of the West." A limestone MONUMENT (L), erected by the Missouri Press Association in 1919, commemorates the *Missouri Intelligencer and Boon's Lick Advertiser*, Missouri's first country weekly west of St. Louis, established at Franklin in 1819 (*see Newspapers and Radio*).

At 1.8 *m.* on State 87, which is the approximate route of the old Santa Fe Trail, is a junction (L) with an unmarked graveled road, which the route follows (straight ahead). Along this road hastily armed men and boys rode one morning to join the Confederate forces at Boonville, only to return in the evening defeated. The hemp and cotton crops of earlier days have been replaced by corn, wheat, and alfalfa. Ozark families, displaced from their farms by the construction of the Lake of the Ozarks, have brought new names to the region.

A cluster of broken tombstones at the rounded crest of the bluff (R) marks the COOPER CEMETERY *8.8 m.* Here is the GRAVE OF COLONEL BENJAMIN A. COOPER, patriarchal leader of those who came to settle in the Boon's Lick Country in 1810. From this hilltop may be seen to the south, on the river bank, the SITE OF JOHN HARDEMAN'S GARDEN, destroyed a century ago by the changing course of the river. Famed as perhaps the first garden and plant experiment station in the Mississippi Valley, it consisted of ten acres formally planned with a center maze, ornamental beds, pools, and "shell-lined paths."

At 9 *m.* is the crossroads settlement of PETERSBURG, informally known as "Cooper's Chapel," at the junction with another unmarked graveled road.

1a. Left here 0.9 *m.* to the SITE OF COOPER'S FORT (R), designated by a red-granite marker (L), largest and most important of the Boon's Lick forts during the War of 1812. At the outbreak of the war, Governor Benjamin Howard warned the settlers of possible Indian attacks, and advised them to move near St. Louis. "We have maid our Hoams here," Colonel Cooper wrote in reply, "& all we hav is here & it wud ruen us to Leave now. We be all good Americans, not a Tory or one of his Pups among us, & we hav 2 hundred Men and Boys that will Fight to the last and we have 100 Women & Girls whut will tak there places wh. makes a good force. So we can Defena this Settlement wh. with Gods help we will do. So if we had a fiew barls of Powder and 2 hundred Lead is all we ask." According to the Fayette *Advertiser* of October 15, 1869, Fort Cooper was attacked by a large number of Indians. Captain Braxton Cooper and the few men who were in the fort at the time debated the possibility of sending to Fort Hempstead, some six miles to the east, for help. Since none of the men could be spared, Mildred Cooper asked her father if she could go. He consented, although the circle of Indians seemed impregnable, and lifting her to the saddle, asked if there was anything she wanted. "Only a spur, father," was her reply. The spur was produced, the gate of the fort drawn open, and "like the arrow-strung bow, Milly and her good steed flew beyond its portals, and away in the deep and intricate forest she sped on her mission." Her sudden appearance surprised the Indians; the shrill war whoop "rang from a hundred savage throats, the sharp, clear report of as many rifles." Hours passed. That Mildred had been killed seemed certain. Then "the shout of friends was heard above the din of strife, the firing rapidly ceased," and the rescue party appeared before the fort, with Mildred at their head.

1b. Ahead from Petersburg 0.1 *m.* on the unmarked graveled road to a county road, which the route follows (L) 1.9 *m.* to another unmarked graveled road; right here 1.2 *m.* to the WALTER MUNDY FARM (L) (*open upon request*) on which is the BOON'S LICK SPRING. The brackish salt waters of the Lick, bubbling from surface springs, have stained the bare earth a grayish white. The curving hillside (R) is shaded with giant trees; near the top is a broken monument to the memory of "Joseph L. Morrison, son of Major James Morrison of St. Charles, Born Jan. 9, 1817, and died August 10, 1833." Local tradition claims young Morrison fell into a kettle of boiling salt water and was scalded to death.

The springs were included in a Spanish grant of 400 arpents to James Mackey, May 21, 1797, who surveyed the claim in 1804. It is believed that Daniel Boone visited the springs soon after 1800 and made salt here, and that the name, Boon's Lick, was given for that reason. Whether or not this be true, it is known that his sons, Nathan Boone and Daniel Morgan Boone, together with the Morrisons of St. Charles, bought a dozen 20-gallon salt kettles at St. Louis in 1806, transported them to the Lick, and began the manufacture of salt. With these, and with 40 additional kettles bought the following year, 6 men were able to extract 100 bushels of salt a week. A keelboat brought supplies every two weeks and returned to St. Louis with the salt. Indian Phillips, thought to have been one of Mason's gang of robbers from the lower Mississippi, supplied game for the salt boilers. William Becknell was in charge of the operations here before the beginning of his overland journey to Sante Fe in 1821.

Cheap transportation destroyed the Boon's Lick salt market. Thirty years of spasmodic attempts failed to revive the industry. Eventually, W. N. Marshall, said to have been "a sea faring man," suggested that the springs be dammed to form a lake in which oysters and salt water fish could be raised for Middle Western markets. Unfortunately for local epicures, the venture collapsed because—this was the reason given—"no fresh water could be found near by in which the oysters could spawn." The low mound near the springs is a relic of the "oyster plan."

2. Left from US 40 on the unmarked dirt road to RIVERCENE (*open 8-5; adm. 25¢*), 0.3 m. (L), a three-story, gray-brick house with mansard roof and cast-iron trim, built by Captain Joseph Kinney (1810-92), who made a fortune from freight and passenger steamboats. Kinney began his river career with the building of the *W. H. Russell* in 1856—the realization of a dream toward which he had worked as teacher, surveyor, pork packer, and shoe merchant. Other boats followed, many among the finest on the Missouri River. When Kinney built the first stern-wheel boat he was called a fool, and insurance companies refused him coverage. In 1869 he was again called a fool for building his mansion so close to the river that his boats could dock at the front gates. River men nick-named the house "Kinney's Folly," and predicted that the river would soon claim it.

The house contains its original furniture, glass, and china, and a notable group of portraits by A. J. Conant and George Caleb Bingham. The parlor appears much as it did in 1869, except that the wallpaper was replaced in 1882. Mrs. Cora Hurt and Mrs. Margaret Ravenel, daughters of Captain Kinney, maintain the house as a museum.

US 40 crosses the Missouri River and enters BOONVILLE, 26.5 m. (675 alt., 6,089 pop.), built on the crest of the bluffs and encircled by hills that mark the eastern end of the prairie upland. In the residential section are ante bellum brick residences with generous rooms, wide halls, and modest Classic-Revival details; flamboyant houses of the "gingerbread" era; and modern cottages and bungalows. Boonville's first settler was the widow, Hannah Cole, who, with her nine children, built a cabin on the bluffs in the early spring of 1810. Neighboring settlers enlarged and palisaded the subsequent settlement as a fort during the War of 1812. When Cooper County was organized in 1818, Boonville became the county seat.

Because of its location on the Missouri River at the point where the western plains break south and east to form the Ozark upland, Boonville was from the first the port of entry and market for southwestern Missouri. White-hooded prairie schooners creaked up the long cobblestone hill from the river ferry, and turned westward for the overland journey. Tall brick and frame warehouses lined Main Street and the water front. Very shortly, the town had private schools, churches, an annual fair (the first State Fair), and a Thespian Society. The pattern of social, religious, and economic life developed by the early Kentucky and Virginia settlers was altered by a large German immigration between 1840 and 1870.

The first land battle of the Civil War was fought four miles below Boonville June 17, 1861. State troops commanded by the Confederate Colonel, John S. Marmaduke, were routed by Federal forces under

Captain Nathaniel Lyon. Military historians consider that this victory was important in preserving Missouri for the Union. With the coming of peace, river trade declined when railroad development (which Boonville business men had refused to encourage) spread elsewhere, sapping the back-country markets. Eventually, local industries and modern highways revived a portion of the town's earlier trade importance.

A formal group of red-brick buildings around an open court forms the center of KEMPER MILITARY SCHOOL (*open*), Center Ave. and Third St., which offers high school and junior college courses. Founded in June 1844, by Frederick T. Kemper, it is the oldest boys' school and military academy west of the Mississippi River. The alumni includes the late Will Rogers, whose student pranks are among the many school legends. The annual enrollment numbers about 450. Dress parade is held each Sunday at 2 p.m., weather permitting. THESPIAN HALL, NE. corner of Main and Vine Sts., now known as the Lyric Theatre, is a two-story structure of Greek-Revival design with a four-columned Doric portico. Built 1855-57 by the Thespian Society, a frontier dramatic group established about 1838 (*see The Theater*), it is said to be the oldest surviving theater building west of the Allegheny Mountains. During the Civil War, the building was fortified and used as a military supply station, barracks, hospital, and prison.

CHRIST EPISCOPAL CHURCH, NE. corner Vine and Fourth Sts., a brick structure of Gothic-Revival design, was built in 1846 and is thought to be the oldest surviving Episcopal church west of the Mississippi River. In WALNUT GROVE CEMETERY, in the southeastern part of Boonville, a limestone obelisk marks the GRAVE OF DAVID BARTON (1783-1837). Barton, a native of Tennessee, came to Missouri before 1812, served during the War of 1812, held various offices under the Territorial government, and was elected president of Missouri's Constitutional Convention of 1820. Elected United States Senator by this convention, he made possible the election of Thomas Hart Benton as his colleague. Later, he and Benton became estranged. Barton served in the United States Senate from 1821 to 1831, and in the State senate during a portion of the session 1834-35. Late in 1836 he came to Boonville, and on September 28, 1837, died hopelessly insane at the home of his friend, William Gibson. Barton's original monument is now preserved near the Thomas Jefferson monument on the campus of Missouri University in Columbia. The present monument was erected by the State of Missouri in 1856.

The SENATOR GEORGE G. VEST HOUSE (*private*), 745 Main St., originally a one-and-a-half-story red-brick building, has been altered by the addition of a second story and a modern porch. The interior woodwork and fluted pilasters flanking the entrance, however, are original details of Classic-Revival design. Vest (1830-1904), a native of Frankfort, Kentucky, came to Georgetown, Pettis County, Missouri, in 1854. Two years later he moved to Boonville. In 1860 he was elected as Representative to the Missouri general assembly, where he played an important part in the seccession activities of the Jackson legislature. Vest served in the Confederate Congress 1862-65 as both representative and senator. After the fall of the Confederacy, he returned to Missouri to resume the practice of law, first at Sedalia, and later at Boonville. He moved to Kansas City in 1877 (*see Tour 4, Warrensburg*).

The SITE OF THE SECOND BATTLE OF BOONVILLE, east end of Morgan St., is a long river-bluff slope, at the crest of which is St. Joseph's Hospital. Hannah Cole's cabin (*see above*), which served as the first courthouse when Howard County was organized in 1816, was on this hill. During the 1850's, the Boonville Agricultural Fair, which from 1853 to 1855 was also the State fair, was held here. Along the ridge can still be traced the line of trenches used in the Second Battle of Boonville, September 13, 1861. In 1879, John I. West, a tramp who had killed a man for 35¢, was hanged here in the last Cooper County public hanging.

The MISSOURI TRAINING SCHOOL FOR BOYS, E. Morgan St., an informal group of red-brick buildings in a landscaped setting, was opened in 1889 as a correctional school for boys under 21 years of age; recently, the age limit has been reduced to 17. Without walls or cells, the school is operated largely on the honor system. The institution cares for 500 boys.

The KURTZ MEMORIAL DOGS, at the entrance of the high school (L), SE. corner Main and Locust Sts., are of cast metal, and were given by Jay Gould to Joseph L. Stephens, Boonville banker in the 1860's. The dogs stood before the old Boonville National Bank Building until 1937, when they were moved to their present site as a memorial to Frederick Kurtz and his wife. Kurtz was janitor of the Boonville Central School for more than 50 years.

West of Boonville, US 40 leaves the river and crosses the upland that becomes the great western plains. Originally, the region, almost treeless, was carpeted with grass and flowers.

The DAVIS-JOHNSON-PATRICK COMMISSION CO. SALES PAVILION (*regular sales each Wed.; horse and mule sales each Thurs., Sept. to March*), 31.5 m. (L), is a long white frame structure with a green roof. The weekly sales here, averaging $15,000, are said to be the largest of their kind in Missouri.

At 34 m. is a junction with State 41, a black-topped road.

Right on State 41 across the Lamine River to an unmarked graveled road, 1.1 m.

Right here 0.7 m. to a dirt road; R. 0.8 m. to a farm lane; L. 0.3 m. to a one-story, white frame farmhouse. Northwest of the house, on the crest of a high bluff above the Missouri River, is an Indian mound containing the marked GRAVE OF GENERAL WILLIAM HENRY ASHLEY (1778-1838), a prominent fur trader, who came to Missouri in 1803. Ashley's exploits in the Rocky Mountains brought him fame. Keelboats and steamboats were named in his honor, and "Ashley Beaver" came to signify an extra-fine quality of fur. He was elected lieutenant governor of Missouri in 1820, and between 1831 and 1837 served as a member of Congress. He died March 26, 1838, and by his own request was buried here, on land he had purchased two years before.

Ahead on State 41 to ARROW ROCK, 12.5 m. (650 alt., 247 pop.), its white frame and dull red-brick houses peacefully lodged against a green hillside. Arrow Rock has been a Sante Fe Trail town, a river port for overland commerce, a county seat, and the meeting place of men significant in the history of the West. According to legend, the name Arrow Rock is derived from a contest between a group of young Indian warriors who assembled on a sand bar opposite the cliff to compete with bow and arrow for the hand of the chief's daughter. The winner shot his arrow so far that it lodged in the bluff. The site was a popular rendezvous with the Indians, for at this point an ancient East-West transcontinental trail crossed the Missouri. The bluff was named *Pierre à Flèche* (Fr., arrow rock) as early as 1723, when Dumont de Montigny mapped the area. William Clark noted it as a good site for a fort when he came through in 1808. When Fort Osage was abandoned in 1813, the post was moved to Arrow Rock and trade continued during the winter of 1813-14, with George C. Sibley as factor. When the danger of Indian attack made the site untenable, Sibley and his men returned to St. Louis.

After the peace treaty of 1815, Arrow Rock was important as a river crossing on the overland route to the West. Ferry service was begun about 1817, and in 1819 the Cooper County court ordered a road established from Arrow Rock to Fort Osage.

On May 23, 1829, a town was laid out and called New Philadelphia, until the derision of the inhabitants for such an imposing name caused the older one to be resumed in 1833. Growth was slow, and when, in the spring of 1830, John Beauchamp Jones (*see Literature*) established the first store here, the village site was a tangle of "bushes, brushes and trees." The only residents were a Canadian-French employee of General Ashley's fur trading company, who, with his American wife, occupied an 8- by 10-foot "mud shanty," and "an amiable" family from Virginia, living in a log house with their slaves in a row of huts. As the back country was settled, the town became a thriving river port. For a few months during the period 1839-40, Arrow Rock was the temporary county seat. The one-and-a-half-story log house, now weatherboarded, which served as the COURT HOUSE (*open by permission*), near the southwest corner of Main and Third Sts. has been relatively unchanged during the past century.

The OLD TAVERN (*adm. 25¢, except for dinner and overnight guests*), on the main street, was built by Joseph Huston about 1834. To the original four rooms with walnut floor boards, generous open fireplaces, paneled doors, and ladder-like stairways to second-floor bedrooms, other rooms have been added at different periods. Present furnishings include walnut, maple, and stenciled chairs, and canopied beds, many of them more than a century old. The tap room, believed to have housed the store which Huston operated, contains a collection of portraits, firearms, and personal objects associated with Dr. John Sappington, Governor Meredith M. Marmaduke, and other early residents of the community. Above the tap room, and of equal size, was the ballroom, now divided into bedrooms, in which public meetings and dances were held. During the 1850's, Miss Amanda Crutcher, lately arrived from the East, attended a dance here. It was fashionable at that time for ladies to make several changes of dress during an evening's entertainment. Miss Amanda's changes from black brocaded silk to pink tarlton, to yellow tarlton, to white, and, when departing, to a blue cloth traveling dress, made her the belle of the evening and helped win her a husband.

On the roof of the tavern, beneath a curiously designed weathervane in the form of a fish, is a bell said to have been taken from a river steamboat more than eighty years ago. Ordinarily, its brisk, clear tones ring for tavern meals, but at moments of civic emergency its voice rallies the townspeople.

The tavern is at the entrance to ARROW ROCK STATE PARK (*picnicking, shelter house*), where 32 acres have been landscaped and made accessible by graveled scenic drives. ARROW ROCK SPRING provided a water supply for Indian tribes, travelers to the Far West, and early villagers. The gray two-story frame ARROW ROCK ACADEMY BUILDING (*open; inquire at tavern*) housed a girls' school established in 1842. It is now partially furnished with ante-bellum objects. The one-room ARROW ROCK JAIL, said to have been built in 1871, has formidable limestone walls and a heavy iron door of open grille-work. Legend says the only prisoner kept in it "hollered and raised such a racket they just had to let him out." In the park is a white, one-and-a-half-story brick house, originally the GEORGE CALEB BINGHAM HOUSE (*open; inquire at tavern*) (*see Art and the Crafts*). Bingham purchased the lot in July of 1837, a year after his marriage, from Claiborne F. Jackson. He apparently built the house soon after, but occupied it only during brief visits to Arrow Rock. He sold it May 1, 1845. The house has been purchased by the State and reconstructed to appear as it did during Bingham's time. It has its orig-inal floors, paneled doors, and carved walnut mantelpiece, but is unfurnished (1941).

Left from Arrow Rock 0.7 *m.* on an unmarked graveled road to ARROW ROCK CEMETERY, in which are buried relatives of Bingham, and Joseph Huston (1784-1865), builder of the tavern. South of the cemetery is the WILLIAM B. SAPPINGTON HOUSE (*open by arrangement*), 3.7 *m.* (L), a red-brick mansion with a two-story portico. Built in 1844 by a son of Dr. John Sappington, it is an important example of Classic-Revival architecture in Missouri. Dr. John Sappington, who lived here with his son during the closing years of his life, came to Missouri from Tennessee about 1817. He early experimented with quinine, then little used, as a treatment for malaria, the most common of frontier diseases, and his "Sappington anti-fever pills" achieved a national sale. He wrote a vigorous book on *The Theory and Treatment of Fevers,* published at Arrow Rock in 1844, and considered by medical authorities an important contribution to American medicine. The doctor's activities also in-cluded Western trading ventures, large-scale farming, and politics. He was the father-in-law of Meredith Miles Marmaduke, governor of Missouri in 1844, and of Claiborne Fox Jackson, governor 1860-62, and the grandfather of John S. Marmaduke, governor 1884-87. He was also the great-great-great-grandfather of the Hollywood actress, Ginger Rogers.

According to legend, Dr. Sappington purchased his coffin several years before his death and kept it under his bed, with apples and nuts in it for his visiting grandchildren. It is also said that when Claiborne F. Jackson, twice married to Sappington girls, asked the doctor for the hand of his third daughter, the doctor replied: "You can take her, but don't come back after the old woman."

Southwest of the Sappington house is the SAPPINGTON CEMETERY (*inquire locally route and road condition*), enclosed with a stone wall topped by a cast-iron fence. Here are buried Dr. John Sappington (1776-1856), his wife Jane (1783-1852), and their numerous relatives, including the two Missouri Governors, M. M. Marmaduke (1791-1864) and Claiborne F. Jackson, and their families.

At 35.3 *m.* on US 40 is a junction with an unmarked graveled road.

Left here to CHOUTEAU SPRINGS (*adm. 10¢, swimming 25¢*), 0.9 *m.* (R). Giant sycamore and oak trees shade the narrow valley whose mineral-water springs were used for medicinal purposes before 1840. The springs and 30,000 arpents of land in the vicinity were granted by the Osage Indians to Pierre Chouteau of St. Louis, March 19, 1792. "As thou hast, since a long time," the grant reads, "fed our wives and our children . . . we do give it to thee, and no one can take it from thee, either today or ever . . . and if some nation disturbs thee, we are ready to defend thee." The grant was con-firmed by Spanish authority in 1799. The United States recognized it in the 1830's, and shortly afterwards William Henry Ashley purchased the land at $1.25 an acre. The springs were soon popular in central Missouri, and by the time of the Civil War a hotel had been built on the hill overlooking the valley. For many years "Uncle" Johnny Whistletrigger, with his sad-faced horse and ramshackle wagon, supplied Boonville families with "Shoooo-toe watah . . . jegs o' Shoooo-toe watah . . . !"

Muddy LAMINE RIVER, 38.5 *m.*, is the largest stream between the Osage and the Kaw. In 1714, Sieur de Bourgmond, who later established Fort D'Orleans on the Missouri, wrote that the "Indians take lead from a mine" on the river. This is thought to be the origin of the name Lamine. In 1720 maps of the region called it Rivière de la Mine. On June 8, 1804, Lewis and Clark found "the Mine river . . . navigable for boats eighty or ninety miles. . . . It forks about five or six leagues from the Missouri and at the point of junction are some very rich salt springs. . . . The French report that lead ore has been found on different parts of the river." The salt springs and lead mines were worked for a time by early Boon's Lick settlers.

West of the river the upland prairie rolls monotonously. Generally fertile and well drained, the area is devoted to corn and wheat, cattle, mules, and hogs. Of the native grasses and flowers which made "these immense natural meadows like a rich carpet," only a few of the more vigorous types remain.

At 52.5 *m.* is a junction with US 65 (*see Tour 9*). At 64.5 *m.*, is a junction with black-topped State 127.

Left here to SWEET SPRINGS, 1 *m.* (675 alt., 1,413 pop.), once known as the "Saratoga of the West." John Yantes, a Presbyterian minister, settled here in 1826, and in 1848 laid out a town. In 1876 Darwin W. and Leslie Marmaduke, wealthy sons of Colonel Meredith M. Marmaduke, became interested in Sweet Springs; the following year they built a hotel with accommodations for more than 400 guests. When country spas went out of fashion, the hotel was converted for a brief period into the Marmaduke Military Academy (1893). In 1906 the building was burned. The SWEET SPRING, in a tree-shaded park at the south edge of the town, flows seven gallons a minute; the lake near the center of the park is fed by an artesian well flowing 350 gallons a minute. The SWEET SPRINGS CREAMERY (*open*), Bridge and Miller Sts., is one of several co-operative creameries in this area.

CONCORDIA, 72.5 *m.* (782 alt., 1,077 pop.), is a German community of prim white homes with peony, rose, and dahlia gardens in front, and neat orchards and vegetable plots in the rear. Concordia's first settler was Heinrich Dierking, called *Troester,* or Comforter, who came to Lafayette County about 1839. Relatives and friends followed, and the farming community slowly developed schools and churches. The town was platted in 1868. The Concordia Band, which gives Saturday evening concerts during the summer, and the three-day Concordia Fall Festival, held in September, are characteristic of the community and its interests. The CONCORDIA CREAMERY COMPANY (*open*), west end of Second St., established in 1892, is the oldest co-operative creamery in this part of Missouri. The form of organization makes it possible to pay the individual farmer several cents a pound more for butter fat than is paid by commercial creameries. ST. PAUL'S COLLEGE (L), occupying a 20-acre tract bordering US 40, was opened as a Lutheran theological academy for young men on January 3, 1884.

In 1905 a junior college was added to the four-year high school course. In 1939, besides the theological students, 110 lay students were enrolled. At 81.5 *m.* is a junction with State 13, a concrete road.

Right here to City Route 13, 5.6 *m.;* R. on this road, through HIGGINS-VILLE, 6.6 *m.* (800 alt., 3,533 pop.), the self-designated "seed corn capital of the United States," to the CONFEDERATE HOME OF MISSOURI (R), 8 *m.,* established in 1891 by former Confederate soldiers, and deeded to the State in 1897. Wide-balconied dormitories house 36 Confederate veterans and widows of Confederate veterans.

ODESSA, 93.2 *m.* (932 alt., 1,881 pop.), platted by A. R. Patterson and John Kirkpatrick in 1878, after the construction of the Chicago and Alton Railroad through this area, was called Kirkpatrick until its founder objected, saying: "It never will amount to anything and I don't want it named for me." T. B. Blackstone, president of the railroad, suggested the name of Odessa, explaining that the gently rolling wheat fields reminded him of the country near Odessa, Russia. Contrary to Kirkpatrick's expectations, the town has become an important agricultural trading and shipping point. A local canning company has operated since 1890.

West of LAKE VENITA (*cabins, meals, boats, fishing*), 93.7 *m.,* are hillside apple orchards, and bluegrass pastures.

SNI-A-BAR FARMS, 106.8 *m.* (*open; apply at manager's office*), consists of several groups of white, red-roofed farm buildings near the center of 2,700 acres in the green Sni-A-Bar Creek Valley. Established under the terms of William Rockhill Nelson's will, the farm is to be used for 30 years for the "material and social betterment of the public and particularly the people of Sni-A-Bar township, and to promote and instill a better knowledge among them . . ." of stock breeding and raising. Mr. Nelson began experimenting with shorthorn cattle, and by selective breeding showed, over a period of years, how an average herd of cattle can be improved.

At 111 *m.,* US 40 becomes a four-lane highway.

Four stone posts form the gateway to the SALVATION ARMY CAMP (*open*), 111.2 *m.* (R), founded in 1924. Indigent mothers and children from Jackson County, in groups of approximately 140, enjoy ten-day vacations here during the summer. The camp, under the supervision of the Salvation Army, is supported by the Community Chest and the Penny Ice baseball game. White frame cottages and a dining hall are surrounded by campgrounds which contain a swimming pool, ball diamond, and other recreational facilities.

US 40 enters Kansas City on the east on Linwood Blvd.; R. on The Paseo; L. on Admiral Blvd.

KANSAS CITY, 128.8 *m.* (748 alt., 399,178 pop.) (*see Kansas City*).

Continuing in Kansas City on Admiral Blvd., L. on the Sixth Street Trafficway, US 40 crosses the KANSAS LINE at 133.8 *m.,* in Kansas City, Kansas.

Tour 1A

Junction with US 40—Augusta—Warrenton; 57.2 *m.,* State 94, State 47.

Graveled road, except asphalt strip between junction with US 40 and junction with County N.

From its junction with US 40 (*see Tour 1*), 0 *m.,* 1.6 miles west of St. Charles, State 94 branches southward to the Missouri River. The land through which the road passes varies from rolling prairie and wooded valleys to Missouri River bottomland. Time and the industry of the people have combined to create here a rich and unusual landscape. Settled first in the more accessible valleys by the French, and developed by Anglo-Americans under the leadership of the Boone family, the region has been coaxed and groomed to an abundant agricultural maturity by the German followers of Gottfried Duden. Fields of alfalfa, wheat, and corn stretch between tree-shaded fences and creeks. Many of the farmhouses, built before the Civil War, are one-and-a-half-story red-brick cottages with long, sloping, shingled roofs that end abruptly over generous porches with white posts and slender spindled balustrades. Occasional red-brick country schoolhouses, many of them a half-century old, nestle in the shadow of tall-spired churches.

FRIEDENS CHURCH (R), 1.4 *m.,* a red-brick structure of late Gothic-Revival design built in 1867, occupies the site of one of the first two Evangelical churches in Missouri—the other being the Femme Osage church in Warren County. Both were established in the winter of 1834-35 by Hermann Garlichs (1807-65), a young German of wealth and education who had settled on the frontier as a gentleman-farmer. When his neighbors requested that he serve as their minister, he returned to Germany and was ordained. For 13 years he was pastor of the German communities in St. Charles and Warren Counties.

At 8.2 *m.* is a junction with County N, a graveled road.

Right here to a granite marker that indicates the SITE OF KOUNTZ FORT (R), 0.3 *m.,* a log structure built near here by John and Nicholas Kountz (or Coontz) about 1812. The two men, Germans, are said to have come to St. Charles County about 1790. After the War of 1812, Nicholas kept a tavern on the Boon's Lick Trail, at the old fort, where he, "though 'rough and wicked,' hospitably entertained the preachers."

COTTLEVILLE, 1 *m.* (517 alt., 136 pop.), was established by Lorenzo Cottle in 1840. The town was settled very largely by German immigrants during the period 1840-60. The scattering of stores and houses along the old road is dominated by the substantial spires of St. Joseph's Church (Roman Catholic) and St. John's Evangelical Church. Long, gray frame houses with friendly stoops and benches hold a suggestion of leisurely summer evening conversations.

West of the junction, State 94 continues through the rolling upland. The courses of adjacent country lanes are marked by cedar trees; white leghorn chickens roam the alfalfa fields; deep-red barns add color to the hills.

WELDON SPRING, 12.3 *m.* (470 alt., 100 pop.), named for John and Joseph Weldon, early residents, and settled by German families about 1849, is at the eastern edge of Howell's Prairie, an irregular upland tract which takes its name from John Howell, a North Carolinian who settled here about 1800. Howell built a band mill and a cog mill on his land, and, as these were the first in the community, his farm became a local meeting place. Musters and military drills were held here, and Indian agents stopped for supplies.

At 12.5 *m.* is a junction with US 61 (*see Tour 7*).

Westward, the highway again follows the curve of the upland, where the country is broken by deep creek valleys. DEFIANCE, 21.5 *m.* (470 alt., 90 pop.), introduces the Boone country.

Right from Defiance on an unmarked graveled road to a junction with a similar road, 0.8 *m.;* L. here 0.3 *m.* and R. again 0.3 *m.* to a junction with another graveled road; L. 0.3 *m.* on this road, and left again, winding along the valley of the Femme Osage Creek, to the two-and-a-half-story, stone NATHAN BOONE HOUSE (*private*), 3.2 *m.* (L). The house, of "blue" limestone quarried on the farm, is well placed on a gentle rise above the creek and near a good spring. In design and construction it is similar to other local buildings of the period before 1820. A central hall and three rooms are on the first floor, and two rooms and a hall on the second. The woodwork is walnut throughout; Daniel Boone is said to have carved the seven mantels with their sunburst details. Although Daniel Boone was never a permanent resident, he often visited here with his son. He occupied a little room to the right of the main hall on the first floor, in the northwest corner of the building. It was partitioned off from the kitchen-dining room, and was entered by a single door opening into the larger room. Boone's last visit was in the summer of 1820, when he came to recover from a severe attack of fever. Here, on September 26, after a three days' illness, he died.

Northwest of the house is the JUDGMENT ELM, the giant tree beneath which Daniel Boone is said to have held court as syndic of the Femme Osage district during the Spanish regime.

Nathan Boone, the youngest and perhaps the most distinguished son of Daniel, was born in Kentucky in 1781, and at the age of 18 followed his father to St. Charles County, bringing with him his 16-year-old bride, Olive van Bibber. He was a major in the Missouri Mounted Rangers during the War of 1812, served as a delegate to the Constitutional Convention of 1820, fought in the Black Hawk War in 1832, and then entered the regular army as captain of the First United States Dragoons, commanded by Colonel Henry Dodge. After serving in many Western campaigns, he retired in 1853 to the home he had built in Greene County (*see Tour 5*). There he died in 1856.

MATSON, 23.3 *m.* (479 alt., 65 pop.), is at a junction with an unmarked dirt road.

Right here to the entrance to the DANIEL BOONE FARM (*private*), 0.2 *m.* South of the two-story, white-brick Abraham G. Matson farmhouse, which dates from about 1840, is the supposed site of the Daniel Boone cabin. The kitchen door of the farmhouse, of thick walnut planks with long, hand-wrought iron hinges, is said to have come from the cabin. A similar door, with similar hinges, is set in the stone wall of a springhouse, said to date from the period of Boone's ownership. Spring water, flowing through a shallow basin in the floor of the old building, serves as a primitive refrigerant for milk, eggs, and butter kept in jars and crocks.

In the autumn of 1799, Daniel Boone, then in his sixty-fifth year, his wife Rebecca, and their younger children came to St. Charles County. Heavily in debt, his Kentucky lands lost because of defective titles, Boone had been drawn to Missouri as much by the promise of Spanish grants and honors as by the favorable accounts of his son, Daniel Morgan Boone, who had preceded him in 1796. He settled on this farm, a Spanish grant of 1,000 arpens (845 acres). Later, an additional 10,000 arpens were granted him. On July 11, 1800, Boone was appointed syndic (judge) of the Femme Osage district, a position he held until the cession of Louisiana to the United States in 1804. Under Spanish law, this appointment placed him in more or less complete administrative charge of all matters civil and military.

Boone's title to the larger tract of land was never cleared, but Congress, by a special act in 1814, confirmed his title to the 1,000-arpen claim. His Kentucky creditors immediately pounced upon him, and in 1815 he was obliged to sell his property to satisfy part of their claims. The remainder he paid off over a period of years by the sale of furs. His huge canoe, with housing over the cargo, was a familiar sight on the Missouri River. Following the death of his wife, Rebecca Bryan Boone, in 1813, Boone hunted and trapped, or lived with his children in St. Charles and Warren Counties. In 1819, Chester Harding visited the old hunter at Callaway Post to paint his portrait. He found Boone alone in a cabin, roasting a steak of venison on a ramroad. Harding asked him if he had ever been lost during his wanderings. "No," Boone replied, "I was never lost, but I was bewildered once for three days."

West of Matson the highway turns abruptly from the bottom, twists to the crest of a high bluff, and then follows a ridge to a junction with the Augusta Road, 28.8 m.

Left on this graveled road to AUGUSTA, 0.6 m. (621 alt., 252 pop.), whose low, white frame houses, with green shutters and stoops, are scattered along the abrupt Missouri River bluffs. Laid out in 1836 by Leonard Harold, it was first named Mount Pleasant, then changed to Augusta in honor of Harold's wife. The many followers of Duden who settled in the neighborhood made Augusta a center of German cultural traditions for many years. In 1856 the Augusta *Harmonieverein* was established, "to cheer up life through vocal and instrumental music as well as by promoting social intercourse through friendship and congeniality." Two years later, a library was organized. Today, the village is a small, neat trading center and shipping point for near-by German farm families.

DUTZOW, 36.9 m. (491 alt., 73 pop.), almost hidden in its narrow valley, was founded by the Berlin Emigration Society in 1832. The settlers included the Von Martels, Herr von Bock, and other aristocratic and professional men, who brought with them a rich background of liberal German culture. In 1834 they were joined by Paul Follenius, Friedrich Muench, and other members of the Giessen Society. At the eastern limits of the village is a junction with the graveled Lake Creek Road.

Right here to the SITE OF THE GOTTFRIED DUDEN HOUSE (L), 0.9 m., on a low hillside. Here lived the man who was largely responsible for the German settlement in Missouri. As Proctor of State for the district of Muehlheim, Germany, he became interested in social problems, and decided that "most of the evils from which the inhabitants of Europe and especially of Germany are suffering, arise from the effects of an excess of population . . . and all the endeavors of the intellectual forces of society must necessarily end in making the state nothing but a great prison-house." Obtaining a furlough for further study, Duden, together with his friend Louis Eversmann, an agriculturalist, came to Missouri in October 1824. Duden lived in Warren County until his return to Germany in 1827. He made a careful study of the frontier, and his observations, published in 1829, were widely circulated in Germany. His reports were highly colored by his favorable impression of America, but they were written with a keen insight into German conditions and influenced many Germans to emigrate to Missouri between 1830 and 1870.

The FRIEDRICH MUENCH HOUSE (*open by permission*), 1.2 *m.* (R), is a gray, one-and-a-half-story building near a buff-colored stone barn and a modern, white farmhouse. Friedrich Muench (1798-1881), a Protestant Lutheran minister, organized, partly from his church members in Germany, the *Giessener Gesellschaft* (Giessen Society) for emigration to Missouri. The group arrived in St. Louis in 1832, and there disbanded. Many, including their leader, came to Warren County, and developed farms in the region where a decade earlier Duden had lived. Muench, the political as well as spiritual leader of his community, served both as minister to his congregation and as State senator. He wrote many books recommending German settlement in Missouri, as well as volumes and pamphlets urging racial and religious toleration.

The house, purchased by Muench, consists of three rooms. The two end rooms are of American horizontal-log construction. The connecting room was added later by a German owner. It is of half-timbered construction, with the exposed portions between the timbers plastered with a mud-and-lime mixture over a split-hickory, basket weave frame. The sloping roof projects several feet beyond the wall of the building (*see Architecture*).

At 37.5 *m.* is a junction with State 47, a graveled road, which leads south (L) four miles to Washington (*see Tour 4*). The tour continues north (R) on this highway, traversing fertile bottom lands settled by French and American families before 1800. Near the Missouri River in this area, a small log fort, San Juan del Misuri, under the command of. Antonio Gautier, a lieutenant of the Spanish militia, was maintained for a few years at the end of the eighteenth century. Later, a village of Creole and Anglo-American settlers developed in the vicinity. In 1804 this village, known as *La Charette* (the cart), consisted of "seven small houses and as many poor families who have fixed themselves here for the convenience of trade." The site was eventually washed away by the river.

At 39 *m.* is a junction with an unmarked graveled road.

Right here to the BRYAN-BOONE CEMETERY (R), 0.9 *m.,* where a large granite boulder marks the site of the original graves of Daniel Boone (1735-1820) and Rebecca Bryan Boone (1737-1813). When Mrs. Boone died, she was buried by her husband on the crest of this low hill overlooking the Missouri River bottoms, on land belonging to her nephew, David Bryan. Seven years later, Daniel's body was laid beside hers. Fragments of the original small gravestones, inscribed "Daniel Boon" and "Rebecca Boon," cut by John B. Wyatt, a local blacksmith, are preserved in the Central College Museum at Fayette (*see Tour 1*). In 1845, despite the fact that Boone had once written from Missouri that he would rather lay his head on the block than set foot on Kentucky soil again, the bodies were removed to Frankfort, Kentucky.

One of Boone's favorite visiting places in his last years was the FLANDERS CALLAWAY HOUSE (*open by permission*), 40.3 *m.* (L), a two-story log structure, now weatherboarded and painted white. The house is said to have been built about 1800, and was the home of Boone's daughter and son-in-law, Jemima and Flanders Callaway. According to Reverend John Mason Peck, Baptist missionary who visited here December 16, 1818, Callaway Post was "a cluster of cabins," rather than a single house, and Daniel Boone's room was at that time "part of a range of log cabins." It is not certain, therefore, that the house remaining is the one in which Boone lived. The frontiersman at the time of Peck's visit was "slightly bald, and his silvered locks were combed smooth; his countenance ruddy and fair. . . . His voice was soft and melodious." Peck, like other missionaries, hoped to get from the old pioneer a profession of faith. Boone received him courteously, but was not interested in his theology. The most Peck could get from him was the simple declaration, "I always loved God ever since I could recollect."

West of the Callaway house, the highway turns north into the upland.

MARTHASVILLE, 41.3 *m.* (321 pop.), scattered along the abrupt slopes of the bluffs, was platted by John Young in 1817. The proprietor of the new settlement advertised that it was near the Missouri River, on the river road from St. Louis to Boon's Lick, a half-mile from old Charette village and Charette Creek, "a bold, lasting stream." As a final attraction, he added that a Dr. Jones, who practised "Physic, Surgery, Etc.," resided there.

In the eastern portion of Marthasville are the gray frame GERMAN EVANGELICAL CHURCH (built 1864), the two-story, red-brick HARVEY GRISWOLD HOUSE (*open by arrangement*), built about 1840 by a pioneer merchant of the community, and the long, gray frame AUGUSTUS FERDINAND GRABS HOUSE (*private*). Grabs, a cultivated German, settled in the bottom in 1834. Ten years later the floods drove him into the uplands, and he purchased a log cabin which he subsequently enlarged into the present structure. The exposed beamed ceilings, woodwork of German design, and fine strap hinges on an exterior door, are of interest. Grabs was both merchant and postmaster, and the lower west room housed his post office and store. The room above was used by a daughter as a schoolroom. The remaining rooms were occupied by his family as living quarters.

Following Grabs' death about 1865, the store was closed, and soon afterwards, the school. Both rooms remain today essentially the same as they were when closed; the shelves and counters and much of the unsold merchandise are still in the store. The maps hang on the schoolroom walls, and the original books are on the shelves. The house is owned and occupied by Grabs' descendants.

North of Marthasville, the highway crosses a broken upland of scenic interest, and reaches the western junction with US 40 (*see Tour 1*) at WARRENTON, 57.2 *m.* (943 alt., 1,254 pop.) (*see Tour 1*).

Tour 2

(Quincy, Ill.) — Taylor — Florida —Paris — Brunswick — Lexington — Independence — Kansas City — (Kansas City, Kans.) ; US 24. Illinois Line to Kansas Line, 220 *m.*

Concrete roadbed except for oil-mat and gravel sections between Paris and Brunswick.
Chicago, Burlington & Quincy R.R. parallels route between Illinois Line and Monroe City; Wabash R.R. between Moberly and Carrollton; and Missouri Pacific R.R. between Waverly and Kansas City. Accommodations only in towns.

Between Taylor and Keytesville, the prairie landscape is varied by occasional valleys cut by shallow streams. Farms, with their barns, silos, and minor outbuildings, occur at regular intervals. The towns tend to follow a pattern, with elm and maple arched residential streets leading to a central Main street. West of Keytesville, the highway crosses the Missouri River at Waverly, and from there west to the State Line it winds among rolling loess hills along the old Santa Fe Trail.

This central Missouri area was settled mainly by Protestant families from Kentucky, Virginia, and Tennessee during the period 1810-30. It is an agricultural region of moderate-sized farms, where conservative social and religious traditions have been preserved. The many preparatory schools and colleges in the area attest a widespread interest in education.

US 24 crosses the MISSOURI LINE, 0 *m.,* on the Quincy Memorial Bridge (*toll: car and passengers 50¢, car and trailer 75¢, including round trip*) over the Mississippi River from Quincy, Illinois. For a short distance, the highway traverses the Mississippi River bottoms.

At TAYLOR, 5.6 *m.* (491 alt., 60 pop.), a farming center, is a junction with US 61, with which US 24 is united for 14 miles (*see Tour 7*). At 23 *m.* is a STATE WEIGHT STATION at a junction with US 36 (*see Tour 3*), which unites with US 24 for 14 miles.

ELY, 31 *m.* (28 pop.) a roadside village (R) sometimes known as West Ely, was established in 1836 by the Reverend Ezra Stiles Ely, a Pennsylvanian, as the seat of the preparatory department of Marion College. The college, chartered in 1831 and located at Philadelphia, some 12 miles to the northwest, was conceived by the Reverend David Nelson as a training school for Presbyterian ministers. Students were permitted to pay their expenses by working on the College farm. William Muldrow, as General Agent, made the school an integral part of his promotion schemes (*see Tour 7a*). He collected large sums of money in the East for its advancement and gathered together an interested faculty, so that both the college and the preparatory school at Ely flourished. The institution became involved, however, in theological controversies and antislavery activities. When Muldrow's schemes collapsed about 1837, the school also failed. In 1841 the Masonic Lodge of Missouri purchased the school property and established at Philadelphia in 1844 the first Masonic College in the world. Two years later this school was moved to Lexington (*see below*).

At 33.2 *m.* is a MARKER calling attention to Daniel Ralls (1785-1820), for whom the county was named. Ralls' fame rests chiefly upon the last political act of his life. In 1820, during the election of Missouri's first two United States Senators, David Barton won without contest, but Thomas H. Benton's election was strongly opposed. Daniel Ralls, representative from Pike County, lay seriously ill at his lodging place, but learning of Benton's plight, he had four husky Negroes bear him on a stretcher to the assembly hall. "If I should faint," he ordered, "recover me there, and by no means take me out before I have given my vote." He cast his vote, important in the election of Benton, and died in Benton's St. Louis home, October 30, 1820. A few weeks later, the legislature named Ralls County, newly formed from Pike County, in his honor.

MONROE CITY, 37 *m.* (748 alt., 1,978 pop.), northeastern Missouri's major shipping point for poultry and eggs, consists of brick and frame cottages set well back on tree-shaded lawns. The brick business buildings along Main Street are mostly one or two stories in height. Many of the town's people originally came from Kentucky or Tennessee. They keep the Southern customs, and honor the South's three traditional enthusiasms: fine horses, fox hunting, and good shooting.

The town is a product of the pre-Civil War railroad building era. Platted in 1857 by E. B. Talcott as a shipping point on the Hannibal & St. Joseph Railroad, it developed as a grain and livestock market for settlers who planted the surrounding prairie in bluegrass and began a profitable business of breeding horses. During the Civil War, the population was sympathetic with the South, but the town was early dominated by Federal troops. It was incorporated in 1869. In 1898, Jasper Henderson organized the Henderson Produce Company and began the development of the poultry industry. Extensive operations in general produce were carried on, and geese were raised for shipment to the East; today, the town sends approximately 50,000 geese to Eastern cities for the winter holiday season. In keeping with the inhabitants' inherited love of sport is the breeding of Spalding-Norris foxhounds, a strain developed here by Victor Spalding, authority and judge of national bench shows and field trials.

ST. JUDE'S EPISCOPAL CHURCH, Main St. between Second and Third Sts., one of the first church buildings in Monroe City, was begun in 1866 and occupied for worship the following summer; it is a mellowed, ivy-covered edifice enclosed by a wrought-iron fence. Of

Gothic-Revival design, the building is L-shaped, with an open belfry on the eastern ell to balance the tower containing the entrance.

The MONROE SEMINARY BUILDING, Third St. diagonally across from the church, is a large, two-story red-brick structure with wide porches across the front and one side. Erected in the summer of 1860, the building was the scene of a Civil War battle in which not a drop of blood was shed on either side. On July 11, 1861, a small detachment of Confederate troops laid siege to the seminary, then occupied by a few Federal soldiers. The Confederates supplemented rifle fire with a few rounds of shot from an antiquated cannon. After an effective hit or two had been registered, U. S. Grant, then colonel of an Illinois regiment, brought his troops into Monroe City and routed the Southerners. This is said to have been Grant's initial field command.

At Monroe City, US 24 branches southwest from US 36, crossing a prairie region of grain and livestock farms.

At 46.6 m. is a junction with State 107, a marked graveled road.

Left here, across the north fork of Salt River, to FLORIDA, 6.3 m. (680 alt., 200 pop.), the birthplace of Samuel Langhorne Clemens (Mark Twain). In the center of town, amid four stores and a few houses, is the MARK TWAIN MONUMENT, a metal bust of the humorist on a white stone base.

In 1835, the Clemens family, then living in Tennessee, received a letter from James Quarles, a relative of Mrs. Clemens, urging that they move to the four-year-old village of Florida. Genial "Uncle James," whom Mark Twain later portrayed as Colonel Mulberry Sellers in *The Gilded Age,* was perhaps the wealthiest man in the village; he had a store, a good farm, and some 30 slaves. When the Clemens family arrived, he offered John Clemens a partnership in the store, and encouraged him to renew his law practice. The village was growing. Before long it boasted three mills, four or five distilleries, a pottery, a hemp factory, and, in 1837, the Florida Academy. Its early promise was never fulfilled, however; other communities soon surpassed it.

In 1837 or 1838, Quarles and Clemens dissolved their partnership. Clemens established a store of his own and continued to practice law. About this time he was elected Justice of the Peace. The family were still poor, however, and after the death of their daughter Margaret in the summer of 1839, they moved to the more promising town of Hannibal (*see Hannibal*).

Although Florida has exchanged its log cabins for frame houses, the village is still much as Mark Twain remembered it. "It had two streets, each a couple of hundred yards long; the rest of the avenues were mere lanes, with rail fences and corn fields on either side. Both the streets and the lanes were paved with the same material: tough mud in wet times, deep dust in dry." In pleasant weather, the children roamed over the countryside, as Albert Bigelow Paine, Mark Twain's biographer, recalls, "hunting berries and nuts, drinking sugar water, tying love knots in love-vines, picking the petals from daisies to the formula 'Love me—love me not,' always accompanied by one or more, sometimes half-a-dozen, of their small darky followers." Even after the family moved to Hannibal, many of Sam's summers were spent on his uncle's farm. Part of his short service as a Confederate volunteer during the summer of 1861 was also spent in Florida.

Ahead on State 107 is MARK TWAIN STATE PARK (*fishing, bathing, picnicking, camping, horseback riding*), 6.8 m., an improved 1,083-acre tract of rolling woodland on the banks of the south fork of Salt River. The Park was conceived by the Mark Twain Park Association which purchased 100 acres within the present area in 1924, and presented it to the State, the first land in Missouri to be acquired through public subscription. Immediately within the park gates, beneath a white, open-sided shelter (L), is the MARK TWAIN

BIRTHPLACE (*free*), which was moved here from its original site in Florida in 1930. The small frame structure consists of two rooms with a lean-to kitchen. It was occupied by the Clemens family upon their arrival in 1835, when it was probably almost new. Here Sam was born, November 30, 1835. During 1836, John M. Clemens built a larger house, now destroyed, which the family occupied until their removal to Hannibal in 1839.

The house, now maintained as a museum, is devoid of architectural pretentions. It is furnished with a carved four-post bed, spinning wheel, organ, candlesticks and molds, and split-bottom chairs—furnishings such as the Clemens family might have had. Within the carriage house is a carriage used by Mark Twain.

PARIS, 59.2 *m.* (673 alt., 1,473 pop.), a farm trading center, was platted as the seat of Monroe County during the summer of 1831. Almost immediately, its transplanted Kentucky and Tennessee families re-created here something of the social pattern of their native regions. They laid out a race track west of the town; Reuben Frigate's "Tom" and the Buford's "Charlemagne" made local racing history here. At regular intervals, military musters were held at the track. The Courthouse Square and the Tavern were the centers of community life. Perhaps the best remembered of the community's native sons has been Tom Bodine, later editor of the Paris *Mercury,* who achieved national fame without leaving the town in which he was born in 1870.

The PARIS MERCURY BUILDING, on Caldwell St., a half block west of Main St., houses one of the oldest newspapers west of the Mississippi River. Established by General Lucian J. Eastin in 1837 as the *Missouri Sentinel,* the paper has been published continuously since that date. Its name was changed to the *Mercury* in 1843. It achieved fame under the editorship of Tom Bodine, a former printer, whose comments in "The Scrap Bag," an editorial column, were widely quoted throughout the country. When Bodine died, July 29, 1937, his relative and partner, Paul Alexander, assumed ownership of the *Mercury.* Bodine had wished to "go with his boots on," but the wish had not been realized. Alexander, however, had the body laid in state in the *Mercury* office, while the force prepared a full-page obituary.

The COVERED BRIDGE, three blocks northeast of the courthouse, was built across the Salt River in 1857, and is still in use. Constructed of braced arches of quarter-sawed oak, the bridge was one of five built by Robert Elliott, an Illinois engineer.

Between Paris and Madison, the route crosses the northern section of Missouri's bluegrass region, where the majority of the farms breed and train saddle horses, though a number of outstanding draft animals have also been produced.

MADISON, 71.5 *m.* (801 alt., 625 pop.), centered about the intersection of US 24 and Broadway, is characteristic of the bluegrass region, for it draws its largest revenue from livestock and poultry shipments, but gives its heart to saddle horses. The town was settled by Kentuckians in the late 1830's. It has been the home of several famous horses, including Sagwaw, a trotter that sold at public auction in Madison Square Garden for $7,100. On the southeastern edge of town are the ATTEBURY STABLES (*open*), and on the southwest are the WEBB AND RAGSDALE STABLES (*open*).

Right from Madison on an unmarked dirt road to the H. CLAY BRYANT STABLES (*open*), 1.5 *m.*, long noted in Missouri for well-trained gaited and show horses.

Between Madison and Moberly, US 24 crosses the eastern portion of the Randolph County coal fields. The first of a series of shaft and strip mines is at 78.4 *m.* At 84.2 *m.* is a junction with US 63 (*see Tour 8*). West of the junction, US 24 skirts MOBERLY (872 alt., 12,920 pop.) (*see Tour 8*), passing between slack piles that line each side of the highway for approximately 14 miles. Coal in Randolph County ranked with agriculture in importance until the 1930's, when production was materially reduced.

The SINCLAIR MINING COMPANY MINE (*open by permission*), 88.9 *m.* (R), its tipple and conveyor rising three stories above the Wabash Railroad tracks, is of the strip type. Coal from a vein near the surface is scooped up with huge shovels, hauled in small cars to the top of the tipple, and dumped on screens that grade it into "slack," "nut," and "lump." During the winter of 1938-39, the mine loaded 35,000 tons of coal a month. The number of miners employed is determined on the basis of a daily production of three-quarters of a ton a man.

At 90.1 *m.* is a junction with County C, a marked black-topped road.

Right here to HUNTSVILLE, 0.8 *m.* (808 alt., 1,739 pop.), the seat of Randolph County, platted in 1831 and named for Daniel Hunt, one of the first settlers in the vicinity, and one of the donors of the town site. The many coal mines in the community once gave the city a busy, industrial appearance, but their decline—so realistically described by Jack Conroy in his novel *The Disinherited* (*see Literature*)—has again made the town dependent upon agriculture.

At RANDOLPH SPRINGS (L), 95.3 *m.*, Dr. William Fort began the manufacture of salt in 1823; for many years he supplied local needs. Following the Civil War and the building of the Wabash Railroad, the "curative virtues" of the springs were promoted. A 27-room hotel was opened on June 1, 1881, and, according to an advertisement, "no pains were spared to render the springs, to all who seek them, whether for recreation, pleasure or health, unexcelled as a summer resort." The spa enjoyed a mild boom which soon passed, leaving its 11 forlorn frame buildings empty. Only the largest spring still flows.

KEYTESVILLE, 113.7 *m.* (643 alt., 854 pop.), platted in 1830 by the Reverend James Keyte, is the seat of Chariton County. PRICE PARK, near the center of town, is a small, landscaped memorial to the town's most distinguished citizen, Confederate General Sterling Price (1809-67). Near a broken fieldpiece is the STERLING PRICE MONUMENT, a heroic bronze statue of the general in Confederate uniform, by Allen G. Newman of New York. Born in Virginia, Price moved to Missouri in 1831, later buying a farm near Keytesville. He was elected to Congress in 1844, but resigned in 1846 to accept a commission as colonel in the Mexican War, during which he was promoted to major general. In 1852 he was elected governor of Missouri. Although a "Douglas Democrat" and an advocate of slavery, Price was at first a staunch Unionist. When hostilities began, however, he accepted a Confederate commission of major general of the State Home Guards, and assisted in the defeat of General Nathaniel Lyon in the Battle of Wilson Creek (*see Tour 6*). He then advanced north to Lexington (*see below*). In October 1864, Price was defeated at Westport, his last campaign in Missouri. After the Civil War he was granted a tract of land near Cordova, Mexico, by Emperor Maximilian, and endeavored to establish a colony there for ex-Confederate soldiers. With the overthrow of Maximilian the project failed, and General Price returned to Missouri in 1866.

BRUNSWICK, 124.8 *m.* (652 alt., 1,749 pop.), a farm trading center, once gave promise of becoming a great port. The town was laid out in 1836, one mile below the mouth of Grand River, by the Reverend James Keyte, and named for his former English home, Brunswick Terrace. At first an important distributing point for back-country hemp, tobacco, livestock, and grain, it grew rapidly in the period 1840-56. Then the building of the railroads to the north cut off its markets, and the Civil War ruined many of its citizens. In 1875 the ever capricious river suddenly changed its course and left Brunswick a mile inland. The "launching ways" of the old boatyard remain.

Brunswick citizens established the State's first INDIVIDUAL MEAT DEPOSITORY, east end of Main St., a white building equipped with a refrigeration unit and rows of individual lockers in which farmers place their freshly butchered meat to preserve it throughout the year, a vast improvement on the old method of smoking or salting meat.

The GRAND RIVER, crossed at 125.8 *m.*, is the largest river north of the Missouri. Below the bridge, the river curves south of Brunswick through an old Missouri River channel. Called by the French as early as 1723 *la grande riviére,* it lay in a valley popular with the Indians as a hunting ground. Along the east bank ran an ancient trail, later known as Field's Trace, which extended from the Missouri to the headwaters of the Grand, where it joined another long-traveled route which ran northwest across the plains to the Rockies. Fox, Sauk, and Pottawatomi generally used this trail when they went on the war path into the Osage country south of the Missouri River. A Fox and Sauk village at the bend of the Grand River was occupied until after 1817. Near by two French traders operated a trading post for many years, and some six miles upstream, Joseph Robidoux is said to have maintained a post for Indian trade. Daniel Boone hunted along the stream for at least one winter after his removal to Missouri (*see Tour 1A*).

At the mouth of the Grand River, on both the north and south banks of the Missouri River, were Missouri and Little Osage villages during the early part of the eighteenth century. Because the site offered commercial as well as geographical advantages, Sieur Etienne Veniard de Bourgmond established Fort D'Orleans in the Missouri River bottom just west of the mouth of the Grand River in 1723.

This fort was the earliest French effort to secure military control of the Missouri River. In 1720 the Spanish had attempted to send a military expedition of about 60 soldiers from New Mexico into French Upper Louisiana. The soldiers were massacred by Indian allies of the French near the mouth of the Platte and Loup Rivers. De Bourgmond built the fort to keep out the Spaniards, and established alliances with the various bands of plains Indians. In 1725 De Bourgmond returned to France, and three years later the fort was evacuated (*see History and Government*). The changing course of the river has destroyed all trace of the building, but the approximate SITE OF FORT D'ORLEANS is indicated by a red-granite marker, 127.3 *m*. (L).

DE WITT, 131.5 *m*. (647 alt., 314 pop.), was Carroll County's center of activity during the Mormon War of 1838. During that summer, a year after the river town had been platted, Mormons from Far West, Caldwell County, began to buy lots in De Witt with the hope of making it a Mormon port for their back-country settlements. Within a few months, the friction between the Saints and their gentile neighbors flared into civil war. On September 10, 1838, a Carroll County delegation notified the Mormons to leave the county within ten days. When Colonel G. M. Hinckle, leader of the group, prepared to resist eviction, troops from Saline, Ray, Howard, and Clay Counties joined those in Carroll County and laid plans to attack the village. On the eve of the expected battle, Judge James Earickson, and William F. Dunnica, of Glasgow, interceded and secured a Mormon surrender on terms which included an agreement that the Mormons would leave Carroll County by the following morning (*see Tours 3 and 10A*).

At De Witt is a junction with State 41, a graveled road (*see Tour 9*).

At 147 *m*. is CARROLLTON (665 alt., 4,070 pop.) (*see Tour 9*), at the northern junction with US 65 (*see Tour 9*), with which US 24 is united to WAVERLY, 157.6 *m*. (684 alt., 876 pop.) (*see Tour 9*).

West of Waverly, US 24 parallels the Missouri River and follows the route of the old Santa Fe Trail. The land is planted in many commercial varieties of apples and is best seen in the spring, when the trees are in blossom.

DOVER, 167.6 *m*. (677 alt., 233 pop.), the second settlement in Lafayette County, was platted in 1835 in the *Terre Beau,* or *Terre Bonne,* Grove, so named by French traders either for its beauty or for its trading advantages. The creek below the village was given the same name, but American settlers soon shortened it to the present Tabo Creek. A point one mile north of town, now marked by a railroad depot, was once a well-known river packet stop. Annually, for over

THE FARMLANDS

Townsend Godsey

MISSOURI MULES

**HORSE SHOW AT THE AMERICAN ROYAL HORSE
AND LIVESTOCK PAVILION, KANSAS CITY**

CATTLE BUYING, KANSAS CITY STOCKYARDS

Townsend Godsey

FARM AUCTION

HEREFORDS

WHEAT FIELD

Piaget Studio

Farm Security Administration; Rothstein

SILOS ON OSAGE CO-OPERATIVE FARMS

CHOPPING COTTON ON A SOUTHEAST MISSOURI FARM

SHARECROPPER CABINS

Farm Security Administration; Rothstein

FARMER

TOBACCO BARN

IN THE COTTON FIELD

a century, a religious revival known as the August Meeting has been held at Dover by the Christian Church.

LEXINGTON, 177.4 *m.* (688 alt., 5,341 pop.), has been the seat of Lafayette County since 1823. Many of its houses are old, with Classic-Revival architectural details and iron grille work that recall the traditions of the South. Lexington grew up around William Jack's Ferry, established in 1819, and was a community of importance long before many counties in the region were settled. In April 1822, the town was platted, and named for Lexington, Kentucky, former home of many of its settlers. The platted tract, now referred to as Old Town, is some ten blocks southeast of the present business district. In the same year, John Aull, who had come from Delaware to try his fortune on the frontier, opened a store. In 1825 his younger brothers, James and Robert, joined him, and the three developed a profitable business outfitting travelers. They established branch stores in other Missouri frontier towns and dabbled in manufacturing and banking, and the commission and forwarding business. Soon Lexington was a prosperous commercial center for the river and overland trade and the rich back-country farms. Edward Pancoast, a Quaker who lived in Lexington during the 1840's, found the population a mixture of prosperous merchants from all parts of the Nation, mechanics and laborers from Kentucky and Virginia, and a shifting group of gamblers, slave traders, and speculators. So great were the profits from hemp, cattle, and tobacco that the near-by farmers, or planters as they preferred to call themselves, raised almost no dairy or garden products. Lexington merchants sent to St. Louis for such commodities.

Even in frontier days, Lexington was interested in education, and in the course of its history has been the home of five colleges: Baptist Female College, Elizabeth Aull Seminary, Masonic College, Central Female College, and Wentworth Military Academy.

In April 1852, Lexington was the scene of one of the worst steamboat accidents in Missouri history. The side-wheeler *Saluda,* carrying 250 Mormons en route to Salt Lake City, met heavy ice and a strong current on the north side of the river, and was forced to return to Lexington for the night. The next day the *Saluda* again tried to round the point and was forced back. The captain then ordered all steam possible, and made a third attempt. When the boat, loaded with passengers, was about 30 feet from shore, the boilers exploded. Passengers were blown to bits and scattered over the river and banks. Only 100 were ever accounted for.

The LAFAYETTE COUNTY COURTHOUSE, on the square near the center of town, is a two-story, white-painted brick structure of Classic-Revival design. A clock tower surmounts the four-columned Ionic portico. Imbedded in the east column is a cannon ball fired during the Battle of Lexington (*see below*).

This Courthouse, one of the most important examples of ante bellum architecture remaining in the State, was designed by William Daugherty, a local architect, and built between 1847 and 1849.

CHRIST EPISCOPAL CHURCH (*open by arrangement*), NE. corner of Thirteenth and Franklin Sts., is a red-brick Gothic-Revival chapel with an octagonal tower, built in 1848 and consecrated in 1850. The architect is unknown, but he may have been the Reverend A. D. Corbyn, then pastor of Christ Church in Boonville. The interior is finished in black walnut, and the ceiling is ornamented with a Gothic truss-arch. The few original "painted glass" windows remaining in the building are perhaps the oldest of this type in the State. Immediately north of Christ Church is the PUBLIC LIBRARY AND HISTORICAL ASSOCIATION BUILDING (*open*), 112 S. Thirteenth St. A two-story frame structure of Classic-Revival design, it was built to house the Cumberland Presbyterian Church. The first floor was constructed about 1840 and the second floor added in 1846-7. Later the building passed into other hands; in 1875 James Lane Allen (1849-1925) established a private school in part of it. Finding the venture unsuccessful, Allen soon returned to Kentucky, where he later wrote *The Kentucky Cardinal* (1894) and other books. In 1924 the building was purchased for a public library.

WENTWORTH MILITARY ACADEMY, Eighteenth St. and Washington Ave., is a standard institution of high school and junior college grade with an average enrollment of 250 students. The physical equipment includes 8 red-brick and stone buildings extended across the front of a 52-acre tract. Wentworth was founded by Stephen G. Wentworth in 1880, and is under the supervision of the Evangelical churches of Lexington.

COLLEGE PARK (R), northern edge of town on Sixteenth St., is a landscaped area on the Missouri River bluff owned and maintained by the city. Within the park is the open-sided MEMORIAL BUILDING, in which are benches, a fireplace, memorial plaques, a map of the Lexington battlefield, and pictures of historic scenes. The cannon in front of the building is from the U.S. Frigate *Constitution*. The memorial is on the site of the first Masonic college in the world, and is, in part, a small-scale reproduction of the white-columned college hall which stood here from 1848 to 1932, when it burned. Masonic College was moved to Lexington in 1846, and closed in 1859. In 1871, after an unsuccessful attempt to establish a State school here, the property was deeded to Marvin Female Institute, later Central College.

Approximately 200 yards west of College Park on Sixteenth St., which becomes a winding drive, a sheet-metal sign in the form of an ox-drawn covered wagon commemorates the association with Lexington of William H. Russell, Alexander Majors, and William B. Waddell, pioneer freighters and co-founders of the Pony Express (*see St. Joseph, and Kansas City*).

A short distance from the memorial, on Sixteenth St., are the marker and gates of the LEXINGTON BATTLEFIELD (*open*), an 80-acre area purchased by the county in 1928. The Battle of Lexington was fought in September 1861, between General Sterling Price's Confederate troops and Colonel James A. Mulligan's Union forces. Prior to the battle, Lexington, like other Missouri River ports, was held by Union troops to prevent the northern and southern branches of the Confederates from joining. To break this chain of posts, General Price, after the battle of Wilson's Creek, August 10, 1861 (*see Tour 6*), moved toward Lexington. The Union soldiers were engaged in throwing up earthworks (still visible) when they learned that the Confederates were upon them. Placing his troops on three sides of the Union entrenchment, Price demanded surrender. Colonel Mulligan refused. Intensive firing began on the morning of September 18, and continued without pause for 52 hours. On the morning of September 20, the Confederates constructed a movable breastwork of hemp bales soaked in water to withstand heated shot, and under this cover advanced to within 50 yards of the Union line. Colonel Mulligan's report of his soldiers "dying from thirst frenziedly wrestling for water in which the bleeding stumps of mangled limbs had been washed and drinking it with a horrid avidity" gives a glimpse of the nature of the battle. By nightfall the situation was hopeless; a white flag was raised, and the Battle of Lexington ended in Confederate victory. General Price took approximately 3,000 prisoners, stores of supplies, and ammunition. The site of General Price's headquarters is marked at the entrance of a three-story building on the north side of Main St. between Ninth and Tenth Sts.; the site of Colonel Mulligan's headquarters is marked on a stone gateway of the old Masonic College.

The ANDERSON HOUSE (*adm. 10¢*), around which the battle of Lexington was fought, is a three-story, red-brick structure erected by Colonel William Oliver Anderson in 1853. The front has a white, one-story porch, and an ell at the back has a two-story gallery. The entrance opens into a large central hall with a circular walnut stairway. The woodwork is of unpainted walnut and each of the 18 rooms contains a fireplace.

During the battle, the house was first occupied by the Federals as a hospital, being some 20 yards west of the outer line of their entrenchments. About noon on September 18th, the house was captured by a Confederate detachment. It was retaken by the Federals some two hours later and captured again by Confederate troops about four o'clock. Both parties suffered heavy loss of life in the attacks.

The house was purchased by Lafayette County in 1928, and the two lower stories were restored. On the second and third floors, is a MUSEUM, in which are relics of the 1860's: furniture, pictures, guns, swords, flags, pistols, and army equipment. A hive of Italian bees is said to have been kept by Colonel Anderson on the third floor, and a hole was left in the wall for their convenience.

The PIONEER MOTHER MONUMENT (R), a cast-stone statue 18 feet high, stands at the north edge of town. It is the work of Frederick C. Hibbard, Chicago sculptor, who was born in Canton, Missouri. Unveiled in 1928, it is one of 12 similar monuments placed in each of the States through which the National Old Trails Road passes.

In the spring, the bluffs and neighboring hills here are yellow with mustard blossom, and mustard greens are part of the native diet. The plant is said to have been unintentionally bestowed upon the town by Alexander Chapman, a druggist, who failed in business during the early 1870's. After the public sale, he found a jar of mustard seed left in his store, and scattered it over the bluff.

At Lexington, US 24 descends a long hill and winds along the foot of the Missouri bluffs past a WORLD WAR MEMORIAL (L), 178 m., a 75-foot concrete stairway ascending the bluffs. The memorial was erected in 1925.

At the memorial is a junction with concrete-paved State 13.

Right here, crossing the Missouri River and passing through HENRIETTA, 4.4 m. (694 alt., 544 pop.), to RICHMOND, 8.8 m. (890 alt., 4,240 pop.), seat of Ray County, an area effectively combining agriculture and coal mining. Richmond was platted in 1827, and named for Richmond, Virginia. Two years later, it succeeded Bluffton as the county seat.

Ray County was organized November 16, 1820, and named for John Ray, Howard County member of the Constitutional Convention of 1820, who died in St. Louis during the convention. Because the county originally embraced all of Missouri west of the Grand River and north of the Missouri (now 12 counties), it was nicknamed the "Free State of Ray." It was settled early, and its citizens almost from the first took an interest in public affairs and the development of the West. "Ringtail Painter" Palmer, a Ray County member of the first Missouri legislature, signed the Texas Declaration of Independence. Captain Israel R. Hendley (1807-47) was killed in the Mexican War battle of Moro. Major Robert J. Williams, veteran of the Mormon and Mexican Wars, served in the Civil War with his faithful mule, "Old Juley," whom he later buried in the Williams family cemetery, four miles northwest of Richmond.

The ALEXANDER WILLIAM DONIPHAN MONUMENT, at the west side of the courthouse, is a ten-foot bronze statue of Colonel Doniphan by Frederick C. Hibbard, erected by the State of Missouri in 1918. Doniphan (1808-87), a native of Kentucky, came to Lexington, Missouri, in 1830, where he was admitted to the bar. Three years later he moved to Liberty. During the Mormon troubles of 1838, in which he served as Commander of the First Brigade under General Lucas, he dramatically refused to obey the order of his superior officer to court martial Joseph Smith and the other Mormon leaders who had surrendered. In May of 1846 Doniphan organized the First Regiment of Missouri Mounted Volunteers for the Mexican War, and as colonel of the group led the overland march that military authorities consider "one of the most brilliant long marches ever made; the force, with no quartermaster, paymaster, commissary, uniforms, tents or even military discipline, covered 3,600 miles by land and 2,000 by water, all in the course of 12 months." Following the Mexican War, Doniphan held many public offices. He opposed Missouri's secession when the Civil War broke out, but took no active part in the conflict. He lived in St. Louis from 1863 until 1868, when he moved to Richmond. There he died, August 8, 1887. He is buried in Liberty.

The OLD RAY COUNTY COURTHOUSE (not open), S. College St., one block south of the square, is an ante bellum brick structure of Greek-Revival design, which was moved to its present site in 1914, when the new courthouse was begun. The original round brick columns were replaced with the present square ones, but the elaborate pediment and heavy cornice are original.

The RICHMOND CEMETERY, N. Thornton St., about four blocks northwest of the courthouse, contains the unmarked grave of Captain Bill Anderson (see Tour 1), Confederate guerrilla who was killed at the Battle of Old Albany in Ray County, October 27, 1864. After the war, when the Cole Younger Circus and Wild West Show played Richmond, Cole Younger, who had fought with Anderson, learned that no funeral had accompanied his friend's burial. He hired a preacher, had his circus band provide music, and conducted ceremonies at Anderson's grave. The cemetery also contains the graves of Colonel Benjamin P. Brown, killed at the Battle of Wilson's Creek (*see Tour 6*); Austin A. King, goverver of Missouri 1848-49; and David Whitmer and Oliver Cowdery, two of the three witnesses of the Book of Mormon. Cowdery was the scribe who recorded the words of the Golden Plates from which Joseph Smith is said to have translated the text.

The highway west from Lexington follows the old route of the Santa Fe Trail. First marked west from Arrow Rock to Fort Osage in 1819, the trail was improved three years later by the Lillard (later Lafayette) County Court, but in 1839 it was still so rough that the French traveler Victor Tixier complained of being thrown repeatedly "in the bottom of the carriage."

WELLINGTON, 177.3 *m.* (716 alt., 656 pop.), platted in 1837, tiny WATERLOO, 190 *m.,* settled in 1905, and NAPOLEON, 193.2 *m.* (750 alt., 132 pop.), laid out in 1836 as "Poston's Landing" and given its present name sometime before the Civil War, form an associa‧ tion of names which local residents cannot explain.

At BUCKNER, 196.6 *m.* (749 alt., 571 pop.), which began as a station on the Missouri Pacific railroad in 1875, is a junction with County 20E, a concrete road.

Right here to SIBLEY, 3.2 *m.* (746 alt., 200 pop.), an early Jackson County settlement named for Major George C. Sibley, early factor of Fort Osage and a surveyor of the Santa Fe Trail.

The route crosses a railroad overpass to a junction with an unmarked graveled road, 3.9 *m.;* R. on this road, which terminates on top of a bluff overlooking the Missouri River, to Sibley School and the old Sibley Cemetery, 4.1 *m.* Behind the small white schoolhouse is the probable SITE OF FORT OSAGE, established in 1808 under the direction of William Clark, of the Lewis and Clark Expedition, as a military and trading post. George Champlin Sibley was appointed factor of the fort, May 17, 1808. After the blockhouses were erected, Clark made a treaty with the Osage in the vicinity whereby, in return for all of Missouri east of a line running south from Fire Prairie to the Arkansas Line, the United States guaranteed protection to the Indians. Temporarily abandoned during the War of 1812, the fort was a government trading post until the system was discontinued in 1822. It then served as a government storehouse until superseded by Fort Leavenworth in 1827.

Along the LITTLE BLUE RIVER, 203.1 *m.,* were fought some of the bitterest battles of the so-called Border War (1857-58). During the Civil War, its waters were again bloodied by Quantrill's guerrillas and Jamison's "Redlegs" alike. After the war, when Kansas City had established itself as a center of wealth, capitalists took over much of the land along its banks for the establishment of "gentlemen's farms." Many of these have Georgian mansions or English half-timbered houses, and impressive barns, silos, and cross-fenced fields.

The MCCUNE HOME FOR BOYS (*open by permission*), 203.9 *m.* (L), consisting of 8 stone buildings on a 299-acre tract, is an institution for delinquent boys, named for Henry L. McCune, first judge of Jackson County Juvenile Court. The home is under the supervision of the Kansas City Board of Education.

At 208.9 *m.* is a junction with a marked black-topped road.

Right here, following arrows, to DICKSON LAKE (L), 0.5 *m.*, a group of five pools fed by springs and stocked with bass, perch, and crappie. Privately owned, it is open to fishermen the year around (*$1 a day for men; accompanying women free*).

INDEPENDENCE, 209.6 *m.* (949 alt., 16,066 pop.), one of the seats of Jackson County (Kansas City is the other), was the scene of much of the Mormon War, and for many years bore the scars of Civil War guerrilla raids. Today (1941) it has 19 industries, and is the headquarters of the Jackson County Farm Bureau, employing the largest staff of its kind in the State, and the center of the Reorganized Church of Jesus Christ of Latter Day Saints.

Daniel Morgan Boone (*see Tour 1A*) is credited with being the first white man to visit the site of Independence. Permanent settlers did not arrive until 1825, when the Indian title was relinquished to the United States. In December 1826, Jackson County, named for Andrew Jackson, was organized, and the following year Independence was platted as the seat of government. In 1830, Samuel Weston opened a blacksmith shop and wagon factory at what is now Liberty St. and Kansas Ave. Independence succeeded Franklin (*see Tour 1*) as the jumping-off place to the West and the Southwest.

In 1831, five elders of the Mormon faith, sent by Joseph Smith, prophet of the sect, from his Kirtland, Ohio, headquarters, came to Independence. Shortly afterward, Smith and other officials arrived. Announcing that this section of Missouri had been revealed as the promised land of the Mormons, they bought 40 acres of land and laid the cornerstone for a temple, which, however, was never erected. The Mormon newspaper, *The Evening and the Morning Star,* was established in June 1832, and by the following year the Mormon population numbered more than 1,200, or about one-third of the total population of the county. As their influence increased, resentment against them grew. Minor persecutions and personal conflicts led to mob violence, until, in 1834, the Mormons agreed to move to Clay County. It is said that nearly 300 Mormon houses were burned when the group, then numbering 1,500, fled from Jackson County (*see Tour 3*).

The gold rush of 1849 brought new color and life to Independence. Weston's blacksmith shop became a focal point for the assembling of wagon caravans to California. Large covered wagons with deep bellies and high wheels stopped while Weston and his helpers fitted iron shoes on the mules or molded iron braces for the oxen's yokes. In May 1846, the first overland mail stagecoach lines into the Far West were started from Independence to Santa Fe, and in 1850 Samuel H. Woodson received the government contract to establish a monthly mail stage service to Salt Lake City. The routes taken by the stagecoaches had already gained fame as the Santa Fe and Oregon Trails. In the late 1850's the City of Kansas (Kansas City) began to overshadow Independence in importance, but rivalry was interrupted by the Civil War.

Almost from the beginning, Independence became the objective of Charles W. Quantrill and his band of guerrillas. Twice during the war the city was held by Confederate troops, each time for one day only. On August 11, 1862, a battle took place in which Confederate Colonel John T. Hughes was killed. The Union leader, Lieutenant Colonel James T. Buell, from Fort Leavenworth, surrendered the town. A second battle took place October 20, 1864, when General Sterling Price occupied the town for a day. After Price was defeated in the Battle of Westport, October 21-23, Independence again became a Federal stronghold. It was in the district affected by Order No. 11 (*see Tour 10*), which forced an exodus of Southern sympathizers from western Missouri. George Caleb Bingham (*see Art*) swore to make General Thomas Ewing, instigator of the order, "infamous with pen and brush," and later did so by painting his famous picture, *Order No. 11*.

After the war, Kansas City became the great livestock market and packing center of the Middle West, and Independence was relegated to the economic background. Today (1941) it is virtually a suburb of Kansas City.

The first JACKSON COUNTY COURTHOUSE (*open weekdays 8-6*), 107 W. Kansas Ave., is a small, one-story log house containing two rooms, with restored stone chimneys at each end. The courthouse was erected in 1827 at a cost of $150. Its white oak and walnut logs were cut by Sam Shepherd, a Negro slave. It was built at the southeast corner of Lynn St. and Lexington Ave., but in 1916 was moved to its present site. Today (1941) it houses the headquarters of the Community Welfare League. The CHRISMAN-SAWYER BANK BUILDING, Liberty St. and Lexington Ave., a three-story, plain brick structure painted a light tan and trimmed in brown, was built in 1857 and used as a fort by Union soldiers in 1862. The walls bear scars and bullet holes. The WORLD WAR MEMORIAL BUILDING (*open*), Maple Ave. and Pleasant St., is a two-story, flat-roofed structure of red brick with white limestone trim, erected in 1926. Its assembly hall seats 1,800.

The AUDITORIUM (*open 9-5 daily; guides*), Walnut St. between S. River Blvd. and S. Grand Ave., is the great convention hall and office building of the Reorganized Church of Jesus Christ of Latter Day Saints, the largest religious group in Independence. Begun in February 1926, the building is of modern functional design. One hundred and four reinforced concrete columns carry the elliptical dome that rises 130 feet above the ground and has an outer surface area of 27,000 feet, covered by two inches of granite. The main auditorium seats 7,000 persons and can be emptied through 60 exits in less than 3 minutes. A smaller auditorium seats 3,000 persons. Offices of the world's headquarters of the sect are at present in the south wing, awaiting completion of the office wing. The denomination is under the leadership of Frederick Addison Smith, grandson of Joseph Smith. On the opposite side of the street, just north of the auditorium, is the site revealed to the Mormon prophet for the building of the Temple of Zion.

MOUNT WASHINGTON MEMORIAL CEMETERY (*open*), 212.9 *m.* (L), contains the graves of many notable pioneers, among them James Bridger (1804-81) fur trader, frontiersman, and scout. Bridger, a native of Virginia, came with his parents to Missouri in 1812. Ten years later he joined General Ashley's expedition to the West. During the remainder of his life, he was identified with the Northwest Territory as an employee of or partner in various fur trading expeditions. He was the first white man known to have visited the great Salt Lake (in the fall of 1824), and he served as guide for various government expeditions. In 1868 he retired to a farm which he had purchased near Kansas City in the early 1850's, and there he died in 1881. The cemetery also contains the grave of William Rockhill Nelson, founder of the Kansas City *Star* (*see Kansas City, and Newspapers and Radio*).

From KANSAS CITY, 218.6 *m.* (748 alt., 399,178 pop.) (*see Kansas City, and Tours 1, 4, and 10*), US 24 crosses the KANSAS LINE, 220 *m.*, to Kansas City, Kansas.

Tour 3

(Shepherd, Ill.)—Hannibal—Macon—St. Joseph—(Troy, Kan.) ; US 36.
Illinois Line to Kansas Line, 198 *m.*

Roadbed hard-surfaced, two and three lanes wide.
Chicago, Burlington & Quincy R.R. parallels route.
Usual accommodations throughout.

US 36 cuts directly across northern Missouri, following the course of the Old State Road used by pioneers before the Hannibal & St. Joseph Railroad was completed in 1859. West of the Mississippi River bluffs, between Monroe City and Macon, the route passes through bluegrass country. From Macon to the Missouri River is a gently rolling prairie region, with occasional stretches of flat land where the rivers have cut wide shallow valleys. The towns, many of which contributed to the opening of the West, are agricultural shipping points, with only a slight development of manufacturing.

From Illinois, US 36 crosses the MISSOURI LINE, 0 *m.*, on the Mark Twain Memorial Bridge (*toll 35¢ one way, 50¢ round trip*) over the Mississippi River to HANNIBAL, Missouri (498 alt., 20,865 pop.) (*see Hannibal, and Tour 7*).

Left on Main Street, which becomes County AA, to Fulton Avenue, 0.9 *m.*

1. Right on Fulton Avenue, 0.8 *m.,* to the entrance (L) to MOUNT OLIVET CEMETERY, immediately south of the city limits, which contains the graves of many members of the Clemens family: John Marshall Clemens (1798-1847); his wife, Jane Langhorne Clemens (1803-90); their sons Henry (1838-58), and Orion (1825-97); and Orion's wife, Mary E. (1836-1904).

2. Left on County AA, an all-weather road, to graveled Mark Twain Cave Road, 2.3 *m.* Right here 0.3 *m.,* to MARK TWAIN CAVE (*open daily; admission 50¢ for 30-minute conducted tour*), which was discovered in the winter of 1819-20 by Jack Sims, a hunter. At first it was called Big Saltpetre Cave, because a large quantity of saltpetre was manufactured from the bat guano found in it. Later it was called McDowell's Cave for Dr. E. D. McDowell of St. Louis, who unsuccessfully experimented with placing the body of a child in the cave to see if it would petrify. It was he who erected the first doors to the cave.

Sam Clemens was never lost in the cave, as described in *Tom Sawyer,* but the incident of Indian Joe was based, at least partially, on fact. The Indian, a "dissolute reprobate," was lost there once and was living on bats when they found him.

South of the Mark Twain Cave Road junction County AA becomes the Scenic Mississippi River Drive, paralleling the river, to the FEDERAL LOCKS AND DAM at SAVERTON, 7 *m.*

RIVERVIEW PARK (R), 1.4 *m.,* is a beautifully landscaped bluff crest from which there is a breath-taking 30-mile view of the Mississippi River, its islands, and the Illinois shore. The view is best from the red-granite look-out balcony perched on the edge of the bluff, approximately 200 feet above the river. Across the river one mile southeast is Jackson Island, where Tom Sawyer, the Black Avenger of the Spanish Main, Huck Finn, the Red Handed, and Joe Harper, the Terror of the Seas, foregathered to become pirates. At an eastern point in the park, Frederick C. Hibbard's bronze STATUE OF MARK TWAIN gazes across the river of which Mark Twain wrote. The park was a gift to the city of Hannibal from Wilson B. Pettibone in 1926.

HANNIBAL-LA GRANGE COLLEGE (R), 2.5 *m.,* a Baptist co-educational institution established at La Grange, Missouri, in 1858 (*see Tour 7*), was moved to Hannibal in 1929. The three principal buildings are grouped in a semicircle on a hill overlooking the river and town. Constructed of red brick, with white stone trim, they show the influence of modern institutional design. At the college is a junction with US 61 (*see Tour 7*).

INDIAN MOUND PARK (*swimming and roller skating; nominal charge*), 3.4 *m.* (R), a public recreational center, contains numerous Indian mounds. The HILLCREST GOLF COURSE (*nominal greens fee*), 4.7 *m.* (L), has nine holes. Between the links and Monroe City, the route enters the northern prairie, an agricultural land of small grains and livestock.

At the STATE WEIGHT STATION (R), 9 *m.,* a small frame structure, all trucks, busses, and other commercial vehicles traveling US 36 and US 24 are officially weighed. The weight which a vehicle may carry is established by law in order to prevent damage to the pavement.

Here is the eastern junction with US 24 (see *Tour 2*), with which US 36 is united to Monroe City, 23 *m.* (see *Tour 2*).

Between Monroe City and Brookfield, the route passes through Missouri's bluegrass country, a prosperous, well-drained farming area. Settlers recognized in this fertile, easily cultivated expanse, free of heavy timber and almost level, the farmsites they were seeking. Because the majority of them were from Kentucky, they began to breed the fine saddle horses for which Missouri has become famous (see *Tour 15*). Today, the farmsteads are marked by extensive white frame and native stone barns, silos, and livestock corrals.

Near the SALT RIVER RAILROAD BRIDGE (L), 31.5 *m.,* U. S. Grant, commanding the Twenty-first Illinois Infantry, was stationed in July 1861 to guard the bridge, then being rebuilt after its destruction by Confederates. From here he was to advance upon Colonel Thomas Harris, who had retreated to Florida, Missouri, from Monroe City. Referring to this order in his memoirs, Grant observed: "It occurred to me at once that Harris had been as much afraid of me as I was of him. This was a view of the question that I had never taken before, but it was one I never forgot."

Corn is the principal grain cultivated in this area. In summer each side of the highway is bordered by great yellow fields, broken only by thin strips of green along the streams and by patches of blue-green pastureland. In late fall, the stalks, stripped of their ears, are cut and stacked in a tepee-like manner. Although some corn is sold, most of it is used locally as livestock feed.

SHELBINA, 40 *m.* (779 alt., 2,107 pop.), platted in 1857 by Major Josiah Hunt, land commissioner of the Hannibal & St. Joseph Railroad, is a prosperous agricultural shipping point. The town clusters about a depot and the COMMUNITY SALES PAVILION, a remodeled livery stable at which auctions are held each Wednesday. Not everybody who comes has something to sell or exchange; many of them "just like the sociability of it all." Singly and in groups, the objects are offered: livestock, household furniture, chickens, blooded horses, eggs, plants "ripe for settin' out," and so on.

1. Left from Shelbina on State 15, a black-topped road, to the BROAD-ACRES HORSE FARMS (*open*), 1 *m.,* a nationally known breeding and training stable consisting of three large well-equipped white barns. Established by H. A. Greenwell, the farm is under the supervision of his son, Welch, who has raised and trained some of America's champion saddle stock, among them Easter Cloud, twice winner of the $10,000 Kentucky State Fair Stake, and Rex Monroe, by the famous Rex McDonald. The farm has developed no particular strain of its own, but has concentrated rather on training and breeding horses owned by others. Approximately 60 animals were prepared for show in 1939.

2. Right from Shelbina on State 15, past the SHELBY COUNTY FAIRGROUNDS (R), 0.7 *m.* to SHELBYVILLE, 8 *m.* (999 alt., 756 pop.), seat of Shelby County, organized January 2, 1835, and named for Isaac Shelby, a Revolutionary War soldier, and governor of Kentucky. Shelbyville was established by County Commissioners as the seat for the county, and the first lots were sold March 31, 1836.

According to tradition, the county was visited by bands of peaceful Sac and Fox Indians as late as 1835. Panicky settlers in the area once sent to Palmyra for aid against these "foes." Captain John H. Curd, responding to the call, found the citizens calmly going about their business, and not a warring Indian in sight. In his fury over this false alarm, Curd got himself drunk, and ended by fighting the neighbors he had come to rescue.

BETHEL, 13.2 m. (967 alt., 217 pop.), is a German community of vine-covered brick houses, once the scene of a famous experiment in communal living. In 1845 Dr. William Keil, a Prussian religious zealot, mystic, and social reformer, came here with 500 followers whom he had converted in Pennsylvania and Ohio to his religious and social theories. Title to the 3,500 acres of the settlement was vested in a few selected leaders. There was no constitution or written law. Dr. Keil's word was final in all social, religious, and legal matters. Each family was given a house; each individual did some work. The wives did the housework and cooking, and made the girls' clothes; the girls worked in the shops; the men and boys farmed or ran the business houses. The community owned a water mill, a tailor shop which made the men's clothing, glove and shoe factories, and a tannery. It was famous particularly for its buckskin gloves, which took first prize in the New York World's Fair of 1858. The BIG HOUSE (open by permission), a long, two-story brick structure near the center of the village, served as hotel and dormitory for members who had no families. A formidable brick structure with a tower served as combination church and school, but marriages were performed in the homes. Each Saturday night food was distributed from stores in the basement of the Big House. Every spring and fall a special overseer checked the clothing needs of each family, and saw that they were supplied. A treasurer was appointed to care for the community funds. The settlement existed harmoniously in this manner for over 30 years.

When other families settled near Bethel, Dr. Keil began to fear the contamination of his group. In 1851 a branch settlement was established at Nineveh, in Adair County. Soon plans were made to establish a new colony in the Far West which would gradually supplant the Missouri colony. Keil had promised his son William that he could accompany the first group of immigrants to the new colony, and although William died before the journey was begun, his father's promise was fulfilled. The body was placed in an iron casket full of alcohol, and when the procession of wagons began, the first carried William's remains. Months later when the group had reached its destination in Oregon's Willapah Valley, William was buried.

Later Dr. Keil moved to the Oregon colony (named Aurora in honor of his daughter), and for more than 20 years directed the affairs at Bethel by letter, holding the group together by the sheer force of his personality. Soon after his death in 1879 the Bethel colony broke up. Each man received his original contribution, plus approximately $29 for each year he had lived in the community; each woman received half this amount. Many of the present Bethel residents are descendants of these colonists.

Right from Bethel 1.5 m. on an unmarked dirt road to ELIM (open), the large, three-and-a-half-story brick mansion of Dr. William Keil. The site was selected by the leader of the colony so that he might remove himself from the "little squabbles" of the villagers. Massive in proportion, and almost completely lacking in ornament, the house, dating from about 1850, is reminiscent of eighteenth century Pennsylvania-German architecture. The third floor was originally the ballroom. A recent tornado destroyed the original attic and roof, and the addition of porches along the front and side have altered the appearance of the structure.

The main side route turns L. at the southern outskirts of Bethel on County M, a graveled road, passing through LEONARD, 22.2 m. (143 pop.), to County C, 25.2 m., a marked graveled road. Right on County C past the small white frame MENNONITE CHURCH, 27.1 m., to CHERRY BOX, 28.1 m. (838 alt., 44 pop.), a German community settled in 1868. The inhabitants are members of the Church of the Brethren, locally called Dunkard, a corruption of the German word *dunker,* meaning to dip or immerse. Twice each year the congregation observes a "love feast." This is usually held in the evening, with perhaps 40 members seated around a table, the men on one side, the women on the other. Bread and wine are passed, each member partaking. This is followed by a foot-washing ceremony in which each person bathes the feet of the one sitting on his right. A bowl of broth is then placed in the center of the table, and each person serves himself. The ceremony derives from the Biblical account of the Last Supper.

West of Shelbina, where the land has the slow-rolling character of the Grand Prairie, is the divide between the Mississippi and Missouri Rivers.

CLARENCE, 52 *m.* (825 alt., 1,157 pop.), was at one time the largest grain and livestock shipping point between St. Louis and Kansas City. Platted in 1857 by John Duff, a railroad contractor, the town is said to have been named for one of his children. Old settlers refer to the surrounding country as Clarence Prairie. The town ships large quantities of soy beans, wheat, oats, corn, and hay.

Westward the country is more rolling, with gray rugged bluffs along the Chariton and Salt Rivers. Through this section run Missouri's extensive coal veins, which at one time made it possible to supplement agriculture by mining. Coal production has decreased considerably in recent decades, and is today of slight importance in terms of the number of men employed. Macon County, once first, in 1938 ranked third among Missouri's coal-producing counties.

At 63 *m.* is a junction with US 63 (*see Tour 8*), on the northern edge of MACON (874 alt., 4,206 pop.) (*see Tour 8*). At 63.3 *m.* is a junction with an unmarked graveled road.

Right here to MACON'S MUNICIPAL PARK (*picnicking, free; fishing, nominal charge*), 0.7 *m.*, a landscaped area centered by a large Y-shaped lake. Although built primarily as Macon's water reservoir, the lake is stocked with game fish.

The BROADCASTING STATION (*open*), 63.4 *m.,* housed in a buff-brick building, is operated by Troop B of the Missouri Highway Patrol. The station is one of six transmitting units maintained by this State department. The two-story red-brick manor house overlooking the surrounding valley from the summit of a small knoll, 64.2 *m.* (R), is OAK HILL (*private*), the summer home of Theodore Gary, utilities magnate and former resident of Macon.

MACON DAM (R), 65.5 *m.,* impounds the waters of Duck Creek, forming Macon Lake (*see above*). Between the dam and Bevier are abandoned coal mine shafts and derricks, and great gray-black piles of tailings. This region, once booming with mining activities, is slowly turning to agriculture.

BEVIER, 68 *m.* (791 alt., 1,105 pop.), with small, neat houses and well-kept streets, still makes small shipments of coal. Near here Alex Rector discovered coal in 1860, while digging a well. Mines were developed, and the railroads and individual operators became wealthy. In 1930 mining on a large scale became unprofitable, so that at present only a small number of mines operate, and these in a comparatively small way.

CALLAO, 71 *m.* (818 alt., 398 pop.), platted in 1858, was named, it is said, by the first postmaster, who, seeking an outstanding name for the village, placed his finger haphazardly on a map of South America and landed on the Peruvian seaport. The town was incorporated in 1889; it was destroyed by fire the following year. West of Callao, US 36 dips into the valley of the CHARITON RIVER, crossing the stream at 74 *m.*

NEW CAMBRIA, 77*m.* (855 alt., 318 pop.), formerly called Stockton, was settled in 1864 and had its name changed by Welshmen who came here in 1880. In 1875 the reported discovery of gold in the vicinity caused a mild boom. When it was learned that the "gold" was merely a worthless glacial deposit, the prospectors departed, leaving the village to small-scale coal mining and farm trade.

At 88 *m.* is the eastern junction with State 5, a concrete highway.

Left on State 5 is MARCELINE, 3.2 *m.* (858 alt., 3,206 pop.), a freight division point on the Atchison, Topeka & Santa Fe Railroad. The town formerly divided its activity between the coal industry and railroading, but now agriculture is gaining in importance. Marceline is perhaps best known as the boyhood home of Walt Disney (b. 1901), author of animated cartoons. The first Disney drawings to attract attention are said to have been those he painted with tar on his grandfather's white barn door when he was about ten. Disney later attended art school in Kansas City and worked for several years as a cartoonist. In 1928 he created Mickey Mouse.

BROOKFIELD, 97 *m.* (910 alt., 6,174 pop.), in what was once called the Locust Creek Country, is a division point for freight on the Chicago, Burlington & Quincy Railroad, and a manufacturing town. Railroad tracks divide it into northern and southern sections, linked by Main Street, east and west of which are the residential sections.

James Pendleton and Joseph Newton, of Howard and Chariton Counties, were among the first white men to visit the broad fertile stretch of land along Locust Creek. Several farming communities developed, but no town was platted until 1859, when Major Josiah Hunt had Brookfield platted as a shipping point on the newly constructed Hannibal & St. Joseph Railroad. After the completion of the railroad, a large number of Irishmen who had been employed on the job moved their families to the town. This ample labor supply, plus the town's central location, caused the railroad to locate its shops and roundhouses here in 1859. Later, because of labor difficulties, the shops were moved to Hannibal, but the introduction of small industries and the increasing farm trade provided new types of employment.

At 102 *m.* is the western junction with State 5, a concrete highway.

Right here to LACLEDE, 1 *m.* (791 alt., 642 pop.), the boyhood home of General John J. Pershing. One block north of the town square, marked by a sign on a tree in the front yard, is the PERSHING HOUSE, a plain, two-story white frame building with ells on each side and a small front porch. A detached summer kitchen is at the rear. John J. Pershing was born near Laclede, September 13, 1860. After graduating from West Point in 1886, he served in the Apache Indian campaign in New Mexico and Arizona. During the Spanish-American War he was stationed in the Philippine Islands, where he remained 15 years. In March 1916, Pershing was given command of an expedition into Mexico with orders to capture Pancho Villa. A year later, when the United States entered the World War, Woodrow Wilson named him commander-in-chief of the American Expeditionary Forces. After the war, General Pershing retired from active service.

At 103 *m.* is a junction with a marked dirt road.

Left on this road is PERSHING STATE PARK, 1 *m.,* now under development (1941), named in honor of General John J. Pershing and informally dedicated December 31, 1930. The park consists of 1,800 acres, which include an extensive tract of virgin prairie grass. Cutting through the grounds is Locust Creek. Within the park is a cottonwood tree locally claimed to be the largest in the world.

At 119.3 *m.* is a junction with an unmarked dirt road.

Right on this road are the Chicago, Burlington & Quincy Railroad tracks, 1 *m.;* eastward down the tracks approximately 80 yards is the HANNIBAL & ST. JOSEPH RAILROAD MARKER, a tall concrete slab enclosed by an iron fence. On it a bronze tablet is inscribed with the legend that here in 1859 was driven the last spike—a golden one—in the construction of the road, which had begun simultaneously at Hannibal and St. Joseph. The spike was driven by Joseph Robidoux, founder of St. Joseph. Directly south of this point, but unmarked, was poured the last concrete in the construction of US 36, September 20, 1930.

At 122 *m.* is a junction with US 65 (*see Tour 9*), with which US 36 is united for two miles.

MOORESVILLE, 133 *m.* (920 alt., 170 pop.), a farming community named for W. B. Moore, a Kentuckian who surveyed the site in 1860, gained national attention when the waters from a near-by mineral spring, now unused, were awarded a medal at the Chicago World's Fair in 1893. The medicinal properties of the spring were discovered by E. J. Moore when his pigs, which habitually drank the water, survived a cholera epidemic. About 1880, Dr. Theophilus Fish built a sanatorium, the Mineral Springs Hotel, on the site. The hotel was operated for nearly 30 years.

BRECKENRIDGE, 137 *m.* (927 alt., 728 pop.), platted in 1858 and named for John C. Breckenridge, Kentuckian, Vice President under Buchanan, 1857-61, and candidate for President against Lincoln, 1860, is a farm trading center with a centrally located city park. In the northeast corner of the park is an old MILLSTONE, commemorating the Mormon Massacre at Haun's Mill, October 30, 1838. A small body of Mormons took refuge in the mill and blacksmith shop on the approach of some 200 militia from Livingston County. About 18 Mormons (some being women and children according to the Mormon account) were killed during the attack, or following their surrender. The militia refused the Mormons permission to bury their dead, and threw the bodies into a well. Haun's Mill is considered one of the many Mormon shrines in this section.

At 139 *m.* is a junction with a graveled road.

Left here to the SITE OF HAUN'S MILL, 4 *m.* Visiting Mormons have carried away all traces of the mill as relics of their sect's early difficulties in finding a place to settle.

The J. C. PENNEY MISSOURI FARMS (*open*), 145.8 *m.* (R), are devoted to horse breeding. The huge stable of corrugated iron has 37 stalls with modern equipment, including automatic water and feeding troughs. Expert trainers supervise the breeding of Percheron and Belgian draft horses, thoroughbred and saddle stallions, and champion mammoth jacks. Many of the animals have won national prizes in their class.

James Cash Penney (b. 1875), founder of the J. C. Penney Company and a large landholder in the county, was born on this farm and spent his boyhood here. One of 12 children, he was but 16 years of age when his father died. After graduating from high school, he started his business career, at the age of 20, as a clerk in a Hamilton general store. His health failed, and he went to Denver, Colorado, where he secured a job at $6 a week. Later he moved to Kemmerer, Wyoming. In the fall of 1898, he opened his first store in a wooden building 25 by 40 feet. On a capital of $500 he made a profit of $8,514 the first year. He organized the J. C. Penney Company in 1902. Other retail stores were opened, and he developed the principle of giving an interest in the business to the men who became managers. In 1937 he had in operation 1,744 stores in 44 States, with annual sales well in excess of $100,000,000. Mr. Penney is now chairman of the board, with headquarters in New York City.

HAMILTON, 148 *m.* (996 alt., 1,655 pop.), founded in 1855 and incorporated in 1868, is a grain and livestock center.

Left from Hamilton on State 13, a black-topped road, to KINGSTON, 8.9 *m.* (1,005 alt., 394 pop.), named for Judge Austin A. King, governor of Missouri 1848-52. The business section of the town forms a square about the three-story CALDWELL COUNTY COURTHOUSE, a massive red-brick structure with native stone trim and cupola. The county, organized in 1836, was named, it is said, by General Alexander W. Doniphan for Colonel John Caldwell of Kentucky, a noted Indian scout and hunter.

Left from Kingston on an unmarked dirt road to the SITE OF FAR WEST, 5 *m.,* one-time seat of Caldwell County and Mormon stronghold in Missouri. Driven out of Ohio, the Mormons came to Missouri in large numbers in 1831, settling first in Jackson County. On December 29, 1836, Caldwell County was established by the State legislature as a Mormon refuge. Within a few months, most of the Saints had moved into the area, where they established Salem at the mouth of Log Creek, two miles south of Kingston, and Far West, the county seat. At the latter, Elders W. W. Phelps and John Whitmer were joined by Joseph Smith and Brigham Young, and a city was laid out in magnificent proportions. The square was 396 feet wide, and the four main streets were 100 feet wide; the other streets measured 82½ feet. In 1837, a temple site in the great center square was selected, and an excavation 110 by 80 feet was made. Within a year the population of Far West grew to more than 4,000.

Friction soon developed between the Mormon residents of Caldwell County and their gentile neighbors. Quarrels and shooting frays increased in violence until nervous State officials condemned the Saints as dangerous to the public good, and troops were dispatched to quell them. The massacre at Haun's Mill (*see above*) made clear to the Mormons the hopelessness of their situation. When the State militia arrived at Far West, they surrendered. The leaders were tried by court martial and ordered shot. General Samuel D. Lucas, in command of the State troops, is said to have commanded General A. W. Doniphan to execute the sentence the following morning in the square at Far West. Doniphan replied: "It is cold-blooded murder. I will not obey your order. . . ." The execution did not take place. The prisoners were taken to Independence, and eventually committed to the jail at Columbia. On the way there, most of the prisoners (including Joseph Smith) got away; the others later escaped from the jail, and fled to Illinois (*see Tour 10A*), where they joined the main forces of their sect, who had left Missouri during the winter of 1838-39 under order of Governor Boggs. After the Mormons left, the houses of Far West were torn down, although the town remained nominally the county seat until Kingston was platted in 1843. Today, a cornfield marks the site of the once prosperous community.

In CAMERON, 161 *m.* (1,036 alt., 3,615 pop.) (*see Tour 10A*), is a junction with US 69 (*see Tour 10A*).

The GREAT LAKES PIPELINE TERMINAL STATION (L), 167 *m.,* a two-story red-brick structure, is flanked by a number of large storage tanks and enclosed by a high wire fence. Here, serving nine companies, is housed the machinery that pumps oil from the fields of the Southwest into Chicago.

The PLATTE RIVER is crossed at 188.2 *m.* Called by the French *Petite Rivière Platte* (little shallow river), and by Lewis and Clark the Little Platte River, the stream gave its name to the Platte Purchase (September 17, 1836), whereby Missouri acquired from the Indians its six northwest counties.

The CORBY MILL RUINS, 190.7 *m.,* consists of a stone foundation and a large forebay. Constructed in 1851 by John Corby, the mill was reputedly one of the finest in the State, with a daily capacity of 200 barrels of flour. Adjoining the mill, a wooden dam 5 feet high reached across 102 River, impounding its waters as a reservoir. The water flowed beneath the mill through the forebay, which has a 20-foot arched stone span on which is chiseled the initials of the contractor and the date of erection, R. K. 1851.

Between the mill and St. Joseph, the highway follows the winding route of an old stagecoach line. On the BRIDLEWREATH FARMS (*open*), 192.3 *m.,* estate of Karl Goetz, are bred saddle horses of national fame. One of the horses, Bridlewreath Peavine, took the five-gaited saddle-horse futurity stakes at the Missouri State Fair in 1938.

From ST. JOSEPH, 197 *m.* (829 alt., 75,711 pop.) (*see St. Joseph and Tour 10*), US 36 crosses the KANSAS LINE, 198 *m.,* on the Missouri-Kansas Free Bridge.

Tour 4

(East St. Louis, Ill.)—St. Louis—Jefferson City—Sedalia—Kansas City—(Kansas City, Kans.) ; US 50.
Illinois Line to Kansas Line, 277 *m.*

Concrete-paved, two and three lanes wide.
Missouri Pacific R.R. parallels route.
Accommodations at frequent intervals; hotels chiefly in larger towns.

US 50 between St. Louis and Kansas City is a less direct, more leisurely and scenic route than US 40. Swinging easily along the course of the old State Road to Jefferson City, the State capital, through the northern fringe of the Ozark upland, the highway follows forested ridges and dips into numerous, carefully tilled valleys. Between Jefferson City and Kansas City, the route crosses a rolling prairie region of prosperous livestock and grain farms.

Section a. ILLINOIS LINE *to* JEFFERSON CITY; *131 m. US 50*
Between St. Louis and Jefferson City are two distinct cultural areas, each representative of the people who developed it. East of Gray Summit the towns were largely settled by the Anglo-American families who moved into the area before 1840. West of Gray Summit, the farms, houses, and many of the towns recall the great German migration just prior to and after the Civil War.

US 50 crosses the MISSOURI LINE, 0 *m.,* on the St. Louis Municipal Bridge (*toll, used for relief purposes, 10¢ for passenger cars, 15¢ commercial vehicles; pedestrians and passengers free*) over the Mississippi River from East St. Louis, Illinois, to ST. LOUIS, Missouri (413 alt., 816,048 pop.) (*see St. Louis*).

Manchester Road, over which US 50 leaves the city, was at one time called the Rue Bonhomme for Joseph Hebert, nicknamed "Bonhomme," or good man, whose farm was on the road. Later it was called Market Street Road. In 1835 it became part of the State Road which the general assembly established to Jefferson City. For 15 miles the highway passes through suburbs and subdivisions.

MAPLEWOOD, 8.6 *m.* (520 alt., 12,875 pop.), one of the large suburban centers of the St. Louis area, occupies part of a Spanish land grant made in 1785 to Charles Gratiot. The neighborhood was once called Sutton in honor of James C. Sutton, a St. Louis ironsmith who bought part of the grant in 1825. In 1890 the Maplewood Realty Company purchased several hundred acres of land from the Sutton heirs

389

for development as a subdivision, and in 1908 Maplewood was incorporated.

BARTOLD'S INN (*open*), intersection of Manchester and Hanley Roads, is a rectangular brick house three-and-a-half stories high. Dormers break the steep pitch of the roof. It was built in 1849 by Frederich Bartold, a German immigrant, to replace the log inn he had built in 1830.

BRENTWOOD, 10.2 *m.* (490 alt., 4,383 pop.), a residential development adjoining Maplewood on the east, was originally three subdivisions: Berry Place, Maddenville, and Brentwood. The three were incorporated under the present name at the turn of the century.

Left from Brentwood on North and South Road to WEBSTER GROVES, 2.8 *m.* (507 alt., 18,394 pop.). Prior to the Civil War, Artemus Bullard erected a stone building on a 150-acre tract of wooded land, and founded in it Webster College, a boarding school for boys. Later, the Missouri Pacific Railroad established a station named Webster. When the post office was established in 1884, the second part of the name was added. The town was incorporated in 1896, made a city in 1914, and in 1918 adopted the commission form of government.

EDEN THEOLOGICAL SEMINARY, 475 E. Lockwood Ave., is a graduate school maintained by the Evangelical and Reformed Church. The five red-brick buildings of the seminary are of late English-Gothic design; the tower of the administration building, which forms the center of the group, is patterned after the Oxford Tower in England. The seminary, founded by the Evangelical Association of the West in 1848 and opened in 1850, was first near Marthasville, Missouri, then in St. Louis. In 1924 it was moved here. WEBSTER COLLEGE, 470 E. Lockwood Ave., not to be confused with the school established by Artemus Bullard, is a standard four-year Catholic college for women, the first in the State to be admitted into the North Central Association of Colleges. The school, housed in two five-story red-brick buildings, was opened as Loretto College in 1916, and later renamed Webster College as a compliment to the community. It is under the supervision of the Sisters of Loretto. The LOCKSLEY OBSERVATORY, maintained by the institution (*open Tues. and Thurs. nights, 8-10, adm. 25¢*), has an observation booth and a 12-inch reflecting telescope. Unusual astronomical occurrences and public lectures are announced through the local press.

KIRKWOOD, 13.1 *m.* (640 alt., 12,132 pop.), is a business and residential suburb. In 1853, after construction of the Missouri Pacific Railroad had begun, a group of St. Louis businessmen purchased 240 acres here and platted a town which they planned "as a suburban home for families who desired pure air and to rear their families away from the contaminating influence of a large city." The town was incorporated in 1865 and named in honor of James P. Kirkwood, then chief engineer of the railroad. In Kirkwood is a junction with US 61-66-67 (*see Tour 7*).

MANCHESTER 19.1 *m.* (512 alt., 600 pop.), is the first non-suburban town west of St. Louis. The settlement, probably named for "old Mr. Manchester" who lived in the vicinity as early as 1795, was selected as a tax collection point in 1823. Five years later lots were sold, but the town's growth was slow. In 1838 it boasted only "12 log houses, 1 tavern and 2 stores."

ELLISVILLE, 24.4 *m.* (730 alt., 288 pop.), named for Vespuccio Ellis, onetime United States Consul to Venezuela, was settled by Captain Harvey Ferris, who came from Kentucky about 1836. The town was later developed by Ellis. The old HUTCHINSON HOUSE (*open by permission*), half-hidden by foliage and trees, is a two-story brick building (L) erected by Captain Ferris in 1842. Georgian in character, with chimneys at each end, the house is reminiscent of central Kentucky's ante bellum homes. It changed hands many times before it was bought by Captain Hutchinson, who built fine stables on the estate, raised thoroughbred horses, and maintained a race track that was famous in its day.

POND, 28.6 *m.* (800 alt., 150 pop.), settled in 1825, was named for an adjacent millpond.

Right from Pond on a marked graveled road to the DR. EDMUND A. BABLER MEMORIAL STATE PARK (*picnic grounds and shelter houses*), 3.5 *m.*, an 868-acre recreational center donated to the State by Jacob Babler, St. Louis capitalist and former Republican national committeeman from Missouri. The park, with elevations varying as much as 380 feet, has 8 miles of roads and 3½ miles of foot trails. A $2,000,000 trust fund established by Babler is used for the care and development of the park, a memorial to the donor's brother, Dr. Edmund A. Babler, St. Louis physician and philanthropist.

At GRAY SUMMIT, 41 *m.* (633 alt., 215 pop.), two of the State's oldest highways crossed—the Wagon Road (*see Tour 5*) and the State Road to Jefferson City. Later the Missouri Pacific Railroad formed a junction with these, and the present town developed. It was named for Daniel Gray, who settled here in 1845, and was called "Summit" because it is one of the two highest points on the railroad route between St. Louis and Kansas City. There is but one other town in Missouri that has a railroad tunnel underneath it (*see Tour 8*).

Right from Gray Summit on an unmarked graveled road to the RALSTON PURINA COMPANY EXPERIMENTAL FARM (*open 9-5, guides*), 1 *m.*, where tests are made of concentrated commercial feed for animals and poultry. The farm, which consists of 540 acres, has 36 buildings for experiments: 11 for chickens, 4 for ducks, 3 for turkeys, 2 for pigeons, 3 for hogs, 6 for beef cattle, 8 for dairy cattle, 1 for horses and mules, and 2 for furbearing animals. Rabbits, mink, silver fox, and the extremely rare chinchilla are housed in the last. Feeding tests are made under average farm conditions. About 100 people are employed.

The Anglo-American settlements west of Gray Summit all but lost their identity when the heavy German immigration into the section began in the 1830's. The thrifty and industrious Germans put under cultivation most of the rocky hills and broken upland prairie. Many individuals of Anglo-American descent remain in the area, but it is the German influence that dominates.

At 41.5 *m.* is the junction with US 66 (*see Tour 5*), with which US 50 is united for 6.5 miles, passing the MISSOURI BOTANICAL GARDEN ARBORETUM (*see Tour 5*), 41.8 *m.* At 43.7 *m.* is a junction with State 100.

Right on State 100, a marked asphalt road, to WASHINGTON, 10.9 *m.* (546 alt., 6,756 pop.), a tranquil German community on the Missouri River with a distinct Old-World flavor. Narrow streets line the hillsides that rise sharply from the river front. The red-brick houses, built flush with the sidewalk, have white trim and green shutters and are noteworthy for their simple brick-work cornices and good proportions. Some of the more pretentious houses are definitely in the German Classic tradition, with brick pilasters, casement windows, wrought- or cast-iron balconies, and recessed entrances. In summer, side-yard gardens blaze with red and orange geraniums, four o'clocks, roses, and deep purple clematis. German is often spoken on the streets.

From its adoption by the Germans in 1833 until the coming of the railroad in the 1850's, the town was a river port. Then the railroad, the increase of population during the period 1850-70, and the careful development of the rather poor back country by thrifty German and Polish settlers, made it a shipping point of some importance, and the social unity that had characterized the city's growth was destroyed.

The town was platted by William G. Owens in 1828. Its first German settlers came in October 1833, purely by chance. Twelve families from Hanover, Germany, arrived in St. Louis and, finding no boat leaving for the Illinois country, their anticipated destination, decided to go up the Missouri River in search of a home. En route, one of the group, having read Duden's book describing the region around Marthasville, Warren County (*see Tour 1A*), suggested they make that vicinity their home. They landed at Washington, then little more than a tavern and ferry crossing. During the 1850's these were joined by other Germans. Social and cultural life came to be centered about the *Theaterverein* (Ger., dramatic society) and, later, the *Turnverein* societies. The theater group was organized in October 1854, by two German residents of Hermann, who later brought all their scenery and costumes to Washington and improvised a stage on the upper floor of the city hall. A theater (*see below*) was built in 1855. Later, the *Dramatischen Sektion* (Ger., actors' group) of the *Turnverein*, (Ger., athletic society group) presented plays at Turner Hall. The *Turnverein,* organized in 1859 and inactive during the Civil War when many of its members enlisted in the Union Army, was a vital force in community life until 1932, when it disbanded.

Many of the German customs survive. On Christmas Eve, some of the old families serve herring salad, a concoction of chicken, herring, apples, beets, eggs, pickles, onion, nuts, and spices—because "if you eat this dish you will never be in want." Decorated blown eggs are exchanged at Easter time, and weddings are celebrated with feasting and dancing, sometimes followed by a *charivari.*

Many of the early settlers were skilled leather workers, who brought fame to the community for the shoes they produced. In 1868, Henry Tibbe, a native of Holland, began the manufacture of corncob pipes. Securing a patent in 1878, he increased production and quality, and developed an international business. Today, two pipe factories and a shoe factory provide employment for many residents.

The LOUIS WEHRMAN HOUSE (*private*), 212 Jefferson St., is distinguished by its imposing German Classic-Revival façade with brick pilasters and capitals. A two-story structure, built before 1860, it was gutted by fire about 1869, and rebuilt, using the original walls, the following year. The lower floor originally was used as a store, the second as living quarters. The WASHINGTON HOTEL BUILDING (*open*), southwest corner Main and Jefferson Sts., was built by C. A. and Bernard Fricke before the Civil War, replacing Bernard Fricke's log tavern in which the first German families stayed after landing from the river boat. The five-story red-brick building is typical of the simple country hotels of its period. The Roman Catholic CHURCH OF ST. FRANCIS BORGIA, Main St., a red-brick structure with a spire that dominates the Washington landscape, was built 1866-69. LIBERTY HALL (*open by per-*

mission), Second St. near Jefferson, was built in 1855 by members of the *Theaterverein*, and used by them until 1866. The stage has been removed and the building converted into a residence.

The MISSOURI MEERSCHAUM PLANT (*open 8-4 workdays; guides*), SW. corner Front and Cedar Sts., processes white Collier corncobs which the company buys from Missouri and Illinois farmers. The cobs are seasoned in bins for two to five years, then sawed to proper lengths, bored in the center to form the bowl, and placed on lathes and shaped by hand. The pipe is coated with plaster of Paris and, after drying, is sanded, scoured, and shellacked. A hole is then bored, a stem inserted, and the "Missouri Meerschaum" is ready for the market. The HIRSCHL-BENDHEIM PLANT (*open 8-4 workdays; guides*), 320 W. Front St., employs a similar process.

The FRANZ SCHWARZER ZITHER FACTORY (*open by permission, 8-4 workdays*), 207 E. Main St., is the only plant in the country where zithers are made by hand. The instruments, of selected wood, have 30 to 45 strings, and a tone range of 6½ octaves. The factory also makes violins, mandolins, and guitars. It was established in 1864 by Franz Schwarzer of Olmutz, Austria. In 1873, the company's zither won a gold medal at the Vienna (Austria) Exposition. A. W. Schepp, foremost American authority on the zither, designs the instruments.

Four miles north of Washington on State 47 is a junction with State 94, which leads eastward eight miles to Augusta (*see Tour 1A*).

West of the junction with State 100, US 50 passes through a rugged country, and at 48 *m.* reaches its western junction with US 66 (*see Tour 5*).

UNION, 53.5 *m.* (568 alt., 2,125 pop.), clustered about the square of its three-story, Bedford-stone courthouse, was platted in 1826 by a commission appointed to locate the center of Franklin County and there establish the county seat to succeed Newport, the original seat. The majority of the population engage in farm trade or work in the shoe factory.

Westward, the highway crosses a rough countryside covered with second-growth oak. At 85.7 *m.* is a junction with State 19, a paved road.

Right on this scenic route through a partially timbered upland, which slips with breath-taking suddenness into the picture-book valley of HERMANN, 18.5 *m.* (520 alt., 2,308 pop.). Here everything looks freshly scrubbed, dusted, and swept, and the wide market place, and prim red-brick houses along the sidewalks (sometimes paved with flagstones), remind one of Rhine Valley towns.

On August 27, 1836, the German Settlement Society of Philadelphia was organized for the purpose of establishing a colony in some portion of the United States, preferably the Far West. Members in Philadelphia were distressed by the thought of their children forgetting the language and customs of the Fatherland, and felt that in partial isolation they would enjoy both the advantages of America and the cultural life of their home country. The society, accordingly, sent scouts to Illinois, Indiana, Missouri, and other places to select a site. Missouri was chosen, probably because it was the home of Friedrich Muench and Paul Follenius (*see Tour 1A*), leaders of the *Giessener Gesellschaft* (Settlement Society of Giessen), which had hoped to found a German State within the limits of the Union.

The first settlers arrived at Hermann during the winter of 1837. The town had been planned in Philadelphia on a grand plan, with four squares, one in each quarter of the chosen site, to be used as public recreation centers. The next year more colonists arrived. Before long the colony grew tired of remote-control government from Philadelphia, and in 1839 it separated from the society. Pre-Civil War growth was fairly rapid. Grape culture, begun in 1844, brought fame when a Hermann citizen received the New York State Fair award in 1853 for the best Catawba wine made west of the Mississippi River. Other citizens made fortunes in river trade.

Social interests were expressed by the *Theaterverein,* the *Erholung* (Ger., recreation society) and, after the Civil War, a *Turnverein.* There was a *Musik Chor mit Blech Instrumenten* (Ger., choir with brass instruments) as early as 1839, and, of course, a good band. Sundays were, and still are, busy days. Until closed by the governor in 1905, the stores stayed open, and the country folk came in to purchase as well as to pray. The *Maifest* (Ger., May Day Festival) celebrated by school children parading through the streets to the picnic ground, the *Schutzenfest* (Ger., shooting contest), and the county fair are all held on Sunday. On *Fast-Nacht* (the last night before Lent) the young people masquerade and go from house to house begging *fast-nacht* cakes (doughnuts without holes) and other sweets.

The STONE HILL FARMS (*open; guides on Sunday*), on the hilltop at the western edge of town, uses the cellars of the old Hermann Wine Company for mushroom cultivation. The building is a massive red-brick structure with turrets and walls a foot thick. The 20 cellars, some of them 200 feet long and 100 wide, open into the hill below the house. Approximately 65 tons of mushrooms are grown here annually. MUSIK HALLE (*open*), E. Second near Market St., a two-story red-brick structure built about 1852, has German-type casement windows, and an interesting brickwork cornice. The CONCERT HALL (*open*), Front St. near Schiller St., was built in 1878. It is an elaborate, three-story brick building with a long second-story cast-iron balcony; the gable end of its roof faces the street. The GENTNER HOUSE (*open*), Market St. near Front St., is an imposing two-story brick house with a formal eighteenth-century-type façade whose projected center portion is capped by a pedimented gable. The cornice woodwork is in Greek-Revival design. The house was built about 1850.

The STREHLY HOUSE (*open by permission*), W. Second St., is in two sections. The older one-and-a-half-story brick portion was built prior to 1845, when it was purchased by Edward Muhl. The two-story red-brick addition was erected shortly before the Civil War by Carl Procopius Strehly, brother-in-law of Muhl. The gabled end facing the street has doors sufficiently wide to admit wine casks. The sidewalk is of old flagstones; the front door step is a block of lithographic limestone originally used in the adjoining print shop. Within the house is an interesting collection of German furniture, glass, and china, brought over by the ancestors of the present owner. The old garden at the back of the house is typical of the better home gardens of Hermann. Among the tulips, roses, and other flowers is a grapevine planted in 1855, a 40-year-old asparagus bed, and a giant cherry tree. Strands of bright cloth tied to branches in the spring frighten the birds from the beds of young lettuce and from the cherries. Edward Muhl (1800-54), publisher of the Cincinnati *Licht Freund,* came to Hermann in 1843 with Carl Strehly. He brought his printing press with him, and began publishing a paper. In 1854 the paper was discontinued, and there was issued in its stead the Herman *Volksblatt.* Carl Procopius Strehly came from Prague, and was an expert in the dyeing and block-printing of cloth. His manuscripts on the making of dyes and designs, and his original wood blocks, are in the possession of Miss Rosa Strehly, owner of the house.

North of Hermann, across the Missouri River, State 19 forms a junction (R), 20 *m.,* with a graveled road marked "To Case," and (L) with County M, a graveled road.

1. Right on road "To Case" 3.9 *m.,* across Loutre Island, to an unmarked dirt road; L. 0.6 *m.,* crossing Loutre River and passing a two-story log house (R), now weatherboarded, said to have been built by Lewis Callaway in 1812,

to an OLD BRICK CHURCH (*open; inquire first house to the north*). Built by slave labor and given to the community in 1841 by William Talbot, the building has double entrance doors, 12-paned window sashes, and paneled shutters. It is said to be one of the oldest Missouri churches still standing, and has its original pews, pulpit, and cast-iron stove. Only the candle sconces, stolen from the walls, are missing. The church and adjoining cemetery are maintained by an association which meets here each August for services and a picnic.

2. Left on County M 6.9 *m.*, to the village of STARKENBURG, home of the SHRINE OF OUR LADY OF SORROWS and ST. MARTIN'S CHURCH. Pilgrimages to the shrine, on the third Sunday of May and the second Sunday of September, annually attract thousands. In 1888, August Mitch, nephew of the pastor, found stored in the rectory the small white statue of Our Lady Helper of Christians, which had served as the main altar figure until replaced in about 1883. He built a rude shrine on the hillside beneath a flowering dogwood tree for the "White Lady," and the pious farm folk came here to make their May devotions. Later a log shrine, still standing, was built. In 1891 the first public pilgrimage was made. The present shrine, south of the church, was built 1907-10 and is dedicated to Our Lady of Sorrows. Of stone in a Romanesque design, it contains numerous plaques attesting favors granted pilgrims.

A stone cottage (R) enclosed by a low stone wall, 87.1 *m.*, is one of the many houses of Rhine Valley type which early German settlers built along US 50. Referred to locally as the NEESE HOUSE (*private*), the cottage was erected in the early 1850's. The older portion has a sharply peaked roof with small, low-set dormers. The interior has a central hallway and three lower rooms. The rough-plastered walls of the hallway are painted. On the parlor ceiling, almost obscured by a later coat of paint, are the outlines of a "hex mark" (*see Architecture*).

MOUNT STERLING, 96.5 *m.* (592 alt., 50 pop.), once the seat of Gasconade County, is today (1941) a small fishing resort (*cottages, boats, and guides*) on the Gasconade River.

LINN, 110.2 *m.* (897 alt., 676 pop.), stretching for a mile on each side of the highway, is the seat of Osage County. Linn was created by the county court in 1842 as Linville; later its name was changed the more clearly to honor United States Senator Lewis F. Linn. The town has preserved a vigorous individuality, expressed through the columns of the *Unterrified Democrat*. This name originated with a Civil War editor, who asserted that his paper would remain Democratic, "unterrified" by threats which he had received.

At LOOSE CREEK (R), 116.1 *m.* (800 alt., 200 pop.), is the junction with County A, a marked graveled road.

Right here, following a winding, heavily wooded ridge, to BONNOTS MILL, 6.8 *m.* (552 alt., 250 pop.), a cluster of white frame buildings in a tiny valley on the bank of the Missouri River. The settlement was once known as Dauphine, and its French origin is recalled by the names of many of the present inhabitants. In 1852, Felix Bonnot established a mill and laid out the settlement. Once a minor river port, the village is now a farm trading center served by the Missouri Pacific Railroad.

Plainly visible directly across the intervening Osage and Missouri Rivers, which join a short distance east of Bonnots Mill, is a long, narrow ridge,

CÔTE SANS DESSEIN (Fr., hill without design), which rises from the wide Missouri bottoms. Here a French village was established in 1808 by Jean Baptiste Roy, a French-Canadian trader of St. Charles, to exploit the Osage River Indian trade and to farm the fertile bottom. On April 4, 1815, while the men of the village were battling a group of Sauk and Fox Indians near by, the fort was successfully defended against a surprise attack by the women and an old man. Following the organization of the State, the town was suggested as the site for the capital, but the plan was defeated by land speculators (*see Jefferson City*).

At 119.5 *m.* is the eastern junction with US 63 (*see Tour 8*), with which US 50 is united to Jefferson City.

West of the junction, US 50 winds into the Osage River Valley, crossing the stream at 120 *m.* on an open-span steel bridge. When river traffic was active, a boat had only to signal with three long blasts of the whistle, and the span was lifted. Now the Secretary of War has ordered that 24 hours' notice be given the State Highway Commission. The river affords good fishing (*boats available*). Named for the Osage Indians, who once, according to French maps of 1700, lived near its mouth, the river was for two centuries an important trade route of the Ozark region. When Du Tisne, the French explorer, visited the Osage in 1719, he found them living on the upper portion of the river, where they maintained their villages until about 1837, when they left Missouri. Steamboats traveled on the river during the 1840's and 1850's, going upstream as far as Osceola, but the service was dependent on high water, and therefore irregular.

At 120.4 *m.* is a junction with a marked graveled road.

Left here to another graveled road, 0.2 *m.;* L. to a third graveled road, 3 *m.;* L. again through partially wooded hill country to OSAGE LOCK AND DAM No. 1 (*open 6-6*), 5.3 *m.,* a concrete dam across the Osage River, completed in 1900, and maintained by the Federal Government. The locks are operated by hand. Fishing below the dam is exceptionally good in February and March.

SCHUBERT, 122.6 *m.* (720 alt., 18 pop.), is a German settlement named for Henry Schubert, who built a store here (R) before the Civil War. The store, of yellow frame, has been operated by the Schubert family for three generations. Near by is a junction with an unmarked graveled road.

1. Left here to TAOS, 1.3 *m.* (710 alt., approx. 75 pop.), a scattering of "cotton stone" houses, heavy log buildings, and modern structures along a ridge crest. When Father Helias D'Huddeghem, born in Ghent in 1796, came here from Belgium as a Jesuit missionary in 1838, he found a colony of 200 Hanoverian and Bavarian immigrants in the region west of the Osage River. After four years of service among them (*see Tour 8*), he gave up his missionary duties and settled in Taos, where in 1840 he had built a stone church, financed partly by his mother, the Countess of Lens, and by the Canon de la Croix of Ghent and the Leopoldine Association of Vienna. In 1874 Father Helias died and was buried in the local cemetery (L); his grave is marked by a tall marble shaft, simply inscribed in Latin.

His stone church was replaced in 1883 by the present CHURCH OF ST. FRANCIS XAVIER, a sharp-spired, red-brick structure of Gothic-Revival design. Above the altar hangs a painting of uncertain date, *The Scourging*, bordered by smaller paintings of St. Francis Xavier and St. Francis of Assisi, attributed to an unknown South American artist, and thought to have been the gift of the Countess of Lens. Near by is an old stone convent and school building. Above the doorway of the school is a simple wrought-iron cross which Father Helias is supposed to have brought from the mission at Côte Sans Dessein (*see above*).

In 1847, largely through the efforts of Father Helias, 50 Belgians under the leadership of Pierre Dirckx, settled at Taos. They were trained craftsmen, and contributed much to the prosperity of the community. Their descendants, who form the majority of the present inhabitants, preserve many religious customs not generally practiced in other parts of Missouri. On the afternoon of November 1, which is both All Saints Day and the eve of All Souls Day, a procession, headed by a cross-bearer and acolytes, follows the winding road from the church to the cemeteries, where the graves are blessed by the priest. On December 6, the Feast of St. Nicholas, a member of the congregation dresses as St. Nicholas, with a bishop's mitre, cope, and staff, and, accompanied by a costumed retinue, goes from house to house, asking parents how their children have behaved during the year, and distributing candy, fruits, and nuts. On Christmas Day, after early Mass, pistols, guns, and firecrackers are shot off in the churchyard.

2. Right on the graveled road to the entrance gate, 2.9 *m.*, of the ALGOA FARMS INTERMEDIATE REFORMATORY (*open daylight hours, inmates may be visited 9-11 a.m., 1-3 p.m.*), a modern reformatory operated by the State for first offenders between the ages of 17 and 25. Without bars, and with the surrounding farmlands enclosed by an ordinary wire fence, the institution has the appearance of a well-planned college. The two-story buildings, completed in 1932, are built of limestone quarried on the 780-acre farm.

JEFFERSON CITY, 131 *m.* (577 alt., 24,268 pop.), (*see Jefferson City*), is at junctions with US 63 (*see Tour 8*) and US 54 (*see Tour 15*).

Section b. JEFFERSON CITY to KANSAS LINE; 146 m. US 50

Between Jefferson City and Kansas City, US 50 crosses a high rolling prairie developed in grain and livestock farms. Early settlement followed the streams, shunning the treeless prairie as worthless (*see Agriculture*); consequently, this section was slow to develop. With the invention of the steel plow and the construction of the Missouri Pacific Railroad (1855-65), settlement became general. Towns sprang up as shipping points for prairie-grown wheat and corn, and, before the development of Kansas City as a cattle shipping center, long droves of cattle, dusty from the trek from the Southwest, were loaded at Sedalia and other points along the railroad.

West of JEFFERSON CITY, 0 *m.*, US 50 follows a new right of way to Centertown, then gradually enters the prairie, where towns are distinctly Anglo-American. Many bear the scars of pioneer battles and border warfare.

Typical of the ante bellum communities of this section, CALIFORNIA 23 *m.* (889 alt., 2,525 pop.), seat of Moniteau County, is a long, rambling town, disjointed during the late 1850's by the building of the Missouri Pacific Railroad almost a mile south of the square. The community dates from an earlier settlement adjoining it, and named, it is said, for one "California" Wilson, who gave a demijohn of liquor to perpetuate his nickname. When Moniteau County was organized in 1845, fifty acres were donated for the county seat, called Boonesborough. The post office was moved here from the old town, and two years later Boonesborough was renamed California.

At first a minor political and trading center, the community had a steady growth following the building of the railroad. Small, local industries developed, including a paper and a woolen mill. At the annual Moniteau County Fair, said to be the oldest in Missouri in point of continuous existence, many fine saddle horses, locally bred and trained, are displayed. The Classic-Revival design of the two-story, brick MONITEAU COUNTY COURTHOUSE, built in 1867, is accented by a semicircular portico of brick columns. Small-paned windows and the original interior woodwork make the building one of the most interesting of the surviving early Missouri courthouses.

TIPTON, 35 m. (922 alt., 1,219 pop.), is named for Tipton Sealey, who donated land for the townsite, platted in 1858. The young town gained a brief importance as the terminus of the Pacific Railroad in 1858, and the starting point of the Overland Mail (see Transportation). During the Civil War, Tipton suffered little from successive occupations by Confederate and Federal troops. After the war, Jesse James is said to have operated a livery stable here for about a year. The INDUSTRIAL HOME FOR NEGRO GIRLS (open), in the northern part of Tipton, is under the jurisdiction of the State Board of Penal Commissions. The institution, which accommodates 70 girls, provides training in domestic science and practical nursing. At Tipton is a junction with State 5 (see Tour 15A).

SYRACUSE, 40.5 m. (913 alt., 262 pop.), on the Missouri Pacific Railroad crossing of the old State Road from Boonville to the Southwest, was planned as the freighting and forwarding center for the southwestern portion of Missouri, and for Arkansas and "the Indian country." Laid out in the early spring of 1859, the town had more than 100 houses before the first train puffed into it during the summer. Overnight, Syracuse was swept by the prosperous, boisterous atmosphere that arose with the arrival of the railroads in the West. Business houses extended for a mile along the tracks. Colonel Brayton, one of the promoters, built a hotel of 30 rooms. The Overland Mail Company, and other stage lines running north, south, and west, established terminals here. Then, in 1861, the railroad was extended to Sedalia, and the bottom dropped out of Syracuse.

Westward, the highway is bordered by great, gently rolling farms, their deep soil an oily black when wet. In midsummer, the harvesters move in, cutting and threshing by machine.

SMITHTON, 53.5 m. (887 alt., 404 pop.), was platted by William E. Combs in 1859, and named in honor of General George R. Smith, founder of Sedalia. Before the World War, Smithton won fame as the home of Colonel Louis M. Monsees, onetime leading jack breeder of America. Colonel Monsees' stock drew the highest prices then on record; in 1910, 80 jacks brought him $67,750. One jack, Bell Boy, brought $3,700. At the St. Louis Exposition in 1904, Colonel Monsees' jack stock received the major awards, with cash premiums totaling $10,000. It was at this fair that the term "Missouri Mule" originated (see *Tour 15*).

SEDALIA, 62 *m.* (907 alt., 20,428 pop.), is a railroad town and the seat of Pettis County. On the northeast are the Missouri-Pacific shops and on the southwest are the Missouri-Kansas-Texas shops; south and west of them are the main residential sections. The majority of the old red-brick houses were torn down shortly after 1900 and new ones of more modern design were built. The streets are lined with magnificent maples, elms, and oaks.

In 1852, George R. Smith, who had come from Kentucky a decade earlier, tried to interest the citizens of the near-by community of Georgetown in diverting the Pacific Railroad from its proposed course and attracting it to their town. Georgetown, however, showed little interest in the matter. As a member of the State legislature, Smith was appointed to the board of directors of the railroad, and succeeded in having the tracks follow the inland route across the prairie; to assure this, $412,000 was raised by public subscription. On November 30, 1857, Smith bought 1,000 acres along the right of way at $13 per acre. He recorded the plat of a town, which he named Sedville in honor of his daughter Sarah, whom he called "Sed." On October 16, 1860, General Smith filed a second plat, including the original Sedville, and called it Sedalia. The first passenger train arrived January 17, 1861, and for a short time Sedalia functioned as a railroad terminal. Merchants came from Otterville, Syracuse, Georgetown, and other places, and established businesses. Before a town government was organized, the Civil War began, and Sedalia became a military post, which it remained until the latter part of 1864. The town was then incorporated, and by an act of legislature the county seat was moved here from Georgetown. General Smith was the first mayor. Growth was steady, and the town became the social and economic center of the area. In 1905, the Missouri Pacific Railroad moved its general shops here.

Aside from the State fair, Sedalia is best known, perhaps, for the number of distinguished newspapermen and writers it has produced. W. F. Brooks is Associated Press correspondent in London; Wilson Hicks is one of the editors of *Life;* Raymond Brandt, winner of a Rhodes scholarship, is Washington correspondent of the St. Louis *Post-Dispatch;* Casper Yost is editorial writer on the St. Louis *Globe-Democrat;* Charles P. Nutter, formerly with the State fair publicity department, was an Associated Press correspondent covering the Spanish Civil War, and is now bureau manager of the Associated Press in New Orleans. All of these men, with the exception of Nutter, were born in Sedalia and worked at some time for Sedalia papers. Another Sedalian, Charles G. Finney, now with the Tucson *Star* (Ariz.), is the author of *The Circus of Dr. Lao,* chosen the most unusual book of 1936, and of *The Unholy City.* Bernarr MacFadden, founder of the MacFadden Publications, promoted wrestling matches in Sedalia for several years, and Vincent Carroll, vice president of the Bell Telephone Company, once worked on the Sedalia *Capital.*

The MISSOURI STATE FAIRGROUNDS, south end of State Fair Blvd., 326 acres, has had more than a million dollars expended on its 54 permanent buildings, 23 of which are of brick and steel construction. At the fair, held late in August, are exhibited Missouri products of farm, field, forest, mine, factory, and fisheries. The harness races are a national attraction. The fair is under the supervision of the State Department of Agriculture.

At Sedalia is a junction with US 65 (*see Tour 9*).

Between Sedalia and Kansas City, US 50 passes through three of the State's most prosperous farming counties. The land is gently rolling prairie developed into extensive fenced and cross-fenced farms. Corn, wheat, and oats are the principal grains. Livestock yields a considerable part of the income. Johnson County produces large amounts of sorghum; Jackson County is one of the State's three leading producers of Irish potatoes.

MONTSERRAT RECREATIONAL AREA (*open*), entered at 82 *m.* (L), a 3,441-acre tract of woodlands, was developed by the National Park Service in co-operation with the Missouri State Conservation Committee for the use of organizations wishing to establish recreational and educational camps. In 1939, two camps were completed, each providing facilities for 96 campers and a supervisory staff. Before a camping permit is issued, the applying organization must be certified by an advisory committee. Applications are made to the Council of Social Agencies, Kansas City. Within the park is a DAY USE AREA (*open*), providing parking space for a hundred cars. Eighty-five combination tables and benches are scattered in groups, each with an outdoor oven, over 40 acres. Hydrants and drinking fountains are at convenient points. The park was established in 1935.

WARRENSBURG, 91 *m.* (803 alt., 5,868 pop.), seat of Johnson County, is one of the oldest towns on the western prairie. The section called New Town, whose business district extends from the Missouri Pacific station south to the courthouse square, developed after the building of the railroad in 1864, when merchants deserted Old Town, the original village, for business locations nearer the tracks. For many years Old Town, in the western part of the city, has contained only the old courthouse, a store, and a scattering of Negro homes.

In 1833, Martin Warren, a Revolutionary War veteran from Kentucky, settled on the present site of Warrensburg. The following year, Johnson County was organized and named for Colonel Richard M. Johnson of Kentucky, "the slayer of Tecumseh," and Vice President of the United States, 1837-41. In 1836, county commissioners selected the site of Warrensburg for the county seat, and the town was named for Martin Warren, its first settler. Wetmore, in his *Gazetteer of the State of Missouri* (1837), speaking of the "judicious location" of the town, suggests that "fountains of pure water in and near it promise cool milk and sweet cream as the accompaniments of strawberries, with which the prairies of Johnson are spotted every season in luxurious crimson." At the outbreak of the Civil War both Cockrell's Confederate Brigade and Foster's Union troops drilled in the town. The completion of the Pacific Railroad to Warrensburg in 1864 introduced a period of rapid growth. The central Missouri State Teachers College was established here in 1871, and, together with farm trade and the administration of county justice, has been one of the town's major attractions.

Probably the oldest building in Warrensburg is the OLD COURT-HOUSE (*open by permission*), Main St. south of W. Gay St., a square, two-story brick structure, built 1838-42. The exterior has been painted yellow, and the interior remodeled, but the general lines of the building remain unaltered. A bronze plaque at the entrance states that here, on September 23, 1870, George Graham Vest delivered his so-called "Eulogy to the Dog." The speech, a classic of American oratory, came as the climax of one of the most interesting trials in Missouri history.

The case began in 1869. Charles Burden, a hunter, had a black and tan hound named Old Drum, which was so well trained to trail man or beast that Burden felt "money could not buy him." "He never lies," Burden would say. "I can always tell the kind of game he is chasing by his bark." Leonidas Hornsby, brother-in-law and neighbor, having had several sheep killed, notified his neighbors that he would kill the next dog caught on his property. On the night of October 28, Old Drum was shot and killed on the Hornsby farm. Burden filed suit for $100 damage. After two trials he was awarded judgment for $25, whereupon Hornsby appealed the case and the decision was reversed. Burden, however, secured another trial, and employed attorneys Wells H. Blodgett, George G. Vest, and John F. Philips; Hornsby engaged Francis M. Cockrell and Thomas T. Crittenden.

Vest delivered the closing argument to the jury. Making no reference to the testimony, he quoted the Biblical story of Lazarus, recited a poem by Byron, and reviewed historical instances of the fidelity of dogs to man. He next argued that a man's friend, son, daughter, reputation, money—all he holds dear—can, and often will, forsake him, but that his dog is faithful throughout life. Even in death, he ended, it is a man's dog that lingers beside the grave, "watchful, faithful, and true." Burden won the case.

In later years the lawyers engaged by Burden and Hornsby achieved considerable success. Crittenden became governor of Missouri, and Blodgett president of the Wabash Railroad. Vest served 24 years in the United States Senate, and Philips, who had been made a brigadier general during the Civil War, became a member of Congress and later United States District Judge for western Missouri. Cockrell, who had been promoted through the ranks to brigadier general in the Confederate Army, was elected in 1875 to the United States Senate, where he served continuously for 30 years—a record equaled only by Thomas Hart Benton. Defeated for a sixth term by the Republican landslide of 1905, he was nevertheless appointed by President Theodore Roosevelt to the Interstate Commerce Commission, on which he served until 1910, when he resigned at the request of President Taft to settle the boundary dispute between Texas and Mexico.

The FRANCIS M. COCKRELL HOUSE (*open by permission*), 205 E. Market St., is a stately old building with side walls half covered by ivy. Built in 1871, the house is L-shaped, and two stories high. Four large rooms and a hallway are on each floor. The stairway and interior woodwork are of walnut. On the east lawn is an unused swimming pool of early date. Still owned by the Cockrell family, the house contains many of its original furnishings: an ebony square piano, a grandfather clock, imported mahogany tables and settees, four-poster bedsteads, mirrors, bookcases, silver and china. Francis M. Cockrell was born in Johnson County, Missouri, October 1, 1834, and commenced the practice of law at Warrensburg in 1855. During the Civil War he gained recognition as the leader of "Cockrell's Brigade," a Missouri unit that won fame in many battles. In competitive drill at Mobile, Alabama, the brigade placed first, and was awarded a flag as one of the best disciplined, best fighting, and most efficient units in the Confederate Army. Cockrell began his political career in 1874, when he was defeated as Democratic nominee for governor. The following year he was elected to the United States Senate. He died in Washington, D. C., December 13, 1915.

CENTRAL MISSOURI STATE TEACHERS COLLEGE, South and Taylor Sts., is a co-educational school established in 1871. Its five principal buildings, constructed since 1915, are of English Renaissance design, and are built of limestone quarried near Warrensburg. The average enrollment is 1,000, a figure which is nearly doubled during the summer term. The new buildings on the campus, a library and gymnasium, were opened in August 1939.

South from Warrensburg on State 13, a marked concrete road, to PERTLE SPRINGS (*open*), 1 *m.*, principal county meeting place for church assemblies, political conventions, and chautauquas since 1887. The 80-acre park, owned by the Christopher family of Warrensburg, is equipped with cabins, outdoor ovens, picnicking and boating facilities, and a dance pavilion (*nominal charge*). Among persons who have delivered addresses here are William Jennings Bryan, Richard P. Bland, Francis M. Cockrell, George G. Vest, M. E. Benton, John J. Ingalls, Bill Nye, and Carrie Nation. On August 6, 1895, the park was the locale of the now famous "one-man" State Democratic convention, called and presided over by Congressman Richard P. Bland. The convention was held in an "off-year," 15 months prior to the national election. It proved of Nation-wide significance when its free silver platform was adopted later by the Democratic Party at the national convention (*see Tour 5*).

PITTSVILLE, 107 *m.* (860 alt., 84 pop.), was settled in 1858 and named for the Reverend Warren Pitts.

Left from Pittsville on State 131, a graveled road, to HOLDEN, 9 m. (844 alt., 1,818 pop.), a tree-shaded ante bellum town whose oldest citizens still spin yarns of the militant prohibitionist, Carrie Nation (1846-1911). She came to Holden in November of 1867 as the bride of Dr. William Gloyd, a physician whom she had married at Belton (see Tour 10b). The doctor proved an habitual drunkard, and the villagers were soon familiar with the pitiful sight of Mrs. Gloyd hurrying frantically along the streets, searching for her husband. Her appeals to the Masonic Lodge to save him were as fruitless as her efforts to have the church people pray for him; nor did the Lord direct His might against the saloon-keepers, who laughed at her pleadings not to sell him more liquor. In the summer following their marriage (1868), her parents took her home to Belton, where her daughter, Charlien, was born. Six months later Gloyd died of alcoholism, and after a period of study at the State Normal School in Warrensburg, Mrs. Gloyd returned to Holden to teach in the public school. Here she remained for four uneventful years, until she was discharged over an argument about the pronunciation of the letter "a." In 1877 she married David Nation, an editor, minister, and lawyer, then living in Warrensburg. A short time later the couple moved to Texas.

Between Pittsville and Lone Jack, US 50 enters Jackson County, one of the most fertile, prosperous, and well-developed counties in the State. During the Civil War, some of the most bitter and brutal episodes in American history took place here between Kansas Jayhawkers and Redlegs, and Missouri slave owners. Even before the war broke out, the fury of conflicting views had resulted in armed struggles. The fight began as one of opinion; it ended as one of revenge.

The little town of LONE JACK, 118 m. (1,010 alt., 350 pop.), received its name from a blackjack tree near a spring which served as a prairie landmark. The town has changed little since the late afternoon of August 15, 1862, when Major Emory S. Foster, out to prevent recently arrived Confederate forces from recruiting in the neighborhood, marched his command of 985 cavalrymen and 2 pieces of artillery into town, forced the Confederates to withdraw, and established himself at the Cave Hotel. Early the next morning the hedgerows near the town concealed detachments of Confederate soldiers under the command of Colonels Cockrell, Thompson, and Coffee, supported by Charles Quantrill's guerrillas: Coleman and James Younger, Frank and Jesse James, George Todd, David Pool, John Jarrette, and other very young men. At five o'clock a gun was fired and house to house fighting began. The hotel served as a hospital, until it became the center of the battle. After five hours the Federals were obliged to retreat.

Union and Confederate dead were buried in separate trenches in the SOLDIERS CEMETERY (open). The names of the dead were not obtained and there are no individual identification marks. The grave of the Confederates, on the site of the blackjack tree, is marked by a marble shaft approximately 26 feet high. An eight-foot pillar of concrete blocks marks the Union grave, from which the bodies were exhumed in 1867 and removed to Leavenworth, Kansas.

LEES SUMMIT, 129 m. (1,050 alt., 2,263 pop.), another town marked by Civil War tragedy, is near the former home of Dr. Pleasant Lea, who was kidnapped by an unknown group of men and shot near the site of the present Missouri Pacific Railroad station. When William B. Howard laid out the town in October of 1865, the railroad is said to have provided a boxcar for a depot. Painted on its side was "Lees Summit," in commemoration of Dr. Lea, and of the fact that the town is on one of the highest points between St. Louis and Kansas City. The mis-spelling was never corrected. For several years the town was known as "the headquarters of some of the worst bandits in the State," but a vigilance committee was formed by law-abiding citizens and "after the death of a few and the scattering" of the other outlaws, the town secured peace.

The JOSIAH N. HARGIS HOUSE (*open by permission*), 207 W. Third St., a white two-story frame building, was built in 1858 by the town's first banker.

UNITY FARM (*grounds and drives open to public*), 131 *m.* (R), a 1,200-acre farm, and a school of religious instruction and spiritual healing, is a department of the Unity School of Christianity. The grounds and buildings are carefully planned. Facing the entrance is the buff stone and stucco campanile, a square, seven-story tower of Italian Renaissance style with a 100,000-gallon water tank concealed in the top. Scattered over the extensive grounds are the buildings of the training school, also of Italian Renaissance design. The school apartment buildings on the north, near the swimming pool, are of Cotswold design. The dining room and terrace tea room (*open by reservation for vegetarian meals*) overlook the amphitheater. On Sunday evenings in summer, band concerts are given in the poplar-rimmed amphitheater (*free*). On the grounds are a 22-acre lake and 20 oil and gas wells. The outlying farmlands are developed into orchards, vineyards, and vegetable gardens (*berries, fruits, garden produce, eggs, and milk for sale at greenhouse*). The Unity School of Christianity is an undenominational religious movement founded by Charles and Myrtle Fillmore in 1899, and based upon the assumption: "I am a child of God, and therefore I do not inherit sickness."

At 136.2 *m.* is a junction with County 5E, a marked concrete road.

Right here to RAYTOWN, 1.3 *m.* (1,030 alt., 500 pop.), onetime postal station and assembly place for wagon trains on the Santa Fe Trail, and today a cross-roads trading village. Between 1870 and 1890 the town was an active center of the Ku Klux Klan.

From KANSAS CITY, 144.5 *m.* (748 alt., 399,178 pop.) (*see Kansas City*), US 50 crosses the KANSAS LINE, 146 *m.*, to Kansas City, Kansas.

Tour 5

(East St. Louis, Ill.)—St. Louis—Rolla—Springfield—Joplin—(Galena, Kans.) ; US 66.
Illinois Line to Kansas Line, 317 *m.*

Concrete roadbed throughout, two and three lanes wide.
St. Louis-San Francisco Ry. parallels route throughout.
All types of accommodations; hotels in larger towns.

US 66, principal highway between Chicago and the Southwest, crosses Missouri diagonally from the Mississippi at St. Louis to the high plains southwest of Springfield. As it cuts through the Ozarks, the highway follows approximately the route of a stage line established by the United States Government two decades before the Civil War. During the war, the road was an important military thoroughfare, traveled by the Federal commands of Frémont, Phelps, and Bliss, and by the Confederate troops of Price, Bains, Hindman, Parsons, and Slack. The Federal Government at that time put in a telegraph line along the road with stations at St. Louis, Rolla, Lebanon, Marshfield, Springfield, and Fort Smith, Arkansas, and the route was known as the Old Wire Road. The Confederates frequently cut the wires. After the war, the government took down the wires, leaving the poles gray and gaunt along the roadside. The country is generally rough to rolling, with slightly more than half the area in hardwood forests. Between St. Louis and Rolla, recreational areas have been developed. Around Joplin is the Missouri section of the great Tri-State lead and zinc fields. US 66 carries more out-of-State traffic than does any other highway in Missouri.

Section a. ILLINOIS LINE to ROLLA, 115 m. US 66

For the first 30 miles, US 66 is an urban and then a suburban thoroughfare. West of the junction with State 100 is the northern fringe of the Ozark Highlands, a recreational and agricultural area of rolling hills, fertile valleys, and occasional sharply broken limestone bluffs. The scene is rural, with valleys patterned in corn and small grains, hillsides and plateaus fenced and cross-fenced into pastures for dairy herds. In the apparently solid sides of many of the bluffs along the river banks, extensive caverns have been eroded by subterranean streams.

US 66 crosses the MISSOURI LINE, 0 *m.,* on the St. Louis Municipal Bridge (*toll, used for relief purposes, 10¢ for passenger cars,*

15¢ commercial vehicles; pedestrians and passengers free) over the Mississippi River from East St. Louis, Illinois, to ST. LOUIS (413 alt., 816,048 pop.) (*see St. Louis*).

For 30 miles west of the city limits, the highway is bordered by the HENRY SHAW GARDEN-WAY, a section planted in native flowers and shrubs. Intermingled with hickory, oak, and a few pines are hawthorn, redbud, and dogwood trees. This improvement, developed by a local association with the assistance of the National Park Service and the Missouri State Highway Commission, commemorates Henry Shaw, founder of the Missouri Botanical Gardens (*see St. Louis*). The hilltops along this section afford magnificent panoramic views of the country side.

At 11.1 *m.* is a junction with the Laclede Station Road.

Right on this concrete road to KENRICK SEMINARY (R), 444 Kenrick Road, 0.8 *m.*, a Roman Catholic school for young men preparing for the priesthood. The buildings are imposing brick structures of Norman-Gothic design. The school was opened in 1893, and named for Peter Richard Kenrick (1806-96), the first archbishop of St. Louis.

Right 0.4 *m.* on Weil Avenue to the ST. LOUIS PREPARATORY SEMINARY, an educational institution which prepares junior candidates for the diocesan priesthood. The buildings, built around a court, are of Spanish monastic design and were completed in 1931.

At 16 *m.* is a junction with US 61 (*see Tour 7*).

SYLVAN BEACH, 18.6 *m.*, is a privately operated amusement and recreational park on the Meramec River, with free picnic grounds, baseball diamonds, and parking facilities (*swimming, riding, and boating at nominal charge*). The Meramec River, rising in the south-central part of the State and winding northwestward to the Mississippi, is one of Missouri's most popular fishing and boating streams. Father Gravier recorded in his journal on October 10, 1700: "We discovered the River Miaramegoua, where the very rich lead mine is situated, 12 or 13 leagues from its mouth." Rumors carried to France that these and other Missouri mines contained silver and gold are said to have given rise to John Law's famous promotion scheme, the Mississippi Bubble (*see History and Government*). Today, the river serves as a weekend playground for city dwellers, and its banks are lined for great stretches with cabins perched high on stilts to clear spring floods.

EUREKA, 32.9 *m.* (461 alt., 530 pop.), a crossroads trading center, is said to have been named by the surveying engineer of the Missouri Pacific Railroad, who found that a route through this valley would eliminate many cuts and grades. When a construction camp was established in 1853, it was gleefully called Eureka. The post office, established after the road was built, retained the name. The town was laid out in 1858.

Right from Eureka on an unmarked graveled road to CAMP WYMAN (*open June, July and Aug.*), 3 *m.*, for underprivileged St. Louis children and their mothers. Equipment includes a swimming pool, crafts shop, dining hall, assembly hall, sleeping cottages, and shelter house for visitors. The camp was established in 1897 as an industrial farm for boys. Since 1928, it has been supported by the St. Louis United Charities.

PACIFIC, 38.9 m. (467 alt., 1,687 pop.), clustered about the junction of the Missouri Pacific and the St. Louis-San Francisco railroads, was platted as Franklin in 1852. Seven years later, when the town was incorporated, the name was changed to Pacific. Silica mines, tunneling into the St. Peter sandstone bluffs (R), furnish employment for many of the town's residents.

West of Pacific, US 66 climbs slowly from the valley. At 39.5 m. (R), if one watches sharply, the southeastern mouth of the railroad tunnel that passes beneath the village of Gray Summit (see Tour 4) can be seen in the distance. At 41.5 m. is a junction with US 50 (see Tour 4), with which US 66 is united for 6.5 miles.

The MISSOURI BOTANICAL GARDEN ARBORETUM (greenhouses open 9-5, free), 41.8 m. (L), consists of 1,600 acres on the Meramec River. In twelve greenhouses, each 100 feet long and 25 feet wide, are grown what is said to be the largest publicly owned collection of orchids in the world. Here are cultivated the plants shown each year at the Botanical Gardens in St. Louis, many of them hybrids developed from parent stock obtained in the American tropics by Superintendent George H. Pring.

One of the principal purposes of the Arboretum is to preserve for the future a typical example of Ozark landscape. Several hundred acres of woodland and meadow along the Meramec were set aside from the first for wild flower gardens. The tract affords possibilities of glade, cliff-side, meadow, and woodland gardens, and consequently it has been possible to introduce wild flowers, shrubs, and trees from many sections of the State to combine with the more than 500 species found in the area. The effort has been toward natural effects, and a comprehensive collection of Missouri plants. It is anticipated that in 1941 these gardens will be opened to the public.

At 43.7 m. is a junction with State 100 (see Tour 4). West of the junction, the highway rides a curving ridge that descends into the Bourbeuse River Valley. Approaching the river, the highway divides into one-way lanes and crosses the river on twin steel and concrete bridges.

At 48 m. is the western junction with US 50 (see Tour 4).

Between the junction and St. Clair, US 66 continues along the approximate route of the Old Wire Road, and traverses the wide, rolling plateau that separates the valleys of the Meramec and Bourbeuse Rivers. Occasional narrow points afford fine glimpses of the level floor and steep, bordering cliffs of the Meramec Valley (L).

ST. CLAIR, 56 m. (770 alt., 1,410 pop.), has the red-brick stores and rambling frame residences typical of rural trading centers. The town was settled by B. J. Inge in 1843 and was known as Traveler's Repose until the citizens tired of its being mistaken for a pioneer cemetery or a wayside tavern. The name was changed to St. Clair in 1859, honoring a resident engineer of the Southwestern Branch Railroad.

Between St. Clair and Bourbon the Ozark foothills become sharper, their sheer sides exposing a variety of strata. The lower beds are of hard, grayish-white limestone; the upper, of soft red clay, with an occasional layer of pink limestone. Numerous wayside stands exhibit specimens of native rock.

STANTON, 67 *m.* (872 alt., 200 pop.), was named for Peter Stanton, who operated a powder mill in the vicinity in the 1850's.

Left from Stanton on a marked graveled road (*slippery when wet*) that winds downward onto the narrow floor of the Meramec River gorge to MERAMEC CAVERN (*open day and night; adm. 40¢ and 25¢; guides*), 3.8 *m.* The electrically lighted first room of the cavern contains parking space for 300 automobiles, and a large dance floor. Reversing the usual direction of caves, this one tunnels upward through the river bluff to a height of 240 feet. It is naturally divided into four floors, through which graveled walks have been laid. The interior formations, often grotesquely shaped, have been given names such as the Natural Stage, 68 feet in height and of 5 different colors; the Wine Table, in what is called the Wine Room; and the Echo Room, in which the sound of one's voice rebounds from formation to formation for several seconds. At the entrance of the cavern is La Jolla Springs, with a flow of 4,700,000 gallons daily. The entrance to the cavern is said to have been discovered by Spaniards about 1760. It was not open to the public, however, until explored by professionals in 1936.

At 73 *m.* is a junction with State 114, a graveled road.

Left here to MERAMEC STATE PARK, 1.2 *m.,* one of Missouri's major recreational areas. The park, which consists of approximately 7,500 acres of rolling woodland drained by the Meramec River, is provided with rustic shelter houses, overnight cottages, and a dining lodge. Along the river are a bathing beach, a playground, and a small zoo. Hiking and bridle trails wind through the entire area. In MERAMEC STATE NURSERY (*follow signs*) various trees are propagated for reforestation purposes. The nursery, using the latest equipment, including an overhead sprinkling system, is planted with approximately 3,500,000 seedlings each year.

FISHER'S CAVE (*adm. 35¢; guides*) is entered through an opening in a bluff on the Meramec River. The first quarter of a mile is a narrow, low-roofed passageway, through which flows a shallow stream. At the end of the passage is the first chamber, an auditorium-like room with a vaulted ceiling 75 feet high. Adjoining the large central chamber by passageways are many smaller ones in which are curiously formed stalactites and stalagmites. Near the end of the cave, approximately one mile from the entrance, is a pool of clear water into which flows Dripping Spring.

In COPPER HOLLOW, northeast corner of the park, are the half-obscured remains of an open-pit copper mine and the ruins of an old smelter. The mine is said to have been opened by Peter Stanton (*see above*). In 1855 the mine was acquired by Reverend Henry I. Coe, who organized a company of ministers and came from St. Louis to take charge of operations. The following year, Dr. Silas Reed, also of St. Louis, bought out Coe's interests. In 1868 the copper ore was exhausted. The major portion of the old copper mining area is within the park. Also on park property is the SITE OF A LEAD MINE, on Thomas Hill (*follow signs*), which Henry Rowe Schoolcraft, a geologist, investigated in 1819. Schoolcraft reported that the mine had been operated since 1796.

SULLIVAN, 73.3 *m.* (971 alt., 2,517 pop.), on the hills left of the highway, lives on its farm trade and two shoe factories. The town was established as Mt. Helicon in 1856, but the officials of the St. Louis-San Francisco Railway changed the name in 1860 to honor Stephen Sullivan, who had donated the right of way through the village. Sullivan came to the Meramec River country from Kentucky in 1800, and made a fortune in tobacco, and lead and copper mining. Although records do not verify the story, legend says that he manufactured gunpowder for the Confederacy and was executed by Federal troops. In Sullivan was born George Hearst (1820-91), California mining engineer and United States Senator, and father of William Randolph Hearst, publisher. George Hearst married Phoebe Apperson, school teacher, at Steelville, Missouri (1862).

The GENERAL WILLIAM SELBY HARNEY MANSION (*open*), in the southwestern part of Sullivan, was built by the Mexican and Civil War veteran about 1870. Two-and-a-half stories in height, with a long rear wing and tan limestone walls, the house contains 35 rooms, of which 25 are bedrooms. The entranceway has wide double doors and a fanlight reminiscent of eighteenth century designs, but in general the house is of modified Swiss chalet type.

At 85 *m.* is a junction with County H, a paved road.

Left here to LEASBURG, 2.1 *m.* (1,023 alt., 173 pop.), beyond which are three caves. CATHEDRAL CAVE (*adm. 40¢; guides*), 2.7 *m.* (R), is an immense cavern with an opening at the base of a high bluff. Many of the stalagmites and stalactites are unusually white.

The MISSOURI CAVERNS (*adm. 55¢; guides*), 6.9 *m.* (R), have an indirect lighting system arranged to emphasize the spectacular colors and shapes of the rock formations. The colors vary from clear crystal to jet black, and include the pinkish-red of onyx. Passage through the cavern is over graveled paths. Some of the formations are the Musician's Balcony, the Cathedral Room, the Live Oak, and the King's Canopy. At the bottom of the cavern, 200 feet down, is Lost River, a clear, subterranean stream that has eaten its winding, rocky way through the bluffs to the Meramec River.

ONONDAGA CAVE (*adm. 40¢; guides*), 7.4 *m.*, at the end of County H, Missouri's pioneer tourist cavern, is entered by flat-bottomed boats that follow the winding channel of Lost River for approximately 900 feet. Beyond, passage is made by graveled paths, with the river sometimes in sight, sometimes only a murmuring sound. Coleman lanterns are used by both guides and visitors. Some of the formations weigh several tons; others are small and delicate. The common shades of onyx (red, brown, and tan) are interspersed with white. A few of the formations have been named: the two Lily Rooms, in which onyx in the form of lily pads appears to be floating on the river; the Cathedral Hall; Onyx Forest; and the Wonder Room. The formations in the Wonder Room developed under water and are so creamy white they look like rolls of fleece. The water, ordinarily 10 feet deep, is siphoned from the room for use.

CUBA, 92 *m.* (1,035 alt., 1,033 pop.), with its business center slowly abandoning a location near the railroad tracks for a new one on US 66, began as a farming village and shipping point in 1857, when M. W. Trask and W. H. Ferguson, anticipating by one year the construction of the St. Louis-San Francisco Railway, surveyed a townsite. The nearest house was then half a mile away, on what was known as Simpson's Prairie. Old residents say the town was given its name by two former gold miners from California, who wished to perpetuate the memory of a holiday they had spent on the "Isle of Cuba."

At Cuba is a junction with State 19 (*see Tour 14*).

ROSATI, 99 *m.* (1,074 alt., 200 pop.), a sprawling community of small farm sites rather than a town, had its beginning about 1900, when a group of 100 Italian families from Arkansas settled here. They had been taken from Chicago by a cotton planter, but had left Arkansas because of bad working conditions. They named their new home for Bishop Joseph Rosati, first bishop of St. Louis.

The ROSATI WINERY (*open weekdays 8-5*), northeastern edge of the community, produces a sweet natural wine under bond. The one-story gray brick building has a capacity of 120,000 gallons, stored in glass-lined concrete tanks. Grapes are bought from a local growers' co-operative association, the members of which also own the winery, and the wine is sold wholesale on the open market. Co-operating with the winery, the government is sponsoring a series of experiments designed to increase the quality of the vintage.

Between Rosati and Rolla, US 66 crosses the Big Prairie, a gently rolling plateau broken by small farm sites and patches of hickory, elm, oak, cedar, and pawpaw trees. Josiah Isbell, the first settler, entered a claim to land here in 1836. Other families followed, and divided their time between farming, cattle raising, and manufacturing gunpowder from the saltpetre in the numerous caves. Later, Welsh, Irish, and English families moved in to develop the clay and iron deposits, and French families from the Swiss border came to farm. The mining and powder-making industries are gone, but the section breeds fine Jersey, Holstein, and Guernsey herds, and cultivates extensive berry patches and orchards. Twice each year the people gather to exhibit their cattle, berries, vegetables, canned fruits, and quilts—at Rolla in May and at St. James in September.

ST. JAMES, 105 *m.* (1,069 alt., 1,812 pop.), sprawling across US 66, has a charm that belies its comparative youth. The main business street is at right angles to the highway. East and west of it are the residential streets, which end abruptly at the town's edge or wind off into the low hills as country lanes.

The town is the business and commercial center of the Big Prairie. From here are shipped berries and truck and dairy products. Oak, hickory, cotton wood, and elm cut from the surrounding hills are here converted into staves. The town also has a small distillery and a women's garment factory.

St. James was platted in 1859 by John Wood in anticipation of the extension westward of the St. Louis-San Francisco Railway. It was intended as a shipping point for the near-by Meramec Iron Works, which heretofore had shipped by wagon train. First called Scioto, its name was changed within a year. During the Civil War, a detachment of German volunteers, encamped near the town, were so impressed with the location that after their enlistment had expired they brought their families here. When the depression of the 1870's closed the iron mines, St. James turned to lumber, agriculture, and wine making. It was incorporated as a town in 1870, with a mayor and city council. In 1921, Mrs. Mayme H. Ousley was elected mayor of St. James. Each September, St. James holds a Grape Festival and Homecoming.

The STATE FEDERAL SOLDIERS HOME (R), northern edge of town, was founded in 1896 by the Woman's Relief Corps and the Grand Army of the Republic, and sold the following year to the State for $1. The institution is for the care of aged veterans and their wives and widows, and is maintained by the United States Government and the State of Missouri. In 1939, 123 men and 102 women were in residence. The administration building, a massive three-story brick structure with many wings, porches, towers, and gingerbread decorations, was once the home of Thomas James.

Left from St. James on State 68, a graveled road, to a junction with a dirt road (*slippery when wet*), 2.4 *m*. Left here 1 *m*. to the ST. JAMES NATURAL TUNNEL, a passageway through a rock bluff, 150 feet long and 30 feet wide. A small spring rises from the tunnel's center and drains in both directions. In winter the tunnel is often used as a shelter for cattle.

At 4.5 *m*. on State 68 is a junction with State 8, a graveled road. Left here 3.1 *m*. to MERAMEC SPRINGS, a charming rustic scene. The spring is in a tiny wooded valley at the foot of a high, rock-studded cliff, and issues from a circular basin in a wide stream that rushes over an old rock dam, passes swiftly beneath an arched bridge, and flows onward into the Meramec River, approximately one mile away. The maximum flow is 271,000,000 gallons daily. At one time the water power was used to serve an iron mine, blast furnace, and gristmill. Today (1941) a small power plant, housed in a frame and native-stone building that blends with the wooded hillsides, uses the stream to develop electricity for a near-by dairy farm.

About the time of the cession of Louisiana to the United States (1804), Lewis Rogers and his band of Shawnee Indians (*see Archeology and Indians*), established their village near this spring. The site proved unhealthful and several Indians died. The remainder of the group, believing they had intruded "upon the dominion of a Matchee Monito, or Evil Spirit" moved to "Indian prairie, in Franklin county, a few miles south of Union."

Near the spring is the SITE OF THE MERAMEC IRON WORKS, established by Thomas James and Samuel Massey in 1826. Only one of the old open-hearth furnaces still stands, a monumental pyramid of cut stone. The ore was mined in the near-by banks of the Meramec, lime for flux and wood for charcoal came from the surrounding hills, and the great spring provided water power. Thomas James, owner of the mines and iron works, was born in Maryland in the 1770's. According to well-founded tradition, he learned of the Missouri iron deposits from a band of Shawnee Indians who visited his Brush Creek furnace in Adams County, Ohio. In 1826, with his foreman, Samuel Massey, and a force of miners, he began work. The village which he developed included a store, a blacksmith shop, and a gristmill. No saloons were allowed. The smelted iron was hauled to Washington and St. Louis until the construction of the St. Louis-San Francisco Railway through the region about 1860, when St. James became the shipping point. The furnace was operated until 1873 and the mine until about 1891.

At 113 *m*. is the northern junction with US 63 (*see Tour 8*), with which US 66 is united through ROLLA, 115 *m*. (1,120 alt., 5,141 pop.), an educational center and the seat of Phelps County. Pine

Street, following a slight ridge, is the business district; east and west, and climbing the hills that surround the town, are the residential streets.

The city had its beginning in 1855, when a group of contractors engaged in the construction of the St. Louis-San Francisco Railway selected a site near the home of John Webber on the Old Wire Road and erected an office and several warehouses. The prospect of a railroad created a mild boom. Within 6 months, 600 persons had moved there. In 1857, Phelps County was organized, and "the child of the railroad," was made the seat of government. The next step was selecting a name. According to legend, John Webber, who had tilled the land and should have known whereof he spoke, wanted to call the town Hardscrabble; E. W. Bishop, resident official of the railroad, wanted it called Phelps Center; George Coppedge, nostalgic for his North Carolina home, asked that it be named Raleigh. This last proposal was accepted and the name was spelled as Coppedge pronounced it, Rolla.

On January 1, 1861, a great crowd of people came from the hills to see their first train. With bells ringing and whistle blowing, a diamond-stacked locomotive puffed up to the new frame station, snorted a gust or two of wheezing white steam, and stopped.

As the western terminus of the section's only railroad, Rolla achieved considerable importance. Here, west-bound supplies from St. Louis and the East were transferred from freight car to wagon train. Here, too, persons en route to the Ozark highlands to homestead bought their equipment and supplies. When the Civil War began, its position made the town one of the first military objectives of the Union Army. Almost overnight a great Federal military encampment came into existence; trenches were dug and earthworks were constructed. On the north and south were two great forts (*see Tour 8*).

Merchants, professional men, and laborers flocked to the town. Families moved in from the hills for protection and supplies. Then, in the midst of the war boom, the railroad was extended west and, shortly afterward, the war ended. Rolla not only lost its strategic importance, but the completion of the Salem & Little Rock Railroad cut off a former trade territory. In 1871, however, it had a rebirth in the opening of the Missouri School of Mines. Today, its economic interests are divided. Each May, Rolla sponsors the Ozark Folk Festival.

The MISSOURI TRACHOMA HOSPITAL (*open 9-5*), southwestern edge of town, is one of two hospitals in the United States devoted to the treatment of this eye disease. The two-story fireproof building is equipped with 70 beds, facilities for visual training, a recreation and assembly room, a dining room, and a children's playroom. Completed in 1939 at a cost of $137,000 the building was financed by State and Federal funds. The grounds were a gift of the Rolla Chamber of Commerce.

Missouri, with 18,000 known cases, is one of the principal trachoma centers of the country. The disease consistently occurs in many Ozark localities, and is also prevalent among the tiff miners of Washington

County (*see Tour 13*). Although it may be alleviated, there is as yet no cure. State records reveal that about 1 case in 27 results in total loss of sight. The State expends $200,000 a year for cases of blindness caused by the disease, and carries on a continuous campaign of prevention. According to Spencer R. McCulloch, writing in the St. Louis *Post-Dispatch,* an estimated total of 1,000 persons in the State are blind because of trachoma, while hundreds of others are unable to earn a livelihood, but still are not eligible for State pensions.

The E. W. BISHOP HOUSE (*open by permission*), southwest corner of Eighth and Park Sts., set among wide-spreading oaks on a lot that is almost a city block, is said to have been the second house in Rolla. Diagonally across the front lawn is the slightly sunken trace of the stagecoach route between St. Louis and Springfield. The house was built by E. W. Bishop prior to the Civil War, and served during the conflict as a military hospital.

The PHELPS COUNTY COURTHOUSE, Main and Third Sts., overlooks the town from a hilltop in the southwestern section. A two-story red-brick building with white stone trim, it was begun in 1859 and completed about 1862. The front roofline of the main portion is surmounted by a cupola; on each side are low wings. Sheltering the entrance is a small iron balcony supported by slender iron columns. During the Civil War it was converted into a hospital for Federal troops.

The MISSOURI SCHOOL OF MINES, Twelfth and Pine Sts., a college of the University of Missouri, is on a 32-acre T-shaped campus shaded by groves of oak, elm, and maple trees. The dozen or more buildings are of brick and stone, two- and three-stories high. The driveway through the campus crosses a sunken garden.

In 1862 the Congress of the United States passed a bill granting a tract of public land to such States as would establish colleges especially equipped to train students in "agriculture and the mechanic arts." Eight years later Missouri passed a bill providing for the establishment of an agricultural and mechanical college at and connected with the State University at Columbia, and for a school of mines and metallurgy to be located in the mineral district of the State in the county that would give the largest bonus to the school. The Phelps County bid, totaling $130,000, exceeded the second highest bid by $17,000, and Rolla, the largest town in the county, was chosen as the site. That was in June 1871; the college opened in November of the same year. Its real development dates from 1890, however, when most of its buildings and equipment were added. Recognized as an outstanding institution of technology, the school offers courses in various branches of mining and metallurgical industries, including petroleum, electrical, chemical, and ceramic geology. The Mississippi Valley Experimental Station of the United States Bureau of Mines, the State Geological Survey, and the United States Geological Survey, Water Resource Division, all maintain headquarters at the school.

The MINERAL MUSEUM (*open weekdays*), third floor of Norwood Hall, is the foremost of its kind in the State. It was begun in 1904, when the Missouri mining exhibit at the St. Louis World's Fair was assigned to the school. In the same year the government of Mexico donated the Mexican exhibit, and later the Canadian government gave a collection of Canadian minerals. To these have been added the Missouri mineral exhibit from the Chicago Century of Progress Exposition, and numerous specimens acquired by purchase, exchange, and gift. Approximately 2,500 specimens are exhibited.

Section b. ROLLA to KANSAS LINE, 202 m. US 66

In southwestern Missouri the highlands of the Ozarks merge with the time-worn plateau of the Springfield area. The hill country, of flat-topped ridges, narrow stream valleys, and small sheltered farmsteads, gives way to the Western Plains, a land of broad gentle valleys and extensive fields of wheat, truck, and pasture. When Schoolcraft traveled through this region in 1819, he found the Ozark ridges "nearly destitute of forest, often perfectly so." This lack of trees was probably the result of the Indian practice (continued by many white settlers) of burning off the land each autumn, which left the soil thin and infertile. On the Springfield plateau, however, Schoolcraft found the soil rich and deep, and observed that "the purest springs gush from these hills . . . the atmosphere is fine and healthful." As the highway nears the Kansas Line, great piles of crushed grey rock indicate a once extensive mining area.

Between ROLLA, 0 *m.*, and Arlington, there is a drop of 425 feet as the highway cuts through rock bluffs and crosses the valleys of the Little Piney and Gasconade Rivers.

At 1 *m.* is a junction with an unmarked graveled road.

Left here across the railroad tracks to a small IRON MINE (*open by permission*), 0.6 *m.*, owned by the Missouri School of Mines and Metallurgy and used as a laboratory by students.

One of the many large springs in this region is MARTIN'S SPRING (L), 3.2 *m.*, enclosed within a squat stone house, with a daily flow of approximately 840,000 gallons. The water forms a small stream that empties into Little Beaver Creek.

At 6.9 *m.* is a junction with County T, a black-topped road.

Left here to NEWBURG, 2.2 *m.* (712 alt., 1,056 pop.), a railroad division point. The car repair shops of the St. Louis-San Francisco Railway are housed in a group of low, red frame buildings strung along the tracks between the main street and the Little Piney River. The site was settled by William Coppedge, who brought his wife, four sons, and two daughters here in 1823 and began manufacturing powder, using saltpetre from a near-by cave. No village was formed until Captain C. W. Rogers platted a town in 1883, in anticipation of a change in the railroad's division points. In 1894 the shops were moved here, thus giving Newburg an industrial life unusual in a region devoted almost exclusively to agriculture and recreation.

ARLINGTON, 13.2 *m.* (695 alt., 34 pop.), at the confluence of the Gasconade and Little Piney Rivers, is typical of the hamlets of the region. Through the redrawing of county lines, it has been successively in St. Louis, Gasconade, Crawford, Pulaski, and Phelps Counties, and was even for a short time seat of Crawford County. It also served briefly as a terminal of the St. Louis-San Francisco Railway. At present, it is an outfitting point for fishermen on the Gasconade and Little Piney Rivers (*boats and guides available*).

The small one-and-a-half-story log cabin, 13.5 *m.* (R), is the JAMES HARRISON HOUSE (*open*), one of the best examples of pioneer construction in Missouri. Placed on a low ridge, with its back to the present highway, the cabin's unpainted logs and handhewn shingles have weathered a dull gray. The mud chinking has acquired the appearance of cement; the windows have solid shutters. Said to have been erected in 1812, the cabin has been a pioneer home, a stagecoach station, and the courthouse of Crawford County. The storeroom served as the courtroom, and the grand jury "considered their presentments" in a near-by grove. James Harrison, the builder, was an energetic 200-pound Virginian, who with his sons, Robert and Thomas, was among the first men of affairs in Pulaski and Phelps Counties.

At 13.7 *m.* is a junction with County D, a graveled road.

Right here, crossing the clear, gravelly Gasconade River, to JEROME (692 alt., 195 pop.), 0.7 *m.*, a sprawling fishing resort (*boats and guides for fishing and float trips on the Gasconade and Little Piney Rivers*).

Westward, the highway climbs the more rugged ridges of the highlands, the true Ozark country, densely wooded with oak, hickory, elm, ash, dogwood, redbud, and hawthorn. The deep blue-green valleys are cut by swift, cold streams that offer excellent fishing. Sparsely settled by families from Virginia, Kentucky, and Tennessee during the restless era following the War of 1812, it remained a frontier until shortly after the Civil War, when timber interests moved in and built a few fair-sized towns. But the commercial timber was soon cut, and the people, unemployed, were forced to pioneer again. This time they turned to agriculture, but their denuded hillsides were washed from under them. Later, fishing resorts were developed here, and, with government aid, erosion-control areas, game preserves, and fish hatcheries.

STONY DELL (*cabins, picnicking, swimming*), 14 *m.*, is typical of the many privately operated resorts that have sprung up beside Ozark highways.

At 17.4 *m.* is a junction with an unmarked graveled road.

Right here, past two large sinks, to ONYX PARK AND CAVE (*adm. 35¢; cabins*), 0.9 *m.* (R). The roof of the cave rises sharply to form a large room. A small stream flowing diagonally across the floor into the Gasconade River is crossed on a fallen stalactite. From the first room the cavern winds into the hillside, forming a horseshoe-shaped tunnel nearly a mile long.

Within recent years the Ozark hill folk have become aware of the commercial value of their handicraft. Many have abandoned their small farm patches and settled along the principal roads. Such a group are the OZARK BASKET WEAVERS (L), 17.7 m., whose bright, clean baskets, strung on wires paralleling the highway, are in sharp contrast with their drab, listing shacks. Methods handed down for generations are used in weaving the cane and hickory splits into baskets. Such tools as are used are largely home-made.

HOOKER, 21 m. (713 alt., 120 pop.), is a focal point for fishermen on the Big Piney, Gasconade, and smaller streams. The highway passes through a mountainous section where second-growth oaks are dwarfed by the few primeval giants lumbering men have left. An occasional fertile valley is under cultivation.

The BIG PINEY RIVER, crossed at 22.7 m., plunges and twists its way from the south, entering the Gasconade River approximately two miles north of this point. The river offers good fishing for perch and smallmouthed and largemouthed bass. Its name had its origin in the short-leaf pine forests along its banks, which provided the first important commercial timber in the State.

DEVIL'S ELBOW, 22.8 m. (15 pop.), is a group of tourist and weekend cottages on a bend of the Big Piney River. The bluffs have been listed by the State Planning Commission as one of the seven beauty spots of Missouri. Legend says the name, Devil's Elbow, was given to the point by lumberjacks who feared and cursed the log jams that formed inevitably at the bend. A trailer camp is among the accommodations.

At 25.4 m. is a junction with State 28, a graveled road.

Right here to a junction with an unmarked graveled road, 2.2 m., which leads R. 0.9 m. to the entrance of POSSUM LODGE, a long-established fishing camp. Near by is a wagon ford used by pioneers. Many legends are connected with the site. One story tells of a wealthy Forty-niner who became ill at the ford on his way back East, and buried gold worth $60,000 in the near-by hills. Another legend has Jesse James and his robber band using the ford as a rendezvous and the hills as a hideaway.

At 3.7 m. (R) on State 28 is a good view of the narrow valley of the Gasconade River. Across the valley, rimming the river, are magnificent bluffs.

Crossing the Gasconade River, State 28 climbs the northern bluffs to PORTUGUESE POINT, 5.3 m., a high elevation formed by two large rocks jutting from the cliff's wall and overhanging the river. The valley circling the point is a popular subject for artists and photographers. It was originally settled by Portuguese farmers, who made a good living raising cattle and sheep.

At 28.9 m. is a junction with State 17, a graveled road.

Left here to the entrance to the GASCONADE DIVISION OF THE MARK TWAIN NATIONAL FOREST, 2.1 m., a 114,587-acre unit established in 1933 under the supervision of the National Park Service (see Tour 14). The forest authorities are restoring, protecting, and using natural resources to furnish employment and pleasure to the people of the State. Of the gross receipts from all forest revenues, such as grazing permits, timber sales, and the lease of recreational areas, 25 per cent is given to local counties for roads and schools.

At 12 *m.* is an unmarked graveled road, which leads L. 3.4 *m.* to BIG PINEY (100 pop.), a tiny crossroads village. Left 3.1 *m.* on an unmarked road, and R. at each fork, is MILLER SPRING, issuing from the foot of a massive cliff. The spring, one of the largest in the State, has attracted scientific attention because of its curious ebb and flow; the amount of water gushing forth measures from 3,000,000 to 13,000,000 gallons daily. The creek formed by the spring drains into Big Piney River a quarter of a mile away. Near by in the bluff is MILLER CAVE (*free; no guides or improvements; inquire at house*), investigated by representatives of the Smithsonian Institution and believed to have been the dwelling of a primitive people. Basing their opinions on the mortars, pestles, bone awls, animal and human skeletons, and other objects uncovered here, archeologists advance the theory that the cave was continuously occupied for several thousand years. Many artifacts found here are displayed at the Smithsonian Institution in Washington, D. C.

WAYNESVILLE, 32 *m.* (806 alt., 468 pop.), at the foot of variegated rock cliffs and all but surrounded by serpent-like Roubidoux Creek, is the most venerable of Pulaski County towns, and is, as might be expected, the county seat. It has a leisurely atmosphere, unmarred by the smoke of industry and the impatient panting of trains, and but little jarred by farmers' Saturday visits or meetings of the county court. Hill people buy their blue denim and flour, their coffee, salt, and sugar with unhurried deliberation. Between purchases they talk. All are called by first names, except the very old. These receive the title of "uncle" or "aunt," and are always referred to by both given name and surname, as "Uncle Jim Corbin."

Waynesville's county court has been in existence for over a hundred years. G. W. Gibson "squatted" on the townsite early in the year 1831, when the near-by spring was a watering place on the Kickapoo Trace (later known as the Old Wire Road). In 1835 James A. Bates opened a store that served also as a temporary courthouse. More people moved in, and in 1839 the town was platted. Harvey Wood secured the post office and named it for "Mad Anthony" Wayne.

About the time Pulaski County was organized, the "ill-famed Counterfeit bank of Niangua" set itself up with a president, cashier, clerks, and a "grave board of directors." The enterprise, described by Wetmore in his *Gazetteer of the State of Missouri* (1837), flourished until "Mistress Missouri Anne Amanda Jemina Skidmore," widow of a director who had been denied his share of the profits, "sharpened her fingernails afresh, and with the extreme violence of female passion, declared a war of extermination against the counterfeiters." With her assistance the United States Marshal broke up the ring.

During the Civil War, town and county were for the South. The courthouse flew the Confederate flag, until Federal troops marched down the Old Wire Road and took over the town on June 7, 1862. A small fort was built as a base on the Federal supply line between Rolla and Lebanon. Since the war, Waynesville has tried lumbering and agriculture and at present is looking with interest upon the ever-increasing tourist trade.

1. Left from Waynesville on an unmarked road to WAYNESVILLE SPRING, 0.5 *m.*, boiling from the rocks at the edge of the road, which is protected by

a concrete retaining wall. After heavy rains the flow of the spring increases from a normal daily flow of 7,000,000 gallons to 104,000,000 gallons. The water empties into Roubidoux Creek, which at high stages submerges the spring.

2. Right from Waynesville on State 17, an asphalt highway, to PIKE'S PEAK CAVE (*adm. 35¢; guides*), 2.4 *m.*, a large cavern with a wide, high entrance in a bluff overlooking the junction of Roubidoux Creek and the Gasconade River. There is a dance floor in the entrance chamber. Fishing in both streams is good.

The highway crosses the northwestern boundary of the Gasconade Division of the Mark Twain National Forest at 36 *m.*, and at 40 *m.* forms a junction with County P, a graveled road.

Right here to a junction with County A, a graveled road, 1.2 *m.;* R. on County A, along a high, narrow ridge and across the Gasconade River, to the OZARK SPRING RESORT (*overnight accommodations*), 5.5 *m.* From the resort a graveled road leads 2 *m.* to TURKEY RIDGE, a plateau-like elevation approximately 4 miles wide and 15 miles long, named for the wild turkeys there. On the ridge is POOR MAN'S CHANCE, developed by E. A. Steckel, who, after being pronounced an incurable cripple, was given 80 acres here by a friend. Steckel, in gathering native ferns for eastern markets, regained his health. In gratitude, he divided his land into ten-acre plots, which he sold to poor farmers at a nominal price. A community of neat houses and profitable orchards has been the result.

HAZELGREEN, 48 *m.* (64 pop.), a trading center and fishing resort, is bounded on three sides by the ever-twisting Gasconade River (*boats and guides for fishing and float trips*). Along the highway and on side roads marked by signs are many resorts equipped for the convenience of fishermen and their families.

At 53 *m.* is a junction with County T, a graveled road.

Right here to WET GLAIZE, 13 *m.* (32 pop.), site of the OZARK FISH HATCHERY (*open*), one of the country's largest hatcheries for the exclusive propagation of goldfish. The fish are reared in a hundred small ponds fed by a large spring.

LEBANON, 65 *m.* (1,265 alt., 5,025 pop.), the seat of Laclede County, is the only urban center on US 66 between Rolla and Springfield. A sprawling town of tree-shaded streets and frame and native-stone houses, Lebanon reflects the agricultural prosperity of the surrounding plateau. It is a shipping point for wheat, corn, oats, and hay; within the last decade, the value of its dairy products has increased from $2,000 a year to $2,000 a week. An overall factory supplements this agricultural income.

Although Jesse Ballew is said to have been the first man to cross the hills and settle in the vicinity, supposedly in 1820, Lebanon had its beginning when Laclede County was formed October 1, 1849. During the Civil War, the community gained strategic importance through its location on the military road between St. Louis and Springfield, the line of march for both armies. It was occupied alternately by the North and the South. At the end of the war, the town's badly disrupted economy was further demoralized by the coming of the railroad in 1868 and the re-location of the town. It is said that railroad officials, denied free land and a depot in town, built their station a mile from the village center. Lebanon picked itself up and moved to the new site. As Harold Bell Wright says in *The Calling of Dan Matthews,* the residents "left the beautiful, well drained site chosen by those who cleared the wilderness and stretched themselves along the sacred right of way." Lebanon has grown and thrived on the mud flat, with depot, yards, section house, and water tanks dominating her business district. It was in Lebanon, as pastor of the First Christian Church, that Harold Bell Wright, the novelist, began his literary career.

The RICHARD PARKS BLAND STATUE, SW. corner of the courthouse square, commemorates Lebanon's most distinguished citizen. Bland was born in Hartford, Kentucky, August 19, 1835, and came to Missouri from Nevada in 1865. After practicing law for four years in Rolla, he moved to Lebanon. In 1872 he was elected to Congress, where he so distinguished himself that he was returned to office 12 times. He suffered political defeat in his district only once, in 1894. Called "Silver Dick" for his 16-to-1 free-coinage stand in 1877, he was co-author of the unsatisfactory Bland-Allison Act. In 1890 Bland renewed his fight for unrestricted coinage of silver. In 1896 he was leading candidate for the Democratic presidential nomination, until William Jennings Bryan unleashed his oratory at the national convention. On June 15, 1899, Bland died at his farm near Lebanon.

JOSEPH W. McCLURG MEMORIAL, Lebanon Cemetery at the northern edge of town, is a simple granite shaft erected by the State in honor of another notable Missourian. Joseph W. McClurg, pioneer builder and merchant, began his political career as deputy sheriff of St. Louis County at the age of 20. Emerging from the first year of the Civil War with the rank of Colonel, he was elected to Congress in 1862, and served three terms. As governor (1868-70), he was largely responsible for the establishment of the Missouri School of Mines and Metallurgy, the agricultural college at the University of Missouri, and the State normal schools at Kirksville and Warrensburg. McClurg died in 1900.

The BLICKENSDERFER INDIAN RELIC COLLECTION, in Joe's Delight Barber Shop, Commercial St. between Jackson and Monroe Sts., contains more than 1,500 Indian arrowheads, tomahawks, mortar stones, skinning knives, and other articles found in the vicinity.

Right from Lebanon on State 64, an asphalt highway, to a fork at 10.8 *m.;* L. here 1.2 *m.* to BENNETT SPRING STATE PARK (*cabins, hotels, camping grounds, trout fishing, hiking, horseback riding, swimming, and one-day float trips*), a major recreational area. Comprising 574 acres of hilly, wooded lands, and cut by the blue-green Niangua River, the park includes the former hamlet of Brice, settled by James Brice in 1837. Here, separated by landscaped lawns, are shelter houses, a post office, store, and tavern—all constructed of native stone in modern design.

BENNETT SPRING, the sixth largest in the State, rises quietly from a circular basin with an average flow of about 95,000,000 gallons of water daily. The spring stream tumbles over a six-foot dam, passes beneath a rustic stone bridge, and crosses approximately a mile of rock ledges and gravel bars before entering the Niangua River. At the dam, a part of the water is diverted into a millrace, which is divided into sections and used as a FISH HATCHERY for breeding rainbow trout, clearly visible in the water. The hatchery raises 200,000 fish annually, with which it restocks the State's streams. Muskrat and mink, protected by park attendants, are plentiful along the waterway, and are quite tame. BENNETT'S MILL, a three-story red frame gristmill on the stream's bank, is the "Gordon's Mill" of Harold Bell Wright's *The Calling of Dan Matthews*. The old miller was a friend of Wright's, and the author spent much time here while writing the book. The Niangua River and the small pool above the dam are two of the best fishing spots in Missouri.

MARSHFIELD, 96 *m.* (1,487 alt., 1,764 pop.), half-hidden among the hills and valleys (L), was named in honor of the Massachusetts home of Daniel Webster. The business district is built about the two-story, brown-brick Webster County courthouse, an imposing structure erected in 1870, with twin cupolas and an arched passageway through the center. Marshfield is a shipping point for corn, oats, and barley, for chickens and dairy products, and for tomatoes—the latter the all important crop, for Webster County is one of the largest tomato producing areas of the State. The fruit must be picked as soon as it is ripe, and wrapped, packed, and shipped immediately. The processing is done in Marshfield, where everyone is concerned about prices and weather, since livelihood depends on these.

The Flannagan family, who arrived in the early 1830's, are said to have been the first white settlers within the present limits of Marshfield. The town was not surveyed until 1856. During the Civil War the village suffered numerous raids. In 1878 and 1880 it was visited by tornadoes which killed 87 persons, injured 200, and removed the second story of the courthouse. Since then things have gone fairly quietly, with only the rise and fall of farm prices to affect the town's tranquillity.

Between Marshfield and Strafford the highway passes from the highlands into the Old Plains or Springfield Plateau. The land is gently rolling and adapted to cultivation. Peculiarly isolated in pioneer days because of its distance from large streams and the difficult country to the east, its history is more meager than that of other border sections. Prior to the War of 1812 it was known as the Osage Country. Some time during or immediately after the war, a band of Kickapoo Indians moved into the area, causing it to be known as Kickapoo Prairie. The land, settled comparatively late, has lent itself to development in large farms for dairy herds, wheat, and oats.

STRAFFORD, 110 *m.* (1,478 alt., 175 pop.), is a crossroads hamlet on land that was once a Kickapoo Indian reservation. By the Treaty of Edwardsville, Illinois (1819), the Kickapoo Indians ceded lands in Illinois and Indiana to the United States in exchange for these lands in southwest Missouri. In 1832, by the Treaty of Castor Hill, St. Louis County, this was again exchanged for lands west of the Missouri State line.

Left from Strafford on an unmarked graveled road, taking first road R., then L. at fork, to the DANFORTH HOUSE (*open by permission*), 2.7 *m.*, an excellent indication of the prosperity and culture developed on the Old Plains shortly before the Civil War. Erected in 1839 and enclosed by a low stone fence, the house is a two-story white structure of Georgian design. The brick of which it is built was fired on the place by slaves, and the deep-set stone of the foundation was dug from quarries in the vicinity. On the lawn is a millstone shipped from France to Natchez by way of New Orleans, and thence across the river and overland by wagon. On an opposite hill is the site of the plantation slave quarters and graveyard. The house was built by Josiah Danforth, and, it is said, was once used as a wayside tavern. It is occupied by a descendant of the builder.

SPRINGFIELD, 121 m. (1,345 alt., 61,238 pop.) (see *Springfield*), is at a junction with US 65 (*see Tour 9*) and US 60 (*see Tour 6*); with the latter, US 66 is united for seven miles.

West of Springfield the highway crosses thickly settled country. The farms are smaller, but the yield is greater than in the region to the east. The principal crops are wheat, oats, strawberries, dairy products, and poultry, with orchards providing a supplementary source of income.

At 137.4 m. is a junction with County F, a graveled road.

Right here to ASH GROVE, 9 m. (1,048 alt., 1,101 pop.), a prosperous farm trading center settled and named by Colonel Nathan Boone, the youngest son of Daniel Boone. R. from Ash Grove 1.8 m. on County V, a graveled road, to (R) the NATHAN BOONE HOUSE (*open by permission*), a "double" cabin built by Colonel Boone in 1837, when he moved his family to Greene County. The exterior logs have been weather-boarded and a new roof has been added, but otherwise the cabin is unchanged. The wide plank flooring is held in place by wooden pegs. The house has four rooms divided by a simple hallway. At each end of the house is a native-stone chimney. Near the cabin is the family cemetery, containing the graves of Nathan Boone and his wife, Olive van Bibber Boone (*see Tour 1A*).

At HALLTOWN, 140 m. (1,143 alt., 168 pop.), is a junction with an unmarked dirt road.

Left here to CHESAPEAKE STATE PARK (*picnic grounds*), 3 m., a 117-acre tract on which is maintained a State fish hatchery for bass, crappie, goggle-eye, and bluegill.

CARTHAGE, 179 m. (941 alt., 10,585 pop.) (*see Tour 10*), is at a junction with US 71 (*see Tour 10*). Westward are the famous Tri-State lead and zinc fields, centering about Joplin and embracing the border counties of Missouri, Kansas, and Oklahoma. When the mines were in full operation, the district produced one fourth of the world's zinc. The contemporary scene, however, is characterized by great piles of chat, dusty-looking buildings, and smokeless chimneys, in sharp contrast with the carefully cultivated wheat, oats, and dairy farms that surround them.

CARTERVILLE, 188 m. (1,003 alt., 1,582 pop.), reflects the desolation that descended on Missouri's great lead and zinc mining area when the mines were closed shortly after the World War. Once a vigorous, prosperous city of 12,000 persons, the town now stretches between great white mounds of chat, and its main street, built unusually wide to carry a heavy traffic, is all but empty.

Carterville was surveyed in August 1875, shortly after John C. Webb had discovered lead in the vicinity (*see below*) and W. A. Daugherty had erected the first house. The following year a hotel was built, and in 1877 the town was incorporated. The World War demand for zinc caused a boom in Carterville as it did in Webb City and other towns of the district. Laborers, professional men, salesmen, and adventurers poured in. New dwellings and business houses were erected, streetcar lines and additional railroad tracks were laid. Then the war ended, production fell off, and, one by one, the mines shut down. Most of the miners moved away. Those who remained have drained several of the mines, however, and, in groups of two or three, are reworking the veins.

Between Carterville and Webb City the mounds of chat and abandoned shafts are continuous.

WEBB CITY, 189 *m.* (1,003 alt., 7,033 pop.), in contrast to Carterville, checked the rapid decline that set in at the death of its principal industry by developing new sources of income. The T-shaped business district retains at least a semblance of its former activity, and only a few of the pre-World War commercial buildings are vacant. The residence sections are shady and clean; the houses are kept in repair.

Until 1873 the site of Webb City was part of the fertile acres belonging to John C. Webb, whose corn and wheat farm consisted of a quarter-section bounded on the east by the Carter farm. In the summer of 1873, as Webb was following his team over the fields, his plowshare hit a hard, half-submerged chunk of lead. Webb put the specimen aside until fall when his corn had been harvested. That winter he showed his discovery to W. A. Daugherty, who immediately became his partner. The winter's work brought little success, however, because of water in the mine. After the second year Webb became discouraged, and sold his interest to C. P. Ashcraft, an experienced miner, who promptly dynamited the shaft. The explosion threw lead in all directions, and opened the greatest mining era Missouri has known.

Some of the miners and promoters who flocked to the area settled to the east, establishing Carterville on Mr. Carter's farm; others settled to the west, on Webb's land. In July 1875, Webb platted the town of Webb City. In the 1880's, discovery of commercial uses for zinc expanded local mineral production. A large semicircle of mines half surrounded the town; the population doubled almost over night. Between 1894 and 1904 the mines produced approximately $23,000,000 in mineral wealth, yet did not reach their peak until 1917-18, when crews worked night and day filling World War orders. At the end of the war Webb City turned its attention to agriculture, and textile and processing plants were opened. Today (1941) two large factories produce work clothes and other wearing apparel, and an enterprising gravel company turns the chat of abandoned mines into road-construction material. Two hospitals further contribute to the resources of the community.

Right from Webb City on an unmarked black-topped road to ORONOGO, 3.8 *m.* (975 alt., 593 pop.), a dilapidated, ghostlike reminder of Jasper County's lead and zinc mining industry. Here is the ORONOGO CIRCLE MINE (*open weekdays 8-4; guides*), famed for the production of some $30,000,000 worth of lead and zinc ore during the last half century. The mine, all but hidden by mounds of chat, operates in an open pit approximately 200 feet deep. Said to have been bought in 1854 for $50, the 10-acre circular tract was at one time the scene of operations for 20 mining firms. The initial purchaser, who bought the land before ore was discovered, operated by lease at a reported $9,000,000 profit. He then sold his title to another firm, which also leased the building and mining rights for a substantial fee. Since the 1890's, the original $50 land purchase has made a dozen or more millionaires.

Between Webb City and the Kansas Line are continuous mounds of chat left by former smelting and mining operators and now being processed by smaller firms who recover as much as 5 per cent of lead and zinc concentrates. These tailing mills have produced approximately 25 per cent of the output of the district in recent years.

At 196 *m.* is JOPLIN (1,008 alt., 37,144 pop.) (*see Joplin*).

US 66 crosses the KANSAS LINE, 202 *m.*, 58 miles northeast of Vinita, Oklahoma.

Tour 6

(Cairo, Ill.)—Poplar Bluff—Cabool—Springfield—Neosho—(Vinita, Okla.) ; US 60.
Illinois Line to Oklahoma Line, 374 *m.*

Concrete paved roadbed.
Missouri Pacific R. R. parallels route between Mississippi River and Poplar Bluff; St. Louis-San Francisco (Frisco) Ry. parallels route between Poplar Bluff and Oklahoma Line.
All types of accommodations in larger towns; limited elsewhere.

In one great westward sweep US 60 reveals all the geographic variations of southern Missouri. It crosses first the broad southeastern lowland where cotton is king and the tenant system is general, then climbs, almost imperceptibly, to the forested highlands of the Ozarks. Westward are the mining districts and the high plains, where dairying, grain farming, and poultry raising share the economic scene. Much of the country through which the route passes is sparsely settled; its chief attractions are the scenery, the fishing streams, and the people.

Section a. ILLINOIS LINE to CABOOL; 203 m. US 60

Between the Mississippi River and Poplar Bluff, the route traverses Missouri's great alluvial plain, an extensive flat land of sluggish bayous, lakes, and connecting drainage ditches.   Often referred to as a land of cotton, it is in reality an area in which the four principal crops of the Nation—cotton, corn, wheat, and legumes—grow in adjoining fields. In late summer, as the cotton and grain ripen, the area is a checkerboard of white and yellow.   The small towns follow a single pattern; each has its group of cotton gins, grain warehouses, loading platforms, filling stations, and low brick stores.   West of Poplar Bluff the magnificently timbered Ozarks offer varied recreational opportunities.

US 60 crosses the MISSOURI LINE 0 *m.,* on a toll bridge (*$1 one way, $1.50 round trip*) over the Mississippi River from Cairo, Illinois. The bridge was designed by the New York firm of Waddell and Hardesty, and was completed in 1929 at a cost of $3,100,000.

At the Missouri approach to the interstate bridge is the scattered community of BIRD'S POINT (318 alt., 118 pop.), near which, about 1800, the first settlement in Mississippi County was made.   The Bird family, who developed a lively mercantile business at the junction of the two rivers, were receiving and forwarding agents for shippers breaking their cargoes at this point.   Here, boats on the New Orleans-St. Louis run unloaded goods destined for Ohio River towns and picked up consignments from the East for delivery at Mississippi ports.   Thus an early record mentions Abraham Bird, in 1811, as "agent at Bird's Point near the mouth of the Ohio," loading and unloading Christian Wilt's flatboats from St. Louis, or his keelboats that plied the Ohio.   Wilt was a leading St. Louis merchant (*see Industry, Commerce and Labor*).

A short distance upstream from the bridge approach is the JOHN A. BIRD HOUSE (*open*), a story-and-a-half frame building erected in 1822 and now weathered to a condition of semi-decay.   During the Civil War, Federal troops took over the house and plantation, arrested Bird for alleged participation in anti-Federal activities, and seized his ferryboat, the *Manchester.*

For several miles the highway rides the setback levee that cuts diagonally across Mississippi County to form the NEW MADRID FLOODWAY.   Left of the levee is an extensive basin constructed to impound the flood waters of the Mississippi and Ohio Rivers and to protect Cairo and towns to the south.   The land in the basin is extremely fertile and has been the source of much litigation with respect to damage caused by the flooding of the basin.

At WYATT, 7 *m.* (320 alt., 417 pop.), is a junction with County E, a graveled road.

Left here to County U, another graveled road, 11.2 *m.;* L. again, crossing an old levee, to the BELMONT BATTLEFIELD, 16.9 *m.,* marked by a giant cottonwood that had its top shot away by artillery fire.   On November 5, 1861, four thousand Federal soldiers under the command of U. S. Grant embarked on transports at Cairo, their headquarters, and were convoyed down the river. Early next morning, they landed within three miles of Belmont, Missouri, and marched toward the Confederate camp. Grant, according to his memoirs, intended to make a demonstration, not to fight a battle. His men, however, were tired of drilling and zealously attacked the Confederates. The Southerners, greatly outnumbered, took advantage of the woods and marshlands and fought for four hours before retreating. Even then they kept up a desultory fire along the river bank. The Federals, however, considered the battle won. The men sacked the Confederate camp; the officers made political speeches. Meanwhile, reinforcements reached the Confederates, who reopened the battle, forcing the Federals to retreat to their transports. The Confederacy lost 642 men, the Union, 480. Born of the battle is the legend that as General Grant forced his horse down the transport's gangplank, a lean hunter from the hills drew a bead upon him, then, without firing the shot that might have altered the Civil War, lowered his rifle. When questioned concerning his hesitancy, he explained, "Well, I wasn't right certain it was Grant on that horse." Hill people never waste lead on shots they cannot call.

CHARLESTON, 15 m. (327 alt., 5,182 pop.), is the capital of this cotton country and a shoe manufacturing city of consequence.

In May 1837, John Rodney surveyed on Matthew's Prairie slightly more than 16 acres belonging to Thankful Randol, Joseph Moore, and W. P. Bernard, and platted the town of Charleston. The prairie had been popular with the Spanish and Anglo-Americans because of the buffalo herds it supported. As families from Tennessee and Kentucky developed cotton plantations in the lowlands, Charleston grew as a trading and shipping center. When Mississippi County was created, February 14, 1845, from part of Scott County, Charleston became the county seat. During the Civil War the local bank was robbed of $100,000, but was spared an additional $55,000 loss by a quick-witted cashier, who hid the money in a trash barrel. After the war, the town resumed its business of trading with and financing cotton farmers.

Cotton determines the life and manners of much of the southeastern Missouri delta. Between January and March, when the farmer prepares for spring planting, crop production loans are arranged. The landowner makes his working and seed loans, and contracts with a local merchant for his tenants' supplies. In turn, the tenants strike bargains with the landlord and sign share agreements. The marketing season, usually from late August through November, is tense until the price of cotton, always erratic, has been set.

BERTRAND, 21.1 m. (321 alt., 377 pop.), on the Missouri Pacific Railroad, was laid out in 1859 by H. J. Deal. SIKESTON, 29 m. (318 alt., 7,944 pop.) (see Tour 7), is at junction with US 61 (see Tour 7).

MOREHOUSE, 36 m. (287 alt., 1,598 pop.), established as a shipping point for lumber on the Cairo branch of the Iron Mountain Railroad (Missouri Pacific), had a prosperous career while the commercial timber of the area lasted. Today, its only industry is a wood-working plant, which employs 200 men in the manufacture of table tops, radio cabinets, mop handles, and the like.

West of Morehouse the route crosses the LITTLE RIVER DRAINAGE DISTRICT, one of the largest drainage developments ever undertaken without State or Federal aid. A prosperous land of corn, wheat, cotton, oats, and other crops, the district comprises an area of approximately 550,000 acres. Near the close of the last century lumbering interests bought great acreages at low prices. After the timber had been cut, they found themselves the owners of a swampy, unhealthful marsh, where travel was difficult, and community life almost unknown. Otto Kochtitzky, representative of one of the lumber companies, proposed organizing the area into a single drainage district. By 1905 sufficient interest had been created for the State legislature to pass an enabling act under the provisions of which a company was formed with Kochtitzky as chief engineer. The total cost of $13,000,-000 was met by benefit assessments ranging from $4 to $40 an acre. The drainage system consists of a great headwater diversion canal, three detention basins in which flood waters are temporarily impounded, and 899 miles of lesser channels spaced at one-mile intervals. Similar drainage plans have reclaimed more than 2,000,000 acres in southeastern Missouri.

DEXTER, 53 m. (323 alt., 3,108 pop.), on the peak of Crowley's Ridge, a dissected *cuesta* extending from Cape Girardeau to Helena, Arkansas, is at the crossroads of the Missouri Pacific and Cotton Belt Railroads. Laid out in 1873, Dexter supports a variety of industries: a large flour mill, a cotton gin, a shirt factory, and a poultry packing plant. At Dexter is a junction with State 25 (*see Tour 11*).

The ST. FRANCIS RIVER, 67.5 m., crossed on one of the largest steel and concrete bridges in the State, is an important drainage and fishing stream. On the western bank is FISK, 68 m. (334 alt., 386 pop.), an important rice shipping point.

Right from the west end of Fisk's main street on a graveled road to another graveled road, 0.8 m.; L. here to the ROY UTLEY RICE FARM (*open*), 0.3 m., probably the most successful in the State. Here, the cereal that the Oriental plants, cultivates, and harvests by hand is raised entirely by machine. Great fields, underlaid by hardpan, are marked off by dirt dikes 12 to 18 inches high. Between April 25 and May 15, the seed is drilled into the dry soil. When the plant puts forth three leaves, the fields are flooded and the land kept under water for approximately 100 days, or until the kernel has hardened. The field is then quickly drained and dried, and the grain is harvested. In 1938 the farm produced an average yield of 80 bushels an acre, at a production cost of about 40¢ a bushel.

Between Fisk and Poplar Bluff, the highway continues through a partly wooded country, crossing the innumerable drainage ditches that run north and south over the whole eastern half of Butler County. At 76.9 m. is a junction with County T, a marked graveled road.

Right here to the WAPPAPELLO DAM, 18 m., under construction (1940) across the St. Francis River. The $6,656,000 project is part of an extensive program of flood control covering this area and adjoining parts of Arkansas.

US 60 crosses the BLACK RIVER, 79.5 m., on a steel and concrete bridge. This popular fishing stream follows a lazy course across the lowlands on its way to Arkansas and the Mississippi.

POPLAR BLUFF, 80 *m.* (436 alt., 11,163 pop.), on the outer fringe of the Ozark highlands, above the Black River and the alluvial plains of southeastern Missouri, is the seat of Butler County. Main Street, crossing US 60 at right angles, follows a ridge that is part of the bluffs which give the town its name. In an angle formed by Main Street and a bend of the Black River is the business district, with factories, woodworking plants, stave mills, and produce houses on the river front. Slightly north of these are the division shops of the Missouri Pacific. Downstream are numerous camping, fishing, and bathing resorts.

The region was a favorite one with the Indians and their predecessors, who left more than 1,800 mounds in the area. Hunters from Tennessee and Kentucky probably visited it in pre-settlement days. Solomon Kittrell, said to have been the first resident of the county, emigrated from Kentucky in 1819, and cleared a farm on Cane Creek, where he built a distillery and tan yard. Development of the isolated, unhealthful area was slow. The "shakes" and other swamp fevers killed many of the settlers, and debilitated those who survived. Nonetheless, by 1849 sufficient land had been cleared and settled for Butler County to be formed from Wayne County; it was named for General William O. Butler of Kentucky, an officer in the Mexican War, and Democratic candidate for Vice President in 1848.

Poplar Bluff was founded in 1850 by a commission appointed to select a site for a county seat. The land chosen was a grove of poplar trees on the low bluffs that outline Black River, the last high ground on the river's downstream course toward the Arkansas border. The town grew slowly, and during the Civil War was almost entirely depopulated by guerrilla warfare. In 1873, the completion of the Iron Mountain Railroad ushered in great lumbering activity. For the next forty years Poplar Bluff mills cut timber into railroad and bridge dimension stock, and finished materials for houses, furniture, barrels, wagon and automobile wheels, tool handles, and oil well sucker rods.

As the timber fell from the hillsides, farming activities slowly expanded. The lowlands were drained, and Poplar Bluff, determined to survive the decline of its single industry, set about building storage and shipping facilities for the farmers, and developing other industries to supplement the remaining woodworking plants. Another railroad, part of the present Frisco system, was built through Poplar Bluff, and rail transportation, combined with the highway system developed in recent years, has made Poplar Bluff a wholesale as well as a retail center for southeastern Missouri and part of northeastern Arkansas. Shortly before 1900, large deposits of ceramic clays were discovered in the environs of the town; the mining of these and of iron ore has provided additional revenue.

The BUTLER COUNTY COURTHOUSE, Courthouse Square, houses in the office of the probate judge (*open by permission*) a collection of Indian relics from mounds near Poplar Bluff.

The A. L. HINRICHS TOTEM POLES, 137½ B St., are "histories carved in wood." One, for example, tells the story of Missouri: from prehistoric days to the time of the Spaniards on one panel, from the arrival of Daniel Boone to the present on another. On another pole is carved a biography of Mark Twain, in 25 tableaux. The artist selects the trees he wishes to carve, saws and squares them, then, with a pocketknife and a few homemade tools, carves the designs.

MUNICIPAL UTILITIES PARK, three blocks north of US 60 on Second St., a landscaped plot containing a swimming pool, surrounds the impressive, municipally owned power and water plant. On the highway, as it approaches the western edge of the city, is the two-story, yellow-brick FIELD HOUSE (R), which serves Poplar Bluff as high school gymnasium, civic auditorium, and recreational center. Adjacent is a modern concrete stadium.

At 80.8 m. is the southern junction with US 67 (see Tour 12).

West of Poplar Bluff the highway enters the true Ozarks, a wild, fragrant region where night falls swiftly and white herons rest in willow thickets. Lanes wind from the highway past cabins whose dooryards are overgrown with dog fennel, pennyroyal, and Queen Anne's lace, and past white frame churches set high off the ground. The primeval quiet of which Schoolcraft wrote in 1819 still lies over these hills, disturbed only by the tinkle of a sheep-bell or the baying of a hound.

On a wooded knoll, 81.3 m., is the DISTRICT FOREST RANGERS HEADQUARTERS (R). The administrative offices, under the direction of a district ranger, and the fire-fighting equipment are housed in four dwelling-type buildings with green roofs and shutters. Beyond is the northern junction with US 67 (see Tour 12).

West of the junction, US 60 becomes a winding scenic drive through the WAPPAPELLO DIVISION OF THE CLARK NATIONAL FOREST. The 347,592-acre tract is one of eight national forest divisions in southern Missouri and was established only after a long and bitter legislative fight between opposing State factions (see Tour 14). The hill folk who owned and lived on the land followed the proceedings with mixed emotions. Some welcomed the arrival of the college-trained forest rangers and their corps of trained helpers; others would have no "truck" with them, saying, "They talked right smart enough, all right, but 'til yet I ain't seen one who kain tell by a hound dawg's bay whether it's a coon or 'possum he's got treed." The sale of land was optional. Many who lived in the forest accepted a fair price, some with tongue in cheek, others because "what's a man wantin' with a piece o' land if there's gonna be a bunch o' smart alecks runnin' around in green britches and shiny boots a-telling yuh what yuh kain and kain't do?" By 1938, however, one and all—the efficient ranger, the scientist endeavoring to control erosion, the recreation leader, and the native—were trying to contribute to the social and economic rehabilitation of the area.

The charming one-story cabin (R), 85 m., advertised as the OZARK DOG KENNEL, is the home of R. E. Koontz, nationally known dog trainer. Behind the cabin are the kennels where Koontz keeps his hunters, and where he boards the many pointers and setters that are brought to him each year for training in the field.

Along the banks of CANE CREEK, 85.8 *m.*, ran the first national road in this part of the country. Constructed during Jackson's administration, it was used by Indian tribes moving to the Southwest, then by stagecoaches and wagon trains. At a point near the bridge, the first settlers of Butler County, Southerners and slave owners, built cotton gins, tan yards, blacksmith shops, and taverns.

Between Cane Creek and Cabool, steep hillsides of oak, pawpaw, hickory, and cottonwood alternate with small clearings made by tractor-run sawmills. The impress of the pioneer remains both in the architecture of the region and in the unpretentious manner of the people, descendants of Scotch-Irish families who moved from Kentucky in ox-drawn wagons (1830-40), and built their cabins around log or white frame churches.

AT ELLSINORE, 107 *m.* (710 alt., 267 pop.), a sawmill town within the national forest, is a junction with County A, a graveled road.

Right here to a LOOKOUT TOWER, 1 *m.*, a steel structure 80 feet high, where forest rangers keep a constant watch. Fire control operations are explained to those who climb to the tower box.

Past the western boundary of the Wappapello Division of the Clark National Forest, 115.2 *m.*, the dense timber continues as the route ascends successive hills. At 111 *m.* is the southern junction with State 21 (*see Tour 13*), with which US 60 is united for 12 miles through a section of the Big Springs country, a land of steep ranges, swift rivers, and innumerable springs. Divided into almost equal parts by the Current River, the area is perhaps the best fishing region in the Ozarks (*see Tour 14*).

VAN BUREN, 131 *m.* (1,345 alt., 458 pop.), is a Current River fishing resort and the seat of Carter County. The town lies in a narrow valley between precipitous hills, with its central business district forming a square about the newly built native-stone courthouse. The chief economic asset of the town is the Current River, widely known for its fighting smallmouthed bass. Almost every other house offers tourists accommodations, and several boat lines operating on the river offer fishing and float trips.

Carter County was organized March 10, 1859, and named for Zimri Carter, the county's first settler, who had built a cabin a few miles south of Van Buren in 1812. County commissioners selected Van Buren as the center of government in 1859. The town had formerly been the seat of Ripley County, and its old log courthouse was used by the courts until 1867.

Left from Van Buren on State 103, a black-topped road, to BIG SPRING STATE PARK (*cabins, dining lodge, and bathhouse, nominal fees; camping and picnic grounds, free*), 3.6 *m.*, an area of 4,416 wooded acres varying in altitude from 450 to 910 feet above sea level. Across Big Springs Branch from the park's recreational center is BIG SPRING, one of the largest springs in America. Surging impatiently from an immense basin at the bottom of a 250-foot limestone cliff, the pale blue water drops from a ledge, rebounds in a spray from the boulders that break its fall, and rushes off to the Current River. One day's flow from the spring could supply the town of Van Buren with water for half a century. From the park, an excursion boat makes several trips daily to Van Buren (*fare $3; $1 for parties of three or more*). Shorter trips are available in smaller boats (*fare 25¢*).

West of Van Buren, the route winds upward, around sharp limestone bluffs and through dense timberlands that are part of the FRISTOE DIVISION OF THE CLARK NATIONAL FOREST, 466,655 acres.

At 132.7 *m.* is a junction with an unmarked graveled road.

Right here to ONYX CAVE (*adm. 50¢; 35¢ for groups*), 0.2 *m.*, operated by Lui Ring, hill-billy fiddler and author of Ozark sporting articles, who refers to himself as Ozark Bill, and specializes in tall tales of southern Missouri. The ebb and flow of a subterranean stream, making the cavern alternately dry and damp, gives many of the formations a soft glowing quality that Ozark Bill advertises as "the only live glowing radium to be found anywhere in a mineral formation."

WINONA, 152 *m.* (983 alt., 480 pop.), is at a junction with State 19 (*see Tour 14*). US 60 continues through the National Forest, entering the heart of the Ozark lumbering district and climbing to yet higher altitudes, until at 159 *m.*, it leaves the forest and enters a small valley. BIRCH TREE, 161 *m.* (990 alt., 495 pop.), named for a large birch that stood on the bank of a creek near the site of an early post office, operates four lumber mills and is considered an unusually good "work town" for this region.

At 165 *m.* is a junction with County M. a graveled road.

Right here to its end, 3.7 *m.*, at a junction with an unmarked graveled road; L. on this road (*narrow, rough, and steep*) to RYMERS RANCH, 6.6 *m.*, on Jack's Fork River, famed for its bass fishing, and one of many resorts in the Big Springs country (*boats and guides for day fishing or float trips; nominal charge*). Beyond the ranch, at 6.9 *m.*, are the two largest EBB-AND-FLOW SPRINGS in Shannon County, on the grounds of the Shannon County Hunting and Fishing Club (*grounds open, clubhouse private*). The waters emerge from dual openings at the base of a rough limestone hill, gushing forth every ten hours at a measured rate of from 8,000 to 10,000 gallons a minute, then diminishing to about 2,200 gallons.

Westward the highway follows ridge crests to ever-higher elevations. Following the great post-Civil War lumbering era, when large timber interests slashed through the hills, smaller lumbering concerns entered the region. The cut of these mills was not great; they nibbled at the forests, and, content with gleanings, have survived. The towns that sprang from their activities are small, fairly prosperous "work towns," such as MOUNTAIN VIEW, 172 *m.* (1,123 alt., 725 pop.), whose mill has been producing railroad ties, staves, and finished lumber since 1878.

At 187 *m.* is a junction with US 63 (*see Tour 8*), with which US 60 is united for 16 miles.

WILLOW SPRINGS, 190 *m.* (1,238 alt., 1,530 pop.), has successfully combined the region's two major means of livelihood in a dairy and poultry market; it also has a tannery, and three sawmills. The five stone buildings (R), 190.5 *m.*, are the DISTRICT FOREST RANGER HEADQUARTERS. The rangers are in charge of the GARDNER DIVISION of the MARK TWAIN NATIONAL FOREST, a total of 1,970,396 acres, the northeastern tip of which is traversed by US 60.

On the eastern edge of CABOOL, 203 *m.* (1,244 alt., 1,069 pop.), is the northern junction with US 63 (*see Tour 8*). Here several produce houses do a year-round business, one of them clearing as high as 60,000 pounds of poultry a month, and 1,800 cases of eggs and 15,000 pounds of butterfat a week. The vicinity is one of the most productive dairying and poultry regions in the central Ozarks.

Section b. CABOOL to OKLAHOMA LINE; 171 m. US 60

Following a circuitous route across the great Ozark uplift, US 60 traverses a hilly, wooded country between Cabool and Springfield. Although this is an agricultural region, the land has retained a primeval quality. The Ozark farmer does not try to conquer the wilderness; he makes friends with it and is content with bits of pasture and small clearings. Beyond Springfield the land is fairly level and free of timber, and great fields of strawberries, grains, and grasses flow on either side of the highway. West of Aurora, the fields often are broken by piles of chat and mining tipples.

West of CABOOL, 0 *m.*, almost every farmstead has its orchard and flock of white leghorn chickens. The fruit brings in the extra cash, the chickens and eggs the regular income; for, as the farmers say, "You cain't never tell about fruit. Frost or blight is apt to get it. But not a hen. A hen works right on, rain or shine."

The STATE POULTRY EXPERIMENT STATION (*open*), 9.6 *m.*, on the eastern edge of Mountain Grove (L), was established in 1911. Here infectious diseases and breeding problems are studied in modern laboratories and poultry yards. In connection with experiments in breeding, the station conducts the Missouri-National Egg Laying Contest, which begins the first day of October and lasts 51 weeks. The station also maintains pens of pheasants, white Chinese geese, mallard ducks, and bantams.

MOUNTAIN GROVE, 10 *m.* (1,463 alt., 2,431 pop.), is the trading and business center of a poultry, fruit, and dairying region. The city had its origin on a near-by site as Hickory Springs, where a post office was established in 1851. The settlement prospered, stores were opened, and Mountain Grove Seminary was built in 1857. When the railroad missed the town in 1883, merchants moved their stock and buildings to the present site, and three years later established Mountain Grove.

Right from Mountain Grove on County A, a graveled road, to the MISSOURI
STATE FRUIT EXPERIMENT STATION (*open*), 1.5 *m.*, where experimental work
and research in fruit culture is conducted on 180 acres of land with more than
1,000 varieties of fruit, including 600 varieties of apples and 300 of grapes.
Twelve international exposition medals have been awarded the station in recognition of its development of new fruit varieties.

Between the junction with County A and Springfield, the route
continues to wind among the deeply rolling hills. The small fields
breaking through the woodlands are kept clean by Angora goats that
eat the sprouts as fast as the stumps produce them.

HICKORY RIDGE FARM (*open by permission*), 26.7 *m.* (L), is the
childhood home of Rose Wilder Lane, whose books *Hill Billy, Cindy,*
and *The Old Home Town,* are among the very few works that have
caught the feeling and character of the Ozarks and its people (*see
Literature*). Near by is the author's summer home.

MANSFIELD, 28 *m.* (1,476 alt., 922 pop.), prototype of Rose
Wilder Lane's *The Old Home Town,* was platted in 1884. A pleasant place, it takes an active interest in its farm trade, cheese factory,
and creamery.

At 34 *m.* is a junction with an unmarked graveled road.

Left here to the tiny village of CEDAR GAP, 1.7 *m.* (1,687 alt., 135 pop.),
scene of the annual Cedar Gap Singing Convention during the first week of
June. Families from the surrounding hills bring their baskets of food for dinner on the grounds, and sing the old-time hymns and ballads from morning
until sundown (*see Music, and Tour 14*).
The area about Cedar Gap is commonly referred to as the Ozark Divide.
North from it flow the creeks and spring-fed streams that form the Gasconade
River; southward flow the tributaries of the White River. A grove of oak
trees half a mile east of town marks the highest point on the plateau, from
which, it is claimed, the distant Three Brothers Knobs are visible. CEDAR
GAP LAKE, a half mile west of the village, offers excellent bass fishing.

Breaking the forest hardwoods between Mansfield and Diggins are
extensive and prosperous apple, peach, and cherry orchards.

SEYMOUR, 40 *m.* (1,642 alt., 751 pop.), on a high plateau in
the center of an extensive clearing, was surveyed for Ralph and Frances
Walker in 1881, when it became certain a railroad would be built
through this point. The farm products of the surrounding region are
prepared for market here in a milk condensery, two vegetable canneries,
and a flour mill. Seymour ships apples each month of the year—freshly
picked fruit in the summer and fall, and stored fruit in the spring and
winter.

In the midst of the State's greatest fruit, tomato, and berry areas,
FORDLAND, 50 *m.* (1,592 alt., 331 pop.), has chosen to be economically dependent upon nuts. This is because of W. A. HAGEL's
NUT EXCHANGE. Hagel began a local trade in black walnuts and
pecans in 1931, and now fills orders for 60,000 pounds of nut meats
a year. During the rush season in fall and winter, approximately 200
Fordland people, employed on a piece-work basis, earn a weekly pay

roll of $1,500. Nuts are trucked in from Kentucky, Tennessee, Oklahoma, and Arkansas.

For 20 miles as it approaches Springfield, US 60 crosses an important livestock area. At 68 *m.* is a junction with US 65 (*see Tour 9*), with which US 60 is united to SPRINGFIELD, 77 *m.* (1,345 alt., 61,238 pop.) (*see Springfield*). Here is a junction with US 66 (*see Tour 5*). The two highways are united for seven miles.

Cutting southwest from the western junction with US 66 (*see Tour 5*), 84 *m.*, US 60 follows a zigzag course across the Springfield Plateau. The land is a high, rolling prairie underlaid with thick limestone beds. The principal industry is agriculture; fruits, vegetables, and berries are the major crops.

REPUBLIC, 93 *m.* (1,311 alt., 790 pop.), in the heart of an extensive fruit and vegetable district, ships large quantities of apples, strawberries, grapes, and tomatoes. The highway crosses the principal street at right angles, dividing the business district into halves. At the southern end of Main Street is a huge apple storehouse.

Left from Republic on an unmarked graveled road, passing several fine apple orchards, vineyards, and strawberry patches, to an unmarked dirt road, 4 *m.;* L. here, and L. again at 4.5 *m.* to a rough, rocky, private road marked by a white frame church (R), 5 *m.;* L. on this road, which is paralleled by a neat hedge-row, to a barbed-wire gate, 5.4 *m.;* through the gate to WILSON'S CREEK BATTLEFIELD, now a part of the McClure farm and open by courtesy of the owner. The battlefield is dotted with a number of small knolls, and takes its name from the creek that flows through the small valley approximately 500 yards east. The Battle of Wilson's Creek, perhaps the most important fought in Missouri, occurred on the morning of August 10, 1861, between Federal troops under General Nathaniel Lyon and an army of the Missouri State Guard under General Sterling Price, co-operating with a Confederate force from Arkansas under General McCulloch. The previous night, Lyon, with about 5,000 men, had sent General Franz Sigel to form a semi-circle about the 12,000 Confederates encamped on Wilson's Creek. He planned that Sigel should attack on the flank and rear while he advanced on the front. But at daylight the Confederates routed Sigel, and the remaining Federals were unable to withstand the superior forces. Lyon fought doggedly, but was killed during a last desperate charge. His army then retreated toward Rolla, leaving the field to Price. Federal casualties were approximately 1,139; Confederate losses, 1,245. In a rock-strewn clearing on the summit of a ridge, marked by a metal flag pole and a limestone slab, is BLOODY HILL, where Lyon was killed.

Between Republic and Verona, the route continues through excellent farming lands, raising strawberries, fruits, and grains. The ground is well drained, fenced, and planted in soil-conserving crops of grain and pasture grasses. Each farm unit has a stone or concrete silo and a massive steep-roofed barn. The towns were established in lead mining days.

One of the many little communities existing on the strawberry crops is BILLINGS, 101.6 *m.* (1,366 alt., 452 pop.), on a southern branch of the St. Louis-San Francisco Railway. In late April, a wave of berry pickers starts in the South; from the Gulf Coast States, these migratory workers move northward with the ripening crops, reaching the Arkansas Ozarks in late April and May, and Missouri in early June. Crouched over the bright green rows, their hands reaching expertly for the fruit, they swiftly strip the vines. As a picker fills a basket he places on it a symbol, usually a piece of paper stamped with his number. These are removed by the checker, who tabulates them and pays the picker accordingly. The baskets are conveyed to the local shipping shed, where the berries are pan-graded, marked for quality, and crated for shipment.

MARIONVILLE, 109.5 m. (1,351 alt., 1,127 pop.), was first settled about 1854. It has been a prosperous flour and sawmill town, and has experienced the heady excitement of a short-lived mining boom. Today (1941) it is the home of a brewing company that advertises the "sparkling Ozark water" of which its beer is made.

AURORA, 115 m. (1,351 alt., 4,056 pop.), reflecting the prosperity of the farms and small industries in the area, has wide, shaded streets, a well-kept retail district, and comfortable houses. Platted in 1872, Aurora boomed in 1887 as a center of lead and zinc mining. Many of the ore bodies were "circles," round shallow deposits quickly exhausted. When the industry died shortly after 1900, the town turned to agriculture and manufacturing. Principal industrial plants are a large floor and feed mill, and a shoe factory. Unusual enterprises are the Midwest Map Company, W. Olive and Washington Sts., housed in a modern white stucco building enclosed by a hedge; and Tasope, foot of E. Elliot St., a school of photo-engraving that uses its cable address as a name. The school offers resident and correspondence classes, and sells and installs photo-engraving equipment in newspaper offices.

The community of VERONA, 120.5 m. (1,273 alt., 405 pop.), is a strawberry shipping point on Spring River, which offers good fishing for smallmouthed bass. The village was platted as a shipping point on the railroad in 1868. Seven years later, the first of a colony of about 40 Waldensian families settled in the neighborhood. Under the leadership of a Mr. Solomon they had traveled from Piedmont, Italy, to South America, and then to the United States.

MONETT, 129.7 m (1,302 alt., 4,395 pop.), its main street a part of US 60, is the largest settlement between Springfield and Neosho. Incorporated in 1887 as a railroad town, Monett developed as the shipping center of the berry-growing region. In June, the sheds along the railroad south of the business district are the scene of great activity, as berries are brought in by truck and wagon, crated, and loaded into freight cars. Most of the annual shipment of 1,000,000 quarts is handled through the Ozark Fruit Growers' Association, a co-operative. During the shipping season both the Federal and State Governments maintain market news service in Monett.

Left from Monett on State 37, a concrete road, to an unmarked graveled road, 1.4 m.; L. here to the STATE HORTICULTURE EXPERIMENTAL FIELD (*open*), 2.2 m., under the direction of the University of Missouri College of Agriculture. The station is devoted to the development and improvement of tomatoes, strawberries, and grapes.

At 17.7 m. on State 37 is a junction with a marked graveled road. Left here, following arrows, to the CRYSTAL CAVERNS (*open May-Nov.; adm. 25¢ and 40¢; guides*), where 6 large chambers, 120 feet below the earth's surface, are fantastically decorated with varicolored stalagmites and stalactites.

Ahead on State 37 is CASSVILLE, 18.6 m. (1,410 alt., 1,214 pop.), huddled in a square about a white stone courthouse, erected in 1913. A fishing center, and a shipping point for livestock, poultry, and dairy products, Cassville was platted in 1845 as the seat of Barry County, organized in 1835. In the vicinity are some of the State's best fishing streams. Boats and guides for fishing and float trips are available.

Confederate members of the Missouri general assembly, fleeing before Union troops, held a session in Cassville, October 31 to November 7, 1861, during which the ordinance of secession, approved at Neosho by 11 senators and 44 representatives, was rewritten by Senator George Vest (*see Tour 4, Warrensburg*). Both the ordinance and act of affiliation to the Confederate States were signed here. During the war, the city was attacked first by one side, then the other. The old courthouse, torn down in 1910, surrounded by a deep ditch and "portholed" as a fort, was almost destroyed after the Battle of Pea Ridge in Arkansas.

Cassville is famed for its railroad, the Cassville & Exeter, the "shortest regulation, broad-gauged railroad in America." The length of the line, 4.8 miles, was determined by the Interstate Commerce Commission, which sent a representative to measure the track. If the railroad had measured five miles or more, it would have been placed under interstate regulations. It was incorporated in 1919 to haul farm produce to the St. Louis-San Francisco main line, and has one official—Dave Dingler, president—and five employees.

At Cassville is a junction with State 112, a black-topped road. Left here across a lofty, sparsely settled region to ROARING RIVER STATE PARK, 7.2 m., a 2,690-acre recreational center developed on land donated to the State in 1928 by the late Dr. T. M. Saymen, St. Louis soap manufacturer. The highway enters the park over a mountain top, then makes a winding descent to a hill-cupped valley. Roaring River, fed by a spring-flow of 20,000,000 gallons daily, pours out of a small lake over twin waterfalls, then rushes through the hills with a terrific roar. In the valley, a dam impounds the river to form BASS LAKE (*fishing, bathing, 25¢*). Overlooking the lake are rustic frame and stone overnight cottages (*nominal charge*). Near the modern native-limestone hotel (*open Mar. 1-Nov. 1*), are picnicking and camping grounds. The RAINBOW TROUT HATCHERIES (*follow markers*) consist of nine propagation ponds. In the surrounding woodlands are deer, fox, quail, and turkey (*hunting prohibited*). The park was developed by the National Park Service, co-operating with the Missouri State Game and Fish Department.

Between Monett and Granby, the highway winds through heavily timbered areas, dips into two deep valleys, and passes a number of chat piles (L).

GRANBY, 148.2 m. (1,142 alt., 1,455 pop.), centered by a public square enclosed by a low limestone wall, is subsisting on local farm trade until the abandoned mines and smelters on the west side of town resume operations. It is the oldest lead and zinc mining town in southwestern Missouri. Two years after William Foster, a Cornish miner, discovered lead here in 1853, the "Granby stampede" began. The lead ore, found from 10 to 75 feet below the surface, was raised in buckets by windlass and crank, or by the "whip," which utilized ox power. More than 3,000 prospectors, miners, gamblers, land speculators, and smelter operators poured into the town, and a period of hectic activity followed.

Christmas was celebrated with fireworks and pranks. Few had Christmas trees in their homes, for gifts were distributed beneath the church tree. One miner, who struck it rich just before Christmas, is said to have used two wagons to haul the presents for his family. During the 1880's, the town's first exuberance was somewhat curbed, but life was still far from dull. One man who made a profession of hunting down criminals for whom rewards were advertised used to dump the bodies of his victims in the main street of Granby "to be identified." Stealing, however, was almost unknown. The miner who demanded "hard money" rather than treasury notes took his pay home in a water bucket unmolested. It was not unusual for a group of miners who worked as partners to sit down on Main Street and carefully divide the bucket's contents, repairing to the corner saloon "to get a drink and change" when the dollars did not come out even.

Miners' language, generally unprintable, was varied by such novel expressions as "Posey-check," an I.O.U. named for the local pool hall keeper, and "an Alex Watson load" of ore, one so small as to be only a "shirt tail load." A local resident was nicknamed "Navy" because, looking through glazed eyes at a print of the *Battle of Manila Bay,* he imagined himself in conflict, drew his pistols, and "sank every ship in the Spanish fleet." Fritz Looney, an itinerant bow and arrow maker, answered all questions in rhyme. All mine tragedies were credited to "Blind Tom," a folklore character who worked on the "graveyard shift" from midnight to morning, and weakened timbers, and started cave-ins.

After the Civil War, the mineral deposits along Joplin Creek diverted mining interests from Granby. The value of zinc was discovered in the 1870's, but it was not until the World War brought a demand for it that Granby experienced fresh prosperity. When the war ended, profits ceased, and the mines and smelters closed.

At 152 *m.* is a junction with Alt. US 71 (*see Tour 10*), with which US 60 is united to NEOSHO, 156 *m.* (1,039 alt., 5,318 pop.), called by the Osage Indian word for clear water because of the large spring near the center of the town. A native-stone courthouse, wide streets, great trees, and scattered parks give the city a spacious, old-fashioned appearance.

Neosho was platted by James Wilson in 1839 and made the seat of Newton County. By July 1850, at least three lead mines had been opened in the vicinity. The most productive was that of Mosely, Oldham & Company, five miles northwest of Neosho on Shoal Creek. Like others in the vicinity, this firm found difficulty in shipping its product to market. Overland hauling costs to Boonville, the nearest Missouri River port, were prohibitive, and shipping on the Grand River was made dangerous by unfriendly Indians. However, the industry developed rapidly and Neosho grew with the mining boom.

On October 21, 1861, the secession members of Missouri's general assembly met here and adopted an act "Declaring the ties heretofore existing between the United States and the State of Missouri dissolved." The approach of Federal troops caused the House and Senate to adjourn, to meet ten days later at Cassville. In 1863 Neosho was garrisoned by Federal troops, and a part of the time by Indian soldiers. General Joseph Shelby attacked the town October 4, 1863, and shelled the courthouse, which was garrisoned as a fort. Captain McAfee, in command of the Federal troops, surrendered. In 1866 Neosho was rebuilt and reincorporated. Since then its growth and economy have been based upon the processing of local farm produce in dairy plants and a flour mill.

Neosho was the home of Colonel Maecenas E. Benton long a Missouri representative in Congress, and the boyhood home of his son, Thomas Hart Benton, painter, and author of *An Artist in America* (1937). Thomas Benton explained in his book that his father was not really a colonel; he was only called so as he "grew portly and substantial." He says his father "stopped long enough in St. Louis after the war to get admitted to the Missouri bar. He hung his shingle out of a Neosho window and . . . became . . . a prominent factor in the Democratic councils of the neighborhood." Civil War veterans, "with imprecise triangles of old men's tobacco spit staining their white or grizzled beards," would congregate in Benton's office, the Confederates talking with a fellow veteran who had served with Forrest in Tennessee, and the Union men discussing pensions. At the family table gathered such famous politicians as William Jennings Bryan, who ate "poached eggs set on the halves of potatoes—half a potato and an egg at the bite." Colonel Benton served in Congress from 1887 until 1903, when Republican protective tariff advocates defeated him.

Congressman Benton's oldest child, Thomas Hart Benton, was born in 1889 and named for his great-uncle, who, although a Tennessee man, was one of Missouri's first two senators (*see History and Government*). Young Benton spent his early winters in Washington, D. C., and his summers riding over the southwestern Missouri hills with his father. While yet in his 'teens he left home for the then booming mining town of Joplin. Though he had never made a drawing from life, he was hired by the Joplin *American* to make sketches of prominent citizens. Benton later attended art school in Chicago and studied for five years in France. It was after his return to America in 1913 that he first won recognition as an interpreter of the Midwestern scene. He is now (1941) director of the department of painting at the Kansas City Art Institute (*see Art*).

The FEDERAL FISH HATCHERY (*open 8-5*), foot of E. McKinney St., has six-and-one-half acres of water divided into numerous rearing ponds for largemouthed bass, crappie, rock bass, and rainbow trout. Established in 1887, it is the headquarters for Federal hatcheries in Missouri, Kansas, Oklahoma, Louisiana, and Arkansas. CITY PARK, two blocks west of the square, is a three-acre tract containing a wading pool for children and Big Spring, one of the largest springs in the southwestern area. The NEOSHO FRUIT EXCHANGE BERRY SHEDS (*open 8-5 workdays*), foot of Brooks St., are used in sorting and grading locally grown berry crops. The long open sheds, extended along the railroad tracks, are especially active in June and July, when strawberries and raspberries are being shipped.

SENECA, 170.5 *m.* (865 alt., 1,091 pop.), a group of frame and stone cottages scattered about a massive stone grinding mill, was platted in 1868. Since 1869 it has been important as the center of the country's only tripoli deposits of great commercial value. Tripoli, used originally for scouring and polishing purposes, has proved to be an excellent filter stone for city water systems, and a good filler for hard and substitute rubber compositions. In 1919 the Seneca deposits were purchased by the Barnsdall Tripoli Company, a subsidiary of the Barnsdall Corporation, which seven years later found that a suitably prepared grade of tripoli was a satisfactory admixture in concrete. In the BARNSDALL TRIPOLI GRINDING MILL PLANT (*open 8-4 workdays*), tripoli is artificially dried, crushed, ground, pulverized, and packed for shipment. Technically, it is a soft, friable, porous, double-refracting silica of the chalcedony variety. It occurs in horizontal beds, which may measure 12 feet in thickness. Because of the absorption of iron from descending surface water, the color varies from a very light cream to a dark rose.

Right from Seneca on an unmarked graveled road, which runs along the Oklahoma State Line, to a group of TRIPOLI DRYING SHEDS, 0.7 *m.,* long V-shaped open-sided buildings used for weather-drying tripoli. Two are in Missouri, one in Oklahoma. Ahead, at 0.9 *m.,* are 37 drying sheds (R) belonging to the Barnsdall Tripoli Company. Here also are the TRIPOLI QUARRIES, great open holes resembling gravel pits. The stone is blasted out, sorted, graded, and hauled to the drying sheds.

US 60 crosses the OKLAHOMA LINE, 171 *m.,* 41 miles northeast of Vinita, Oklahoma.

Tour 7

(Keokuk, Iowa)—Canton—Hannibal—Bowling Green—Kirkwood—Bonne Terre—Farmington—Jackson—Sikeston—New Madrid—Caruthersville—(Blytheville, Ark.); US 61.
Iowa Line to Arkansas Line, 412 *m.*

Concrete paved roadbed throughout.
Route paralleled by Chicago, Burlington & Quincy R.R. between Iowa line and St. Louis; by St. Louis & Hannibal R.R. between Hannibal and St. Louis; by

St. Louis-San Francisco Ry. between St. Louis and Crystal City, and between
Cape Girardeau and Arkansas Line; by St. Louis, Iron Mountain & Southern
R.R. (roughly) between St. Louis and junction with US 67; and by Mississippi
& Bonne Terre R.R. between Crystal City and Bonne Terre.
Accommodations of all kinds available; hotels chiefly in larger towns.

US 61, following but seldom overlooking the Mississippi River, cuts
through an economic and social cross section of eastern Missouri. Between the Des Moines River and the St. Louis suburbs, the highway
traverses the low-rolling river country made famous by Mark Twain.
South of the St. Louis area, the hills are steep and the countryside retains the influence of the French and German settlers who played such
an important part in Missouri history.

Section a. IOWA LINE to KIRKWOOD; 173 m. US 61

In its northern section, US 61 parallels the Mississippi, crossing a
region in which corn, small grains, cattle, and horses are the principal
farm products. The prairies, glacial in origin, stretch limitlessly from
the west, breaking in weathered bluffs above the Mississippi bottomland. Anglo-American farmers, chiefly from the South, have settled
here, and have built upon the fertile soil a stable economy little disrupted by industrial problems. The water-front settlements along the
route, once bustling with river trade, have been drained of vitality by
railroads and highways. Many of the towns bear the classical names
popular in the empire-building era—Athens, Antioch, Alexandria, Hannibal, Troy—or such ambitious titles as Moscow Mills, New London,
Philadelphia, and New Hartford. The Indian and French history of
the region is recalled by Kahoka, and the Des Moines, Wyaconda,
Fabius, and Cuivre Rivers.

The tract of land extending approximately ten miles south of the
Des Moines River was both the cause and scene of the so-called Honey
War between Missouri and Iowa. In 1839 Governors Lilburn W.
Boggs of Missouri and Robert Lucas of Iowa established conflicting
State boundaries. In attempting to collect taxes within the areas specified, Sheriff Uriah Gregory of Clark County, Missouri, was arrested
by Sheriff Sheffelman of Van Buren County, Iowa, charged with usurpa-
tion of authority, and imprisoned. Both governors ordered soldiers to
the disputed territory, and public meetings were held in the opposed
States. Judgment was secured against a Missourian in an Iowa court
for cutting bee trees in what he thought was Missouri. A satirical
poem, "The Honey War," by John I. Campbell, which appeared in
the *Missouri Whig & Advertiser* (Palmyra), December 26, 1839,
produced a wave of laughter and helped to quiet the excitement. Sung
to the tune of "Yankee Doodle," the verses ridiculed the heroics of the
two governors, suggesting: "If the Governors want to fight, just let
them meet in person." The issue, so settled, would make no widows
and leave "no orphans unprotected." Furthermore:

> Our honey trade will then be laid
> Upon a solid basis;
> And Governor Boggs
> Where'er he jogs
> Will meet with smiling faces.

US 61 crosses the IOWA LINE, 0 *m.*, on a free bridge over the Des Moines River, a stream named for the Illinois Indian villages, *Mouingouinas*, or, *Moingona*, which early French explorers found at the head of the rapids, on the south bank, and at the beginning of a trail to the mouth of the river. This name seems to have been a corruption of the Algonquin word *mikonany*, meaning, "at the road." The name was abbreviated in characteristic Creole parlance to *la rivière des Moins*.

ALEXANDRIA, 0.3 *m.* (498 alt., 631 pop.), is on a levee-protected bottom at the junction of the Des Moines and Mississippi Rivers. The site of the town was first settled by a Mississippi River ferryman in 1824-25, and in 1839 the place was named in his honor. Between 1848 and 1872, Alexandria almost rivaled St. Louis and Chicago as a pork-packing center. In the peak year of the industry (1869-70), 42,557 hogs were slaughtered and packed, and droves reaching 1,000 were driven in from as far away as 100 miles. Like the cowboys, who quiet their cattle with low-sung lullabies, the hog drivers developed sing-song chants. One ran something like this:

> Hog up. Hog up.
> Forty cents a day and no dinner.
> Straw bed and no cover.
> Corn bread and no butter.
> Hog up. Hog up.

At Alexandria is a junction with State 4, a graveled road that becomes an oil mat surface at Wayland.

Right here to KAHOKA, 16.3 *m.* (697 alt., 1,781 pop.), platted 1856, which derives its name from that of the Gawakie Indians—"the lean ones." Kahoka is a grain center and the seat of Clark County, which was organized in 1836 and named for William Clark, Territorial Governor of Missouri and member of the Lewis and Clark Expedition. Because it is near the Iowa and Illinois borders, the county was formerly a rendezvous for criminals, who conveyed stolen goods over the State lines. As a protection against these marauders, Major David McKee (1823-96) of Kahoka, with Hugh Allen Stewart and others, organized the Anti-Horse Thief Association in 1854. A grand lodge was formed in Clark County in 1863 and McKee was made president. The organization—whose motto is "Protect the Innocent and Bring the Guilty to Justice"—still claims a membership of approximately 50,000. The annual Clark County Fair, one of the most elaborate in northeastern Missouri, is held in Kahoka each August.

CANTON, 26.3 *m.* (494 alt., 2,125 pop.), oldest town (1830) in Lewis County, is named for Canton, Ohio, and extends from the high bottomland along the Mississippi River to the bluffs on the west. Here was the home of Jesse W. Barrett (1822-86), Methodist preacher and educator who established in 1862 the Canton *Press,* a Democratic weekly, "Pledged but to truth, to liberty and law, no favor swings us and no fear shall awe." In 1864 Barrett was made Grand Master of the Independent Order of the Odd Fellows, and three years later he assisted in the organization of the Missouri Press Association of which he was president from 1867 to 1870.

CULVER-STOCKTON COLLEGE, on the western side of Canton, is a four-year co-educational school with an enrollment of 400 students. The college buildings, of Greek-Revival design, are grouped in a semicircle on a bluff facing the river. The landscaped campus affords an excellent view of the city and valley. Founded by the Disciples of Christ, the school was chartered as Christian University in 1853, the first college west of the Mississippi to receive a charter as a co-educational institution. Its first president was James Shannon, ex-president of the University of Missouri. During the Civil War the school was used as headquarters for Union soldiers and during the World War as a training camp. The present name was adopted in 1917.

Between Canton and La Grange, US 61 approximates the route of the Salt River Road laid out in 1823 between St. Charles and the Des Moines River. The WYACONDA RIVER, 31.7 *m.*, bears a Sioux Indian name meaning a place often visited by the Great Spirit.

LA GRANGE, 32.8 *m.* (484 alt., 1,222 pop.), at the confluence of the Wyaconda and Mississippi Rivers, was platted in 1830 and incorporated in 1838. The business district lies along the bank of the Mississippi, and the residential section is scattered westward over rolling bluffs. Godfrey Le Sieur, the first settler, established a trading post at the mouth of the Wyaconda when the region was under Spanish control. Archives in St. Louis reveal that he was a licensed trader "at the Weaucandah, on the upper river" in 1795. The ruins of his four cabins were here when John Bozarth came from Kentucky in 1819 and erected a cabin two miles south of the present site of La Grange. Many settlers came to La Grange from Kentucky and Tennessee, and the village grew rapidly. Pork packing plants, cooper shops, distilleries, a flour mill, tobacco factories, and other industries were developed, furnishing outlets for the products of the back country and the basis for a heavy river trade. Houses of dignified Greek-Revival design were built about a village green and on the hills above the river.

In the square is the UNION SOLDIERS MONUMENT, a marble shaft bearing the great seal of Missouri, erected in 1864 to the memory of those soldiers of Lewis County who fell "in defense of their country." Although never captured during the war, La Grange suffered an ultimate ruin more complete than many battle-scarred towns, for the war disrupted its credit system, and the railroads built after the war took away its river trade. The MARSHALL HOUSE (*open*), near the corner of Third and Jefferson Sts., is a two-story yellow frame structure erected in the 1850's. From about 1858 until October of 1860 it was the home of Thomas Riley Marshall (1854-1925), governor of Indiana 1908-12, and Vice President of the United States during the administrations of Woodrow Wilson. His "What this country needs is a really good five cent cigar" added a new catch line to the American idiom. His father, Daniel M. Marshall, a country doctor, was an abolitionist who antagonized a dangerous group of Southern sympathizers in the community. Fearing an attack would be made on his life, he returned with his family to Indiana, their former home. The La Grange Male and Female College, founded 1857-58 by the Baptist Church, has been moved to Hannibal (*see below*).

TAYLOR, 41 *m.* (491 alt., 60 pop.), a small farming community, is at the northern junction with US 24 (*see Tour 2*), with which the route is united for 14 miles.

At the southern edge of Taylor, US 61 crosses the NORTH FABIUS RIVER, and at 44 *m.* the FABIUS RIVER, referred to by early historians as the Jeffron or Jeffreon River. Where the combined branches of the Fabius empty into the Mississippi three or four miles east of here, three abolitionists from Quincy, Illinois, were arrested in July 1841. The men, George Thompson and James E. Burr, ministerial students, and Alanson Work, an older friend, determined to help a group of Missouri slaves gain their freedom. The slaves, however, betrayed their would-be rescuers. Their testimony was admitted in evidence at the trial in Palmyra, though such a procedure was illegal and the men were sentenced to from three to five years imprisonment at Jefferson City. Before their terms ended, however, they were pardoned by Governor John C. Edwards. Later, Thompson published *Prison Life and Reflections* (1847), describing the treatment the men received from the time of their arrest to that of their release, and revealing the abominable conditions then existent at the State prison.

Although the abolitionist efforts of Alanson Work were abortive, his crusade was continued by a son, Henry Clay Work, who, as composer of "Marching Through Georgia" and other campaign songs of the Civil War, played a potent role in the antislavery movement.

A marker (R), 50 *m.*, indicates the GRAVE OF GEORGE SHANNON, in an old cemetery on a hill 100 yards from the road. Shannon, born in Pennsylvania in 1787, served as a private on the Lewis and Clark Expedition (1804-06), and after the return of the party was wounded in the leg by Indians. The leg was amputated at St. Charles, and Shannon became known as "Peg-leg." Returning to Philadelphia to study law, he assisted Nicholas Biddle in the editing of the Lewis and Clark journals. Later he was admitted to the Kentucky bar and returned to Missouri, where he served as State Senator and United States District Attorney. He died suddenly at court in Palmyra, August 30, 1836.

PALMYRA, 51.6 *m.* (652 alt., 2,285 pop.), Marion County seat, presents a leisurely appearance, with wide lawns, fine old trees, and early houses that suggest the Southern origin of many of its early settlers. The town was platted in 1819 and named for the Syrian city built by King Solomon, probably because it, too, was founded in the wilderness. The settlers built their homes around a large, clear spring in the center of the village, immediately south of the present Palmyra power plant. Stone steps to the spring remain, but the water is piped to the plant, leaving the spring bed dry. The PALMYRA MASSACRE MONUMENT, on the courthouse lawn, was erected in 1907 to the memory of the victims. On September 12, 1862, Confederate forces under Colonel Joseph C. Porter raided Palmyra and captured Andrew Allsman, a Union spy. Two days later, Union troops under Colonel John McNeil stampeded Porter's forces, and on October 8 warned the Confederates that unless Allsman was returned unharmed within ten days, ten prisoners from Porter's command would be shot. Unfortunately, Allsman was not available; his fate has never been definitely established. On October 18, McNeil ordered ten of the "worst rebels," that is, those of prominence and rank, to be shot. The selected men were taken to the fair grounds and placed before a firing squad of 30 Federal soldiers. The executioners did poor work, however; only 3 men were killed instantly, and a second squad had to step forward to finish the slaughter.

In the GREENWOOD-PALMYRA CEMETERY, northern edge of town, is the GRAVE OF WILLIAM H. RUSSELL, hailed as the "Napoleon of the West" when he founded the Pony Express in 1860. Russell, a native of Vermont, worked for a while in a bank at Richmond, Missouri, then, in the late 1840's, secured government contracts for freighting. In 1854 he formed a partnership with Alexander Majors and W. B. Waddell, and when the Central Overland California and Pike's Peak Express Company was organized in 1860, he was made president. To prove that their route to the Pacific by way of Denver was practicable, Russell and Majors started the Pony Express in April 1860 (*see St. Joseph, and Transportation*). Unfortunately, the venture was ruinously expensive. When Russell went to Washington for payment on his contracts, he was given bonds illegally diverted from the Indian Trust Fund; he was later obliged to return them, but was absolved of blame. Congress was expected to provide other payment, but in the excitement of the Civil War the case was forgotten. The adverse publicity left Russell's venture in high disfavor. In April 1861, Bela M. Hughes succeeded Russell as president of the company, and, with the completion of the overland telegraph in October, the Pony Express came to an end. In 1862 the company was sold to Ben Holladay (*see Tour 10*).

The red-brick FIRST METHODIST CHURCH, dating from the early 1820's, won fame as the place where ministers assembled in 1866 to revive the Methodist Episcopal Church South in the country devastated by the Civil War. The Palmyra *Spectator,* whose office is on Olive Street (L), is probably the oldest paper in Missouri continuously owned by the same family. It was founded in 1839 by Jacob Sosey, grandfather of the present owner. In 1903, Frank H. Sosey, son of Jacob, published *Robert Devoy,* a novel dealing with the Palmyra Massacre and the Civil War.

Left from Palmyra on State 56, a graveled road, to an unmarked dirt road, 3.5 *m.;* L. here, on the bank of the Mississippi River, to the SITE OF MARION CITY (*marked*), 7.5 *m.,* a town that Colonel William Muldrow (1797-1872) launched in 1835 as the future metropolis of the Middle West. The river bottom at this point is three miles wide and subject to annual inundations. Muldrow, however, regarded the location as ideal for a "gateway to western transportation." At times the river filled a slough west of the proposed city, making the site an island, and Muldrow planned to deepen this into a canal for steamboat traffic. The first railroad to be surveyed in Missouri was laid out and partially graded from Marion City to near-by Philadelphia in the fall of 1835; branches were planned to Palmyra and Ely. As originally designed, the road was to extend westward to the Pacific Coast.

Plans for the city were carried forward, and immigrants were beginning to arrive, when, in the spring of 1836, the Mississippi completely flooded the site. Promoters said they would erect a levee to keep back the water, but disillusioned settlers left in large numbers. Uninformed newcomers continued to arrive, however, and soon various commercial buildings were under construction. Marion City became a busy shipping point, with a daily hack line to Palmyra and other towns. In 1850, it was one of the principal hog markets in northeastern Missouri. But high waters in 1844 and 1851 put a definite stop to the city's growth. Gradually the community was abandoned and fell into decay. Today, the Mississippi flows over the eastern part of the townsite, and swamps claim the western portion.

Marion City was supposedly the "Eden" of Charles Dickens' *Martin Chuzzlewit*. William Muldrow had promoted the scheme with fine maps that depicted a well-developed community of spacious streets, banks, churches, hotels, wharves, even a theater and a newspaper office. However, when Easterners who had purchased lots arrived, they found Marion City very like the "Eden" of Dickens' account:

There was not above a score of cabins in the whole; half of these appeared untenanted; all were rotten and decayed. The most tottering, abject and forlorn among them was called, with great propriety, the Bank and National Credit Office. It had some feeble props about it, but was settling down deep in the mud, past all chances of recovery. In some quarters a snake or zigzag fence had been begun, but in no instance completed; and the fallen logs, half hidden in the soil, lay mouldering away. Three or four meagre dogs, wasted and vexed with hunger; some long-legged pigs wandering away into the woods in search of food; some children, nearly naked, gazing . . . from the huts; were all the living things he saw.

Muldrow's finances became hopelessly involved, and he left in 1849 for California. There, in partnership with John Sutter, he purchased a large tract of land from the Russian Fur Company. The United States government, however, refused to confirm title to the land, and Muldrow eventually returned to Marion County, where he died in 1872.

South of Palmyra, US 61 winds through rolling farmlands to form at 55 *m.* the southern junction with US 24 (*see Tour 2*). At 62.5 *m.* is a junction with US 36 (*see Tour 3*), on the outskirts of HANNIBAL (489 alt., 20,865 pop.) (*see Hannibal, and Tour 3*).

The approximate SITE OF BATES' TRADING POST (R), 63 *m.*, is indicated by a low granite marker almost hidden by roadside planting. The post was established by Moses D. Bates, who acquired an interest in Hannibal when the town was platted in 1819, built the first house there, and operated the first store (*see Hannibal*).

The HATCH DAIRY EXPERIMENT STATION (*open*), 64.8 *m.* (R), with cross-fenced fields, massive barns, tall round silos, and substantial employees' houses, looks like a wealthy man's hobby. The farm was formerly Strawberry Hill, the home of William Henry Hatch, "the father of agricultural experiment stations." Born in Kentucky in 1833, Hatch came to Hannibal in 1845 to practice law. After service in the Civil War, he was elected to Congress for eight successive terms. Under his leadership, the Bureau of Animal Husbandry was created in 1884, and in 1887 the Hatch Act provided for a system of government-supported agricultural experiment stations. By the terms of this act and the complementary Adams and Purnell Acts (1906, 1925), Congress appropriates $90,000 annually to each State for these stations. It was also through the efforts of Hatch that the cabinet position, Secretary of Agriculture, was authorized. Hatch died December 23, 1896, and his estate was bequeathed to the State University by his daughter, Sarah Rodes Hatch, for use as an experiment station.

Placid SALT RIVER, 70.9 m., is known through the frontier expression, "to row a man up Salt River," which came to mean to defeat him or make him otherwise uncomfortable, particularly in reference to political candidates. The expression supposedly originated with reference to a Missourian who, repeatedly beaten at the polls, moved farther and farther up Salt River, either as evidence of his discomfiture or in the expectation of finding more friendly voters.

NEW LONDON, 72.5 m. (600 alt., 1,005 pop.), founded in 1819 by William Jamieson, an English engineer, is a trading and shipping point for farm produce. A majority of the homes were built in the 1860's and 1870's, though a few are older. The limestone RALLS COUNTY COURTHOUSE in the center of town, built in 1857-58, was chosen to represent Missouri courthouses at both the New York and San Francisco world fairs in 1939. Its Classic-Revival façade of four Tuscan columns supporting a pediment surmounted by an octagonal cupola was reproduced on the façade of the Missouri Building at each fair. Each room contains a large fireplace, originally the only means of heating the building. The wings, designed in the style of the original building, are recent additions. The former Century Hotel or PURDOM TAVERN (private), on the highway south of the courthouse, was erected in 1829; a long two-story brick building (R), it is said to have been the stopping place of many important travelers. Senator Thomas Hart Benton stayed here often and spoke on many occasions from the hotel balcony.

At 92.5 m. is a junction with US 54 (see Tour 15).

BOWLING GREEN, 93 m. (876 alt., 1,975 pop.), Pike County seat, was platted in 1826 and named for the Kentucky home of many of the town's early residents. The CHAMP CLARK STATUE, west courthouse lawn, is a bronze figure, by Frederick C. Hibbard, of James Beauchamp Clark (1850-1921), nationally known as "Champ." Clark came here from Kentucky in 1876. From 1893 until his death in 1921, with the exception of the term 1895-97, he was a member of the House of Representatives. He served as Speaker of the House for eight years and in 1912 was a serious contender for the Democratic Presidential nomination. HONEY SHUCK (open by permission), College St. three blocks east and one block south of the square, a rambling white frame house set on a tree-shaded lawn, was Clark's Bowling Green home. The JOHN WALTER BASYE HOUSE (*open by permission*), across the street from the Clark place, a low-lying white frame structure, is the oldest house in the city. Part of the dwelling was built of logs in 1829.

Pike County, settled about 1808 and organized in 1818, was named for Brigadier General Zebulon Montgomery Pike, discoverer of Pike's Peak. The slang term "Pike" or "Piker" derives from this place. As the *Knickerbocker Magazine* in 1857 explains: "Our only neighbor was a squatter, and a Pike of the pikiest description. There may possibly be some untutored minds, who do not understand the meaning of the term 'Pike.' It is a household word in San Francisco, originally applied to Missourians from Pike County, but afterwards used to designate individuals presenting a happy compound of verdancy and ruffianism."

Two songs sung by successive generations of Americans made Pike County a symbol. The tale of the tribulations of love-torn "Joe Bowers," and the related ballad of "Sweet Betsy from Pike" and her lover Ike contain the essence of frontier humor. They gave to American literature "a new character, a western type distinguished by his ruggedness, impetuosity, profanity and big-heartedness." Pike County residents maintain that "Joe Bowers" originated on a trek to California which 200 "Pikers" under the leadership of Captain McPike made in 1849. Joe Bowers, an ox driver, hoped to get gold enough from the trip to support his love, Sally Black. Frank Swift, another member of the group, made up a few verses concerning Joe and Sally. In 1856 these were printed and sung by Johnson's Minstrels. From this grew the ribald tale of Joe's returning with a lucky strike only to find Sally the wife of a red-haired butcher and mother of a red-haired baby.

At 115.3 *m.* is a junction with County B, a graveled road.

Left here, winding between tree-crowned hills, to the FEDERAL NURSERY AND EXPERIMENT STATION (*open*), 10.2 *m.* (R). Established in 1934 by the United States Department of Agriculture, the farm consists of 237 acres, two-thirds of which are used for the production of plants and seeds to supply Federal agencies and private individuals with various grasses, vines, and plants suitable for checking erosion, for reforestation, and for wild life food and cover. The remaining area is used for experimental work. Approximately 6,000,000 plants are raised annually.

Southward, the prairie country gives way to timbered ridges and sharply cut creek valleys, tributary to the CUIVRE RIVER, crossed at 124.1 *m.* The Creole name, *Rivière au Cuivre* (Fr., Copper River), is thought to come from the belief that there was copper along the stream's course. Today the name is locally pronounced "quiver." Land in the fertile bottoms along the river's gravel-choked course was granted to Americans by the Spanish government as early as 1791, although permanent settlement does not seem to have been made until ten years later. During the war of 1812, Fort Howard, named for Governor

Benjamin Howard, was built at the mouth of the Cuivre to protect the settlers from Indian attacks.

At 125 *m.* is a junction with State 47, a graveled road.

1. Left on State 47 to an unmarked graveled road, 3.4 *m.*, L. to the CUIVRE RIVER RECREATIONAL AREA (*fishing, boating, swimming*), 5.6 *m.*, a tract of 5,000 acres developed by the National Park Service and the Conservation Commission of Missouri. Summer and weekend camps for social service groups and civic organizations from industrial centers have been established. Winding graveled roads lead through forested valleys and over grassy hill-tops. Along the Cuivre River and Sugar Creek, a tributary which flows through the area, are a number of clear, gravel-bottomed pools.

2. Right on State 47 to TROY, 0.8 *m.* (573 alt., 1,493 pop.), Lincoln County seat, platted in 1819 and named for Troy, New York, by Joshua N. Robbins. Placid, tree-shaded streets, white-frame and red-brick houses, the sharp-spired Christian Church (built 1859), and the courthouse (built 1870), suggest a history unaffected by economic boom or collapse. The SITE OF WOODS' FORT, erected during the War of 1812, is marked at the corner of Main Street and State 47.

Lincoln County, lying partly on the Mississippi bluffs and partly on the prairie, was organized in 1818. In 1828 the county seat was moved to Troy. The earliest settler of the county is said to have been Major Christopher Clark, who came from Winchester, Virginia, and settled four miles north of the present site of Troy in 1801. During the War of 1812, he erected Clark's Fort, which he stocked with 7,000 pounds of cured pork, among other items, for the use of refugee families. When the Territorial Legislature organized the county in 1818, and the question of a name was presented, Major Clark said with dramatic brevity: "I was born, sir, in *Link-horn* County, North Carolina. I lived for many years in *Link-horn* County, in old Kaintuck. I wish to live the remainder of my days, and die in *Link-horn* County, in Missouri; and I move, therefore, that the blank in the bill be filled with the name of Link-horn." His motion was carried unanimously. During the early 1840's, when organized bands of counterfeiters and horse thieves operated in various parts of the State, Lincoln County settlers were protected by a group of vigilantes called the Slickers, a title adopted by a similar organization in Benton County in 1841. The name originated from the form of punishment usually inflicted: whipping with hickory "slickings" (switches).

Ahead on State 47 is HAWK POINT, 8 *m.* (721 alt., 279 pop.), a small Bohemian community in the rough timber lands of the Cuivre River Valley. In the early 1840's, six families bought land here, built shelter for their stock, erected log cabins chinked with clay and straw, and turned themselves to the task of working the land for subsistence. They were thrifty and hard working, and many of them prospered. Attracted by their success, other Bohemians joined the group from time to time, until today the colony numbers some 300 or 400 persons and includes the near-by community of Mashek.

MOSCOW MILLS, 129 *m.* (461 alt., 347 pop.), platted 1821, is a farm village overlooking the Cuivre River from a hilltop. The COMMUNITY CENTER (*open*) occupies one side of a two-story stone house erected by slaves in the 1830's. The exact date of construction is not known, but its one-time magnificence is indicated by walls 18 inches thick, hand-carved walnut woodwork, and a massive, curved stair rail. Behind the house is an old slave cabin.

WENTZVILLE, 140 *m.* (624 alt., 752 pop.), bordering the high-way (R), is at a junction with By-Pass US 40 (*see Tour 1*) and US 40, which unites with US 61 to its junction with US 66.

Southeast of Wentzville the highway enters the Missouri River Valley, where pasture lands, trim fence rows, and winding rocky creeks give the country a park-like appearance. At 150.6 *m.* is a junction with State 94 (*see Tour 1A*); south of the junction the highway crosses the MISSOURI RIVER, 154 *m.*, on the free DANIEL BOONE BRIDGE. It was in this vicinity and near Marthasville that Daniel Boone spent the last period of his life (*see Tour 1A*).

Between the river and Kirkwood, the farm scene slowly gives way to one typical of the outskirts of a great American city. Roadside cafés, tourist camps, roadhouses, and filling stations appear, first in scattered groups, then surrounded by commuters' cottages and homes belonging to well-plotted, often incorporated, suburban towns.

In KIRKWOOD, 173 *m.* (423 alt., 12,132 pop.), a St. Louis suburb, is a junction with US 50 (*see Tour 4*).

Section b. KIRKWOOD to JACKSON, 127 m. US 61

In its middle section, US 61 follows the approximate route of the Spanish King's Highway through the oldest settlements of Missouri. The lead deposits of the Meramec, Big River, and Mine La Motte areas were known to French explorers in the early decades of the eighteenth century and seasonal mining activities were developed, but, with the exception of Ste. Genevieve, permanent settlement was delayed until the close of the century. Today, the mines of the Flat River region, said to be the richest lead producing area in the world, are the modern realization of John Law's "Mississippi Bubble" (*see History and Government*). With the purchase of the Louisiana Territory in 1803, and the heavy American immigration that followed, new mines and smelters were opened and farms and towns developed. During the period 1800-60, large groups of German immigrants found homes in Cape Girardeau, New Hamburg, Kimmswick, and other communities, making the area as diverse in racial heritage and agricultural economy as in geography and modes of livelihood.

South of KIRKWOOD, 0 *m.*, US 61 is a landscaped, four-lane highway skirting St. Louis and its principal suburban areas. At 1 *m.* is a junction with US 66 (*see Tour 5*). MEHLVILLE, 7 *m.* (789 alt.), is hardly more than a crossroads store and school.

Left (straight ahead) from Mehlville on an unmarked macadam road to the stone entrance gates of JEFFERSON BARRACKS (*open Sunday 7-5 only*), 2 *m.*, home of the Air Corps Detachment for the training of air corps recruits. Grouped about the wide parade grounds are the personnel and administration buildings. The site, selected in 1826 and named in honor of Thomas Jefferson, consists of 1,702 wooded acres. The post supplanted Fort Bellefontaine, which was established on the Missouri River in the northern portion of St. Louis County in 1806. It served as a distribution point for troops and munitions destined for scattered frontier garrisons. Many persons famous as military or political leaders have been stationed at Jefferson Barracks, among them General William Selby Harney (1800-89), whom Jefferson Davis called "the finest man I ever saw," and whom Indians honored as a swift runner of foot races; General Henry Atkinson (1782-1842), veteran of the War of 1812, commander of the famed Yellowstone expedition to the Rocky Mountains (1819-20), and commander of Jefferson Barracks (1827-32). Lieutenant Jefferson Davis (1808-89), following his graduation from West Point in 1828, came to the Barracks with a Negro slave as body servant; after the Black Hawk War he brought the captive Chief Black Hawk back here. Colonel Robert E. Lee (1807-70), who had done engineering work on the St. Louis water front in the 1830's, assumed command of the post in 1855. Lieutenant Ulysses S. Grant (1822-85) was sent here in 1843, and it was at near-by "Whitehaven" that he met Julia Dent, who later became his wife. Other officers from Jefferson Barracks who later gained fame during the Civil War include the Union generals W. T. Sherman, Don Carlos Buell, W. S. Hancock, and J. C. Frémont, and the Confederate generals James Longstreet, Joseph E. Johnston, G. B. Crittenden, D. M. Frost, A. A. Pope, and J. B. Hood. The UNITED STATES NATIONAL CEMETERY (*open*), west of the parade grounds, is enclosed by a stone wall with an impressive gateway. The landscaped grounds are patterned by rows of small white marble crosses marking the graves of 16,000 soldiers.

South of Mehlville, US 61 follows a route first marked as El Camino Real by Spanish order in 1789. In 1808 Territorial Governor Meriwether Lewis ordered the old highway remarked and the timber cleared for a width of 25 feet. As far south as New Madrid, US 61 follows in general this old road.

The MERAMEC (Ind., catfish) RIVER, crossed at 12.3 *m.,* has a restless current that winds through farm lands, past irregular clumps of giant oak, sycamore, and elm trees, and between bluffs that vary from sloping hillsides to abrupt gray crags. The stream has long been a weekend attraction (*swimming, boating, fishing*) for St. Louisans, and numerous private and public cabins are scattered along the crests of the bluffs or perched on stilts in the bottoms. Penicaut's mention in 1700 of "a mine of lead fifty leagues from the river" drew the first white settlers to the region, beginning the river's long history as the highway for French and American trade and settlement. John Hildebrand cleared a farm and built a cabin on the Meramec in 1774. Jean Baptiste Gomache is said to have established a ferry, the first in Missouri, across the river near its mouth in 1776.

The "OLD HOUSE" (*open*), 16.9 *m.* (R), identified by the wooden figure of a horse near the driveway entrance, is a two-story, green-shuttered log structure, weatherboarded on three sides and painted white. Its construction, date unknown, suggests that it originally contained two rooms divided by a "dogtrot." Its history has been established as far back as 1831, when Chris Rayburg added a second story and built the log wing in the rear. Later, the Widow Rayburg is said to have operated the house as a tavern at which stagecoaches made regular stops. Stories are told of Ulysses S. Grant coming here with fellow officers while he was stationed at Jefferson Barracks.

At 19.6 *m.* is a junction with County K, a graveled road.

Left here to KIMMSWICK, 0.8 *m.* (409 alt., 172 pop.), which, like many other villages tucked along the Mississippi, had its origin as a river port. Laid out in 1857 by Theodore Kimm, it found a modest prosperity as a smelting and shipping point for iron mined at Pilot Knob and Iron Mountain until

1882, when the smelter was closed. It is now a farming center and a popular weekend resort and artist colony.

A notable example of Missouri-German half-timber construction is the FRANZ A. HERMANN HOUSE (*open by permission*), a one-and-a-half-story dwelling (R) almost hidden by a grove of old trees and a fence matted with honeysuckle. Built in the manner of medieval German houses, the building is supported by a framework of carefully pinned hewn-oak beams, the interstices plastered. Begun in 1859, it was but partially completed when the Civil War broke out and Union soldiers moved in for a period of occupation. An immense stone-vaulted beer cellar extends into the hillside below the house.

At 26 *m.* is a junction with the Herculaneum Road, a concrete highway.

Left here to HERCULANEUM, 0.7 *m.* (407 alt., 1,800 pop.), center of all roads from the mining district to the south. Located at the mouth of Joachim Creek's long valley and dwarfed by a semicircle of Mississippi River bluffs, stores and houses are overshadowed by the gray bulk of the St. Joseph Lead Company smelters. Reverend John Clark preached the first Protestant sermon in Missouri from a rock in the Mississippi just off this shore in 1798. The value of the site as a shipping point for lead mined at Potosi and Old Mines was recognized in 1808, when Moses Austin and Samuel Hammond platted the town and gave it its fanciful name.

The ST. JOSEPH LEAD COMPANY SMELTER (*open; apply at office*), a great rambling plant of steel and glass in the center of town, contains blast furnaces, a refining furnace, and a calcining furnace. At the time it was built, following the completion of the Mississippi River and Bonne Terre Railroad in 1890, it was considered the largest lead smelter in the United States. Ore is shipped here from the mines at Bonne Terre, Desloge, and other points (*see below*). SHOT TOWER BLUFF, marked by a bronze tablet in the southeastern part of town, is the site of a shot factory established in 1809. The tower erected in that year by J. N. Maclot was the first in the Missouri area. The following year a second tower was built by Moses Austin; when Henry Rowe Schoolcraft visited Herculaneum in 1817, three shot towers were in operation. The shot manufactories consisted of small wooden towers erected at the edge of the 100-foot bluff, the upper portion of which overhung the base. The lead, mixed with an arsenic alloy, was melted in an iron pot in the upper part of the tower and poured through a copper sieve into a cistern below, large shot being dropped 140 feet, small shot, 90 feet. The shot was then polished in a revolving barrel. One man could cast 4,000 or 5,000 pounds of shot a day, but it took 9 days to polish this amount. During the 18-month period ending in June 1817, 668,350 pounds of shot, valued at more than $50,000, were produced here.

CRYSTAL CITY, 30.2 *m.* (420 alt., 3,417 pop.), skirted by the highway, is a planned, factory-owned town in the wide valley cut through the Mississippi River bluffs by Plattin Creek. In the center is a small park and the gray stone, Gothic-styled Grace Presbyterian Church. Adjoining the park are the numerous buildings of the Pittsburgh Plate Glass Company, more modern than when Walt Whitman visited Crystal City in 1879 and expressed his surprise in a letter to a friend. "What do you think I find manufactured out here and of a kind the clearest and largest, best, and most finished and luxurious in the world . . . ? Plate glass!" The "inexhaustible and peculiar sand— the original white gray stuff in the banks" that Whitman spent most of a day examining was discovered by Forrest Shephard, geologist, in 1843. Glass production was begun about 1872.

The PITTSBURGH PLATE GLASS COMPANY PLANT (*open 8-4 work-days; guides*), on a 75-acre tract east of the central park, consists of industrial-designed brick and steel buildings that date in the main from 1925 and 1926. Although machines have replaced many of the opera-tors since Whitman's visit, 2,500 men are employed, and the processing of the silica sand, soda ash, and other ingredients remains essentially the same. Whitman was apparently impressed when he "saw the melt-ing in the pots . . . a wonderous process, a real poem . . . all glowing, a newer vaster study for Colorists, indescribable, a pale red-tinged yel-low, of tarry consistence all lambent . . . sometimes sun striking it from above with effect that would have filled Michel Angelo with rapture."

In Crystal City is a junction with State 21A (*see Tour 13*), and approximately one mile south of it is a junction with State 25 (*see Tour 11*).

The operator of the Hillcrest Filling Station (L), 52.8 *m.,* will give directions for hiking to the SAM HILDEBRAND CAVE, 0.5 *m.,* in the bluff overlooking Big River. The cave was named for a Civil War outlaw, who used it as a hide-out. According to Sam's *Autobiography* (1870), he was born in the vicinity in 1836, and lived quietly as a farmer until the tension of the Civil War fanned a neighborhood quar-rel into murder and retaliation. From that time until the close of the war, Hildebrand lived as an outlaw, hiding in the cave between forays throughout southeastern Missouri, robbing on occasion but generally directing his efforts toward "aiding the Southern cause" and killing his enemies. The latter must have been numerous, for there were "eighty notches" on the stock of his gun, "Kill-Devil." At the end of the War, Hildebrand left Missouri with a price on his head. Family tradition states that he was shot in Illinois by a relative who wanted the reward. When asked to identify the body, however, Hildebrand's two sisters swore it was not that of their brother rather than let the relative collect. Hildebrand is buried in Flat River. For many years local children were disciplined by the threat, "Sam Hildebrand'll get you if you aren't good."

In the abrupt, meagerly cultivated hills along Big River and its winding tributaries—Hazel Run, Pike Run, Bee Run, and others—many early traditions and superstitions have survived. Even recently it was popularly believed that several persons in the area were witches. If a pot of soap spoiled, if a cow gave bloody milk, or if someone suddenly "fell ill," it was the hand of the witch. Love potions were used, charms were laid, and the wise were careful to burn their clip-pings of hair or nails, for in the hands of the witches "powerful and dangerous magic" could be made of these.

Between BIG RIVER, crossed at 53.6 *m.,* and Farmington, moun-tainous piles of gray chat are signposts of the largest lead producing area in the world. Where the scene has not been changed by modern industry, the country appears much as described by Schoolcraft in 1819: "sterile, though not mountainous; the lands lie rolling, like a body of water in gentle agitation. . . . The soil is a reddish coloured clay, stiff and hard, and full of fragments of flinty stone, quartz and gravel." Much of the area, as now, was covered by a "stinted growth of oaks . . . here denominated *post oaks.*" The ore deposits consist of galena (lead sulphide), disseminated usually in the lower stratum of the Bonne Terre formation, a deposit of dolomitic limestone 500 feet thick found in horizontal beds in the northern part of the county. Although early French miners seemingly knew that the mineral existed here, mines were not developed extensively until after the close of the Civil War. The French called the area *La Bonne Terre,* "the good earth," in reference to its mineral wealth.

At 56.3 *m.* is a junction (R) with County J, a graveled road.

Right here to BONNE TERRE, 0.9 *m.* (828 alt., 3,730 pop.), the oldest of a series of closely spaced lead-mining towns. Here among surrounding mine shafts is a modern community of wide, tree-shaded streets, a library, churches, hospital, and brick and frame dwellings. The greatest single economic factor of the community is the St. Joseph Lead Company. Incorporated in 1864, the company began operations the following year on a 964-acre tract. Mining was of the surface type until the introduction of the diamond drill in 1869. The holdings were increased by purchase of other mines. In 1890 the Missouri River and Bonne Terre Railroad was built between Bonne Terre and Riverside, the junction with the Iron Mountain Railroad, one mile south of Herculaneum. A smelter was erected at Herculaneum (*see above*), and Bonne Terre became the mining and shipping center for innumerable small mines. After a decade of consolidation, the St. Joseph Lead Company, with its subsidiary, the Doe Run Lead Company, emerged in 1900 as the largest of the four principal lead mining companies operating in southeastern Missouri. The St. Joseph Lead Company Office Building, Main and Allen Sts., is a two-and-a-half story brick structure of early English design. From the office are directed the vast lead-mining interests of Bonne Terre, Desloge, Leadwood, Flat River, River Mines, and Elvins.

At 63 *m.* is a junction (R) with State 32, a concrete road that leads through a series of mining towns.

Right here to FLAT RIVER, 3.3 *m.* (796 alt., 5,401 pop.), sometimes called the "lead capital of the world." The first mine shaft here was sunk in the fall of 1870, but the venture failed, and it was not until 1890 that the boom began. The first period of Flat River's history was one of rough-and-tumble activity; outside of the mines, life centered about the Blue Goose, the Black Bear, the Klondike, and the Moonlight saloons. Then the St. Joseph Lead Company bought the mines, and order was established. Today, Flat River is an efficient, almost model town, with the Flat River Junior College, housed in a group of modern brick buildings in the southeastern part of town, as evidence of its achievement. The college was founded in 1922.

The vicinity of what is now FARMINGTON, 69 *m.* (973 alt., 3,738 pop.), seat of St. Francois County, was known as the "Murphy Settlement" during the last years of the Spanish regime. About 1798, William Murphy, said to have been a Baptist minister, visited here, armed with official permission to settle. He then returned to Tennessee, where he died. In 1799 his son William settled here; he was joined during 1802 and 1803 by various friends and members of his family, including his mother, Sarah Barton Murphy. Although not platted until 1823, Farmington became the county seat when St. Francois County was organized in 1821. The first county court met at the home of David Murphy, but in 1824 a brick courthouse was built. The Ste. Genevieve, Iron Mountain and Pilot Knob Plank Road was built about 1854. The St. Louis & Iron Mountain Railroad was completed in 1858, and during the decade 1865-75, other railroads were constructed through the county, but all missed Farmington. In 1901 the St. Francois County Electric Railway Company was formed by Farmington investors, and its tracks, connecting with the St. Louis & Iron Mountain Railroad at De Lassus, gave Farmington additional commercial importance.

STATE HOSPITAL NO. 4 (*open daily*), west end of Columbia St., an institution for the treatment of mental and nervous diseases, was opened in 1903. The two- and three-story, red-brick and white-stone buildings scattered along a shaded drive were one of the first cottage-plan groups in the United States. The institution has approximately 1,500 patients. LONG MEMORIAL HALL, SE. corner of West Columbia and South Franklin Sts., a two-story brick structure built in 1925, houses the public library, the city administration offices, and the COMMUNITY MUSEUM (*open Saturday 1-5 p.m.*), which contains an exhibit of pioneer domestic articles from Farmington and St. Francois County. The TOM V. BROWN HOUSE (*open by arrangement*), NW. corner of Washington St. and Murphy Ave., a two-story white house with a long veranda across the front, is said to have been built by one of Reverend Murphy's sons soon after 1800. Records reveal that the county court rented one of the rooms from 1822 to 1823. In the northeast corner of the MASONIC CEMETERY, Henry St. five blocks S. of the square, is a white marble shaft marking the site of a log church in which "the first Sunday School west of the Mississippi River was organized and taught by Sarah Barton Murphy in the year 1805." Mrs. Murphy is said to have gone about on horseback, asking parents to send their children to her on Sundays. She kept them all day, fed them, and taught them Bible lessons, singing, reading, and writing. Mrs. Murphy's grave is a few yards south of the shaft. David Barton, Missouri's first United States Senator, was a nephew of Sarah Barton Murphy.

South of Farmington, agriculture replaces mining. The highway passes through a rolling valley devoted chiefly to fruits, small grains, and livestock, and winds among the wooded hills that form a break in the valley south and east of Fredericktown.

MINE LA MOTTE, 83.7 m. (838 alt., 200 pop.), a scattering of faded frame houses, a store, a church, and a school in a shallow valley under large elm and oak trees, has acquired the appearance of "a town that used to be." Yet no Missouri community has a longer history. It was here that the first lead "diggin's" in Missouri was opened by Sieur Antoine de la Mothe Cadillac, governor general of Louisiana, when he visited the site in 1715. Eight years later, Phillipe François Renault was granted lead-producing areas on the Meramec and at Mine La Motte, which he worked until 1744, when other individuals took over. Henry Schoolcraft, who visited Mine La Motte 1817-18, estimated the annual production at approximately 800,000 pounds. Schoolcraft was the first to note that cobalt and other minerals occurred here in combination with the lead ore.

Almost the only tangible remains of the town's rich history are the RUINS OF THE WHITE HOUSE (L), crowning the low hill above the creek and hidden by a tangled growth of trees and vines. The date and builder are unknown, but the massive, rough plastered brick walls are impressive even in ruin.

At 87.4 *m.* is a junction with US 67 (*see Tour 12*), and at 125.1 *m.* with State 34, a graveled road.

Right on State 34 to BURFORDVILLE, 5.4 *m.* (385 alt., 79 pop.), on the Whitewater River. At the eastern edge of the village, on the river's bank, is the BOLLINGER MILL (*open*), with a first story of stone, built about 1800, and three later stories of brick. A gambrel roof was added in 1868. The water wheel that formerly furnished power has disappeared, but the Whitewater still pours over the stone dam, rebuilt in 1858. At the time of its construction, the mill was the largest in the District of Cape Girardeau, and settlers came as far as 100 miles to have their wheat and corn ground. Its energetic builder, Major George Frederick Bollinger, came into the colony with a group of North Carolina German families who settled along the fertile valley of the Whitewater and its tributaries about 1800. Their tradition of thrift and careful farming is still evident. About the dam is the BURFORDVILLE COVERED BRIDGE, of sturdy hewn timbers carefully pinned together, and supported by two massive stone piers.

JACKSON, 127 *m.* (429 alt., 3,113 pop.), is at a junction with State 25 (*see Tour 11*).

Section c. JACKSON to ARKANSAS LINE, 112 m. US 61

Between Jackson and the Arkansas Line, US 61 crosses one of the most diversified farming areas of the State, then drops abruptly from the low hills into the flat, fertile acres of lower southeastern Missouri, a land of cotton and corn and extensive plantations cultivated by tenant farmers. Here, on reclaimed bottomlands, is Missouri's latest agrarian frontier.

South of JACKSON, 0 *m.,* US 61 passes through an open country of hillside pastures, carefully tilled fields, and compact farm buildings that is part of Cape Girardeau County. Here the thrifty descendants of early German farmers have refused to abandon their diversified crops for cotton. A part of each years' profit is regularly put into farm improvement, so that the hillsides show little or no signs of erosion and the barns and silos are brightly painted structures of good proportions.

At 0.8 *m.* is a junction with the graveled McKendree Chapel Road.

Left here to MCKENDREE CHAPEL, 2.4 *m.*, built about 1819, the oldest existing Protestant church building in Missouri. The carefully restored gray chapel with hewn-poplar log walls sheathed with weatherboarding, has stern utilitarian lines. The massive stone chimney, small windows, thick batten doors, and roof of hand-split shingles were characteristic of frontier churches. A grove of trees and a spring made the site an early Methodist camp meeting ground, and here the first Methodist Church west of the Mississippi was organized about 1806. Among its early ministers were "Rough and Ready" Watts, who preached hell and damnation, and "Slick and Easy" Watts, not a relative, who preached "heaven and happiness." On one occasion, when a member of "Rough and Ready's" audience annoyed him by interrupting, he laid down his Bible, put the pistol he always carried beside it, and announced that he would have to "Lick a man before he could proceed." He did, and services continued.

At 8 *m.* is the northern junction with Alt. US 61, which leads L. 3 miles to CAPE GIRARDEAU (356 alt., 19,426 pop.) (*see Cape Girardeau*).

Southward, the uplands slowly lose themselves in the almost unbroken sweep of the Mississippi flood plain. The land was formed by deposits of silt from the Ohio and Mississippi Rivers, and by a series of earthquakes (*see below*) that lowered and shifted the surface, leaving great swampy areas, now for the most part drained. Not only did the mosquito-infested swamps breed malaria, but travel was slow and circuitous, and farming was impossible except on a few higher tracts. "On leaving the uplands at Cape Girardeau," wrote D. T. Madox, a Kentucky traveler, in 1817, "we enter what is the great swamp; though it does not properly possess that character. The timber is not such as is usually found in swamps, but consists of fine oak, ash, olive, linn, beech, and poplar of enormous growth. The soil is a rich black loam. In the fall it is nearly dry . . . but during high water it is extremely dangerous and disagreeable to cross. The horse sinks at every step to the belly in water and loose soil; and . . . the unwary traveler, but for the marks on the trees, would be in danger of being lost in the trackless morass." Isolated higher portions attracted scattered settlements of Germans and Anglo-Americans during the generation preceding the Civil War, but the great migration down the Ohio shunned the region for more hospitable, if more distant, Missouri lands. After the war, the lumbering companies moved in, cutting the forests and clearing the land. In 1905 the Little River Drainage System was inaugurated (*see Tour 6*), and the country rapidly filled with one-time sawmill employees, Southern cotton planters, Ohio corn farmers, Middle Western wheat farmers, and the largest Negro rural population in the State. For approximately 30 years the land has produced great crops of wheat, cotton, corn, and melons.

At 21.8 *m.* is the junction with County A, a marked graveled road.

Right here, passing through an upland of corn, wheat and oat fields, and brightly painted farm buildings enclosed by well-tended fences, to NEW HAMBURG, 2 *m.* (460 alt., 137 pop.), a German community dominated by the tawny bulk of the St. Lawrence Roman Catholic Church. The close-packed, square, one- and two-story white frame houses are owned by descendants of German immigrants who settled here in 1846. Because of their isolation, they remained a racial, religious, and economic unit until a comparatively recent date. On New Year's Eve, masked villagers in fancy dress go from house to house, singing old German songs and being treated to wine and cakes. Belief in witchcraft is common. Spells are laid, the future is told, and charms are often worn. Most serious is the hex or curse placed on individuals by their enemies. If one wishes to dream of a future mate, he need only sleep with nine different kinds of leaves beneath the pillow. Signs and omens are carefully observed before planting or reaping crops, or undertaking any other important venture. St. Lawrence Church is a landmark visible for miles. The main portion of the building, with stuccoed stone walls and painted glass windows, dates from 1859. The unornamented, functional simplicity of the walls blends easily with the sturdy, Romanesque-type steeple and façade, built in 1907. Behind the larger church is the village's first church, built of logs about 1847 and later weatherboarded.

BENTON, 23.6 m. (440 alt., 408 pop.), with a two-story brick courthouse giving a modern note to the central square, is the seat of Scott County. The community was platted on land owned by Captain William Mayers in 1822 and named for Senator Thomas Hart Benton. In 1864 an act of the general assembly moved the county seat from Benton to Commerce, where it remained until it was returned to Benton by popular vote in 1878. The wild life that once made the region a hunter's paradise has disappeared to a large extent, but ducks, geese, and quail are still found in the undeveloped areas. In 1938 bobcats proved a sufficient menace to cause the organization of a "drive." The high point of Scott County's social year is Neighbor Day, held at Benton each October and featuring a chicken-calling contest, a baby show, the display of farm produce, and the crowning of "Queen Geneva."

In a neglected family cemetery, 27.1 m., on a hilltop 100 yards from the highway and accessible only by foot, is the Grave of General Nathaniel W. Watkins. General Watkins, a half-brother of Henry Clay, was born in Virginia in 1796. After service in the War of 1812, he moved to Jackson, Missouri, in 1819, and became prominent as a lawyer. He served several terms in the Missouri legislature, and in 1861 was appointed commander of the Southeast Missouri District by Governor Claiborne Fox Jackson. General Watkins resigned after a short period to retire to his home, "Beechwood," which stood near the cemetery. Here he died in 1876.

SIKESTON, 40 m. (325 alt., 7,944 pop.), generously proportioned, is one of the economic and cultural centers of Missouri's great cotton region. The oak- and magnolia-shaded homes of wealthy landowners are as characteristic of its life as the railroad tracks and red-tiled depot in the heart of the business district. As the town's commercial importance increased, the residential streets were extended north and south, and the industrial property east and west. On the eastern edge of town are several compresses and a cottonseed oil plant; outlining the western edge are bright, corrugated-iron cotton gins.

Settlement was made in the vicinity prior to the Louisiana Purchase in 1803, but early attempts to build a town were not successful. Sikeston was platted by John Sikes in 1860. Like other communities in southeastern Missouri, it experienced a period of activity during the lumbering era that followed the Civil War. Cheap lands bred large plantations, which, with the drainage of the lowland areas, brought rapid agricultural development. This wealth was expressed in ginger-bread mansions with fenced lawns and cast-iron fountains, a great yellow brick, pseudo-Baroque Methodist church, and the trim lines of white grain elevators and squat cotton compresses. Between 1910 and 1920 cotton was king, and only recently has the large-scale cultivation of such crops as alfalfa, melons, grains, and potatoes been introduced.

At Sikeston is a junction with US 60 (*see Tour 6*). Southward the land is low and flat, the cotton fields broken here and there by acres of corn and patches of wheat and oats.

At 60 *m.* is a junction with the New Madrid Road, a marked concrete highway.

Left here to NEW MADRID, 1 *m.* (298 alt., 2,450 pop.), seat of New Madrid County and a Mississippi River port. The great earthen levee crowds upon a succession of lackadaisical river-front shacks, several blocks of brick and frame commercial buildings in the style of the 1890's, and a fringe of residences. Unlike the usual county-seat town, the central square, with its bleached gray-brick and stone courthouse, is but an incidental part of the town plan. The town's main streets are at right angles to the river. Unconsciously the city expresses the interest of its citizens, who keep one eye on the Mississippi and the other on the hills.

Modern New Madrid is the descendant, four or five times removed by flood and the changing course of the river, of a fur-trading establishment founded about 1783 by François and Joseph Le Sieur, Canadian trappers and traders in the employ of Gabriel Cerré of St. Louis. The site of the post was near a large Delaware Indian town on the margin of an extensive prairie upon which were several other Indian villages. Traders were soon attracted, and "L'Anse à la Graise" (Fr., Greasy Bend, or, Fertile Cave) became a seasonal rendezvous.

The close of the Revolutionary War brought the American colonies to the boundaries of Spanish territory, and in an effort to prevent further American expansion, the Spanish authorities agreed to a tentative plan for a buffer colony. Settlers were to be offered liberal grants of land, religious freedom, local self-government, and the creation of a port of entry which would eliminate the necessity of carrying goods to New Orleans. Spain was to donate 15,000,000 acres for this project, which had been suggested by, and was under the control of, Colonel George Morgan, an American Revolutionary War veteran.

Early in 1789, Morgan selected the site of New Madrid as his "capital," and the town was laid out on a rectangular plan extending four miles along the river. Sites for schools, churches, and market places were provided, and in the center of the town a generous driveway was platted around a lake. No trees along the streets or in the parks of the new town were to be cut without official permission, and game in the surrounding country was protected by law.

The project aroused great interest among American colonists, who considered Morgan's plan a better means of attracting settlers to the West than any suggested by Congress. But the scheme conflicted with the ambitions of General James Wilkinson of Kentucky, and perhaps of Estevan Miro, governor of Louisiana, who had plans for a Spanish Mississippi Valley empire that would include Kentucky. Miro, prompted by Wilkinson, ended Morgan's project, but confirmed the grants made to settlers, and New Madrid continued as an agricultural and trading village. Many of Morgan's group returned to their homes, but other settlers came to the country, and a commandant was appointed. The close of the Spanish regime, and the years immediately following the transfer of the territory to the United States in 1804, saw a rapid increase of population in the area. The fertile bottom lands were well suited to farming, and New Madrid prospered despite the dangers and losses from river pirates, who hid in secluded coves and on the islands along the Ohio and Mississippi Rivers, to rob and murder the unprotected traveler.

It was a natural catastrophe that most seriously retarded the town's development. Shortly after two o'clock on the morning of December 16, 1811, the settlers were awakened by the groaning and creaking of their houses and the falling of furniture. They hurriedly groped their way into the open where, with the ground trembling in a succession of shocks, they stood through the winter's night. Daylight brought other shocks, and for almost two years scarcely a day passed without a disturbance. The ground rose and fell, accompanied by loud rumbling noises and the discharge of gases. Great cracks formed in the earth, and trees were bent until their branches interlocked. Landslides swept down the bluffs and hillsides; areas were pushed up, and still larger areas sank, in some instances as many as 25 feet. Great waves churned the bed of the Mississippi, washing boats high on the shore and sweeping thousands of trees into the river. Banks caved in and sand bars and islands disappeared.

The great fault zone beneath the area had produced similar disturbances at earlier periods (notably in 1776, 1791 or 1792, and 1795), but those of 1811-12 were the most violent of the past two centuries. They restricted development for more than 50 years, for people fled the country. In 1816 Congress provided that the sufferers be granted land in other parts of the State. By that time, however, those who had remained were accustomed to the changed environment, so that only 20 of the grantees occupied land elsewhere, and the majority of the claims were purchased by St. Louis land speculators. To add to the woes of New Madrid, a band of religious zealots, the Fanatical Pilgrims, arrived at this time in search of Jerusalem. Gaunt and ragged, they did not wash their bodies, own property, perform labor, or bury their dead. Their food was mush and milk served in a wooden trough and sucked through hollow cornstalks. In addition to these social disadvantages, they had a disconcerting habit of bursting into private homes chanting, "Praise God! Praise God!" or "Repent!"

Despite the constant shifting of the river channel, which forced the moving of New Madrid some three or four times before the Civil War, subjected it to intermittent floods and gave it a swamp unhealthiness, the community continued a slow growth as an agricultural and shipping center. The strategic value of the site was recognized by the building there of the Confederate fortification of Island No. 10, to block Federal control of the river. On March 3, 1862, General Albert A. Pope attacked New Madrid. Finding it strongly defended by Confederate gunboats, he laid siege to the town. On the thirteenth he opened a heavy artillery fire, and during the night the Confederate forces evacuated New Madrid, which opened the way for Pope's attack on and capture of Island No. 10. Following this interlude, the town again became a county seat village concerned with local problems of farming and trade. In the mud of the river lies the wreckage of a steamboat, *Sporty Days;* on the banks of the levee, among a conglomeration of shacks, a fish house displays the crudely painted sign, "Let Friendlyness Prevail."

South of the junction with the New Madrid Road, US 61 cuts a comparatively straight line close to the twisting Mississippi River. The flat land is black and fertile. Farm holdings are extensive, but the farm buildings are not as substantial as those to the north; for Missouri's "boot heel" sinks deep into the cotton kingdom, where farm labor is done by tenants who work on shares. In Pemiscot County, the cotton fields are broken by fields of corn almost equally great. But farther south on US 61 cotton is predominant.

PORTAGEVILLE, 76 *m.* (271 alt., 2,107 pop.), has well-kept stores and houses along Main Street, indicative of the prosperity of good cotton years. Here is the sprawling red-frame PORTAGEVILLE COMPRESS AND WAREHOUSE COMPANY PLANT (*open by permission*), in which bales of ginned cotton are reduced in size under hydraulic pressure and stored for shipment. Hauled to the compress from the gins, the baled cotton is unloaded by Negro handlers, who pitch it to another group of Negroes who "bust" the bands with a "band breaker" and throw it into the press. The Negroes work rhythmically, shouting at one another above the snorts and puffs of the compress.

HAYTI, 90 *m.* (256 alt., 2,628 pop.), with its business district across the railroad (R), gins and ships cotton.

Left from Hayti on State 84, a concrete road, to CARUTHERSVILLE, 6 *m.* (225 alt., 6,612 pop.), seat of Pemiscot County. Built on a bend of the Mississippi River and protected from floods by an earthen levee surmounted by a concrete wall, the town is the center of a cotton, corn, melon, and alfalfa area. It is also a shipping point for wood products, sand, and gravel. Caruthersville had its origin in La Petite Prairie, a French trading post whose site, near that of Caruthersville, has been washed into the river. It was settled about 1794 by François Le Sieur, the fur trader, who a decade earlier had established a post at New Madrid. The settlement on the wide, fertile bottom attracted John Hardeman Walker and his family from Tennessee in 1810. The violence of the New Madrid earthquake desolated the settlement in 1811-12. Seven years later, when the Reverend Timothy Flint traveled through the region, traces of the catastrophe were still evident; crevics where the earth had divided, sand covering the region to the depth of two and three feet, the surface red with oxidized pyrite. Only two families remained, and "the tokens of former cultivation and habitancy, were now mementos of desolation and desertion."

The Walker family was one of those that remained. In 1818 Walker, learning that the proposed southern boundary of the State would not include his land, began a vigorous campaign to include all land south to the thirty-sixth parallel, between the Mississippi and the St. Francis Rivers. To Walker Missouri thus owes its "boot heel." In 1857, with George W. Bushey, he platted a town on a portion of the Walker plantation and named it Caruthersville, in honor of Samuel Caruthers (1820-60), Madison County lawyer and judge. The town had a slow growth, until it became the eastern terminus of the St. Louis, Kennett & Southern Railroad; about 1900, it succeeded Gayoso as the county seat.

Right 3.5 *m.* from Caruthersville on an unmarked concrete road to a cluster of houses and stores called STUBBTOWN; L. 1.7 *m.* on the marked Cottonwood Point Road to a great INDIAN MOUND (L), the largest in southeastern Missouri. Rising like a low hill from the surrounding flat plain, the mound is 400 feet long, 250 feet wide, and 35 feet high, with a southern approach to the summit. The sides originally were covered with two layers of burned clay, three to four inches thick, with split cane laid between each layer. This and other mounds in the vicinity indicate a numerous and sedentary people, interested in agriculture and more advanced in civilization than the migratory Indians living in the area at the arrival of the white men. Early settlers used the mound as a refuge during flood.

CANADY, 96 *m.* (79 pop.), is a cotton growing community whose trade center is at STEELE, 105 *m.* (244 alt., 1,585 pop.), which like most towns in this section, began as a cluster of cabins on a plantation and found its impetus for growth in the construction of the St. Louis-San Francisco Railway in 1901. HOLLAND, 107 *m.* (242 alt., 390 pop.), a cotton shipping point, also exports large quantities of alfalfa, corn, and melons.

US 61 crosses the ARKANSAS LINE 112 *m.*, about six miles north of Blytheville, Arkansas.

Tour 8

(Bloomfield, Ia.) — Macon — Moberly — Columbia — Jefferson City —Rolla—Cabool—(Mammoth Spring, Ark.) ; US 63. Iowa Line to Arkansas Line, 355 *m.*

Concrete-paved highway between Kirksville and Rolla; elsewhere black-topped surface, except for 11-mile stretch south of Rolla.
Wabash R.R. roughly parallels route from Iowa Line to Columbia; St. Louis-San Francisco Ry. between Cabool and Arkansas Line.
Hotels and tourist camps in larger towns; lesser accommodations in southern region.

US 63, between the Iowa Line and the Arkansas Line, divides Missouri almost into halves. Topographically, however, Missouri is divided not north and south but east and west. Between the Iowa Line and the Missouri River the land along US 63 is gently rolling prairie; south of the Missouri River, the highway winds along the sharp ridges and dips into the narrow river valleys of the Ozark highlands.

Section a. IOWA LINE to JEFFERSON CITY, 153 m. US 63

US 63 crosses the MISSOURI LINE, 0 *m.*, 37 miles south of Ottumwa, Iowa, and enters Missouri's great corn, wheat, and livestock region.

LANCASTER, 5.2 *m.* (979 alt., 886 pop.), publicized as the birthplace of Rupert Hughes, has been seat of Schuyler County since its organization in 1845. A neat little town, well-secured in its position as a horse and poultry center, its heart is the public square, centered by a two-and-a-half-story, red-brick courthouse; at the northeast corner is a one-story log building, erected as a tavern by James Bryant in 1846.

The RUPERT HUGHES BIRTHPLACE (*private*), W. Washington St., is a small gray stucco house (R) trimmed in white. Rupert Hughes was born January 31, 1872. He spent his boyhood in Keokuk, Iowa, and received a master's degree from Yale University in 1899. He was editor on *Godey's Magazine, Current Literature, The Criterion,* and the *Encyclopaedia Britannica.* His published works include novels, juvenile books, and plays. He now (1941) resides in California.

The WILLIAM P. HALL HORSE BARNS (*open*), two blocks north of the square, a group of seven large unpainted two- and three-story structures with steeply pitched roofs, belong to one of the most active horse and mule dealers in the Nation. The business was established in 1890 by Colonel William P. Hall, who also owned a circus. During the Boer War, the establishment developed an extensive South African trade which helped to make Lancaster prominent as a horse market. One day's orders have totaled as much as $55,000. Between two of the structures is a red railroad coach said to have been one of the cars in Abraham Lincoln's funeral train. The largest barn (L) formerly housed the elephants and big cats of Colonel Billy Hall's Circus.

In QUEEN CITY, 14.5 *m.* (1,003 alt., 646 pop.), opposite the northeast corner of the park, is the SITE OF GLENN FRANK'S BIRTH-PLACE, now occupied by a two-story gray stucco house. The original frame building burned several years ago. For a number of years, the Frank family lived at Green Top, a few miles south of here. Glenn Frank, born October 1, 1887, entered the ministry at the age of 16 and for several years was an evangelist on the Chautauqua circuit, in which capacity he became known as a speaker, writer, and editor. At 38 he became the "boy president" of the University of Wisconsin. From 1937 to his death in 1940 he wrote and lectured extensively on politics and economics.

GREEN TOP, 18.7 *m.* (991 alt., 254 pop.), a small railroad shipping point, gained notice in 1935 by electing an entire ticket of women to civic offices.

KIRKSVILLE, 29 *m.* (969 alt., 10,080 pop.), seat of Adair County and home of the State's first normal school, is one of the largest towns in north central Missouri. Economically, Kirksville is well entrenched, with six factories, four wholesale houses, five banks, and many lesser establishments that contribute to an annual pay roll exceeding $1,500,-000. The surrounding country is largely devoted to grain farming and the raising of livestock and poultry. Until recent years, coal mining was important.

Kirksville was founded in 1841 as the seat of Adair County, which was organized in that year. According to tradition, Mr. and Mrs. Jesse Kirk gave the commissioners a turkey dinner on condition that the town be named for them. The Kirks conducted a tavern on what later became North Centennial Street. Many of the early settlers were from Kentucky, and Kirksville's sympathies were divided during the Civil War. Although the county furnished men for both armies, the relatively unimportant Battle of Kirksville was the only engagement of any size in the area. On the morning of August 6, 1862, a thousand Federal soldiers, commanded by Colonel John McNeil, routed 2,000 poorly armed Confederates under Lieutenant Colonel Joseph C. Porter and Captain Tice Cain.

Kirksville was the home of one of Missouri's outstanding educators, John R. Kirk (1851-1937). Born on a farm in Bureau County, Illinois, Kirk entered Kirksville Normal School in 1873, graduating in 1878. He became president of the normal school in 1899, after four years' service as State superintendent of schools. During the 26 years of his presidency, he worked continually for the advancement of normal school endeavors, and received national recognition for instituting and promoting many of the methods now generally accepted. He pioneered in the development of the rural-school system and established experimental schools to demonstrate his theories. He fostered music in schools and better physical equipment. The consolidated school, so common today, was advocated by Kirk for many years before its establishment.

MEMORIAL PARK, Hickory St. between Mulanix St. and Florence Ave., a block-square playground, is the site of the Union assault on the Confederate position during the Battle of Kirksville. The park is also the original site of the teachers' college; a rough boulder bearing a bronze plaque commemorates the Cumberland Academy (built 1860-61), which housed the institution. The building burned in 1872. In 1932 the city and county purchased the grounds and improved them for recreational purposes.

NORTHEAST MISSOURI STATE TEACHERS COLLEGE, E. Normal Ave. between Marion and Mulanix Sts., occupies 8 red-brick buildings grouped in an open quadrangle on a 15-acre campus. In the center of the campus, atop a white stone pedestal, is a life-size metal statue of Joseph Baldwin, founder of the college, designed by Leonard Crunelle, a pupil of Loredo Taft. The school, a fully accredited co-educational institution, has an average enrollment of 870 students. In the spring of 1867, Professor Baldwin came to Kirksville from Indiana, where he had conducted private normal schools. On September 2, 1867, he opened the Normal School in the Cumberland Academy building, where it remained for six years. During this time the name was changed to Missouri Normal School and Commercial College. In 1870 the school was accepted as a State institution and renamed First District Normal School of Kirksville. It took its present name in 1919. General John J. Pershing was a pupil of the school.

The KIRKSVILLE COLLEGE OF OSTEOPATHY AND SURGERY, W. Jefferson St. between Fifth St. and Osteopathy Ave., is housed in five plain red-brick buildings, two and three stories high, and a large two-story frame dwelling converted to academic use. Two of the buildings house free clinics; the others are devoted to instruction. A hundred yards north of the buildings, in a natural amphitheater, is Laughlin Bowl, whose wooden seats accommodate 8,000 spectators. Left of this, in a small park, is the STILL CABIN, a small one-room log structure in which Dr. Andrew Taylor Still (1828-1917), founder of the school, was born. The cabin was shipped here from Jonesboro, Virginia. The college, the largest of its kind in the United States, offers a four-year course. The average enrollment is 600. Dr. Andrew Taylor Still came to Missouri as a boy and, later, moved to Kansas, where in the practice of medicine he evolved a new theory of healing. He returned to Missouri and devoted the rest of his life to developing this theory. In 1892 he established the American School of Osteopathy.

LA PLATA, 43.2 m. (930 alt., 1,421 pop.), at the junction of the Wabash and Santa Fe railroads, was laid out in 1855. ATLANTA, 52.5 m. (902 alt., 397 pop.), on a great prairie that extends southward in unbroken fields of grain, was platted in 1858.

At 63 m. is a junction with US 36 (see Tour 1) on the outskirts of MACON, 64 m. (874 alt., 4,206 pop.). Known as the "City of the Maples," Macon stands in a forest of old trees, given to the city long ago in lieu of taxes. It is the seat of Macon County, first settled in 1827, and organized in 1837. The town's growth was delayed until the Hannibal & St. Joseph Railroad was built through here in 1858, providing an outlet for agricultural products. The two towns that formerly stood on the site—Macon (1856) on the east, and Hudson (1857) on the west—were incorporated as Macon City in 1859. In 1863 the county seat was moved from Bloomington to Macon, which was named, as was the county, for Nathaniel Macon (1757-1837), Revolutionary War soldier and United States Senator from North Carolina.

Much of Macon's development was brought about by Colonel Frederick William Blees and Theodore Gary. In 1892 Colonel Blees purchased the St. James Military Academy, established in 1875. After conducting the school for five years, ill health and the pressure of other business caused the colonel to close the institution, but two years later the cornerstone of a new school, the Blees Military Academy, was laid. Colonel Blees died in 1906, and his widow continued to operate the school for three years, finally selling the buildings to the Still-Hildreth Sanatorium. Colonel Blees also built a Catholic church in Macon, established a carriage and chair factory, and defrayed the expense of the greater part of the sewerage and street paving in the town. Theodore Gary, Macon's other benefactor, projected the plans for the city water supply, paving improvements, coal-land development, telephone plant, and public library. He also provided for the improvement and care of Oakwood Cemetery, and the building and equipping of the Samaritan Hospital. Gary served as chairman of the Missouri State Highway Commission from 1921 to 1926.

The IMMACULATE CONCEPTION SCHOOL, Rollins and Union Sts., formerly St. James Academy, is a memorial to Colonel Blees, who remodeled the large two-story brick structure as a residence and later turned it into a parochial school and chapel. A round tower surmounts the corner of the building.

The STILL-HILDRETH SANATORIUM (R), 65.2 m., an osteopathic institution comprising several buildings amid campus-like grounds covering 400 acres, was established in 1914 under the direction of three pioneer osteopaths—Arthur G. Hildreth, and Charles E. and Harry M. Still, sons of the founder of osteopathy. The sanatorium specializes in the treatment of neuroses.

JACKSONVILLE, 74 m. (851 alt., 181 pop.), named for Hancock Jackson, pre-Civil War Governor of Missouri and Randolph County resident, was established as a railroad stop in 1858. CAIRO, 80 m. (864 alt., 250 pop.), was platted two years later for the same purpose. At 86.2 m. is a junction with US 24 (see Tour 2).

In MOBERLY, 87 m. (872 alt., 12,920 pop.), which was laid out in 1866 on the watershed between the Mississippi and Missouri Rivers, are the shops of the Wabash Railroad, a large shoe factory, a hosiery mill, a hay-press factory, and other manufacturing plants, which provide employment for several thousand persons. Six coal mines are near by. The town is a division point of the Wabash Railroad; trains enter its Union Station from five directions.

In 1858, the great railroad building year, a charter was granted the Chariton & Randolph County Railroad to construct a line from a point in Randolph County to Brunswick, in Chariton County. One mile north of the present town of Moberly was the village of Allen, but the railroad officials decided to found a city more convenient to their proposed route. In 1861 the inhabitants of Allen were invited to move to the new site. The railroad even offered to move the houses and to allocate to each landholder as much ground in the new town as he owned in the old. Only one resident, an Irishman named Patrick Lynch, complied. He jacked his one-story frame house onto rollers, hitched it to a yoke of oxen, deposited it upon the new townsite, and settled into a long residency as the solitary citizen of Moberly. When the Civil War blocked prospects of building, Lynch, who was tired of waiting, plowed up the stakes marking the lots, and planted a garden along the west side of the railroad tracks, where the business section of Moberly now stands. After the war, the franchise of the Chariton & Randolph County Railroad passed into the hands of the North Missouri Railroad, and Moberly again was considered as a potential railway center. In 1866 lots were sold, and Patrick Lynch, in consideration of his services in "holding the city through war without the loss of a life or a house," was presented with deeds to two lots. The town was incorporated in 1873. During the eighties and nineties, the development of near-by coal mines made the village the colorful center and weekend rendezvous of miners from outlying camps.

In 1916 Moberly celebrated its golden jubilee. Prominent citizens wrote letters to children of the town and left them in a metal strongbox, which was placed in a bank vault, to be opened and read during the centennial celebration in 1966. More than 700 letters were written. Moberly is the home of Mrs. J. J. Gasparotti (Elizabeth Seifert), winner in 1938 of the Dodd, Mead-Red Book prize of $10,000 for her novel, Young Doctor Galahad. ROTHWELL PARK, Rollins St. at the western edge of town, is a 240-acre tract containing a 40-acre lake, a lighted beach (open May-Sept.; free), a bathhouse of gray stucco, and amusement facilities. Asphalt drives extend through the wooded hills bordering the several arms of the lake.

At 101 *m.* is a junction with State 22, a black-topped road.

Left here to CENTRALIA, 11.8 *m.* (884 alt., 1,996 pop.), whose principal industry is the A. B. Chance Manufacturing Company, specializing in the production of telephone-pole anchors. The town was established in 1857 on the proposed route of the North Missouri Railroad, which was completed to this point in 1859. It was named for its central position on the railroad between St. Louis and Ottumwa, Iowa. At Centralia, during the Civil War, occurred the Centralia Massacre. On the morning of September 27, 1864, 80 Confederate guerrillas, led by Bill Anderson, part of a band of 350, entered the town, plundered the two stores and the dozen or more homes of food and supplies, and then held up the stagecoach from Columbia, robbing the passengers. James S. Rollins, the United States Congressman, and James H. Waugh, sheriff of Boone County, both strong Union sympathizers, were in the coach, but the attention of the guerrillas being diverted by the approach of a North Missouri train from St. Louis, they were not recognized. Placing ties across the railroad track to stop the engine, the guerrillas opened fire, wounding the fireman. Of the 150 people on the train, 23 or 24 were unarmed Federal soldiers, either discharged or on furlough. The bandits robbed the passengers, took $3,000 from the baggage-car safe, and rifled the baggage, one piece of which yielded $10,000. They then stripped the Federal soldiers of their uniforms, evacuated the train, and set fire to it. The engineer was forced to open the throttle, and the blazing train traveled two or three miles west before it was entirely burned. Anderson then commanded that the Union soldiers be taken to the south side of the railroad and placed in line. A German, wearing a military blouse and cap, protested in his native tongue that he was not a soldier, but he was lined up with the others. The guerrillas formed a squad, with Arch Clements in charge, and fired with revolvers at about 20 paces. Half the Union men fell at the first volley; others staggered about and were shot again and again until they were dead. Most of them were from the First Iowa Cavalry and the First Missouri Engineers. The depot was burned, and the guerrillas returned to their near-by camp with the spoils, including large supplies of whisky which they had stolen from the stores.

That same afternoon, a Union force of 175 men, under Major A. V. E. Johnson of the Thirty-ninth Missouri Infantry, arrived at Centralia. Major Johnson, believing that the size of the main force of the guerrillas had been overestimated, determined to pursue them. He gathered about 120 men in the open prairie, leaving a guard of 35 in Centralia. Meanwhile, the guerrillas sent out a small scouting party under Dave Poole, for the purpose of luring the Union men to the guerrilla camp. Major Johnson and his men fell into the trap and were attacked. The battle was short but furious. The troops, mostly raw recruits, were poorly mounted, while the guerrillas were trained marksmen, equipped with fresh horses and well armed. Probably not more than 12 Union men escaped. Major Johnson was killed, some say by Jesse James.

At 122 *m.* is a junction with US 40 (*see Tour 1*), with which US 63 is united through COLUMBIA, 123.5 *m.* (713 alt., 18,399 pop.) (*see Columbia*).

DRUESDALE FARMS (*open*), 125 *m.* (R), is a public riding academy and earthen show ring, enclosed by a whitewashed fence. Here Druesdale three- and five-gaited saddle horses are for sale. The stables maintain 40 horses for public use (*50¢ per hour*). The Christian College Annual Horse Show, held here during June commencement week, is an all-girl affair.

Opposite Druesdale Farms, and forming a junction with the highway, is the Ashland Pike, an early-day toll road that connected Columbia with Jefferson City by way of Ashland.

The BONNE FEMME CHURCH (R), 130 *m.,* is a small red-brick building, with four sharply sloping gables over arched, art-glass windows. This structure, built in 1843, replaced a log church erected in 1819. The church name comes from its location on the north bank of Petite Bonne Femme (Fr., pretty little women) Creek. Near here was the Bonne Femme Academy, opened in 1829 with Warren Woodson as teacher. The school boasted a "very commodious brick building with two rooms of 22 feet square." An unusually large millstone is in front of the church.

ASHLAND, 136.5 *m.* (900 alt., 434 pop.), a scattering of frame houses, several of which have second-story galleries above small front porches, is on the western edge of Two-Mile Prairie, a favorite land mark of pioneers in the early decades of the last century. The town was founded in 1853. A story, mostly legendary, has been handed down from Civil War days concerning the Battle-That-Didn't-Take-Place. A troop of Confederates was encamped on the river near Ashland, when Federal soldiers headed for Jefferson City arrived. The commanders of the two contingents, who were friends, previously had made a gentleman's agreement that they would avoid battle. The groups came together at night, and both sides prepared for conflict, but they agreed to wait until daylight for the encounter. When morning came and the two commanders recognized each other, the Confederate troops were ordered to retreat to the west, the Federals to the east. Charges of neglect were made against both commanders.

At 150.3 *m.,* US 63 passes between the fields of STATE PRISON FARM No. 2 (*open by permission*), 1,100 acres on which a large portion of the foodstuffs used in Missouri's penal institutions is raised by convict labor.

At 151.5 *m.* is a junction with US 54 (*see Tour 15*), with which US 63 is united to JEFFERSON CITY, 153 *m.* (557 alt., 24,268 pop.) (*see Jefferson City*), where there is a junction with US 50 (*see Tour 4*).

Section b. JEFFERSON CITY to ARKANSAS LINE, 202 m.
US 63

Between Jefferson City and Rolla, US 63 follows a zigzag route across the deeply rolling foothills of the Ozark Highlands. Settled by German families during the period 1830-50, the land is developed in grain and livestock farms, and the small, neat villages are clustered about imposing Roman Catholic churches. South of Rolla to the Arkansas Line, the hills are steeper and the stream valleys narrower. Much of the land is covered by second-growth forest, though dairy farming is an important occupation.

IN THE HIGHWAYS
AND BYWAYS

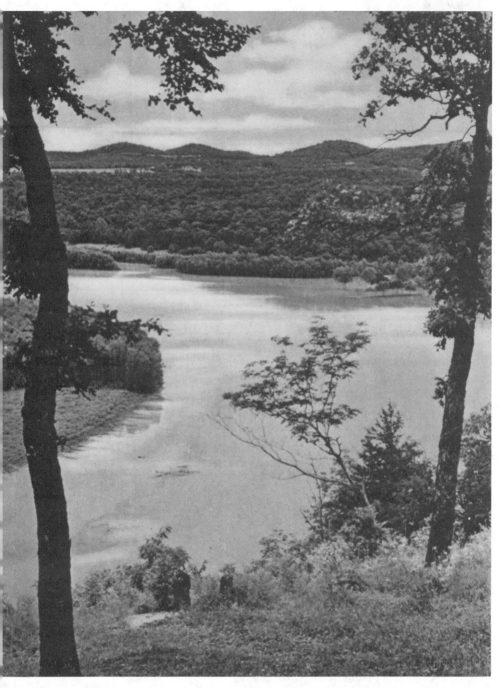

Townsend Godsey

LAKE TANEYCOMO IN THE OZARKS

**THE SWIMMING HOLE, BENNETT SPRING
STATE PARK**

GREER SPRINGS

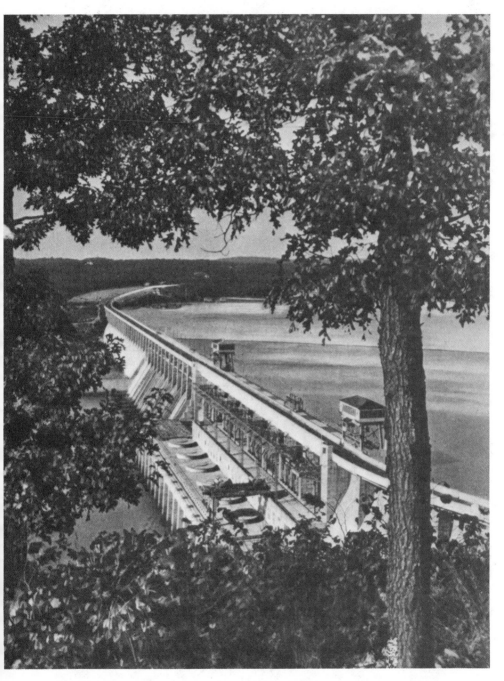

Missouri Writers' Project

BAGNELL DAM AND THE LAKE OF THE OZARKS

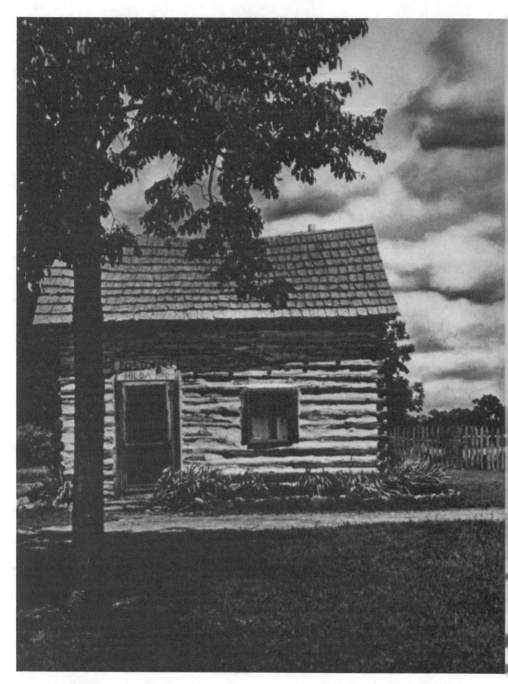

Townsend Godsey

POST OFFICE, HILDA

U. S. Forest Service

CABIN IN THE OZARKS

BAPTISING AT BENNETT SPRING

Townsend Godsey

SAWING COBS FOR CORN-COB PIPES, WASHINGTON

St. Louis Post-Dispatch

STRIPPING CYPRESS TREE IN "SWAMPEAST" MISSOURI

St. Louis Post-Dispatch

**WEAVING A COVERLET, THE
SCHOOL OF THE OZARKS,
POINT LOOKOUT**

School of the Ozarks

OZARK POTTERY MAKER

Piaget Studio

READY FOR AN OZARK FOX HUNT

At JEFFERSON CITY, 0 *m.*, US 63 unites for 11.5 miles with US 50 (*see Tour 4*), then turns southward. Pastured slopes whose crests are feathered with timber, and carefully tilled bottomlands, are evidence of the wisdom of the early German settlers, who learned to protect hillsides against erosion and to supplement their staple crops of corn and wheat with a herd of cows, some sheep, a garden, and an orchard. Mellowed stone houses of Germanic design, more recent brick and freshly painted white frame houses, and solid red barns accent the natural beauty of the countryside and indicate the stability of its economy.

Prim stone and frame buildings crowd the main street of WEST-PHALIA, 15.3 *m.* (750 alt., 374 pop.), which winds from the valley to the crest of a bluff, crowned by the sharp spire of St. Joseph's Catholic Church.

In the summer of 1835, a small group of Westphalian families settled along the Big Maries River. Two of the group, Dr. Bernard Bruns and a Mr. Bartman, located on the bend of the river near the present site of the town and, in the following year, opened a store. Lack of funds, the difficult task of clearing the land and preparing it for cultivation, and disease and loneliness discouraged many. A few who had the means to do so returned to Germany, but other immigrants continued to augment the group that remained, and conditions slowly improved. In the spring of 1837, a log chapel was built, and in it, a year later, Father Ferdinand Benoit Marie Guislain Helias d'Huddeghem celebrated Mass. Father Helias named the log chapel in honor of St. Joseph, patron saint of Belgium.

Soon after his arrival, Father Helias purchased 40 acres from Francis Geisberg and laid out the town of New Westphalia—now Westphalia. From this village, Father Helias conducted his missionary activities throughout central Missouri. Indefatigable in his work, he was often very outspoken and so antagonized many of his parishioners. In the spring of 1842, he returned to St. Louis, leaving affixed to the church door a Latin distich of his own composition. Translated, it read:

> Why should the man who courts hardships hie
> to the dusky Indies?
> Let him come to Westphalia and he will find
> hardships aplenty.

Within a few months, however, he became the resident priest of Taos (*see Tour 4*), where he remained until his death 30 years later.

In 1848, the log chapel was replaced by the present ST. JOSEPH'S CHURCH, a buff stone structure in modified Romanesque design. The present spire was added in 1883. In the sacristy are preserved a small antique painting, said to have been sent to Father Helias by his mother, the Countess of Lens, antique silver religious vessels, and an elaborately embroidered cope that was once used by Pope Boniface VII.

At 18.6 *m.* is a junction with a marked dirt road.

Right here to CAMP MARIES, 1.6 m., five cabins and a one-story white frame commissary on a knoll above the Maries River. During the summer months, the camp serves the Lake of the Ozarks Council, Boy Scouts of America.

At 21.3 m. is a junction with County E, a graveled road.

Left here to RICH FOUNTAIN, 3.2 m. (300 pop.), typical of the many small, off-the-main-highway German communities sprinkled through this section. The town consists of a few houses and stores scattered across a steep, rocky hillside. Overlooking the town and the valley farms are the impressive Roman Catholic Church and school. The atmosphere is one of neat, rural simplicity. The settlement was called Rich Fountain by Father Helias, because of the many clear springs in the neighborhood. One of these, near the present site of the town, was purchased by John Strumpf from John Burns about 1839. Strumpf built a water mill here, which he soon changed to a treadmill worked by oxen, and, in 1856, to a steam mill.

The 250 Bavarian families who settled in the vicinity about 1842 had come to the United States to escape oppressive government restrictions which "made it impracticable for them to conform to the marriage laws of the church." Many of these couples were married by Father Helias. The CHURCH OF THE SACRED HEART, at the northern edge of town, enclosed by a low stone wall, is of buff-colored stone, with a black slate roof surmounted by a clock tower and spire. Narrow oval-arched windows break the sidewalls. Left of the church are the parochial schools, nuns' residence, and parish house. On August 17, 1938, Rich Fountain celebrated the centennial of the parish established by Father Helias d'Huddeghem.

FREEBURG, 27.1 m. (802 alt., 395 pop.), dominated by the imposing red-brick Church of the Holy Family, is one of the youngest of the German communities. Although listed as a post office in 1884, it was not until the building of the Rock Island Railroad in 1902 that the town assumed some importance as a shipping point. The railroad, however, does not pass through the town; it runs beneath it. Engineers thought it easier to tunnel through the ridge than to grade it to a proper level. Gray Summit (*see Tour 4*) is the only other town in the State under which a railroad tunnel runs.

VIENNA, 37.1 m. (433 pop.), seat of Maries County, is built around a square containing a small, plain, two-story brick courthouse. The community was settled in 1855 by German and Irish families, who purchased land in the vicinity during a widely advertised sale of cheap lands. Dr. E. G. Latham, the presiding judge of the county court, wanted the commissioners to name the town Vie Anna, in honor of a young woman of his family who had recently died. Vienna was accepted as a compromise.

South of Vienna, US 63 rides a high, narrow ridge that offers a sweeping panorama of timbered valleys. The road is an excellent example of good highway engineering, with the multitudinous curves all banked. The GASCONADE RIVER, crossed on a high steel and concrete bridge at 43.3 m., is a winding, blue-green stream famed for its fishing (*jack salmon, black bass, trout, and crappie*).

A HIGHWAY TURNOUT (*picnicking facilities*), 49.5 m. (R), affords a widespread view of Spring Creek Gap and its forested hills and valley.

VICHY, 51.8 m. (1,112 alt., 210 pop.), named for the famous

French resort, was once a popular spa. At the northern end of the village, in a ravine (R), the single surviving mineral spring plays a stream of water through a half-inch pipe. The town, platted in 1880, was destroyed by a tornado in 1886.

Left from Vichy on a dirt road to the CHURCH OF GOD CAMP GROUNDS, 2 m., a 40-acre tract, with a square, white-painted, frame tabernacle that seats more than 500 persons. A rectory and a long, two-story frame dormitory complete the equipment. Here are conducted each year a series of old-time camp meetings, to which many come prepared to stay from one to ten days. The meetings usually begin during the first week in August, and are conducted by evangelists. They are joyous affairs, where all the participants soon know each other. The hymns are old, the singing whole-hearted; the preaching, simple and direct, is, interspersed with lengthy prayers.

South of Vichy, US 63 winds through valleys planted in grain and hemmed in by tree-covered hills. At 63 m. is the northern junction with US 66 (see Tour 5), with which US 63 is united through ROLLA, 65 m. (1,120 alt., 5,141 pop.).

The RUSSELL BROTHERS CIRCUS WINTER QUARTERS (open), 65.9 m. (L), is a series of corrals, white frame barns, and low-roofed stone stables, grouped about a low hill. At the end of the season, the circus breaks up, and the artists—acrobats, bareback riders, aerialists, and clowns—go their separate ways. Only a few employees remain, to feed and care for the animals and rolling stock. In late winter the whole crowd shows up again for a period of intense practice and training. The entertainers perfect their acts, the animal handlers get their charges sleek and in condition for travel, the painters brighten up the parade wagons, and the trainers put the big cats, elephants, and ponies through their paces. In spring, when the circus begins its tour, everything is spic and span. There is new canvas for the "big top," the elephants' toenails are manicured, and the bands' instruments are polished. The troupe travels in 70 motorized units and covers approximately 16,000 miles each year. Mrs. Pauline Russell Webb, only woman circus director in the United States, is in complete charge.

The circus's winter quarters are on the SITE OF FORT WYMAN, erected during the Civil War for Union troops. The original structure, 400 feet square, was surrounded by trenches and a moat. The outside log walls were slanted, to make the Minié balls glance off and upward. The fort was one of a series erected to protect Rolla, in which was a cantonment and 20,000 troops (see Tour 4). The center of the stockade contained a shelter, and close by was a well.

Southward, US 63 crosses rolling hill country of second-growth forest. In summer, the hillsides are cool and bright with the foliage of oak, pine, and cedar trees; on the lowlands, the deep greens of pasture lands are broken by the yellows of wheat and corn. In winter, the fields are bare, and the walnut trees cast a smoky black against the brown of post oaks on hills of ever-changing color.

The village of EDGAR SPRINGS, 84.7 m. (150 pop.), has not forgotten how to celebrate the Fourth of July in the old-time way.

Early on the morning of the holiday, a crowd gathers from the hills as if by magic: old folk who remember when the big lumber mills operated and there was an abundance of money; young people who know only that the land has been washing away ever since the mills "cut out," and that the crops are poor; and, of course, a speaker, who addresses the milling crowd from a flag-draped platform. The speaker knows that his listeners believe emphatically, as did their fathers before them, in democracy and individualism, and it is of these he talks. After the speech, there is a barbecue, at which everyone helps himself to anything he wants. The women visit, discussing rural news or exchanging recipes, and the men engage in hog-calling contests and horse-shoe tournaments. The boys try to win the admiration of the girls by climbing a larded pole or catching a greased pig.

The LICKING NURSERY (*open*), 96.5 *m.* (R), operated by the United States Forest Service in co-operation with the State Conservation Commission, consists of 40 acres and several utility buildings, including barracks for laborers employed during the rush seasons. Forty different species of trees and shrubs, used chiefly for reforestation purposes in the Clark and Mark Twain national forests, are raised here. Some of the trees are sold to Missouri farmers at production cost, to help them control drainage and reduce erosion. The nursery, established in 1934, produces 1,500,000 trees a year.

LICKING, 101 *m.* (598 pop.), surveyed in 1878 and named for a buffalo lick a quarter of a mile east of town, boasts a giant oak, two blocks south of the business district, which is believed to be more than 150 years old. The trunk of the tree, measuring 14 feet in circumference, has been carved with hearts and initials by several generations.

John Baldridge and Barney Low, the first settlers in the vicinity, built cabins near the lick about 1826. An enormous treasure of silver is thought to be hidden somewhere in the hills, and, as late as 1889, local residents reported that the Indians who formerly lived here returned secretly each year to visit the cache.

At 113.6 *m.* is a junction with State 17, a graveled road.

Left here to YUKON, 4.8 *m.* (50 pop.). R. from Yukon on State 137, a graveled road, to the OUTLAW LOOKOUT TOWER, 5.4 *m.*, an 80-foot wooden observation platform, adjacent to an 18-room cream-colored stucco dwelling; both were built in 1930 by Harry Getchie, alias Harry Watson. Watson, as he was known in the vicinity, spent money lavishly in the building of the house and tower, and on other improvements. The mystery surrounding his movements caused an investigation by the Texas County sheriff, who found that a man answering Watson's description was wanted for mail robbery. Watson was convicted by a Federal court and died in prison. The large estate is unoccupied.

HOUSTON DEPOT (L), 119.8 *m.*, a dilapidated one-story concrete structure with glassless windows and doors, has occupied the site since 1921, although no railroad has ever approached closer than 15 miles. In 1921, a Houston druggist, Dr. P. A. Harrington, promoted the building of a hydroelectric plant on the Big Piney River. His success in raising money for the project led him to undertake the building of an electric interurban railroad between Houston and Rolla, a distance of 55 miles, to connect at the latter point with the St. Louis-San Francisco Railway. His plan was to enlarge the hydroelectric plant to supply power for the interurban line. He raised $33,000 for the project and had the depot built. Five miles of grade had been completed when a flood washed away the dam and destroyed the power plant. This catastrophe so disheartened the supporters of the plan that they refused to contribute any more money, and the project was abandoned.

HOUSTON, 120 *m.* (820 pop.), seat of Texas County, the largest in Missouri, is the center of a dairying and recreational region. The county, 1,159 square miles in area (larger than the State of Rhode Island), was established in 1845. In the following year the county seat was platted and named for General Samuel Houston, first president of the Texas Republic. During the Civil War, Houston was twice destroyed, and when peace came not a citizen remained. Postwar reconstruction was accompanied by bitterness, but in 1872 the town was incorporated. The Houston *Herald,* a weekly established in 1878, has been published continuously since that year.

At 120.2 *m.* is a junction with State 17, a graveled road.

Right here to a narrow graveled road, 5.8 *m.;* L. 2.2 *m.* to a similar road; L. 1.2 *m.* to White Rock Bluffs. A quarter of a mile along a footpath that descends to the base of a 100-foot bluff is a farmhouse, east of which are a group of red and yellow INDIAN PAINTINGS. The work of some prehistoric tribe, the drawings represent both human and animal forms. A story handed down from early settlers is that one of the first white men to enter the region asked an old Indian chief if he knew who put the paintings on the bluff. The chief answered that they were there when his people came, "many, many moons ago." Artifacts recovered here indicate that the site was once occupied by an Indian village.

South of Houston are many stacks of cut white-oak timber, the product of several small sawmills that nibble away at the second-growth forest. The mills are seldom stationary, but are moved from place to place by trucks. The stacks await shipment to larger mills, where they are converted into barrel heads and staves.

CABOOL, 138 *m.* (1,244 alt., 1,069 pop.), is at a junction with US 60, with which US 63 is united for 16 miles (*See Tour 6*).

At 167 *m.* is a junction with State 14, a graveled road.

Right here to a LOOKOUT TOWER (*open*), 10 *m.* (L), a 110-foot structure overlooking a division of the Mark Twain National Forest. Left from the tower 1.2 *m.* on a marked graveled road to SILOAM SPRINGS (54 pop.), a small mountain resort with a few white frame cottages scattered across the side of a hill. In the valley, at the edge of the forest, are a nine-hole golf course (*green fee, 50¢*) and a concrete swimming pool (*adm. 25¢*).

WEST PLAINS, 173 *m.* (949 alt., 4,026 pop.), seat of Howell County, and the only town of size for many a hilly mile, is built on diversified agriculture. Five creameries handle the milk from surrounding dairy farms; livestock is fed, sold, and distributed to both State and out-of-State buyers; and large quantities of small grains are stored and shipped. Because of its auction sales, West Plains has two big days each week—Monday, when the sales are held, and Saturday, the usual busy time for agricultural centers. Hardly has the last grain or dairy farmer left on Saturday night before the livestock breeders begin to arrive, bringing with them cattle, horses, sheep, and hogs. Scores of trucks line the streets, and hotels and rooming houses are filled. Between Monday morning and Monday night, $40,000 to $50,000 and hundreds of animals change hands.

Among the first residents of the county was Josiah Howell, of Tennessee, who settled one mile west of the present site of West Plains in 1840. When the county was organized in 1857, it was named in his honor. The county seat, laid out a year later, was named for its level site. During the Civil War, the residents of the county suffered from the raids of the opposing armies; at the close of the war not more than 50 families remained.

In 1873, when the community was little more than a backwoods village, Cornelius Bolin announced that he had bought a piano—the first in the region—for his daughter Alice. Few believed it would survive the 100-mile wagon trip across the hills from Rolla. When it did come, the village turned out, and a one-time music teacher—the only individual in the region who could play the instrument—proudly rendered "My Old Kentucky Home." The "excitement of the assemblage knew no bounds."

In later years, Charles T. Aid, perhaps remembering the impression made by the first instrument, placed an electric piano in his store and reserved a space for children to listen. Profiting by his location next to the church, he put a full-length mirror in the display window, "so that women folks could see themselves in Sunday array." A short time later, a national magazine included "Uncle Charlie" among the 12 "big country merchants" of the United States. He was doing a business of $250,000 a year, drawing farm trade from a radius of 85 miles.

The JOSEPH AID GUN COLLECTION, in the Aid Hardware Store, 200 Court Sq., includes several guns more than 100 years old, approximately 50 rifles and shotguns, mostly of the cap-and-ball type, a Sharps buffalo gun, and 25 pistols. The WEST PLAINS AUCTION BARNS, 16 St. Louis St., a group of large stone and frame buildings, are the center of the region's livestock industry.

BRANDSVILLE, 186 m. (941 alt., 224 pop.), and KOSHKONONG, 191 m. (958 alt., 358 pop.), are farmers' villages on the St. Louis-San Francisco Railway. At 198 m. is a junction with State 19 (see Tour 14).

THAYER, 199 m. (518 alt., 1,692 pop.), built on a hill, is a division point on the railroad and an important shipping center for timber and dairy products. The city, brought into being by the St. Louis-San Francisco Railway, is the home of approximately 350 employees of the railroad.

US 63 crosses the ARKANSAS LINE, 202 m., 150 miles northwest of Memphis, Tennessee.

Tour 9

(Des Moines, Iowa)—South Lineville—Carrollton—Waverly—Sedalia—Preston—Buffalo—Springfield—Hollister—(Little Rock, Arkansas); US 65.
Iowa Line to Arkansas Line, 339 *m*.

Concrete and oil-mat paving throughout, two and three lanes wide.
Route paralleled roughly by Chicago, Rock Island & Pacific R.R. between South Lineville and Trenton; by Chicago, Milwaukee & St. Paul R.R. between Trenton and Chillicothe; by Missouri Pacific R.R. between Sedalia and Warsaw and between Branson and Arkansas Line; and by St. Louis-San Francisco Ry. between Springfield and Ozark.
Hotels in larger cities; tourist and trailer camps, and numerous resorts, especially on southern part of route.

US 65, as it runs the length of western Missouri, crosses in turn the northern prairies, the valley of the Missouri River, the fertile upland south of the river, the Lake of the Ozarks, and the rolling hill country in which lie Springfield and Lake Taneycomo.

Section a. *IOWA LINE to SEDALIA, 155 m. US 65*

Farmers from Kentucky, Tennessee, Virginia, and the Carolinas settled Missouri's northern plains and developed great farms on the rich prairie. Here are bluegrass pastures and fields of corn, wheat, and oats, and farms where some of the best dairy cattle, horses, and mules in the State are raised. On the bluffs along the Missouri River are apple orchards and sheep pastures. South of the river are prairie pastures brilliant in midsummer with orange butterfly weed, and in early fall with goldenrod and Spanish needle. The region was settled a generation before the Civil War by people who appreciated the feel of wide acres. Their industry and profits are expressed in barns and farm buildings that dwarf the neat, solidly constructed houses.

US 65 crosses the MISSOURI LINE, 0 *m.*, 75 miles south of Des Moines, Iowa, and enters SOUTH LINEVILLE (1,094 alt., 82 pop.), a cluster of garages, filling stations, and small residences. Before the Iowa-Missouri boundary was established in 1896, neither the village nor its larger Iowa counterpart was sure of its official location. A story persists that at least one politician profited by this uncertainty, serving first as a member of the Missouri general assembly, and later as a representative in the Iowa legislature.

The business district of PRINCETON (R), 14.5 *m.* (839 alt.,

473

1,584 pop.), is located on a high promontory, separated from the residential area by valleys on the north and south. One- and two-story brick mercantile houses enclose an open square once occupied by the courthouse. Platted in 1846 and incorporated in 1853, Princeton is the seat of Mercer County, named for General Hugh Mercer, who fought with Washington in the Battle of Princeton (New Jersey). The name of the city commemorates the battle, which took place January 3, 1777, and ended in British defeat.

Best known, perhaps, of early-day Princeton residents is Martha Canary (1850-1903), who, as a scout for the United States Army during its campaign in the Black Hills in 1872, won the soubriquet "Calamity Jane." Martha was born in Princeton, the eldest of six children. About 1863 her parents moved to Montana and soon after died, leaving Martha with the responsibility of the family, until about 1870, when she was "left to follow her own inclinations." She became a scout, wearing the buckskins, chaps, and spurs of her male associates. "She took the greatest pride in her ability to out-chew, out-smoke, out-swear and out-drink most of her masculine companions. Her profanity, in particular, was so rich in metaphor, and so varied, that it was a source of delight to discriminating audiences. . . ." Her career as a scout ended with the final defeat of the Sioux in 1891. She is buried beside Wild Bill Hickok (*see Springfield*) in Mt. Moriah Cemetery, Deadwood, South Dakota.

AXTELL HOSPITAL (L), southern end of town, is a two-story white frame structure fronted by four large columns. Bright green shutters shield the windows, and a wooden railing extends around the roof. The building was once the home of Ira Hyde (1838-1926), member of Congress (1872-74), and was the home of his son, Arthur Mastick Hyde (b. 1877), until his removal in 1912 to Trenton, Missouri, where he has since made his home. Mr. Hyde served as Governor of Missouri (1921-25), and as Secretary of Agriculture (1929-33). PRINCETON PARK (R), 15.9 *m.,* is a small recreational area (*swimming pool, 15¢ and 25¢*).

Southward to Trenton, the highway parallels a tributary of the Grand River. Farms are closely spaced and intensively cultivated. In the spring, tractors crawling across the wide landscape appear as red and green dots against the dark brown of freshly plowed fields, their motors swelling to a roar as they climb the top of a rise, or diminishing to a low hum as they drop from sight behind a hillock. The crops sown on these deep glacial soils support the livestock and feeding industry, which is the principal source of income for many northern Missouri farmers. Among the more prominent farms of the region is the KATHANS HEREFORD FARM, 37.5 *m.* (R), equipped with mammoth white barns, corrals, and a huge silo. The farm is known for its pedigreed Hereford bulls, among them Prince Domino XXIV, Anxiety, Jr., and Dominick XIV.

TRENTON, 39.4 *m.* (822 alt., 7,046 pop.), centered by the massive Bedford-stone Grundy County courthouse, is dependent primarily on agricultural and railroad activities. The principal streets converge at "Five Points" in the heart of the business district. Settled about 1834 by families who drifted into the region from Howard and Randolph Counties, and first known as Bluff Grove or Lomax's Store, Trenton was made the seat of justice in 1841, when Grundy County was organized, and was platted in the same year. It was probably named for Trenton, New Jersey.

From approximately 1897 until 1905, the city was the scene of a co-operative experiment in education and business. Walter Vrooman, heading a group of socialists, purchased the property of Avalon College, which had closed in 1891, and established Ruskin College as the American branch of the Ruskin Hall movement in England, a movement inspired by the social theories of the English author and lecturer, John Ruskin (1819-1900). The group soon "undertook to run not only the school but the town as well on the socialistic principles." In 1902-03, "The Multitude Incorporated" was formed to act as trustee for the co-operative businesses the group had acquired, and with which it was expected to support the college, or university, as it was then called. The project was locally unpopular and the venture collapsed because of internal dissension.

MOBERLY PARK (*free camp grounds*), Eighteenth St. and Tindall Ave., is marked at its entrance by a SOLDIERS AND SAILORS MEMORIAL ARCH, beneath which a sealed box, imbedded in concrete, contains the life histories of 27 men of Grundy County who were killed in the World War. Left of the arch are 27 elm trees, dedicated in 1920 to the memory of the "silent victors."

Right from Trenton on State 6, a concrete highway, past the CROWDER MEMORIAL STATE PARK (R), 4.4 *m.*, approximately 650 acres of rugged, heavily wooded land being developed (1940) as a recreational area, to EDINBURG, 5.7 *m.* (110 pop.), boyhood home of Enoch Herbert Crowder (1859-1932). Crowder's varied career included service in the United States and the Far East preceding his appointment in 1911 as judge advocate general of the United States Army, in which capacity he made sweeping changes in the administration of military justice. When the United States entered the World War, he presented a comprehensive plan for the creation of a great military force. His Selective Service Act (the Draft) was adopted May 18, 1917. In 1923 Crowder was appointed the first United States ambassador to Cuba. The SITE OF GRAND RIVER COLLEGE (R), Main St. and State 6, is indicated by crumbling ruins. Here Crowder, who graduated from West Point, once attended classes. The college, which pioneered in higher education in northwest Missouri, was operated from 1850 to 1893.

Somewhere in the general area between Trenton and Chillicothe is the mythical country of Poosey, which cannot be exactly located. It is described by local residents as "Just across the road there," or "Just t'other side of our east forty." Distances in Poosey are measured by "hollers" rather than miles. The name probably originated in connection with a group of settlers from Posey County, Indiana, who won the aversion of their Missouri neighbors by their aloofness. According to Earl A. Collins in his *Folk Tales of Missouri* (1935), children were forbidden to "have any tripe with them Pooseyites," and today the name carries something of a suggestion of disgrace. To be called a Pooseyite is the equivalent of being called a Bristle Ridger or a Bald Knobber.

SIMPSON PARK (R), 61.6 *m.*, a 10-acre recreational area on the northern edge of Chillicothe, with a swimming pool and other facilities (*adm. 10¢; children under 16 free, except Sundays and holidays*), was presented to the city by Dr. and Mrs. Arthur J. Simpson.

At 62.1 *m.* is a junction with County A, a graveled road.

Right on County A, known as the Ben Hur Highway, through the Grand River hills to the Graham Mill Road, a country lane, 3.8 *m.;* R. to the GRAHAM COVERED BRIDGE (*open to pedestrians only*), 4 *m.*, across the Grand River. Many of the heavy oak timbers in the bridge structure were hand-hewn and hauled here by oxen. Built in 1866, the bridge replaced a similar one burned by Confederate soldiers during the Civil War. Livingston County is preserving the bridge for its historical value.

Left from the bridge, upstream 100 feet, is the GRAHAM MILL SITE, indicated only by the ruins of its foundations. Erected by John M. Graham and his father, James Graham, in 1866, the mill served a large territory, in a day when "going to mill" was a social event. Like the country store, the mill was a neighborhood meeting place, where the men, waiting their turn to have their grain ground, aired their views on politics and religion. Others stood about, gossiping, inspecting the machinery, or watching the movement of the water-wheels. The miller generally received one-eighth of the ground grain for his labor.

At 62.4 *m.* is CHILLICOTHE (798 alt., 8,012 pop.), the seat of Livingston County, whose prosperity is well founded in supplying the wants of some 3,000 collegians, a wide farm trade, and many industrial plants.

The town was platted in 1837 and named for Chillicothe, Ohio. The name is Shawnee Indian for "the big town where we live." Although Chillicothe became the county seat in 1839, it remained relatively unimportant until the completion of the Hannibal & St. Joseph Railroad in 1859 boomed the development of the area. Later, the city gained additional advantages by pioneering in the movement for better roads.

Chillicothe has been the home of several people of note, among them Earl Sawyer Sloan (1848-1923) and his brother Foreman Sloan, both natives of Ohio. The brothers operated a livery stable on Elm Street and bought and sold horses between 1870 and 1872. During this time, Earl Sloan compounded a liniment to relieve sprains and bruises in horses, and found it to be also effective for human beings. He returned to Ohio, and his product, marketed as "Sloan's Liniment," became world famous. A tablet in the south wall of a drugstore, northeast corner of Locust and Jackson Sts., marks the SITE OF THE BROWNING HOTEL. Here died Nelson Kneass (1823-69), who wrote the music for the poem, "Ben Bolt," in 1847. Kneass had come to Chillicothe with a small dramatic and musical troupe. He was buried by friends in Edgewood Cemetery, where a gray-granite memorial has been erected in his honor.

CHILLICOTHE BUSINESS COLLEGE, 1220 Monroe St., established in 1890 by Allen Moore, is the largest business college in America. On the 20-acre campus is COMMERCE HALL, a 2-story red-brick building which houses a model banking department, operated on the scale of the average small-town bank. TELEGRAPH BUILDING, a remodeled three-story structure with a mansard roof, has classrooms for students of commercial and railroad telegraphic communication. Fully equipped offices are used in teaching business subjects.

The STATE INDUSTRIAL HOME FOR GIRLS, Third and Dickinson Sts., at the western edge of town, occupies a group of red-brick buildings, including five cottages, a high school, an administration building, and a laundry. Delinquent girls, placed here for education and rehabilitation rather than for punishment, are disciplined under the merit system. Complete high school training is offered, including courses in commercial subjects and home economics. The home was built in 1888. The number of occupants varies from 150 to 200.

At 63.4 *m.* is a junction with US 36 (*see Tour 3*), with which US 65 is united for two miles. GRAND RIVER, crossed at 65 *m.,* carried an uncertain river traffic about the middle of the last century. The last recorded trip upon its waters was made by the steamboat *Bonita* in 1857.

CARROLLTON (R), 95.2 *m.* (665 alt., 4,070 pop.), seat of Carroll County, occupies a high bluff overlooking the Missouri River bottom. In November of 1819, John Standley, his seven sons, and John Trotter, settled within the present limits of the city. When Carroll County, named for Charles Carroll, a signer of the Declaration of Independence, was organized January 2, 1833, John Standley donated land for the county seat, which was platted and had its first sale of lots March 31, 1834. Carrollton had a slow growth, until the completion of the Wabash, St. Louis & Pacific Railroad (now the Wabash) after the Civil War provided the community with needed transportation facilities.

The GENERAL JAMES SHIELDS MONUMENT, east side of the courthouse lawn, is a life-size bronze statue on a high red-granite base. General Shields was born in County Tyrone, Ireland, May 12, 1806, and came to America in 1826. While serving as State auditor of Illinois in the late 1830's, anonymous charges were made against him which were traced to Mary Todd and a friend, Miss Jayne. Abraham Lincoln shouldered some of the responsibility. Shields promptly challenged him to a duel, but the matter was compromised and Lincoln and Shields became warm friends. Shields represented three States in the United States Senate: Illinois (1849-55), Minnesota (1857-59), and Missouri (January-March, 1879), and was a veteran of the Black Hawk, Mexican, and Civil Wars. He came to Carroll County in 1866, and died at Ottumwa, Iowa, June 1, 1879. He is buried in St. Mary's Cemetery, northeastern edge of Carrollton, where a monument erected by the Federal Government marks his grave.

The STATE CHILDREN'S HOME, western edge of town, housed in a group of cottages of Tudor design, cares for an average of 150 dependent and neglected children. Since its founding in 1921, the institution has placed 1,584 children in private homes. Of this number, 306 have been adopted.

At Carrollton is a junction with US 24 (see Tour 2), with which US 65 is united for ten miles. At 100.6 m. is a junction with an unmarked dirt lane.

Left on this lane, through treeless fields, 2 m., to the WILLIAM BAKER HOUSE (L), a large, white frame, plantation-type structure, with double-deck porches on the west and south sides. Built in the 1850's by William Baker, a river captain, and once used as a hotel for steamboat travelers, it is known locally as the River House. In 1865 three former Union soldiers invited themselves to a New Year's Eve party at this house. When ordered to leave, they challenged any or all of the guests to duels. Three merrymakers accepted, but only one duel was fought. James McMurtry, one of the intruders, was killed, and his opponent seriously wounded. Because the spirits of the combatants are said to haunt the house, it has long been shunned as a residence.

Southward, the route crosses the broad bottomlands of the Missouri River, passing numerous sloughs and oxbow lakes left by floods before United States Army engineers succeeded to some extent in keeping the river in the desired channel.

The MISSOURI RIVER, crossed, 104.8 m., on the lofty steel and concrete Waverly Bridge costing $585,000, has been variously described. Thomas Hart Benton was fairly accurate when he said, "The Missouri River is a little too thick to swim in, and not quite thick enough to walk on." Albert D. Richardson, pre-Civil War reporter for the New York *Tribune*, described it as follows:

By daylight the broad current is unpoetic and repulsive—a stream of liquid brick-dust or flowing mud, studded with dead tree-trunks broken by bars and islands of dreary sand, and inclosed by crumbling shores of naked soil. Its waters will deposit a sediment an eighth of an inch thick upon the bottom of a tumbler in five minutes. Though at first unpalatable and medicinal, one soon finds it a pleasant, healthful beverage. I have seen errant Missourians so partial to it, as to urge that the pure waters of the Rocky Mountains were unfit to drink because of their clearness. . . . Only in the day's full flare is the stream revolting. Morning twilight, while the east is silvery, late evening when the west is blood-red, and moonlit night, all mellow and idealize it. Then every twig and leaf is penciled sharply upon clear sky, the turbid waters sheeny and sprinkled with stars, and the environing woods dreamy and tender. Often they are exquisitely tinted; and the night pictures of the despised Missouri, rival in beauty those of the familiar Hudson, and the far, stupendous Columbia.

Disliked as it was by some, the treacherous, shifting channel of the Missouri offered a natural means of transportation which played a vital part in the opening of the West.

WAVERLY, 105.2 m. (684 alt., 876 pop.), high on the southern bank of the Missouri River, was formerly an important river port. First platted as Middletown in 1845, it was renamed Waverly three years later. John Brown, famed abolitionist, is supposed to have stopped here on his trek to Kansas. The story goes that one of his children died and was buried here, but that Brown returned a few years later and exhumed the body, being unwilling to leave any of his family in the soil of a slave State.

Brown may have had a particular distaste for Waverly because it was the home of General Joseph Orville Shelby from about 1852 until the beginning of the Civil War. Shelby (1830-97) was born and educated in Lexington, Kentucky, and came to Waverly to operate a rope factory. During the Kansas-Missouri border troubles, he led a company of Kentuckians against the Abolitionists. By 1861 he was known as one of the wealthiest slave and land owners in Missouri. At the outbreak of the war, he joined the Confederate forces and is said to have raised his first command in the red-brick WAVERLY METHODIST CHURCH, in the western portion of Waverly. After the Civil War, he offered his services to Maximilian in Mexico. When the Emperor died, Shelby returned to Missouri, settling in Bates County. He is buried in Forest Hill Cemetery, Kansas City, Missouri.

Waverly is at the southern junction with US 24 (see Tour 2).

On the bluffs south of the river, apples and small fruits are cultivated. Here is one of the most extensive loess areas in the State. The brown, porous soil lies in a narrow strip along the banks of the Missouri River. It is a wind-blown deposit formed at the close of the Ice Age.

GRAND PASS, 109.4 m. (665 alt., 115 pop.), was so named for the narrow bluff "pass," from 100 to 500 yards wide, between the valleys of Salt Fork Creek and the Missouri River. This natural roadway was followed by the Santa Fe Trail, commemorated by a granite marker (L).

Between Grand Pass and Malta Bend, the highway crosses the southern edge of the broad lowlands that extend north to the Missouri River. French explorers and fur trappers called the area Les Plaines des Petites Osages (Fr., the plains of the Little Osage), for the Indians who once lived here. Time has so corrupted the name that the area today is known as the 'Tit (teet) Saw Bottoms.

MALTA BEND, 114 m. (652 alt., 355 pop.), a shipping point for farm and orchard products, was named for the river steamer Malta, a sidewheeler which, under Captain Joseph W. Throckmorton, sank with a cargo of furs in the bend two and a half miles north of town, in August 1841. The settlement was platted in 1867.

At 124 m. is the junction with State 41, a graveled road.

Left here 7.3 m. to FAIRVILLE, an unincorporated village. Here is a junction with County 122, a graveled road; L. to VAN METER STATE PARK, 12 m. (shelter houses, picnic facilities, camp grounds, nature trails), a 546-acre conservation and recreational area, donated in 1933 by Mrs. Annie van Meter. The park extends over the densely wooded 'Tit Saw Bottoms (L) and into the rugged bluffs bordering the Missouri River (R). The State plans to preserve the natural features and wild life of the park. Sixty-seven species of birds and 44 kinds of trees have been identified. North and east of the shelter house, foot trails lead to a high plateau that extends northward in a series of fingerlike ridges. Encircling the plateau is an earthen mound, 2,700 feet in length, popularly known as the OLD FORT and thought by archeologists to be of prehistoric origin (*see Archeology and Indians*). The north and south ends of the breastwork, which is roughly elliptical, are on the tableland; the sides curve along the east and west slopes at various distances below the summit. The outer wall is augmented by a complicated arrangement of minor embankments and trenches. It is thought that the place was accessible only through the southern end, where two small mounds guard the entrance. The fingerlike ridges north of the fort, called the PINNACLES, once marked the south bank of the erratic Missouri River. East of the fort, approximately half a mile, is an INDIAN VILLAGE SITE, occupying a T-shaped tract along numerous ravines. The ground once was strewn with potsherds, bones, and pieces of flint implements, many of which have been placed in museums.

MIAMI, 13.2 *m.* (275 pop.), sprawled along a winding bluff ridge overlooking the wide Missouri River valley, was platted as Greenville in 1838, and five years later received its present name. Near here, at the foot of the bluffs, a group of Miami Indians established a village before 1810. Although these Indians were probably not responsible for the attacks and murders attributed to them by the white settlers of the Boon's Lick Country, they did commit a number of acts of petty thievery. In 1814, General Henry Dodge, commanding 3 companies of Missouri militia, and Colonel Benjamin Cooper, commanding the local company of Boon's Lick militia, together with a force of about 50 friendly Shawnee warriors, swam their horses across the Missouri River at Arrow Rock and followed an old Indian trail to the Miami village, which they planned to attack. The Indians, however, had fled at the approach of the troops. About 31 men, 112 women, and a few children were hunted out of the woods where they had hidden and stood cowering while the Boon's Lick men begged to be allowed to reclaim the goods stolen from them, and to avenge themselves for the murder of their comrades. Dodge, however, commanded that the Miamis, together with the stolen goods found in their possession, be sent to St. Louis for trial. "By God, Sir," Cooper roared, grabbing Dodge by the collar with one hand and waving his sword over the General's head with the other, "If you attempt to enforce that order, your head will fly off your shoulders like pop-corn off a hot shovel." Other officers succeeded in parting the men, and the matter was finally settled according to Dodge's order.

By 1840, Miami was a river port of considerable importance, shipping large quantities of hemp and other produce. The white frame CHRISTIAN CHURCH (*open by permission*), on the main street of the town, was built in 1854 and is typical of the less pretentious Missouri "meeting houses" of the period.

The Missouri River is crossed at 14.4 *m.* on a new (1940) bridge (*toll; 30¢ for car and driver, 5¢ for each additional passenger*).

North of the Missouri, the route crosses the wide, fertile river bottom to join US 24 at 18.4 *m.*, one mile west of De Witt (*see Tour 2*).

MARSHALL, 125 *m.* (779 alt., 8,533 pop.), Saline County seat, depends primarily on corn and wheat, but is supported in part by a shoe factory, a milk-processing plant, Missouri Valley College, and a State institution for the feeble-minded. The water and light plants, representing an investment of more than a million dollars, are municipally owned, and the revenues derived from their operation have made possible improvements that place the city considerably above the average in civic progress.

Marshall, settled in 1839 by immigrants from Virginia, Tennessee, and Kentucky, on a site known as Elk's Hill, was named for John Marshall, Chief Justice of the United States Supreme Court (1801-

35). Because of its inland location, the town grew slowly, since the better lands along the Missouri River on the northern and eastern borders of Saline County were occupied first. The Civil War seriously hampered the town's expansion, for after 1862 the place was occupied almost continually by Federal troops. On October 13, 1863, the Confederate general, Joseph Shelby, was defeated near the city by Federal troops under the command of General E. B. Brown and Colonel John F. Philips. In 1870 the town had a population of only 924, but by 1881, three years after the arrival of the Chicago and Alton Railroad, it numbered 3,000. Its subsequent growth has been gradual.

Saline County, named for its numerous salt springs, was organized in 1820. Settled by persons of Southern antecedents, who came to the Arrow Rock country soon after 1810, it has produced some of the State's most remarkable leaders (*see Tour 1*).

The GEORGIA BROWN BLOSSER HOME FOR CRIPPLED CHILDREN (*open by permission*), 828 E. Eastwood St., is a two-story, red-brick structure in the shape of a large V. The institution, which cost $60,000, was founded under provisions of the will of the late Mrs. Louis P. Blosser, who left $500,000 to establish and maintain the hospital. The GEORGIA BROWN BLOSSER HOME FOR AGED WOMEN (*open by permission*), 840 E. Eastwood St., a two-and-a-half-story, red-brick building with terra-cotta trim, cares for aged Methodist women. The construction cost of $40,000 was provided for in the $300,000 willed by Mrs. Blosser to the institution.

MISSOURI VALLEY COLLEGE, Redman St. and College Ave., a four-year co-educational institution, is identified by its massive, three-story red-brick administration building, erected in 1888. Seven other brick buildings of two to four stories are scattered over the 40-acre campus. Organized in 1888, the school has been under the supervision of the Missouri Synod of the Presbyterian Church since 1906. The average enrollment is 350.

The MISSOURI STATE SCHOOL FOR FEEBLE-MINDED AND EPILEPTIC, E. Slater St. and N. Lincoln Ave., housed in 14 connected brick and stone three-story buildings, was established on a tract of 288 acres in 1899. The school now (1941) represents an investment of nearly $2,000,000, and accommodates 1,300 white and Negro patients, approximately 300 of whom are epileptic. The school operates a large farm north of the campus.

INDIAN FOOTHILLS PARK (R), at the eastern city limits on Eastwood St., is a 110-acre, fully equipped recreational area (*swimming pool, 10¢ and 25¢*). The name of the Park was suggested by traces of an Indian village formerly discernible here.

At 137 *m.* is a junction with US 40 (*see Tour 1*).

OSAGE FARMS, 144 *m.*, is a 5,329-acre project of the United States Resettlement Administration, operated under the Farm Security Administration. The tract is divided into small farm units, which are sold on long-term agreements to farmers otherwise unable to buy or rent farm lands. Approximately 31 families, each with its own house and utility buildings, farm the land under a community arrangement. Those eligible to participate are "tenants who are self-dependant but who do not have tenure arrangements which afford them sufficient security, tenants or owners living on submarginal land, and young couples who cannot accumulate adequate resources to start farming as tenants." The project has been in operation since March 1938.

At a sweeping curve of the highway, 149 *m.*, a perpendicular rock bluff (L) rises 100 feet above the road. On the summit of the bluff is BOTHWELL LODGE (*private*), a rambling, 29-room yellow-stone structure. Turrets and corner towers suggest a castle of the Middle Ages. John R. Bothwell, St. Louis and Sedalia attorney, began its construction in 1898, using it first as a country house and later as a permanent residence. Since his death a number of years ago, it has served as a clubhouse.

SEDALIA, 155 *m.* (907 alt., 20,428 pop.), is at a junction with US 50 (*see Tour* 4).

Section b. SEDALIA to ARKANSAS LINE, 184 m. US 65

South of SEDALIA, 0 *m.*, the prairie gives way to wooded hills where the damming of the Osage River has created the Lake of the Ozarks, Missouri's most ambitious recreational enterprise. Farther south is Springfield, the State's fourth largest city. Deep in the Ozarks, near the Arkansas Line, is the beautiful Shepherd of the Hills country.

LINCOLN, 24 *m.* (970 alt., 379 pop.), incorporated in 1869, is the outgrowth of an older settlement that developed about Wiley Vincent's tavern on the Springfield Road.

HANGING HOLLOW, 31 *m.*, obtained its name from a hanging that did not take place. On a bright, sunny morning many years ago, a young man of the vicinity, convicted of robbing and murdering one of the older settlers, stood beneath the limb of a tree, a rope about his neck. As the deputies were about to carry out their work, a messenger from the sheriff rode madly into their midst to tell them they had the wrong man—the true murderer had just confessed.

At 34 *m.* is a junction with State 35, a concrete highway.

Right here to WARSAW, 1.6 *m.* (687 alt., 957 pop.), an historic town that has been changed almost overnight from a staid agricultural community to a lively tourist center. On the banks of the impounded Osage River, it is now at the head of the Lake of the Ozarks, its business district fronting the water.

Warsaw became the seat of Benton County in 1837, when county commissioners, refusing the bids of Frisco Town and Osage, decided to plat a new town for the seat of justice. The town soon became an important shipping point, for it was near the head of navigation on the Osage River and at the crossing of the important Springfield Road. Tons of freight were shipped up the Osage to Warsaw and from here distributed throughout a region equivalent in area to 15 counties. Downstream were shipped pork, hides, tallow, furs, and grain. The most exciting phase of the town's history was the "Slicker War," waged 1841-45 between the law-abiding citizenry and the counterfeiters, horse thieves, and cattle rustlers that infested the region. The townspeople and farmers formed an organization popularly known as the "Slickers," and made it their business to "slick" with hickory switches all suspected lawbreakers. But thieves and counterfeiters managed to join the organization and soon brought it into bad repute. Charles Pancoast, whose "Journal of Adventures on the American Frontier" is incorporated in *A Quaker Forty-Niner* (1930), describes one of the leaders, the six-foot-eight-inch, dark eyed, and eagle nosed "Tom Turk," whose hair hung in black curls down his back. "He wore lye-colored Pants, girded with a red Belt and silver Buckles, and high Boots, from which the handle of a Bowie Knife peered out; another knife was in his shirt at the back of his neck; a pistol was in his belt, and a rifle in his hand."

The "Anti-Slickers" were soon organized to combat these desperadoes, and war broke out between the two factions. A veritable reign of terror began; murders, shootings from ambush, public whippings, night rides, raids, indictments, and trials were common. Nine persons lost their lives, and much blood was shed before the trouble ended.

After the decline of river traffic in the 1870's, Warsaw settled into the quiet ways of a rural village, until the building of Bagnell Dam (1929-31) made it a popular fishing resort (*guides, boats, tackle, and bait at nominal prices*).

The WARSAW DISCIPLES OF CHRIST CHURCH (*open*), one block east of the courthouse, is a one-story red-brick structure with a white wooden cupola, built in 1840. The church served as headquarters for Union forces during the Civil War, receiving about $600 in payment from the United States Government in 1926. The OLD UNION HOUSE (*open by permission*), on Main St. opposite the courthouse, a two-story brick building, painted yellow, was a favorite lodging place for rivermen and travelers in steamboat days. Double-deck porches extend across the front. The rooms have walnut woodwork fastened with wooden pins. The building, which housed Federal officers during the Civil War, is now a funeral home.

US 65 crosses an arm of the LAKE OF THE OZARKS (*see Tours 15 and 15A*), 36.5 m., on a steel and concrete bridge, and traverses a series of hills and small valleys covered by cedar, oak, and black-walnut forests.

CROSS TIMBERS, 53.6 m. (950 alt., 250 pop.), was named in 1871 for the near-by intersection of two timber belts. Lost Silver Mine, a legendary shaft, is supposedly near here. The mine, according to legend, was known as Old Brooksie Mine and was producing silver when the Civil War began and Union troops took the county. The operator, unwilling to let the Federals seize his silver, is said to have dammed the Pomme de Terre River, thereby flooding the shaft and obscuring the location. It is believed that the site is still under water, at a point about three miles southwest of Cross Timbers.

At 60 m. is a junction with US 54 (*see Tour 15*). Southward, the timber thins and farmlands are productive. Cattle is a principal source of income, but in the vicinity of Springfield much of the land is devoted to fruit, strawberries, and truck.

CRYSTAL CAVE, (*adm. 25¢*), 107.8 m. (R), is located at the bottom of a great sink 75 feet deep. The entrance is reached by native stone steps. Sunk deeply into the hills, the cavern's tunnel is perpetually cool. Within are stalactite and stalagmite formations resembling thrones, cascades, draperies, and pillars. In a walnut grove immediately south of the cave entrance is a small park equipped with picnic tables (*free*).

SPRINGFIELD, 113 *m.* (1,345 alt., 61,238 pop.) (*see Springfield*), is at a junction with US 66 (*see Tour 5*) and US 60 (*see Tour 6*) ; with the latter, US 65 is united for 9 miles.

The U.S. HOSPITAL FOR THE CRIMINAL INSANE (*open 9-5*), 115 *m.*, is one of the most modern prison hospitals in the world. Completed in 1933, the institution consists of 10 buildings on a 445-acre tract enclosed by a high wire fence. The principal buildings, joined to form a large U, with the administration building facing the highway, are two- and four-story brick structures trimmed with white stone. The staff numbers 250. There are approximately 150 working prisoners and about 675 patients, of whom approximately one-third are insane. The inmates are received by transfer from Federal penitentiaries and reformatories. The hospital, which has a capacity of 1,000 beds, has every necessary modern device. Among prisoners treated here was Gaston B. Means, who died in December 1938.

The NATIONAL CEMETERY (*open*), 117 *m.* (R), was established by the Federal Government in 1869 and improved in 1911. Here are buried 2,347 Union and 569 Confederate soldiers. This is the only place in the United States where a Union and Confederate cemetery adjoin each other. Several years ago a bill was introduced in Congress to make a gateway between the two, on the theory that there should no longer be barriers between the North and the South. Opponents of the bill argued that as the soldiers had been in life, so they should be in death—apart. Nevertheless, the bill was passed, and the gateway was opened with formal ceremony.

SEQUIOTA STATE PARK (L), 119.8 *m.*, the smallest of Missouri's State parks (14.6 acres), contains a fish hatchery and a cavern. The hatchery consists of 11 rearing pools, a hatchery building, and a small lake. Smallmouthed bass and bluegill are propagated. CAVE RIVER CAVERN (*adm. 25¢*) is approximately 75 feet behind the hatchery building and about 30 feet from a spring that flows 12,000,000 gallons daily. The trip through the cave is made by boat and requires 20 to 30 minutes. The tunnel is well lighted.

The JAMES RIVER, crossed at 121.8 *m.*, is one of the Ozark's better fishing streams (*boats and guides for fishing or float trips at nominal cost*).

At 122 *m.* is the southern junction with US 60 (*see Tour 6*).

OZARK, 130 *m.* (1,177 alt., 961 pop.), trading center of a tomato-growing region, is built around the three-story, red-brick Christian County courthouse. The town was platted in 1843. Although its population was only 100 by 1850, it boasted an excellent academy, the Ozark High School, which pioneered in higher education in the region and drew students from a wide area. In 1887 Ozark gained national prominence when justice was served upon the Bald Knobbers, a band of vigilantes secretly organized at Forsyth (*see below*) in 1884, who had turned into a marauding horde of night riders. Murders, whippings, and general disorder were charged to the organization. In 1887 the enraged citizens of the district organized a widespread man hunt, which ended with the arrest of 30 men. Of this number, four were tried on charges of first degree murder and sentenced to hang. During subsequent legal appeals three of the four escaped. Posses captured two of these, and the three condemned men were hanged May 10, 1889, ending the reign of terror.

Between Ozark and the Arkansas Line, US 65 winds among wooded hills that are largely given over to recreation. Bordering the road are numerous tourist camps, filling stations, and stands selling Ozark pottery and articles of woodcraft. At 140.4 *m.* is a junction with an unmarked graveled road.

Right here to the MONTAGUE TROUT HATCHERY (*open*), 2.5 *m.*, privately operated, which utilizes the waters of a spring that flows at the rate of 7,000 gallons a minute. Approximately 300,000 rainbow trout are propagated annually. The fish, which are raised on a diet of cooked cereals, meat, and cod liver oil, are sold to hotels and restaurants. Fishing is permitted (*fee: 45¢ a pound*).

At 151.3 *m.* is a junction with a marked graveled road.

Left here to the OLD SPANISH CAVE (*adm. 50¢; guides*), 0.3 *m.*, approached by a rustic foot bridge across a deep ravine. The cave, which consists of 6 large rooms that extend 1,600 feet into the limestone hill, was "rediscovered" in 1892 by persons using a "Spanish treasure chart." Although the cavern was searched thoroughly, and three shafts were sunk in likely places, no buried treasure was found.

At 159 *m.* is the southern junction with State 76, a black-topped road.

Left here, along a narrow ridge crest, into the valley of Bull Creek, through the village of WALNUT SHADE, 5.7 *m.* (758 alt., 50 pop.), and up a heavily wooded slope to a junction with State 76A, 7.4 *m.*, a graveled road. R. 2.6 *m.* through groves of cedar and scrub oak, to ROCKAWAY BEACH (110 pop.), on the shore of LAKE TANEYCOMO. A fully equipped resort (*hotels and cabins; riding, tennis, golf, hiking, boating, and fishing*), Rockaway Beach is one of the most attractive of southern Ozark villages. Native wood, rough finished and stained, and varicolored local rocks have been used extensively as building materials.

At 11.2 *m.* on State 76 is a junction with a marked graveled road, which leads R. 0.5 *m.* to CEDAR POINT (*cabins; hiking, swimming, boating; guides*). a lakeside resort backed by wooded hills.

The SHEPHERD OF THE HILLS ESTATE (*hotels and cottages; golf, fishing, boating, and swimming*), 13.2 *m.*, is a real estate development extending from the highway to the water's edge. At 14.2 *m.* is a junction with County V, a graveled road.

Right here 0.9 *m.* to POWERSITE DAM, 1,700 feet long and 52 feet high, which impounds the waters of White River to form 24-mile-long Lake Taneycomo. The dam was completed in 1912 by the Empire District Electric Company, a subsidiary of Cities Service. On a hillside opposite the dam is ELECTRIC PARK (*cabins, boats, and guides*), a small fishing resort. OZARK BEACH, 1.1 *m.*, and EDGEWATER BEACH, 1.7 *m.*, are other resorts on County V (*hotel, cabins, boats, and guides*).

Ahead on State 76 to FORSYTH, 14.8 *m.* (696 alt., 290 pop.), a farming and recreational center and the seat of Taney County. It was once the headquarters of the Bald Knobbers, an organization formed July 4, 1884, on the summit of Bald Jess, one of the bare-topped hills overlooking the village. The band was composed at first of honest citizens but upon the withdrawal of the majority of its members at the request of the State's attorney general, it was taken over by a group of young ruffians. Crimes were committed against "tie whackers," who cut timber and shaped logs into railroad ties; squatters, who paid no taxes; and homesteaders, who restricted grazing on the land that once had been a free range. Not until the countryside rose up in arms was the band finally dispersed (*see Ozark, above*).

CHULA VISTA (L), 164 *m.*, is a roadside turnout offering one of the best views in the region. From an observation tower (*free*) surmounting a hotel, it is possible to see more than 70 miles southwest and 65 miles northeast.

The OWEN BOATLINE (R), 169.6 *m.*, maintains the largest fleet of fishing and pleasure boats in the Lake Taneycomo area (*boats, guides, tackle, and bait*).

BRANSON, 170 *m.* (723 alt., 1,011 pop.), on Lake Taneycomo, is predominantly a resort town. Tourist and fishing camps, hotels, and boat docks line the shaded lakeshore. The business district is filled with cafés, taverns, drug stores, and novelty shops.

Right from Branson on State 80, an asphalt road that follows high, winding ridges through the country described in Harold Bell Wright's *Shepherd of the Hills* (*see Literature*), to DEWEY BALD, 7 *m.*, the 1,341-foot peak frequently mentioned in the novel. From the summit, the White River, 400 feet below, appears so close at hand that visitors invariably try to throw stones across it.

MATT'S CABIN (R), 7.2 *m.*, was the home of "Old Matt" and "Aunt Molly," two of the principal characters in the book that has given its name to this region. The cabin is a typical frame and log, early Ozark structure, with a steep-pitched shingle roof. At one end is a large field-stone chimney. The cabin overlooks Mutton Hollow, Sammy's Lookout, and other settings used in the novel.

INSPIRATIONAL POINT (R), 7.5 *m.*, is a small circular drive on the summit of a high hill. The panorama that spreads below is one of the most appealing in the Shepherd of the Hills country. Westward, the highway follows the ridges or descends by easy grades to the valley floors.

MARVEL CAVE (*adm. $1.15*), 10.2 *m.* (L), is one of the largest of the many limestone caverns in Missouri. The entrance, a short distance from the dwelling that serves as an office, leads downward into a great chamber 350 feet long and 200 feet high. Within the chamber is Pike's Peak, a massive rock formation 175 feet high. A trip through the ten miles of passageways that have been explored usually takes nine hours, but the majority of visitors do not attempt to see more than a third of the attractions, which include the Cathedral Room, the "highest natural unsupported dome in the world," Harold Bell Wright's "Devil's Head," still on the wall of Mad Howard's Room, 420 feet underground, the Grand Canyon, Lost River, and the Egyptian Room.

UNCLE IKE'S POST OFFICE, 10.3 *m.*, is a small, crib-like frame building, described by Wright as "the little old post office at the forks." The office, still doing a business of "from $50 to $100 a year," contains the odd fixtures so well described by Wright. "Uncle Ike," the postmaster characterized by the author, is buried near the small town of Notch.

At the southern limits of Branson, US 65 crosses Lake Taneycomo on a 1,155-foot concrete bridge.

HOLLISTER, 172 *m.* (735 alt., 370 pop.), the southernmost of the Lake Taneycomo resorts, is a planned village, often referred to by sociologists as "a good example of the possibilities of the American rural town." The commercial buildings are of the English half-timbered type and are constructed of stone, stucco, and wood. Building restrictions and the prohibition of factory construction have preserved the town's original plan. Hollister was platted in 1906 by William J. Johnson, a landscape architect, whose plan drew upon the natural beauty of the limestone hills by means of terraces, parks, and supporting walls of stone. When the impounded waters of White River formed Lake Taneycomo, the village became a water-front resort (*cabins, fishing, boating, swimming, and riding*).

At 173.6 *m.* is a junction with County P, a graveled road.

Right here, following a narrow ridge above deep valleys, to the SCHOOL OF THE OZARKS, 0.3 *m.*, sponsored by the Presbyterian Church. The physical equipment consists of a group of academic buildings of native stone, arranged in a quadrangle, and a number of red-brick and stucco-like utility houses. Frame buildings are perched on the edge of the bluff-like plateau that forms the campus and looks out across the White River Valley. Founded through the efforts of the Reverend James Forsyth, the institution was opened at Forsyth in 1907, with an enrollment of 35 pupils. At first only grade school work was offered, but as no accredited high school existed in Taney or adjoining counties, high school work was added and the first diploma presented in 1913. At present (1941) the school is an accredited high school offering vocational training as well as academic courses. It was moved to its present location in 1915. Many of the buildings are gifts from wealthy Missourians. The students earn part of their tuition fees by working 16 hours a week in the school's cannery, dairy, print shop, or power plant, or on the school farm. The remainder of the $150 fee is paid for each student by a sponsor, either an individual or a group, who "adopts" the student for a year. From the waiting list of 550 or more, 50 new students are admitted each year, keeping the enrollment at 250.

The COMO CRAFT POTTERY (*open 8-6 daily*), 174.5 *m.* (R), housed in two white frame buildings, was established by Harold Horine, who holds patents on the manufacturing process. In the display room is a collection of 17 oil paintings by Charles Harold Coleman. The collection is owned by Rose O'Neil, artist, writer, and originator of the Kewpies. A few of Miss O'Neil's original magazine sketches are on display.

US 65 crosses the ARKANSAS LINE, 184 *m.*, 175 miles northwest of Little Rock, Arkansas.

Tour 10

(Council Bluffs, Iowa)—Maryville—St. Joseph—Kansas City—Harrisonville — Butler — Rich Hill — Nevada — Lamar — Carthage — (Fort Smith, Ark.) ; US 275 and 71.
Iowa Line to Arkansas Line, 350 m.

Concrete highway, two and three lanes wide.
Route paralleled by the Chicago, Burlington & Quincy R.R. between Maryville and Kansas City; by Missouri Pacific R.R. between Kansas City and Carthage, and from Diamond to junction with St. Louis-San Francisco Ry.; by St. Louis-San Francisco Ry. from junction with Missouri Pacific R.R. to Neosho; by Kansas City Southern Ry. to Arkansas Line.

The opening of the Santa Fe Trail in 1821, and the subsequent growth of steamboat traffic, attracted public attention to western Missouri. The Osage Indians relinquished their title to the lands south of the Missouri River in 1825, and in 1836 the Fox and Sauk and other tribes traditionally occupying the lands north of the river were moved westward. With the region open, settlement was rapid. Lively, bustling towns grew up along the river, and in the fertile valleys hemp and tobacco, cultivated by slave labor, was profitably introduced. North and south across the prairies, Kentucky, Tennessee, Ohio, and Indiana families developed grain and cattle farms, fencing their treeless acres with the curious Osage orange, or *bois d'arc* of the Indians. When Kansas became a mecca for anti-slavery groups in the 1850's friction with slave owners of the Missouri border was inevitable. The conflict of ideas became a war of retaliation, and after the outbreak of the Civil War no portion of the Nation suffered more heavily. Whole towns were razed, and great numbers of citizens were killed or driven from their farms. The difficulties of social and economic readjustment after the war were reflected in the careers of the Younger brothers, Belle Starr, and others of the outlaw era. Before long, however, cattle and grain again supplied the basis for a stable economic growth. Later, the culture of small fruits and berries, and poultry raising, dairying, coal, lead, and zinc mining, and marble quarrying gave the area an increasing prosperity.

Section a. IOWA LINE to KANSAS CITY; 150 m. US 275

The northwestern corner of the State produces a considerable portion of Missouri's corn, oats, tobacco, alfalfa, horses, hogs, and chickens. The highway, parallel to, but seldom approaching the meanderings of

488

the upper Missouri River, is a glorified farm-to-market road carrying grains and livestock to St. Joseph and Kansas City.

US 275, which the route follows to St. Joseph, crosses the IOWA LINE, 0 *m.*, 55 miles south of Council Bluffs, Iowa. In the rich bottom lands to the right of the highway, the Missouri River has changed its course many times, creating problems of State boundaries and land ownership. At present some 4,000 or more acres of land on the east, or Missouri, side of the river, is considered a portion of Nebraska, because until recently it was on the Nebraska side of the stream.

ROCKPORT, 17.5 *m.* (935 alt., 1,406 pop.), was platted in the spring of 1851 as the seat of Atchison County to succeed Linden, some five miles to the north. Among the early residents of the county were a group of Germans who came from St. Louis in 1845 under the leadership of Harmon Schubert to establish a socialist community near present-day Rockport. Disaster accompanied the first crop, however, for the mill leased by the settlers was washed away by high water. Soon afterward the colony disbanded.

At 24 *m.* is a junction with US 59, a hard-surfaced road.

Left here to TARKIO, 1.6 *m.* (916 alt., 2,114 pop.), advertised as the "center of the corn belt." The business district in the eastern part of town spreads over the bottom lands of Big Tarkio River. Tarkio was laid out in August of 1880. The name is Indian for "walnut," or "a place where walnuts grow." Before the town was two years old, its citizens began agitating for the removal of the county seat from the older town of Rockport. Without waiting for the election, they built a courthouse. This proved a mistake, for the county voted to leave the seat of justice where it was. The citizens, left with a fine empty building, decided to use it as a college, and in 1883 they established the Tarkio Valley College and Normal Institute. TARKIO COLLEGE, near the northwestern edge of town, an accredited Presbyterian co-educational institution, developed from these unusual beginnings. On a slight knoll in the midst of a tree-shaded campus are the administration building, erected in 1930, and the men's and women's dormitories, three-story, red-brick structures trimmed with stone. The average enrollment is 250.

Southward are endless fields of corn. During planting time, the countryside is dotted with tractors and teams of horses moving slowly along the parallel rows, pulling machines that drop and cover the seed with a single mechanical stroke. In summer the land is hidden by a great green wave higher than a man's head—save in those years when drought takes the crop.

In 1902 the Atchison County farm of David Rankin—some 30,000 acres in all—was considered the largest corn farm in the world. Rankin raised annually more than 1,500,000 bushels of corn, much of which he used to fatten livestock for market. In 1939 corn production in Atchison County totaled 4,358,200 bushels.

MOUND CITY, 50 *m.* (877 alt., 1,606 pop.), which has survived four fires and as many floods to become the largest town in Holt County, is a shipping point for fruit, grain, and livestock. In 1840 Thomas Ferguson purchased land at the mouth of the south fork of Davis Creek and built a double log cabin in which he started a tavern.

Four years later he sold the building to Andrew P. Jackson. The site became known as Jackson's Point and was a regular stopping place on the stage route from St. Joseph to Council Bluffs. Here a post office was established, which was moved in 1855 to the store of Galen Crow on the north bank of Davis Creek. This store, and the blacksmith shop of E. Peter Forbes, were the first buildings on the present site of Mound City, which was platted in 1857. The name is derived from a low mound or hill upon which a portion of the town is built.

Right from Mound City on State 118, an asphalt road, to BIG LAKE STATE PARK (*cabins, hotel, campgrounds, boating, fishing, and picnicking*), 9.2 *m.*, a 100-acre recreational area on Big Lake. Adjoining the park on the west is the SQUAW CREEK NATIONAL WILD LIFE REFUGE (*fishing permitted*), a Federal migratory wildfowl sanctuary established in 1935. The 5,000 acres of waterway that extend four miles northward along the east bluffs are often covered with ducks in the fall. Innumerable islets punctuate the quarter-mile width of the lake.

OREGON, 65 *m.* (1,094 alt., 978 pop.), dominated by its massive gray-brick courthouse, is a grain and livestock center and the seat of Holt County. Settled first by families from Indiana and later in the northwestern section by Germans, Holt County was organized February 15, 1841. Oregon was laid out as the seat of justice in June of that year, and named in honor of the Oregon country, which was then attracting the first of a long procession of immigrants.

The village had cause to remember for a long time a "heavenly manifestation" on the evening of July 8, 1851. A bolt of lightning struck the hotel, a six-room log structure, and exploded a barrel of brandy, one of alcohol, and one of whisky. The burning liquid flooded the barroom and only one of the seven men who were at the bar survived.

Right from Oregon on State 111, an asphalt road, to FOREST CITY, 3.3 *m.* (858 alt., 548 pop.), a quiet farm trading center that was brought into being and then abandoned by the capricious Missouri River. Laid out in 1857, Forest City was for a decade an important river port. At times as many as 13 steamboats were moored at the town's docks, and trade amounted to $300,000 annually. Then in 1868 the river flooded; when the waters receded, the new channel was far to the west. J. W. Zook's shipment of 3,700 sacks of corn in August 1868, was the last cargo to leave Forest City by boat.

East of Oregon, US 275 crosses the eroded bluffs of the Nodaway River Valley, a fertile land settled by farmers from Ohio, Indiana, Kentucky, and Tennessee immediately after its purchase by the United States in 1836. The name of the stream is a corruption of *Nadowe-is-iw,* the Chippewa name for the Sioux, meaning "enemy." John Bradbury, English botanist, called the stream the "Naduet." On April 17, 1811, he met here Wilson P. Hunt's party which had spent the winter at the mouth of the river in preparation for a spring journey up the Missouri. Hunt's expedition was immortalized by Washington Irving in *Astoria.*

At 81 *m.* is a junction with US 71, a concrete highway.

Left here across the gentle hills of Nodaway County to PUMPKIN CENTER, 17 *m.;* on a farm near by the author and lecturer, Dale Carnegie, spent the formative years of his life. Born November 24, 1888, at Maryville, the future teacher of effective speaking and applied psychology gained his early education at a school to which he rode three miles on horseback. He arose at three each morning, studied by coal-oil lamp, and fed his father's pedigreed hogs. At 19, he was graduated from the State Teachers College, Warrensburg, and in 1911 went to New York to win friends and influence people. He has lectured in the principal cities of the United States, Canada, and Europe, and has written a number of books, including the best seller by which he became known internationally.

Nodaway County is famed for its hogs; in 1939, it had 104,110. Hog raising is no longer as simple as it was in the last century, when the beasts rooted for their food and "hawg killin' time" was a social event. Today's hog represents a large financial investment. The farms are equipped with great frame and concrete barns, squatty, round silos, and especially fenced pastures. Although the larger consignments are still made in the months of October, November, and January, hogs are now shipped by trucks throughout the year to St. Joseph and Kansas City, where big packing plants do the killing and dressing.

When the site of MARYVILLE, 25 *m.* (1,036 alt., 5,700 pop.), was selected for the seat of newly organized Nodaway County in September of 1845, it was named in honor of Mrs. Mary Graham, the first white woman to live within the limits of the town. Her husband, Amos Graham, a politician and lawyer, was the dominant power in the village for many years. In November of 1846, a visitor found Maryville a straggling settlement of six houses, of which Graham was "county clerk, collector, assessor, and everything but the judge.'" About 1856 Graham formed a law partnership with Albert P. Morehouse (1835-91). Morehouse established *The Nodaway Democrat* in 1869, served as State representative in 1877-78, and also in 1883-84. Elected Lieutenant Governor in 1884, Morehouse served as Governor of Missouri, 1887-88, after the death of Governor John S. Marmaduke. Forrest C. Donnell, Republican candidate for Governor of Missouri in 1940, was born near Maryville, August 20, 1884. He graduated from the Maryville High School, attended the University of Missouri, and after completing his law studies moved to St. Louis to practice law.

The NORTHWEST MISSOURI STATE TEACHERS COLLEGE, at the northwestern edge of Maryville, was founded in 1905, and became a four-year institution in 1919. On the 72-acre campus are a red-brick, three-and-a-half-story administration building of modified English-Tudor design, a residence hall for women, a training school building, a gymnasium, and other buildings. A 248-acre farm provides food stuffs for college use, as well as experimental ground for horticulture and agriculture classes.

Right from Maryville on State 4, a black-topped road, crossing the 102 River at 1.8 *m.* The name of the stream originated in the fact that an early-day military road through northwest Missouri crossed this stream 102 miles north of its starting point at the Missouri River.

At 15.4 *m.* is a junction with County P, a graveled road.

Right on this road 1.5 *m.* to the BENEDICTINE CONVENT OF PERPETUAL ADORATION, built in 1881-82, a massive, three-story, red- and yellow-brick structure surmounted by spires. The convent was established December 6, 1875 by the three Benedictine nuns, the Reverend Mother Anselma Felber, Sister M. Beatrice Renggli, and Sister M. Engster. In 1880 the sisters opened the present school for girls and young ladies. The stone German-Romanesque CHAPEL designed by the late Father Lukas Etlin, and built in 1909, contains art glass windows and a series of mosaics depicting the Christian life. The mosaic above the altar measures 27 feet in height and, like the others, was made in Bavaria.

CONCEPTION, 16.9 *m.* (100 pop.), a quiet country village, was established in June of 1860 by leaders of the Reading Colony, a settlement of Irish Catholics who had emigrated from the vicinity of Reading, Pennsylvania. The colony grew out of the efforts of Owen and Peter O'Reilly, contractors of the Lebanon Valley Railroad, their paymaster William Brady, and the local priest, Father James A. Power, to provide a livelihood for railroad workers thrown out of employment by the depression of 1857. The 58 members of the original colony contributed a fund of $20,000 with which to purchase lands in the West. Father Power, Owen O'Reilly, and Anthony Felix entered claim to a large acreage in the vicinity of Conception, and the first families arrived here in 1858. Ten years later the settlement had grown to 75 families, and the first shanties of "posts filled in between with sod and roofed over with boards" had been replaced by more comfortable and permanent dwellings. CONCEPTION ABBEY (*open*), established in September of 1873 by the Benedictine Fathers Frowin Conrad and Adelhelm Odermatt, formerly members of Engleberg Abbey, in Switzerland, is housed in a group of three-and-a-half-story red-brick buildings. These, together with the Abbey Church, form an open square, and are of the modified German-Romanesque design common to the order in the United States. The Abbey is decorated with frescoes in the Beuronese style, painted by a German artist with the help of Brothers Hildebrand and Ildephonese of the Abbey. This style of painting was first developed in the Benedictine Abbey of Beuron, Germany, during the middle years of the nineteenth century. The ABBEY CHURCH, built 1882-88, and dedicated in 1891, was designed by Brother Adrian, a Franciscan monk. The church proper measures 206 by 66 feet, the transept 104 by 34 feet. The interior height is 56 feet. The church has been created a minor Basilica, an honor conferred on only one other church west of the Mississippi (at St. Paul, Minnesota). In the RARE BOOK ROOM (*open*) of the Abbey Library is a collection of early manuscripts and printed books, largely gifts from Engelberg Abbey. These include 34 manuscript fragments in Latin on vellum dating from the tenth to the fifteenth centuries, as well as 22 volumes printed before 1500.

The Abbey maintains a boarding high school for boys, and a Junior College established in 1883. The high school has an average enrollment of 75, and the College of 40. Most of the students are preparing either for the order or the priesthood.

SAVANNAH, 84 *m.* (1,115 alt., 2,108 pop.), is the seat of Andrew County. One- and two-story, red-brick commercial structures are centered about the courthouse square. On the western side of town is an extensive, well-platted residential section, developed since 1911 by wealthy St. Joseph commuters.

Savannah, near the geographical center of the county, was platted in 1841, the year Andrew County was created. It was named for Savannah, Georgia. Prior to the Civil War, two newspapers, the *Northwest Democrat* and the *Plain Dealer,* were published here. The former was fervent in its support of the pro-slavery cause, the latter just as extreme in support of the Union. Immediately after the war began, Federal troops rode into town and destroyed the plant of the *Northwest Democrat.* A short time afterward, Confederate troops took the type of the *Plain Dealer* and molded it into bullets.

ST. JOSEPH, 96 *m.* (829 alt., 75,711 pop.) (*see St. Joseph*), is at a junction with US 36 (*see Tour 3*).

For several miles south of St. Joseph, US 71 follows the roadbed of the old Jefferson Highway, once referred to as the Pine and Palm Tree Highway. The route passes through deep cuts in the bluffs of the Missouri River.

The small, unadorned, white frame SPARTA CHURCH (R), 99.5 *m.*, is all that remains of the town of Sparta, onetime (1840-46) seat of Buchanan County (*see St. Joseph*).

At 102.7 *m.* is a junction with County H, a black-topped road.

Left here to AGENCY, 4.1 *m.* (838 alt., 361 pop.), once known as Agency Ford because the agency of the Sac and Fox Indians was located at this point, where the road from Clay County to the Blacksnake Hills (*see St. Joseph*) crossed the ford. In 1839 Robert Gilmore established a ferry here. The present town was platted in 1863—long after the Indians had been driven westward. Today (1941) it is noteworthy for the RATCLIFFE MANUFACTURING PLANT (*open weekdays 8:30-4:30*), a three-story, red frame building (R) in which are manufactured wooden stirrups sold internationally. The factory was opened in the late 1870's, and in the following decades consumed all the willow trees on the near-by river bottom. Today wood is imported. Many of the machines used in cutting and shaping the stirrups were designed by the plant's founder.

Some five miles south of the century-old village of FAUCETT, 108.5 *m.* (947 alt., 150 pop.), US 71 enters Platte County, the only county in northwestern Missouri where tobacco is extensively cultivated. Almost every farm has its tobacco field and its group of tobacco barns. The barns have steeply pitched roofs, and a series of narrow doors along each side, used as ventilators for drying the tobacco, which is hung from multiple rafters inside. White Burley is the principal variety grown; it is sown in February or March and transplanted between May 1 and June 20, when the plants are four to six inches high. Harvesting generally begins when the middle leaves turn yellow, at which time the plant will yield a leaf of maximum weight and good color, and will not damage readily while drying. The grown plant, or stalk, is "split" or "speared" on painted tobacco sticks, and left to wilt in the sun before being hauled to the barns.

In curing White Burley, growers usually hang six plants to the stick, with the sticks placed eight inches apart on rails in the barns. Color, flavor, and aroma depend in large measure upon the curing process. Drying is gradual; the ventilator doors are kept partly closed for several days, until the tobacco is thoroughly wilted. As the leaves turn brown, faster drying is desirable, and the doors are opened wide.

The next process is that of stripping and grading. This is done preferably in cloudy or foggy weather, when the leaf holds just enough moisture to be handled without breaking. With ventilators again opened—this time to allow the entrance of moisture—crews of six strippers to a table work the leaves. The first man removes the "flyings," the thin chaffy leaves at the bottom; the next takes off the "trash," the two to four leaves that are longer and more solid than flyings, but very light; a third man removes the "lugs", still another takes off the "bright leaf"; then the "red leaf" at the top comes off. The "tips" are two or more short red leaves, the very topmost. The sorted leaves are then made into "hands" of approximately 25 leaves each, held together by a piece of leaf bound around their butts. Hands are hung on sticks and bulked to retard drying. The tobacco is then hauled to the warehouse on wagons or trucks, approximately 400 sticks to the load.

At 114.9 *m.* is a junction with County Z, a black-topped road.

Right on County Z to DEARBORN, 2.1 *m.* (881 alt., 456 pop.), annually the scene of operations of a fox hunters' association. The association's bench shows and field trials attract dog fanciers from Platte and Buchanan Counties, who come with tents and kennel cars, and make a holiday of the three- or four-day event. High spot of the meet is a fox hunt, which begins just after dark and often lasts the better part of a night. The hunters sometimes follow the pack, but usually they gather on a convenient hilltop and follow by sound. Each man knows the voice of his hounds, and without seeing either dog or fox, can tell the course and progress of the hunt, from the picking up of the scent to the kill.

At NEW MARKET, 115.5 *m.* (870 alt., 75 pop.), a village founded on the banks of Bee Creek in 1843, is a junction with County H, a graveled road.

Right on County H, a highway deep cut in the almost regular folds of the loess hills. Sombre, unpainted tobacco barns crown nearly every ridge, and dwarf the well-kept farm houses beside them; their gaunt lines give the region an unusual character. WESTON, 11.3 *m.* (773 alt., 1,121 pop.), an important tobacco market, is half-hidden in a pinched little valley between Missouri River bluffs. Modern store fronts contrast with older buildings along the single business street, but the adjoining hillside streets are virtual museums of pre-Civil War domestic architecture. Most distinctive are the one-and-a-half-story rose-brick houses with Classic-Revival porticoes. Jutting over the roofs of the houses from one of the bluffs is HOLY TRINITY CHURCH, a native gray-stone structure of Gothic design with twin spires. The church was built in 1911, succeeding one erected in 1844 by Father Ruthowsky, a Polish Roman Catholic.

Weston had its beginning when Joseph Moore staked a claim in 1837, laid off a few streets, and sold some lots. The following year he sold a half interest in his claim to Bela M. Hughes, who laid out the present town and actively promoted its growth. Within a year the population had increased to 300, and shipping advantages on the Missouri River made the town a port for much of the growing overland traffic. Among those who prospered by this commerce was Ben Holladay (1819-87), a native of Kentucky whose parents had brought him to western Missouri during his early boyhood. Holladay ran a store and hotel in Weston, and did a little trading with the Indians in Kansas. In 1849 he built a large, two-story Classic-Revival house at 600 Short Street (*still standing; private*). Following the Mexican War he entered the overland freighting business, gradually succeeding the firm of Russell, Majors, and Waddell (*see Kansas City, and Tour 7a*). Under his direction the overland stagecoach service reached its peak.

By 1849 Weston merchants had shipped 1,577 tons of hemp, and huge quantities of pork, lard, peltries, wheat, and tobacco, but this commerce was abruptly ended in 1857, when the shifting course of the Missouri River left the town several miles inland. The population dwindled to a fraction of its boom total. In 1894, however, tobacco culture, which had declined after the Civil War, was encouraged by the excellent prices a local firm, Berry & Hawkins, obtained in Kentucky. Production increased. About 1910 J. B. Doran built the first Weston warehouse where sales were made by independent buyers and speculators. In 1928 five million pounds of tobacco were sold at Weston for an average price of $28.67 a hundred pounds. Now two warehouses, with some 130,000 feet of floor space, are devoted to the sale of White Burley leaf Platte County tobacco. Shipments are also made here from other sections of

Missouri, as well as from Kansas and Arkansas, making Weston the biggest loose-leaf tobacco market west of the Mississippi.

During the winter months, when tobacco is graded and sold, great farm wagons and trucks, loaded high with the year's crop, crowd the highway and winding dirt roads. Buyers for Eastern tobacco companies descend on the village, and everyone is interested in the quantity, quality, and expected prices of White Burley. Activity centers about the TOBACCO WAREHOUSES (*open 8-5 weekdays*), two large, corrugated-iron structures on Main Street. Here the baskets of tobacco are placed in long rows, forming aisles for the auctioneer and buyers. The auctioneer moves slowly, chanting his peculiar, sing-song jargon. About him are the buyers, examining the tobacco leaves and indicating their bids by a wink, a nod, or some other sign known only to the initiated. Approximately a quarter of a million pounds of Burley tobacco are sold each day, until the three- to five-million-pound crop is exhausted. Then the auctioneer, the buyers, and the trucks disappear. The tense atmosphere is dispelled, and the town sinks once again into its quiet ways, waiting for next year's crop, when prices will surely be good.

The HOLLADAY DISTILLERY (*open 8-4 weekdays*), on a dirt road at the southern edge of town, adjoins a government warehouse in which 5,000 gallons of whisky are placed each week for aging. The plant was begun about 1856, when Ben Holladay's brother, Major David Holladay, who operated a mill on the site, discovered that the four near-by springs contained limestone water ideal for the manufacture of Bourbon whisky. The business flourished until the passage of the Volstead Act. In 1937 it was revived by the Singer Brothers of Kansas City.

Approximately 20 yards from the highway is a large INDIAN MOUND (R), 120.1 *m.*, believed to have been used for burial purposes. It is oval in shape, and approximately 100 feet long and 30 feet high.

"OLD FLINTLOCK" BAPTIST CHURCH (R), 120.7 *m.*, is a low, sagging, one-story log house, built about 1840 on land donated by Captain Andrew Johnson, a veteran of the War of 1812. Vine-covered and rapidly falling into decay, the hand-hewn walnut logs, pegged together, still hold chinks of mortar and stone. The origin of the church's nickname is unknown.

TRACY, 125 *m.* (778 alt., 230 pop.), on the north bank of the Platte River, is the scene of the Platte County Fair, an annual event since 1888.

Crossing the Platte River on a concrete and steel bridge, US 71 enters PLATTE CITY, 126 *m.* (805 alt., 675 pop.), a tobacco and grain center dominated by the red tin roof of the Platte County courthouse. Soon after the military road from Liberty Landing in Clay County to Fort Leavenworth was laid out in 1828, Zadoc Martin established a ferry at the Platte River crossing of that road. Soon afterward, he built a flour mill at the falls near the present highway bridge, and the settlement which grew up was called Martinville in his honor. In 1839 the settlement was selected as the seat of Platte County, and renamed Platte City.

Platte County and Platte City have much in common. Both gained national notice in the Mexican War, when Missouri furnished more troops than any other State, and Platte County served as their point of departure. At the outbreak of the Civil War, the county was strongly in sympathy with the South. Hundreds of men from the vicinity joined the Confederate Army. On December 16, 1861, Union troops burned Platte City. On the following day two citizens were killed by soldiers. On July 15, 1864, Union troops burned again the several buildings that had been rebuilt.

A number of Platte County men helped make Western history. Peter Hardeman Burnett was captain of the first wagon train over the Oregon Trail to the Pacific Coast, and the first Governor of California. General A. W. Doniphan led Missouri troops on their march to the sea during the Mexican War. Ben Holladay (*see Tour 7*) developed the overland stage that served the West before the coming of the railroads. David Rice Atchison, 16 times president pro tem of the United States Senate, is alleged to have been President of the United States for a single day (*see Tour 10A*).

At 137.2 *m.* is a junction with State 9, a concrete road.

Right on State 9 to PARKVILLE, 3.1 *m.* (754 alt., 671 pop.), a college town tucked away in a long narrow valley. In the early 1840's, this was one of the most important towns on the Missouri River, ranking with or even surpassing Kansas City. In the 1850's, when the slavery question caused unrest and bloodshed all along the Kansas border, the citizens of Parkville were active on both sides. The *Industrial Luminary,* a paper of considerable influence, was edited by two of the most outspoken abolitionist editors on the border—W. J. Patterson and George S. Park, the latter the founder of the town and, despite his sentiments, a slaveholder. The office of the paper was in Park's recently opened stone hotel, an imposing edifice truthfully described by its owner as the largest and most commodious hotel west of St. Louis.

On April 14, 1855, members of the Platte County Self-Defensive League rode into town, entered the newspaper office, seized the presses, type cases, files, and office equipment, and moved them into the street, where a large crowd quickly gathered. Park was in Kansas at the time, but Patterson was seized and might have been badly manhandled had not his wife clung to him hysterically. It was agreed that he should leave the county at once and remain away permanently. The leader of the group then mounted the steps of the hotel and read a resolution drawn up by the league, declaring the *Industrial Luminary* a nuisance, inimical to public welfare, and naming the editors as traitors to the State and country. The resolution also announced that the Northern Methodist Church, because of its abolitionist views, would not be tolerated in Platte County. Then, accompanied by the unwilling Patterson, the raiders carried the printing equipment across White Alloe Creek to the foot of Main Street, where they dumped it into the Missouri River. Patterson left immediately for Montreal, Canada, where he became a wealthy man. Park went to Illinois, but returned at the request of the Parkville community, which seems not to have sympathized with the league's action.

PARK COLLEGE, located on an 80-acre hilltop campus at the eastern edge of town, is a 4-year co-educational institution. Adjacent to the campus is the college farm of 1,200 acres, of which 300 are under cultivation. The college plant includes nine dormitories, five classroom buildings, library, observatory, commons, heating plant, printing shop, carpenter and electrical shops, laundry, dairy, greenhouses, and an orchard. With the exception of many-turreted MACKAY HALL, completed in 1893, which houses the administrative offices, most of the buildings are of modified Tudor-Gothic design in brick or native limestone.

The college, established in 1875 and chartered four years later, is the outgrowth of a desire on the part of George S. Park to provide an education for students without funds, by permitting them to earn part of their tuition and board by working in one or another of the school's enterprises. Since its inception, the college has graduated more than 2,400 students, and thousands more have taken courses there.

At 142 *m.* is a junction with US 69 (*see Tour 10A*).

NORTH KANSAS CITY, 146 *m.* (746 alt., 2,688 pop.), an industrial town on the north bank of the Missouri River, was founded by the North Kansas City Development Company. The company, which purchased the site in 1912, constructed residential and business buildings, paved streets, laid water and gas mains, installed street lights, landscaped several parks, and erected waterworks before offering lots for sale. Today (1941) the company still controls municipal policies and will sell or lease building sites only to selected types of business. The houses, designed for factory employees, are frame structures, one and two stories in height.

At 147 *m.* is a junction with a narrow, unmarked graveled road.

Right here to the KANSAS CITY MUNICIPAL AIRPORT, 0.5 *m.*, a 687-acre field with 4 hard-surfaced runways, 9 hangars housing commercial and private aircraft, and a post office for clearing mail. Fronting the field is the airport terminal, a one-story, buff-brick building trimmed with stone. The airport serves three major airlines (*see Kansas City*).

At 147.5 *m.* US 71 crosses the Missouri River on a free bridge and enters KANSAS CITY, 150 *m.* (748 alt., 399,178 pop.) (*see Kansas City and Tours 2, 3, and 4*).

Section b. KANSAS CITY to CARTHAGE; 145 m. US 71

South from KANSAS CITY, 0 *m.*, US 71 crosses a high, rolling prairie drained by shallow, gravel-bottomed streams, a land of cattle and poultry farms, producing sizeable quantities of corn, wheat, barley, and, in particular, sorghums. Between Carthage and the Arkansas State Line, the prairie gives way to the Ozark foothills, where diversified farming and mining, and the increasing tourist trade have served to develop the area, even during the lean depression years.

HICKMAN MILLS, 16.7 *m.* (1,005 alt., 200 pop.), was once a leading town of the region. Founded in 1836, it was a center of activity for both Union and Confederate soldiers during the Civil War. When Order No. 11, issued by Brigadier General Thomas Ewing in August 1863, compelled all citizens, except those who could prove their loyalty to the Union and who resided within one mile of specified towns, to vacate their property, Hickman Mills' population grew beyond the town's capacity. Hundreds poured in, bringing with them only the simplest necessities. A year later the destitute and harassed Confederate army of General Sterling Price pillaged the town. Hickman Mills never recovered.

1. Right from Hickman Mills on County 10S, an asphalt road which winds through one of the most efficiently developed farm areas in the State, to the SOUTH RIDGE GOLF CLUB AND PICNIC GROUNDS (*picnics and tennis, 25¢; greens fee, 50¢*), 1 *m.* (R), containing a rambling stucco club house. At the crossing

of the BIG BLUE RIVER, 2.6 *m.*, the deep-worn roadway of the Santa Fe Trail is visible (R).

At 4.3 *m.* on County 10S is a junction with County 3W, a paved road.

Right here 5 *m.* to DALLAS (870 alt., 104 pop.), formerly a trading station on the Santa Fe Trail. DALLAS MILL (*open*), on a low rocky ledge along Indian Creek, is said to be one of the oldest mills in continuous operation in the State. A dilapidated two-story structure, the mill's frame side walls and wooden shingles have weathered to a drab grayish color. John Fitzhugh built the stone basement and installed the forebays of the mill in 1830. Seven years later the building was leased to Anthony B. Watts, who eventually became its owner. Just prior to the Civil War, Watts added a towering superstructure which became a local landmark. Anthony Watts' son, Stubbin, who took time off from work at the mill to serve in the Confederate Army, was known locally as the "fiddling miller of Dallas." DALLAS PARK, in a bend of Indian Creek immediately south of Watts' Mill, is a 35-acre recreational center. On an island in the lagoon are a bathing beach, a dance hall, and amusement concessions.

Left 1.5 *m.* on County 3W to NEW SANTA FE, a tiny hamlet that has seen both better and worse days. The village developed about the farm of John Bartleston, who erected a cabin in the forest along the Santa Fe Trail in 1833 and subsisted on hominy and potatoes. Within a few years, a community known as Little Santa Fe developed. Wagon caravans laden with merchandise for the Mexican and California trade paused here before pushing Westward. In 1851 Little Santa Fe was incorporated as New Santa Fe. About this time the village's troubles began. Located on the line between a free and a slave State, it suffered from the Border War of 1855-60, the Civil War, and the depredations of the bands of outlaws who came after the war. Finally, the isolation of the village from the railroad reduced it to little more than an historic site.

2. Left from Hickman Mills on 10S, an asphalt road, to LONGVIEW FARMS (*open weekdays; guides*), 11.8 *m.*, one of the outstanding horse and dairy-cattle farms of America. The owner's residence is a two-story stucco building overlooking a large sunken garden and 120 acres of landscaped grounds. The 1,700-acre farm is divided into four divisions—floral, dairy, horse, and hog—each directed by a superintendent. In the floral unit, gardenias and roses are raised for the Kansas City market. The dairy herd consists of approximately 525 cows, of which 450 are always fresh. South of the dairy is the horse unit. In the largest of three barns is a training and show arena used during wet weather. East of it is a private race track, one-half mile in length, with a grandstand and clubhouse for guests. Almost 100 hackney horses are stabled here; 15 or 20 are ready for show at all times. Included in the stables are the famous hackneys, Captivation and Evasion, and Adoration and Admiration; the latter won 17 of their first 18 showings. Perhaps the all-time favorite of the farm was the great horse, Revelation. Dave Smith, nationally known trainer, is superintendent of the horse unit. The hog unit is in the southeastern portion of the farm, and is equipped with modern facilities. The farm stores approximately 40,000 tons of silage and 1,000 tons of alfalfa each year. Developed by R. A. Long, the late Kansas City lumber magnate, Longview is now the property of his daughters, Mrs. Lula Long Combs and Mrs. Hayne Ellis, wife of Rear Admiral Ellis. The property represents an investment of $2,750,000.

Between Hickman Mills and Harrisonville, US 71 continues through a prosperous region of stock and grain farms. Victor Tixier, French author, traveling here in 1839, observed that the prairie becomes wider and the woods scarcer and thinner. "The grass," he wrote, "low and thick, covered a series of small wooded hills and plains crossed by many brooks . . . we encountered small troops of five or six deer, prairie hens, woodcocks with long tails. . . . In the woods huge flocks of parrots flew away as we approached, uttering discordant cries. . . ."

BELTON, 21.4 *m.* (1,106 alt., 971 pop.), all but missed by the highway, was platted in 1871, and is best known as the home of Carry Nation, the militant prohibitionist. Carry Nation was the daughter of George and Mary Campbell Moore. She was born in Garrard County, Kentucky, and lived in a dozen counties of Kentucky, Missouri, and Texas before her family settled permanently in Belton in 1867. A few months later, Carry married Dr. Charles Gloyd, a young physician, and with him moved to Holden (*see Tour 4b*). It was soon obvious that Gloyd was an incurable drunkard, and Carry spent many months of "literal Hell" with him before her parents took her home to Belton, where her daughter Charlien was born. When Gloyd died six months later, Carry entered the State normal school at Warrensburg and obtained a teacher's certificate. She taught the first grade in Holden until she was dismissed four years later over an argument about the pronunciation of the letter *a*. Left with no means of support, Carry prayed to the Lord to send her a husband. Ten days later, she met David Nation, lawyer, minister, and editor. Shortly they were married, to spend 24 miserable, disapproving years together. For the first ten of these years Carry supported the family by operating cheap hotels in Texas towns, but in 1889 Nation became pastor of the Christian Church in Medicine Lodge, Kansas. Here Carry began her crusade against the three things which she believed had ruined her first husband—drink, tobacco, and the Masons. Since saloons were illegal in Kansas, there was no penalty for destroying their property; Carry Nation began with stones and bricks, and progressed to her famous hatchet, which she first used in Wichita in 1900, when she destroyed the Hotel Carey bar. In 1901 David Nation divorced her on grounds of desertion, and for the next ten years her life was a series of dramatic experiences compounded of violence and visions. In the course of her last public speech, January 13, 1911, she faltered, hesitated as though bewildered, and whispered, "I—I have done what I could." Five months later, she died and was buried in the family plot in the Belton cemetery. Her grave remained unmarked until 1924, when friends erected a granite shaft inscribed:

Carry A. Nation
Faithful to the Cause of Prohibition
"She hath done what she could"

According to Herbert Asbury in *Carry Nation* (1929), PECULIAR, 30.5 *m.* (1,006 alt., 206 pop.), received its name when a group of spiritualists under the leadership of Mrs. Jane Hawkins came to Cass County in search of a home. George Moore, Carry Nation's father, took Mrs. Hawkins and some of her followers to look at a farm for which he had the agency. As they came over a hilltop and saw the valley below, Mrs. Hawkins exclaimed: "That's peculiar! It is the very place I saw in a vision in Connecticut." Thus, when the spiritualists bought the farm and laid out a town in 1868, they named it Peculiar.

At 38.4 *m.* is a junction with a marked graveled road.

Left here to LUNA LAKE (*cabins, swimming, and fishing; nominal charge*), 4 *m.*, a recreational center developed about a lake stocked with fish from State hatcheries.

HARRISONVILLE, 39 *m.* (904 alt., 2,322 pop.), the seat of Cass County, is the economic capital of a prosperous farm area centered by a three-story buff-brick and stone courthouse in a large square.

Nowhere was the bitterness of border warfare more keenly felt than in Cass County, and no family was more closely associated with the lawlessness and brutality of the period than the Youngers. According to the autobiographical *Story of Cole Younger* (1903), Colonel William Henry Younger purchased a large farm near Harrisonville in 1858. Here he lived and raised cattle until he moved into the town, where he started a livery stable, bought an interest in two large stores, and received a United States Government mail contract. His sympathies, when the war broke out, were with the Union.

One evening, his daughter and his son, Cole, then 17, attended a dance at the home of Colonel McBee, a Southerner. During the evening, a group of Union soldiers, among them Captain Irvin Wally, forced their way in to the party. When Cole's sister refused to dance with the Captain, he and Cole fought. The next day Wally attempted to arrest Cole as a spy, but Cole escaped, and soon after joined Quantrill's band. Thus, inadvertantly, Colonel Younger came under suspicion as a Southern sympathizer. On July 20, 1862, he was waylaid on his way home from Kansas City, robbed, and shot dead. In September of 1863, the Younger home in Harrisonville was burned by Union forces. When Mrs. Younger moved to her country home, that too was burned.

After the war, Cole Younger and Frank James seem to have organized the group which, under the leadership of Jesse James, was to become the most notorious band of outlaws in American history. For the next ten years Cole was associated with nearly all the spectacular robberies perpetrated by the band. Cole was usually accompanied by his brother James, and frequently by another brother, Robert; a third, John, was shot to death March 16, 1874, at the beginning of his apprenticeship. James, Robert, and Cole Younger, the James boys, and three other men robbed the bank at Northfield, Minnesota, September 7, 1876. In the ensuing fight two citizens and the three other robbers were killed. The James brothers escaped, but the Youngers, all wounded, were captured and sentenced to life imprisonment. Robert died in the Minnesota penitentiary in 1889; James and Cole were eventually paroled. James committed suicide in 1902, and the following year, after a long campaign, Cole was pardoned. He returned to Missouri, where he made a living lecturing. Later, he toured in a

Wild West show with Frank James. He died near Lee's Summit, Missouri, in 1916.

Between Harrisonville and Butler, US 71 traverses a rolling country where the farms are smaller and support more landowners and fewer tenants. Comfortably secure in well-constructed, modernly equipped houses, the farmers raise livestock, poultry, and wheat.

ADRIAN, 56.2 m. (868 alt., 868 pop.), a shipping point for grain and poultry, was founded in 1880 and named for the Michigan home of some of its settlers.

BUTLER, 66.1 m. (866 alt., 2,958 pop.), platted in 1854 and named for William O. Butler, officer in the Mexican War, became the seat of Bates County in 1856. The quiet streets hardly recall the holocaust of 1861, when the courthouse and many other buildings were burned by a squad of cavalry sent from Kansas under orders of Colonel James Montgomery. During the succeeding years of the war, it is said, most of the remaining buildings in the town were burned to prevent Southern sympathizers from harboring rebels. After the war, Butler was gradually rebuilt. Each August the town attracts as many as 20,000 visitors for the Little Bit and Bridle Show, a horse show often referred to as the "Little American Royal." At the BUTLER COMMUNITY SALES PAVILION (*open weekdays*), a low, white frame, barnlike structure with a bright tin roof (R), and the BATES COUNTY SALES PAVILION (L), a similar building, livestock auctions are held each Tuesday and Thursday respectively.

RICH HILL, 78 m. (805 alt., 1,994 pop.), named by the first postmaster, E. W. Ratekin, for the town's location on a hill underlaid with coal, is a faded memento of mining days near the Marais des Cygnes (Fr., the Marsh of the Swans) River. In 1880 the site was part of a cattle range; in 1883 it was a well-constructed city of 8,000, with an imposing parkway and sturdy brick buildings. As mining activities declined after 1900, the population of the community decreased.

At Rich Hill is a junction with an unmarked dirt road.

Left here to PAPINSVILLE, 7 m. (85 pop.), platted in April, 1847, and named for Melicourt Papin, St. Louis Indian trader. Papinsville was the seat of Bates County 1848-56. In the fall of 1861, most of the town, and the bridge, were burned by troops commanded by General James Lane of Kansas, to prevent General Sterling Price from crossing the river at this point and using the town as a base.

Harmony Mission was established three or four miles upstream in August of 1821. Sponsored by the United Foreign Mission Society of New York and encouraged by the United States Government, the project originated with the Osage Indians then living in this area (*see Archeology and Indians*). In 1820, Chief White Hair and a delegation of Osage Indians went to Washington and requested President Monroe to establish a mission for them similar to Union Mission at Fort Gibson, Oklahoma. Forty-one persons responded to the Mission Society's call for volunteers, including a carpenter, a shoemaker, a wagon maker, 2 farmers, 15 women, and 16 children, and the ministers, Nathaniel B. Dodge, Benton Pixley, and William B. Montgomery. The Osage in council granted land for the mission, and government workmen aided in the construction of the log building for the settlement. William S. Williams (d. March 1849), better known as "Old Bill," later a colorful trapper, trader, and explorer in the Far West, aided the missionaries in preparing a dictionary of the Osage language and part of a grammar. A school was begun about January of 1822, with 12 Indian children as pupils. Reverend Pixley confided to his diary that he found them "as interesting and active as the generality of children among the whites, and I have sometimes thought them more so." The missionaries, however, failed to achieve any real success in their work because of their inability to understand the primitive mind, and their unbending insistence upon an Osage adoption of New England morality. Williams soon tired of the impossible situation. The crisis came when, contrary to the advice of Williams, the minister preached a sermon on Jonah and the whale, at the end of which an old chief arose and declared, "We have heard several of the white people talk and lie; we know they will lie, but that is the biggest lie we ever heard." Soon afterwards, Williams "laid aside his Christianity and took up his rifle and came to the Mountains." The Indians, tiring of their guests, chose to ignore them. The mission continued until the Osage were moved west of the Missouri State Line in 1837, but the missionaries failed to convert a single adult Osage. After the mission was closed, the United States purchased the property for $8,000. A few settlers remained, and in 1841 a post office, the first in the county, was established here and called Batesville.

Among the legends associated with the mission is that of the young Marquis Auguste Letier of France. Letier came to America in search of his father, who had left France during the French Revolution to become a fur trader. At Harmony Mission the young Marquis learned that his father had died there only three weeks before. He was consoled, however, by the love of Degninon, a young Osage girl from the mission whom he married and took back to France. Less romantic is the story of the young missionary and his wife who went to Fort Osage for supplies. The horses having strayed while the couple were eating supper, the man went off to find them. No sooner had he gone than wolves surrounded their covered wagon. The woman fought them off with an axe until her husband returned several hours later with his gun.

Between Rich Hill and Nevada, US 71 passes through a wheat and cattle country dotted with the black tipples and waste piles of small coal mines, a majority of which have been abandoned.

The RED STAR COAL COMPANY MINE (L), 82.7 m., operates a small, deep-shaft mine. Brought to the surface on chain conveyors, the coal is broken mechanically and passed through a "shaker screen." The dust is carried by another belt conveyor a short distance from the tipple and dumped in much the same manner as sawdust from a lumber mill. The OSAGE COAL COMPANY MINE (R), 83.1 m., is a similar shaft.

At HORTON, 86.8 m. (776 alt., 98 pop.), is a junction with an unmarked dirt road.

Left here to BLUE MOUND, 7 m., an oval-shaped Indian mound with a base area of approximately 150 acres, connected with a smaller mound by a large, earthen, wall-like section. The origin of the mounds is unknown, but the Osage Indians used Blue Mound as a burial place within historic times. When Chief White Hair, one of a series of notable Osage chiefs bearing the same name, died about 1825, he was buried in the Blue Mound.

At 95.3 m. is a junction with an unmarked cinder and rock road.

Right here to STATE HOSPITAL No. 3, 0.8 m., an eleemosynary institution established by the general assembly of 1885 for the treatment of mental diseases. The main building is an elaborately trimmed, four-story, red-brick structure, with mansard roof and numerous turrets and dormers—the ultimate in rococo. Other buildings include a surgical hospital, an employees' dormitory, a patients' cafeteria, and an employees' cafeteria. The institution is on a 520-acre tract, of which 92 acres compose the building sites, grounds, and park. In addition, the State leases approximately 1,500 acres for gardening, farming, and grazing. The number of patients averages about 1,800.

NEVADA, 97 *m.* (874 alt., 8,181 pop.), on the boundary between Missouri's western prairie and southwestern plateau, draws economic advantages from both. It is the region's largest shipping point for wheat, corn, livestock, poultry, and prairie hay. The business district forms a square about the Vernon County courthouse, a three-story, Carthage-limestone structure with a red-tile roof, corner turrets, and a clock tower.

Nevada was settled almost wholly by families from Kentucky and Tennessee. It was platted in 1855 and named by Colonel DeWitt C. Hunter, the first permanent resident, for Nevada City, California. During the early years of the Civil War, the little town was the headquarters of several detachments of Confederate troops, and was known as the "Bushwhackers' Capital." On Tuesday, May 26, 1863, a company of Federal militia from Kansas marched into the town under the command of Captain Anderson Norton. The inhabitants were told that if they needed help in removing their furniture, the soldiers would assist them, for within 20 minutes the town would be burned. Thereafter, until the close of the war, Nevada consisted of an ash heap and two log cabins spared through some oversight. Nevada became a division point of the Missouri-Kansas-Texas Railroad in 1870.

The WILLIAM JOEL STONE MONUMENT, on the courthouse grounds, sculptured by Irvin D. Wight of Kansas City, is an heroic bronze on a granite base. William Joel Stone (1848-1918) was born in Madison County, Kentucky. When he was 15, he went to live with his married sister in Columbia, Missouri, where he attended the University of Missouri for three years. He was admitted to the bar in 1869, and two years later settled at Nevada, where he served as prosecuting attorney of Vernon County (1872-74). After serving three terms in the State legislature, Stone was elected Governor of Missouri (1892-96), and in 1903 was chosen to succeed Vest in the national Senate—an office which he filled until his death. COTTEY COLLEGE, northwest corner of W. Austin and S. Chestnut Sts., is a privately endowed junior college for girls. Grouped about the ornate administration building, a three-story, rambling red-brick structure (built 1884), are the four principal buildings of the ten-acre campus. The school, established as Vernon Seminary by Virginia Alice Cottey in 1884, was chartered as Cottey College in 1887. Since 1927 the college has been owned and operated by the P.E.O. Sisterhood; it has an average enrollment of 125 students. RADIO SPRINGS PARK, foot of S. College St., is a health and recreation center with two lakes (*swimming, 25¢*) and a golf course (*greens fee, 50¢*).

CAMP CLARK, 100.3 *m.*, entered through a gray-stone archway (L), is the summer training quarters of the Missouri National Guard. Approximately 2,500 militiamen are gathered here each August for military training and maneuvers.

At 123 *m.* is a junction with US 160, a concrete road.

1. Left on US 160 to LAMAR, 1 *m.* (980 alt., 2,992 pop.), the seat of Barton County. Founded in 1856, and named for Mirabeau B. Lamar, President of the Texas Republic, (1838-41), the town is the eastern terminus of the Fort Scott Military Road. Lamar is perhaps best known for the Lamar *Democrat,* one of the most widely quoted newspapers in the State. Founded sometime before the Civil War, which disrupted its publication, the paper has been owned and edited since 1900 by Arthur Aull.

2. Right on US 160 to a junction, 9.9 *m.,* with State 43, a graveled road; R. to County K, 14.5 *m.;* L. to LIBERAL, 17.1 *m.* (885 alt., 771 pop.), founded in 1880 by G. H. Walser (1834-1910), a disciple of Robert C. Ingersoll. Walser, born in Indiana, served in the Civil War, and lived for a time in Rockport before moving to Lamar, where he conceived the idea of establishing a refuge for free-thinkers. Walser purchased land and platted Liberal. Within a few months, a settlement of enthusiasts, ranging from "out and out Agnostics to the more spiritual minded Deists and Spiritualists," developed. According to *Camp's Emigrants' Guide* of May 1883, the citizens of Liberal "boast . . . they have no church, no preacher, or priests, no saloon. . . . They have no hell, no God, no devil, no debauchery, no drunkenness. They believe in but one world at a time, and a heaven of their own making." Although they "practiced the art of doing good, being happy, industrious, sober and independent," the community aroused opposition locally and nationally. Unperturbed, Walser built the Universal Mental Liberty Hall, "to provide a place where any person could come and speak on any subject," and established in 1884 the Liberal Normal School, advertised as providing an education free "from the bias of Christian theology," which announced in 1885 that it had 113 students representing 7 States. Walser's semimonthly magazine *The Orthopoedian* was published until 1900. In 1881, "an addition" to Liberal was established by H. H. Waggoner, who invited only orthodox Christians to move in. The Liberalites answered by erecting a barbed wire fence between the two settlements "to keep the Christians out," and in 1883 Walser bought the Christian suburb outright. Meanwhile he had become interested in spiritualism, and seances were regularly held until about 1887, when a fire exposed the spiritual manifestations as a fake. The last spiritualistic camp meeting in Liberal was held in Catalpa Park in 1899. Since Walser's death in 1910, the community has lost much of its original character. The FRED SACKETT COLLECTION (*open 8-5 weekdays*), office Municipal Light and Water Company, Main St., contains approximately 4,000 Indian relics, the majority of which are of Osage and Sauk origin.

Southward to Carthage, the route enters the Springfield plateau, an area in which dairying is a major industry. Few if any of the herds are large, but nearly all are of improved stock (*see Agriculture*).

The Carthage area is underlaid with marble and limestone, as well as lead, zinc, and other minerals. "Carthage White Marble" came into prominence in 1880, when C. W. Fisher, a stonecutter, exhibited a highly polished specimen, and in time secured a national market. Marble quarried in the area has been used by architects in some of America's best-known buildings, including the Macy department-store building, New York, the Field and Rosenwald museums in Chicago, and the Rust Building, San Francisco.

At 134.5 *m.* is the junction with a graded dirt road.

Right here 1 *m.* to the SITE OF THE BATTLE OF CARTHAGE. Here on July 5, 1861, a Union force of 1,100 infantry, with 8 pieces of artillery, commanded by Colonel Franz Sigel, attacked 4,000 Missouri State Guardsmen, armed with 7 pieces of artillery, and 2,000 unarmed recruits under the command of General Claiborne F. Jackson. The Union column had been sent from Springfield to intercept the Confederate forces, which were moving south to join General Ben McCulloch's troops near the Arkansas State Line. Finding his command outnumbered, Colonel Sigel began an orderly retreat to the south, engaging in a succession of rear-guard skirmishes until he reached Carthage; here he moved eastward. When darkness halted the fighting, he marched his men all night and escaped. The Union losses were 13 killed and 31 wounded, 5 of the latter being taken prisoner. The State Guard's loss was 35 killed, 125 wounded, and 45 captured.

At 143.8 *m.* is a junction with Quarry Drive, an unmarked graveled road.

Right here to the CARTHAGE MARBLE CORPORATION PLANT (*open weekdays 8-4; apply at office for guides*), 0.7 *m.* The process of cutting and finishing the stone is an elaborate one. The corporation employs approximately 175 people, and ships about 2,500 carloads of marble yearly.

CARTHAGE, 145 *m.* (941 alt., 10,585 pop.), high on the south bank of winding Spring River, is the region's largest marketing and shipping point and one of the principal manufacturing cities of south-western Missouri. Flour mills, machine works, and shoe and clothing factories are among its enterprises.

Henry Piercey is said to have built the first house in Carthage; George Hornback opened the first store. The town, which was selected as the seat of Jasper County, was platted in 1842 and named for the ancient commercial center of northern Africa. Twenty-two years later, Confederate guerrillas burned the courthouse, the business section, and most of the residences. After the Civil War, a lead and zinc mining boom in the Joplin area brought the town a share of prosperity. When the marble quarries were opened in the 1880's, its economic base was firmly established. The importance of dairying in the region has stead-ily increased, largely as a result of the "Missouri Dairy Club" plan, originated by E. G. Bennett, and first organized at Carthage in 1916, when 105 head of high-grade Holstein heifers were purchased to im-prove local herds. Under the plan, this purebred cattle has gradually replaced the original scrub stock.

In the latter part of the nineteenth century, Carthage was known throughout the Nation as the home of two widely publicized women, Belle Starr and Annie Baxter. Belle Starr (1846-89) was born Belle Shirley, the daughter of Judge John Shirley, a Carthage resident of wealth and standing, and a Southern sympathizer. When Edward, Belle's brother, joined Quantrill's band, his sister gave him regular information as to the movement of Federal troops. She was an excel-lent rider and pistol shot, and after Edward was killed she herself became a member of Quantrill's bushwhackers. In 1866 Judge Shirley moved to Texas, where Belle eloped with Jim Reed, one of the old Quantrill gang. Reed was shot by a friend who hoped to gain the reward offered for his capture, but Belle frustrated this plan by refusing to identify the body as her husband's. Later she married Sam Starr, a Cherokee, and with him established a ranch on the Canadian River in Indian Territory. The ranch became a notorious bandit hideout, and the headquarters for Belle's band of "eight men who rode under her orders." Here she was shot by Edgar Watson, wanted in Florida for murder.

Mrs. Annie Baxter enjoyed fame of an entirely different nature. She was clerk of Jasper County. Elected in 1890, she was prevented from taking up her duties on the grounds that women did not have the right to hold office. Mrs. Baxter carried the case to the State Supreme Court, where she won a favorable decision. Her resolution in fighting for her rights brought such widespread attention that she was made a colonel on the governor's staff.

MEMORIAL HALL (*open 9-5 weekdays*), Oak St. and the highway, houses a collection of artillery, machine guns, rifles, and other relics of the various wars in which the United States has engaged. MUNICIPAL PARK (*tennis and picnicking*), Seventh St. and the highway, is equipped with a nine-hole golf course (*greens fee, 50¢*) and a swimming pool (*adm. 10¢ and 15¢*).

Carthage is at a junction with US 66 (*see Tour 5*).

Section c. CARTHAGE to ARKANSAS LINE; 55 m. Alt. US 71

Between CARTHAGE, 0 *m.*, and Neosho, the route follows Alt. US 71 (at Carthage, the main branch of the highway swings west from its north-south route to pass through Joplin). As the State Line is approached, the rolling Springfield Plateau gives way to the Ozark Highland, a land of trout streams and mountain resorts, of wooded hillsides and rocky caverns. An early-day hunter, said to have been Edmund Jennings, a Tennessean, visited this area and was so impressed with the great springs that he later described it as the country of the "six boils" or springs. His pronunciation of "boils" was interpreted as "bulls," and thus the southwest Missouri region is now known as the "country of the six bulls."

DIAMOND, 12.8 *m.* (1,169 alt., 486 pop.), is near the birthplace of George Washington Carver, famed Negro educator and agricultural chemist. Born of slave parents about 1864, Carver was stolen and carried to Arkansas with his mother, who was never heard of again. In Arkansas he was exchanged by his captors for a race horse valued at $300. He was later returned to his former home, then known as Diamond Grove. After working his way through high school in Minneapolis, Kansas, he was elected to the faculty of Iowa State College of Agriculture and Mechanics, where he devoted especial attention to bacterial laboratory work in systematic botany. In 1896 he became a teacher at Tuskegee Institute, winning international fame for his discovery of industrial uses for agricultural products. Dr. Carver has found more than 300 by-products of the peanut, making it one of the most important commercial crops in the South. He is now (1941) director of the Department of Agricultural Research at Tuskegee Institute.

At 20.1 *m.* is a junction with US 60 (*see Tour 6*), with which Alt. US 71 is united to NEOSHO, 24 *m.* (1,039 alt., 5,318 pop.) (*see Tour 6*).

KELLY SPRINGS, 35.7 *m.*, on a small lake (R), and BEAVER SPRINGS, 40.1 *m.*, are trout fishing resorts (*overnight cabins; fishing and equipment at nominal charge*).

ANDERSON, 41.8 *m.* (904 alt., 938 pop.), an outfitting point for fishing parties, once boomed with the excitement of a gold rush when "pay dirt" was reported found at Splitlog, a crossroads settlement some four miles to the northwest. In 1887, a group of men, posing as mining promoters, interested Matthias Splitlog in financing a McDonald County gold and silver mining venture. Splitlog was a Wyandotte Indian who had made a fortune in Kansas City real estate, although unable to read or write. With his financial backing, events moved fast. The Splitlog Silver Mining Company was organized, the city of Splitlog laid out, and a daily stageline begun to Neosho. Assay reports claiming heavy deposits of gold and silver threw the countryside into a fever of mining excitement. The roads were lined with white-topped wagons labeled "bound for Splitlog." A railroad company was capitalized at $3,000,000, and Splitlog was made treasurer of the construction company. He drove the first spike—a silver one—with appropriate flourish, "after music by the Indian band from the territory." But the railroad venture, like the mining boom, collapsed when the promoters overplayed their hands. People became suspicious and the bubble burst. The promoters fled in time to escape punishment, but Splitlog was ruined. The railroad later became a portion of the Kansas City Southern lines.

Between Anderson and Noel the highway winds among rugged wooded hills where the soil is too thin for anything but small plots of corn, apple orchards, and patches of strawberries or tomatoes. Summer tourists bring this section most of its money, spending it for recreational purposes and equipment, and for the pottery, woven-cane baskets, and hooked rugs that natives make during the winter.

LANAGAN, 45.3 *m.* (854 alt., 340 pop.), a cluster of one-story frame, brick, and rock buildings and several modern tourist camps, owes its existence to a well of gushing sulphur water that attracts visitors during the summer months.

At TRUITTS' CAVE (*restaurant*), 45.7 *m.* (R), an electrically lighted cavern in a great limestone bluff, is a junction with State 88, a black-topped road.

Left here to PINEVILLE, 4.8 *m.* (524 pop.), a hill town established in 1847, which shed its provincialism when Tyrone Power, Henry Fonda, a large cast of supporting actors, cameramen, technicians, and directors, moved in from Hollywood in the summer of 1938 to film *Jesse James.* Under the influence of Hollywood's magic, Pineville took on the appearance of a ripsnorting town of

Missouri's outlaw years. Tons of yellow clay concealed the four paved streets; the squat, red-brick stores retired behind false fronts; and the Dixie Belle Saloon preempted a corner of the courthouse square. The town assumed daily the activity and character that heretofore had been reserved for court day; the streets were alive with horses and vehicles, the sidewalks and courthouse lawn packed with people. When hillman met hillman, he no longer spoke of weather, crops, or politics, but of how a man wearing shiny brown boots and new khaki pants had driven up to his cabin door and offered him $20 to let Jesse James be chased by a posse across his field, or of how he had been signed to act in the picture and told to grow a beard. At the completion of the film, workmen removed the clay from the streets and restored the town to something of its former appearance.

GINGER BLUE, 47.3 *m.*, an Elk River resort, is one of the oldest of Ozark fishing camps. Southward, the highway passes through a magnificent, heavily timbered section of the Ozarks. Flinty limestone bluffs rise abruptly, over-shadowing the roadbed. They are known as Cliff Dwellers' Bluffs, for they are lined and often tunneled with small caverns which show evidence of prehistoric habitation.

In a bend of the Elk River, crossed at 51 *m.*, is NATIONAL PARK, a fishing resort at the foot of a limestone bluff. NOEL, 51.5 *m.* (828 alt., 515 pop.), borders the Elk River, here damned to form a small lake, stocked with trout (*fishing, boating, swimming; nominal charge*).

BLUFF CAVE (*adm. 35¢; guides*), 53.3 *m.* (R), is an electrically lighted cavern deep in the hills. Within the cave is a lake, 75 feet wide and 500 feet long.

US 71 crosses the ARKANSAS LINE, 55 *m.*, 120 miles north of Fort Smith, Arkansas.

Tour 10A

(Des Moines, Iowa)—Bethany—Pattonsburg—Plattsburg—Excelsior Springs—(Kansas City, Kan.) ; US 69.
Iowa Line to Kansas Line, 124 *m.*

Roadbed hard surfaced throughout.
Route paralleled roughly by the Chicago, Burlington & Quincy R.R. between Andover and Bethany; by the Chicago, Rock Island & Pacific Ry. between Altamont and Cameron; by the Chicago, Milwaukee, St. Paul & Pacific R.R. between Lawson and Excelsior Springs; by the Kansas City, Clay County & St. Joseph R.R. and roughly by the Chicago, Milwaukee, St. Paul & Pacific R.R. between Excelsior Springs and Liberty; by the Kansas City, Clay County & St. Joseph R.R. between Liberty and Kansas City.
Hotels and tourist camps in the larger cities.

US 69, principal highway between Des Moines and Kansas City, crosses Missouri's northwestern plains, connecting the several agricultural and livestock centers of the region with the markets and shipping facilities of Kansas City. Besides the farmlands and villages, the principal scenes of interest are the historic sites of Mormon activity during the 1830's, and the locale of the Jesse James legend.

The highway crosses the IOWA LINE, 0 *m.*, 75 miles south of Des Moines, Iowa, and for 24 miles pursues an uninterrupted course over a rolling prairie where few trees break the winter winds or screen the earth from the parching heat of summer. In some years the corn fires and the pastures burn, and the rains, if they come at all, arrive too late. But usually the rains come when they should, and the land is bright and green, the grain rich, and the cattle fat. Each farm has its herd of blooded beef and dairy cows, its flock of chickens, its squatty, round silos and massive barns. When prices are good, northwestern Missouri farmers are perhaps the most prosperous in the State; when prices are low, their crops, and even their stock and land, may pass under the auctioneer's block.

BETHANY, 23.8 *m.* (916 alt., 2,682 pop.), seat of Harrison County, derives its principal income from agricultural trade and shipping. Each week's activities come to a climax on Tuesday, when everyone who has a sheep or hog, chicken or horse to swap or sell appears at the old NORTHWEST MISSOURI FAIRGROUNDS, southwestern edge of town, and takes part in the community sale. The trading is mostly in livestock, but one can barter for or buy practically anything: halters, furniture, hay mowers, eggs, poultry, milk, or butter.

The countryside around Bethany has been so highly developed during the past century that it little resembles the rolling, grass covered prairie which John Seehorn Allen found when he settled north of the present town in 1840. During October, a few months after their arrival, both John and his wife fell ill. One day their young daughter smelled smoke, and to her horror discovered that the coarse prairie grass surrounding their cabin was a wall of flame. Two men answered her cries for assistance, however, and together they started a back fire which checked the blaze.

Land in the present county was surveyed and opened for entry in 1842; three years later Harrison County was organized and named for Albert G. Harrison, Missouri congressman. County commissioners selected for the county seat the site which Allen platted. Allen later served as Circuit and County Clerk, and as a delegate to the State Convention of 1861, where he declared for the preservation of the Union, expressing the point of view of his predominately anti-slavery, and anti-secession country.

As a child, Edgar W. (Ed) Howe (1853-1937), later famous as the "Sage of Potato Hill," was brought to Harrison County from Indiana in a covered wagon. His father, a farmer, schoolteacher, and Methodist circuit rider, built a church on his Missouri homestead and preached in it every Sunday. Later, he organized a company of Union soldiers and served as its captain, until he was incapacitated; he then returned to Bethany, where he started a newspaper. It was here that Ed, then 12 years old, began his journalistic training. Howe later moved to Atchison, Kansas, established the Atchison *Globe* (1877), and became noted for his philosophical writings and pungent paragraphs. *The Story of a Country Town* (1883) is one of his several books (*see Literature*).

PATTONSBURG, 41.8 *m.* (799 alt., 1,017 pop.), strung along the Grand River bottoms, operates five small creameries, a sawmill, and a vegetable canning plant. The word "creamery" is used in this area to cover several activities, but not the one usually implied by it. The plants do not make butter and other dairy products, but are receiving stations to which farmers bring their whole milk, eggs, and poultry. The creameries ship the produce to St. Joseph, Kansas City, and Springfield. The well-equipped canning plant is operated by the farm women of the vicinity for their own use. Surplus canned goods are sold on the local market.

Pattonsburg was platted two miles north of its present site in 1845, but when the Chillicothe & Omaha Railroad was being built through the county in 1871, the residents moved to meet it. The township, in fact, subscribed $20,000 to bring the rails within its reach.

At 52 *m.* is a junction with State 6, a graveled road.

Left here to GALLATIN, 8.7 *m.* (931 alt., 1,642 pop.), seat of Daviess County, on the south bank of Grand River. Platted in 1837 and named for Albert Gallatin, Secretary of the Treasury (1801-13), the town now huddles about its three-story brownstone courthouse with a serenity that belies its turbulent youth.

In the autumn of 1831, three years before the last Indians left the present limits of Daviess County, William Peniston, the first permanent white settler in this area, established a camp on Splawn's Ridge. The following spring his party was joined by more members of the Peniston family, and soon other settlers moved in. R. P. Peniston, the head of the clan, built a horse-mill to grind flour and meal for the settlers and this became the nucleus of a village platted as Mill Port. In 1836 Daviess County was organized and named in honor of Joseph H. Daviess, a Kentucky soldier in the War of 1812. Gallatin was platted to serve as the county seat, and with its growth the village of Mill Port, some three miles to the east, declined. The county's development was, almost immediately thereafter, given an unexpected turn by the arrival of hundreds of Mormon families. Harried from Jackson, Clay, and Ray Counties, the Mormons still hoped to find a haven in the Missouri Zion which the Prophet, Joseph Smith, had revealed to them. A "stake" laid out some four miles north of Gallatin as Adam-ondi-Ahman was a thriving town when the county seat was a straggling row of "ten houses, three of which were saloons." Friction soon developed between the Saints and the Gentiles whom they outnumbered. When a group of unarmed Mormons came to Gallatin to vote on August 6, 1838, they were met by a mob encouraged by Colonel William P. Peniston, whose election the Mormons opposed. Brittle tempers snapped when a village drunkard picked a quarrel with a Mormon leader, and the fight became general.

"Pistols were not used," Major Joseph H. McGee reported; but "rocks and clubs were in demand, and an occasional butcher knife slipped in. Men dropped on all sides." Major McGee saw a Mormon pursued by two Missourians. "He had a butcher knife sticking between his shoulders." His attackers kept after him, but another Mormon "seized a big club and rushing between them and their victim . . . felled them both to the earth." The Mormons retreated, but on October 11, 1838, they captured Gallatin, and sacked and burned Stollings' storehouse, and the tailor shop.

State 6 continues to a junction with State 13, a graveled road, 10.7 *m.;* L. here to a dirt road, 13.9 *m.;* L. again, crossing the railroad tracks, and R. to another dirt road, 15.5 *m.;* L. here, then R. at 16.1 *m.* to a white frame cottage (L), 16.8 *m.;* R. 200 yards from the cottage, along a trail, to the SITE OF ADAM-ONDI-AHMAN. Here, on the great bend of the Grand River, Lyman Wight, a soldier in the War of 1812, and an Elder of the Mormon Church, settled in 1837 and established a ferry. On May 19, 1838, the Prophet Joseph Smith and other members of the Church visited Wight's settlement, and selected it as the site for a "stake." The Lord had revealed to Joseph Smith that the place was named Adam-ondi-Ahman, which "in the Reformed Egyptian language," means "Adam's Consecrated Land." In explaining the religious importance of the site, Elder B. H. Roberts in his *The Missouri Persecutions* (1900), says that this is the Valley of Adam-ondi-Ahman, where three years before his death Adam gathered all the patriarchs—Seth, Enos, Cainan, Mahalaliel, Jared, Enoch, and Methuselah—and gave them his final blessing, and "even as he blessed them, the heavens were opened and the Lord appeared. . . . " Here, too, Smith prophesied, " 'Ancient of Days,' Adam, will come . . . when the books will be opened and the judgment shall sit . . . the Son of Man will appear . . . and issue a decree . . . that his dominion shall be everlasting. . . .'" At the brow of the hill above the village, Smith announced the discovery of the ruined stone altar where the patriarchs had worshipped.

The settlement's growth was rapid. By October 1838, nearly 200 houses had been built, and 40 more families were living in wagons awaiting the construction of dwellings. As the Mormon War spread in violence and the Gentiles became more determined to drive out or "exterminate" the Saints, Adam-ondi-Ahman became a sort of armed camp. On November 8, 1838, shortly after the surrender of the Mormons at Far West (*see Tour 3*), Brigadier General Robert Wilson was ordered to Adam-ondi-Ahman to hold an inquiry into the alleged Mormon outrages. After a three-day hearing, every Mormon was acquitted, but Wilson ordered the town evacuated within ten days, permitting the Mormons to spend the winter in Caldwell County, but requiring that they leave the State during the following spring. The prosperous community, thus abandoned, fell into ruin, and only a dilapidated log structure on the hillside —said to be the home of Lyman Wight—remains.

On the night of July 15, 1881, as the Chicago, Rock Island & Pacific R.R. pulled out of WINSTON, 54.8 *m.* (1,044 alt., 381 pop.), a shipping point for one of the few coal mines in this area, four men boarded the train. Each wore a red bandanna around his neck, partly concealing his features. Two similarly masked men had got on at Cameron a short time before. As William Westfall, the conductor, began to take up tickets, the largest of the strangers rose and shouted "All Aboard," as a signal to the others. Then, drawing his pistol, he cried, "You are the man I want," and shot Westfall dead. A passenger, John McCulloch, was shot as he tried to escape. The train was stopped, and the bandits robbed the baggage car of between $8,000 and $10,000. They then rode off on their horses, which had been tied near by. Frank and Jesse James were charged with the holdup. In 1882, Frank James, who had voluntarily surrendered to Governor T. T. Crittenden, was indicted as a participant and tried at Gallatin. According to Paul I. Wellman, in the Kansas City *Star,* General Joseph Shelby, beloved Confederate leader, appeared dramatically at court as the principal witness for James. Shelby had commanded James during the Civil War, and his arrival served to reawaken many memories in this predominately Southern community. "The Bonnie Blue Flag" and other Confederate songs were played on the streets while the trial went on with its oratory, table pounding, fine language, and frenzied appeals. With Jo Shelby as a witness, and the Lost Cause as an issue, there could be only one verdict. Frank James was acquitted.

CAMERON, 65.2 *m.* (1,036 alt., 3,615 pop.), was platted in 1855 and named for Colonel Elisha Cameron of Clay County, father-in-law of Samuel McCorkle, one of the town's founders. Two garment factories help to balance Cameron's agricultural economy.

Cameron is at a junction with US 36 (*see Tour 3*).

At 71.8 *m.* is a junction with State 121, a graveled road.

Left here to WALLACE STATE RECREATIONAL AREA (*fishing, picnicking, camping, swimming, cabins*), 1.7 *m.*, 120 acres improved by the State Park Board in 1933.

At 80 *m.* is the southern junction with State 116, a black-topped road.

Right here, past a number of mule and horse breeding farms, to LATHROP, 5.1 *m.* (1,071 alt., 1,049 pop.), a town internationally known since the Boer War, when the British government sent a number of buyers here to purchase mules for its army. During the World War, too, buyers from several nations were stationed here, purchasing both army mounts and draft animals.

PLATTSBURG, 12.1 *m.* (953 alt., 1,915 pop.), is a typical county seat, with low, flat-roofed commercial buildings forming a square about the Clinton County courthouse.

A few families from Clay County settled in the southern portion of Clinton County in 1826, and were soon followed by groups from Kentucky and Tennessee, as well as from many of the New England States. The county was organized January 2, 1833, and commissioners selected a site along Horse Fork Creek for the location of the county seat. A sale of lots was held a year later. After being named Concord, then Springfield, the town became Plattsburg in 1835, after Plattsburg, Clinton County, New York. John Livingston, who had settled near by three years before, was the town's first citizen. During his first winter, it is said that he killed 48 black bears, 22 of them on a large elm tree which stood on the site of the present courthouse. The wild life departed, however, as settlers moved in, and Plattsburg profited from the location here of the United States Land Office (1843-59). In this office government lands in northwest Missouri were sold, and squatters' claims filed.

Plattsburg is principally known for its associations with three men: David Rice Atchison, O. O. McIntyre, and J. Breckenridge Ellis.

The ATCHISON MONUMENT, on the courthouse lawn, is a life-sized metal figure on a red-granite base. An inscription reads: "David Rice Atchison, 1807-1886. President of U. S. one day. Lawyer, statesman and jurist." It is argued that Atchison, president pro tem. of the Senate, was President of the United States the day of March 4, 1849, which fell on Sunday, thus delaying by 24 hours the inauguration of Zachary Taylor. Atchison's last years were spent on his Clinton County farm.

The BIRTHPLACE OF O. O. McINTYRE (*open by permission*), 208 Maple St., is a two-story frame house with a double-decked porch. O. O. McIntyre (1884-1938), a Missouri boy "who made good in the city," never forgot his home town. In his famed column, first to be syndicated in New York, he often referred to his cornsilk-smoking days in Plattsburg. McIntyre went to the metropolis after holding various editorial posts in Ohio, and in 1912 began the briskly phrased jottings on the Gotham scene which brought him fame, not only as one of the highest paid newspaper writers in the world, but also as one of the few New Yorkers able to retain a small-town perspective. He is said to have interpreted New York as "provincials" wished it interpreted.

"ELLISAN" (*private*), northwest corner of Fourth St. and State 116, a one-story frame house with many gables and two deep bays, is the home of John Breckenridge Ellis. On the side lawn is a small summerhouse in which the author often works. Ellis was born near Hannibal, February 11, 1870, and after attending several schools and colleges, at one of which he obtained a good musical education, became a professor of English. He began his literary career in 1902. Ellis is the long-time president of the Missouri Writers' Guild and the author of several books, among them *Little Fiddler of the Ozarks* and *When the Light Burned Low*.

At 90.5 *m.* is a junction with a graveled road.

Right here to a junction with a farm lane (L), 1.6 *m.*, which leads ·1 *m.* to the WALTUS LOCKETT WATKINS MILL (*open 9-5 daily, adm. 41¢*). Entering the 1,400-acre Watkins farm, the road passes between two ponds which formerly supplied water for the steam boilers of the four-story, red-brick mill (L). On the first floor is the office, the brick-paved blacksmith shop, and the flour mill. The walls of the shop are hung with harness, rope, and tools used in operating the plantation. The ponderous wooden machinery still holds in place the stone burrs between which the grain was ground, and the long, silk-covered frame in which the flour was bolted. The cloth-making equipment, made by Furbush & Page of Philadelphia and patented in 1853, is still on the upper three floors of the building: machines that cleaned the wool, spindles that twisted it into yarn, great weaving looms, dyeing vats, and the napping and fulling machines that gave the cloth body and finish. Half-used sacks of dyewood remain, and curious personal items, such as the journals, pencils, desks, and chairs of the foremen.

Waltus Lockett Watkins (1806-84) was born in Kentucky and came to Missouri in 1832 with little money but possessing an expert's knowledge of the steam engine, which was then being developed for industrial use. He patented about 5,000 acres of land in 1839, and ten years later built an ox-driven flour and woolen mill. In May 1861, at the outbreak of the Civil War, his three-and-a-half-story brick steam-driven mill was completed. Forty mill employees, directed by workmen from the East, produced serviceable woolen cloth until about 1886, when cheaper Eastern woolens usurped the market. The building remains much as it was when the workmen left their machines.

Above the mill, on the crest of a tree-shaded hill, is the WATKINS HOUSE, a two-and-a-half-story, red-brick structure of Classic-Revival design, built in 1850. To the rear is a brick summer kitchen with a cavernous fireplace for cooking, near by are a fruit-drying house, and a smokehouse which includes among other accessories a giant brine vat made of a sycamore log. South of the house is the Watkins cemetery, surrounded by a low stone wall.

East of the mill, and near the entrance road, is the brick MOUNT VERNON MISSIONARY BAPTIST CHURCH, built in 1870-71, and the octagonal brick FRANKLIN SCHOOL BUILDING, built about 1852. Both buildings were given to the community by Mr. Watkins, and, long unused, have reverted to his estate. Efforts are being made (1941) to interest the State in purchasing Watkins' farm and maintaining it as a museum.

At 93.2 *m.* is a junction with State 92, a graveled road.

Right here to another graveled road, 5.8 *m.*; R. to a similar road at a schoolhouse, 7.3 *m.*; R. to the entrance of the ROBERT JAMES FARM (*adm. 50¢*),

8.2 m., once the home of Frank and Jesse James. The front part of the T-shaped, white frame and log house dates from 1893; the log ell at the rear was built about 1822 by Jacob Gromer, and purchased by Robert James in 1845. Inside, the floors and ceilings sag, and the doors slant at crazy angles on the warped walls. The door into the kitchen is little more than five feet high, and the fireplace, once bombed in an attack on the James' home, has fallen in. In the front room of the newer portion are photographs and relics of the James family, including a sampler which the mother of the James boys worked as a student in St. Catherine's Academy, Lexington, Kentucky, and the diploma granted Robert James by Georgetown College, Georgetown, Kentucky.

The Reverend Robert James, with his wife, Zerelda, arrived in Clay County shortly before the birth of Frank James, January 10, 1843. Two years later, they purchased this farmstead, where, in the back room, Jesse was born, September 5, 1847. James was pastor of the New Hope Baptist Church for seven years and a member of the first board of trustees of William Jewell College at Liberty. In the spring of 1850, he went with a wagon train to California, where he died that August. Several years later, Mrs. James married Dr. Reuben Samuels. At the outbreak of the Civil War, Frank, then 18, joined the Confederate forces under Price, and later became a member of Quantrill's guerrilla band. In 1863, following Quantrill's raid on Lawrence, Kansas, a squad of Federal soldiers came to the farm, hanged Dr. Samuels to a tree in the orchard, manhandled Mrs. Samuels and her daughter, Susie, and lashed Jesse with the rope lines from a horse until they thought him dead. Mrs. Samuels and Susie cut down Dr. Samuels, resuscitated him, and dressed Jesse's wounds. Soon afterward, Jesse, a boy of 15, mounted his horse and rode away to join his brother among Quantrill's guerrillas (*see Tour 2*).

After the Civil War, Frank and Jesse, like many other young Missourians who had ridden under the black flag during the war, were declared outlaws by the Government. Facts concerning Missouri's outlaw years are meager, but legend of the James boys is rich and widespread. Jesse James became a traditional figure, a Robin Hood of the lawless West who lived for 18 years by the aid of his gun.

According to the James family, Frank and Jesse, soon after their marriages in 1874, moved to Tennessee, where Jesse lived until he returned to St. Joseph in 1881. In the middle of the night of January 26, 1875, a railroad detective, accompanied by six other men, slipped up to the James' farmstead and threw a bomb wrapped in rags through the kitchen window, expecting the explosion to drive Frank and Jesse from the house. The brothers, however, were not there, and someone in the family, thinking the smoking rags on the floor were intended to set the house on fire, kicked the bomb into the fireplace. The explosion killed Jesse's little half-brother Archie Samuels, and tore off Mrs. Samuels's right arm. On April 3, 1882, Jesse, living quietly in St. Joseph, under the name of Howard, was killed by his pretended friend, Bob Ford, who received the major portion of the $10,000 reward offered by railroad companies (*see St. Joseph*). His body was brought to the farmstead and buried near the house. In 1902, it was removed to Mount Olivet Cemetery at Kearney.

After Jesse's death, Frank surrendered to Governor T. T. Crittenden. Tried and acquitted of all charges, he returned to the family farm, where he lived until his death in 1915. The farmhouse is now occupied by his widow and his son, Robert J. James, who bears the name of Jesse's father, the Baptist minister who crossed the river to break the prairie and preach Christianity to a turbulent frontier.

During June of 1880, some harvesters, finding a spring in the little valley of Fishing River, observed that it had a mineral taste. A Negro who had long suffered from scrofula overheard their conversation and later began drinking the water. Soon he was cured. The news spread throughout the countryside and other inhabitants came to the spring, finding relief there from rheumatism and a wide variety of ailments. The spring from which they drank is known today as Old Siloam Spring; the field, ringed about with timbered bluffs, has become Missouri's principal spa, EXCELSIOR SPRINGS, 95 *m.* (801 alt., 4,864 pop.).

Within a few months after the discovery of the spring's curative powers, Reverend V. B. Flack, a Missouri City minister, advised the owner of the land, A. W. Wyman, to lay out a town. The site was surveyed September 1, 1880, and a mild boom began the following spring. Other springs were developed; Saratoga, the Relief, and the Empire. In 1887 the Chicago, Milwaukee & St. Paul Railroad opened its line between Chicago and Kansas City via Excelsior Springs, and this encouraged the organization of the Excelsior Springs Company, which spent more than half a million dollars in developing the town as a health and recreation center. Growth has been steady. Beginning in September 1935, the city obtained through the Public Works Administration a series of loans and grants, totaling, in 1939, $870,700, with which to purchase and develop the water resources of the community. Today (1941) the waters are dispensed from a central plant under the supervision of the Mineral Water System, a division of the city government. Four general types of water are piped into the plant; saline, calcium, sodium bicarbonate, and ferro-manganese. The ferro-manganese springs in Excelsior Springs are said to be the only two of that type in the United States. At Excelsior Springs are held each year the Midwest Bridge Tournament, in May; an invitational golf tournament, in May or June; and the popular "Mulesta," an elaborate fair, in September.

SILOAM PARK, near the center of town, is a well-developed recreational area on Fishing River. HALL OF WATERS (*open 6:30 a.m.-9 p.m.*), in Siloam Park, completed in 1938, is a modern three-story building of stone and concrete, with an 85-foot tower of structural glass. The recessed main entrance has monumental bronze doors bordered by bas-reliefs in a Mayan motif, and elaborate bronze grilles. The interior is ornamented by variegated tiles inlaid on composition walls. In the east wings are baths (*open 8-5 daily*), massage parlors, and hydrotherapy departments. On the lowest level of the building is a bottling plant, which ships waters from the springs to all parts of the United States. The Hall of Springs, a southern extension of the building, is a large glass-enclosed lounge where the mineral waters are sold from a glorified "soda fountain." Beneath this room is the MINERAL POOL (*open 1:30-9:30 p.m.; swimming, 35¢*). Offices of the city and of the Chamber of Commerce are in other parts of the building. MAURER LAKE PARK (*open in summer*), on the southern edge of town, is a shaded 50-acre tract equipped for recreational purposes (*swimming, boating, fishing, riding, camping; nominal charge*).

Left from Excelsior Springs on State 10, a black-topped road, to a junction with an asphalt road, 0.8 *m.;* right here to the 225-acre EXCELSIOR SPRINGS GOLF

CLUB, 1.6 *m.*, a member of the Trans-Mississippi and Western Golf Association. The 18-hole course is one of the best in the Middle West. A visitor's card (*$1 a day, $5 a week*) entitles the holder to all privileges, including the use of the clubhouse, which is built around a log cabin erected in 1835.

At 105 *m.* is the Liberty Cutoff, an unmarked concrete highway.

Left here to LIBERTY, 2.6 *m.* (850 alt., 3,598 pop.), the seat of Clay County. The town is on a gentle slope rising to the north, with the courthouse and the business district at its approximate center. At the foot of the slope, and flowing out onto the prairie, are railroad yards, produce houses, and grain elevators. East, west, and on the hilltop are residential sections, where aged elms shade modern cottages and nineteenth-century houses.

On January 2, 1822—less than two years after the first permanent settlers entered the region—Clay County was organized with a population of about 1,200. Liberty was platted soon after, and the first sale of lots was held July 4, 1822. The new town boomed. Colonel Sheebael Allen's Landing on the Missouri River a few miles to the south was the main port for northwest Missouri during the period 1829-41, and Liberty was the outlet for much of the trade to the northwest Missouri area, and to the Far West. Southern settlers had introduced slavery into the county, and as hemp, tobacco, and the overland trade proved increasingly profitable, an aristocracy of planters and merchants, intensely pro-slavery, developed.

Like other Missourians who engaged in the overland commerce, Clay County residents, long covetous of Mexican territory to the Southwest, greeted with delight the announcement of war with Mexico. On May 30, 1846, Liberty held a public "war meeting" to raise a company of mounted volunteers. By June 6 the roll was filled, and the group departed for the regimental assembly point at Fort Leavenworth, where a Clay County man, Alexander W. Doniphan, was elected colonel (*see Tour 2*). Oregon and California provided further outlets for Clay County energies.

Later, when friction with the abolitionists of Kansas developed, young Clay Countians enthusiastically joined in the conflict. The outbreak of the Civil War, however, was received with mixed feelings. A public meeting held in Liberty, April 22, 1861, advocated secession; another meeting on the 23rd pleaded for maintenance of the Union. The older and more sober residents prepared for the conflict with foreboding, and the Liberty Home Guard was organized. On September 16, 1861, Lieutenant Colonel John Scott, commanding a Federal force of 500 men, was ambushed near Blue Mills, some 4 miles southeast of Liberty, by 700 State Guards commanded by Colonel J. P. Saunders. The Federal loss was about 17 dead and 80 wounded, to the State Guard's loss of 5 killed and 18 wounded.

Other battles and skirmishes occurred in Clay County during the war, but none proved as dangerous to public welfare as the rising swarm of guerrillas. A public meeting attended by 1,500 Clay County residents at Liberty on July 20, 1864, condemned the guerrillas as "ravenous monsters of society," who were "fighting against the government and . . . their peaceable and loyal neighbors." The following spring, Dr. Reuben Samuels and family (Jesse and Frank James' stepfather, mother, and other relatives) were among those banished from the county for "treason and notoriously disloyal practices."

In 1866 the Clay County Savings Association in Liberty (*see below*) was robbed in broad daylight, the crime being generally attributed to the James boys and their associates. The incident was perhaps the closing act of violence in Liberty's turbulent period of growth. Peace brought a new security, with the frontier gone and the old trails superseded by the railroads. Liberty slipped easily into a mellowed old age; lacking industries, it has divided its interests among farm trade, courthouse politics, and the activities of William Jewell College. The recent development of the highway system has placed the community within a network of bustling traffic. In 1872 the "First Monday" community sales were inaugurated in Liberty. On this monthly occasion, cattle, grain, household furnishings—anything anybody wants to sell—are brought to town for the auction or for "trading off beforehand." Colonel George W. Neat, the first auctioneer, used to boast: "I've sold mo' stuff than any man livin' . . . niggers, land, goods, hemp, whiskey, steamboats, an' a few coffins."

On February 27, 1849, the State legislature chartered WILLIAM JEWELL COLLEGE, a co-educational institution named for Dr. William Jewell (1789-1852) of Columbia, Missouri, who gave the Missouri Baptist General Association $10,000 in land as a nucleus for the development of the school. The college was opened to students January 1, 1850. The two- and three-story red-brick buildings of the college, of modified Georgian and Classic-Revival design, overlook the town from a 100-acre campus on "Old Hill," at East Franklin and North Jewell Streets. The average enrollment is 500. WILLIAM JEWELL HALL, one of the most important Classic-Revival buildings surviving in the State, is a three-story structure of red brick with white trim. Rococo cast-iron window lintels, and the three square-brick Doric columns of the recessed center portico, are interesting features. This building, designed by J. O. Sawyer, Cincinnati architect, was begun in the fall of 1850 and entirely completed in 1858 (a portion of the structure had been completed as early as 1853). Between 1861 and 1868, the college was virtually suspended. When Federal troops retreating from the Blue Mill disaster entered Liberty September 17, 1861, they converted the second and third floors of this building into a hospital, and, it is said, used the first floor as a stable for their horses. The following August, Federal troops again occupied the building and the college grounds for several weeks. The structure now contains recitation and lecture rooms and houses the music department. The CARNEGIE LIBRARY (*open 7:45 a.m.-6 p. m. daily except Sat. afternoons, Tues. and Thurs. evenings 7-9:45 p.m.*), on the college campus, is housed in a two-story, red-brick building with a low, silvered dome. It contains the Charles Haddon Spurgeon collection of 7,000 volumes of Elizabethan and Puritan literature; the Ted Malone collection of modern poetry; and the Louis Mertins collections of holographs of modern American authors. The library also houses the archives of the Missouri Baptist Historical Society, an important depository of early manuscripts and imprints.

In MOUNT MEMORIAL CEMETERY, north of and adjoining the college campus, is the broken tombstone of James McFarland (1820-58), a circus performer, whom a hotel proprietor in Liberty stabbed to death to prevent his forcing his way into the room of his estranged wife. The stone is succinctly inscribed "Died in Liberty, Mo., May 27, 1858. For loving not wisely but too well." The OLD POST OFFICE (*private*) rear of the present post office building on Main St., one-half block south of the square, is a one-story structure of hewn logs with saddle-notched corners. It was built in the early 1830's and served as the second post office building in Liberty. A redwood tree at the southeast corner of the two-story, red-brick MADISON MILLER HOUSE (*private*), at 124 N. Gallatin St., is said to have grown from a seedling which Miller brought from California in 1851. Miller's home, a rambling Classic-Revival structure with a modern porch, was built in 1840. North of the Miller home is the BISHOP HOUSE (*private*), northwest corner of Gallatin and Mississippi Sts. It was built by Dr. Ware S. May before 1840—the first brick house in Liberty. It is a one-story structure of red brick set in Flemish bond, with a center cross-paneled door. The windows, with nine panes of glass in the upper sash and six in the lower, are original. The MAJOR ALVAN LIGHTBURNE HOUSE (*open upon application*), 307 N. Water St., is an imposing Classic-Revival two-and-an-attic-story structure now occupied by the Sigma Nu chapter of William Jewell College. Major Lightburne came to Liberty from Kentucky in 1832, established a hemp factory, speculated in land, and became one of the wealthiest men in the community. Although the interior of the house has been considerably altered, the exterior is original except for the removal of the front portico.

The CLAY COUNTY SAVINGS ASSOCIATION BANK BUILDING (*open*), northeast corner of Water and Franklin Sts., is a two-story, red-brick structure with stone trim, dating from the 1850's, and now housing a clothing shop. Early on the morning of February 14, 1866, according to Buel's *The Border Outlaws,* some 12 men entered Liberty by different routes and met in the square. Nine patrolled the front of the bank while two "presented pistols" at the heads of Mr. Bird, the cashier, and his son, and forced them to hand over some $72,000 in specie and currency. As the bandits rode off, Bird shouted to George Wymore, a 12-year-old student on his way to school, that the bank had been robbed. When the boy took up the cry, he was promptly shot. A posse attempted to follow the bandits but lost their trail; the loot was never recovered. Clay County residents believed that Cole Younger and the James Boys were implicated in the robbery.

The SITE OF THE OLD CLAY COUNTY JAIL (*open*), 210 N. Main St., is occupied by a two-and-an-attic-story frame house, now owned by the Reorganized Church of Jesus Christ of Latter Day Saints (*see Tour 2, Independence*). The southwest portion of the basement floor is formed of large, rough-hewn flagstones which, together with a portion of a wall, are said to be part of the original one-story stone jail. This jail, built in 1833 and occupied as a jail until about 1853, survived until replaced by the present house in 1900. On December 1, 1838, the Mormon leaders, Prophet Joseph Smith, his brother Hiram Smith, Lyman Wight, Alexander McRae, Caleb Baldwin, and Sidney Rigdon, were committed to this prison. Wild rumors were spread of poisoning attempts, gruesome punishments, lynching threats, and attempted escapes. The prisoners denounced loudly such townspeople as came within shouting distance; Joseph Smith had revelation after revelation. Of the prisoners, Rigdon was paroled; the other five remained in the Liberty jail until April 15, 1839, when they were transferred to Daviess County for further trial.

South from Liberty on Leonard Street to a junction with By-Pass US 71, 1 *m.*, a marked concrete highway; L. here, crossing the Missouri River bluffs, to an unmarked dirt road, 3.5 *m.*; R. to the SITE OF THE UNITED STATES ARSENAL (L), 3.8 *m.*, on the S. P. Boggess & Sons farm. Only scattered ruins remain of the fortifications, the quarters for the men, and the storage rooms for guns and ammunition. In the center of the enclosure was a powder house with a single door, and near by was a deep cistern. The arsenal was established here in 1836, and was occupied as such until about 1869. The land reverted to farm use in the 1880's, and the last of the brick buildings was razed soon after 1900.

On the afternoon of December 4, 1855, a volunteer force of about 100 men, mostly Clay Countians, surprised the arsenal, placed under arrest Major Luther Leonard, the commanding officer, and his small staff, and removed three cannon, harness, rifles, pistols, revolvers, and other military supplies. The Clay County group had been raised under the command of Major Ebenezer Price to aid pro-slavery Kansans capture the Free State town of Lawrence, which was then in rebellion against territorial authorities. The "Wakarusa War," as the struggle was called, soon ended; the Clay Countians returned home, and eventually the arsenal recovered all but $400 worth of its stolen supplies. The second capture of the arsenal on April 20, 1861, was more serious. Early in the morning, while Major Nathaniel Grant was at breakfast, 200 Clay and Jackson County secessionists, commanded by Colonel Henry L. Routt, surrounded the arsenal and demanded its surrender. With a staff of only two men, defense was impossible, and the garrison was held prisoner for about a week while all the stores were removed. Most of the arms and ammunition were hauled in wagons to Liberty and distributed to the "minute men" of Clay and surrounding counties. This was the first overt act by citizens of Missouri against the Federal Government at the outbreak of the Civil War.

At 107.3 *m.,* is a junction with By-Pass US 71, a concrete paved road.

Right here 0.2 *m.* to a junction with an unmarked graveled road. L. 3.9 *m.* to a second graveled road; R. 1.1 *m.* over a road which becomes dirt (*impassable in wet weather*) to another dirt road; R. again 0.5 *m.* to MULTNOMAH (*private*). Built 1853-54, the square, two-story, red-brick structure is crowned by a low, glass-enclosed "Belvedere," and has a long, one-story ell at the rear. The monumental proportions of the house are given added interest by a two-story portico with four round, plastered-brick Ionic columns arranged in pairs. A small, cast-iron balcony—not attached to the columns—is at the second-floor doorway. The windows have cast-iron lintels. The main portion of the house contains two halls measuring 20 by 40 feet each, and 8 rooms, 18 by 20 feet each.

Multnomah (Ind., running water) was the country home of Major John Dougherty (1791-1860), a native of Kentucky who came to Missouri in 1808 and almost immediately became an employee of the St. Louis Missouri Fur Company, working as trader and trapper in the Far West. After a few years, he was made United States Indian sub-agent, and about 1827 he became agent of the Upper Missouri tribes. Dougherty and a half-breed Indian wagered as to which had the most endurance. According to legend, they set out one morning on foot, armed only with knives, covered some 40 miles, and killed 23 elk. They returned to their starting point the same day. "The Indian never recovered from the tremendous effort, but Major Dougherty suffered only temporary inconvenience." About 1837 Dougherty resigned as agent, and moved to this Clay County farm. From about 1839 until 1855 he was associated with Colonel Robert and William Campbell of St. Louis (*see St. Louis*) as United States sutler and freighter. Dougherty is generally credited with having been a vital force in arranging the Platte Purchase (1836), which added six full counties and portions of others to northwest Missouri.

In a park near his home, the major kept a herd of buffalo, which increased to 23 before they were sold in St. Louis in the 1850's. Southeast of the house is a redwood tree grown from one of the seedlings which Madison Miller brought from California in 1851 (*see above*).

The Dougherty heirs sold the estate about 1881. In recent years, the stately old house has been occupied by tenant families. Unrepaired and unpainted, it is rapidly falling into ruin.

At 111.9 *m.* are junctions with State 10, a concrete paved road (L), and an unmarked graveled road (R).

1. Left on State 10 0.5 *m.* to a black-topped road; R. here 0.1 *m.* to BROAD-ACRES FARM (*open by arrangement*), the estate of J. A. Bruening, which has specialized in the breeding of Clydesdale horses since its development about 1930. The modern two-and-an-attic-story white frame "Colonial" house, set on a landscaped lawn, can be seen for several miles.

2. Right on the unmarked graveled road 2.6 *m.* to a graveled road; L. here 0.7 *m.* to BIG SHOAL BAPTIST CHURCH, a one-story, red-brick structure with double entrance doors. The church was organized May 21, 1823, by the Elder William T. Thorp, pioneer frontier minister. The present building was constructed in 1851. Beginning in 1827 and continuing for more than 80 years, the second Sunday in May (the date of the Annual May Meeting) was known as "Bonnet Sunday." On this day the ladies of the congregation mixed piety with vanity in the display of their new spring bonnets. Services are no longer held in the church and it is rapidly falling into ruin.

The SHELLCREST FARM (*open*), 114 *m.* (L), specializes in the breeding of fine Percheron horses, Holstein cattle, and Duroc hogs.

At 121.5 *m.* is a junction with US 71 (*see Tour 10*) south of which US 69 crosses the KANSAS LINE, 124 *m.*, on the Fairfax Bridge over the Missouri River to Kansas City, Kansas.

Tour 11

Junction US 61—Jackson—Dexter—Cardwell—(Paragould, Ark.); State 25.
Junction US 61 to Arkansas Line, 210 *m.*

Roadbed concrete or blacktop paved.
Route paralleled by St. Louis-San Francisco Ry. between junction with US 61 and St. Mary's, and between Dutchtown and Cardwell.
Hotels in larger towns.

North of Jackson, State 25 winds among abrupt hills and narrow valleys, where French Creole farmers more than two centuries ago introduced the agricultural methods of medieval France. Between Jackson and Dexter, the highway enters upon wide valleys and a succession of low ridges; at Dexter, it shoots over a last ridge and drops dramatically to the Mississippi bottoms, where the cottonfields of Arkansas meet those of Missouri.

Approximately one mile south of CRYSTAL CITY, 0 *m.* (*see Tour 13*), State 25 branches southeast from US 61 (*see Tour 7*), and follows a course removed from, but parallel to, the Mississippi River. In Ste. Genevieve County, it crosses low limestone hills and carefully tilled valleys, where cattle and small grains are raised, and where neat white farm buildings accent a scene of quiet beauty.

At 4.5 *m.* is a junction with a graveled road.

Left here, passing through the white gates of the W. O. Shock farm (R), 0.6 *m.*, to SELMA HALL (*private*). The house, patterned after North Italian Renaissance country houses, was designed by George I. Barnett, English-trained St. Louis architect, for Ferdinand Kennett, Mississippi River steamboat operator. Probably the finest ante bellum home in Missouri, it was built in 1854 at a cost of $125,000, and popularly called "Kennett's Castle." Its gray limestone walls and square, four-story tower crown a succession of terraces which, to the east, overhang the Mississippi River and, to the west, overlook landscaped grounds which include a formal garden. The house was gutted by fire in March 1939, but has been restored by the firm of Nagel & Dunn to approximately its original appearance.

At the crest of a hill, a forest opening (R) reveals the FOURCHE A DUCLOS (Fr., Duclos' Fork) Valley, 18.7 *m.*, and the hillside village of BLOOMSDALE, 20 *m.* (500 alt., 210 pop.). Known in the 1830's as La Fourche à Duclos, the settlement was rechristened in 1874. Tall-spired ST. PHILOMENA CHURCH (R), with buff-stone walls and stark Romanesque lines similar to other Roman Catholic churches of Ste. Genevieve County, introduces the old French District of Ste. Genevieve, of which the Bloomsdale region is a northern sector.

Within the old district, contemporary life has eaten at the fabric of the earlier, more leisured culture; but working on the hillside farms, in the lime quarries, and in the stores and gasoline stations, are men and women with mellow French names, many of whom speak a curious Creole French and preserve fragments of Creole custom and tradition.

At 27 *m.* is a junction with the graveled Zell Road.

Right here to ZELL, 1 *m.* (615 alt., 350 pop.). A cluster of white frame houses and a store with a cellar that extends into a hillside cavern form the secular part of the "German Settlement," as Zell was called before the Civil War. Cruciform ST. JOSEPH'S CHURCH, with its unornamented stone walls, grew under the direction of Father Angelo Hyppolite Gandolfo, pastor of Ste. Genevieve, who laid the cornerstone in 1845. Recessed entrance doors and a steeple (added in 1918) relieve the gaunt simplicity of the nave. A wrought-iron cross in front of the church commemorates the mission conducted here by the Redemptorist Fathers in October 1868. Not so old as the church, but of the same enduring structure, are the PARISH SCHOOL AND NUN'S RESIDENCE, and the square, two-story PRIEST'S HOUSE. Marking the sunken graves in the CEMETERY are wrought-iron crosses and gray tombstones of Gothic and Baroque designs, with faded inscriptions in German.

At 32 *m.* is a junction with a black-topped road.

1. Left here 1 *m.* to STE. GENEVIEVE (401 alt., 2,787 pop.) (*see Ste. Genevieve*).

2. R. to the MISSISSIPPI LIME COMPANY PLANT (*open 8-4 workdays*), 0.3 *m.* (L); the PEERLESS WHITE LIME COMPANY PLANT (*open 8-4 workdays*), 1.4 *m.* (L); and the BLUFF CITY LIME AND STONE COMPANY PLANT (*open 8-4 workdays*), 2.8 *m.* (L), each factory a succession of lime-dusted buildings with irregular rooflines broken by crusher tipples and kilns. Back of the plants are the quarries—great tunnels bored into the side of a 75-foot limestone bluff. The deposit is Spergen limestone, and tests approximately 98.6 per cent calcium carbonate. The life of the supply here is estimated at considerably more than 100 years. The stone is removed from the mines in great chunks, called "rock," which are first burned in vertical kilns at a temperature of 2,000°, to drive out the carbon dioxide, leaving calcium oxide (quicklime), and then powdered for use in the building industry, in agriculture, and in chemistry.

Southward, the highway curves sharply from the uplands and dips into the wide, fertile bottoms bordering the Mississippi River. Here, about three miles below the present town of Ste. Genevieve, on what was once the river's bank, is the SITE OF OLD STE. GENEVIEVE (*see Ste. Genevieve*).

On the crest of the bluffs (R), 36 *m.,* is the SITE OF NOUVELLE BOURBON, established in 1793 by Baron de Carondelet, Governor of

Louisiana, for a group of French royalist refugees whose settlement at Gallipolis, Ohio, had failed. Pierre de Hault De Lassus de Luzière, friend of Carondelet and member of the landed aristocracy of Flanders, who had served on the Council of Louis XVI before the Revolution, was placed in command of an area extending west from Nouvelle Bourbon to Mine La Motte and the Murphy settlement (later Farmington). He was authorized to exercise a limited civil and military jurisdiction and to issue permits to settlers. When Moses Austin visited Nouvelle Bourbon in 1797, he found it to consist of about 20 houses and to include among its residents Jean René Guiho, lord of Legand and a native of Nantes, Jacques de Mun, and other members of the exiled French aristocracy. The village, however, was too near Ste. Genevieve to prosper and gradually was absorbed by the larger settlement. The last remaining house was destroyed about 1920.

At 38.5 *m.* is a junction with the Ozora Road, a marked graveled highway.

Right here to the SALT SPRINGS (L), 0.2 *m.*, around which developed Missouri's first white settlement. French settlers of Kaskaskia, across the river, manufactured salt on the site as early as 1700. This important frontier commodity was produced by the simple process of boiling the saline water until nothing but the salt remained. In 1807, the salt works had 46 kettles, holding about 25 gallons each, which yielded 15,000 bushels of salt annually. The industry was continued until well into the nineteenth century, supplying a valuable item of export.

The vigorous Romanesque lines of the SACRED HEART CHURCH (L), 5.4 *m.*, a buff-stone building completed in 1925, dominate the village of OZORA (540 alt., 554 pop.), a farming community isolated from the main highways by steep hills and winding valleys.

At 5.7 *m.* is a junction with an unmarked graveled road. R. 1.6 *m.* to CAMP WRATHER (R), used by the University of Chicago for summer field courses in geology. The camp was begun in 1915 by the late Dr. Stuart Weller, who discovered an unusual range of rock formations in the surrounding area. The OZORA MARBLE QUARRIES, ahead and L., were discovered by Dr. Weller. The upper quarry is of rose-veined, the lower of golden-veined marble.

ST. MARY'S, 41 *m.* (389 alt., 605 pop.), platted about 1847 by Miles A. Gilbert, a New England merchant, is a milling and farming center.

Between St. Mary's and Brewer, the highway leaves the river and crosses a rolling upland. The land surface is pitted at times with sinkholes; springs are numerous.

At 54 *m.* is a junction with State 51, a concrete highway.

Right here to PERRYVILLE, 0.6 *m.* (570 alt., 3,907 pop.), seat of Perry County. In the midst of the town is the two-and-a-half-story, red-brick courthouse, its square central tower overshadowing the business district. Platted as the county seat in 1822, Perryville became the center of an area that had been settled by Americans since 1801, when Isadore Moore developed a farm near the forks of Cinque Hommes and Saline Creeks. The first merchant in the village was Ferdinand Rozier, former partner of John James Audubon, artist and ornithologist (*see Ste. Genevieve*). On the northeastern corner of the courthouse lawn, the UNION MEMORIAL, a figure of a Union soldier on a pedestal of gray Vermont granite, commemorates the 1,800 Union soldiers from

Perry County who served in the Civil War. Across the northwestern corner of the square, indicated by a red-granite marker, ran the King's Highway, extended by Spanish authority from New Madrid to St. Louis in 1789.

West from the square to County T, 1.1 *m.*, a graveled road; R. to St. MARY'S-OF-THE-BARRENS (*open, inquire at office*), 1.4 *m.* (L), a Roman Catholic seminary. The four-story brick administration building, erected in 1848, contains offices and reception rooms. The CHURCH OF THE ASSUMPTION (R), a stone and stuccoed structure, was begun in 1827 under the direction of the venerable Angelo Oliva, an Italian lay brother, who cut the stone for the building, superintended its erection, and found time also to contribute considerable labor to the churches of St. Louis and Ste. Genevieve. The Church of the Assumption was planned as an exact reproduction of the mother church of the order, the Church of Monte Citorio in Rome. This task proved too great, however, and a scale one-third that of the original was adopted. The dome, rising 45 feet above the floor of the sanctuary, the simple arching and Tuscan details of the interior, and the "grand altar of stone elegantly painted to represent green marble," were much admired by the 41 clergymen who assisted in the consecration, March 9, 1837. The original Tuscan façade was replaced in 1913 by one of Romanesque design. Right of the main altar is the French Chapel, used in early days by families who wished to hear sermons in French. A sundial on the south wall of the church and a carved stone sacrarium dated 1830 are items of interest preserved from the church's beginning. The LIBRARY (*open by appointment*) includes a group of fifteenth- and early sixteenth-century books, an illuminated Flemish Book of Hours, and a thirteenth-century Bible, the latter two in manuscript. The BISHOP EDWARD T. SHEEHAN MEMORIAL MUSEUM (*open by appointment*) houses Oriental art objects, curios, and personal relics of Bishop Sheehan. Southwest of the church, almost hidden by a grove of trees, is the one-room log cabin long known and preserved as BISHOP ROSATI'S SACRISTY, said to have been built for Father Rosati in 1818.

St. Mary's-of-the-Barrens, Missouri's oldest college, and mother house of the Congregation of the Missions (Vincentian Fathers) for the western province of the United States, was established in 1818, through the efforts of Bishop Louis William Du Bourg. In 1815, soon after his appointment as Bishop of Louisiana, Bishop Du Bourg went to Rome to seek assistance in the care of his "truly desolate diocese." A group of priests and brothers, under the charge of Father Felix de Andreis, were sent to St. Louis, and were subsequently invited by the 35 Catholic families of Perry County to establish a seminary at the "Barrens." The offer was accepted, and the buildings were erected on a 640-acre tract of wooded land. During the period 1820-40, students came to the seminary from California, Mexico, and South America. Father de Andreis died in 1820; in 1837, his body was reinterred beneath the pavement of the Chapel of St. Vincent, and the burial place was marked by a marble tablet.

South of the junction with State 51, the highway crosses the Perry County "Barrens," a name brought from the small prairies of southwestern Kentucky. The land has a rolling sweep, with shallow winding valleys, occasional sinkholes, and a general air of rural well-being. Several limestone houses with wide chimneys are sturdy remnants of early settlement.

Fifty feet R. on a farmhouse lane, 56.8 *m.*, are the RUINS OF THE CHEVEAUX SHRINE, erected in 1851. Carved on the stone base and almost obliterated by time are various religious insignia and pious inscriptions in French. The wooden cross is gone.

UNIONTOWN, 65.5 *m.* (577 alt., 235 pop.), is dominated by the tall spire of its Lutheran church.

Left from Uniontown on County A, a graveled road, to ALTENBURG, 9 *m.* (577 alt., 264 pop.), spiritual and economic center of Perry County's Lutheran settlement. Friendly cottages with tile roofs and luxuriant gardens crowd the roadway at informal angles. On a hilltop street are Altenburg's two Lutheran churches, Emanuel and Trinity. In the surrounding hills are trim valley farms producing cattle, sheep, and hogs, as well as grains, hay, fruit, and poultry. Local craftsmen in wood, leather, metal, and clay have until recently satisfied the community's needs.

Perhaps the only settlement in early Missouri created for purely religious reasons, Altenburg occupies a peculiar place in the educational and religious history of the State. In 1839, more than 600 Saxon Lutheran emigrants, under the leadership of Martin Stephan, former pastor of St. John's in Dresden, bought 4,472.66 acres of Perry County land with a communal fund of $9,294.25. Much of the soil was poor and had to be cleared of timber before it could be cultivated. The majority of the settlers were students or professional men unfamiliar with heavy farm work, and the first years were difficult. More discouraging, however, was the expulsion of the community's leader, Martin Stephan, who, accused of voluptuous living and dictatorial conduct, was rowed silently across the Mississippi River and deposited on the Illinois shore, an exile. But the people were "of a will," and modest houses and stores, with half-timbered, neatly plastered walls and red-tile roofs—made in local kilns—slowly replaced the crude log huts.

The FIRST HOME OF CONCORDIA SEMINARY (*apply to pastor of Trinity Lutheran Church*), in the park facing Trinity Lutheran Church, is a square, one-story log building, dedicated December 9, 1839. The college opened with seven male students and offered courses in "Religion, Latin, Greek, Hebrew, German, French, English, Geography, History, Mathematics, Physics, Natural History, Elements of Philosophy, Music, Drawing." Girls were admitted shortly after the opening. In 1849 the college was placed under the supervision of the Evangelical Lutheran Synod of Missouri and moved to St. Louis. The log cabin, mother institution of all the junior colleges and seminaries of the Missouri Synod, was moved to its present site in 1915 and covered by a protective shelter. It is now used as a museum, and contains examples of early furniture, books, pewter, and farming implements.

TRINITY LUTHERAN CHURCH (*open weekdays by appointment*), a limestone structure with slender white steeple and recessed doorway, was built in 1867, replacing an older building now used as a school. The interior has a barrel-vaulted ceiling, long side galleries supported by Doric columns, and a small round pulpit with hood set high in the wall.

OLD APPLETON, 67 *m.* (401 alt., 119 pop.), is a single, irregular street of neatly fenced white frame houses and a cluster of stores. The community assumed the character of a village in the early 1820's, after parties of Roman Catholic families from Kentucky and a group of German immigrants from Baden settled the hillsides and developed farms. The APPLETON MILL, on Apple Creek on the edge of town, has a comparatively new superstructure, but the stone forebay and dam constructed by Alfred McClain in the 1820's are still in use.

On a hill west of Old Appleton approximately 400 Shawnee Indians established a village after the Indian migration from Ohio and Indiana in the period of 1784-97. The Indians constructed their houses in the French manner, setting the logs in the ground perpendicularly and filling the interstices with clay. In Spanish times, a path known as the Shawnee Trace extended from the residence of Don Luis Lorimier (*see Cape Girardeau*) to this "Big Shawnee village" and thence to Ste. Genevieve and St. Louis. The Shawnee war chief at this time was Peter Cornstalk, a fluent orator, son of the celebrated Cornstalk of the Dunmore War. In 1825, the Shawnee sold the land granted them by Spanish authority and moved farther west.

JACKSON, 85 m. (497 alt., 3,113 pop.), seat of Cape Girardeau County, is platted on a broad, low hill. At the crest of the slope is a two-and-a-half-story, gray-stone courthouse, from which radiate the tree-shaded village streets. The hill was selected as the site of the new county seat in February 1814. Platted as a town and named for General Andrew Jackson, the settlement quickly superseded Cape Girardeau (then involved in clearing the land titles of its first settlers) in political and commercial importance. In 1818 Jackson was described as "a considerable village on a hill, with the Kentucky outline of dead trees and huge logs lying on all sides." The population was 300. The following year the town was incorporated, and Tubal E. Strange established there the *Missouri Herald,* one of the first five newspapers in the State.

By 1849 Cape Girardeau had untangled its land titles, and the third branch of the State's bank had been moved there from Jackson. A cholera epidemic struck Jackson the same year, and "before the third week nearly every person able to do so had fled, scarcely enough remaining to care for the sick and bury the dead." During the Civil War, the town suffered from the divided loyalties of its citizens and from frequent occupation by military forces. Following the war, Jackson developed as a trading and milling center for a wide farming area.

Cape Girardeau County, organized October 1, 1812, had its origin as the Spanish District of Cape Girardeau, established in 1794, with Don Luis Lorimier as commandant (*see Cape Girardeau*). Large numbers of American immigrants came into the district prior to the Louisiana Purchase in 1803, and about 1800, many German families came here from North Carolina under the leadership of George Frederick Bollinger. The church they established was the first Protestant church in Missouri. When Missouri became a State in 1821, Cape Girardeau County had a population of 7,852.

The annual Jackson Homecoming, held in early September, began in 1908, when the COLONEL WILLIAM JEFFERS MONUMENT was dedicated, a tall limestone obelisk in the city cemetery, three blocks south of the public square. Colonel Jeffers (1827-1903), who had served in the Mexican War, enlisted in the Missouri cavalry of the Confederate States at the outbreak of the Civil War. The CAPE COUNTY MILLING COMPANY (*open 8-4 workdays*), in the eastern part of Jackson, is representative of a local industry that has been important for more than 50 years. Here, in 1902, an electrical process of bleaching flour was developed by J. N. Alsop. The JULLIETTE GRANGER RESIDENCE (*open by appointment*), 209 W. Main St., is a gray two-and-a-half-story frame structure; its one-story wing was built about 1818 by Joseph Frizzell, early Jackson merchant. The main part of the house dates from the 1830's, and was built by Charles Welling, a native of New Jersey who established himself in Jackson as a merchant in 1831.

At Jackson is a junction with US 61 (*see Tour 7*).

The lowlands between Jackson and Dexter have been reclaimed for agricultural purposes by an extensive drainage system that extends, roughly, from Cape Girardeau to the Arkansas Line. Before the vast network of canals was dug across the low flood plain, the land was all but uninhabited. It is now one of the most fertile areas of the State, producing bumper crops of wheat, barley, oats, and corn.

At 85.6 *m.* is a junction with an unmarked graveled road.

Right here 0.5 *m.* to the W. A. LOWES FARMHOUSE (L). A dirt road continues 0.5 *m.* through the Lowes farm (*inquire at house for directions*) to the BETHEL BAPTIST CHURCH SITE AND CEMETERY, indicated by a marker. Bethel Church, the mother of all Baptist Churches west of the Mississippi River, was organized by the Reverend David Green on July 19, 1806. In the fall of 1812 a hewn-log "meeting house," 30 by 24 feet, was built, with a plank floor, a stone fireplace 4 feet wide opposite the pulpit, and 3 glass-paned windows. The pulpit was "kind of box shaped" and made of planks. The seats were of split logs without backs. The "Rules of Decorum" drawn up by the Church forbade, among other things, whispering, or going from the meeting "without leave." Hunting or trading on Sunday, card playing, attending or giving "frolics and balls," and similar diversions were frowned upon. In June of 1814 the church invited the courts to meet in the building until the Cape Girardeau County courthouse was built. On November 9, 1816, a resolution was passed allowing Sister Hannah Edwards "to wear gold ear rings for the benefit of her eyes." Four years later it was agreed that if "a member is constrained to shout," the church would bear with him.

Bethel Congregation was absorbed by the Jackson Baptist Church about 1867, and the old church was subsequently destroyed.

The DIVERSION CHANNEL, 96 *m.,* is one of the main channels of the Little River Drainage District (*see Tour 6*). Before the huge ditch was dug, the Castor, Blackwater, and Little Rivers, rising in the Ozark foothills, often overflowed their banks. Today, the waters of these streams are diverted by the channel directly into the Mississippi.

DELTA, 101 *m.* (337 alt., 320 pop.), a group of buildings near the base of a timbered upland, is a farming community and shipping point.

South of ADVANCE, 113 *m.* (614 pop.), the route crosses the lowlands of the old Castor River, whose circuitous channel has been straightened by a broad earthen levee and the Diversion Channel. Green fields of corn and wheat are broken by the purple and red of clover pastures. Almost every farmstead has a small orchard and a flock of chickens. A boulder before a farmhouse bears the notice: "Bibles For Sale. Bibles for Christmas."

At 131 *m.* is a junction with County E, a graveled road.

Right here to BLOOMFIELD, 0.4 *m.* (383 alt., 1,208 pop.), seat of Stoddard County and center of a farming, dairying, and poultry region. The business district surrounds a yellow-brick courthouse, erected in 1909 on the public square. Bloomfield is on the site of a Shawnee village whose chief, Wapepillese, fought with a group of braves under General Henry Dodge during the War of 1812. The town was platted in 1835; lumbering and milling developed shortly thereafter, and the Bloomfield Seminary was established. During the Civil War, Bloomfield was made a military post by the United States Government, and was virtually destroyed. For many years after the war, the rivalry between Bloomfield and Dexter was strong. Failing to accomplish the removal of the courthouse, the people of Dexter finally secured, in 1895, the enactment of a law declaring that four terms of circuit court should be held each year in Stoddard County, two at Bloomfield and two at Dexter. But the arrangement proved unsatisfactory, and the law was repealed.

The EVANS POTTERY (*open daily*) (R), 135 m., one of the few surviving potteries of Missouri, was established sometime before 1851 by Thomas Simmemon, a potter from Marietta, Georgia. The original log cabin still houses a part of the works, including the old-fashioned foot-feed, or "kick," potter's wheel. Descendants of the founder operate the pottery.

DEXTER, 137 m. (323 alt., 3,108 pop.), is at a junction with US 60 (*see Tour 6*).

South of Dexter, State 25 drops from a ridge top to the endless flatness of southeastern Missouri, as different from the upland region in its cultural and economic life as in its topography. Scattered over the rich land are Tennessee and Kentucky sawmill "hands," deep-South cotton planters, Ohio corn farmers, and Missouri's largest rural Negro population.

BERNIE, 147 m. (303 alt., 1,160 pop.), is a community of neatly painted brick and frame houses gathered about a small business center and cotton gin.

MALDEN, 155 m. (294 alt., 2,673 pop.), is a cotton-ginning center and a shipping point for large quantities of cotton, melons, and corn. Near here, Howard Moore built a house in 1829; some time later, a store was established. Malden as a town dates from 1877, when it was platted under the direction of Major George B. Clark, construction engineer for the Little River Valley & Arkansas Railroad, and named for Malden, Massachusetts. Malden's location on the railroad—at first a narrow-gauge line, on which cars bobbed up and down as they crossed the cotton rows—gave it a commercial advantage over neighboring villages and made it, for a time, the largest town in the county.

South of Malden, "King Cotton's" dominion meets the horizon with a monotony that is broken only by occasional clumps of trees in a brush-choked swamp. The gray loam becomes black when wet and is so rich that it often appears greasy. There was a time when great quantities of corn and wheat were raised here, but since cotton has usurped the land, grain production has steadily decreased. The coming of cotton and the downhill trek of former sawmill workers from the Ozark region were coincidental. The hillman, first a tenant farmer, then a sharecropper, is now in process of becoming a day laborer, employed only for planting and picking.

CLARKTON, 163 m. (273 alt., 733 pop.), was platted in 1860 and named in honor of Henry E. Clark, one of the contractors of the old Weaverville-Clarkton plank road, sometimes called the "Devil's Washboard." Before the building of the county's first church in 1846, outdoor services were held in Clarkton. The pulpit consisted of "two blackjack poles driven in the dirt floor with a cypress board pinned to their tops." Once, when tallow candles were scarce, "lamps" were made of eggshells, by draining them, filling them with bear's oil or 'coon grease, and inserting twisted cotton wicks.

Writing of HOLCOMB, 169 m. (269 alt., 388 pop.), in 1895, Mrs. Mary Smyth-Davis said that, in 1880, "one could not see over a quarter of a mile in any direction on account of the heavy timber, and deer roamed the woods in the neighborhood even in the daytime." The sawmills soon moved in, however, and today the fertile black land is divided into productive, well-cleared farms. Platted about 1870, the village was named for Louis Holcomb, an early settler. It is a shipping point for cotton, melons, and strawberries.

KENNETT, 182 m. (258 alt., 6,335 pop.), has been the business and legal center of Dunklin County since the first settlers accepted the overnight hospitality of the Indian chief, Chilletecaux, whose village stood near the site. Later, the chief's pole house was bought by Howard Moore, who built one of the first gristmills in the county; when the town was platted in 1846, it was named for him. In 1849, however, the name was changed to Butler and, a few years later, to Kennett, in honor of Dr. Luther M. Kennett, Mayor of St. Louis (1849-52).

Kennett is essentially a cotton town. Cotton is responsible for its new, substantial houses and its encircling belt of bright corrugated-iron gins and dull brick and frame warehouses. Cotton dominates its social and economic life. Banks lend most of their money at planting time (early spring) and collect it during ginning season (late fall). Merchants open charge accounts, payable when crops have been "made." In early spring, the town is tense: landowners must make arrangements for production loans and for their tenants' food supply; tenants and sharecroppers begin drawing rations and other necessities upon the basis of future work. In fall, the highways are lined with trucks and wagons with their sides temporarily heightened, and the streets are crowded with mules, horses, and motor trucks, all pulling loads of cotton to the gin, where they await their turn to drive upon the scales and have the cotton weighed and sucked into the gin's mechanism. If the crop has been good and the price is "right," everybody is momentarily affluent. If conditions are unfavorable, there is only the hope for "next year."

SENATH, 195 m. (250 alt., 1,261 pop.), a typical cotton town, was established by its first postmaster, A. W. Douglass, in 1882, and named for his wife, Mrs. Senath Hale Douglass.

ARBYRD, 202.7 m. (268 alt., 489 pop.), crowds closely about the sprawling, dull-red frame sheds and central building of the area's compress. Every town does not have a compress—there is not cotton enough for that. Instead, areas defined by the vicinity's yearly baled-cotton yield are established, with one compress in each area. In the ARBYRD COMPRESS (open by permission), bales of cotton collected from surrounding farms are compressed under steam to facilitate storage and shipment.

CARDWELL, 206 *m.* (270 alt., 913 pop.), was platted by the Burtig brothers of Paragould, Arkansas, in 1896, and named for Frank Cardwell, cashier of the Bank of Paragould. Important as an early timbering center, it changed in less than a year's time from "the forest home of the bear, deer, coon and turkey . . . to a thriving little railroad town of 150 inhabitants."

West of Cardwell, State 25 crosses a low, swampy area, and ends at the ARKANSAS LINE, 210 *m.,* on a free bridge over the St. Francis River, 35 miles east of Walnut Ridge, Arkansas.

Tour 12

Junction with US 61—Fredericktown—Greenville—Poplar Bluff— (Corning, Ark.) ; US 67.
Junction with US 61 to Arkansas Line, 91 *m.*

Concrete roadbed except for ten miles of black-top north of junction with US 60.
Route paralleled by St. Louis, Iron Mountain & Southern R.R. between junction with County O and Arkansas Line; by St. Louis-San Francisco Ry. between junction with US 60 and junction with State 14.
Hotels principally in larger towns; cabins and camping facilities throughout.

US 67, which north of Fredericktown is coincident with US 61 (*see Tour 7*), crosses in its southern section the eastern fringe of the Ozarks, a region of rocky hills and small, cultivated valleys. South of these are the wedge-shaped lowlands that form the northernmost portion of the Gulf Coastal Plain. Here frequent flooding by the St. Francis and Black Rivers has· deposited a rich alluvial soil that appears in sharp contrast to the rocky lands of the hills. Profligate cutting of forests has curtailed the lumber industry and established an agricultural economy for almost the entire area.

South of the junction with US 61, 0 *m.* (*see Tour 7*), US 67 crosses the wide valley of Saline Creek, and enters FREDERICK-TOWN, 1 *m.* (722 alt., 3,414 pop.), half hidden by old trees and secure from the flood waters of Castor (Fr., beaver) and Saline Creeks. Wooded hills and knobs of igneous rock form an arc to the south. In the town's center is the two-and-a-half-story, red-brick MADISON COUNTY COURTHOUSE, built in the modified Romanesque design of the early 1900's. The business buildings on the square, and the prosperous, well-kept homes indicate a county seat with economic resources somewhat above the average.

In 1800 a group of 13 Creoles erected a number of log houses on a Spanish grant in the bottomland north of Saline Creek, within the present limits of Fredericktown, and called the village St. Michael. They cultivated farms in the valley and occasionally worked Mine la Motte for lead. In 1811-12, the "Year of the Great Shake," the St. Michael area survived the New Madrid earthquake (*see Tour 7*) with little damage, but in June 1814, flood waters of Saline and Castor Creeks almost destroyed the community. In 1818 Madison County was organized, and the following year Fredericktown, established on the south bank of Saline Creek, was made the county seat. Gradually Fredericktown expanded to include the site of St. Michael. The community's growth was slow until the St. Louis, Iron Mountain & Southern Railroad was extended from Pilot Knob into Arkansas in 1872, affording shipping facilities for the timber and mineral industries of the region. The valley farms, many of them specializing in dairying, have given the county a certain stability of income, increased sporadically by the production of local mines. Lead is the chief mineral product, but appreciable amounts of copper, bismuth, zinc, iron, manganese, antimony, arsenic, nickel, tungsten, and cobalt are also mined. Granite and marble outcroppings near Fredericktown afford a supply of stone for local building, but the rock has not been quarried to any great extent on a commercial basis.

ST. MICHAEL'S CATHOLIC CHURCH, two blocks west of the courthouse, is a red-granite structure of modified Romanesque design, erected in 1927. Father Lewis Tucker, in charge of the parish from 1845 to 1880, made plans in 1846 for a new Church of St. Michael to replace the log church dating from about 1800. The Reverend John Rothensteiner, in his *Chronicles of an Old Missouri Parish* (1917), records that "Father Tucker had ordered a marble slab to be placed above the church-door, bearing the inscription of Matthew 21:13: 'My house shall be called a house of prayer.' The sculptor, on opening the Bible at the place indicated, read the entire verse: 'My house shall be called a house of prayer, but you have made it a den of thieves,' and so he chiseled it all in the patient stone. . . ." The unwanted words were filled in with putty, but, as the years passed, the putty became whiter than the surrounding stone so that for nearly a century pious worshippers passed beneath this withering indictment. Since the razing of the building in 1927, the stone has been preserved in the parish school adjoining the present church. In the parish house is a painting, *The Holy Family,* which tradition says was sent to Upper Louisiana by a king of France.

Right from Fredericktown on State 70, a marked graveled road, through the winding valley of the Little St. Francis River, to an unimproved dirt road, 6.3 *m.;* L. 4.4 *m.* to a SILVER MINE, worked for many years for its silver, but known today for its production of tungsten. The occurrence in Missouri of the tungsten-bearing mineral, wolframite, has been known since 1870, but not until

1918 was its economic importance realized. At that time, demands for the metal as a steel alloy caused producers to investigate the known tungsten localities and the amount of wolframite at the old silver mine was found to be sufficient for working. The deposit is a typical fissure vein ranging from 12 to 36 inches in width and dipping southwest at an angle varying from 45 to 60 degrees. The ore is mined through two tunnels and a 200-foot inclined shaft.

South from Fredericktown, US 67 winds across the valleys between ridges of the St. Francois (pronounced "Francis") range of the Ozark Highlands 6 *m.* to the ST. FRANCOIS DIVISION OF THE CLARK NATIONAL FOREST, comprising at present (1941) 40,057 acres. The timber is predominantly oak, pine, and cedar, and the irregular surface of the country is drained by clear, spring-fed streams. In the valley of Twelve Mile Creek are occasional isolated farmhouses, some of pioneer hewn-log construction with stone chimneys. Appearing infrequently are large barns of weathered, unpainted lumber, with bonnet-like gables and wide side roofs covering oak frameworks stuffed with the season's hay.

The highway crosses the southern boundary of the St. Francois Forest at 13.1 *m.*, and winds through COLDWATER, 22.7 *m.* (502 alt., 78 pop.), a trading community in a district of sparse settlement.

At 29.4 *m.* is a junction with County K.

Right here to CAMP LEWALLEN, 2.1 *m.*, a 270-acre recreational and training camp for the Southeast Missouri Council, Boy Scouts of America. The woodland borders the Little St. Francis River.

At 31.4 *m.* is a junction with State 34, a hard-surfaced road.

Right here to State 101, 4.1 *m.*, a graveled road; R. to the main entrance of SAM A. BAKER STATE PARK (*camp grounds, cabins; fishing, bathing, boating, riding*), 3.2 *m.*, a recreational area of 4,718 acres between the Big and Little St. Francis Rivers. The park was named for the late Sam A. Baker, governor of Missouri 1924-28, who was a native of Wayne County, in which the park is located. The entrance gates, cabins, dining lodge, and other buildings are stone structures of rustic type. The entrance drive follows for almost a mile the meandering course of the St. Francis River, a stream known to the Indians by the Choctaw word Cholohollay, meaning "smoky water." Big Creek and Mudlick Creek, excellent fishing streams for bass, swirl through narrow granite shut-ins beneath precipitous cliffs.

US 67 enters the WAPPAPELLO DIVISION OF THE CLARK NATIONAL FOREST, 123,866 acres of woodland, where grape, red plum, persimmon, cherry, blackberry, whortleberry, crab apple, and innumerable other wild fruits grow in abundance.

GREENVILLE, 39.9 *m.* (381 alt., 572 pop.), Wayne County seat, sprawls on the banks of the St. Francis River with careless irregularity, its nondescript frame buildings reflecting the prosperity of the community during the lumbering boom near the close of the last century. The town, which dates from about 1819, might be expected to proceed indifferently about its affairs, for a dam is being constructed at Wappapello, 20 miles southeast on the St. Francis River, and the lake created by the dam will inundate the town, so that its citizens are now making plans for a new, thoroughly modern Greenville on near-by higher land.

Left on an unmarked dirt road from Greenville to a similar road, 1.7 *m.*; R. to the BLUE SPRING (*cabins, meals*), 8.4 *m.* (R), a giant Ozark spring colored a curiously vivid blue even on a cloudy winter day. From the base of a high bluff, the spring pours approximately 31,400,000 gallons of water daily into the St. Francis River, a popular fishing stream (*equipment for float trips available*).

The highway crosses the BLACK RIVER at 56 *m.*, and at 56.5 *m.* forms a junction with an unmarked graveled road.

Right here to KEENER CAVE AND SPRING (*adm. to park and beach, 25¢; adm. to cave, 10¢ and 25¢*), 3.6 *m.*, in a tree-covered bluff above the Black River. The cave, electrically lighted, is explored by boat. A submarine light, 40 feet under water, casts weird shadows on the walls and on the stalactite-covered ceiling. The water in the cavern is approximately 75 feet deep, but marks indicate that the depth was once greater. Suspended on the cavern wall is an INDIAN DUG-OUT CANOE, found in the cavern waters in 1937. The boat, 39 feet long, 18 inches wide, and 9½ inches deep, is carved from a large log, and marks of the flint axes used in hollowing and shaping it are plainly discernible. The canoe had been under water possibly 300 years.

Southward, US 67 traverses the southern part of the Wappapello Forest. The sharp ridges and narrow valleys of the Black River country are succeeded by a rolling, almost prairie upland. POPLAR BLUFF, 68.9 *m.* (436 alt., 11,163 pop.), is at a junction with US 60 (*see Tour 6*).

US 67 descends from the upland ridge country and enters the flat lowlands of southeastern Missouri. Between here and the Arkansas Line, only occasional patches of cypress, maple, and gum trees remain of the dense forest that once covered the region. Most of the timber has been cut within the past 50 years; the swamps have been drained and the land is increasingly used for agricultural purposes. The best lands lie along CANE CREEK, 74.5 *m.*, where Solomon Kittrell, probably the first settler in this neighborhood, is said to have made his home in 1819.

NEELYVILLE, 86 *m.* (307 alt., 280 pop.), founded as a timber shipping point on the Missouri Pacific Railroad in the early 1870's, is now a center of cotton, truck, and rice production. Timber resources in the county were rapidly depleted during the last quarter of the nineteenth century, and construction of drainage ditches was begun about 1908 to open the area to agriculture.

In the vicinity of Neelyville, several hundred prehistoric earthen mounds have yielded well-preserved artifacts, and Missouri archeologists have declared that in this corner of the State was one of the most densely populated settlements of the mound builders. Bones and pottery have been unearthed in large quantities, though much investigation remains to be done before the survey of the area is complete.

US 67 crosses the ARKANSAS LINE, 92 *m.*, 50 miles northeast of Walnut Ridge, Arkansas.

Tour 13

Junction US 61—Festus—De Soto—Potosi—Centerville—Doniphan —(Pocahontas, Ark.) ; State 21A and State 21.
Junction US 61 to Arkansas State Line, 182 *m.*

Graveled road, except concrete-paved stretches between De Soto and Glover, between N. and S. junctions with US 60, and between N. and S. junctions with State 14.
Route paralleled roughly by St. Louis, Iron Mountain & Southern R.R. between Hematite and Glover; by Missouri Southern R.R. between Ellington and junction with US 60; and by St. Louis-San Francisco Ry. between Hunter and Grandin.
Hotels principally in larger towns; numerous tourist cabins and camp sites, especially on southern part of route.

Beginning on the southeastern fringe of the Ozark Highlands, the route follows a twisting southward course through some of the State's oldest settlements and past some of America's oldest lead mines; skirting the highest peaks of the Ozarks, it ends in a recently developed recreational area. Almost a century before Missouri became a State, Frenchmen worked the lead deposits in what is now the Old Mines-Potosi area. In these villages the language and customs of the Old World have lingered through many generations. Between Potosi and Arcadia, families still dig for barite and lead as their forefathers did. Farther south, Federal and State agencies have established great forests and park areas in a region stripped of its timber prior to 1910. Here are valleys developed in dairy, poultry, fruit, and grain farms. The steep-wooded slopes are stocked with wild turkeys and other upland game birds. The waters of the Black and Current Rivers flow cold and clear, and are known throughout the country for their fighting bass and trout.

At the western limits of CRYSTAL CITY, 0 *m.* (420 alt., 3,417 pop.), State 21A branches southwest from US 61 (*see Tour •7*). FESTUS, 0.1 *m.* (395 alt., 4,620 pop.), is the commercial and residential neighbor of industrial Crystal City. The story goes that when Festus was platted in 1878 it was called Tanglefoot—either for the gait of homeward-bound roisterers, or for the town's principal product, which caused it—but that as the village grew in size and dignity, a more respectable name was demanded. The village fathers consequently opened a Bible at random, intending to adopt the first proper name they saw. "Then Agrippa said unto Festus, I would also hear the man myself," is the passage upon which the searching finger came to rest. Why "Festus" was favored over "Agrippa" not even the oldest citizen can now recall.

533

HEMATITE, 6.3 *m.* (434 alt., 213 pop.), scattered along the side of a low hill, was named for a small iron mine formerly operated in the vicinity Dairying is the principal occupation of the area, although small grains, cotton, and tobacco were produced in appreciable amounts in earlier days, and the community was of importance as a shipping point for flour, lumber, ties, and building stone. William Null and a group of other American immigrants are said to have settled here on Spanish grants about 1800, but the town was not platted until 1861.

VICTORIA, 9.2 *m.* (468 alt., 162 pop.), was founded in 1859, two years after the St. Louis & Iron Mountain Railroad was extended through this region. George Hammond is said to have arrived prior to 1776, but a whitewashed stone marker, in the eastern part of the village, commemorates Thomas L. Bevis as the first settler (1802). Bevis' wife, Prudence, was known as "Queen Bevers, the Witch." For 28 years after her husband's death in 1826, most of the misfortunes that befell the neighborhood were attributed to her. Among the many tales of her powers was the claim of Aaron Cook that Queen Bevers turned him into a horse one night and rode him to a ball. What seems particularly to have annoyed Cook is that she left him tied to a plum bush. Henry H. Jones eventually freed the community of her malice. Enraged by a spell she had cast over his gun—it would no longer shoot deer—he made an image of the witch and blasted it with a shot from the jinxed weapon. The old woman soon developed a sore leg, and the gun once more brought home the venison. This established Jones as a witch charmer, and he soon enjoyed a good business counteracting Queen Bever's black magic.

DE SOTO, 12.7 *m.* (509 alt., 5,121 pop.), advertised as the "Fountain City" because of its many artesian wells, lies partly along the valley of Joachim Creek and partly across several abrupt limestone hills. Stone quarried from the hills has been used to pave the streets and build many of the houses, the rather pretentious designs of which indicate that De Soto's most rapid growth took place in the 1880's. Isaac van Metre built the first house on the site of De Soto in 1803, but the town was not founded until 1857, when the St. Louis & Iron Mountain Railroad was completed through Jefferson County. De Soto soon became a shipping point for lead mined in the vicinity. In later years, railroad shops, and shoe, hat, and stave factories were established. Eight or more artesian wells, which now provide the city's water supply, yield waters of such purity that they were selected for use at the Louisiana Purchase Exposition at St. Louis in 1904.

The two-story white frame THOMAS C. FLETCHER HOUSE, 610 N. Main St., has been altered until the main portion has little in common with its original columned façade. Fletcher (1827-99), born at Herculaneum, was the State's first Missouri-born (and its first Republican) governor (1864-68).

South of De Soto the route follows State 21, passing, at 22.4 *m.* (R), the main entrance to WASHINGTON STATE PARK (*tourist accommodations*), an improved area of 694 acres on the southern bank of the Big River. Almost all species of flora and fauna common to the Ozarks are found here. The log and stone concession building was erected by the Civilian Conservation Corps. At convenient intervals along the graveled park roads and footpaths are shelter houses, trailside lookouts, and rustic bridges. A hillside fault (*follow arrows to marker*) reveals strata of geological interest. A cavern, reached by a marked footpath up the steep side of a bluff overlooking the Big River, contains a variety of rock formations. A group of petroglyphs (*follow arrows*) are excellent examples of early Indian art.

Between the park and Caledonia, State 21 traverses one of the oldest settled areas of the Midwest, a section little changed since the first Frenchman began to work the shallow lead deposits with pick and shovel. These implements are still used for mining in the local "diggin's," small, shallow holes pockmarking the rust-red hillsides.

Houses with low-pitched roofs and whitewashed *galéries,* the rosered walls of St. Joachim's Church, and several gasoline stations strung along the highway identify OLD MINES, 31.7 *m.* (821 alt., 416 pop.), a Creole lead and tiff mining community all but surrounded by shallow diggings. Here for nearly 150 years have lived people of French descent, united by nationality, religion, and their own social and economic practices, and almost completely isolated from the main currents of American life. Perhaps 90 per cent of them speak a French dialect, combined with certain Spanish, American, and a few African words. Strange nicknames for individuals, common during Colonial days here as well as in France, are in general use. For instance, during the Civil War Joseph Boyer was called "a diamond in the rough." Since then, he, his children, and their children have been called "Ghiam" (from *ghimant,* Can.-Fr. for diamond). Records of the period mention "Joseph Boyer dit (called) Ghiam." So persistent is the use of nicknames that often the original family name is hardly remembered.

The modern Creole works his garden plot desultorily, for his chief labor is digging ore. With the aid of his wife and children, he digs a shallow surface pit and from it scrapes enough tiff to support a meager existence. When the ore is exhausted, or when the pit grows too deep to be worked by this primitive method, the spot is abandoned for a new one. Often the miner gathers enough ore during the first half of the week to permit him to hunt or fish or doze upon his *galérie* until the following Monday. French ballads and folk tales of the Middle Ages are popular, especially on holidays. On New Year's Eve, the young people stroll about the village, stopping at the homes of friends and singing "La Guignolée." The host usually serves cookies and wine. If he has nothing to give, his daughter must dance with the visitors.

Old Mines, which was accumulated rather than founded, is the center of an area of lead mines that have been worked for more than 200 years. Although the early history of the industry is confused, it seems likely that the "old mines" on a branch of the Meramec west of the present village were discovered and worked by miners and Negro slaves under the direction of Philippe François Renault. Sent to develop the Missouri mines by the Company of Indies about 1720, Renault remained in the area until around 1744. He established lead mining as Missouri's first industry, and probably attracted to the State its first permanent settlers. With the discovery of richer lead deposits five miles south, about 1773, Renault's old mines were temporarily abandoned. According to Moses Austin, who wrote a history of lead mining in Missouri in 1804, fifteen French families settled near the old mines in February 1802, and formed a village. Their descendants inhabit the community today.

St. Joachim's Church (R) achieves beauty through simplicity and good proportions. Cruciform in shape, with Palladian details, its design is related to that of the Roman Catholic churches built during the same period (about 1830) at Perryville and Ste. Genevieve. Inside are straight-backed box pews, a decorative white altar railing, and a copper baptismal font that has been in use for more than 100 years. Above the altar hangs an early painting of the Virgin Mary, the work of an unknown artist. Some of the silver altar vessels were brought from Canada during the first part of the last century. On special occasions the priest wears vestments of rich brocade and cloth-of-gold brought from France for use in the log church erected on this site in 1802. Scattered over the hillside in St. Joachim's Cemetery, south of the church, are many wrought-iron crosses of early French origin. The impressive large stone "box" monuments of Marie Louisa Lamarque (1799-1868), who was "eminently munificent toward the sustainment and propagation of Religion," and of her husband, Étienne Lamarque (1785-1851), a native of France, are enclosed by an ornate cast-iron fence.

Sprawled over the banks of a creek which winds through its center, POTOSI, 38.4 m. (905 alt., 2,017 pop.), seat of Washington County and formerly a lead-mining town, is the center of the largest barite district in the United States. Contrasted with its neon-lighted business section, where Saturday crowds pack the narrow streets, are the quiet residential sections of weathered frame and brick houses, many dating from pre-Civil War boom years.

The lead deposits at Potosi were discovered about 1773 by François Azor, nicknamed Breton for his birthplace in Brittany, France. Breton (pronounced and often spelled "Burton") had been an employee of Renault (see above). As news of his strike spread, some of the older mines in the vicinity were gradually abandoned. Recurrent Indian raids and the expense of hauling the smeltered ore to Ste. Genevieve, however, restricted the development of Mine a Breton until near the close of the century. When Moses Austin visited these mines in 1797, he found that they were worked by residents of Ste. Genevieve and New Bourbon, chiefly during the period after harvest in August until just before Christmas. During the remainder of the year, "but few hands are employed."

This leisurely industry was completely disrupted by the bustling Austin, who in 1797 received a grant of one league square which contained most of Mine à Breton. He built the first reverberatory furnace west of the Alleghenies, a shot tower, a plant for making sheet lead, a sawmill, a flour mill, a store, and an imposing home for his family. The embryonic Creole settlement soon grew into a healthy village, which defended itself against Indian attacks in 1799 and in 1804. By this latter date, 14 American and 12 French families, totaling more than 200 people, were living here. Austin estimated that Mine à Breton produced $21,933 worth of lead in 1804, compared with a total of $40,100 for all the mines of Missouri. Between 1798 and 1816, some 4,680 tons of lead were smelted in the Mine à Breton area alone.

When Washington County was organized in 1813, Austin donated 40 acres and John Rice Jones 10 acres for a county seat, immediately north of Mine à Breton village, across Mine à Breton creek. A town was laid out and named for the Mexican silver mining city of San Luis Potosi. In 1826 the two adjoining villages were consolidated under the name of Potosi.

Lead mining declined in Washington County in the latter part of the nineteenth century, partly because of the exhaustion of the deposits and the diminishing value of lead, but especially because of the discovery of uses for barite. Previously barite, or "tiff," was regarded as gangue, and it was not until after the Civil War that it was found to be of worth as an inert pigment and filler. As new uses of barite were discovered, old lead diggings were reopened and new ones developed. The United States, although sometimes surpassed by Germany in annual production of crude barite, is the world's largest consumer of the mineral. From 50 to 60 per cent of the national production comes from Missouri, and of this, 94 per cent is mined in Washington County. The greatest tonnage is produced by scooping ore from pits with pick and shovel, as was done two centuries ago, although steam shovels are increasingly used. Mechanization has proceeded slowly. The average pit miner, living rent-free on company land, at present rarely earns as much as $20 a week—and that only with the aid of his entire family.

In the Presbyterian cemetery, one block northwest of the courthouse, is the GRAVE OF MOSES AUSTIN, marked by a plain box-like monument. Austin was born in Durham, Connecticut, October 4, 1761, and part of his boyhood was spent at Middletown, Connecticut, where there were important lead and smelting operations during the Revolutionary War. Later he became a merchant in Philadelphia and Richmond. In 1789 he acquired lead mines in southwestern Virginia. In 1796-97 Austin explored the mines of Missouri, and after obtaining the Mine à Breton grant he became Missouri's first industrialist, and a leading citizen of the Territory. The depression following the Napoleonic Wars, and the collapse of the Bank of St. Louis in 1818, bankrupted him. The following year he conceived the plan of forming a colony in Texas, and discussed the idea at Durham Hall, his Potosi home, with his son Stephen Fuller Austin (1793-1836), who later, as "the Father of Texas," carried out their plans. In 1820 Moses Austin rode by horseback to San Antonio, where he was granted permission to settle 300 American colonists in Texas. The hardships of the return journey destroyed his health and he died near Potosi, at the home of his son-in-law, James Bryan, June 10, 1821. In April 1938, Texas attempted to remove his remains to the State cemetery in Austin, where his son, Stephen F. Austin, is buried, but Potosi refused permission. The VALLÉ-PERRY HOUSE (*open by arrangement*), on Jefferson St. (R), is a two-story frame structure facing Mine à Breton Creek. Its one-and-a-half-story log wing, built by Basile Vallé about 1795, is probably the oldest building in Potosi.

At 48.4 *m.* is a junction with County M, a graveled road.

Left here through IRONDALE, 6.9 *m.* (811 alt., 446 pop.), once a mining town, to the IRONDALE BOY SCOUT CAMP (L), 7.1 *m.*, one of the largest and best-equipped scout camps in the United States. Founded in 1914 by the St. Louis Council, Boy Scouts of America, the camp consists of 210 acres, on which are 165 buildings, including a large amphitheatre and auditorium. A log cabin built in 1866 houses a wild life collection.

CALEDONIA, 51.7 *m.* (924 alt., 139 pop.), a picture-book community on the banks of Goose Creek, was established in 1819 by Alexander Craighead. Its two most pretentious homes are the JANE THOMPSON HOUSE, a two-story brick building with a Classic-Revival doorway, erected in 1848, and the MARTIN RUGGLES HOUSE, also a two-story brick dwelling with Classic-Revival details, built in 1852 to "surpass the grandeur" of the Thompson house. The PRESBYTERIAN CHURCH (L), on a hilltop across Goose Creek, is a red-brick structure with white trim and green shutters, which shows both Gothic and Classic-Revival influence in its arched windows and entrance and in the frame cupola breaking the roofline. The church was built about 1872. The DOCTOR JAMES HUGH RELFE HOUSE, east of the church, is a long, two-story, white frame building with massive stone and brick chimneys. Relfe (1791-1863), a Virginian, was a Representative in the State legislature 1835-44, served in the Black Hawk War, and was United States marshal for the District of Missouri in 1841. He represented his district in Congress from 1843 to 1847.

Left from Caledonia on State 32, a graveled road, to a PRESBYTERIAN CEMETERY (L), 0.8 *m.*, the site of the first Presbyterian service held west of the Mississippi River. The service was a sunrise prayer meeting conducted by a group of Scotch Presbyterians from North Carolina on December 1, 1807.

South of Caledonia the highway winds through Bellevue Valley, named for the vista of surrounding hills, distant forests, and large granite boulders. BUFORD MOUNTAIN, second highest peak in Missouri (1,760 feet), extends southward for several miles on the left.

GRANITEVILLE, 62.2 *m.* (1,139 alt., 600 pop.), scattered across the summit of Granite Hill, is a company-owned town belonging to the A. J. Sheahan Granite Company. Most of the buildings, including the modern commissary, office building, church, and school, are of red granite quarried in the neighborhood. Pneumatic drills and derricks are used to cut and lift the stone from the open pit quarries, which cover approximately 1,200 acres. The quarries were opened in 1868 by B. G. Brown, governor of Missouri 1870-72, and Thomas Allen, founder of the St. Louis & Iron Mountain Railroad Company. On the northern side of Graniteville, reached by a short footpath, are the ELEPHANT ROCKS, great masses of stone that have been carved by the erosive forces of wind and water into gigantic pieces of crude statuary. Balanced Rock is a tremendous boulder so nicely adjusted on a pivot the width of a hand that it may be easily tilted.

At 63.4 *m.* is a junction with County W, a concrete highway.

Left here, crossing Arcadia Valley, to IRON MOUNTAIN, 3.9 *m.* (1,077 alt., 350 pop.), a former mining community. For almost a century, the town roared with activity; but when the richer deposits thinned out, and the price of iron dropped, the mines were no longer profitable. Today (1941) the all-but-empty little village consists principally of a hotel built about 1860, a commissary, a church, a school, an office building, and a handful of miners' shacks scattered about an abandoned mill.

Northeast of the town is IRON MOUNTAIN, a loaf-life formation once thought to be composed of solid iron and proclaimed the "largest and richest mass of iron upon the globe." The hill, which rises 200 feet above the valley floor, has a base area of 500 acres. The deposits were first developed by the Missouri Iron Company, organized in 1836, which invested $5,000,000 in the exploitation of Iron Mountain and Pilot Knob (*see below*). The company failed, and in 1845 was succeeded by the American Iron Company. In 1851-54, a plank road 12 feet wide was built between Iron Mountain and Ste. Genevieve, a distance of 42 miles. The ore was carried by oxcart over this road until the St. Louis & Iron Mountain Railroad was completed to Pilot Knob in May of 1858. Between 1848 and 1860, the company employed 1,200 men at an average wage of from 90¢ to $1.10 for each 12-hour day. All houses and stores were owned by the company, and employees, paid in script, were forced to trade at the commissary.

The mines were open pits formed by drilling, blasting, and scooping out the ore. The iron was reduced by placing crude blocks of it on a foundation of logs in alternate layers of charcoal, and exposing it for a month to as hot a fire as the ore could endure without melting. This process expelled impurities and permitted the ore to be easily broken into small pieces which, when mixed with limestone and charcoal, were ready for the blast furnaces. Five million tons of ore, 50 to 60 per cent of which was iron, were mined before the deposits began to give out. By 1884 activity was greatly reduced. When post-World War prices cracked, making iron mining unprofitable even at low wages, the company stopped operations, and the miners either drifted to other localities or remained to farm the surrounding Arcadia Valley.

At 4.9 *m.* on County W is a junction with an unmarked graveled road. Right here 1.2 *m.* to IRON MOUNTAIN LAKE (*fishing, boating, camping; nominal charge*), artificially created to provide a reservoir for Iron Mountain and the mines.

Between the junction and Ironton, the highway continues through winding Arcadia Valley, a wide, fertile plain outlined by Iron and Shephard Mountains and Pilot Knob. The knobs in this part of the State are for the most part igneous intrusions stripped of their sedimentary cover by centuries of erosion.

PILOT KNOB, 66.2 *m.* (951 alt., 426 pop.), at the foot of the cone-shaped hill for which it was named, is another mining town forced by circumstances to turn to agriculture. The hill, PILOT KNOB (L), is approximately 600 feet high. Like Iron Mountain, it was once thought to be composed of solid iron, and was worked for half a century before the deposits were discovered to be comparatively shallow surface layers. Albert D Richardson, correspondent of the New York *Tribune,* visited the area just prior to the Civil War and described both the knob and the mines:

> The sides of the mountains are covered with oak, hickory and ash saplings. The summit is a mass of enormous boulders 50 feet high, and upheaved into every conceivable position. Some stand erect, sharply defined pillars. Two, a few feet apart, form a gigantic natural gateway. Another huge slab leaning against a solid wall constitutes a picturesque cave. . . . Miners were digging horizontally into the mountain, drilling, blasting, and prying off great fragments of rock which fell crashing over a little precipice. In the pit below, some were breaking up these fragments with sledge hammers; others loading them into cars which conveyed the ore by an inclined-plane railway to furnaces at the base.

South of Pilot Knob, an iron marker (L) indicates the RUINS OF FORT DAVIDSON, 66.5 *m.,* its battle-scarred earthworks overgrown with trees and underbrush, yet plainly visible from the highway. The fort was erected by Federal troops during the Civil War to protect the Pilot Knob and Iron Mountain mineral deposits. During September of 1864, Confederate General Sterling Price entered southeast Missouri with a force of between 12,000 and 20,000 men, intending to capture St. Louis. Only General Thomas Ewing and a Federal force of approximately 1,000 men at Fort Davidson lay between the Confederates and their destination. On September 27, Price directed a bloody assault on Fort Davidson with two of his three divisions, but was repulsed with a loss of about 1,500 men and retired, planning to repeat the attack at daybreak. That night Ewing, hopelessly outnumbered, spiked his cannon and slipped away, leaving two soldiers to blow up the powder magazine. The Confederates did not detect the escape until an explosion shook the hillside, showering earth and rocks for hundreds of yards. Price wasted three precious days in futile pursuit, permitting St. Louis to be so strongly reinforced that he dared not attack.

IRONTON, 68.5 *m.* (919 alt., 1,083 pop.), sprawled across the base of Shephard Mountain, is more concerned with its tourist trade and its activities as the seat of Iron County than with mining. The town was founded when the county was organized in 1857. On August 8, 1861, shortly after receiving his commission as brigadier general, U. S. Grant, at the head of the 21st Illinois, his old regiment, arrived at Ironton to assume command of the district. Four days later he wrote to his sister Mary that he had about 3,000 volunteer troops, nearly all infantry, stationed at Ironton. Soon afterwards he was relieved by General B. M. Prentiss and placed in command of the District of Southeast Missouri, which included southern Illinois. Grant moved his headquarters to Cape Girardeau, then to Cairo, Illinois. The IRON COUNTY COURTHOUSE, center of town, is a two-story brick structure with Greek-Revival cornices, entrance, and interior trim.

Erected in 1858, the building was used as a refuge for Union soldiers retreating before General Price after the attack on Fort Davidson. The walls of the building still bear the scars of Confederate gun fire.

Right from the Ironton courthouse on an unmarked graveled road to a similar road, 1.5 *m.;* right on this road to SHEPHARD MOUNTAIN LAKE (*cabins, boating, fishing, swimming*), 1.9 *m.,* at the base of Shephard Mountain.

At 69.2 *m.* is a junction with State 70, a concrete highway.

Left here, cutting across Stouts Creek Valley past the four-story, red-granite building of the MISSOURI BAPTIST OLD FOLKS HOME (R), 1 *m.,* and the RIFLE RANGE (R), 2 *m.,* used by soldiers from Jefferson Barracks, to LAKE KILLARNEY, 2.8 *m.* (R), an artificial lake impounding the waters of Stouts Creek. Fishing is especially good for smallmouthed and largemouthed bass, crappie, goggle-eye, and perch (*cabins, golf, tennis, riding, boating, and swimming*).

ARCADIA, 69.5 *m.* (926 alt., 346 pop.), platted in 1849, is a resort village surrounded by swift mountain streams and quiet woodlands. The METHODIST ASSEMBLY GROUNDS (*tennis, golf, swimming*) on Arcadia Heights (L), are used by the Southeastern Missouri Conference of the Methodist Church during their annual three-week session, which usually begins near the end of June. The ARCADIA WEAVERS (L), on the highway, were organized in 1936 as a project of the Works Progress Administration to revive the art of weaving. Many of the women employed continue work during "off hours" and offer their handicraft—coverlets, blankets, linens, carpets, and other articles—for sale. The wool used is carded, spun, dyed, and woven by hand. The URSULINE ACADEMY (L), southern part of town, is a Roman Catholic school for girls. Established as a high school by the Reverend J. C. Berryman of the Methodist Episcopal Church South in 1849, it was reorganized in 1870 as the Arcadia Seminary. In 1871 it was transferred to the Ursuline Sisters.

Between Arcadia and Glover, the highway climbs into the highest peaks of the Ozarks. First ascending HOGAN RANGE, it rides the summit along the so-called "Sky Ride of the Ozarks," and at 73.1 *m.* crosses TIP-TOP (1,500 alt.), the drainage divide between Arcadia Valley on the north and Big Creek on the south. From here, the view of Arcadia Valley, surrounded by 7 mountains, is unbroken for 25 miles. Following a mountain ledge bordered by a granite guardwall, the highway curves down into Big Creek Valley through ROYAL GORGE, a canyon-like shut-in with perpendicular walls rising more than 100 feet above the roadbed.

HOGAN, 77.6 *m.* (889 alt., 89 pop.), lies at the foot of Taum Sauk Mountain, the highest peak in Missouri. Guides are available for trips up the mountain.

Right from Hogan on a marked dirt and rock road to the foot of TAUM SAUK MOUNTAIN, 6 *m.* At the end of the road is a footpath that leads through entangling underbrush and across large boulders to the DEVIL'S TOLL GATE, 10 *m.,* otherwise known as "Fat Man's Misery," a narrow passage between two granite boulders in a canyon 700 feet below the peak of Taum

Sauk. The path continues up the mountain. Halfway to the summit is a view of MINA SAUK FALLS, whose waters cascade from a spring over granite ledges, and drop nearly 200 feet. The path winds through almost impenetrable underbrush to the summit of the mountain, 12 m. (1,772 alt.), a plateau approximately a mile and a half long. The mountain and falls received their names from an Indian legend: When the maiden, Mina Sauk, daughter of Taum Sauk, Chief of the Piankishaws, married a warrior of the Osage tribe, the Piankishaw medicine men declared her bewitched. To release her from the spell, they ordered her husband thrown from the mountain to the canyon below.

Mina Sauk, watching the execution of the order, broke from the women holding her, and leaped after her beloved. When the girl's body crashed on the rocks, there was a flash of lightning, followed by a deafening roar, and a stream of clear water poured down the mountain over the bodies of the lovers. Thus was created magnificent Mina Sauk Falls, and the scars of Taum Sauk Mountain. West of Taum Sauk and connected with it by a saddle is WILD-CAT MOUNTAIN (1,757 alt.).

The isolation of this rugged country has been the most important factor in shaping the lives of its inhabitants. Families are large, and the traditions, dialect, folklore, superstitions, and customs of their Anglo-Saxon forebears have lingered persistently. A mild climate, an abundance of fish and game, patches of fertile valleys along springfed streams, and small, portable sawmills sustained the local population, until the recent development of recreation centers in the area (*see Tour 14*).

At LESTERVILLE, 88.7 m. (163 pop.), a trading center in a heavily wooded district, float trips down Black River may be arranged at nominal cost. The floats are small, flat-bottomed boats guided by poles rather than by paddles or oars. Black River, a clear, bright stream that belies its name, is noted for largemouthed and smallmouthed bass, goggle-eye, and jack salmon (walleyed pike).

Downstream from Lesterville on Black River to the B. K. LEACH TURKEY RANCH (*open*), 5 m., where thousands of turkeys are raised each year and sent to State game preserves. Leach, a resident of Kirkwood, has produced a blue-headed wild turkey, graceful and sturdy, in an attempt to propagate birds similar to the native stock. At 7 m. on Black River, in a grotto at the base of a high bluff (R), is WARNER BAY SPRING (*cabins, camping, fishing*), which discharges a maximum of 10,000,000 gallons of water daily into a pool covered with deer moss and water lilies.

The WILLIAM RAYFIELD LOG CABIN (*open*), 92.6 m., is a one-story, vine-covered structure with immense stone chimneys at each end. Erected by Rayfield about 1850, the cabin is an excellent example of pioneer architecture. It is built of unusually large logs, carefully squared and neatly fitted together. A single roof extends over two large rooms separated by a "dog trot," or open space, used as a porch.

Southwestward from the cabin, the highway winds through dense forests of pine and oak, crossing the BLACK RIVER at 93.1 m. and the southeastern tip of the MERAMEC DIVISION OF THE CLARK NATIONAL FOREST at 94.7 m. (*see Tour 14*). Near CENTERVILLE, 97.7 m. (537 pop.), the seat of Reynolds County, are a number of springs and good fishing streams (*cabins, boats, and fishing equipment*).

Left from Centerville on an unmarked graveled road to REED'S SPRING, 0.5 *m.*, where approximately 9,700,000 gallons of water gush from the hillside each day. The water is impounded in a large pool covered with watercress and lilies. The flume and waterwheel of a gristmill that until recently stood beside the dam were part of the Missouri exhibit at the New York World's Fair in 1939.

At ELLINGTON, 116.6 *m.* (670 alt., 849 pop.), a shipping point for fruit, dairy, and poultry, is a junction with State 106, a graveled road.

Right here to another graveled road, 4.5 *m.;* L. to DEER RUN STATE PARK, 5.9 *m.*, a forest and game preserve of 8,160 acres. Within the park, at STILLHOUSE HOLLOW (*follow arrows*), are numerous pens where cottontail deer and wild turkeys are raised for distribution throughout the State.

South of Ellington is a wild rugged land of scattered settlements, most of which were made by Tennessee and Kentucky hillmen during the days of the great lumber industry. After Missouri became a State, the yellow-pine forests that covered this area were sold to large timber interests, often for as little as $1.25 an acre. The companies moved into the area just prior to and shortly after the Civil War, and by 1900 they had all but denuded the Ozarks. Most of their employees were left stranded. Some drifted into the southeastern lowlands and became tenants on cotton farms. Others—whose sagging rail fences and weathered, dilapidated cabins the highway occasionally passes—attempted to farm the hillsides.

At 133.5 *m.* is a junction with US 60, with which State 21 is united for 12 miles (*see Tour 6*). HUNTER, 149.5 *m.* (735 alt., 208 pop.), a one-time lumber camp and sawmill town, has been reduced to a meager rural trade.

In 1887 the Missouri Lumber and Mining Company founded the town of GRANDIN, 154 *m.* (876 alt., 294 pop.), and erected what was said to be the largest lumber mill in the State. After the St. Louis-San Francisco Railway was built through here in 1889, the company enlarged its plant, and the town, with a population of 3,000, prospered for a couple of decades. In 1910 the timber supply began to give out and the company closed its mills. The former employees then built their own mill and continued the industry, but on an ever-decreasing scale.

DONIPHAN, 170 *m.* (344 alt., 1,604 pop.), on the north bank of Current River, is the seat of Ripley County. Settled about 1847, Doniphan was named for Colonel Alexander Doniphan of Mexican War fame (*see Tour 2*). It was made the county seat in 1859, when Ripley County, organized in 1833, was reduced to its present size. In DONIPHAN CITY PARK (*picnicking, fishing, camping*), on the western side of town, a marker on the bluff above Current River indicates the SITE OF THE LEMUEL KITTRELL HOUSE. Kittrell, believed to have been the first settler in the county, built his home here in 1819, and erected a grist and carding mill on the river. Federal troops burned Doniphan during the war, but the mill was saved. Since it was the only gristmill within many miles after the war, it was in constant demand. In 1895 it was abandoned; only a part of the dam remains.

At Doniphan arrangements may be made for boats, guides, and equipment for float trips on Current River, one of the coldest, swiftest, and best fishing streams in the State. The usual procedure is to travel by automobile to Tunnel Bluff (*see below*), board boats there, and float downstream to Doniphan. Agents of the float guides return the automobiles to Doniphan.

Right from Doniphan on a graveled road to TUNNEL BLUFF, 28 *m.,* a natural tunnel through a rock bluff approximately 125 feet above Current River. Southward on the river from Tunnel Bluff are rugged banks and the mouths of tight little valleys. A boat often "strikes blue water," the hillman's expression for entering the quiet, still pools in which fishing is good. At 2 *m.* is the confluence of Barren Creek and Current River. LEWIS CAVE (*adm. 50¢; guides*), 3.5 *m.,* an extensive cavern in the side of a bluff, is improved with electric lights and other facilities. Within the damp recesses of the cave mushrooms are cultivated. Here also are many stalagmites and stalacites, and a small stream inhabited by blind fish. MABREY SPRING, 5 *m.,* forms a millrace that once supplied power for a gristmill. Fish here are abundant, as they are at near-by SILVER SHOAL, which hillmen say is the meeting place for "all the fish in the river." DARK BAY, formed by the confluence of Calven and Buffalo Creeks with Current River, is one of the still, deep pools the natives call "blue water." At BOYLE'S SLOUGH, half-way between Tunnel Bluff and Doniphan, floatmen usually stop for lunch near a spring of excellent drinking water. Downstream, the current is swifter. Boats skim rapidly over PIG'S ANKLE SHOALS. HARGUS SHOALS skirt the 3 sides of DEER LEAP, which towers more than 100 feet above the river. Just north of Doniphan, 28 *m.,* the river makes a quick turn that sends boats rapidly to the dock.

State 21 ends at the ARKANSAS LINE, 182 *m.,* 35 miles north of Walnut Ridge, Arkansas.

Tour 14

Junction with US 66—Cuba—Salem—Eminence—Winona—Junction with US 63; State 19.
Junction with US 66 to junction with US 63, 140 *m.*

Road black-topped except for short graveled stretches; two lanes. The route is paralleled by the St. Louis-San Francisco (Frisco) Ry. between Cuba and Salem, and by the Southwestern and Southern R.R. between Eminence and Winona.
All types of accommodations available; hotels chiefly in larger towns.

Winding southward through Ozark mountain passes into the Big Springs Country, the route penetrates a rugged, half-wild area divided into almost equal parts by the Current River. There is a rough, strong beauty in the mountains and cliffs and narrow valleys. There is much color, too, in the folk life of the section. Along the byways of the route, protected by the rocky hills, are folkways that elsewhere have passed from the American scene.

In CUBA, 0 *m.* (1,035 alt., 1,033 pop.), State 19 branches south from US 66 (*see Tour 5*). The MERAMEC RIVER, crossed at 6.2 *m.* on a steel and concrete bridge, is one of the State's best fishing streams (*see Tour 7*).

At 7 *m.* is a junction with a marked graveled road.

Left on this road, which rides a winding, wooded ridge, to the WILDWOOD CLUB (*overnight accommodations, boats, guides*), 0.5 *m.*, a fishing resort, with a rambling, V-shaped stucco lodge set against the side of a hill. The hill descends to the Meramec River, where there is a boat landing.

At 7.8 *m.* is a junction with State 8, a graveled road.

Right here to the entrance gate of INDIAN SPRING LODGE (*cabin and hotel accommodations*), 2.7 *m.* (R), on a 375-acre resort on the Meramec River. In the manner common to the section, the lodge faces the river from a hillside. It is a rambling, well-planned, stone and frame building, three stories in height. On the grounds are two springs, each with a flow of 75 gallons a minute, tennis courts, a bathing beach, and fishing, boating, and riding facilities.

The highway descends a long winding hill to STEELVILLE, 8.9 *m.* (755 alt., 1,013 pop.), a tree-shaded farm and resort center, and the seat of Crawford County. Although the first settler here was William Britton, who built a log house and a small gristmill on Yadkin Creek in 1833, the village was named for James Steel, who arrived two years later. The house of James Harrison at the mouth of the Little Piney (now in Phelps County) served as the seat of government from the organization of Crawford County in 1829 until it was superseded by Steelville in 1836. As if Steel's name were prophetic, the section immediately entered an era of iron mining and related activities. Iron ore of high grade was discovered in the banks of the region's numerous streams, and capital was invested. Mines were opened north, east, and west of town, and the miners came to Steelville each Saturday night to spend their pay. The era came to an abrupt end, however, when more profitable mines in Minnesota and Michigan were developed, and the majority of Steelville's miners and ironworkers turned to the land for subsistence. Supplementing the town's farm income is a small tourist trade—mostly fishermen.

Left from Steelville on State 8, a black-topped road, to an unmarked graveled road, 1.9 *m.;* R., then L. at the first fork, and R. at the second fork, over as rough a road as lies hidden in the Ozarks, to the CHERRY VALLEY MINE, 4 *m.,* said to be the oldest operating mine in the county. Operations were begun in 1870 by the Sligo Iron and Furnace Company. Of the open-pit type, the mine appears at first to be simply a great excavation in the rusty red hillside. Once down in the pit, however, the shafts are visible. These descend 45 or 50 feet, then extend at right angles into the hills. Sulphur has been discovered here as well as iron, and in 1938 the mine was being worked for both minerals.

At 11.9 *m.* is a junction with a marked graveled road.

Left here winding through isolated valleys and over hills wooded with oak, pawpaw, hickory, cedar, and a sprinkling of shortleaf pine, to the WESTOVER FISHERIES (*fishing from 7 a.m. to 5 p.m., small fee; overnight cabins*), 7 *m.,* a privately operated hatchery for the breeding of rainbow trout. The fish are reared in an old millrace, fed by a spring that issues approximately 8,400,000 gallons of water daily from a basin half-hidden beneath the crags of a hillside. The millrace is divided into several sections, in each of which fish are grouped according to age. Near the head of the improvised stream is a spawning house, a frame structure on a raised concrete foundation. The spawning stock is carried into the house in October. Later, their eggs are placed on the wire mesh bottoms of thin, flat trays. The trays are fitted into racks about six inches above a small stream flowing through the basement. As the fish are hatched, they drop into the stream. Approximately four months elapse between the time the spawning stock is transferred to the house and the day when the baby fish are removed to the first section of the millrace. The young are fed cereal and meat two to five times daily. The waters of the stream are so clear that the fish—approximately 600,000 of them—are plainly visible. Adjoining the fisheries and flowing parallel with the millrace is a shallow creek stocked with trout. It is in this stream that sportsmen are allowed to fish. The hatchery ships trout to hotels in Middle Western cities.

The route enters a deeply rolling land planted in vineyards and orchards. In season, fruit and grapes are offered for sale at small brush-arbor stands along the road. From this point southward, the farms are smaller and more scattered, the houses less substantial.

OZARK TOPS, 26 *m.,* is the official name of a roadside turnout (L), which offers an excellent view of wooded mountains and blue-green valleys. The section, especially south of the turnout, was first settled in the 1820's, when iron was discovered in the area. Development was not extensive, however, until 1835, when the energetic Lewis Dent, legislator from Dent County, arrived and began promoting mining activities and bringing in new families. After the so-called mining boom, lumber interests moved in, taking their toll of natural resources. Money flowed from the region, and several millionaires were made; but, somehow, the natives—those Scotch, Irish, Welsh, and English families who drifted in on the tide of pre-Civil War immigration—never seemed able to get their hands on any of it. Today, agriculture is the region's principal means of livelihood.

At 28.9 *m.* is a junction with a marked graveled road.

Left here to SLIGO, 1 *m.* (70 pop.), a former iron-mining town. A large frame commissary, a hotel, and several dwellings and commercial shops are empty and forlorn. Sadly overlooking the ruins is a rambling frame house, set against a hillside, once reserved for company executives. Between 1881 and 1921, seven blast furnaces operated here, and 1,500 iron molders and 200 "mule skinners" worked, spent their money, and raised their families. In 1921, the furnaces were closed. All save a few of the workers moved away. Those who persistently cling to the village have turned to farming, supplementing their income by hunting and fishing.

A stone gateway, 31.1 *m.* (L), gives entrance to INDIAN TRAIL STATE PARK, a forest and game preserve of 13,256 densely timbered acres. The land is broken by deep valleys and crossed by Crooked and Fish Water Creeks. Near the center is a 2,500-acre game sanctuary enclosed by a high wire fence (*open by permission*). Here, Virginia white-tailed deer and wild turkeys are propagated. Another propagation unit breeds beaver, otherwise extinct in Missouri. Tree culture and timber improvement is under the direction of a resident forester. Approximately 60 miles of graveled roads make all sections of the park accessible, but there are no overnight accommodations. The park was purchased by the State Game and Fish Commission in 1924.

The Meramec River, a continuously winding stream, is again crossed at 31.9 *m.* on a steel and concrete bridge.

SALEM, 44.6 *m.* (1,182 alt., 3,151 pop.), locally referred to as the gateway to the Big Springs Country, was founded in 1851, by Joseph Milsaps. It is the seat of Dent County, organized in February of 1851, and named in honor of Lewis Dent, a Tennessean, who settled there in 1835 and served as its first representative in the Missouri general assembly. While Salem did not suffer as greatly from the Civil War as many other Missouri communities, fires destroyed at least half the town. Following the war, with the coming of the St. Louis-San Francisco Railway, and the opening of the large iron deposits south of the town in Simmons Mountain in 1872, Salem had a steady growth as a mining and shipping center for a large area.

1. Right from Salem on State 72, a black-topped road, to LAKE SPRINGS, 13 *m.* Near the lake is the MOUNT HERMON CHURCH, a small frame structure in which is held the annual convention of the Christian Harmony Singing School, one of the oldest singing organizations in the Ozarks (*see Music*). The present director, D. E. Boyd of Salem, is the nephew of Elisha and Greenberry Hunt, two brothers who came from Virginia to Dent County in 1858 and taught several "singing schools" in the western part of the county. Following their deaths during the early years of the Civil War, their schools were continued by other leaders, one of them a woman. The schools are not confined to any particular church organization, but members are usually Methodists or Baptists, who accept invitations to other churches and community gatherings. The leader, or singing master, goes from community to community, like an old-time circuit rider, teaching the younger generation "tone lengths," "pitch," and "tone shapes," and the songs from *Christian Harmony,* which holds to the ancient "shape-note" songs derived from the musical literature of Elizabethan England.

On the first Sunday in October the various branches of the singing school gather at the Mount Hermon Church for a "sing-feast." This does not mean that they come to sing a mere song or two; they bring their lunches and pallets for their babies, and sing all day. The president opens the meeting with a song, a chapter from the Bible is read, and the minister leads the group in prayer. The leader of the class then "opens singing school" with the aid of a "pitch pipe" or a tuning-fork. The scale of the key in which the song is written is sung, then the notes of the tune, and, finally, the words. This procedure is always followed, for it is believed that "all persons should learn to sing the tune by note before they try to sing the words." Early-day music teachers advised their classes to eat green peas and spinach or other greens as a tonic to strengthen their vocal cords. Without benefit of piano or organ, the "fa, sol, la" notes of the major diatonic scale roll forth. Singing to please themselves, they move from song to song, until the one who has charge of it sends word that lunch is ready. When the meal is over, a leader pitches the tune of "Come All Ye Faithful," and the singing is resumed. Joyfully, they sing one hymn after another, until at last the sun sinking into the forests of distant hills reminds them that there are chores to be done before night sets in.

2. Left from Salem on State 72, a marked graveled road, to SCOTIA POND CHOPPINGS, 14 *m.*, a wooded section used for the annual Dent County Fox Hunt (*no fixed date*). The pond has a surface area of approximately three acres, and offers good duck hunting. The "Choppings" received its name in 1879, when, during the "starving time," or depression, of that year, men earned a living chopping wood here for 50¢ a cord.

At 49.9 *m.* is a junction with County K, a graveled road.

Right here, taking County E at a fork, 5.3 *m.*, to a junction with State 119, 10.9 *m.*, a graveled road. L. on State 119 to MONTAUK STATE PARK (*shelter houses, camping sites, overnight cabins*), 15.8 *m.*, 754 acres of heavily forested mountain land. Within the park are several miles of graveled roads which often ride high ridges and afford excellent panoramic views. Elevations range from 930 to 1,230 feet above sea level. Near the center of the park is the head of Current River, a spring with a maximum flow of 40,000,000 gallons daily. The clear, swiftly flowing water retains a temperature of 55°, making it an excellent fishing stream for trout and black bass. Near the spring, a small dam impounds the waters of the river, forming a lake that is used for fish propagation. In it are bred bluegill, perch, crappie, largemouthed black bass, trout, and channel cat. Forming a bank of the river is a rugged limestone bluff, wooded in pines and oaks. Also on the river, slightly south of the spring, is an old frame flour mill, the waterwheel of which is used to generate electricity for the park.

The SHANNONDALE COMMUNITY HOUSE (R), 66.5 *m.*, is a sturdy, T-shaped, one-story structure built of concrete and native stone. The house is the fruit of work begun in 1929 by the Reverend Paul A. Wobus, pastor of the Evangelical and Reformed Church, as part of the home missions program of that denomination. The church provided the funds, and men from the neighboring hills provided the labor. In addition, the latter have constructed a caretaker's cabin, a log cabin for guests, and the frame co-operative store across the highway. The community house serves the hill people as a recreational and educational center. In the fall of each year, usually in October, a "folk school" is held under the direction of the Reverend Vincent Vucher, resident pastor. There is no conclusive definition of a folk school; what it seems to be is an experiment in co-operative living. The hill folk say the name is a translation of the title given such groups by the Danish originators. "When you ask us what a folk school is, we can only invite you to break bread with us," one of the leaders explained to Dorothy Coleman, feature writer for the St. Louis *Post-Dispatch*. At the school, "shepherd pipes," cut from bamboo poles and tuned to a seven-tone scale by varying the size of the holes bored in the reed, are played, and such folk songs as "Three Little Pigeons," "Come All Ye Campers," and the Czechoslovakian tune, "Morning Comes Early," are sung. National authorities are brought in to lecture on consumers' co-operatives, war and peace, agricultural problems, economics, and politics. Instruction is given in such varied subjects as music, stained glass painting, and hygiene.

Across the highway is the small frame SHANNONDALE CO-OPERATIVE STORE, which has no official connection with the community house, but is an outgrowth of an interpretation of the co-operative teachings of N. F. S. Grundtvig (1783-1872), Danish churchman and educator. The store, an experiment in co-operative distribution, has about 35 members who have bought interests in the profits at $2.50 a share, and who bring the store a weekly business of approximately $200. Once a week the manager of the store drives a pick-up truck over a 30-mile circuit, delivering supplies and collecting cream and eggs; the eggs are taken to the markets in Salem, where they are accepted in barter.

CURRENT RIVER, crossed on a reinforced concrete bridge at 75.3 m., is one of the scenic fishing streams of the State. From its source approximately 40 miles northwest, it winds a turbulent way through the most rugged sections of the Ozarks, and empties into the Black River approximately 160 miles southeast. Above its junction with Jack's Fork, from which it receives 120,000,000 gallons of water daily, it is fed by Montauk, Welch, Cave, Pulltight, and Round Springs. The river takes its name from the swirling, cascading flow produced by its fall, which averages seven feet per mile. Scenic beauty and good fishing for black bass, salmon, and goggle-eye have made the river a popular float stream, and outfitting and conducting floats are local means of livelihood. A float trip is made under the supervision of guides in one or more boats, depending upon the number of persons in the party. The trips usually begin at Round Spring (*see below*) and last from two to six days. The time is spent drifting leisurely with the current and fishing in well-known holes. At night, camps are made on the sand bars which invariably lie opposite the bluffs that mark sharp bends in the river. The most famous of the fishing holes are Twin Rocks, Anthole, Cedar Stub, Spring Hollow, School House, Sugar Camp, Buttermilk Chute, Gravel Spring, Cynthia Chute, Log Yard, Watermelon, Boat's Bend, and Boiling Pot—names that smack of past adventure and homely anecdote.

ROUND SPRING STATE PARK (L), 75.6 m., is a small recreational center built about Round Spring. The spring rises from a basin 80 feet in diameter, with sidewalls 30 feet high; its waters, of a soft, bluish color, catch the wavering shadows of overhead branches and reflect them against gray-limestone bluffs. So still is the surface that one must look at the government gauge to believe that the spring is actually flowing. An average of 18,000,000 gallons of water daily empties into the Current River, approximately a quarter of a mile away. A maximum flow of 336,000,000 gallons daily was recorded in May 1933. The outlet is through a low, natural arch in one of the bluffs. The 77-acre park affords free camping and picnicking grounds, but no overnight accommodation.

ROUND SPRING CAVERN (*adm., 56¢ and 28¢; guides*), 75.8 m. (R), extending into a mountain side, is well improved with bridges and graveled paths. A short distance from the entrance the passageway forks, forming a Y. At the southwestern end of the cave is a 14-foot waterfall, which forms a small stream flowing through the cave.

JACK'S FORK, crossed at 88 m. on a steel and concrete bridge, is a swift, clear fishing stream that empties into the Current River.

EMINENCE, 88.5 m. (875 alt., 417 pop.), is the outfitting point for float trips on the Current River, and the seat of Shannon County, which was organized January 29, 1841, and named for the Honorable George G. Shannon, a prominent Missouri lawyer and politician. The three-story brick courthouse that dominates the town from a central square is new (1941); the old one burned May 23, 1938. About the courthouse, on three sides, are one-story brick and frame stores and shops. On the fourth side are frame cottages that extend up and over the hill that overlooks the town from the west.

About 1837 the first regular copper mining in Missouri was begun within the present limits of Shannon County. These mines, worked intermittently since that time, were producing before the Michigan mines had been discovered.

1. Left from Eminence on State 106, a graveled road that cuts directly eastward into the mountains where six blunt peaks stand in bold relief against the sky, to a junction with a marked graveled road, 5.4 m. Left on this road, which winds downward from the wooded mountainside, to RUSSELL'S RANCH (cabins; boats, tackle, and guides for fishing or float trips), 8.4 m., a fishing camp at the junction of Jack's Fork and the Current River.

2. Right from Eminence on State 106 to ALLEY SPRING STATE PARK (cabins), 5.6 m., a 407-acre recreational area, rough, hilly, and heavily wooded, one of the most unspoiled landscapes in the State. Two central ridges, each approximately 1,200 feet in elevation, cross the area. Near the park's center is ALLEY SPRING, rising in a circular basin 200 feet in diameter and flowing a daily average of 78,200,000 gallons. A maximum flow of 409,000,000 gallons daily was recorded in 1929 and 1933. Near the spring is a three-story frame watermill, built shortly after the Civil War and used by people of the vicinity for grinding corn. Dotted over the area are picnic grounds, camping sites, and shelter houses. Jack's Fork offers good bass fishing.

Southward, the highway continues among the mountains, crossing heavily forested areas broken in places by small sawmill operations and bottom lands developed in fruit orchards and poultry and dairy farms. Much of the land, officially classed as submarginal, has been placed in forest reserves, such as the FRISTOE DIVISION OF THE CLARK NATIONAL FOREST, entered at 96.5 m., one of the eight large timber and game preserves of southern Missouri. The forest contains 279,383 acres at present, and is under the supervision of the National Forest Service.

The story of these great forested areas begins with the cutting of timber for commercial purposes in the 1860's. This reached its peak in 1899, when 723,754,000 board feet were cut. From then on, annual production steadily dropped, until, in 1931, it totaled only 75,000 board feet. Had the cutting been selective, the land would have retained its value, but young trees were destroyed in getting out the older ones, and the hills, when big operations ceased, were all but stripped of their cover.

This destruction, thorough as it was, was carried even further by the several thousand former employees who remained on the land after the lumber companies moved out, attempting to farm the hillsides. Many were squatters; others bought small tracts, but usually lost them within a few years through inability to meet interest payment, and also became squatters. It was all but impossible to earn a living from the land, for, except in the river bottoms, the soil was shallow, four to eight inches in depth. The first few years of tillage provided a meager living, but as the years went by the soil's protective covering washed away, and in most places little except gravel and rock remained. As the fertility of the soil decreased, many of the residents sought opportunities outside of the hills and the population decreased steadily. Today, one sees few young men and women in this portion of the Ozarks.

A soil and timber conservation program was begun in the area with the establishment of the first State parks in the 1920's. These were mainly game preserves, fish hatcheries, and recreational areas. Little attention was given to reforestation until after 1931, when a legislative enactment first permitted the Federal Government to acquire land in Missouri for reforestation purposes. In 1933 the limit which the government was permitted to buy was increased from 25,000 acres per county to 100,000 acres, and in the following year the acreage limit was removed. Conservation work in these national park areas (*see General Information*), which are under the direction of the United States Forest Service, has included the replanting of millions of oak, pine, and other trees, the control of forest fires, and wild life conservation activities.

WINONA, 99.4 *m.* (920 alt., 480 pop.), a railroad shipping point, is at a junction with US 60 (*see Tour 6*).

The ELEVEN POINT GAME PRESERVE (R), 111.6 *m.,* was established in 1934 and is under the supervision of the United States Forest Service. Here, on 13,000 acres, experiments in the conservation of deer, quail, wild turkey, and small game are conducted. The first experiment with wild turkeys proved that a system of close supervision defeated its purpose; the birds soon lost their wild instincts, becoming as tame as chickens. They would nest where wolves, foxes, and other predatory animals destroyed their eggs. Lacking a fear of man, nearly half the stock was shot by hunters. A new plan, called "loose control," was adopted in 1926. Under it the birds have regained many of their original characteristics.

ALTON, 121.1 *m.* (576 pop.), the seat of Oregon County, is a farm trading center. About 1815, Thomas Hatcher, the first permanent settler in the county, located on the Eleven Points River, and a few years later a group of Kentucky families established themselves near by. Supplies were brought by horseback from Ste. Genevieve, 175 miles to the east. The settlers hunted, trapped, raised "a patch of corn," and lived on the most friendly terms with the Indians. By 1841, the population had sufficiently increased to form Oregon County, but for civil purposes the area was attached to Ripley County until 1845. In 1859, Alton succeeded Thomasville as the county seat. To prevent the possible destruction of the county records during the Civil War, Major M. G. Norman hid them in a cave on near-by Piney Creek, where they remained from 1862 until 1865. The precautionary measure proved to be a wise one, for the Courthouse was burned.

State 19 ends at a junction with US 63 (*see Tour 8*), 140 *m.*, 4 miles north of the Arkansas Line.

Tour 15

(Pittsfield, Ill.) — Louisiana — Vandalia — Mexico — Fulton — Jefferson City — Eldon — Camdenton — Hermitage — Eldorado Springs — Nevada — (Fort Scott, Kan.) ; US 54.
Illinois Line to Kansas Line, 280 *m.*

Concrete and oil-mat paved throughout.
Route paralleled roughly by Chicago & Alton R.R. between Louisiana and Jefferson City; by Missouri Pacific R.R. between Jefferson City and Bagnell; and by Missouri-Kansas-Texas R.R. between Eldorado Springs and Kansas Line.
Hotels in larger towns; numerous resorts and tourist accommodations, especially on western half of route.

In Missouri, US 54 crosses three distinct topographic regions, differing in natural resources and in pioneer heritage, yet forming a composite whole loosely described as Middle Western. Along the Mississippi River, in the vicinity of Louisiana, are broken bluffs sheltering narrow valleys adaptable to fruit culture. Southwestward are broad, rolling prairies leveled by the great glaciers that once penetrated the northern portion of the State. A short distance north of the Missouri River, the prairies give way to the Ozark Highlands, which extend south and west to the Kansas State Line. Principal items of interest, other than historical, are the orchards and horse farms of the northeast, and the Lake of the Ozarks country in the southwest.

Section a. ILLINOIS LINE to JEFFERSON CITY; 104 m., US 54

Between Louisiana, Missouri, and the vicinity of Fulton, US 54 zigzags over a rolling prairie country whose soil—at many places thin and underlaid with limestone or clay—is of glacial and loessial origin.

Kentucky, Virginia, and Tennessee families, settling the region in the period 1815-40, found much of the prairie upland a natural pasture well adapted to livestock culture. The raising of fine horses, cattle, and the ubiquitous "hawg," is still the chief industry of the region, although corn, wheat, barley, sorghum, hay, and poultry are cultivated widely. In Pike and Callaway Counties, extensive apple orchards have been developed. The towns support various small industries. Centered at Mexico are several major refractories plants.

US 54 crosses the MISSOURI LINE, 0 m., in the middle of the CHAMP CLARK BRIDGE (*toll, 50¢*) over the Mississippi River, 20 miles southwest of Pittsfield, Illinois. The bridge was completed in 1928 at a cost of $1,000,000.

LOUISIANA, 0.7 m. (469 alt., 4,669 pop.), in a valley at the confluence of Noix Creek and the Mississippi River, is a onetime river port which has turned to agriculture and industry. Like other Mississippi River towns, Louisiana began on the bank of the stream and developed inland, leaving the older sections along Water and Main Streets to be taken over by industries and wholesale business houses. Residences reveal a succession of architectural styles; large, mellowed ante bellum structures stand beside houses adorned with the gingerbread trim popular during the 1880's and 1890's; compact contemporary dwellings reflect the town's recent economic advancement. Laid out by Samuel K. Caldwell and Joel Shaw in 1818, and named for the State of Louisiana, the town served as the seat of Pike County until succeeded by Bowling Green in 1823. Among the industrial plants of the city are a glove factory, and an establishment that manufactures pearl buttons from Mississippi River mussel shells.

The LLOYD C. STARK HOUSE (*open by permission*), northwest corner of Fourteenth and Georgia Sts., is a two-story white frame dwelling with the elaborate trim and wide porches typical of the 1890's. Lloyd Crow Stark, born on a Pike County farm November 23, 1886, was graduated with honors from the United States Naval Academy in 1908, and served four years in the United States Navy. He was later vice president and general manager of the Stark Nurseries, president of the Mississippi Valley Apple Growers Association, and in 1917 and again in 1919 was elected president of the American Association of Nurserymen. He was elected Governor on the Democratic ticket November 3, 1936.

The peak of a bluff in RIVERVIEW CEMETERY, on the northern edge of Louisiana, provides a magnificent view of the winding Mississippi River, and the park-like bottom lands of Pike County, Illinois. On the south and west, partially wooded "camel-hump" knobs sweep in endless procession against the horizon.

Left from Louisiana, State 79, a graveled road, winds among the bluffs close to the Mississippi River. The area it traverses was the earliest settled in this part of the State. At 1.6 m. is a junction with County D, which leads R. 1 m. to the SITE OF BUFFALO FORT, marked by a granite boulder (R). The fort was erected about 1811 to protect 25 pioneer families who had established their homes in the vicinity. Trouble with the Sauk and Fox Indians began about 1811 and continued until the Treaty of 1815 removed the Indians to lands farther west. During the War of 1812, especially, the Indians abetted by the British waged war against the settlers of the Buffalo and Noix Creek valleys.

Southeast on State 79 to CLARKSVILLE, 9.5 m. (461 alt., 879 pop.), a pleasant village scattered over a bluff that rises abruptly above the Mississippi. The settlement dates from 1816. Before 1820, it is said, Territorial Governor William Clark, en route to St. Louis from Prairie du Chien, Wisconsin, spent a winter here with a company of soldiers. In the 1850's rivermen called the place Appletown, because of the quantity of apples shipped each fall. The vicinity of Clarksville was overrun by rattlesnakes in the early days. According to John Davis, who settled in Missouri in 1820 and lived at Clarksville for many years, "snaking frolics" were a favorite pastime. On one occasion Mr. Davis and his neighbors killed 700 rattlesnakes in one day on a knob near the town. This record was surpassed by Miles Price, for 30 years constable and justice of the peace in Pike County. He and his neighbors killed 9,000 rattlesnakes on one of their annual spring snake hunts.

South of Clarksville, in broad Annada Valley, State 79 crosses RAMSAY CREEK, 15.9 m., named for Captain Allen Ramsay, a Revolutionary War veteran stationed at Cap-au-Gris in Lincoln County during the War of 1812. A cluster of houses and a white frame school building (R) mark the village of ANNADA, 17.9 m. (452 alt., 110 pop.), named for Anna and Ada Jamison, daughters of Carson Jamison, an early settler. West of the village rises massive SALTPETRE BLUFF, where Annada pioneers secured saltpetre for manufacturing gunpowder.

Southward, State 79 continues as a recently completed scenic drive to a junction with US 40, 52 m., 7 miles west of St. Charles.

Southwest of Louisiana, US 54 crosses the broken bluffs that outline the western bank of the Mississippi River. The fertile limestone soil is especially adapted to apple culture. In spring, the long symmetrical rows of trees are covered with a mass of pastel-colored blossoms which attract many visitors.

The STARK BROTHERS NURSERY (open), 3 m., extending over large acreages on each side of the highway, is the most important industry in the vicinity of Louisiana, and one of the largest nurseries in the United States. Trees bearing the famous Delicious apple cover the hillside (R), where driveways, bordered by hedges and small, decorative trees, wind through landscaped grounds past the nursery buildings. Left of the highway, beside the railroad spurs, are many packing houses, long, story-and-a-half concrete-block sheds whose sloping black roofs are broken by skylights. Here apples, trees, and shrubbery are graded and packed for shipment. Almost surrounding the sheds are large fields of evergreen trees and shrubs. The nursery was established in 1816 by James Stark, from the "contents of his saddle bags," and is probably the oldest in the Nation. Stark's descendants have maintained and expanded it, establishing branches throughout the country.

At 12.4 m. is a junction with US 61 (see Tour 7).

Between the junction and Fulton, US 54 follows a step design southwestward across the level northern prairie. Several large refractories plants utilizing the extensive clay deposits of the area stand along the road, but grainfields dominate the landscape. The loam of the prairie is particularly adaptable to corn, small grains, and pasture crops. The land has received careful attention since its settlement in the 1820's and '30's, and much of the profits have been turned back to farm development. The farmsteads are fairly extensive, with large barns, silos, and cross-fenced fields of oats, clover and timothy hay, corn, and other crops that can be used for livestock feed as well as for sale. Each farmer has herds of blooded cattle and hogs, and flocks of sheep and poultry.

VANDALIA, 26.8 m. (768 alt., 2,672 pop.), primarily an agricultural community, was laid out about 1871 by Aaron McPike, Judge Caldwell, Amos Ladd, and Colonel Haden, and incorporated in 1874. Small brick business buildings surround STONE STREET PARK, an open square in the center of town. The park's diagonal concrete walks are inlaid with advertisements of local merchants and industries, and compliments to leading citizens. In the northwest corner of the park is a memorial to World War veterans, Vandalia's LIBERTY BELL, which cracked open while being rung in celebration of the Armistice, November 11, 1918. Vandalia manufactures, among other things, wash dresses and clay products.

On the wide prairie, the WALSH REFRACTORIES (L), 34.7 m., consist of a large group of corrugated steel and red-tile buildings, kilns, and derricks. The clay, scooped from great open pits, is transported to the crushers by derricks and there rendered fine and powdery. It is then molded into bricks, tiles, furnace linings, and other fire-clay products, and "burned" at intense heat in the kilns. The products have a national market.

LADDONIA, 39.2 m. (780 alt., 588 pop.), originated as a railroad camp in 1871, and was named for Amos Ladd, one of the founders of the town. Formerly the place was referred to as "Mutton Town" because herds of sheep awaiting shipment were often penned up in its streets.

Between Laddonia and Mexico, US 54 traverses an important part of Missouri's celebrated saddle horse country, whose limestone soil is particularly adapted to bluegrass. Many Kentuckians settled here, and bred and trained horses, some of which achieved great fame. The first of these was C. T. Quisenberry's Missouri Clay; then came Joseph Stanhope's Royal Gold Dust, Robert Edmonston's Artist, and Joseph A. Potts' Artist Rose. International authorities may disagree on the greatest saddle horse of all time, but not Audrain Countians. They are convinced he was Rex McDonald, foaled in Callaway County, trained in Audrain County, and acclaimed world champion so many times that he was eventually barred from ring competition. Belle Beach, trained by Tom Bass, was not only champion high-school mare of the world, but is said to have been the greatest high-school horse in history. Bass, born a slave, was recognized as a horseman without peer. In his youth he worked around Mexico as a stable boy and hostler, but in his later life he and his famous mare were prominent in every major fair and horse show in America. Bass was invited to take Miss Rex, owned by a Colonel Fulton of Kansas City, to Queen Victoria's Diamond Jubilee, but refused because he was afraid to cross the ocean.

The MEXICO COUNTRY CLUB (*greens fee $1*), 56.2 *m.* (R), has a nine-hole golf course adjoining a small lake.

MEXICO, 57.5 *m.* (800 alt., 9,053 pop.), seat of Audrain County, combines brick manufacturing and saddle horse breeding, and modernity and tradition. The business district, dominated by the cylindrical clock tower of the courthouse, is the center of town. Radiating from it are the residential streets, with older homes of Classic and ginger-bread design close in, and modern bungalows and Georgian houses farther out.

A majority of the city's workers find employment in the clay refractories plants or with the railroads, three of which—the Wabash, the Chicago & Alton, and the Chicago, Burlington & Quincy—maintain division shops here. A large number of women are employed in a shoe factory.

The upland prairies of Audrain County were not settled early because of the danger of prairie fires, the difficulty of obtaining wood and water, and the presence of green-head flies. At certain times of the year, the flies made day travel impossible, and even plowing and other farm work had to be done at night. The county was organized in December of 1836, and named for Colonel James H. Audrain (1782-1831), a State legislator from St. Charles County. The present site of Mexico was selected for the county seat in March 1837; it lay in the midst of the so-called Salt River settlement, whose inhabitants were known as Salt River Tigers. The love of fine horses was a tradition among these people; race tracks about 6 feet wide and 600 yards long were laid out on the prairie for regular Saturday afternoon races. When Mexico was platted, Doan's Race Track, which was about two miles north of the townsite, was abandoned, and a new track was laid out at the edge of the town.

By the time of the Civil War Mexico had grown into a sprawling county-seat town. Most of the residents wished to preserve the Union, but when forced to choose sides, they supported the Confederacy. Two or three regiments of Federal troops were quartered in the town in the early summer of 1861. The soldiers were badly disciplined and indulged in thievery and vandalism against the residents, until Colonel U. S. Grant was put in command of the district. Grant came to Mexico in July of 1861, and immediately ordered the protection of property rights. He also introduced more flexible drill tactics, having found the regulation forms unsatisfactory. It was while he was in Mexico that Grant first learned, through a newspaper, that his name had been recommended for promotion to Brigadier General. Soon after, the promotion was confirmed, and Grant was ordered to Ironton (*see Tour 13*).

After the war, the town resumed its quiet life. By the 1890's, the Lee brothers and other Mexico horsemen had established well-equipped stables. In 1908 the first $1,000 trotting- and pacing-race stakes and the first $1,000 and $1,500 show rings ever offered were inaugurated as a part of the Mexico Fair. Today (1941) the great spring and fall saddle-horse auction sales held by the stables attract buyers from all parts of the Nation.

Shortly after 1900, an important deposit of fire clay was discovered directly under the town. Clay refractories were established, and today Mexico is the center of one of the most important fire-clay manufacturing areas in the world. The vein of clay owned by one plant alone has been estimated by the government to be great enough to supply this plant for more than 200 years. Much of the 30,000,000 pounds of freight handled each month in Mexico is composed of fire-clay products.

The LEE BROTHERS STABLE (*open*), northwest corner of Webster St. and West Blvd., an extensive, fully equipped establishment for breeding, training, and exhibiting saddle horses, is operated by George and William D. Lee, two of Missouri's most noted horsemen. Beginning with the saddle gelding, Mascot, winner of gelding classes at the Chicago World's Fair in 1893, the stable has developed many champions, including Nancy Beloved, which sold for $22,000 at a Chicago auction. The JOHN T. HOOK STABLES (*open*), northeast corner of Muldrow St. and West Blvd., is another extensive establishment. Prior to opening these stables in 1935, Hook spent 30 years managing his stables in Paris, Missouri, and the Longview Stables near Kansas City.

The MISSOURI MILITARY ACADEMY, eastern end of E. Jackson St., is an accredited institution for boys between the ages of 6 and 21. The square, barrack-type brick buildings with white stone trim are centered by the more elaborate administration building—distinguished by a white portico with four white columns and a great dome. The academy was established in 1889 under the direction of Charles H. Hardin, governor of Missouri 1874-76. The KING'S DAUGHTERS HOME, southeast corner of Webster St. and West Blvd., a two-and-a-half-story, yellow-brick structure, is the home of aged members of the King's Daughters, an international charitable organization established in 1886. The Missouri circle, founded in 1888, is one of the oldest chapters in the United States. Grouped in a semi-quadrangle beneath large oak trees are the deserted HARDIN COLLEGE BUILDINGS, 1000 S. Jefferson St., where more than 5,000 girls received their education in the period between its founding as the Audrain County Female Seminary in 1858 and the closing of its doors in 1930. The school was renamed in 1873, when Governor Hardin re-endowed it.

THE A. P. GREEN FIRE BRICK COMPANY PLANT (*open 8-4 workdays; guides*), east end of E. Breckenridge St., is one of the largest units of its type in the world. The plant is an extensive group of steel and corrugated-iron buildings, kilns, and sheds. In front of the group, approached by a landscaped drive, is a white-brick office building of Classic design. In the rear are the clay pits and a small lake. The clay, of excellent quality, is scooped from the open pits by steam shovels and hauled to the crusher house in small railway cars. It then passes through an amazingly elaborate system of processing until it reaches the molds and the modern tunnel kilns. Practically every operation, from the digging of the clay to the measuring of "grain size," aging, and testing of finished products, is in charge of engineers. The company maintains a modern laboratory equipped with a self-contained model brick plant. Three types of refractories are made: dry press, stiff mud, and handmade, the last molded in thousands of intricate forms. The molders are men of long experience and have an artisan's pride in their work. Each product is stamped with the name of the molder as well as that of the company. This custom dates back to the days of the guilds; it gives the molders a feeling of responsibility and a pride in workmanship that people who operate machines cannot experience. The A. P. Green Brick Company, founded by A. P. Green in 1910, and employing approximately 500 persons, has what amounts to a world monopoly on many types of fire-clay products. The Mexico Refractories plant is a similar establishment.

The HAMILTON BLUEGRASS FARMS (open), 60 m. (R), is one of the outstanding saddle-horse breeding and training stables in the State. A group of long white frame barns, enclosed by corrals and surrounded by rolling bluegrass pastures, are the center of the farm's activity. Here Jim Hamilton and his sons have bred and trained more champions than has any other saddle stable in the vicinity. Among the outstanding stallions have been Lord Highland, Mexico Admire, and Roxy Highland; the last sold for $27,500. On the front of the sales pavilion is a large portrait in colors of Sweetheart on Parade. Within the pavilion are a show ring and seats for buyers and spectators. Here the farm holds its spring and fall auction sales.

AUXVASSE, 68.5 m. (875 alt., 490 pop.), an agricultural trading center, was founded by J. A. Harrison in 1871. Like all towns in Callaway County, it ships a large number of horses and mules each year.

Callaway County, organized in 1820, has been a leading mule-breeding county since Missouri first made a reputation for the number and quality of its mules. As early as 1823, caravans brought from Santa Fe, Mexico, jacks, jennets, and mules (see Agriculture). By 1830, Callaway owners had begun to breed mules for the market in large numbers, and the industry was so profitable that frequent mention was made of it in the newspapers. One of the earliest notices in Missouri was published by the Columbia Statesman, November 29, 1830: "Mules for sale—For sale at my farm on Grand Prairie, one mile east of Capt. A. Allens, in the neighborhood of Aux Vasse Church, Callaway County, 42 head of mules, 3 years old next spring."

Soon Missouri was raising more mules than it needed, and Missouri mules were carried by steamboat to the Southern States, or driven overland to Independence and St. Joseph for use in wagon trains. During the Boer War, England bought a large number. It was the exposition of Missouri-bred and -reared mules at the St. Louis World's Fair in 1904, however, that proved the supremacy of the Missouri stock, although even before that time the expression "Missouri mule" had gained international meaning. During the World War, a Missouri firm supplied the British Government with large numbers of mules and horses. Mules are generally divided into two classes, "sugar mules" and "cotton mules." The former are bred for use in the sugar-cane fields of Louisiana; the latter for the cotton fields of the Southern States.

The breeding of fine horses in Callaway County was begun by the first settlers. Harry May's race track on May's Prairie, laid out about 1820, was the scene of many early races. On one occasion, the Willinghams and Kilgores of Audrain County borrowed Sanford Jameson's fine racing nag, Janus, filled her mane and tail full of sheep burs, and took her to May's race track to run against a crack pony known as Nick Biddle, which had been brought from Kentucky. The mare presented such a poor appearance that the bets were all against her, but she outran the pony by 250 yards in a run of 600. Mr. Jameson later sold the mare to a Louisiana trainer, who won $80,000 with her.

The CARL GILMAN STABLES (*open*), 69.5 *m.* (L), is a boarding and training school for saddle horses. Many of the stable's horses have won prizes in Middle Western horse shows.

KINGDOM CITY, 74.5 *m.* (855 alt., 12 pop.), is at a junction with US 40 (*see Tour 3*).

FULTON, 81.5 *m.* (818 alt., 8,297 pop.), Callaway County seat, is built about a public square, in which stands a modern red-brick and limestone courthouse. Fulton has a shoe factory, a clay refractories plant, two colleges, two State institutions, and a long-established farm trade. On the first Monday of each month a livestock sale is held one mile north of Fulton, and during the last week of September the town stages a horse and cattle show, enlivened by a street fair.

Fulton was founded as the county seat in June 1825, and named Volney for Count Constantin Volney, French scientist and atheist. Two months later, its name was changed to honor Robert Fulton, American scientist, artist, and marine engineer. George Nichols, who settled here in 1824, donated 50 acres to the county for the townsite. His log house was the first within the present limits of Fulton, and he "had to go ten miles to get men to help him raise it," according to Bryan and Rose in *Pioneer Families of Missouri* (1876). "They came before sunrise on the appointed day, had the cabin completed before the sun went down, and danced in it the same night." The county was named for Captain James Callaway, Warren County resident, who was killed in a battle with Indians in 1815. A monument on the northwest corner of the courthouse square honors his memory. Among the several industries of Fulton is the OVID BELL PRESS, housed in a two-story red-brick building on N. Bluff St., which serves book and magazine publishers in half a dozen Middle Western States.

STATE HOSPITAL NO. 1, E. Fifth and State Sts., is housed in a group of modern brick buildings centered about an administration building designed by Solomon Jenkins and completed in 1851. The institution was established in 1847 and opened in 1849 as the State Lunatic Asylum, the first hospital for mental patients west of the Mississippi River. During the Civil War, the buildings were occupied by Federal soldiers and the work of the institution was discontinued for a few years. The hospital has been partly modernized and equipped out of the $10,-000,000 appropriated by the general assembly of 1935 for the rehabilitation and improvement of State penal and eleemosynary institutions. In 1939 the institution had 2,350 patients, with one physician to each 300 patients. The STATE SCHOOL FOR THE DEAF, northwest corner of Fifth and Vine Sts., consists of 16 three- and four-story, red-brick structures on a 334-acre campus. Founded in 1851, the school has trained approximately 3,500 students under the age of 21. Tuition is free to residents of Missouri, but parents or guardians must furnish clothing and traveling expenses. The school has an enrollment of approximately 370.

WESTMINSTER COLLEGE, Westminster Ave., between Fourth and Sevenths Sts., housed in a group of buff- and red-brick buildings of Classic design on a 40-acre campus, is an accredited 4-year liberal arts college for men. Following the decision of the Presbyterian Synod of Missouri in 1849 to establish a college, the members and officers of the Presbyterian Church of Fulton obtained a charter for Fulton College in 1851 which they hoped would be adopted by the synod. In 1852, the synod, meeting in Fulton, accepted their offer. The institution was rechartered as Westminster College and opened for its first session in May 1853. Commemorating the merger of the northern and southern branches of the Presbyterian Church in support of the college is Reunion Hall, a three-story, buff-brick dormitory erected in 1903. The William Chrisman Swope Memorial Chapel, a Gothic-type structure of red brick trimmed in white stone, a gift to the school, was completed in 1919 at a cost of $57,000.

WILLIAM WOODS COLLEGE, Twelfth and Nichols Sts., an accredited junior college for girls, is housed in 14 buildings on an 85-acre tree-shaded campus. The school is under the direction of the Christian Church, and has an annual enrollment of approximately 300. It was founded at Camden Point, Platte County, as the Orphan's School for Girls of the Christian Church of Missouri. When the building burned, the members of the Fulton Christian Church secured the school's removal to Fulton, where it was reopened in 1890. Later it became Daughter's College, and in 1900, receiving the aid of Dr. William S. Woods, Kansas City banker, it became William Woods College. The MARGARET L. BARBER LOAN COLLECTION (open) is in the upper rooms and corridors of the Academic Building. The collection was established in 1927 and contains, among other articles, oil paintings from Mexico, primitive American portraits, and examples of early American and European furniture.

Right from Fulton on Westminster Road, which becomes County F, a graveled highway winding among low hills, to REED'S LAKE (open year around; fishing 50¢ a day; cabins), 5 m. (L), a private resort. The lake was created by a dam built in 1930, and lies in a natural bowl surrounded by a wall of native stone. Bass, crappie, and perch are abundant, and the surrounding brush has been cleared to permit anglers to use fly rods from the shore. Within the tract of 140 acres, enclosed by high wire fences, are 12 deer and 4 elk; herds of sheep keep the grass at the entrance smooth.

South of Fulton, US 54 crosses a rolling country broken here and there by sharp sandstone hills and small forests of walnut, oak, and ash. The highway follows a lofty ridge for approximately seven miles, then winding down a long hillside, emerges abruptly upon the broad bottom lands of the Missouri River. The view of the State capitol, surmounting the high limestone bluffs that form the river's southern bank, is impressive.

At 102.5 m. is a junction with US 63 (see Tour 8), with which US 54 is united to JEFFERSON CITY, 104 m. (557 alt., 24,268 pop.) (see Jefferson City), which is at a junction with US 50 (see Tour 4).

Section b. JEFFERSON CITY to KANSAS LINE; 176 m., US 54

Following a winding route between Jefferson City and the Kansas Line, US 54 crosses the northern portion of the Ozark foothills and ends on a flat prairie-like plateau. The Ozark region is characterized by sharp, heavily wooded ridges and valleys; it is a thinly populated area where life centers around Bagnell Dam and the Lake of the Ozarks. Farther to the southwest is an occasional mineral spring or fishing resort.

Southwest of JEFFERSON CITY, 0 m., US 54 plunges directly into the sparsely settled Ozark foothills. Although a small plot is cultivated here and there in grain, most of the country is in second-growth timber or pasture. Tie cutting and livestock raising are the principal occupations.

ELDON, 31.6 m. (934 alt., 2,590 pop.), a division point on the Rock Island Railroad, has experienced its greatest period of growth since the erection of Bagnell Dam in 1929. Platted in March 1882, it remained a typical farm trading village until 1903, when the railroad placed a roundhouse and a few shops here. Today (1941) Eldon is characterized by new, flat-roofed red-brick buildings, shade trees, and brick cottages. The town supplements its farm and railroad income with a cheese plant and a men's clothing factory.

The ELDON GOLF COURSE (R), 32.4 m., is a nine-hole course (*greens fee, 50¢*). The caretaker maintains a stable of saddle horses (*50¢ per hour*), and a tanbark show ring; here the Lake of the Ozarks Horse Show is held in late August or early September of each year. The show is open to three- and five-gaited saddle horses.

AURORA SPRINGS, 34.2 m. (125 pop.), platted in 1880 by Abram Fulkerson, was for 20 years the largest town in Miller County and a spa of sectional repute. Now it is a roadside hamlet whose inhabitants offer statuary, pottery, and woodwork for sale.

At 34.4 m. is a junction with State 52, a concrete road.

Left on State 52, which winds down into the Osage River Valley, to TUS-CUMBIA, 9.8 m. (585 alt., 269 pop.), the seat of Miller County. The town is built on several levels. The business section rests on concrete piling along the river's edge; the residences, reached by long, steep flights of steps, are hung perilously on the side of a 175-foot bluff; the massive, silver-domed courthouse surmounts the whole. The single industry, milling, is conducted in a four-story tin building at .the eastern edge of town.

At an early date two brothers, J. P. and J. B. Harrison, both bachelors, built a log-cabin trading-post near a spring on the present site of Tuscumbia. When Miller County was organized February 6, 1837, the house of William Miller near the mouth of Saline Creek was selected as the county seat, but the second court moved the seat to the Harrison brothers' store. Tuscumbia, laid out on land donated by the Harrisons, was probably named for Tuscumbia, Alabama. The word is derived from a Cherokee Indian word, *tash-ka-ambi*, meaning, "the warrior who kills."

Among the first residents of the county was John Wilson, an eccentric Irishman, who, with his family, moved here about 1822. The Wilsons spent their first winter in a cave on Tavern Creek near the mouth of the Barren Fork. Wilson died in 1855, aged 100, and his funeral was carried out according to his instructions, as follows: he was laid in a coffin which he had made in 1842, and salt was packed about him. With a demijohn of good liquor near his head, he was sealed into a small alcove of the cave. A good dinner, with "something to wash it down," was served those who assisted at the interment. Wilson had asked that at the end of seven years his friends meet again, open the tomb, and have a "snort" from the demijohn in his memory. The Civil War intervened, however, and the reunion was never held. Years later vandals broke into the vault.

At 40.5 *m.* is a junction with County V, a graveled road.

Left on County V to BAGNELL, 1.5 *m.* (587 alt., 118 pop.), where development followed the completion of the railroad to this point. The town was named for William Bagnell, the railroad contractor. It achieved local prominence during the building of Bagnell Dam (1929-31), when the village was changed overnight from a quiet ferryboat landing on the Osage River, and the terminus of the Missouri Pacific branch line from Jefferson City, to a boom town filled with workmen. The town gave its name to the dam. At one time, more railroad ties were shipped from Bagnell than from any other point in Missouri.

Between the junction and the Lake of the Ozarks, an increasing number of filling stations, roadside eating places, tourist camps, novelty stands, and brightly painted signs with arrows pointing along winding dirt and graveled roads indicate a widely publicized recreational area.

From a ROADSIDE OBSERVATION POINT (R.), 42.5 *m.*, an improved parking space, is a panoramic view of several miles of the Lake of the Ozarks' jagged shoreline.

At 43 *m.*, is a junction with an unmarked macadam road.

Left on this road, which ascends to the flat, wooded summit of a bluff, to LAKESIDE, 0.4 *m.*, a village built and maintained by the Union Electric Light and Power Company, owner of Bagnell Dam. Rows of white frame cottages (L) are occupied by company employees and their families. The HOLIDAY HOUSE (R) is a two-story, gray frame and stone hotel operated by the company. From LOOKOUT POINT (R), a railed parking space at the edge of the bluff, is a sweeping view of Bagnell Dam and the shining, many-armed Lake of the Ozarks. Within a small, glass-enclosed structure on a corner of the point is a model of a section of the dam. The model demonstrates the operation of the hydroelectric plant and the floodgates.

At 43.5 *m.* the highway crosses BAGNELL DAM, which houses Missouri's largest hydroelectric generating plant and impounds the waters of the Lake of the Ozarks. The dam, constructed of reinforced concrete, is 2,543 feet long and rises 148 feet above the bedrock of the Osage River. The flow of water through the spillway, which is 520 feet wide, is controlled by 12 floodgates, each of which weighs 27 tons and is capable of discharging 101,000 gallons of water a second. The electric power plant, under the dam proper, has eight large and two small structural steel gates, through which water is diverted into the turbines. There are 6 main generators with an initial capacity of 201,-000 horsepower. The generators deliver their power at 13,800 volts, and this, greatly increased by transformers, is sent on transmission lines to the St. Louis area. A modern feature of the plant is that each generator is under a separate, removable roof instead of in an individual building. The plant delivers an estimated average of 400,000,000 kilowatt hours annually.

Work on the dam began August 6, 1929; the hydroelectric plant commenced operation October 19, 1931. Construction of the power plant required the excavation of nearly 1,000,000 cubic yards of earth and 73,000 cubic yards of rock. Approximately 545,000 cubic yards of concrete, 2,300 tons of reinforcing steel, and 1,150 tons of structural steel were used in the dam's construction. Bagnell Dam is owned and operated by the Union Electric Light and Power Company, St. Louis.

The LAKE OF THE OZARKS (R), formed by the impounding of the waters of the Osage River, is one of the largest wholly artificial lakes in the United States. Broken by innumerable coves that give it the shape of an octopus, it is 129 miles long, has a 1,300-mile, irregular shoreline, wooded in oak, hickory, elm, wild crab, and other trees, and covers an area of 95 square miles. The water inundates 17 per cent of the surface of Camden County, and parts of Miller, Morgan, Benton, Henry, and St. Clair Counties. The lake affords excellent fishing for largemouthed black bass, silver bass, crappie, walleyed pike, and perch. It is seen at its best during the summer months, when all of the recreational concessions are open and the surrounding forest is bright with sumach, sassafras, wild grape, and other shrubs and vines.

At the southern end of the dam, an EXCURSION BOAT LIVERY (*open May to Oct.; 20-minute ride, 50¢; also for charter*), 44 *m.* (R), operates a fleet of 38- and 45-foot cruisers. The boats, driven by licensed operators, leave every few minutes during the season. Near by is a graveled bathing beach (*adm. 35¢*).

LAKE OZARK, 44.4 *m.,* composed of a single row of one- and two-story buildings, hotels, restaurants, dance halls, taverns, and shops (R), is a roadside hamlet catering to vacationists. The left side of the highway, too steep to support buildings without expensive foundation construction, is unused.

Southwest of Lake Ozark, the highway is intersected by innumerable winding, rocky roads that lead to fishing and tourist camps and other attractions on the lake front. The resorts in general are of modern

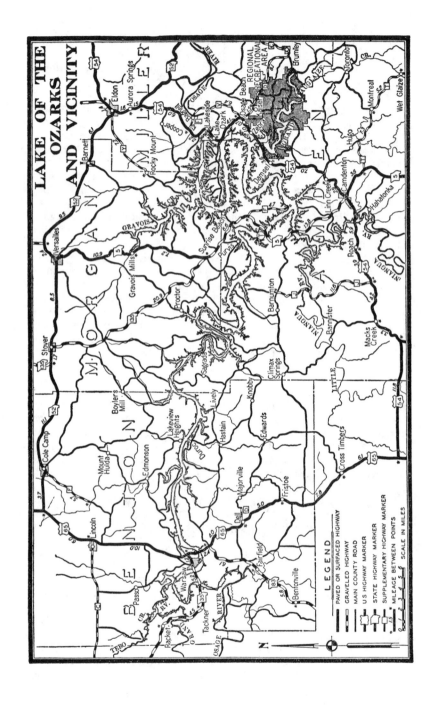

tourist-cottage design, and have a guest capacity of from 10 to 150 persons. An average minimum rate is $1 per person; for groups occupying cabins it is less. Most of the camps have a floating dock, boats, and fishing equipment. Modern conveniences are available in a majority of the cabins, although a few attempt to achieve a "roughing-it" atmosphere. Many maintain a commissary; some offer dining-room service. For the most part, the camps are operated by outsiders rather than native hillmen.

At 45.5 *m.* is a junction with the Horseshoe Bend Road, an unmarked black-topped road.

Right on this road, which rises and falls like a roller-coaster, is an attractive section of lake-front property known as HORSESHOE BEND, a game preserve area. The road terminates in a dead end at 7.2 *m.*

At 46.5 *m.* is the entrance (R) to the ARROWHEAD BEACH TRACT, an exclusive summer residential area. Homes here, while not necessarily large, are required to be of a specified value, and built along lines that harmonize with the general appearance of the community.

At 46.8 *m.* is a junction with a steep, unmarked graveled road.

Right on this road to the GORE BOATYARD, where most of the larger craft on the lake are docked and serviced. Large frame storage sheds line each side of a narrow ravine that extends to the water's edge, where a 17-ton marine railway is used to haul out the larger cruisers. A rustic, two-story building (L) houses a shop equipped to design and build any type of sailboat or power-craft suitable to the lake. Extending into the sheltered bay is a long floating pier on each side of which are covered boat wells.

OSAGE BEACH, 49 *m.,* a tiny resort village, was one of the earliest projects planned by real estate promoters in connection with the lake. A town was platted and a few lots sold when Bagnell Dam was first proposed in 1928. The economic depression halted development after 1930, however, and many lots remain unsold. At the foot of the steep hillside (R) is one of the better, man-made, sand beaches of the lake (*adm. 25¢; free to hotel guests*). On the cove reaching in from the main Osage channel of the lake is an airplane and marine gasoline station.

At 49.1 *m.* is a junction with an unmarked graveled road.

Left on this road to the GRAND GLAIZE FISH HATCHERY (*open*), 0.9 *m.,* which maintains facilities for restocking the lake with fish. In 11 one-acre feeding ponds arranged in a series below a small lake are bred largemouthed black bass and several varieties of perch. By an agreement with the Federal Government, made when the dam was franchised, the Union Electric Light and Power Company established and maintains the hatchery.

Until recently, ZEBRA, 49.7 *m.* (40 pop.), in one of the most fully developed areas on the lake, consisted of a single frame building containing a combination post office and store. The post office has been replaced by a hotel.

Southwest of Zebra, the highway rides a ridge across the Osage bluffs, then descends abruptly to cross the GRAND GLAIZE BRIDGE, 50.2 *m.*, a steel and concrete cantilever structure four-tenths of a mile in length. The term "glaize," as used in this area, is an abbreviation of *au glaize* (locally written *auglaize*), a French phrase meaning "at the clay" or "at the loam." It is applied to the stream and its tributaries because during the spring rise the red clay near the headwaters of the Grand Glaize colors the water a deep red. At the eastern end of the bridge are several fishing barges at which tackle and bait may be obtained. At the bridge's western end is the part-time docking place of the *Governor McClurg,* formerly a ferryboat and now a floating café and dance hall making regular trips on the lake (*mid-May to Sept.; 3-hour trip*).

At 51.9 *m.* is a junction with a marked graveled lake road.

Left on this road to MALIBU BEACH (*cabins, swimming, boating, fishing*), 0.6 *m.,* one of the costliest of the lake developments. Here is a wide, natural beach, and a peninsula that extends one-tenth of a mile into the Grand Glaize arm of the lake.

LINN CREEK, 60.5 *m.* (722 alt., 202 pop.), in a small valley on the banks of a creek of the same name, gained its new buff-brick church (L) and native-stone store (R) from the construction of the lake— but it lost half of its population through the same cause. Old Linn Creek was the seat of Camden County until its valley site on the Osage River, near the mouth of the Niangua, was inundated by 40 feet of water when the lake was created. Linn Creek citizens, faced with the necessity of moving their community, failed to agree upon a new site. One group moved to the site of present Linn Creek; the other, forsaking a valley location, moved to the flat summit of a near-by bluff and founded a new town, which they named Camdenton in honor of the county.

CAMDENTON, 64 *m.,* (893 pop.), established in 1929, is the seat of Camden County and, by virtue of its youthfulness, something of an anomaly in this section of the State. About a large landscaped circle are grouped the business buildings, of modern or pseudo-English half-timber design. The CAMDEN COUNTY COURTHOUSE (L) is a comparatively small, yellow-brick structure distinguished by its modern lines. Camdenton is at a junction with State 5 (*see Tour 15A*).

Camden County, first settled by Reuben Berry and William Pogue in 1827, was created as Kinderhook County in 1841 and given its present name in 1843 in honor of Charles Pratt, Earl of Camden, because of his sympathetic stand on the question of "taxation without representation." The county, well wooded in oak, hickory, and cedar trees, is dependent for its livelihood on small sawmill operations, on a limited production of stock, wheat, corn and potatoes, and on the tourist trade.

At 66.8 *m.* is a junction with an unmarked, narrow dirt road.

Left on this road (*slippery when wet*) to the entrance (L) of HAHA-TONKA (Ind., smiling water) ESTATE, 3.3 *m.*, the country place of the late R. M. Snyder, Kansas City millionaire. On the 3,500-acre grounds of the estate are a river valley, bluffs, a lake, and a spring that gushes from the base of a cliff. The road within the estate crosses NATURAL BRIDGE, a massive rock arch 50 feet in height and slightly wider than the roadbed, spanning a narrow, deep gorge. HAHATONKA TOWER (L), a square, five-story stone structure, originally designed as part of the estate's water system, is on the highest point on the grounds. Its walls are said to be five feet thick. Across the road from the tower is the CARRIAGE HOUSE, a two-story gray stone structure with a gabled roof broken by dormer windows; within are quarters for hostlers.

HAHATONKA CASTLE (*adm. 25¢; lodging*) occupies the flat summit of a crag known as Deer Leap Hill, rising 200 feet or more above the spring branch. The castle is a 3-story, gray limestone, 28-room mansion of modified late Eng-lish-Renaissance design. The slate roof has two gables on each elevation. Balancing the front gables are two dormers, and rising above the whole are four large stone chimneys. The façade is ornamented by the thick columns and rounded arches of the entrance porch. A gravel, grass, and flagstone ter-race leads from the entrance to the edge of a cliff, where supporting stone walls are covered with vines and other vegetation. The house was begun in 1905 and completed in 1922. Snyder imported 20 stonemasons from Scotland, who quarried the limestone from a near-by ledge and transported it to the site on a miniature railroad. The millionaire died before the work was completed, and for nearly 17 years the structure remained unfinished. The estate has been used but little by the Snyder family, who contended before the Missouri Supreme Court that the construction of Bagnell Dam caused great damage to the property.

Directional arrows lead from the castle to HAHATONKA VILLAGE, a small hamlet consisting of three structures, one a weathered, yellow-stone post office. The village is older than the estate. HAHATONKA SPRING, gushing from the face of a rugged, vertical limestone cliff, ranks eleventh among Missouri springs, with an average flow of 48,000,000 gallons of water daily. The clear cold water rushes through a precipitous canyon, splashing itself into foam of robin's egg blue for about 1,000 yards before it empties into what was once the 40-acre HAHATONKA LAKE (*overnight cabins, fishing, bathing, boating; nominal charge*). Since 1931 the waters of the Lake of the Ozarks have reached back into the Hahatonka district and absorbed the smaller lake. It was this that fomented the litigation between the Snyder estate and the Union Electric Light and Power Company.

The crossing of the NIANGUA RIVER, 67 *m.*, affords a view of the southernmost arm of the Lake of the Ozarks. Zebulon M. Pike, who explored the Osage River in 1806, recorded that "the Yungar (or Ne-hem-gar)," as the Niangua was then called, was so named by the Indians because of the many springs at its sources. The stream was famed for the bear in the vicinity, which Pike says were hunted not only by the French, but by the Osage and Creek (Muskogee) In-dians. Westward, the land changes from precipitous to low-rolling hills. The forests are less dense and more land is cultivated. With few exceptions, the towns are rural trading centers, with here and there a mineral spring developed as a spa.

At 93 *m.* is a junction with US 65 (*see Tour 9*).

Overlooking the Pomme de Terre (Fr., potato) River from a hilltop is HERMITAGE, 99 *m.* (1,210 alt., 321 pop.), one of the smallest county seats in Missouri. The first settler in the vicinity was Thomas Davis, who came here before the site was selected as the seat of Hickory County in 1845.

Hermitage, the first platted town in the county, was named for the home of Andrew Jackson, in Tennessee. The nearest mill was at Buffalo, 30 miles away, until W. E. Dorman put up an ox-mill at Hermitage, and ground wheat and corn.

Three or four farm villages intercept the course of the highway as prairies alternate with woodlands, and grain, poultry, and livestock farms become dominant features of the landscape.

At 119 *m.* is the junction with State 13, a concrete paved road.

Right here to OSCEOLA, 13 *m.* (750 alt., 1,190 pop.), an Osage river town and the county seat of St. Clair County. During the winter of 1835-36 Sanders Nance built a cabin here. That spring other settlers moved in and a store was opened. "Finding it a good trading point," the settlers laid out a town, which they named for Osceola, a Seminole Indian chief who was captured in 1837 after a two-year war with the United States. By 1860 the town was one of the most prosperous in southwest Missouri, and controlled a considerable commerce. Steamboats occasionally took advantage of high water to chug up the Osage to this point; Osceola stores were filled with merchandise, and the bank held large deposits of money.

Thus it happened that Jim Lane, Kansas abolitionist seeking a means to retaliate for Missouri forays across the border, determined to take Osceola. An attempt in 1860 failed because the town was well defended, but before long most of the Osceola men joined the Confederate Army. On September 23, 1861, Lane attacked again. The bank, however, had prudently secured most of its funds elsewhere, and Lane was disappointed in his hope of easy loot. He consequently ordered the town sacked, and within the next two days every store and home was stripped. Lane then had the town burned, and rode off with nearly a million dollars worth of goods.

North of Osceola, State 13 crosses Grand River, one of the tributaries of the Osage, to enter CLINTON, 37 *m.* (750 alt., 6,041 pop.), a prosperous farm trading center, and seat of Henry County, which was organized in December of 1834. The site of the present town was chosen for county seat two years later, and the first lots were sold in the spring of 1837. The town grew slowly until about 1870, when the introduction of large-scale dairy and poultry farms, and the opening of coal mines in the vicinity, brought prosperity. More than 225,000 pounds of butter and 735,000 pounds of cheese are made annually in Clinton. Local hatcheries have a setting capacity of 4,000,000 eggs every three weeks.

ELDORADO SPRINGS, 142 *m.* (913 alt., 2,342 pop.), was founded in 1881. The story is that in that year Mrs. Joshua Hightower, being desperately ill, started overland for Hot Springs, Arkansas, but progressed no farther than this spot, where her condition forced her to rest. The papers of the time reported that having drunk freely of the waters of the local springs, she became so improved in health that after two weeks she was able to return home. The incident was widely publicized, and within a short time a small tent city developed on the site. In the fall of 1881, a hotel, a store, and several other buildings were erected. Within five years, a substantial town, with a newspaper and three churches, was doing a good business as a health resort. Today (1941) the town's health equipment includes modern facilities for hospitalization and relaxation. In SPRING PARK, Spring St.

between Main and Jackson Sts., is a chalybeate or "iron" spring. The park is a natural bowl, in the center of which is a concrete basin with a drinking fountain. Paper cups are available for public use. Benches are provided for those who drink the waters, and tennis, croquet, and horseshoe courts may be used without charge. Within the park is a two-story red-brick COMMUNITY BUILDING, which houses a basketball court, an auditorium, and the public library. Near the springs are hospital and bathing facilities.

With the development of Eldorado Springs, several other mineral springs in the vicinity were bought and promoted as health resorts. One of these was NINE WONDERS SPRINGS (R), 143 m., now a group of modern cabins, but in 1887 a well-financed rival of Eldorado Springs. In that year a syndicate bought 700 acres surrounding the 9 springs, enclosed the mineral waters in a large basin, platted a park, and erected a $6,000 amphitheater. It then built a two-story brick store and several frame houses, and established a bank. Though never incorporated, Nine Wonders achieved a measure of success. In time, however, the town was abandoned, and most of the structures were moved to Eldorado Springs. The rough stone basin is still used, but only seven of the springs are active.

Westward to the Kansas Line, the highway crosses Vernon County, a well-developed, prosperous prairie section. Here are large wheat, corn, and livestock farms, with extensive painted barns and white silos that contrast sharply with those in the poorer, less cultivated counties east of Eldorado Springs. Prior to the Civil War, partisan groups participating in what is commonly known as the Border Ruffian War, committed many depredations in Vernon County. Barns and houses were burned, men were killed, and stock was stolen. During the war, the area, settled mostly by pro-slavery families, was the scene of much bitter fighting (*see Tour 10*).

NEVADA, 161 *m.* (862 alt., 8,181 pop.), is at a junction with US 71 (*see Tour 10*).

DEERFIELD, 170 *m.* (784 alt., 165 pop.), dependent on the asphalt mines a short distance west of town, was settled by Abram Redfield, who established the now defunct Deerfield Pottery there in 1871. An ASPHALT REFINERY, on the south side of town, is a cluster of brick and corrugated iron buildings equipped to crush and refine the mineral pitch ore from which asphalt is obtained. The product is used for road construction and roofing.

Right from Deerfield on County H, a graveled road, to a series of AS-PHALT PITS, 0.5 *m.*, where extensive mining has been conducted for a number of years. The mines are large black holes 20 to 30 feet deep, and, like all strip mines in Missouri, are called "diggin's." The brownish-black mineral pitch is scooped up from the pit bottoms with great shovels.

US 54 crosses the KANSAS LINE, 176 *m.*, 175 miles east of Wichita, Kansas.

Tour 15A

Junction with US 54—Camdenton—Gravois Mills—Versailles—Tipton—Junction with US 50; 58 *m.*, State 5.

Roadbed graveled and black-topped.
Tourist and resort camps along route; hotels in towns.

Between Camdenton and Versailles, State 5 is primarily a tourist highway winding among the sharp-walled valleys and wooded ridges of the Ozark hills. Following the construction of Bagnell Dam, which created the Lake of the Ozarks (1931), rocky upland tracts on the new lake shore were converted into resort sites, and villages that escaped the inundation became tourist centers.

North of CAMDENTON, 0 *m.* (1,002 alt., 893 pop.) (*see Tour 15*), is a junction with Old Five, 2.1 *m.*, an unmarked graveled road.

Right here through a grove of scrub oak to a junction with another graveled road, 4.2 *m.*

Left here 0.2 *m.* to LOVERS' LEAP, a sheer, 100-foot bluff from whose crevices gnarled cedars grow. The summit presents a good view of the confluence of the Osage, Niangua, and Linn Creek arms of the Lake of the Ozarks, which enter from the north, west, and south, respectively.

Ahead on Old Five to the GOVERNOR JOSEPH A. McCLURG HOUSE (*open*), 4.5 *m.* (L), a two-story, rubble-rock dwelling draped with vines that almost hide the screened porch and end chimney. At the back is a large two-story stucco ell and a kitchen, both added when the older part was remodeled. Many of the original walnut doorjams and window sills are intact. The house, built by McClurg in 1854, is now a resort hotel. McClurg, who died in 1900, served as Governor of Missouri 1868-72.

The HURRICANE DECK TOLL BRIDGE (*automobile and driver, 40¢; round trip, 70¢; additional passengers, or pedestrians, 5¢ each; automobile, trailer, and driver, 60¢; round trip, $1*), 12.7 *m.*, is a concrete and steel structure, one-half mile long. Designed by L. J. Sverdrup and built at a cost of $655,000, the bridge was awarded first prize by the American Institute of Steel Construction in 1936 as the most beautiful medium-sized steel span erected that year. The traffic way is 65 feet above the Osage arm of the Lake of the Ozarks (*boats, tackle, and fishing guides*).

At 15 *m.* is a junction with Lake Road 20, a graveled road.

Right here, past the entrances to a number of lake resorts, to GREEN BAY TERRACE (*cabins, swimming, boating, fishing*), 3.2 *m.*, a small lakeside community "ruled" by William Green, Sr., the genial, self-styled "Sittin' Bill—Chief of the Ozark Hill-Billies." Sittin' Bill, a living information bureau, spins tales of the region prior to the lake's formation.

At 17.1 *m.* is a junction with an unmarked graveled road.

Left here through a wooded area to HURRICANE DECK, 0.8 *m.*, a mile-and-a-half slice of the great bluff above the Osage channel of the Lake of the Ozarks. The road terminates at a circle in a barren, level crest of tableland offering an excellent view of the lake and upper valley. The name Hurricane Deck is suggestive of the strong wind that sometimes sweeps the edge of the bluff.

A ROADSIDE TURNOUT (L), 17.7 *m.,* is a graveled parkway with picnicking facilities. North of the turnout, the highway crosses a wooded section of shoreline developed by numerous resorts, most of which are some distance off the road. The camps to the right are on the Osage and Gravois arms of the lake; those to the left are on the Niangua River and the upper Osage. The majority of them are modern.

At 19.4 *m.* is a junction with Lake Road 13, a narrow dirt road.

Right here to ST. PATRICK'S CHURCH (L), 1 *m.,* a small chapel with a bright tin roof. In 1858, Thomas Fitzpatrick, seeking a homestead, came to the Ozark wilderness from Ireland. Here, in the cool green of the hills, he staked a claim and built a log house. He then returned to Ireland, and brought back his wife. Soon the couple were joined by other families from County Farmaraugh, Ireland. In 1860 the colony decided to erect a church. Native stone was taken from a quarry a mile away and hauled to the site by oxen. Lime was burned on the grounds. Construction was slow, though all the neighbors helped, Henry Purvis, the one non-Catholic in the group, also assisting his fellow pioneers. When, at last, the exterior was completed in 1863, the priest from Cole Camp came to say Mass. It was 20 years before the interior was finished. With the creation of the lake, the importance of the church increased. The structure was remodeled, and two small rooms were added at the back, one a sacristy, the other lodging quarters for the priest during inclement weather.

At 25 *m.* is a junction with Lake Road 8, a graveled road.

Right here, following directional signs, and L. at the forks, 4.7 *m.* to the GRAVOIS BOAT AND DRY DOCKS, 5 *m.,* at the confluence of the Gravois and Osage arms of the lake. The docks maintain one of the largest pleasure and fishing fleets on the lake. From the large frame and corrugated iron sheds, a small marine railroad extends to the floating wharves. Cranes are used to lift smaller boats to the drydock. The various lake craft are kept in the wells of the floating docks during summer. Practically all types of boats can be rented, including houseboats with accommodations for six to ten persons and a crew.

GRAVOIS MILLS, 29.5 *m.* (673 alt., 59 pop.), an unincorporated village on a long finger of the Lake of the Ozarks, was platted in 1884. Near here, Josiah S. Walton began operating a water-driven gristmill about 1835, taking a percentage of the flour or meal ground as his fee. He did such a ıthriving business that sometimes customers had to camp at the mill several days waiting their turn. All trace of this early mill has disappeared. Near the Walton Mill, the Hume brothers built a woolen mill about 1870 and manufactured woolens for the central Missouri trade. In 1895, Asa Webster purchased the Hume property, added a sawmill, and built the stone dam which forms the Troutdale Hatchery lake (*see below*).

Left from Gravois Mills on Lake Road 4, a graveled road that follows the winding course of the old mill stream, to the TROUTDALE HATCHERY (*open*), 1.1 *m.*, a privately operated rainbow-trout propagation unit consisting of a gray frame hatchery building, a lake, and subsidiary rearing pools. The lake and pools are fed by Collins Spring, which flows at the rate of more than 5,000,000 gallons daily. During spawning season (January and February), the female trout are caught in nets and stripped of their eggs, which are then fertilized and hatched in troughs of water. When the young trout are between five and eight inches long, they are released into the lake. The hatchery was established in 1931, and produces about 200,000 trout annually. The fish are sold on the commercial market. Visitors are permitted to fish in the lake (*small fee*).

North of Gravois Mills, the highway follows the winding Gravois arm of the lake, crosses Big Gravois Creek, and, leaving the lake shore, climbs to the upland.

JACOB'S CAVE (*open 8 a.m.-10 p.m.; 25¢ guide fee; group rates*), 33.5 *m.* (L), is reached over a winding dirt road. The cave consists of four large and several small rooms, the first of which is equipped with picnic tables. A small stream runs through the passageway.

At 34.5 *m.* is a junction with an unmarked graveled road.

Left here through dense timber to a small frame store (L), 0.9 *m.* Two hundred yards left of the store is a NATURAL BRIDGE, a high passageway tunneling 600 feet through the hills. The thick roof connects 2 bluffs that rise 100 feet above the road. Within the passage is a small spring.

The A. B. KIDWELL BRACKET FACTORY (R), 2 *m.*, housed in a rambling unpainted frame structure, converts oak timber of the region into telephone post brackets (the upright, wooden knobs that hold glass insulators). The factory operates on order, and at times employs ten workers, who make the brackets with lathes and saws. From this isolated spot, the company ships its products as far as the Orient.

A small LAKE AND DAM (R), 38 *m.*, in a miniature ravine about 32 feet below the highway, is part of the lake region's roadside beautification program.

VERSAILLES, 41 *m.* (1,037 alt., 1,781 pop.), seat of Morgan County, is the northernmost of the Lake of the Ozarks towns. Built around a public square, in the center of which is the two-story, red-brick Morgan County courthouse, it draws its income from the tourist and farm trades and the administration of justice. The market, elevator, and seasonal cannery of the local farmers' co-operative association, provide improved methods for utilizing or conserving surplus produce, as well as work for members and markets for their products. Goods are sold directly to lake resorts.

Morgan County was organized in 1833 and named for General Daniel Morgan, Revolutionary War patriot. Millville, now extinct, served as the county seat until succeeded by Versailles in 1834. Anglo-American families from Tennessee, Kentucky, and Virginia began settling in the narrow but fertile Osage and Niangua River valleys about 1820, building mills where water power could be utilized, and developing an almost self-sufficient social and economic life. Timber, furs, farm produce, and some lead were shipped to distant markets down the Osage River, the county's early highway. Hunters, trappers, and traders regularly traveled the river, and during the steamboat era small river boats puffed their way up to Warsaw. In 1858 the Missouri Pacific Railroad reached the northern portion of the county, and after the Civil War large numbers of Swiss and German families, many of them Mennonites, opened farms in the prairie uplands.

The MARTIN HOTEL (R), a half-block north of the square, is a plain, two-story, red-brick structure, built by Samuel Martin in 1879 to replace a log inn that the Martin family had operated as a hotel since 1853. Martin and his wife, Elizabeth, ran the hotel jointly until his death in 1906 at the age of 92. For 20 years more, Mrs. Martin, or, more familiarly, "Grandma" Martin, continued taking guests. She died at the age of 103 years, 6 months, and 16 days. Today (1941) an aged daughter, "Miss Lucy," carries on, claiming to be a member of the oldest continuous "hotel family" in one location in Missouri.

TIPTON, 58 *m.* (922 alt., 1,219 pop.), is at junction with US 50 (*see Tour 4*).

PART IV
Appendices

Missouri Chronology

1659   Pierre d'Espirit, Sieur Radisson, and his brother-in-law, Medard Chouart, Sieur des Groseilliers, claim discovery of rivers which may be Mississippi and Missouri.

1673   July. Marquette and Jolliet pass mouth of Missouri River on journey of exploration down the Mississippi.

1682   Feb. 14. Robert Cavelier de la Salle passes mouth of Missouri on voyage of exploration down the Mississippi.
April 6. La Salle reaches mouth of Mississippi.
April 9. La Salle claims Mississippi Valley for France.

1688   Baron La Hontan writes of exploring Missouri upstream to mouth of Osage River.

1693   May. Two French traders accompanied by some Kaskaskia Indians visit the Missouri and Osage villages on the Missouri River; establish trade relations.

1699   Seminarian priests, Fathers Montigny, Davion, and St. Cosme, erect crosses on Grand Tower below present Wittenburg in Perry County, and at Cape de la Croix below present Cape Girardeau.

1700   Le Sueur explores for mines on Mississippi and Missouri Rivers.
Autumn. Kaskaskia Indians settle at mouth of Des Peres River within present limits of St. Louis. Priests establish Mission of St. Francis Xavier there.
Salt reported being made at La Saline, present Ste. Genevieve County.

1702   March. Seventeen Frenchmen leave Des Peres mission to ascend Missouri, and build fort somewhere near present Iowa-Nebraska State line. Attacked by Indians. Probably returned unharmed.
D'Iberville petitions King of France for concession of some lead mines in Missouri area.

1703   Kaskaskia Indians move from River Des Peres to site on Kaskaskia River. Mission abandoned.

1706   Derbanne said to have explored upper Missouri.

1710   Memoir of d'Artaguitte mentions discovery of silver in southeastern Missouri lead deposits.

1712   Missouri Indians from villages in present Saline County relieve French besieged at Detroit.
Antoine Crozat granted 15-year trade monopoly of Louisiana.

1714   Etienne Veniard Sieur de Bourgmond explores Missouri River as far north as mouth of the Platte.
Charles Claude du Tisne shows Governor Cadillac specimens of silver ore said to have come from mine in southeast Missouri.

1715   Cadillac visits Illinois Country to investigate story of silver mines. Opens mine at Mine la Motte.

1717   Crozat surrenders charter after heavy losses.
        August. Company of the West given charter for 25-year trade monopoly of Louisiana. Later merged with "Royal Company of the Indies," with John Law as Director General.

1719   Pierre de Boisbriant arrives at Kaskaskia with party of engineers and workmen instructed to open lead and silver mines in southeast Missouri. Subsequently opens mines at Mine la Motte and on Mineral Fork of Big River. Rumors of silver here continue.

1720   Charles Claude du Tisne, French-Canadian, on order of Governor Bienville, explores southwest Missouri area and visits Osage villages. Philip Renault establishes St. Philippe near Fort Chartres with orders to develop mining operations in southeast Missouri.
        Spanish military expedition of 60 men massacred near confluence of Platte and Loup Rivers in present Nebraska by Indians friendly to French.

1723   Company of the Indies withdraws credit subsidy to Renault. Renault receives concession of southeast Missouri mines.
        Fort d'Orleans begun under direction of De Bourgmond in present Carroll County.

1725   De Bourgmond returns to France with group of Indians from Missouri area.

1728   Fort d'Orleans abandoned.
        Fur trade monopoly on Missouri and Ohio granted for five years to French-Canadians Marain and Outlas by Company of the Indies.

1731   Company of the Indies surrenders its charter.

1739   Mallet brothers and six companions arrive at Santa Fe from Illinois settlements.

1744   Renault sells holdings to government and returns to France.

1745   Joseph des Bruisseau granted exclusive trading privileges on the Missouri. May have built fort at mouth of Osage River.

1750   Earliest known reference to Ste. Genevieve. Village developed shortly before this date.

1752   Provisions made for a Roman Catholic church in Ste. Genevieve—the first in Missouri.

1762   Dec. 3. France, by secret treaty of Fontainebleau, cedes territory west of the Mississippi to Spain.
        July 6. Maxent, Laclede & Co. granted exclusive trading privileges in Upper Mississippi Valley area.

1763   December. Pierre Laclede Liguest selects site of future St. Louis.

1764   Feb. 14. Thirteen-year-old Auguste Chouteau heads party of workmen sent to establish St. Louis.
        Father Sebastian Meurin comes to Ste. Genevieve. First resident priest.

1765   July 17. St. Ange de Bellerive surrenders Fort Chartres to British and moves capital of Upper Louisiana to St. Louis, maintaining control of government until formal transfer to Spanish authorities in 1770.

1768 Spanish officers build fort "El Principe de Asturias, Senor Don Carlos," at the mouth and on south bank of Missouri River. A block house is built on north bank.

1769 Chief Pontiac buried in St. Louis, following murder in Cahokia, Illinois.

1770 May 20. St. Ange formally surrenders possession of Upper Louisiana to Spanish Lieutenant Governor Piernas.

First Catholic Church in St. Louis dedicated.

Hildebrants and other American families settle on Meramec River.

1774 Lead mines at Mine à Breton (later Potosi) discovered by François Azor dit Breton.

1778 General George Rogers Clark's conquest of British Illinois Country aided by Spanish authorities in Missouri.

1779 Pierre Laclede Liguest dies.

1780 May 26. Spanish at St. Louis repulse combined British and Indian attack. *L'Année du Coup.*

1781 Settlement at Les Petites Côtes (later St. Charles) begins.

1784 First Shawnee and Delaware Indians migrate into southeast Missouri.

1785 Great flood on Mississippi and tributary rivers.

Ste. Genevieve relocated on higher ground. Old village site gradually abandoned.

Settlement of St. Ferdinand de Florissant begins.

1788 Madame Marie Josepha Pinconneau dit Rigauche establishes girls' school in St. Louis.

1789 February. Colonel George Morgan founds New Madrid.

May 23. Governor Miro refuses Morgan permission to develop colony plans. New Madrid becomes Spanish post.

El Camino Real marked out, following old Indian trail from New Madrid to St. Louis.

1792 Oct. 6. Pedro Vial and two companions arrive at St. Louis having made overland trip from Santa Fe.

The honey bee is first seen in Missouri.

1793 Nouvelle Bourbon established as haven for royalist refugees.

Louis Lorimier authorized to encourage Shawnee and Delaware immigration into southeastern Missouri.

1794 May 21. Auguste and Pierre Chouteau obtain six-year monopoly of Osage Indian trade on condition they build a fort on Osage River. Build Fort Carondelet in present Vernon County.

Reverend Josiah Dodge preaches first Protestant (Baptist) sermon west of the Mississippi.

Spanish Commercial Exploration Company developed by St. Louis merchants. Subsidized by Spanish government.

1796 Daniel Morgan Boone settles in St. Charles District.

Reverend John Clark, first Methodist preacher, enters Missouri.

1797 January 21-26. Moses Austin granted concession at Mine à Breton.
Captain James Piggott starts ferry across Mississippi at St. Louis.
1798 Americans settle in Bellevue Valley and on Big River.
1799 Military post established at Portage des Sioux against threatened American invasion.
Nathaniel Cook forms American settlement near present Farmington.
Daniel Boone heads group of Kentuckians settling in St. Charles District.
1800 Oct. 1. Spain retrocedes Louisiana to France in Treaty of San Ildefonso.
Thirteen Creole settlers granted lands at St. Michael (Fredericktown).
American settlement at Bird's Point, now Mississippi County.
Daniel Boone made Syndic of Femme Osage.
1801 Murphy settlement begins in vicinity of present Farmington.
1802 Creole settlement made at Old Mines.
Pierre Chouteau induces Big Osage tribe to move to Arkansas River area in order to retain their trade.
James Pursley, an American, with two companions, leaves St. Louis on a hunting expedition and eventually wanders to Santa Fe.
1803 April 30. Treaty of Cession signed by representatives of the United States and France. It cedes the Louisiana territory to the United States for a net purchase price of $15,000,000.
1804 March 9. Formal transfer of Upper Louisiana from France to the United States made at St. Louis.
May 14. Lewis and Clark expedition leaves camp at the mouth of Wood River, opposite the mouth of the Missouri, to explore upper Missouri River and the Columbia River to the Pacific ocean. Return to St. Louis in 1806.
July 4. St. Louis post office, first in State, established in St. Louis.
July. Chief White Hairs of the Osage leads delegation to Washington, D. C.
Oct. 1. Upper Louisiana becomes District of Louisiana, attached to the Territory of Indiana for administrative purposes.
Nov. 3. Sauk and Fox Indians at St. Louis cede northeast Missouri lands to United States. Indians later claim treaty was made by unauthorized representatives.
1805 March 3. Territory of Louisiana created, independent of Territory of Indiana. General James Wilkinson appointed Governor. St. Louis made the capital.
Board of Land Commissioners created to examine French and Spanish land grant claims.
Baptist congregation, said to be first in Missouri, organized in Tywappity Bottom.
1806 Fort Bellefontaine established.
July 16. Zebulon Pike's expedition leaves Fort Bellefontaine for Southwest via Missouri and Osage Rivers. Returns 1807.
Methodists establish church at McKendree, near Jackson.

Nathan and Daniel Morgan Boone, and the Morrisons of St. Charles, start manufacturing salt at Boon's Lick.

Kentucky families settle on Loutre Island.

1807 Louisiana Lodge No. 109, first Chapter of the Masonic Order in Missouri, chartered in Ste. Genevieve.

Louisiana Academy organized in Ste. Genevieve. Chartered by legislature following year.

1808 March 20. First issue of the *Missouri Gazette,* first newspaper in Missouri, appears in St. Louis; some months later, Joseph Charless, its editor, publishes first book in Missouri, *The Laws of the Territory of Louisiana.*

St. Louis incorporated. First election held July 3.

Fort Osage, in present Jackson County, established as government factory under direction of General William Clark.

By treaty made at Fort Osage, Osage Indians cede to United States all lands north of the Missouri River, and all land south of the river lying east of a line running south from Fort Osage.

1809 St. Louis Missouri Fur Company organized. Reorganized 1812; dissolved 1814.

Hostility of Indians on frontier increases.

April. Governor Lewis orders riflemen to relieve Fort Madison (Wisconsin), besieged by Indians. Appoints committee to superintend building of blockhouses from Mississippi to Missouri Rivers.

April 21. General order for muster of territorial volunteer companies.

John N. Maclot builds first shot tower in State at Herculaneum.

1810 Population of Territory of Louisiana 19,976.

Massacre of members of Cole party near Loutre Island by Indians.

Families from Loutre Island settle in Boone's Lick Country.

1811 March. The "Astorians," headed by Wilson P. Hunt, leave St. Louis for expedition to mouth of Columbia River.

Dec. 16. New Madrid earthquake begins.

1812 Counties organized: Cape Girardeau, New Madrid, St. Charles, Ste. Genevieve, and St. Louis.

March 3. Nathan Boone's company of Mounted Rangers mustered. Begin patrol from Salt River on Mississippi River to mouth of Loutre River on Missouri River.

July. First United States Army recruiting office west of the Mississippi opens in Ste. Genevieve.

Oct. 1. Territory of Louisiana becomes Territory of Missouri, with a governor, a legislative council, and a house of representatives.

Dec. 7. First Territorial General Assembly meets in St. Louis.

Robert McKnight, James Baird, and Samuel Chambers leave St. Louis on trading expedition to Santa Fe. Are imprisoned in Santa Fe by Spanish authorities.

Horse races held on Mamelle Tract near St. Charles.

1813 Washington County organized.

Indian danger causes temporary abandonment of Fort Osage.

1814   May 1. Force of territorial militia commanded by General William Clark leaves St. Louis for upper Mississippi. Takes Prairie du Chien; builds fort which surrenders to combined English and Indian attack on July 20.

July. Missouri Fur Company established. Continues through various reorganizations until about 1830.

August. Three volunteer companies raised. Major Zachary Taylor builds Fort Johnson near mouth of Lemoine River in present Iowa. Major Henry Dodge leads force for relief of Boon's Lick settlement.

Dec. 24. Treaty of Ghent.

1815   Jan. 6. First St. Louis theater opens.

March 7. Captain James Callaway and four of his men ambushed by Indians on Loutre River.

April 4. Indians attack Côte Sans Dessein; are repelled.

May 24. Indians attack Rangers in Battle of the Sink Hole near the Cuivre River.

July 10. Treaty-making conferences begin at Portage des Sioux with William Clark, Ninian Edwards of Illinois, and Auguste Chouteau as United States Commissioners.

Western Journal, second Missouri newspaper, established in St. Louis.

A. P. Chouteau and Julius De Mun organize overland trading expedition from St. Louis to Santa Fe. Imprisoned at Santa Fe and goods confiscated. Released after three years.

Iron furnaces built on Stout's Creek, near present Ironton.

1816   Howard County organized.

April 29. Missouri made territory of the highest rank.

May and June. Treaties signed at St. Louis with the ten tribes who failed to appear at Portage des Sioux. Formal end of War of 1812.

Aug. 12. First Presbyterian Church in Missouri organized at Caledonia.

August 21. Bank of St. Louis chartered with capital of $163,000. Roads opened from Potosi and St. Charles to the Boon's Lick Country in Howard County.

1817   August 9. First steamboat arrives at St. Louis, the *Zebulon M. Pike.*

August 23. Thomas H. Benton kills Charles Lucas in duel at St. Louis.

Thomas McBride organizes Salt Creek (Christian) Church in Howard County. First Christian Church in Missouri.

1818   Counties organized: Cooper, Franklin, Jefferson, Lincoln, Madison, Montgomery, Pike, and Wayne.

Jan. 6. Petitions presented in Congress asking statehood for Missouri Territory.

Sept. Mother Duchesne establishes Order of the Sacred Heart at St. Charles.

Nov. 13. Territorial Legislature adopts memorial to Congress asking for statehood.

Land offices established at St. Louis, Jackson, and Franklin.

Vincentian Fathers establish St. Mary's-of-the-Barrens in Perry County, the oldest collegiate institution in Missouri.

St. Louis Academy, forerunner of St. Louis University, established in St. Louis.

Pine lumbering begun on headwaters of the Gasconade.

1819   March 2. House and Senate fail to concur on Missouri Bill. Indignation meetings held throughout territory.

April 23. First issue of the *Missouri Intelligencer* appears at Franklin.

July 30. In the treaty of Edwardsville the Kickapoo Indians trade their lands east of the Mississippi River for lands in southwest Missouri.

Oct. 7. The Reverend John Ward preaches first Episcopal sermon in Missouri at St. Louis.

Steamboat *Independence* proves the Missouri River navigable.

Depression reaches West.

Expedition up the Missouri to the mouth of the Yellowstone, headed by Major Stephen H. Long, includes the *Western Engineer,* a serpent-shaped steamboat.

Chester Harding paints portrait of the aged Daniel Boone in St. Charles County.

Road marked west from Franklin to Fort Osage.

Arkansas Territory formed from Missouri Territory.

1820   Population: 56,335 free; 10,222 slaves; total 66,557.

Counties organized: Boone, Callaway, Chariton, Cole, Gasconade, Lafayette, Perry, Ralls, Ray, and Saline.

March 6. Missouri Enabling Act passed by Congress and approved by President Monroe.

May 12. Constitutional Convention meets at Mansion House Hotel in St. Louis. David Barton elected president.

July 19. Constitution adopted, taking effect immediately. Barton issues writs for first election held under authority of the "State of Missouri."

August 28. First State election. Alexander McNair elected governor.

September 18. First General Assembly convenes in St. Louis; 14 senators, and 43 state representatives. David Barton and Thomas H. Benton elected United States Senators October 2.

September 26. Daniel Boone dies.

Stagecoach line begins operating between St. Louis and Franklin.

1821   Counties organized: Scott and St. Francois.

Spring. Pierre Chouteau establishes a trading post at mouth of the Kaw.

Congress refuses to accept Missouri Constitution on basis of clause preventing free negroes and mulattoes from coming into State. Antislavery party attempts on this basis to prevent admission of Missouri as a slave state. Compromise effected permitting admission of Missouri, if legislature, by a "solemn public act," should declare that no attempt would be made to enforce this passage.

June 10. Moses Austin dies before plans to colonize Texas are completed.

June 26. Missouri legislature passes "solemn public act."

August 10. Missouri admitted into Union as a State.

September 1. William Becknell starts from Franklin on first successful commercial overland expedition to Santa Fe.

December 31. State capital located at present site of Jefferson City and provisions made for laying out town.

United Foreign Mission Society of New York establishes Harmony Mission in present Bates County for Osage Indians.

Loan offices established to relieve pressure of depression.

1822 Clay County organized.

January 11. State seal adopted.

April 15. William Henry Ashley's party of 80-odd men leave St. Louis for newly organized Rocky Mountain Fur Company's expedition to the Far West.

Western Department branch of American Fur Company established in St. Louis.

1823 May 11. St. Regis Seminary, first such Indian School for boys in the United States, begins operations at Florissant under Jesuit supervision.

Salt River Road laid out from St. Charles to Des Moines River.

Sauk and Fox Indians cede lands north of Missouri River and east of a line running north from the mouth of the Kansas River.

1825 General Lafayette and party visit St. Louis.

Commissioners appointed by Federal government to mark road from western Missouri to Santa Fe.

Big and Little Osage, and Kansas Indians·cede rights to all remaining lands claimed in Missouri. Shawnees also cede remaining lands in southeast Missouri for reservation west of the Missouri State line.

1826 Counties organized: Jackson and Marion.

Jefferson Barracks established.

Springfield Iron Furnace and Forge opened near Potosi.

Thomas James and Samuel Massey begin iron works at Meramec Springs.

Kit Carson runs away from Franklin to Santa Fe, beginning career as hunter, trapper, guide, and Indian fighter in Far West.

Legislature holds first session in Jefferson City.

Legislature abolishes the whipping post, pillory, and stocks as means of punishment in Missouri.

1827 Joseph Robidoux establishes fur trading post on present site of St. Joseph.

William Henry Ashley sells his Rocky Mountain Fur Company to Smith, Jackson, and Sublette, who push fur trade operations beyond Rocky Mountains to Pacific Ocean.

1829   Counties organized: Crawford and Randolph.

Gottfried Duden's *Bericht über eine Reise* published in Germany, precipitating heavy German immigration during following decade.

Branch of the United States Bank established in St. Louis. Operated until 1833.

1830   Population: 115,364 free, 25,091 slaves; total 140,455.

1831   Monroe County organized.

Joseph Smith, Prophet of the Church of Jesus Christ of Latter Day Saints (Mormon) announces Jackson County revealed as site of Zion; Mormon settlement there begins.

St. Louis made a port of entry.

1832   Treaty of Castor Hill, St. Louis County, by which Kickapoos cede Missouri lands for tract west of State line.

Allied Delaware and Shawnee tribes in southeast Missouri area cede remaining lands; are soon removed west of State line.

May-Sept. Black Hawk War.

Cholera epidemic.

St. Louis University chartered.

1833   Counties organized: Carroll, Clinton, Greene, Lewis, Morgan, Pettis, Pulaski, Ripley, and Warren.

First heavy German immigration into State begins.

Mormons driven from Jackson County into Clay County.

Westport platted by John C. McCoy.

1834   Counties organized: Henry and Johnson.

April. Reverend Jason Lee and Nathaniel J. Wyeth leave Independence on overland trip to Oregon.

Reformed Evangelical Churches, first in Missouri, established at Friedens and Femme Osage.

Charter granted to first Missouri lodge of the Independent Order of Odd Fellows. State organization formed soon afterward.

First regular Unitarian services in Missouri held in St. Louis.

The *St. Louis Herald,* Missouri's first daily, established.

1835   Counties organized: Barry, Benton, Cass, Polk, Shelby, and Stoddard.

Oct. 31. First issue of *Anzeiger des Westens,* first Missouri German-language newspaper, appears in St. Louis.

Nov. 30. Samuel Clemens (Mark Twain) born in Florida, Missouri.

Missouri State Penitentiary established.

1836   Counties organized: Audrain, Caldwell, Clark, and Daviess.

January 1. First Jewish congregation in Missouri meets in St. Louis.

April 30. Fifty-nine delegates meet in St. Louis for first Missouri railroad convention. Various lines projected.

Missouri Iron Company organized to develop deposits at Iron Mountain and Pilot Knob.

The Platte Purchase, comprising six northwest Missouri counties, added to State.

Missourians go to Texas to aid in fight for independence.

1837 Counties organized: Linn, Livingston, Macon, Miller, and Taney.
September 28. David Barton dies in Boonville.
October 6. Missouri troops commanded by Colonel Richard Gentry leave Columbia to participate in Seminole war.
November 17. Capitol burns at Jefferson City.
Remaining Osages moved west of State line.
Mormons establish Far West in Caldwell County as religious and administrative headquarters of church.

1838 Counties organized: Buchanan, Newton, and Platte.
June. Adam-ondi-Ahman founded in Daviess County. Mormon settlement.
August 6. Mormon-Gentile riot at Gallatin.
September. Outbreak of open war between Mormons and Gentiles.
September 1. General William Clark dies.
September 11. Third Division of Missouri Militia ordered to seat of Mormon war.
October 11. Mormons besieged at De Witt surrender.
October 18. Mormon force takes Gallatin and burns several buildings.
October 27. Governor Boggs declares Mormons enemies who must be exterminated or driven from State.
October 30. Mormons massacred at Haun's Mill.
October 31. Mormons surrender at Far West.
Fall and winter. Cherokee Indians pass through southern Missouri over Trail of Tears, en route to reservation west of State line.

1839 Saxon Lutheran colonists settle in Perry County. Establish Concordia Seminary at Altenburg.
Mormons emigrate from Missouri into Illinois.
"Honey War" with Iowa over border dispute.

1840 Population: 325,462 free, 58,240 slaves; total 383,702.
Forty newspapers operating in State.
Journeymen bricklayers in St. Louis pledge 10 hour day.
Last antelope seen in Missouri.
McDowell Medical College established as a branch of Kemper College.
Missouri State capitol completed at cost of about $350,000.

1841 Counties organized: Adair, Andrew, Bates, Camden, Dade, Dallas, Grundy, Holt, Jasper, Osage, Ozark, St. Clair, Scotland, Shannon, and Wright.
Legislature removes property qualifications for voters and office holders in municipalities.
"Slickers," vigilante groups, organized in Lincoln and Benton Counties to suppress horse stealing and petty lawlessness. "Slicker War" breaks out.
Classes begin at Missouri University. John Lathrop president.
The daguerreotype is first used in Missouri.
Mechanics and Workingmen's Party formed.
Last great concentration of elk seen in Missouri.

1843   May 22. "The Great Emigration," a party of more than 120 wagons, leaves Elm Grove in western Missouri for Oregon. Group headed by Peter H. Burnett.

Oct. 3. Senator Lewis F. Linn dies. David R. Atchison appointed to succeed him.

Joseph Robidoux plats St. Joseph.

Imprisonment for debt abolished.

1844   F. T. Kemper open boys' school at Boonville, antecedent of Kemper Military School.

Oct. 22. The Millerites await the end of the world at Hannibal.

Missouri Historical and Philosophical Society organized.

Floods on Missouri and Mississippi Rivers.

Howard High School, forerunner of Central College, established at Fayette.

Dr. John Sappington publishes his *Theory and Treatment of Fevers,* advocating use of quinine.

First Masonic College in world established at Philadelphia, Mo.

1845   Counties organized: Atchison, Cedar, DeKalb, Dunklin, Gentry, Harrison, Hickory, Knox, Lawrence, Mercer, Mississippi, Moniteau, Nodaway, Oregon, Putnam, Reynolds, Schuyler, Sullivan, and Texas.

William Keil establishes Bethel, a communistic settlement in Shelby County.

1846   Mercantile Library Association established in St. Louis.

Regiment for the Mexican War raised in Missouri, commanded by Colonel A. W. Doniphan and Colonel Sterling Price. Begins historic overland march.

1847   December 20. Telegraph communication between St. Louis and East established.

1848   September 12-17. François Xavier Aubry makes 800-mile horseback ride from Santa Fe to Independence in 5 days and 16 hours.

1849   Counties organized: Butler, Laclede, and McDonald.

Great fire in St. Louis.

National railroad convention in St. Louis.

State Hospital No. 1 opens in Fulton for treatment of insane.

Pacific Railroad chartered.

Cholera epidemic.

Lead mines in southwest Missouri opened.

Forty-nine plank road companies chartered.

1850   Population: 594,622 free, 87,422 slave; total 682,044.

September 3. Eugene Field born in St. Louis.

Samuel H. Woodson of Independence receives first overland mail contract—Independence to Salt Lake City.

Last buffalo seen in Missouri.

1851   Counties organized: Bollinger, Dent, Pemiscot, Stone, and Vernon.

Missouri School for the Deaf opens at Fulton.

Eli W. Whalen establishes Missouri School for the Blind in St. Louis. Becomes a State institution a few years later.

1852   December 9. Pacific Railroad begins first railroad service in Missouri, from St. Louis to Cheltenham.

1853   February 22. The City of Kansas (Kansas City) chartered.
       February. First high school in State opened in St. Louis.
       State Geological Survey authorized.
       Washington University founded in St. Louis.

1854   April 26. Massachusetts Emigrant Aid Company chartered by Massachusetts Legislature to send free settlers to Kansas.
       May 30. Kansas-Nebraska Bill signed by President Pierce. Precipitates contest between North and South over admission of Kansas on free or slave status.
       July 29. Platte County residents organize the Platte County Self-Defensive Association with object of settling Kansas with pro-slavery men.
       November. Kansas Territorial election scene of first open conflict. Illegal votes by Missourians elect pro-slavery candidate.
       St. Louis Republican issues first Sunday paper in State.
       Anti-Horse Thief Association founded in Clark County.
       United States Patent Office distributes first sorghum seed in Missouri.

1855   Counties organized: Barton, Maries, and Webster.
       March 30. Pro-slavery Missourians, voting illegally in Kansas Territorial election, seat a pro-slavery legislature.
       July 12. Pro-slavery convention held at Lexington, with 25 Missouri counties represented, advocates "just and constitutional measures" to prevent Kansas from becoming a free state.
       November. Wakarusa War. Free-State men entrenched at Lawrence surrender to pro-slavery forces formed principally of Missourians.
       Pacific Railroad completed to Jefferson City. On train's first run, bridge over Gasconade collapses; many killed.

1856   May 11. United States marshal summons a posse to quell Kansas Free-State groups indicted by grand jury. Posse formed chiefly of Missourians. Lawrence entered, hotel and press destroyed. Many houses robbed, and some Free-State leaders arrested.
       May 21. Missouri State Teachers Association organized.
       John Brown "avenges" Lawrence raid by killing five pro-slavery settlers on Pottawatomie Creek. Missouri forces organize. Guerrilla war breaks out.
       Atchison and Doniphan, commanding Missouri troops, drive John Brown from Ossawatomie.
       Sept. 15. Territorial Governor John W. Geary visits camp of 2,700 pro-slavery Missourians marching on Lawrence, and persuades them to return home.
       The Academy of Science founded in St. Louis.

1857   Counties organized: Douglas, Howell, Iron, and Phelps.
       March 6. Chief Justice Roger B. Taney renders Supreme Court decision in Dred Scott case. Declares, in substance, that slavery can-

not be prohibited in the territories of the United States. Decision brings slavery question to crisis.

The *Westliche Post* begins publication in St. Louis.

First Agricultural and Mechanics Fair held in St. Louis.

The Icarians, French socialistic group, settle at Cheltenham, St. Louis County. Experiment ended 1864.

State banking system established; office of Bank Commissioner created.

Collapse of Page & Bacon, St. Louis banking house, precipitates financial panic in Missouri.

1858 April 2. St. Louis and Iron Mountain Railroad completed to Pilot Knob.

April 10. Thomas H. Benton dies.

May 1. John Hockaday begins weekly mail service between Independence and Salt Lake City.

May 14. Kansans begin series of raids into Bates and neighboring counties.

May 31. Missouri's Governor Stewart orders troops to southwest Missouri border.

Sept. 15. John Butterfield's semi-monthly overland stage service between San Francisco and Tipton begins at both ends of the line.

December 19. John Brown heads raid into Vernon County; liberates 11 slaves by force.

December 30. Jayhawkers raid Linn County, destroying property. Residents appeal for military protection.

North Missouri Railroad completed to Mexico, Missouri.

1859 Counties organized: Carter and Christian.

February 13. Hannibal and St. Joseph Railroad completed.

February 24. Governor Stewart approves act "for protection of persons and property on the western border of this State."

Captain John Wise sets balloon record, from St. Louis to Henderson, N. Y., in 39 hours, 50 minutes.

1860 Population: 1,067,081 free, 114,931 slave; total 1,182,012.

April 3. Pony Express service inaugurated simultaneously at St. Joseph and San Francisco.

Dec. 4. Brigadier General D. M. Frost, commanding Missouri Volunteer Militia of St. Louis, arrives at southwest border.

796 miles of railroad track in Missouri.

154 newspapers in State.

1861 Worth County organized.

February-March. State Convention to consider relations with United States Government meets at Jefferson City and at St. Louis. Express hope of compromise.

April 20. Pro-Southern force captures Liberty arsenal.

May 2. Legislature convenes on call of Governor C. F. Jackson. Jackson organizes Missouri State Guards.

May 10. Federal troops capture pro-Southern State troops at Camp Jackson.

June 12. Planters' House Conference in St. Louis. Last hope for compromise ended by Federal Commander General Lyon's declaration of war.

June 17. Federal forces commanded by General Lyon defeat State troops at Boonville in first land battle of Civil War.

July 30. Convention reconvenes at Jefferson City. Deposes Governor Jackson and other officials. Establishes provisional government.

August 10. Battle of Wilson Creek ends in questionable victory for pro-Southern State forces and Confederate allies.

Sept. 18-21. Battle of Lexington ends in Confederate victory.

September 23. Jim Lane, commanding a force of Kansas Jayhawkers, sacks and burns Osceola. Many other cities in southwest Missouri burned during this period.

October 21. "Rebel" legislature convenes at Neosho. Ordinance of Secession passed October 28.

November 7. Battle of Belmont ends in Federal victory.

American Miners Association formed by convention of Illinois and Missouri Miners at St. Louis.

1862 April. Companies formed in southwest Missouri for protection against Jayhawker raids.

June 2-14. State Convention passes law requiring oath of loyalty to Union from voters, officials, jurymen, and attorneys.

August 6. Federal victory at Battle of Kirksville ends Confederate Colonel Joseph C. Porter's recruiting in northeast Missouri.

August 15. Battle of Lone Jack.

October 18. Palmyra massacre.

St. Louis court house finished at cost of $1,199,871.

1863 June. Ordinance of emancipation of slaves after 1870 passed by State Convention.

August 21. Quantrill's bushwhackers sack Lawrence.

August 25. Order No. 11 commands evacuation of Jackson, Cass, Bates, and a part of Vernon Counties, with exception of those living within one mile of certain designated towns.

September 2. Radical meeting convenes in Jefferson City. Denounces provisional government. Sends committee of 70 to confer with Lincoln, who declines most of their important demands.

Numerous battles and skirmishes throughout State.

1864 September. General Sterling Price leads Confederate raid into Missouri.

September 27. Centralia Massacre. General Price defeated at Pilot Knob.

October 21-23. Defeat of Price at Westport ends Confederate effort to carry on campaign in Missouri.

October 27. Bill Anderson, bushwhacker leader, killed in Battle of Albany, Ray County.

1865 January 6-April 10. Constitutional Convention meets in St. Louis; dominated by radicals.

January 11. Slavery abolished in Missouri.

March 13. Board of Agriculture created; authorized by Act of 1863.

July 4. New constitution put in force.

September. Pacific Railroad completed to Kansas City.

Missouri State Dental Association organized.

1866 St. Louis Philosophical Society established.

Missouri Historical Society organized in St. Louis.

Lincoln Institute (now Lincoln University) established in Jefferson City; provides higher education for Missouri Negroes.

1867 May 17. Missouri Press Association organized.

Eight-hour-day law passed by Missouri legislature.

1869 Hannibal Bridge, first across Missouri River, completed at Kansas City.

1870 Population: 1,721,295.

February 24. State College of Agriculture and School of Mines created by General Assembly as branches of the University of Missouri.

May 19. State Board of Immigration created.

Robert E. Lee wins upstream race from New Orleans against *Natchez.*

First stockyards built in Kansas City.

Northeast Missouri State Teachers College opens at Kirksville.

1872 Schools of law and medicine added to Missouri University. Women admitted to all branches of the school.

First zinc shipments made from Joplin.

Radical Republican rule ended by coalition of Democrats and Liberal Republicans.

1873 First national convention of Patrons of Husbandry (the Grange) held in St. Louis.

Miss Susan E. Blow opens first kindergarten in St. Louis.

1874 July 4. Eads Bridge over Mississippi at St. Louis opened.

1875 May 5-August 2. Constitutional Convention.

June 3. Day set apart for fasting and prayer for deliverance from grasshopper plague.

October 30. Constitution adopted.

St. Louis separated from St. Louis County.

1876 Democratic National Convention meets in St. Louis. Nominates James Tilden for president.

1877 Missouri Railroad employees join nation-wide strike.

Richard P. Bland begins his free silver campaign.

1878 Chicago & Alton Railroad Bridge completed at Glasgow.

Second Union Depot in world built at Kansas City.

Veiled Prophet festival started in St. Louis.

Joseph Pulitzer merges *Post* and *Dispatch* to form present paper in St. Louis.

1879 January. General Assembly of Knights of Labor held in St. Louis. Adopts motto, "One for all, all for one."

George C. Bingham dies in Kansas City.

Missouri Bureau of Labor Statistics created.

1880 Population: 2,168,380.

December 29. Missouri Bar Association formed.

William Rockhill Nelson buys Kansas City *Star*.

First Negro newspaper, the St. Louis *Advocate*, begins publication.

St. Louis Symphony Society organized.

1881 St. Louis streetcar workers strike for shorter hours, higher pay.

Bureau of Mines and Mine Inspection created.

1882 April 5. Jesse James killed by Robert Ford at St. Joseph.

1883 State Board of Health created.

First national convention of cattlemen meets in St. Louis.

St. Louis Training School for Nurses, first of its kind west of the Mississippi, founded in St. Louis.

Mark Twain writes *Life on the Mississippi*.

1884 O. O. McIntyre born at Plattsburg. Sara Teasdale born in St. Louis.

Bald Knobbers organize in southwest Missouri.

1885 Railroad strikes.

1886 First Priest of Pallas festival in Kansas City.

1887 General Alexander W. Doniphan dies at Richmond.

Central Labor Union, St. Louis Trades Assembly, and Arbeiter-Verband combine in St. Louis Trades and Labor Assembly.

Missouri Training School for Boys and the State Industrial Home for Girls created.

Local option law on manufacture and sale of liquor passed.

1888 Third Annual Convention of the A. F. of L. meets in St. Louis, Samuel Gompers presiding.

1889 Board of Mediation and Arbitration created to handle strikes.

Norman J. Coleman appointed first United States Secretary of Agriculture.

Henry Shaw dies. Will endows Missouri Botanical Garden as public institution.

1890 Population: 2,679,183.

Last passenger pigeon seen in Missouri.

Sullivan and Adler design Wainwright Building in St. Louis. First "modern" skyscraper.

Charter of First Church of Christ, Scientist, first in Missouri, obtained.

1891 Missouri State Federation of Labor organized in Kansas City.

First automobile brought into the State.

1892 Barnes Medical College founded in St. Louis.

Andrew Taylor Still begins American School of Osteopathy at Kirksville.

1895 August 6. Pertle Springs Democratic Convention makes free coinage of silver a national issue.

1896 March 27. Tornado strikes St. Louis.

Reedy's Mirror begins publication.

Tom Turpin pioneers in modern "jazz" with "Harlem Rag."

First rural mail delivery routes established in Missouri.

Democratic Party nominates Richard P. Bland for president.

1898 May 13-25. First, Second, Third, Fourth, Fifth and Sixth Regiments of Missouri Volunteer Infantry mustered into United States Service.

July 24. Light Battery A starts for Porto Rico.

July 25. Third Regiment of United States Volunteer Engineers organized. Goes to Cuba in December.

The State Historical Society of Missouri founded.

1899 Unity School of Christianity founded in Kansas City.

State School for Feeble-Minded and Epileptic established at Marshall.

1900 Population: 3,106,665.

St. Louis streetcar employees strike.

Democratic National Convention at Kansas City nominates William Jennings Bryan for President.

1901 First Missouri State Fair held at Sedalia.

Driest year on record.

1903 Spring. Heavy floods on Missouri and Mississippi Rivers.

1904 April 30. Louisiana Purchase Exposition opens in St. Louis.

Herbert S. Hadley, Attorney General of Missouri, prosecutes Standard Oil Co., Harvester Trust, and Lumber Trusts, for illegal practices.

1905 Little River Drainage District organized. Rapid development of "Swampeast" Missouri follows.

Last paroquet seen in Missouri.

Walmsley Conservation Law passed.

1907 Missouri State Sanatorium opens at Mount Vernon.

State Highway Engineer appointed to advise counties on road construction.

St. Louis votes tax-supported art museum.

St. Louis Aeronautics Club organized. Sponsors first international balloon races.

1908 National Convention of People's Party held in St. Louis.

Roy Knabenshue makes St. Louis' first dirigible flight.

School of Journalism, first in world, established at University of Missouri.

1909 Game and Fish Department and office of State Food and Drug Commissioner created.

1910 Population: 3,293,335.

April 21. Mark Twain dies.

First international aviation meet held in Kinloch Park, St. Louis.

Second international balloon races held in St. Louis.

1911 February 5. State capitol burns.

October 4. First air mail ever carried flown from Kinloch Park to Fairgrounds Park, St. Louis.

1912 First Missouri Farm Bureau organized at Cape Girardeau.
Powersite dam completed across White River.

1913 Missouri State Highway Commission created.

1914 Missouri Farmers Association organized in Chariton County.
Pageant and Masque of St. Louis given in St. Louis.

1916 First United States Army Aeronautic Corps established at St. Louis.

1917 April 24. State Council of Defense created.
July 17. Governor issues proclamation for organization of Home Guards.
August 5. Missouri National Guard taken into Federal service.
September. First group of drafted men goes to Camp Funston.

1918 May 17. Thirty-fifth Division lands in France.
June. Eighty-ninth Division sent overseas.
New capitol at Jefferson City completed.

1919 Last National Balloon Race held in St. Louis.

1920 Population: 3,404,055.

1921 Centennial Road Law designates a system of State roads and inaugurates modern highway development.
Centenary of Statehood celebrated.
WEW, St. Louis University radio station, starts broadcasting.
Constitution amended to enable women to hold any office in State.

1923 Pulitzer Air Races held at Lambert Field, St. Louis.
President Harding makes first Presidential broadcast at St. Louis.
St. Louis votes $87,000,000 bond issue for civic improvements.

1925 Workmen's Compensation Law passed.

1926 Calvin Coolidge dedicates Kansas City's Liberty Memorial.

1927 Lindbergh flies Atlantic in the *Spirit of St. Louis*.
Wettest year on record.
Tornado strikes St. Louis.

1930 Population: 3,629,367.

1931 Bagnell Dam completed.
Highway patrol begun.

1932 Kansas City Co-operative Orchestra organized. Becomes Philharmonic Society in 1933.

1933 William Rockhill Nelson Gallery of Art and the Atkins Museum of Fine Arts opens in Kansas City.
Missouri State Department of Agriculture created by act of General Assembly.

1934 State Sales Tax law becomes effective.

1935 Lead and zinc miners of southwest Missouri and tiff miners of Washington County strike.
University of Kansas City organized.

1936 Conservation Commission established.
Republican National Convention meets in Kansas City.

1937 June 23. Legislation creates program of old age assistance, aid to dependent children, general relief, and child welfare.

1938 KSD in St. Louis starts experimental broadcasting of facsimile newspapers.

1939 July 9. Governor Lloyd Stark signs Kansas City Police Bill.
Trachoma Hospital at Rolla completed.
United States Government acquires 40-block area on St. Louis
waterfront as site for Jefferson National Expansion Memorial.
Sharecropper demonstration along Highway 61 in Southeast Missouri.

1940 Population: 3,784,664.
May 12. Mother Rose Philippine Duchesne beatified.
Ellis Fischel State Cancer Hospital at Columbia opens.

A Selected Bibliography

NATURAL SETTING

Swallow, G. C. *The First and Second Annual Reports of the Geological Survey of Missouri.* Jefferson City, Mo., James Lusk, Public Printer, 1855. 239 p., illus.

Broadhead, G. C., Meek, F. B., Shumard, B. F. *Reports on the Geological Survey of the State of Missouri, 1855-1871.* Jefferson City, Mo., Regan & Carter, 1873. 323 p., maps.

Branson, Edwin Bayer. *Geology of Missouri.* Columbia, Mo., 1918. (Missouri University Eng. Exp. Station Series 19, Bulletin; Vol. 19, No. 15.) 172 p.

Emerson, Fred Valentine. *Geography of Missouri.* Columbia, Mo., 1912. (Missouri University Bulletin, Vol. 1, No. 4.) 74 p.

Ellis, James Fernando. *The Influence of Environment on the Settlement of Missouri.* St. Louis, Webster Publishing Company, 1929. 180 p.

Buehler, H. A., State Geologist. *Large Springs in Missouri.* Rolla, Mo., Bureau of Geology and Mines, 1929. 13 p.

Fuller, Myron L. *The New Madrid Earthquake.* Washington, D. C., Government Printing Office, 1912. (United States Geological Survey, Bulletin 494.) 119 p., map, diagrams.

Broadhead, Garland C. *Distribution of Trees and Shrubs in Missouri.* Edited by H. L. Walmsley. Kansas City, Mo., c1932.

Rickett, Theresa C. *Wild Flowers of Missouri; A Guide for Beginners.* Columbia, Mo., 1937. (Missouri University, College of Agriculture, Circular 363.) 144 p., illus.

Palmer, Ernest Jesse, Steyermark, Julian Alfred. *Annotated Catalogue of the Flowering Plants of Missouri.* St. Louis, 1935. (Reprinted from Missouri Botanical Garden Annals, Vol. 22, No. 3, p. 375-758, Sept. 1935.) 483 p.

Steyermark, Julian Alfred. *Spring Flora of Missouri.* Published by the Missouri Botanical Garden, St. Louis, and the Field Museum of Natural History, Chicago. 1940. 585 p., illus., map.

Bennitt, Rudolf, and Nagel, Werner O. *A Survey of the Resident Game and Furbearers of Missouri.* Columbia, Mo., 1937. (The University of Missouri Studies, Vol. XII, No. 2.) 215 p.

Bennitt, Rudolf. *Check-List of the Birds of Missouri.* Columbia, Mo., 1932. (The University of Missouri Studies, Vol. VII, No. 3.) 81 p.

Riley, Charles Valentine. *Noxious, Beneficial and Other Insects of the State of Missouri.* (Annual Report of the Missouri State Entomologist, Jefferson City, 1869-1877, Vols. 1-9.)

ARCHEOLOGY AND INDIANS

Fowke, Gerard. *Prehistoric Objects Classified and Described.* St. Louis, Missouri Historical Society, 1913. (Missouri Historical Society Department of Agriculture, Bulletin 1.) 32 p., 15 plates.

—— *Archeological Investigations.* Washington, D. C., Government Printing Office, 1922. (Smithsonian Institution, Bureau of American Ethnology, Bulletin 76.) 204 p.

—— *Antiquities of Central and Southeastern Missouri.* Washington, D. C., Government Printing Office, 1910. (Smithsonian Institution, Bureau of American Ethnology, Bulletin 37.) 116 p., illus., map.

La Flesche, Francis. *A Dictionary of the Osage Language.* Washington, D. C., Government Printing Office, 1932. (Smithsonian Institution, Bureau of American Ethnology, Bulletin 109.) 406 p. (Includes a collection of Osage Indian folk songs, tales, and rituals, pp. 358-406.)

Foreman, Grant. *Our Indian Ambassadors to Europe.* St. Louis, 1928. (Missouri Historical Review, Vol. 5, February 1928, pp. 109-128.)

Peale, T. R. *Ancient Mounds at St. Louis, Missouri, in 1819.* Washington, D. C., Government Printing Office, 1862. (From Annual Report of the Board of Regents of the Smithsonian Institution, 1861, pp. 386-391.)

Burrill, Alfred C. *Missouri Caves Yield Up Their Secrets.* Jefferson City, Mo., 1934. (Missouri State Museum, Bulletin No. 5, February, 1934.)

Gilmore, Melvin R. *Uses of Plants by the Indians of the Missouri River Region.* Washington D. C., Government Printing Office, 1912. (United States Bureau of American Ethnology, Thirty-third Annual Report, 1911-12, pp. 43-194.)

HISTORY AND GOVERNMENT

Conard, Howard Louis (ed.) *Encyclopedia of the History of Missouri.* New York, Louisville (etc.), The Southern History Company, Haldeman, Conard & Company, Prop., 1901. 6 vols., illus.

Williams, Walter, Shoemaker, Floyd C. *Missouri, Mother of the West.* New York, Chicago, The American Historical Society, Inc., 1930. 5 vols., illus.

Stevens, Walter B. *Centennial History of Missouri (The Center State) One Hundred Years in the Union, 1820-1921.* St. Louis, Chicago, The S. J. Clarke Publishing Company, 1921. 4 vols., illus., map.

Violette, Eugene M. *A History of Missouri.* New York, Boston, D. C. Heath & Company, c1918. 500 p., illus., maps.

Switzler, William F. *Switzler's Illustrated History of Missouri, from 1541 to 1877.* Edited and published by C. R. Barns, St. Louis, 1879. 601 p., illus.

Culmer, Frederic Arthur. *A New History of Missouri.* Mexico, Mo., McIntyre Publishing Company, 1938. 592 p.

Houck, Louis. *A History of Missouri from the Earliest Explorations and Settlements until the Admission of the State into the Union.* Chicago, R. R. Donnelley & Sons Company, 1908. 3 vols., illus., maps.
—— *The Spanish Regime in Missouri.* Chicago, R. R. Donnelley & Sons Company, 1909. 2 vols.
—— *Documents Relating to the Attack Upon St. Louis in 1780.* St. Louis, 1906. (Missouri Historical Review, July 1906, Vol. 2, No. 6, pp. 41-54; reprinted from the Canadian Archives, Series B, Vol. 97, pt. 22, p. 290.)
Douglass, Robert Sidney. *History of Southeast Missouri.* New York, Chicago, The Lewis Publishing Company, 1912. 2 vols.
Williams, Walter (ed.). *A History of Northeast Missouri.* New York, Chicago, The Lewis Publishing Company, 1913. 3 vols., illus.
—— *A History of Northwest Missouri.* New York, Chicago, The Lewis Publishing Company, 1915. 3 vols., illus.
Garraghan, The Reverend Gilbert Joseph, S.J. *Chapters in Frontier History; Research Studies in the Making of the West.* Milwaukee, The Bruce Publishing Company, c1934. 188 p., illus., maps.
Gregg, Kate L. *The War of 1812 on the Missouri Frontier.* St. Louis, 1938-39. (Missouri Historical Review, Vol. 33; October 1938, pp. 3-22; January 1939, pp. 184-202; April 1939, pp. 326-348.)
Kretzmann, P. E. *The Saxon Immigration to Missouri, 1838-1839.* St. Louis, 1939. (Missouri Historical Review, Vol. 33, pp. 157-169, January 1939.)
Roberts, Elder B. H. *The Missouri Persecutions.* Salt Lake City, Utah, George Q. Cannon & Sons Company, 1900. 333 p., illus.
Linn, William Alexander. *The Story of the Mormons.* Missouri period, pp. 161-208. New York, The Macmillan Company, 1902. 637 p., illus.
Carr, Lucien. *Missouri, A Bone of Contention.* New York, Boston, Houghton Mifflin Company, 1888. 377 p., map.
McElroy, John. *The Struggle for Missouri.* Washington, The National Tribune Company, 1909. 342 p., illus.
Ryle, Walter Harrington. *Missouri: Union or Secession.* Nashville, George Peabody College for Teachers, Nashville, Tenn., 1931. 247 p.
Trexler, Harrison Anthony. *Slavery in Missouri, 1804-1865.* Baltimore, The Johns Hopkins Press, 1914. 259 p.
Snead, Thomas Lowndes. *The Fight for Missouri, From the Election of Lincoln to the Death of Lyon.* New York, Charles Scribner's Sons, 1886. 322 p., maps.
Britton, Wiley. *The Civil War on the Border.* New York, London, G. P. Putnam's Sons, 1890-1899. 2 vols., illus., maps.
Edwards, John N. *Shelby and His Men; or The War in the West.* Cincinnati, Miami Printing & Publishing Company, 1867. 551 p., maps.
Connelley, William Elsey. *Quantrill and the Border Wars.* Cedar Rapids, Iowa, The Torch Press, 1910. 542 p., illus.
Leftwich, W. M. *Martyrdom in Missouri.* St. Louis, S. W. Book & Publishing Company, 1870. 2 vols.

Miller, Reverend George. *Missouri's Memorable Decade, 1860-1870.* Columbia, Mo., Press of E. W. Stephens, 1898. 175 p., illus.

Clarendon, A. E. *Missouri, Its State and Local Government.* New York, Maynard Merrill & Company, 1897. 187 p.

Barclay, Thomas S. *The Liberal Republican Movement in Missouri, 1865-1871.* Columbia, Mo., The Missouri State Historical Society, 1926. 288 p.

—— *History of Missouri National Guard.* Published by authority of the military council, Missouri National Guard. Jefferson City, Mo., 1934. 283 p., maps.

Edwards, Evan Alexander. *From Doniphan to Verdun; the Official History of the 140th Infantry.* Lawrence, Kansas, The World Company, c1920. 259 p., illus., maps.

Park, Eleanore G., and Morrow, Kate S. *Women of the Mansion; Missouri, 1821-1936.* Jefferson City, Mo., Midland Printing Company, 1936. 435 p., illus.

McGee, Major Joseph H. *The Story of the Grand River Country, 1821-1905.* Edited by R. J. Britton. Gallatin, Mo., The North Missourian Press, 1909. 67 p.

Bell, Ovid. *Côte Sans Dessein. A History.* Fulton, Mo., The Ovid Bell Press, Inc., 1930. 98 p.

Schiavo, Giovanni E. *The Italians in Missouri.* New York, Italian-American Publishing Company, 1929. 214 p.

TRAVEL AND DESCRIPTION

Shea, J. D. G. (ed.) *Discovery and Exploration of the Mississippi Valley with Original Narratives of Marquette, Allouez, Membre, Hennepin, and Anastase Douay.* New York, J. S. Redfield, 1853. 267 p., facsimile of Marquette's map.

Abel, Annie Heloise (ed.). *Tabeau's Narrative of Loisel's Expedition to the Upper Missouri.* Norman, Okla., University of Oklahoma Press, 1939. 272 p.

Larpenteur, Charles. *Forty Years a Fur Trader on the Upper Missouri; the Personal Narrative of Charles Larpenteur, 1833-1872.* Edited by Elliott Coues. New York, F. P. Harper, 1898. 2 vols., illus., maps.

Stuart, Robert. *The Discovery of the Oregon Trail.* Edited by Philip Ashton Rollins. New York, Charles Scribner's Sons, 1935. 391 p.

Stoddard, Major Amos. *Sketches, Historical and Descriptive, of Louisiana.* Philadelphia, Matthew Carey, 1812. 488 p.

Gregg, Kate L. (ed.) *Westward with Dragoons:* The Journal of William Clark on His Expedition to Establish Fort Osage, August 25 to September 22, 1808. Fulton, Mo., The Ovid Bell Press, Inc., 1937. 97 p., illus., maps.

Brackenridge, Henry Marie. *Views of Louisiana; Together with a Journal of a Voyage up the River Missouri, in 1811.* Reprinted from the Pittsburgh edition of 1814 in R. G. Thwaites' *Early Western Travels.* Cleveland, Arthur H. Clark Company, 1904.

Schoolcraft, Henry R. *Journal of a Tour into the Interior of Missouri and Arkansas from Potosi or Mine à Breton in Missouri Territory, in a South-West Direction toward the Rocky Mountains, 1818-1819.* London, Printed for Sir Richard Phillips & Company, 102 p., map.

Flint, The Reverend Timothy. *Recollection of the Last Ten Years Passed in Occasional Residences and Journeyings in the Valley of the Mississippi.* Introduction by the editor, C. Hartley Grattan. New York, Alfred A. Knopf, 1932. 380 p. (Reprinted from edition of 1826.)

Madox, D. T. *Late Account of the Missouri Territory, Compiled from Notes Taken During a Tour Through That Country in 1815, and a Translation of Letters from a Distinguished Emigrant, Written in 1817.* Tarrytown, N. Y., W. Abbatt, 1926. (Reprint of Paris, Ky., edition of 1817.)

Wetmore, Alphonso. *Gazetteer of the State of Missouri.* St. Louis, C. Keemle, 1837. 382 p., illus., map.

McDermott, John Francis (ed.), Salvan, Albert J. (trans.). *Tixier's Travels on the Osage Prairies.* Norman, Okla., University of Oklahoma Press, 1940. 309 p., illus., maps.

Hughes, John T. *Doniphan's Expedition, Containing an Account of the Conquest of New Mexico; General Kearney's Overland Expedition to California; Doniphan's Campaign against the Navajos; His Unparalleled March upon Chihuahua and Durango; and the Operations of General Price at Santa Fe.* Cincinnati, J. A. and U. P. James, c1847. (Senate Reprint, 1914.) 407 p., map.

Flagg, Edmund. *The Far West.* Reprinted from 1838 edition in R. G. Thwaites' *Early Western Travels, 1748-1846.* Cleveland, Arthur H. Clark Company, 1906. Vols. 26 and 27.

Hewitt, J. N. B. (ed.), Jarrell, Myrtis (trans.). *Journal of Rudolph Friederich Kurz; an Account of His Experiences Among Fur Traders and American Indians on the Mississippi and the Upper Missouri Rivers, During the Years 1846 to 1852.* Washington, D. C., Government Printing Office, 1937. (Smithsonian Institution, Bureau of American Ethnology, Bulletin 115.) 382 p.

Clark, Thomas D. *Manners and Humors of the American Frontier.* St. Louis, 1940. (Missouri Historical Review, Vol. 35, October 1940, pp. 3-24.)

Hannum, Anna Paschall (ed.). *A Quaker Forty-Niner; The Adventures of Charles Edward Pancoast on the American Frontier.* Foreword by John Bach McMaster. Philadelphia, University of Pennsylvania Press, 1930. 402 p., illus.

O'Hanlon, John. *Life and Scenery in Missouri, Reminiscences of a Missionary Priest.* Dublin, James Duffy & Company, Ltd., 1890. 293 p.

Hogan, The Right Reverend John Joseph. *On the Mission in Missouri, 1857-1868.* Kansas City, Mo., John A. Heilmann, 1892. 205 p.

Parker, Nathan H. *Missouri As It Is in 1867: An Illustrated Historical Gazetteer of Missouri.* Philadelphia, J. B. Lippincott & Company, 1867. 458 p., illus.

Thorp, Joseph. *Early Days in the West; Along the Missouri One Hundred Years Ago.* Liberty, Mo., Liberty Tribune, 1924. 94 p.

Street, Julian. *Abroad at Home.* New York, The Century Company, 1916. 517 p., illus. (See "In Mizzoura" and "The Beginning of the West" pp. 201-336.)

Ramsay, Robert L., Read, Allen Walker, Leech, Esther Gladys. *Introduction to a Survey of Missouri Place-Names.* Columbia, Mo., 1934. (The University of Missouri Studies. Vol. IX, No. 1.) 124 p.

Darby, Ada Claire. *"Show Me" Missouri.* Kansas City, Mo., Burton Publishing Company, c1938. 142 p. Illustrated by Ellen Word Carter.

INDUSTRY AND COMMERCE

Waterhouse, Sylvester. *The Resources of Missouri.* St. Louis, A. Wiebusch & Son, 1867. 96 p.

Schoolcraft, Henry R. *A View of the Lead Mines of Missouri.* New York, Charles Wiley & Company, 1819. 299 p.

Wright, Clarence A. *Mining and Milling of the Lead and Zinc Ores in the Missouri-Kansas-Oklahoma Zinc District.* (In co-operation with the Missouri Bureau of Mines and Geology, H. A. Buehler, State Geologist.) Washington, D. C., Government Printing Office, 1918. 134 p., illus., tables.

Atherton, Lewis E. *The Pioneer Merchant in Mid-America.* Columbia, Mo., 1939. (The University of Missouri Studies, Vol. XIV, No. 2.) 135 p.

——— *James and Robert Aull—A Frontier Missouri Mercantile Firm.* St. Louis, 1935. (Missouri Historical Review, Vol. 30, October 1935, pp. 3-27.)

——— *Business Techniques in the Santa Fe Trade.* St. Louis, 1940. (Missouri Historical Review, Vol. 34, April 1940, pp. 335-341.)

Jennings, Sister Marietta. *A Pioneer Merchant of St. Louis, 1810-1820; The Business Career of Christian Wilt.* New York, The Columbia University Press, 1939. 219 p.

Chittenden, Hiram M. *The American Fur Trade of the Far West.* New York, F. P. Harper, 1902. 3 vols., illus., map. (Revised edition, New York, R. R. Wilson, Inc., 1936.)

Duffus, Robert L. *The Santa Fe Trail.* New York, London, Toronto, Longmans, Green & Company, 1930. 283 p., illus., map.

TRANSPORTATION

Chappell, Philip Edward. *A History of the Missouri River.* Kansas City, Mo., Kansas State Historical Society, 1905. 98 p., illus.

Gould, Emerson W. *Fifty Years on the Mississippi; or, Gould's History of River Navigation.* St. Louis, Nixon-Jones Printing Company, 1889. 749 p., illus.

Chittenden, Hiram M. *History of Early Steamboat Navigation on the Missouri River; Life and Adventures of Joseph La Barge.* New York. F. P. Harper, 1903. 2 vols., illus., map.

Merrick, George Byron. *Old Times on the Upper Mississippi: The Recollections of a Steamboat Pilot from 1854 to 1863.* Cleveland, A. H. Clark Company, 1909. 323 p., illus., maps.

Petersen, William John. *Steamboating on the Upper Mississippi, The Water Way to Iowa: Some River History.* Iowa City, The State Historical Society of Iowa, 1937. 575 p.

Gentry, North Todd. *Plank Roads in Missouri.* St. Louis, 1937. (Missouri Historical Review, Vol. 31, April 1937, pp. 272-287.)

Overton, R. C. *The First Ninety Years; An Historical Sketch of the Burlington Railroad, 1850-1940.* Chicago, 1940. 40 p.

LABOR

Dacus, Joseph A. *Annals of the Great Strikes in the United States.* St. Louis, Scammell & Company, 1877. 480 p., illus.

Nolen, Russell M. *The Labor Movement in St. Louis Prior to the Civil War.* St. Louis, 1939. (Missouri Historical Review, Vol. 34, October 1939, pp. 18-37.)

—— *The Labor Movement in St. Louis from 1860 to 1890.* St. Louis, 1940. (Missouri Historical Review, Vol. 34, January 1940, pp. 157-181.)

AGRICULTURE

Ashton, John. *History of Shorthorns in Missouri Prior to the Civil War.* Jefferson City, Mo., 1923. (Missouri State Board of Agriculture, Monthly Bulletin, Vol. XXI, No. 1.) 87 p., illus.

Harrison, Jack. *Famous Saddlehorses and Distinguished Horsemen.* Edited by William Rufus Jackson, c1933. 440 p., illus.

Popplewell, Frank S. *St. Joseph, Missouri, As a Center of the Cattle Trade.* St. Louis, 1938. (Missouri Historical Review, Vol. 32, pp. 443-457, July 1938.)

SOCIAL WELFARE

Breckenridge, A. C., and Colman, W. G. *Missouri as a Pioneer in Criminal Court Reform.* St. Louis, 1939. (Missouri Historical Review, Vol. 33, July 1939, pp. 471-476.)

Forman, Jacob Gilbert. *Western Sanitary Commission: a Sketch of Its Origin, History, Labors for the Sick and Wounded of the Western Armies and Aid Given to Freedmen and Union Refugees.* St. Louis, 1864. 159 p.

Goodwin, E. J. *History of Medicine in Missouri.* St. Louis, W. L. Smith, 1905. 284 p.

History Committee of Missouri State Dental Association, E. E. Haverstick, Chairman. *The History of Dentistry in Missouri.* Fulton, Mo., The Ovid Bell Press, Inc., 1938. 600 p., map.

McCain, William D. *The Papers of the Food Administration for Missouri, 1917-1919, in the National Archives.* St. Louis, 1937. (Missouri Historical Review, Vol. 32, October 1937, pp. 56-61.)

EDUCATION

Phillips, Claude A. *A History of Education in Missouri.* Jefferson City, Mo., Hugh Stephens Printing Company, c1911. 292 p.

McMillan, Margaret, and Morris, Monia Cook, *Educational Opportunities in Early Missouri.* St. Louis, 1939. (Missouri Historical Review, Vol. 33: April 1939, pp. 307-325; July 1939, pp. 477-498.)

Chiles, Henry C. *The Masonic College of Missouri: An Experiment in Education.* Published by Grand Lodge of A. F. & A. M. of Missouri, 1935. 48 p., illus.

Dorsey, Dorothy B. *Howard High School, the Outstanding Pioneer Co-educational School in Missouri.* St. Louis, 1937. (Missouri Historical Review, Vol. 31, April 1937, pp. 249-266.)

Viles, Jonas. *The University of Missouri; a Centennial History, 1839-1939.* Columbia, Mo., 1939. 508 p., illus.

RELIGION

Rothensteiner, The Reverend John, S. J. *History of the Archdiocese of St. Louis in Its Various Stages of Development from AD 1673 to AD 1928.* St. Louis, Blackwell-Wielandy Company, 1928. 2 vols., illus., map.

Garraghan, Reverend Gilbert Joseph. *The Jesuits of the Middle United States.* New York, America Press, 1938. 3 vols., illus., maps.

Callan, Louise. *The Society of the Sacred Heart in North America.* New York, London, Longmans, Green & Company, 1937. 809 p., illus., maps.

Schneider, Carl E. *The German Church on the American Frontier.* St. Louis, Eden Publishing House, 1939. 579 p., illus., maps.

Polack, William G. *Fathers and Founders.* St. Louis, Concordia Publishing House, c1938. 79 p., illus.

Douglass, Robert Sidney. *History of Missouri Baptists.* Kansas City, Mo., Western Baptist Publishing Company, 1934. 545 p., illus.

Duncan, R. S. *A History of the Baptists in Missouri.* St. Louis, Scammell & Company, 1882. 1 vol.

Peters, George L. *Disciples of Christ in Missouri.* Kansas City, Mo., Centennial Commission, c1937. 244 p.

McAnally, David Rice. *History of Methodism in Missouri from Date of Its Introduction, 1806, to the Present Day.* St. Louis, Advocate Publishing Company, 1881. 640 p.

Gray, Marcus L., Baker, Ward M. (ass't.). *Centennial Volume of Missouri Methodism, Methodist Episcopal Church, South.* Kansas City, Mo., Press of Burd & Fletcher Printing Company, c1907. 575 p., illus.

ART AND ARCHITECTURE

Bryan, John A. *Missouri's Contribution to American Architecture.* St. Louis, St. Louis Architectural Club, 1928. 286 p., illus., map.

Butts, Porter. *Art in Wisconsin,* with preface by Dr. Oskar F. L. Hagen. Madison, Wisconsin, Democrat Printing Company, c1936. 213 p., illus. (Contains much incidental information about Missouri artists.)

Christ-Janer, Albert. *George Caleb Bingham of Missouri; the Story of an Artist,* with preface by Thomas Hart Benton. New York, Dodd, Mead & Company, 1940. 171 p., illus.

Drumm, Stella M., Van Ravenswaay, Charles. *The Old Courthouse.* St Louis, 1940. (Glimpses of the Past, Missouri Historical Society, Vol. VII, Nos. 1-6, January-June 1940.)

Heilbron, Bertha L. (ed.). *Making a Motion Picture in 1848. Henry Lewis' Journal of a Canoe Voyage from the Falls of St. Anthony to St. Louis.* (Story of John Rowson Smith, John Banvard, Henry Lewis, and other painters of Mississippi River panoramas associated with St. Louis.) St. Paul, Minnesota Historical Society, 1936. 58 p., illus.

Hodges, William Romaine. *Carl Wimar, a Biography.* Galveston, Texas, C. Reymershoffer, 1908. 37 p., catalogue.

Mitchell, Giles Carroll. *There is No Limit; Architecture and Sculpture in Kansas City.* Kansas City, Mo., Brown-White Company, 1934. 162 p., illus.

Peterson, Charles E. *Early Ste. Genevieve and Its Architecture.* St. Louis, 1941. (Missouri Historical Review, Vol. 35, pp. 207-232, January 1941.)

Powell, Mary McEachin. *Public Art in St. Louis.* St. Louis, 1925. 51 p., illus. (Reprint, St. Louis Public Library Monthly Bulletin, July-August, 1925.)

MUSIC AND THE THEATER

Krohn, Ernst C. *A Century of Missouri Music.* St. Louis, 1924. 134 p.

Carson, William G. B. *The Theatre on the Frontier; the Early Years of the St. Louis Stage.* Chicago, The University of Chicago Press, c1932. 361 p., illus.

Ludlow, Noah M. *Dramatic Life As I Found It.* St. Louis, G. I. Jones & Company, 1880. 733 p.

Smith, Solomon Franklin. *Theatrical Management in the West and South for Thirty Years, Interspersed with Anecdotical Sketches.* New York, Harper & Brothers, 1868. 275 p., illus.

LANGUAGE AND LORE

Belden, Henry H. (ed.). *Ballads and Songs.* Collected by the Missouri Folk-Lore Society. Columbia, Mo., 1940. (The University of Missouri Studies, Vol. XV, No. 1) 530 p., music.

Carrière, Joseph Medard (ed.). *Tales from the French Folk-Lore of Missouri.* Evanston and Chicago, 1937. (Northwestern University Studies in the Humanities, No. 1.) 354 p., illus.

Collins, Earl A. *Folk Tales of Missouri.* Boston, The Christopher Publishing House, c1935. 133 p.

Criswell, Elijah Harry. *Lewis and Clark: Linguistic Pioneers.* Columbia, Mo., 1940. (University of Missouri Studies, Vol. XV, No. 2, April 1, 1940.) 316 p.

Dorrance, Ward A. *The Survival of French in the Old District of Sainte Genevieve.* Columbia, Mo., 1935. (The University of Missouri Studies, April 1, 1935.) 133 p., illus., map.

McDermott, John Francis (ed.). *Private Libraries in Creole Saint Louis.* Baltimore, The Johns-Hopkins Press, 1938. 186 p.

Emberson, Frances Guthrie. *Mark Twain's Vocabulary; A General Survey.* Columbia, Mo., 1935. (The University of Missouri Studies, Vol. X, No. 3.) 53 p.

Ramsay, Robert L., Emberson, Frances Guthrie. *A Mark Twain Lexicon* Columbia, Mo., 1938. (The University of Missouri Studies, Vol. XIII, No. 1.) 278 p.

LITERATURE

De Voto, Bernard Augustine. *Mark Twain's America.* Boston, Little, Brown & Company, 1932. 353 p., illus.

Jesse, Richard H., Allen, E. A. (eds.). *Missouri Literature.* Columbia, Mo., E. W. Stephens, 1901. 382 p.

Snider, Denton J. *The St. Louis Movement in Philosophy, Literature, Education, Psychology, with Chapters of Autobiography.* St. Louis, Sigma Publishing Company, 1920. 608 p.

Snoddy, James S. (ed. and coll.). *A Little Book of Missouri Verse.* Introduction by Perry S. Rader. Kansas City, Mo., Hudson-Kimberly Publishing Company, c1897. 200 p.

Spotts, Carle Brooks. *Development of Fiction on the Missouri Frontier, 1830-1860.* Columbia, Mo., 1935. (Reprinted from the Missouri Historical Review.) 70 p.

NEWSPAPERS

Johnson, Icie F. *William Rockhill Nelson and the Kansas City Star.* Introduction by William Allen White. Kansas City, Mo., Burton Publishing Company, c1935. 208 p.

Lewis, Lloyd. *Propaganda and the Kansas-Missouri War.* St. Louis, 1939. (Missouri Historical Review, Vol. 34, pp. 3-17, October 1939.)

Seitz, Don Carlos. *Joseph Pulitzer; His Life and Letters.* New York, Simon & Schuster, 1924. 478 p., illus., map.

Sparlin, Estal E. *The Jefferson Inquirer.* St. Louis, 1938. (Missouri Historical Review, Vol. 32, pp. 156-163, January 1938.)

Stevens, Walter B. *Joseph B. McCullagh.* St. Louis, 1930-34. (Missouri Historical Review, Vols. 25-28, 1930-1934.)

Tasher, Lucy Lucile. *The Missouri Democrat and the Civil War.* St. Louis, 1937. (Missouri Historical Review, Vol. 31, pp. 402-419, July 1937.)

THE OZARKS

Sauer, Carl Ortwin. *The Geography of the Ozark Highland of Missouri.* (Published for Geographic Society of Chicago.) Chicago, University of Chicago Press, 1920. 245 p.

Monks, William. *A History of Southern Missouri and Northern Arkansas; Being an Account of the Early Settlements, the Civil War, the Ku-Klux, and Times of Peace.* West Plains, Mo., West Plains Journal Company, 1907. 247 p., illus.

Schultz, Gerard. *Early History of the Northern Ozarks.* Jefferson City, Mo., Midland Printing Company, 1937. 192 p., illus.

Reminiscent History of the Ozark Region. Chicago, Goodspeed Brothers, 1894. 787 p., illus.

Buel, James W. *Legends of the Ozarks.* St. Louis, W. S. Bryan, 1880. 110 p., illus.

Wilson, Charles M. *Backwoods America.* Chapel Hill, N. C., The University of North Carolina Press, c1934. 209 p., illus.

Randolph, Vance. *Ozark Mountain Folks.* New York, The Vanguard Press, c1932. 279 p., illus., music.

—— *The Ozarks; An American Survival of a Primitive Society.* New York, The Vanguard Press, c1931. 310 p., illus., music.

CITIES

Rothensteiner, The, Reverend John, S. J. *Chronicles of an Old Missouri Parish; Historical Sketches of St. Michael's Church, Fredericktown, Madison County, Missouri.* Cape Girardeau, 1928. 119 p., illus.

Bek, William G. *The German Settlement Society of Philadelphia and Its Colony, Hermann, Missouri.* Philadelphia, Americana Germanica Press, 1907. 170 p., illus., charts.

Ford, James E. *A History of Jefferson City, Missouri's State Capital, and of Cole County.* Jefferson City, Mo., The New Day Press, c1938. 600 p., illus.

Deatherage, Charles P. *Early History of Greater Kansas City, Missouri and Kansas, The Prophetic City at the Mouth of the Kaw.* Kansas City, Mo., C. P. Deatherage, 1927. 3 vols. (Diamond Jubilee edition, 1928.)

Whitney, Carrie Westlake. *Kansas City, Missouri: Its History and Its People, 1808-1908.* Chicago, S. J. Clarke Publishing Company, 1908. 3 vols.

Aikman, Duncan (ed.). *The Taming of the Frontier.* By Ten Authors. New York, Minton, Balch & Company, 1925. 319 p. illus. (See: "Kansas City: Houn' Dawg vs. Art," by Henry Haskell, pp. 201-233.)

Garraghan, The Reverend Gilbert Joseph. *Saint Ferdinand de Florissant.* Chicago, Loyola University Press, 1923. 271 p., illus., maps.

Yealy, Francis J. *Sainte Genevieve, the Story of Missouri's Oldest Settlement.* Ste. Genevieve, The Bicentennial Historical Committee, 1935. 150 p., illus., map.

Uts, Nellie, Wilson, G. Marion. *History of the Growth and Development of St. Joseph.* St. Joseph, c1935. 125 p., mimeographed.

Tracy, W. P. *Men Who Made St. Joseph the City Worthwhile.* St. Joseph, Combe Printing Company, 1921. 150 p.

Scharf, John Thomas. *History of St. Louis City and County from the Earliest Period to the Present Day.* Philadelphia, L. H. Everts & Company, 1883. 2 vols., illus.

Hyde, William, Conard, Howard L. *Encyclopedia of the History of St. Louis, a Compendium of History and Biography for Ready Reference.* Louisville (etc.). The Southern History Company, 1899. 4 vols.

Lionberger, I. H. *Annals of St. Louis and a Brief Account of Its Foundation and Progress, 1764-1928.* St. Louis, 1929. 71 p.

Anderson, Galusha. *The Story of a Border City During the Civil War.* (St. Louis). Boston, Little, Brown & Company, 1908. 385 p., illus.

Steffens, Lincoln. *The Shame of the Cities.* New York, McClure, Phillips & Company, 1914. 306 p. (See: "Tweed Days in St. Louis," pp. 29-59, and "The Shamelessness of St. Louis," pp. 101-143.)

McClure, Eleanor B. *Early History of Washington, Missouri.* Washington, Mo., *The Washington Missourian,* 1939. 48 p., illus.

Musick, James B. *St. Louis as a Fortified Town.* St. Louis, Press of R. F. Miller, 1941. 166 p., illus.

PEOPLE

United States Biographical Dictionary and Portrait Gallery of Eminent and Self-Made Men (Missouri volume). New York, Chicago, (etc.), United States Biographical Publishing Company, 1878. 890 p.

Shoemaker, Floyd C. *Missouri's Hall of Fame; Lives of Eminent Missourians.* Columbia, Mo., The Missouri Book Company, 1918. 269 p., illus.

Bryan, William Smith, and Rose, Robert. *A History of the Pioneer Families of Missouri; with sketches, anecdotes, adventures, etc. relating to early days in Missouri; also lives of Daniel Boone and Black Hawk, with biography and history of primitive institutions.* (Facsimile of 1876 edition.) Columbia, Mo., Lucas Brothers, 1935. 569 p., illus.

Bay, William Van Ness. *Reminiscences of the Bench and Bar of Missouri.* St. Louis, F. H. Thomas & Company, 1878. 611 p., illus.

Bechdolt, F. R. *Giants of the Old West.* New York, London, The Century Company, c1930. 245 p., illus., maps.

Bakeless, John Edwin. *Daniel Boone.* New York, William Morrow & Company, 1939. 480 p., illus., map.

Sabin, Edwin L. *Kit Carson Days, 1809-1868.* Chicago, A. C. McClurg & Company, 1914. 669 p.

Favour, Alpheus H. *Old Bill Williams, Mountain Man.* Chapel Hill, N. C., University of North Carolina Press, c1936. 229 p., illus., map, geneal. tab.

Beckwourth, James P. *Life and Adventures of James P. Beckwourth, Mountaineer, Scout, Pioneer, and Chief of the Crow Nation of In-*

dians (dictated to T. D. Bonner). (London, 1856.) New York, Alfred A. Knopf, 1931. 405 p.

Alter, J. Cecil. *James Bridger, Trapper, Frontiersman, Scout and Guide.* Salt Lake City, Utah, Shepard Book Company, 1925. 546 p., illus., map.

Hafen, LeRoy, Ghent, W. J. *Broken Hand, the Life Story of Thomas Fitzpatrick, Chief of the Mountain Men.* Denver, Colo., The Old West Publishing Company, 1931. 316 p., illus., map.

Frederick, James V. *Ben Holladay, The Stagecoach King; a chapter in the development of transcontinental transportation.* Glendale, Cal., The Arthur H. Clark Company, 1940. 334 p., illus., map.

Meigs, William M. *The Life of Thomas Hart Benton.* Philadelphia, London, J. B. Lippincott Company, 1904. 535 p., illus.

Benton, Thomas Hart. *Thirty Years' View.* New York (etc.), D. Appleton & Company, 1863, 1864. 2 vols., illus.

Phillips, Catherine Coffin. *Jessie Benton Frémont: A Woman Who Made History.* San Francisco, John Henry Nash, 1935. 361 p., illus.

Easum, Chester Verne. *The Americanization of Carl Schurz.* Chicago, The University of Chicago Press, c1929. 374 p.

Paine, Albert Bigelow. *Mark Twain, a Biography; the Personal and Literary Life of Samuel Langhorn Clemens.* New York, London, Harper & Brothers, 1935. 4 vols., illus.

Brashear, Minnie May. *Mark Twain, Son of Missouri.* Chapel Hill, N. C., University of North Carolina Press, 1934. 294 p., illus., map.

Woodward, W. E. *Meet General Grant.* New York, Horace Liveright Publishing Corp., 1928. 512 p., illus.

Grant, U. S. *Personal Memoirs of U. S. Grant.* New York, Charles L. Webster & Company, 1894. 666 p., illus.

Todd, Helen. *A Man Named Grant.* Boston, Houghton Mifflin Company, 1940. 508 p., illus.

Stevens, Walter B. *Grant in St. Louis.* St. Louis, The Franklin Club of St. Louis, 1916. 172 p., illus.

Gresham, Hugh C. *The Story of Major David McKee, Founder of the Anti-Horse Thief Association and the Anti-Thief Association.* Cheney, Kansas, 1937. 80 p.

How, Louis. *James B. Eads.* New York, Houghton Mifflin Company, 1900. 120 p.

Dimmock, Thomas. *Henry Shaw, a Biographical Sketch.* St. Louis, 1890. (Missouri Botanical Garden Report, Vol. 1, pp. 7-25, illus.)

Smith, William E. *The Francis Preston Blair Family in Politics.* New York, The Macmillan Company, 1933. 2 vols., illus.

Crittenden, H. H. (comp.). *The Crittenden Memoirs.* New York, G. P. Putnam's Sons, 1936. 542 p.

Asbury, Herbert. *Carry Nation.* New York, Alfred A. Knopf, 1929. 307 p., illus.

Thompson, Slason. *Eugene Field: A Study in Heredity and Contradictions.* New York, Charles Scribner's Sons, 1901. 2 vols., illus.

Clark, Champ. *My Quarter Century of American Politics.* New York, London, Harper & Brothers, c1920. 2 vols., illus.

Benton, Thomas Hart. *An Artist in America.* New York, R. M. McBride Company, c1937. 276 p., illus. in color.

Hagedorn, Hermann. *Brookings, A Biography.* New York, The Macmillan Company, 1936. 334 p., illus.

BANDITS AND BAD MEN

Edwards, John N. *Noted Guerrillas, or, The Warfare of the Border.* St. Louis, Bryan, Brand & Company, 1877. 488 p., illus.

Buel, James W. *The Border Outlaws: an authentic and thrilling history of the most noted bandits of ancient or modern times; the Younger brothers, Jesse and Frank James, and their comrades in crime.* St. Louis, Historical Publishing Company, 1881. 148 p., illus.

Evans, James W., Keith, A. Wendell, M.D. *Autobiography of Samuel S. Hildebrand, the Renowned Missouri 'Bushwhacker' and Unconquerable Rob Roy of America.* Jefferson City, Mo., State Times Book and Job Printing House, 1870. 312 p., illus.

Dacus, Joseph A. *Illustrated Lives and Adventures of Frank and Jesse James and the Younger Brothers, the Noted Western Outlaws.* St. Louis, N. D. Thompson & Company, 1881. 442 p.

Love, Robertus. *Rise and Fall of Jesse James.* New York, London, G. P. Putnam's Sons, 1926. 446 p., illus.

Triplett, Frank. *The Life, Times, and Treacherous Death of Jesse James; the only Correct and Authorized Edition. The facts and incidents dictated by Mrs. Jesse James and Mrs. Zerelda Samuel, his mother.* St. Louis, Chicago, J. H. Chambers & Company, 1882. 416 p., illus.

Younger, Cole. *The Story of Cole Younger. By Himself.* Chicago, Press of the Henneberry Company, 1903. 123 p., illus.

Morris, Lucille. *Bald Knobbers.* Caldwell, Idaho, The Caxton Printers, Ltd., 1939. 253 p., illus.

STORIES WITH A MISSOURI BACKGROUND

Cannon, Ralph. *Lee on the Levee.* New York, the Saravan House, 1940. 188 p.

Churchill, Winston. *The Crisis.* New York, London, The Macmillan Company, 1901. 522 p., illus.

Clemens, Samuel L. (Mark Twain) *The Adventures of Huckleberry Finn.* London, Chatto & Windus, 1884. 438 p., illus.

——— *The Adventures of Tom Sawyer.* Hartford, Conn., The American Publishing Company, 1876. 274 p.

——— *Life on the Mississippi.* Boston, J. R. Osgood & Company, 1883. 624 p.

Davidson, Lallah Sherman. *South of Joplin.* New York, W. W. Norton & Company, c1930. 200 p., illus.

Dillon (Mrs.), Mary C. (Johnson). *The Rose of Old St. Louis.* New York, The Century Company, 1904. 460 p.

Doneghy, Dagmar. *The Border; A Missouri Saga.* New York, W. Morrow & Company, 1931. 343 p.

Dorrance, Ward A. *Three Ozark Streams; Log of the Mocassin and the Wilma.* Richmond, Mo., The Missourian Press, c1937. 58 p.

—— *We're from Missouri.* Richmond, Mo., The Missourian Press, 1938. 97 p.

—— *Where the Rivers Meet.* New York, Charles Scribner's Sons, 1939. 252 p.

Ellis, J. Breckenridge. *The Little Fiddler of the Ozarks.* Chicago, Laird & Lee, c1913. 308 p., illus.

Hauck, Louise Platt. *The Youngest Rider, a Story of the Pony Express.* Boston, Lothrop, Lee & Shepherd Company, c1927. 245 p., illus.

Howe, Edgar Watson. *The Story of a Country Town.* Boston, J. R. Osgood & Company, 1884. 413 p.

Kantor, MacKinlay. *The Voice of Bugle Ann.* New York, Coward-McCann, Inc., c1935. 128 p.

Lane, Rose Wilder. *Hill-Billy.* New York, London, Harper & Brothers, 1926. 286 p.

—— *Cindy, a Romance of the Ozarks.* New York, London, Harper & Brothers, 1928. 200 p.

Lindbergh, Charles Augustus. *We.* New York, London, G. P. Putnam's Sons, 1927. 318 p., illus.

Magaret, Helene. *Father DeSmet, Pioneer Priest of the Rockies.* New York, Farrar & Rinehart, Inc., c1940. 371 p.

McBride, Mary Margaret. *How Dear to My Heart.* New York, The Macmillan Company, 1940. 196 p., illus.

Montieth, John. *Parson Brooks: A Plumb Powerful Hardshell.* St. Louis, O. H. P. Applegate, 1884. 115 p.

Musick, John R. *Stories of Missouri.* New York, Chicago, etc., The American Book Company, 1897. 288 p., illus.

Neihardt, John G. *Indian Tales and Others.* New York, The Macmillan Company, 1926. 306 p.

Randolph, Vance (ed.). *An Ozark Anthology.* Caldwell, Idaho, The Caxton Printers, Ltd., 1940. 374 p.

Randolph, Vance. *Ozark Outdoors; Hunting and Fishing Stories of the Ozarks.* New York, The Vanguard Press, 1934. 299 p., illus.

Robb, John S. (Solitaire). *Streaks of Squatter Life, and Far West Scenes; a Series of Humorous Sketches Descriptive of Incidents and Character in the Wild West.* Philadelphia, Carey & Hart, 1847. 187 p., illus.

Sosey, Frank H. *Robert Devoy, a Tale of the Palmyra Massacre.* Palmyra, Mo., Press of Sosey Brothers, 1903. 172 p., illus.

Tuck, Clyde Edwin. *The Bald Knobbers; A Romantic and Historical Novel.* Indianapolis, B. F. Bowen & Company, 1910. 325 p., illus.

Weeks, Raymond. *The Hound-Tuner of Callaway.* New York, Columbia University Press, 1927. 277 p., illus.

———— *Boy's Own Arithmetic.* New York, E. P Dutton & Company, c1924. 188 p., illus.

Wright, Harold Bell. *The Calling of Dan Matthews.* New York, A. L. Burt Company, 1909. 363 p., illus.

———— *The Shepherd of the Hills.* New York, A. L. Burt Company, 1907, 1922. 347 p., illus.

Map of
MISSOURI
in Eight Sections

Index to State Map Sections

LEGEND FOR STATE MAP

▬▬▬▬ Concrete, Brick or Oil Mat Pavement	▬▬ ▬ ▬ State Line
▬▪▪▪▪▬ Gravel, Crushed Stone or Oiled Earth	▬ ▬ · ▬ County Line
▭▭▭▭ Graded Earth	▬▬▬ State Park
U.S. Highway	▬▬▬ National Forest
State Highway	○ Town
Supplementary Highway	● County Seat
County Road	Ⓕ Free Bridge
Mileage Between Points	Ⓣ Toll Bridge
Federal Lock and Dam	🄵 Ferry

MAP SHOWING SECTIONAL DIVISION OF STATE MAP

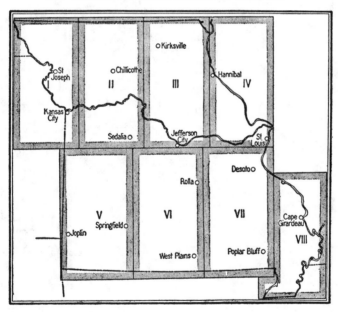

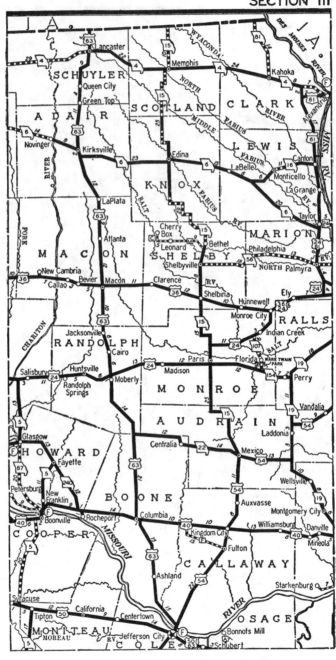

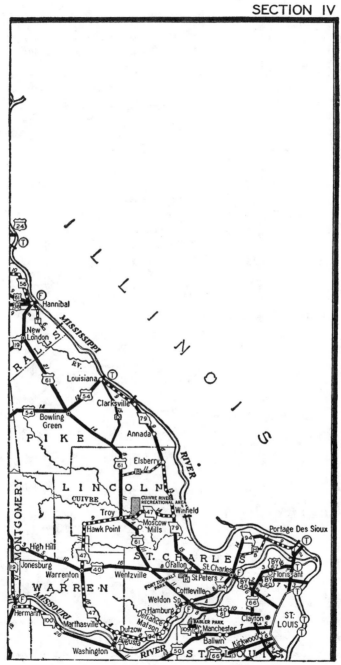

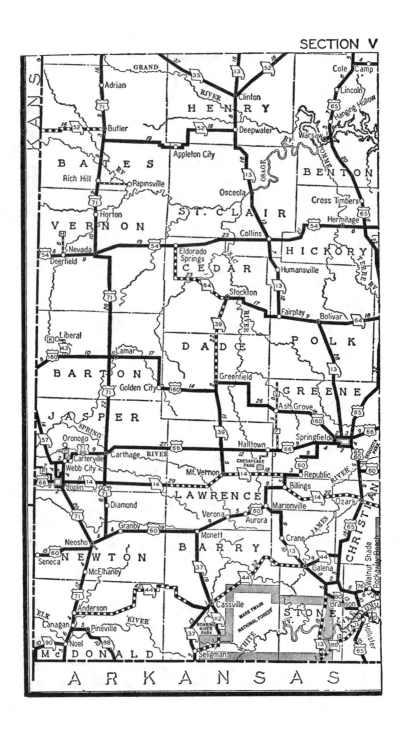

SECTION VI

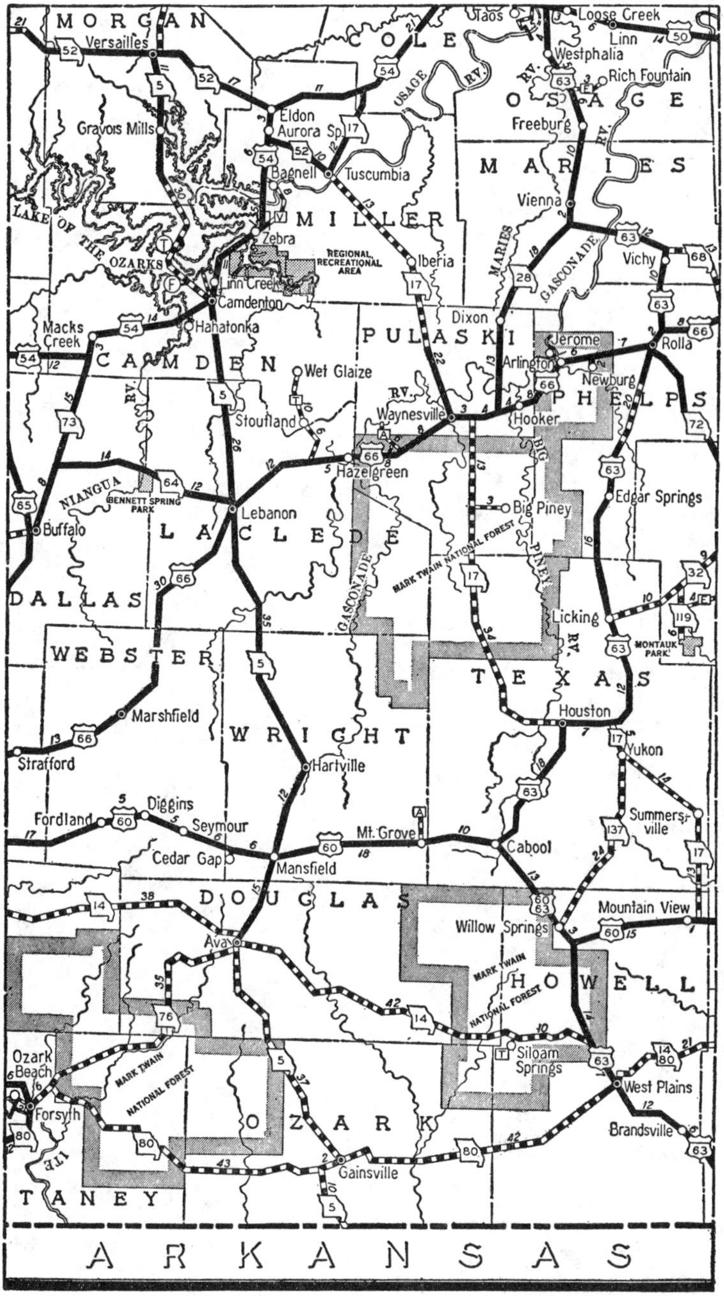
MORGAN
Versailles
COLE
Taos
Loose Creek
Linn
Westphalia
Rich Fountain
OSAGE
Freeburg
MARIES
Vienna
Vichy
Rolla
PHELPS
Newburg
Jerome
Arlington
Hooker
Dixon
PULASKI
Waynesville
Hazelgreen
Big Piney
Edgar Springs
Licking
MONTAUK PARK
TEXAS
Houston
Yukon
Summersville
Cabool
Mountain View
Willow Springs
HOWELL
Siloam Springs
West Plains
Brandsville
Gravois Mills
Eldon
Aurora Sp.
Bagnell
Tuscumbia
MILLER
Iberia
LAKE OF THE OZARKS
Zebra
REGIONAL RECREATIONAL AREA
Linn Creek
Camdenton
Hahatonka
Macks Creek
CAMDEN
Wet Glaize
Stoutland
NIANGUA
BENNETT SPRING PARK
Buffalo
Lebanon
LACLEDE
DALLAS
WEBSTER
Marshfield
Strafford
WRIGHT
Hartville
Fordland
Diggins
Seymour
Cedar Gap
Mansfield
Mt. Grove
DOUGLAS
Ava
OZARK
Gainsville
Ozark Beach
Forsyth
TANEY
MARK TWAIN NATIONAL FOREST
USAGE RV.
GASCONADE
MARIES
BIG PINEY
ARKANSAS

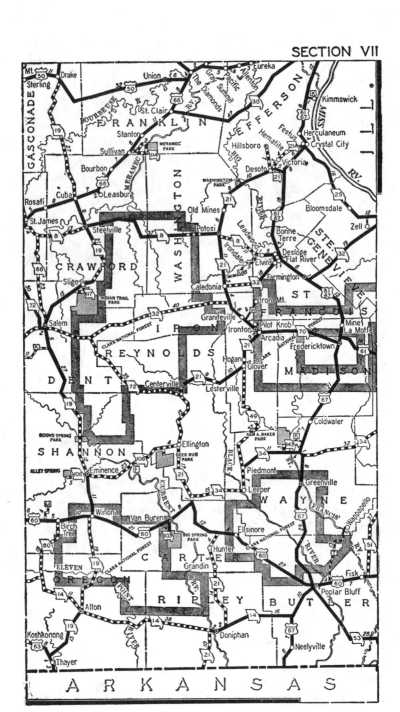

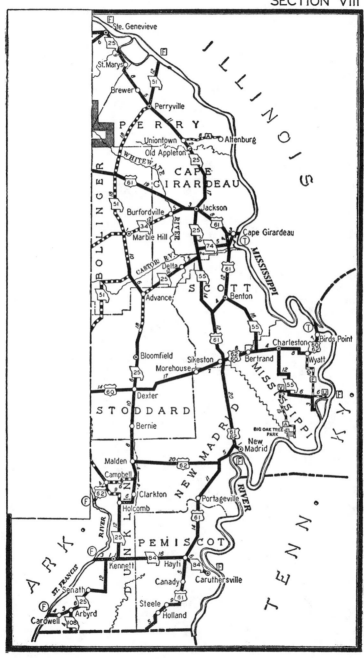

Index

Errata

P. 8, line 12   "McFadden" should read "Macfadden"

P. 110, line 13   *"Westiche"* should read *"Westliche"*

P. 110, line 33   *"L'Quest"* should read *"L'Ouest"*

P. 120, line 14   "Daniel Green" should read "David Green"

P. 143, line 32   "Englemann" should read "Engelmann"

P. 163, line 1   "Haenchen" should read "Haenschen"

P. 200, line 16   *"Cape"* should read *"Cap"*

P. 280, line 43   *"Champ"* should read *"Champs"*

P. 296, line 45   "Vanderventer" should read "Vandeventer"

P. 302, line 33   "Robert L. Lee" should read "Robert E. Lee"

P. 316, line 20   "de Smet" should read "De Smet"

P. 328, line 29   "Pettis" should read "Pettus"

P. 353, line 47   "Mackey" should read "Mackay"

P. 379, line 2   "Charles W. Quantrill" should read "William W. Quantrill"

P. 400, lines 2, 3   "MacFadden" should read "Macfadden"

P. 403, line 36   "Charles Quantrill" should read "William Quantrill"

P. 435, line 32   "Saymen" should read "Sayman"

P. 462, line 29   "Loredo" should read "Lorado"

P. 516, line 15   "Sheebael" should read "Shebael"

P. 536, line 24   "French" should read "Creole"

P. 571, lines 19–20   "Farmaraugh" should read "Farmanaugh"

P. 577, line 17   "Cape de la Croix" should read "Cap de la Croix"

P. 597, line 3   "Agriculture" should read "Archeology"

P. 608, line 21   *"Langhorn"* should read *"Langhorne"*